RIVERS
RUN
THROUGH
US

ERIC B. TAYLOR

RIVERS

A NATURAL AND HUMAN HISTORY

RUN

OF GREAT RIVERS OF NORTH AMERICA

THROUGH

Foreword by MARK ANGELO

US

RMB
rmbooks.com

For information on purchasing bulk quantities of this book, or to obtain media excerpts or invite the author to speak at an event, please visit rmbooks.com and select the "Contact" tab.

RMB | Rocky Mountain Books Ltd.
rmbooks.com
@rmbooks
facebook.com/rmbooks

Cataloguing data available from Library and Archives Canada
ISBN 9781771605113 (hardcover)
ISBN 9781771605120 (electronic)

Edited by Peter Enman
Interior design by Lara Minja, Lime Design
Cover photo iStock.com/benedek

Printed and bound in Canada

We would like to also take this opportunity to acknowledge the traditional territories upon which we live and work. In Calgary, Alberta, we acknowledge the Niitsítapi (Blackfoot) and the people of the Treaty 7 region in Southern Alberta, which includes the Siksika, the Piikuni, the Kainai, the Tsuut'ina, and the Stoney Nakoda First Nations, including Chiniki, Bearpaw, and Wesley First Nations. The City of Calgary is also home to Métis Nation of Alberta, Region III. In Victoria, British Columbia, we acknowledge the traditional territories of the Lkwungen (Esquimalt and Songhees), Malahat, Pacheedaht, Scia'new, T'Sou-ke, and W̱SÁNEĆ (Pauquachin, Tsartlip, Tsawout, Tseycum) peoples.

We acknowledge the financial support of the Government of Canada through the Canada Book Fund and the Canada Council for the Arts, and of the province of British Columbia through the British Columbia Arts Council and the Book Publishing Tax Credit.

To my memory of my father,
Eric Walter Taylor (1920–2015),
who first introduced me
to the magic of rivers

CONTENTS

List of Illustrations/images

List of maps

Foreword

— **Mark Angelo** —

I HAVE BEEN DRAWN to rivers and streams since I was a child; there was just something about moving water that I found captivating. Growing up in southern California, I would spend hours exploring small creeks in the nearby foothills looking for aquatic insects, crayfish or anything else I might find.

Riveted by rivers, I wasn't very old when I began to appreciate the immense importance of waterways as a global resource. Eventually, I also came to realize that my fascination with rivers was widely shared by many around the world, a phenomenon stemming from the key role rivers have played in human development. The reciprocal relationship that exists between the human experience and rivers is explored in depth by Eric Taylor in *Rivers Run Through Us: A Natural and Human History of Great Rivers of North America*.

While writing this foreword, I found myself reflecting on some of my early river journeys that were especially impactful. Among these was a trip as a young paddler on the Rio Grande, and I remember so vividly being awestruck by the beauty of the Rio Grande gorge the first time I saw it. Located near Taos, New Mexico, the walls of this narrow river canyon shot up over 200 metres through layers of volcanic basalt while 500-year-old piñon and juniper trees dotted the landscape. Hidden among the cliffs, scree slopes and large boulders were ancient pictographs scratched into the black basalt, touchpoints of the Rio Grande Pueblos, "the people of the great river."

It was a remarkable stretch of river in every sense, and I could easily appreciate why, to many, this 80-kilometre-long gorge is New Mexico's equivalent to the Grand Canyon.

My journey all those years ago was focused on following the course of the Rio Grande, the second longest river in the continental United States with a length of close to 3000 kilometres.

Upon leaving New Mexico, I drove south to El Paso, Texas, where I spent several more days exploring and paddling other parts of the river. It was a trip I enjoyed immensely, and I came to view many parts of the river as a great oasis amid an otherwise arid landscape. The basin of the Rio Grande comprises a massive area, from its headwaters in south-central Colorado to its terminus in the Gulf of Mexico. Throughout its course, the river plays a vital role in nourishing ecosystems and irrigating agricultural lands in both the United States and Mexico.

In recent years, I returned to El Paso for the first time in over four decades only to find that a stretch of river I had paddled so long ago had completely run dry, an occurrence that has become increasingly frequent due to excessive water withdrawals and climate change. Remembering the river that I had seen so many years before, this was a stunning and sobering sight: a stark reminder that even great rivers can face immense pressures.

In my late teens, I went to the University of Montana, where I got into paddling and fly fishing in a major way. As a student, I also became increasingly fascinated by the natural and human history associated with waterways. During those years, I started paddling nearby rivers like the Blackfoot and Clark Fork (tributaries of the Columbia) and soon developed a passion for travelling by river, both within the continent and elsewhere. I also knew at that point that I wanted to spend my life working to protect and restore rivers.

In the decades since, I've paddled along many of the world's large river systems, ranging from the Amazon to the Nile and from the Ganges to the Zambezi. But I equally enjoy exploring the incredible waterways that exist closer to home, and I feel extremely fortunate to have travelled on and along each of the ten rivers so effectively featured in Eric Taylor's *Rivers Run Through Us*.

Over the years, I have come to believe that rivers are the arteries of our planet; they are lifelines in the truest sense. They have immense natural, cultural, recreational and economic value and have been shaped and influenced over time by both natural and human elements. At the same time, rivers help to shape the lives of those who live within their basins. Understanding these relationships is crucial to our efforts to better care for rivers and, through this book, Taylor makes a significant contribution to that endeavour.

I first met Eric Taylor several years ago at a Pacific salmon forum where he made a very impactful and well-received speech about the need to conserve salmon stocks. As a university professor, he has spent his career in and around rivers, and his lengthy experience and extensive knowledge, coupled with a great passion for rivers, makes him perfectly suited to write this book.

One of the most enjoyable aspects of Taylor's book is the great diversity of topics he covers – from war, to art to salmon – all of which relate to rivers. I believe readers will gain great insight, not only about how humans have impacted rivers, but also the extent to which rivers have affected us.

One of the great rivers examined in *Rivers Run Through Us* is the Fraser River in British Columbia, which, for most of my life, has been my "home river." It is a river I have lived along for close to five decades and it holds a special place in my heart.

The Fraser is an amazing river in so many respects. It's one of British Columbia's dominant features, and whether one walks along the river, paddles it, fishes it or simply admires its beauty, most would say this river adds greatly to the quality of life we enjoy. Further, one cannot talk about a river like the Fraser without also talking about Pacific salmon, an important symbol to many British Columbians, as well as other North Americans. Salmon are ingrained in our culture and, in many ways, help to define our sense of place as explored in several contexts in *Rivers Run Through Us*.

One of the greatest adventures in my life took place in 1975 when I had a chance to paddle the full length of the Fraser. In both kayaks and rafts, our journey covered 1375 kilometres. By trip's end, I remember being so impressed with the river's power, its beauty and its diversity. Ever since, I have looked at this amazing waterway as literally the "heart and soul" of our province.

I believe many who live within the basins of the other nine great North American waterways explored by Taylor (from the Mackenzie to the Hudson) would express similar sentiments about their "home rivers."

My early trips on the Fraser also inspired the idea of creating a provincial event aimed at celebrating the many values of our river heritage. While it took a few years to become reality, the first BC Rivers Day took place in 1980, and its success ultimately led to the establishment of World Rivers Day in 2005, an event now celebrated by millions of people in over 100 countries. To know that the roots of this global celebration of rivers, now one of the biggest environmental events on the planet, come right back to the Fraser basin is something special!

Clearly, each of the great rivers so elegantly described in this treatment by Taylor has its own compelling narrative. As examples of issues explored in *Rivers Run Through Us*, I think of my own travels on rivers such as the Colorado, from its headwaters in the Rocky Mountains, through Arizona's Grand Canyon (one of the world's great paddling trips) to its terminus in the Sea of Cortez. Along the way, the river is literally the lifeline of the southwest, providing water for up to 40 million people along with 5 million acres of farmland, something Taylor elaborates on with great insight.

I also recall my trips on the Yukon, a river that retains so much of its natural glory but also one with a fascinating history in its role as a principal means of transportation during the Klondike gold rush.

As a Canadian, I've had a long-held interest in the St. Lawrence, a river that played such a prominent role in Canada's early history and one that remains a focal point for so many who live in Quebec. The river also continues to be the most important commercial waterway in Canada and the United States.

Or the Mississippi, a river with a north-south axis that at one time was the most important vein of transportation on the continent.

In my youth, it was also a river that ignited my imagination with thoughts about river travel, thanks to the writings of Mark Twain.

The fact is that every great river in North America has its own unique story to tell. Rivers have shaped our land and our history in so many ways, and understanding these elements is important to any strategies that might be developed to manage or restore these waterways. Just as importantly, Eric Taylor's book contains compelling narratives and fascinating stories about great rivers. For readers, it will heighten their awareness of the many values of our waterways while also emphasizing the need to better care for them – something we must do because each of these rivers delivers immense benefits to people, economies and nature.

MARK ANGELO is an internationally renowned river conservationist, paddler and educator. He is the founder and Chair of both BC and World Rivers Day and is the recipient of both the Order of BC and the Order of Canada in recognition of his river conservation efforts. His work has been honoured by numerous international and educational institutions and has been the subject of several feature films. Mark has paddled more than 1,000 rivers and explored countless others in well over 100 countries, perhaps more than any other individual.

Acknowledgements

I CANNOT RECALL when the idea of writing a book about rivers and North American history crystallized in my mind, but I do know that moment was the result of a lifetime of being around, enjoying and working in rivers. My father first introduced me to rivers through the joys and art of canoeing. My chief academic mentors, Drs. J.D. McPhail and P.A. Larkin, intensified my interest in rivers and river biodiversity through the study of fishes. Steve Cox-Rogers, a companion early in graduate school, introduced me, fresh from Ontario, to some wonderful rivers of British Columbia during many fishing trips. It was in the summation of experience from these trips that I first felt a certain "specialness" about rivers. I have enjoyed several fine canoe and fishing trips on spectacular rivers in Yukon and northern British Columbia with Steve Watt, Grahame Arnould, Robert ("Steady") Turner, Scott Tomenson and Tim Falconer. I am especially grateful to Tim, a writer of several fine books, for inspiration, encouragement, advice, comments on the manuscript, making me laugh more times than I can count and for introducing me to "the bell" at Bombay Peggy's in that most magical of towns, Dawson City, Yukon. Robert Turner and Dolph Schluter provided helpful comments on portions of the manuscript. I am also grateful to Andrew Chisholm for providing comments on the manuscript in its entirety and to Steve Watt for reassuring advice. I appreciate the early encouragement of Ruben Boles and his gift of a copy of Mark Twain's delightful *Life on the Mississippi*. I am also very grateful and honoured that Mark Angelo, a great defender of and educator about rivers, took the interest and time for write this book's Foreword.

The Natural Research Council of Canada has funded my research for almost 40 years. The University of British Columbia, the Beaty Biodiversity Museum and the Department of Zoology in particular, have provided a wonderful intellectual, creative and collegial environment – all crucial to the development and writing of this book. Much of the text was written while I was on sabbatical at the University of Queensland, in Brisbane, Australia, in 2014–2015. Long walks along the Brisbane River provided plenty of inspiration, and I thank Dr. Cynthia Riginos for being a wonderful host at UQ. Dr. A.R.E. ("Tony") Sinclair is thanked for inspiration (especially after reading his *Serengeti Story: Life and Science in the World's Greatest Wildlife Region,* 2012), helpful discussions, encouragement and for advising me to "just finish the book and worry about finding a publisher later," which made the writing a lot more fun. Eric Leinberger of the Department of Geography at UBC was a pleasure to work with in creating beautiful maps for this book. Derek Tan of the Beaty Biodiversity Museum was a great help in image acquisition and lent his considerable talents and professionalism to drafting several illustrations – he has the patience of Job. The publisher, Don Gorman, and staff at Rocky Mountain Books are thanked for their tremendous support and patience throughout the publishing process. I also appreciate the careful attention to detail by editor Peter Enman. Overall, researching and writing this book has been an untold pleasure and education – I must also thank all the authors of wonderful books on individual rivers, accumulated and read over the last several decades, all of which helped inspire this volume. Philip Fradkin's *A River No More: The Colorado River and the West* (1996) was particularly impactful in awakening me so many years ago to the power and influence of the water development lobby in the US.

Finally, I thank my family, Meg, Eric, Andy and especially my wife, Nini, all of whom have shared many great moments on rivers and encouraged and nourished this effort through their love and support over the years.

CANIM LAKE, BRITISH COLUMBIA
September 2020

INTRODUCTION

A river is water is its loveliest form; rivers have life and sound and movement and infinity of variation, rivers are veins of the earth through which the lifeblood returns to the heart.

—RODERICK HAIG-BROWN, conservationist, angler and writer,
A River Never Sleeps, 1946

It is an obvious fact of historical geography that large rivers play an important part in the history of the lands through which they flow.

—R.H. WHITBECK, *The St. Lawrence River and Its Part in the Making of Canada*, 1914

Rivers are natural bodies of fresh water that flow within a defined channel and they have promoted and sustained human development for millennia. Rivers have provided myriad benefits: drinking and washing water, animal and plant protein and other products, transportation, power, irrigation, cooling and industrial support, recreation and inspiration. In providing these benefits, rivers have in turn been profoundly influenced by human development (dam and reservoir construction, canals, pollution and biodiversity loss). Rivers have been fundamental to the history and development of ancient and populous countries such as India and China. Human development and especially the control of rivers sought to save India from the failure of monsoon rains (via irrigation) and China from catastrophic floods (through dam construction) and fuelled the power of ancient Rome.[1] The reciprocal relationship between humans and rivers through history suggests, therefore, that rivers and their enveloping landscape represent a fundamental social-ecological unit.[2] This significance of rivers and their interactions with humans and the development of societies is reflected by the emergence of the academic field of "river history" or river historiography.[3]

Sumer (or Sumeria), in the southernmost area of Mesopotamia and encompassing parts of present-day Iraq and Kuwait, is generally considered to be the first human civilization, dating back to ~7,450–5,950 years ago (ya).[4] Sumer eventually encompassed many city-states, all of which were centred in and around the Tigris and Euphrates rivers – perhaps the first manifestation of humans as a "riparian species."[5] These rivers helped to form part of what is known as the "Fertile Crescent" – relatively moist and fertile land within the otherwise desert and unproductive regions of western Asia to northeastern Africa – that laid the groundwork for agriculture and much of subsequent human development.[6] Sumerians are credited with inventing irrigation by building levees to hold back floodwaters and then cutting canals into the levees to flood their fields. The importance of the "Fertile Crescent," and the role of these rivers in producing it, is reflected in another name for his area – the "Cradle of Civilization." Ironically, poor management of a key gift of rivers – irrigation – and resulting salinization of the water was likely an important factor in the demise of Sumer.[7]

In North America, the development of Indigenous civilizations and the civilizations founded subsequently following European colonization were initially based largely on the "highway of rivers" that allowed transcontinental movement of people and goods from the vast interior to the Atlantic to Pacific and Arctic coasts. Even today, the nature and future of rivers profoundly impacts us all. From current major hydroelectric projects ("Site C" in British Columbia's Peace River Valley) to drought conditions in major basins (the Colorado and Sacramento–San Joaquin rivers), to removal of century-old dams, rivers and their attributes present the public and governments with major opportunities, challenges and choices.

Rivers, therefore, are of interest and importance for utilitarian reasons (e.g., providing recreational or power-generation opportunities) and for understanding the history and future of human development.[8]

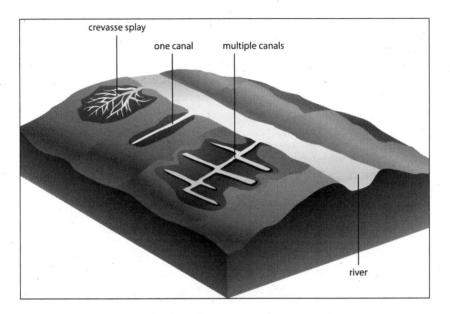

Three stages of Sumerian irrigation: crevasse splay formed when a channel is cut through a river levee and drains downhill; a single confined "spur" canal; and a "herringbone" pattern of multiple lower gradient canals of each spur canal. Adapted from Wilkinson, Rayne, and Jotheri (2015).

Rivers are, however, interesting for at least two other fundamental reasons. First, they are an integral component of the "hydrological cycle"[9] and, therefore, central to the persistence of life on Earth. The hydrological, or water, cycle refers to the continuous movement of water above, on or below the surface of the Earth and its transformation between different physical states: ice, atmospheric water (e.g., rain and mist), fresh water and saline water, even as the total amount of water within the Earth and its atmosphere remains relatively constant. These transformations involve well-studied phenomena such as precipitation, evaporation, transpiration, condensation, sublimation, filtration and surface and subsurface flow, as well as the different states of water: liquid (water), solid (ice) and gas (vapour). Consequently, and given that the typical human is 50–65% water by weight and that water is fundamental to the proper functioning of life's processes, humans simply could not persist without the provision of safe drinking water, which owes its ultimate origin and continual rebirth to the hydrological cycle. In his work *Great River: The Rio Grande in American History*, Paul Horgan described returning water from the land to the sea to maintain the "exquisite balance" of the hydrological cycle as "the work, and the law, of rivers."[10] Simply put, rivers are a focal aspect of the persistence of life on Earth through their vital contribution to the "virtuous cycle"[11] of water.

Second, rivers are of inherent importance to many people – beautiful and powerful systems of tremendous and unquantifiable aesthetic value, part of the well-documented connection between environmental quality and human well-being.[12] There is something about that essential quality of rivers – their "flow" – that reaches deeply into the human consciousness.[13] It may be the energy involved in the flow of rivers or that the flow itself is suggestive of a living entity, something that moves, with a "metabolism."[14] In fact, four rivers of the world (one in New Zealand, one in Colombia and two in India) were recently recognized legally as "persons,"[15] meaning that, under the law, they can be ascribed certain rights that can be enforced. These rivers, under suitable representation, possess the right to sue (and be sued) as they now can have legal standing.

Human fascination with rivers may also stem from the parallels between the network-like structure of rivers and that of the human circulatory or nervous systems.[16] Indeed, in his book *Seven Rivers of Canada*, Hugh MacLennan cited Heraclitus, a pre-Socratic Greek philosopher, who considered "reality" as the state of "flux" where *Everything Flows*[17] (a term common in the later writings of Simplicius, another Greek philosopher, along with Plato and Aristotle to describe Heraclitus's philosophy of reality as "everchanging"). Our fascination with rivers may also reflect both the history of rivers as the source of abundance and devastation for humans and the central place of rivers in human religion, mythology and culture.[18] Literally thousands of songs, books, poems, plays, movies and pieces of art have been created with rivers as central themes, which reflects the deep connection between rivers and human experience.[19] Think of Jerome Kern's "Ol' Man River," Joni Mitchell's "River," the four rivers of Hades in Homer's *Odyssey*, Mark Twain's *Huckleberry Finn*,

Francis Ford Coppola's *Apocalypse Now*, itself a film adaptation of Joseph Conrad's novella *Heart of Darkness,* or Leonardo's *Mona Lisa* with a river as a backdrop. In what is probably the world's largest gathering of humanity, up to 50 million people on a single day, Hindus celebrate Kumbh Mela at four rivers in India every 12 years – a spiritual cleansing dip in the rivers is a central feature of the festival.[20] Rivers, in both their physicality and meaning to humans, are acknowledged as important drivers of national identities, and there are many examples of the idea of a "national river" – the Thames in England, Russia's Volga River and the Hudson River of the US (see Chapter 10).[21] These meanings of rivers for humans were nicely encapsulated by Laurence C. Smith in *Rivers of Power: How a Natural Force Raised Kingdoms, Destroyed Civilizations, and Shapes Our World* when he listed access, well-being, natural capital, territory and a way to express power as fundamental benefits that rivers provide humanity.

With this historical perspective in mind, it may seem that what the term "river" means would be unambiguous, yet this is not necessarily true. Somewhat loosely defined, a "river" is a natural body of water that flows within a defined channel, typically towards another river, a lake or the sea, or sometimes just ends by drying up or disappearing into the earth. Although formal distinctions either do not exist or vary by country, a "river" is commonly distinguished from terms such as "rill," "rivulet," "stream," "brook," "creek" or "kill" by the simple observation that a "river" is larger than any of these other kinds of flowing water. Indeed, these other features are typically considered to be able to flow into a river, but a river, while it may flow into another river, does not flow into a stream or creek. Still, the exact size at which a flowing element of water becomes a "river" is not defined precisely.[22] Luna Leopold, the noted American hydrologist and son of Aldo Leopold, the even more noted philosopher, author and environmentalist, offered a general definition of rivers in his 1994 *A View of the River*. Leopold explained that precipitation delivers more water to the Earth than is lost from it by evaporation or transpiration. Rivers are the means, therefore, by which this excess water is delivered to its ultimate base level in the oceans (water also flows to recharge ground water and springs).[23] The smallest element of what will eventually become a river is a "rill" – that first overland flow of water that results from rainfall, or snowmelt, on a hillslope. To form a rill, the flow must be of a depth sufficient to shield the soil surface from the impact of continuing rainfall and thus prevent the "obliteration" of incipient flow, an ongoing phenomenon that began at least four billion years ago.[24] From such humble beginnings, rills grow into rivulets, rivulets into creeks and streams, and these into rivers. A river, as it flows and interacts with the surrounding topography, thus acts as "the carpenter of its own edifice."[25]

Hydrologists (those who study water on Earth) have developed the so-called Horton-Strahler stream order classification system to describe streams and rivers of different size.[26] The Horton-Strahler system consists of ranks from "first-order" (e.g., tiny headwater streams originating from a glacier or mountain top that have no tributaries) to "twelfth-order" (e.g., the massive Amazon River). Rivers are generally considered to be anything larger than sixth-order in size, but such classification is not always so neatly applied; there is, for example, the ambiguously named "Stonycreek River" in southwestern Pennsylvania, described as a "hybrid large creek and small river."[27] There are cases where a named "creek" may be longer or have greater flow than a named "river," and the terms have no legal meaning.

What are the central aspects of rivers that many find so compelling? Writing now, the answer seems self-evident to someone who has been in (literally) and around rivers his whole life. In fact, I spent much of my first 19 years of life with the Don River, a much-abused tributary of Lake Ontario, flowing through the edge of our Toronto home's backyard. Upon reflection, however, I realized that such self-evidence was not always so. One of my earliest memories of a river was not an entirely pleasant one. My father, a well-practised part-time outdoorsman, took my older sister and me on a first canoe trip on the Burnt River of the Kawartha Lakes system in southern Ontario. At some point on the trip we dumped the canoe while going through a modest set of rapids. The water was warm and not too fast, and, I *think* I was wearing a life jacket, so the only consequences were a wet night and a shortened trip. I thought not much of it and continued to enjoy many other rivers and canoe trips. Thirty-eight years later, I dumped again at a tricky eddy. This time it was on the Big Salmon River, in central Yukon, the water was faster, very cold (~10°C or 50°F), and the consequences could have been much worse given the isolation and conditions. The canoe and gear (except a cherished fly-fishing vest and a box of red wine!) were retrieved, a fire was laid and set, my canoe partner and I warmed up with the help of our four compadres, and we soon set off again to enjoy a memorable trip.

Between those two dunkings, I have come to think much more about rivers, and I am almost embarrassed to admit how much I took them for granted early in my adult life. Three developments have since focused my attention on rivers: I reignited a love of angling, principally fly-fishing; I became a university professor with a speciality in fish biology and conservation; and, finally, I developed an interest in history. The connections between the first two developments and rivers seem obvious: it is almost a necessary precondition to develop an interest in rivers if one fly-fishes (and hopes to be at least modestly successful!). Similarly, if one hopes to understand fishes and contribute to their conservation one simply must appreciate and try to understand their habitats, which, for a freshwater fish person working in North America, means, to a large extent, rivers. Perhaps it is no surprise, then, that our current house rests between two streets named after great rivers – Yukon and Columbia streets in Vancouver, British Columbia. But, *history* – why would an interest in history motivate an interest in rivers?

Ellen Wohl explained it succinctly in *Disconnected Rivers: Linking Rivers to Landscapes*: rivers "reflect a people's history."[28] One simply cannot understand the history of human civilization, or its future, without an appreciation of the role that rivers have played in explaining our current situation on Earth. The observation that at least 84% of the world's 459 cities of more than one million people live along a major river speaks to the intimate connection between rivers and human development.[29] In discussing the importance of the Gulf of Mexico to the development of the US, Jack Davis in *The Gulf: The Making of an American Sea* noted "an intimate and vital connection linking humankind, nature and history."[30] Richard White, in *The*

Organic Machine: Remaking the Columbia River (see Chapter 5) put it succinctly: "We cannot understand human history without natural history and we cannot understand natural history without human history. The two have been intertwined for millennia."[31] If history is a way of knowing how we came to be and where our societies are going,[32] White's summation illustrates the importance of understanding the role of rivers in the development of North America.

There are probably more than 500,000 rivers in North America,[33] many of which have, or merit, their own individual treatments (e.g., Bruce Hutchison's *The Fraser* (1950), part of the 64-volume *Rivers of America* series). With such an abundance of subject matter and with the acknowledgement of the importance of rivers discussed above, how were the systems that are the subject of this book chosen? First, the intent of this work is not to produce an encyclopedic summary of rivers of North America. There are many websites and learned books that treat rivers in this way (e.g., see Natural Resources Canada or Arthur C. Benke and Colbert E. Cushing's *Rivers of North America* [2005]). Rather, my intent is to provide a taste of the diversity of rivers and their geography and to illustrate how such diversity has shaped different aspects of the human experience in North America. Second, for a treatment of North American rivers, I wanted to have at least two rivers that involved Mexico and Mexicans as part of their essential historical or contemporary narrative (see the chapters on the Rio Grande and the Colorado River). Third, I wanted to examine a set of "major" rivers, but not defined as such solely by physical features (e.g., length, area, discharge or sediment load), which is not always immediately straightforward.[34] Rather, I selected the rivers based on their association with some compelling historical and/or contemporary narrative, rivers that in some way "shook" the North American continent, or a large portion of it, which serves as at least one measure of their historical "importance."[35] Readers will notice, however, that there is a large geographic gap between the easternmost river (the St. Lawrence River) and the next river in a northwesterly direction (the Mackenzie River). I offer several reasons (excuses?) for this glaring gap. First, most of the rivers in that arc of land are "shortish" (all the rivers in this book are at least 500 km[36]) and I wanted to cover rivers over the greatest extent of geography. Second, much of the northeastern extremes of North America are sparsely inhabited, probably in no small part owing to their challenging environments and because most of their rivers flow to the north or northeast, towards even more challenging environments of the subarctic and Arctic. These factors likely reduced the potential for general, compelling human narratives to emerge. This in no way devalues rivers in this area, many of which are stunningly beautiful and have played critical roles in the history of Indigenous Peoples or more regional development, as well told in excellent treatments such as *Electric Rivers: The Story of the James Bay Project,* an account of massive hydroelectric development on a series of rivers in northwestern Quebec,[37] or *Samuel Hearne: Journey to the Coppermine River, 1769–1772*, the story of the first European to traverse northern Canada to the Arctic Ocean – 8000 km – by foot![38] One simply has to draw the line somewhere, and while I will certainly not argue that there are no other rivers in North America with important stories to tell, the importance of the rivers that I do discuss is unquestioned. The rivers that are the subject of this book are offered to make a more fundamental point – the critical role of rivers *in general.* Finally, these ten rivers were chosen as an update and extension of Hugh MacLennan's fine book *Seven Rivers of Canada* penned in 1961. That volume, based on a series of articles for *Maclean's* magazine, told the story of seven rivers from the Mackenzie River to the Saint John River as the "rivers that made a nation."[39] We have learned much about these rivers in the ensuing 60 years, thus motivating an update at least from a Canadian standpoint. More recently, in Martin Doyle's *The Source: How Rivers Made America and America Remade its Rivers*, the author states that "rivers shaped the basic facts of America"[40] in terms of topics ranging from federalism to taxation to conservation. Hence, I wanted to expand on MacLennan's and Doyle's idea of how rivers make nations to a continental scale and include rivers in the United States and Mexico and, thus, understand how rivers could "make a continent." In addition, in *Rivers in History: Perspectives on Waterways in Europe and North America*, Christof Mauch and Thomas Zeller describe emerging historical studies of American rivers that focused on water politics and "water wars" in the south-west of the US and contrasted those with the more environmental and cultural aspects of studies of European rivers. The physical nature and human experience of Canadian rivers are, however, also sufficiently distinct from rivers in the US (see Chapter 1) that they need to be included for an understanding of the role of rivers in North American development.

The academic literature of environmental economics of rivers has been dominated by two principal themes concerning rivers and human development. The "reductionist" theme focuses on one-way river-human interactions – the "technological control [of rivers by humans] and social transformation [of humans by rivers]."[41] From another perspective, reductionist explorations can focus on the "ecological fate" (typically one of decline) of rivers based on human-based changes. An alternative theme, one to which this book adheres (see Chapter 12), involves embracing the human-river relationship as a "continuum"[42] of reciprocal interactions, where humans and rivers influence one another simultaneously and such influences must be studied together.

From a literary perspective, great rivers have also been described differently in terms of their relationships with humans. In his Afterword to Mark Twain's *Life on the Mississippi*, Leonard Kriegel of the City College of New York described the Mississippi River, with respect to its relationship with Huck Finn and his friend Jim the Black slave, the main characters in Twain's *Huckleberry Finn*, as "a god ... [acting as a] ... divine mediator between their [Huck and Jim's] desires and the desires of the civilized men and women on shore."[43] Kriegel concludes that Twain only came to understand the Mississippi when he realized that it "did not create itself to serve man."[44] Alternatively, Charles Darwin in his *A Naturalist's Voyage Around the World* (1889) described the "grandeur" of the Paraná River (in Argentina) as being "derived from reflecting how important a means of communication and commerce it forms between one nation and another; to what a distance it travels; and from how vast a territory it drains the great body of fresh water which flows past your feet."[45] Although I would reverse the order of the attributes that Darwin described for the Paraná in terms of their significance, each chapter that follows explores this theme – understanding the significance of each river in terms of both its physicality and its interactions with North Americans.

With a working definition of rivers, some rationale for their importance and interest, and how the ten rivers were selected in mind, the basic tenet of this book is that major rivers of North America have played a central role in the origins, functioning and persistence of human society, a role that is critically dependent on the geographic context: the geography of the drainage basins and how this influences flow, animal and plant biodiversity and other natural resources, transportation and human settlement patterns. By understanding the *geographic* context of rivers, I hope to demonstrate a *functional* link to the associated human experience. This central theme is like the recent spate of single-issue books that have emerged such as *Cod: A Biography of the Fish that Changed the World*, or *Salt: A World History* or *Empire of Cotton: A Global History*. These are books that explore what appear to be simple or one-dimensional themes (one species, a mineral or a commodity), but upon detailed examination reveal myriad complex, profound and broad impacts on humanity that have enhanced our appreciation of their role in human development. It is my hope that I can impart the same appreciation towards rivers. Associated with this theme is the idea that the central role of rivers and their geography in influencing North American human development is underappreciated, and that we ignore the centrality of rivers to our existence and prosperity at our peril.[46]

Consequently, the goals of this book are five-fold. First, I describe the "family tree" of great river systems and their encompassing landscape – watersheds of North America – and how the terrestrial landscape and its history have orchestrated the great flow patterns of North America. Second, I introduce ten great river systems and their physical geography. Third, I describe the major aspects of the human history of each river, particularly because the geographic history of each river extends over such great lengths of time that they can only really be comprehended within the context of the timing of the people who colonized each basin.[47] Fourth, I explore *one* central aspect of

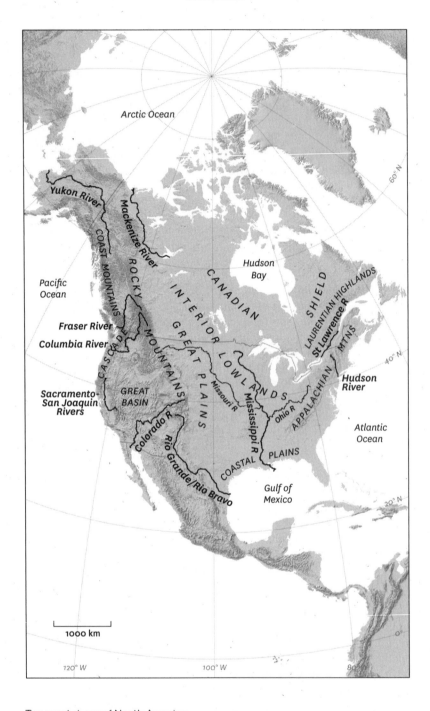

Ten great rivers of North America.

each great river with respect to its influence on human development or experience. Each river discussed, of course, has multiple stories to be told, but by selecting one key story and by replicating across rivers and highlighting different aspects, my goal is to illustrate the incredibly diverse ways that rivers impact humanity. Finally, and in sum, I strive to impart a greater understanding and, thus, appreciation for these ten systems, and of rivers more generally, specifically in terms of their myriad contributions to the history, experiences and the past and future quality of life for all North Americans. Ultimately, I hope this effort towards a greater appreciation will promote the restoration of the most degraded systems and the persistence of them all.

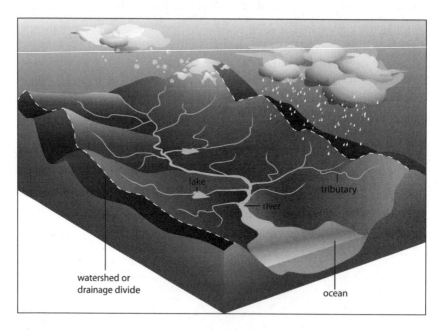

Basic structure of a river and its watershed and associated watershed divides.

— ONE —

The North American Family of Rivers

Rivers reflect a continent's history.

—ELLEN WOHL, *Disconnected Rivers*, 2004

He who hears the rippling of rivers in these degenerate days will not utterly despair.

—HENRY DAVID THOREAU, A Week on the Concord and Merrimack Rivers, 1849

Each of the great multitude of rivers of North America belongs to a great "family" of major watersheds or drainage basins – large areas of landscape within which each river and its tributaries are contained, and with which each river interacts via flooding, weathering, erosion, groundwater recharge, vegetation dynamics, nutrient cycling and geological changes.[1] Drainage basins are separated from each other by heights of land, or drainage divides, that direct water-flow in different directions (e.g., towards the Pacific Ocean vs. towards the Arctic Ocean).

Various classifications of major drainage basins have been proposed depending on whether they include information on biodiversity, climate or direction of flow. The simplest classification includes four major divisions that are based on the final destination of each set of rivers, usually a major ocean basin: Arctic, Pacific, Atlantic and Great Basin. The Great Basin of the southwest US is an internal (or 'endorheic') basin, meaning one that is 'closed' and does not include an outflow to some other body of water. A slightly more complex system is based on six principal hydrological (continental) divides and has seven basins: Arctic, Pacific, Hudson Bay, Laurentian, Atlantic, Gulf of Mexico and Great Basin. Still more complex systems incorporate information on aquatic biodiversity (the totality of diversity of populations, species and ecosystems), resulting in 176 "aquatic ecozones" in North America.[2] In the following, I adopt as the fundamental unit of organization of North America's great rivers the seven-basin model driven by the formation of six major hydrological divides: the Great (or Continental), Laurentian, Arctic, St. Lawrence, Eastern and Great Basin divides.[3]

How did these seven great conduits of water form? The major basins stem from the actions of three basic processes and their interactions: continental drift, orogeny (mountain building) and glaciation. North America began its most recent period as a continent largely physically independent from South America and Europe about 200 million ya when the continents, drifting atop the Earth's crust and mantle as part of great tectonic "plates," began moving towards their current positions, which they have occupied for about 65 million years (my). Consequently, North America achieved (for the time being anyway) its principal north–south axis and the variability in temperature and precipitation that this orientation generates. For much of the previous 140 my, North America had a more southern latitudinal distribution and was tilted in a more east–west orientation. The principal north–south orientation of North America accounts, in part, for the observation that virtually all our great rivers flow in a predominantly northerly or southerly direction.[4] Notwithstanding the principal north–south orientation of North America, the drainage systems obviously do not simply "sprawl out" across the continent like a glass of milk spilled on a flat table, and not all run solely along a north–south axis. Instead, the various continental divides, themselves the result of great upheavals

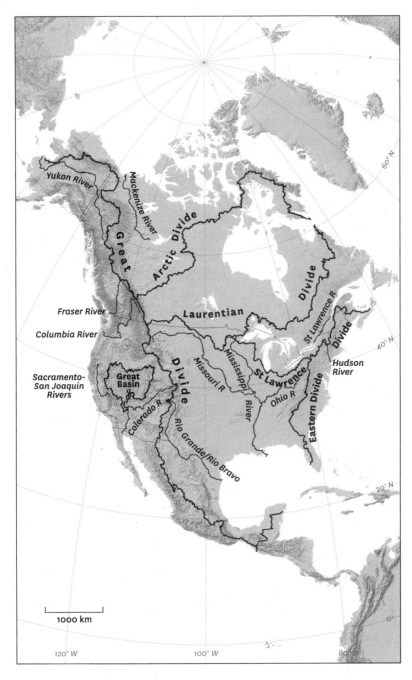

The six continental divides in North America: Great Divide, Great Basin Divide, Arctic Divide, Laurentian Divide, St. Lawrence Divide, and the Eastern Divide.

in the Earth's surface, organize the flow into the seven major basins described above. Essentially, these flows are organized within, as Philip King described in *Evolution of North America*, an "almost ideally symmetrical"[5] continent – the near encircling of the central Precambrian Shield and interior lowlands (the North American "craton") by mountain belts: the Appalachians to the southeast, the Cordilleran system in the west, and the Innuitian and East Greenland systems to the north.

The Appalachian Mountains are a chain of mountains extending from the island of Newfoundland southwest to central Alabama. The chain is composed of local mountain formations such as the Long Rand Mountains in Newfoundland, the White Mountains of New Hampshire, the Blue Ridge Mountains, the Alleghény Mountains and the Great Smoky Mountains. The Appalachians are the oldest mountains in North America; they began forming some 480 million ya when all the continents were drifting, colliding and merging into a series of supercontinents.[6] The uplifting of the Appalachian Mountains caused by these continental collisions and subsequent episodes of mountain building resulted in the splintering of the original flow of river systems into those that now flow northeast to the Atlantic (e.g., the St. Lawrence River system), southeast to the Atlantic coastal plain (e.g., the Hudson River), and south and southwest to the Gulf of Mexico (e.g., the Mississippi River and its eastern tributaries such as the Ohio River). Since the breakup of the most recent supercontinent known as Pangaea beginning about 200 million ya, the Appalachians have undergone substantial erosion such that their relief is much lower than in the past.

The second great mountain chain of North America is, of course, the Rocky Mountains, which form the core of a great western spine, the North American Cordillera, running from the north coast of Alaska through northwestern Canada to central Mexico. Although many of the rocks that comprise the core of the Rocky Mountains are up to one billion years old, the final stage of major uplifting, the Laramide Orogeny, which formed the current Rocky Mountains, began between 80 and 55 million ya,[7] and the current relief is of even more recent origin. The "Rockies" are, therefore, much younger than the Appalachian Mountains. The Rocky Mountains form the core of the western Continental Divide that separates rivers flowing to the Arctic and Atlantic oceans, and to Hudson Bay and the Gulf of Mexico, from those flowing to the Pacific Ocean, including the Bering Sea. The Rocky Mountains and associated mountain chains extend this "Cordilleran effect" north through Yukon and eastern Alaska, driving the Yukon River north and west to the Bering Sea, while the Mackenzie River flows to the Arctic Ocean. Farther south, the Cordilleran effect forces the Missouri (the great western tributary of the Mississippi River) and Rio Grande to the Gulf of Mexico while the Colorado River flows to the Pacific basin.

Two other continental divides have their origins in the Rocky Mountains. Snow Dome Mountain, near the British Columbia–Alberta border in the Columbia Icefields, forms the western apex of the divide between the Arctic, Pacific and Hudson Bay drainages. Farther south in Montana, Triple Divide Peak forms another "hydrological apex" that is the western origin of the boundary among the Pacific, Hudson Bay and Gulf of Mexico drainages. Triple Divide Peak also forms the western margin of the Laurentian Divide, which runs west to east and eventually north to the eastern margin of Ungava Bay in northern Quebec. The St. Lawrence Divide runs along the southern margins of the Great Lakes and the St. Lawrence River. The Eastern Divide (essentially the Appalachian Mountains) runs southwest and south from about midway along the St. Lawrence Divide to the end of the Florida Panhandle. Together, the latter three divides demarcate the divisions among the Hudson Bay, St. Lawrence and Atlantic coastal drainages.[8] The interaction among these mountain ranges and divides explains why that great funnel of the southern half of North America, the Mississippi River, encompasses such a vast watershed, draining 40% of the US from the east slopes of the Rocky Mountains (via the Missouri River) to the western slopes of the Appalachian Mountains (via the Ohio River), and why it flows to the Gulf of Mexico and not the Arctic or Atlantic oceans.[9]

The last major divide, the Great Basin Divide, comprises a circular set of high points formed by the intersection of a series of mountain ranges and plateaus: the Rocky Mountains to the east, the Sierra

Nevada Mountains to the southwest, the Columbia Plateau to the north and the Colorado Plateau to the southeast. This circular set of mountain peaks creates the Great Basin and isolates its interior-flowing, internal drainages (e.g., Great Salt Lake and its tributaries) from those flowing to the Pacific. Clearly, the Rocky Mountain system, and to a lesser extent the Appalachian Mountains, are major organizing forces of the North American river network.

Finally, there is glaciation – the collective historical and contemporary action of the great ice sheets which, in accordion-like fashion, advanced and receded repeatedly up to 20 times over all of Canada and much of the northern United States during the Pleistocene Epoch (~2.8 million ya to 12,000 ya). The ice sheets, up to 3 km thick in places, were composed of the Cordilleran Ice Sheet (covering an area from the Rocky Mountains to the Pacific), the Laurentide Ice Sheet (over areas to the east and north), the Innuitian Ice Sheet (the Canadian Arctic Archipelago) and the Greenland Ice Sheet.[10] These ice sheets were formed by cyclical changes in the Earth's climate and at their maximum extent collectively encompassed well over 10 million km^2 (the area of North America is about 24.8 million km^2).[11]

The repeated advance and retreat of these ice sheets had two principal physical impacts on North America's contemporary river systems. First, their growth and movements along the landscape, and the outflow of water from melting glaciers, helped to scour the large valleys through which today's rivers flow. Second, the melting ice provided, and still provides in many cases, most of the water source for the rivers themselves.[12] For instance, the St. Lawrence River system is the outlet of the Laurentian Great Lakes, which formed as the melting Laurentide Ice Sheet carved great basins into the land and these basins then filled with meltwater (see Chapter 11). The contemporary icefields in the Rocky Mountains of British Columbia provide the ultimate source for the mighty Columbia River as it twists and turns from Columbia Lake some 2000 km to the Pacific Ocean (see Chapter 5). Consequently, these great geographic and climatic processes have sculpted the landscape of North America and provided it with the water and kinetic energy that define the vast aquatic circulatory system of the world's third biggest continent.

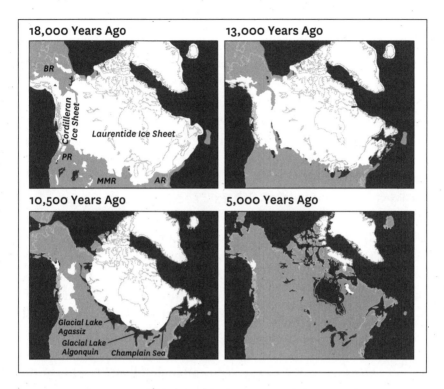

Four stages of Wisconsinan Glaciation from maximum extent (upper left) at 18,000 ya to full recession (bottom right) at 5,000 ya. Proglacial lakes are shown as dark grey along the margins of the ice sheets. BR = Bering Refuge, MMR = Missouri/Mississippi Refuge, PR = Pacific Refuge, AR = Atlantic Refuge. Adapted from Dyke (2004).

Of the seven basins and the ten rivers that will be explored, the Gulf of Mexico encompasses the largest area at 6.2 million km^2 (and the Great Basin the smallest at 0.542 million km^2). The Pacific Basin, however, spans the greatest range of latitude and the Great Basin and St. Lawrence the smallest. The basins with the highest human population densities over much of their area (i.e., > 25 people/km^2) are the Atlantic, St. Lawrence, Gulf of Mexico and southern portion of the Pacific basin; the Arctic, Hudson Bay and Great Basin are largely very sparsely inhabited (< 10 to < 1 people/km^2).[13]

How do the ten rivers to be explored – the Mackenzie, Yukon, Fraser, Columbia, Sacramento–San Joaquin, Colorado, Rio Grande,

Mississippi, Hudson and St. Lawrence – stack up in the "world table" of rivers? There are many ways to measure the 'greatness' of a river: its length, drainage area, volume of water at peak flows ("discharge"), fisheries yield, human population size supported etc. (see Appendix 1). Although river length would seem to be a relatively simple metric, as Hugh MacLennan noted in *Seven Rivers of Canada* it can be a bit more complicated at second glance. Depending on where one locates the source(s) of a river, or where it ends, determining its exact length can be tricky (where, for instance, does the Mississippi River, with its vast delta, end and the Gulf of Mexico begin?). Acknowledging (and delighting in) this uncertainty, most rankings have the Mississippi River (including its major western tributary the Missouri River) listed as the fourth longest river in the world at 6275 km (behind the Nile (6650 km), Amazon and Yangtze rivers). At number 13 in the world list is the Mackenzie River (extending to its western tributary, the Finlay River) at 4241 km. At 3185 km, the Yukon River just falls outside the top 20 (at 21!).

While the major river systems of North America are treated as a group in this book, they have had fundamentally distinct histories and influences on the socio-economic development of Canada and the US during these countries' foundational periods of the 18th and 19th centuries.[14] These distinctions may, in part, stem from the climatological gradient in North America. Canadian rivers are ensconced within temperate to Arctic climates, while those of the US (with the notable exception of Alaskan portion of the Yukon River) are typically found within temperate to subtropical climes. All major US ocean ports are ice-free year-round with easy access to markets in Europe, Asia and the West Indies, but until major exploration and population expansion west of the Mississippi River took off post-1840,[15] the US was largely hemmed in between the Appalachians and the Atlantic seaboard. On the other hand, by the mid-19th century, Canada had achieved some mastery of the St. Lawrence River, especially upstream of the rapids near Montreal, as a conduit to the vast central and western hinterland of Canada (and the US). By the 1850s, the US had developed major commercial centres like New York, Boston, Philadelphia and New Orleans, all with population sizes between 100,000 and 600,000 (by contrast, Toronto and Montreal, now Canada's two largest cities, both had fewer than 60,000 inhabitants in the early 1850s).[16] Furthermore, the US had developed great intellectual capital in personalities such as Benjamin Franklin and Thomas Jefferson, and writers such as Walt Whitman and Henry David Thoreau. Explorations of US rivers were, notwithstanding the westward explorations of Meriwether Lewis and William Clark in the US early in the 1800s, largely confined to the relatively short rivers of the Atlantic coastal plain. By contrast, the river exploration experience of Canadians at the time was described by Hugh MacLennan as more of an "epic"[17] one, with the likes of Louis Jolliet, Jacques Marquette, Alexander Mackenzie, Samuel Hearne, Peter Pond, David Thompson and Simon Fraser exploring the vast interior of the continent and huge rivers such as the Mackenzie, Mississippi, Fraser and Columbia, north, south and west of the Great Lakes made accessible by the fur trade routes branching west from the St. Lawrence River (see Chapter 11). In this sense, the Canadian experience of the great rivers of North America helped to define the great east–west continuum of nationhood – these rivers formed an early "highway of trade" and were critical to the foundational *concept* of a nascent Canada. The great rivers of the US portion of North America, by contrast, were more critical to the *expansion* of the US westward (see Chapters 5–7 on water rights and the "hydraulic West"[18]) expressed so vividly by President Thomas Jefferson's initiating the Lewis and Clark Corps of Discovery Expedition of 1804–1806. Thus, despite the many commonalities in the influences of geography on North American rivers, human–river interactions following European contact have fundamentally distinct origins in Canada and the US.

— TWO —

The Mackenzie River
Two World Views

Ladies and gentlemen, we are embarked on a consideration of the future of a great river valley and its people.

—JUSTICE THOMAS A. BERGER,
Mackenzie Valley Gas Pipeline Inquiry, 1975

Rivers are an obvious component of the natural world, and while this aspect of rivers is surely widely recognized, how we relate to rivers, and Nature in general, is much more variable across different cultures and societies. A fulsome discussion of how different cultures define and relate to Nature is well beyond the scope of this book, but suffice it to say, as Helaine Selin stated in *Nature Across Cultures: Views of Nature and the Environment in non-Western Cultures*, there are "no universals regarding what it means to live in your environment."[1] Fully recognizing that to describe Indigenous and Western views of Nature as opposite, monolithic belief systems is overly simplistic,[2] there is perhaps one fundamental aspect of human concepts of Nature that is often thought to differentiate North American (and other) Indigenous beliefs from Western beliefs: their respective degrees of perceived "difference" between humans and Nature.[3]

Many if not most North American Indigenous cultures view Nature as an "alive and self-conscious"[4] system that must be respected, and of which humans form but one of many interconnected parts. This belief thus connects directly with how many Indigenous Peoples define themselves: the landscape *is* their life, the two are simply inseparable,[5] and persistence of both requires respectful reciprocity. By contrast, the Western concept of Nature, while debated since the classical times of the Greeks, usually centres on some minimum level of "separateness" between humans and Nature. The separation grows with our increasing isolation from Nature in day-to-day activities (~80% of Canadians and Americans live in urban areas), driven largely by our ability to make a living that is not directly tied to the land or water, even though making that living may depend indirectly on exploitation of Nature.[6] This distinction has been recognized in perceptions of water and water development.[7] As a scientist and "student of Nature" as well as one who spends much time in the outdoors, I too typically think of Nature as something "separate." It is something to be studied, understood, appreciated and conserved, but I can't say that I truly feel part of a continuum with Nature, much as I may love it. Indigenous and non-Indigenous "world views" of Nature often come into conflict when urban-based economic activities focus on resource exploitation in non-urban areas, most notably when large infrastructure projects like oil and gas pipelines or hydroelectric dams are proposed for areas encompassing traditional Indigenous territories. The conflicts over the Keystone XL pipeline in the central plains of the US or the Site C hydroelectric dam in northeastern British Columbia are recent examples.

During European colonization of North America, what is now Canada and the US dealt with land use conflicts with Indigenous Peoples (Native Americans in the US) in distinct ways. In the US, treaties between the US government and what were considered "sovereign Indian nations" were created between about 1774 until 1832. Treaty-making continued for "domestic, dependent" Indian nations until 1871, when the US stopped recognizing the treaty process.[8]

In Canada, the British-held territories began making treaties with Indigenous Peoples in 1701, typically involving issues of peace and neutrality (re: conflicts with French colonies in North America).[9] The Royal Proclamation of 1763 formalized the treaty process and often dealt with land purchases from Indigenous Peoples in Canada in exchange for reserve lands and other benefits from the government ("the Crown"). In 1975, the modern era of treaty-making began in Canada and was precipitated by federal supreme court decisions that led to Canada's current "Comprehensive Land Claims" policy. Twenty-five such land claim agreements have been signed since 1975. (A separate process established in 1992 applies to British Columbia.) Such Indigenous Treaty Rights were recognized and affirmed in Canada's Constitution Act of 1982.[10]

The Mackenzie River Valley encompasses the traditional lands of three Indigenous groups broadly defined by language and culture: the Dene (a northern component of the Athapaskan language group, which includes Apache, Navajo and several other groups); various peoples whose names derive from "Inuit" (e.g., Inuvialuit, Inupiat, Cup'ik and Yup'ik); and the Métis (people of mixed ancestry between Indigenous and non-Indigenous Peoples).[11] The Dene and Métis are inhabitants of the inland portions of the subarctic forests while the Inuit occupy the coastal Arctic from the Bering Sea to Greenland. In 1968, fossil fuel reserves were discovered in Prudhoe Bay, off Alaska's North Slope.[12] Proposals to move these resources south to the coterminous US states emerged in the early 1970s and included crossing northern Canada and linking with Canadian fossil fuel reserves along the way, particularly within the Mackenzie River Delta – the very intersection of traditional lands of the Inuit and Dene. This resource movement corridor would then extend southeast through the Mackenzie River Valley to northern Alberta, from where existing linkages would transport the resources to the US. The impacts of these proposals on some of the least industrially developed lands of North America and the peoples that inhabited them were recognized as significant. This chapter recounts the story of the Mackenzie River, the conflicts about pipeline development in the region, and the pivotal role that these conflicts played in the evolution of Indigenous governance and the evolving relationship among Indigenous Peoples, non-Indigenous Canadians and the federal government of Canada.

The geography and origin of the Mackenzie River

THE MACKENZIE RIVER was named for Sir Alexander Mackenzie (1764–1820), a Scottish explorer who was the first European to travel the river to its mouth and the first European to cross North America north of Mexico (see below and Chapter 4). In the Slavey language it is known as "Deh-Cho" or "big river" and in Inuvialuktun, "Kuukpak," or "great river." The Mackenzie River proper flows some 1738 km[13] after emerging from the northwest corner of Great Slave Lake. It flows along the eastern margins of the northern Cordillera to the west and the exposed portions of the Precambrian Shield to the east, entering the Arctic Ocean at the Beaufort Sea. The massive Mackenzie River Delta encompasses a 12,000 km² network of more than 30,000 ponds and small lakes, as well as myriad side channels and wetlands. It is second in size in the Arctic only to Russia's Lena River Delta.

The Mackenzie River drainage, however, also includes some massive tributaries that could justifiably merit their own chapters and together constitute what Leslie Roberts called in *The Mackenzie* "the great sweep of a majestic canvas."[14] Including these tributaries, the Mackenzie River stretches to 4241 km, second only the Mississippi River in North America and the 13th longest in the world. First among its tributaries is the Peace River drainage, whose source (and that, ultimately, of the Mackenzie River itself) is Thutade Lake in the Omineca Mountains of north-central British Columbia. Here, the outlet creates the Finlay River, which flows northeast then south through the Rocky Mountain Trench about 400 km, where it meets the Parsnip River; their confluence forms the Peace River proper. The Parsnip River originates in Arctic Lake in the Rocky Mountains of central BC and flows along a northwest course some 240 km in almost direct opposition to the Finlay River's course. At the confluence of the Parsnip and Finlay rivers, the Peace River (now impounded as Williston Reservoir by the W.A.C. Bennett Dam) cuts *through* the

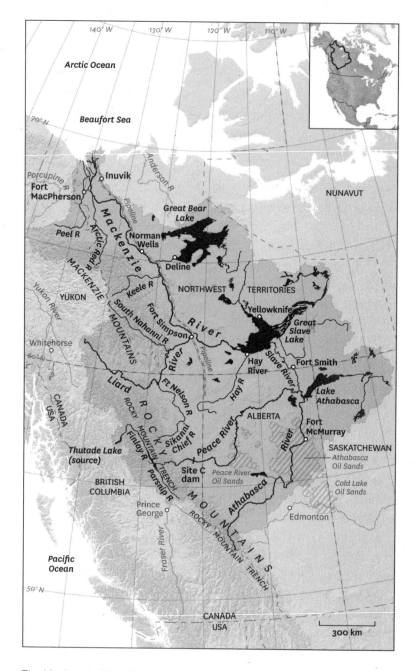

The Mackenzie River Basin including the Peace and Athabasca rivers. The route of the proposed Mackenzie Valley Pipeline of the 1970s is shown as a light grey/white segmented line and major oil sands deposits as hatched areas.

Rocky Mountains to flow east and northeast about 1300 km to the delta of Lake Athabasca. The delta of Lake Athabasca is also formed by the discharge of the second great Mackenzie tributary – the Athabasca River. From its source in the Columbia Icefields in the Rocky Mountains of western Alberta, 370 km southeast of Arctic Lake, the Athabasca River flows 1231 km northeast to Lake Athabasca. Here, the Peace and Athabasca rivers merge to form the Peace-Athabasca Delta at the western end of Lake Athabasca, from which emerges the 415 km long Slave River. The Slave River then flows almost due north to Great Slave Lake, Northwest Territories, from whose westernmost arm issues the Mackenzie River proper. About 300 km downstream from Great Slave Lake, the Liard River joins the Mackenzie River as its largest mainstem tributary. The Liard River flows 1115 km from its source in southeastern Yukon and has a drainage area only about 10% smaller than that of the Peace River. Altogether, the drainage basin of the Mackenzie River is 1,805,000 km², almost 20% of Canada's area and 92% of the size of Mexico, ranking second (to the Mississippi River) in North America and 11th worldwide. The Mackenzie River's average discharge is 10,300 m³/s which is third in North America (behind the St. Lawrence and Mississippi rivers) and 27th worldwide. Between 400,000 and 450,000 people live within the Mackenzie River basin in three Canadian provinces (British Columbia, Alberta, Saskatchewan) and two territories (Northwest Territories and Yukon).[15]

The Mackenzie River is unique among the roster of great North American rivers. Despite its massive size, it is perhaps the least well known by most North Americans, a feature first commented upon in Leslie Roberts' *The Mackenzie* (1949) and which has probably changed little in the ensuing 72 years. The relative anonymity of the Mackenzie River is likely a result of its location in the Canadian subarctic and Arctic and because it flows "down North,"[16] *away* from major population centres, to the Arctic Ocean. Owing to the sparse population in the basin, especially along the mainstem, the Mackenzie River, and perhaps the Yukon River, are the great rivers of North America that have maintained the least altered relationship with their original human inhabitants.

In addition to its large size, the Mackenzie River is notable for its anomalous course. First, it is the only river system in North America that cuts completely through the Rocky Mountains, via the Peace River, in a west to east direction (one of its tributaries, the Liard River to the north, also cuts eastward, but through the gap between the Yukon Ranges and the northern terminus of the Rocky Mountains). Second, from the Saskatchewan River of the Canadian central plains south to the Rio Grande, rivers that drain the eastern margin of the Cordillera generally flow eastward or southeast to the Gulf of Mexico (the Rio Grande), to the Mississippi River or to Hudson Bay (the Saskatchewan River). By contrast, although the Mackenzie River system (via the Peace, Liard and Athabasca rivers) begins in a generally eastward flow, it deviates sharply to the north and west with the beginning of the Slave River and the Mackenzie River mainstem. This "against the grain" flow pattern suggests that some fundamentally different process impacted the Mackenzie River compared to the other major rivers of the eastern Cordillera. In fact, and despite its vastness, the Mackenzie River in its current form is a young river; its final flow pattern was not established until after the final wasting away of the Wisconsinan glaciers a mere 10,000 ya.

Since earlier in the mid-late Cretaceous to the early Paleogene (from about 100–70 million ya) the course of much of the current Mackenzie River lay beneath one of the great inland epicontinental seas, the Western Interior Seaway, which sundered North America into a series of massive islands.[17] The great eastern-flowing Cordilleran rivers began to form when the Laramide Orogeny drove the major uplift of the Rocky Mountains and other Cordilleran ranges about 80 million ya, hence draining the Western Interior Seaway. Eroded rock from mountain building and river drainage formed the gentle piedmont slopes that extended from the base of the emergent mountains to the Canadian Shield and created eastward-flowing drainages such as the Saskatchewan, Missouri and Arkansas rivers. The eastward-flowing Peace and Liard river drainages had already become established through the Rocky Mountain and Tintina trenches. These trenches, essentially wide valleys between mountain ranges, began to form during geologic faulting – the creation of cracks in the Earth's surface rocks and resultant displacement of rocks on either side of a fault. These faults occurred after the uplift of the Columbia and Cassiar Mountains, but before the main period of Rocky Mountain uplift that took place to the east and south of these other ranges.[18] The early Peace River must, therefore, have been of sufficient volume to erode through the Rocky Mountains as they formed. Thus, from about the Paleogene (65 million ya) to the end of the Pleistocene (10,000 ya), the early Peace and Liard rivers were components of a series of rivers that merged into a super, Atlantic-bound system known as the paleo "Bell River" that flowed eastward and emptied into Hudson Strait in the northeast Atlantic. This system included primordial regions of the Mackenzie River mainstem that were located about 100–200 km upstream from the present-day delta and were formed by flows originating from western highland areas.[19] At the same time, but farther to the north, what is now the Peel River (Mackenzie River drainage) and Porcupine River (Yukon River drainage) flowed in a northeasterly direction to the Arctic Ocean somewhere between the present-day Anderson River and the Mackenzie River deltas. The drainage divide between these paleo-Arctic (Peel/Porcupine) and Atlantic (Bell River) drainages was such that both these river systems flowed *across* the present course of the Mackenzie River, with most of the area drained by the current Mackenzie River flowing to the Atlantic. Clearly, then, some major geological event must have disrupted these flows to establish the current integrated Mackenzie River system flowing to the Arctic.

As will be shown in several other chapters, this disruption was provided by the repeated advances and retreats of the Pleistocene glaciers and, in the case of the Mackenzie River, the most recent Wisconsinan glaciation (see Chapter 1). The Laurentide Ice Sheet was at its maximum extent about 25,000–30,000 ya and extended to meet the Cordilleran Ice Sheet along the eastern margins of the current Mackenzie River valley with a lobe of ice extending onto the current Mackenzie River Delta (the Mackenzie Ice Lobe). The advance of the Laurentide Ice Sheet to the south and west, acting like a giant bulldozer, scoured massive amounts of sediments and thus removed the gently sloping divide between the pre-existing Arctic and Atlantic paleo-drainages.

The advance of the ice sheet also cut off the flow of the Porcupine River east to the Arctic basin and backed it up to the Yukon River. The flow of the Porcupine River into the Yukon River was established by about 21,000 ya following erosion of surrounding lands and glacial retreat. By about 13,000 ya, water streaming from melting and retreating glaciers produced extensive flows to the Mackenzie River Delta and to the current Peel and Anderson rivers. Continuing glacial recession to the southeast by 11,500 ya had begun to establish the mainstem Mackenzie River, which drained glacial lakes Mackenzie and Peace. The former would shrink to form an enlarged mainstem Mackenzie River by 11,000 ya. Glacial Lake McConnell, which encompassed contemporary Great Bear Lake and much of Great Slave Lake, formed along the retreating margin of the Laurentide Ice Sheet and by 10,000 ya had grown to be the second largest North American proglacial lake at 215,000 km² (second only to Glacial Lake Agassiz and almost 90% of the area of all our Laurentian Great Lakes). The expansion of Glacial Lake McConnell to the south captured the drainage of Glacial Lake Peace and hence the entire Peace River drainage (which until then flowed to the Mississippi/Missouri drainage). By about 8,500 ya ice recession and land rebound had proceeded sufficiently to separate Lake McConnell into the present-day Great Bear Lake, Great Slave Lake and Lake Athabasca.[20] The pattern of Wisconsinan ice advance and retreat, therefore, had significant implications not only for establishing the present-day course of the Mackenzie River north to the Arctic Ocean but also for altering the supply of fresh water among the Pacific, Arctic and Atlantic oceans' basins with impacts on marine circulation patterns, productivity and climate.[21]

Early human history of the Mackenzie River basin

ICE-FREE AREAS that existed marginal to, or between, the Pleistocene ice sheets are called glacial refugia. Most of these refugia (see map, p.21) existed south of the Cordilleran and Laurentide ice sheets in North America, but at least one major refuge was in northwestern Canada and Alaska. Most of the Yukon River valley, upstream to near Dawson City, Yukon, remained unglaciated throughout the

Pleistocene and even into the older Pliocene glaciations. This unglaciated river valley was part of a much larger refuge known as "Beringia" and included ice-free areas in Siberia and the Bering Land Bridge that connected North America and northeastern Siberia. During the glacial advances, the Bering Sea did not exist, because sea levels dropped by up to 200 m (today, the Bering Sea is mostly less than 50 m deep), so that there was a broad expanse of ice-free land that extended from central Yukon and central Alaska, west to the Chukotka and Kamchatkan peninsulas in Russia. During these glacial advances, the Yukon River Valley was isolated from the rest of North America by the coalescence of the Cordilleran and Laurentide ice sheets. By contrast, connections for terrestrial and freshwater organisms were much more open between the lower to middle Yukon River Valley and Siberia via the Bering Land Bridge.

Movement of animals from Asia to North America is known to have occurred as far back as 55 million ya.[22] The consensus among those who have studied the patterns of timing of human colonization of the New World is that native Amerindians stem from colonists who entered North America from northwest Asia, somewhere east of the Yenisei River in central Russia. The first record of human habitation in eastern Siberia has been estimated at 31,000 ya from finds of stone and animal bone tools.[23] The human prehistory of the Mackenzie River basin involved a complex series of migrations and back-migrations from unglaciated portions of the Yukon River valley and the central North American plains. Given its proximity to ice-free areas of the Yukon River valley, colonization of the Mackenzie River area is at the core of the debates about the number and exact route(s) of the initial human invasion of northwestern North America from northeastern Siberia. The earliest finds of human artifacts (stone microblades and fluted arrow points) in central Alaska suggested that human colonization of eastern portions of North American Beringia from northeast Asia occurred postglacially and no earlier than 13,000–14,000 ya. New discoveries in northwestern Arctic Russia dated to 32,000 ya suggest, however, that parts of northwestern Beringia were occupied *before* the end of the last glacial maximum. Consequently, the most recent origin of North American Indigenous

Peoples may stem from an "out of Beringia" model rather than an "out of Asia" hypothesis.[24] This Beringian-origin hypothesis is supported by genetic, modelling and paleo-ecological data, although evidence of human fossil remains, or proxy archaeological objects dated to more than 13,000 cal ya, remain rare or controversial. Regardless, the current consensus appears to be that the first humans crossed the Bering Land Bridge into North America as they hunted colonizing large mammals perhaps as early as about 16,500 cal ya and moved eastward until they became blocked by ice. Once the ice began retreating (by about 14,000–12,000 cal ya), humans could disperse farther east and south either (or both) along the coast or via the ice-free corridor emerging between the receding Laurentide and Cordilleran ice sheets, perhaps including the nascent Mackenzie River valley. While archaeological finds (e.g., ~15,350 cal ya in Monte Verde, Chile, to 26,500 cal ya in Chiquihuite Cave, Mexico[25]) suggest possible earlier colonization, perhaps via the Pacific coast, the first peoples of the arctic and subarctic lands are considered the result of more recent expansions east and south from Beringia.[26]

The number of migrations into North America has been another source of debate among archaeologists, linguists and geneticists. Within the Mackenzie River basin, the consensus appears to be that today's prevalent Inuit (previously referred to as "Eskimos" and part of the Aleut-Yupik-Inuit language groups) and Dene were likely derived from more recent and separate migrations from Beringia than earlier groups that moved farther south.[27] Other paleo-archaeological finds in central Alaska that have affinities with North American Plains Paleoindian traditions, but not to those of inhabitants of northeast Asia, suggest at least some movement of earlier migrants to North America *back* to northeastern portions of North American Beringia and adjacent areas between 11,700 and 12,900 ya. Consequently, it is likely that the Mackenzie River basin was subject to colonization from two directions, one from eastern Alaska and another by the back-migration of Paleoindians from central North America to the subarctic as the corridor between the Cordilleran and Laurentide ice sheets emerged postglacially. Before the end of the last glacial maximum, the coalesced ice sheets are considered to have been a barrier to colonization of interior North America, including the Mackenzie River valley.[28] Consistent with this idea is the observation of Paleoindian archaeological finds in Charlie Lake Cave, near present-day Fort St. John, BC, on the Peace River, dated to ~11,000 ya. Other artifacts found at Fisherman Lake near the Liard River 216 km southwest of the Liard-Mackenzie confluence have been estimated to be between 7,000 and 8,000 years old.[29] Artifacts found in the Anderson Plain area of the lower Mackenzie River suggest that this area was occupied by at least 5,000 ya, and those found at the Franklin Tanks deposit at the outlet of Great Bear Lake may be as old as 6,500–7,500 ya.[30] Despite this antiquity, the oldest site of continuous settlement dates to about 1,350 ya at the Gwich'in community of Tsiigehtchic.[31] Today the Dene are represented in the Mackenzie basin by at least 11 different Indigenous Peoples (e.g., Gwich'in, Slavey, Beaver, Western Cree).

The lower Mackenzie River Delta on the Arctic coast became ice free between 13,000 and 11,500 ya,[32] and while some groups may have occupied the area from the west as long ago as 5,000 ya, the ancestors of today's occupants, the Inuit, did not enter the region until about 1,000 ya.[33] The Inuit are derived from the Thule culture that arose some 2,000 ya in the eastern Bering Sea area and colonized the western North American Arctic about 1,500 ya, bringing with them a novel whale-hunting maritime tradition. Around 1,000–700 ya, the Thule embarked on a rapid eastward expansion throughout the Arctic (including the Mackenzie River Delta area) as far as eastern Greenland, the exact reasons for which are unclear.[34] Today, the Inuit of the lower Mackenzie River valley are one of eight historically recognized Inuit groups – the Western Arctic Inuit. The Inuit of this area refer to themselves as Inuvialuit.[35]

Perhaps more than any other of the great rivers of this book, the Mackenzie River basin is singularly associated with the post-Contact fur trade. The Mackenzie River became known to Europeans owing to the increasing thirst for furs as regions around the Laurentian Great Lakes and Mississippi River basin became depleted. The first European to explore the Mackenzie River to any extent was Peter Pond (1739–1807), described as a "legend" of Canadian history.[36] Pond was an American fur trader, cartographer and one of the founders of the North West Company, one of two great fur trading companies, the other being the Hudson's Bay Company, that were engaged in a fierce commercial rivalry between 1789 and 1821. At first glance, Pond might seem ill-suited to have made profound contributions to understanding the great northwest; he was initially trained as a shoemaker and hailed from a completely different environment – coastal Connecticut – but contribute he did. In seeking new opportunities west of the Great Lakes, Pond entered the Athabasca region in 1778. Based on his travels and interactions with Indigenous Peoples, Pond produced the first map of the area that laid out the basic relationships among the major rivers and Great Bear Lake, Great Slave Lake, Lake Athabasca, the Rocky Mountains, Hudson Bay and the Arctic Ocean. Pond was, therefore, the first European to formally conceptualize a great drainage basin flowing to the Arctic Ocean that might provide a coveted Northwest Passage to the Pacific Ocean and, eventually, the Orient.[37]

A keen observer of Pond's map was Alexander Mackenzie (1764–1820), a Scot from the island of Lewis in the Hebrides. Hardship steeled Mackenzie at an early age. When he was 10, his family moved to New York City owing to impending economic depression in Scotland. Then, the fear of impacts of the American Revolutionary War motivated a move to Montreal at 14.[38] A year later, Mackenzie was engaged as a clerk with Finlay, Gregory and Company, a fur-trading enterprise in Montreal. Mackenzie is best known for making the first transcontinental voyage across North America north of Mexico. Between 1792 and 1793 he travelled from Montreal to Fort Chipewyan on Lake Athabasca, up the Peace River and crossed the Continental Divide to the upper Fraser River, then moved through the Coast Mountains to the Bella Coola River and the Pacific Ocean. Four years before beginning this epic voyage, however, Mackenzie joined the North West Company and was sent to learn from and eventually replace Peter Pond in the Athabasca country. Ostensibly, his mission was to find a water route to the Pacific in efforts to reduce the costs of transport of furs and trade goods between Britain and the Canadian fur heartland. Working on information from Indigenous Peoples,

Mackenzie entered the outlet of Great Slave Lake at the end of June 1789 and began his descent of the Mackenzie River. With the aid of Chipewyan guides and translators, Mackenzie averaged almost 160 km per day and interacted with many local peoples such as Slavey, Hare and Dogrib who confirmed that he would eventually reach the sea. Indeed, two weeks after leaving Great Slave Lake, Mackenzie's crew detected tides and reached the Arctic Ocean. Although Mackenzie had been the first European to travel the "Highway to the Top of the World,"[39] it did not lead to the Pacific Ocean, a result that is thought to have led to his attaching the moniker "River of Disappointment"[40] to the great system that now bears his name.[41] With the short Arctic summer closing in fast, Mackenzie simply reversed his path and was back at Fort Chipewyan by September 12, 1789, after 102 days' travel to the Arctic Ocean and back.

In the ensuing years, the North West Company and Hudson's Bay Company battled for supremacy in the fur trade in the Athabasca country, including the Mackenzie River, where many trading posts were established along the river or its tributaries such as Fort Simpson, Fort Good Hope, Fort Norman, Fort Providence and Fort McPherson. Eventually, the two companies merged in 1821 and the surviving Hudson's Bay Company continued to exercise its monopoly in the Athabasca country, part of the larger "North-Western Territory," until the latter (and "Rupert's Land" to the east and southeast) was transferred from Britain's control to the Dominion of Canada in 1870. The heart of the Mackenzie River basin was thus contained within the new administrative District of Mackenzie. Eventually the new North-West Territories was whittled away, reconfigured (contributing to all or parts of Yukon, Alberta, Saskatchewan and British Columbia) and eventually renamed as the Northwest Territories in 1906.[42] Throughout this time and until 1954, the Mackenzie area, and the Northwest Territories (and Yukon) in general, was governed by what James K. Smith recounted in *The Mackenzie River: Yesterday's Fur Frontier, Tomorrow's Energy Battleground* as "an almost continuous state of absence of mind."[43] Rather, an "unholy trinity"[44] comprising the Anglican and Catholic churches, the Royal Canadian Mounted Police and the Hudson's Bay Company held sway over the region, about one-third of Canada's land area, until the federal government eventually created the Department of Northern Affairs and National Resources (today's Crown-Indigenous Relations and Northern Affairs Canada) in 1954. The District of Mackenzie as an administrative unit ceased to exist in 1999, but the Mackenzie River valley proper contributes most of the population of the Northwest Territories, which today is about 45,000 people. This, along with Nunavut (created in 1999 and part of which at one time constituted the eastern half of a larger Northwest Territories), are the only two jurisdictions in Canada where Indigenous Peoples constitute the majority (~50.4 and 85.8%, respectively; by comparison Alaska has the highest proportion of Native Americans by state, 14.8%).[45]

A problematic geological legacy:
Mackenzie River Valley hydrocarbons

TWO YEARS BEFORE Alexander Mackenzie entered the eponymous river at the outlet of Great Slave Lake, he noted a phenomenon whose legacy lasts to this very day. While making his way up the Athabasca River 38 km from its confluence with the Clearwater River, he noticed what he referred to as "some bitumenous fountains ... in a fluid state."[46] Mackenzie remarked on the long-known utility of this substance, when mixed with resin from spruce trees, for gumming canoes. He also noted that "in a heated state, it emits a smell like that of sea coal" and "the banks of the river, which are there very elevated, discover veins of the same bitumenous quality."[47] What Mackenzie saw, of course, was what is now commonly referred to as "bitumen," a heavy, black and viscous form of petroleum that can also occur in a semi-solid state. Bitumen, also known as asphalt, has common usage as the "glue" that, when combined with gravel aggregate, is used to make "blacktop" for highways. Its use as a sticky substance useful in construction has been known since the ancients, and the seepages that Mackenzie noted are like the La Brea Tar Pits of California and a 300 ha[48] "lake" of bitumen in Trinidad and Tobago ("Pitch Lake"). Through much of the lower Athabasca River valley, bitumen is mixed in with sand, clay and water to form one of three major deposits in Canada, the "oil sands," encompassing about 142,000 km² in central Alberta and a small portion of adjacent Saskatchewan.[49] The Athabasca oil sands represent the world's third largest source of proven reserves of recoverable petroleum (an estimated 171 billion barrels), behind only those found in Venezuela and Saudi Arabia.[50]

The Mackenzie River basin contains two other notable deposits of conventional and non-conventional (e.g., gas hydrates or crystalline deposits of water that contain gas molecules) fossil fuel. The potential for extensive hydrocarbon resources in different parts of the basin was suspected by the Canadian government since at least the 1880s.[51] The first was discovered in 1920 when workers drilling near oil seepages first noted in 1911 at Norman Wells, on the banks of the main river 150 km south of the Arctic Circle, discovered a major field. The oil field was developed in the 1940s as a response to war-fuelled demand for energy products.[52] Subsequent expansions raised production to a peak as high as 34,000 barrels/day in the early 1990s; today it is about 7,500 barrels/day.[53] The second involves the major oil and natural gas fields in the Beaufort Sea–Mackenzie River Delta Basin (BMB). The BMB resources are distributed mostly (two-thirds) within the Beaufort Sea itself and the remainder inland to the head of the delta; deltaic regions are typically rich in petroleum resources.[54] These petroleum and gas resources are a geological legacy of the massive deposition of organic materials associated with Cretaceous Western Interior Seaway that extended from the Gulf of Mexico to the Arctic between 65 and 145 million ya, and also to earlier events dating to the Devonian.[55]

In the BMB, favourable geological conditions resulted in the first wells being drilled in the early 1960s, with activity picking up after the oil discovery in adjacent Prudhoe Bay, Alaska, in 1968.[56] Within the context of the Middle East oil crises of the 1970s, initial interest was in conventional oil resources, and at least 263 wells have been drilled in the area, revealing as much as 245,229,430 m³ (1.54 billion barrels) of recoverable oil and 349,314,800 m³ of conventional natural gas.[57] Such massive potential prompted discussions to build one or more pipelines to transport Alaskan oil and gas east to the

Mackenzie Delta to join with Canadian sources and transport the accumulated resources along the Mackenzie River valley to northern Alberta and eventually to southern markets. One proposal, the Canadian Arctic Gas Pipeline, put forth by a consortium of 27 US and Canadian companies, was to be more than 4000 km long and cost C$8 billion (~$54 billion in 2021 dollars).[58] A second proposal, the Foothills Pipeline, would have originated in the delta and run south to northern Alberta to service Canadian markets only.[59] As James K. Smith recounted in *The Mackenzie River*, "The key to a northern pipeline is land, land on which live Inuit – with whom Ottawa has never made a treaty –, Dene, and Métis."[60] Obviously, either of these proposals would have massive implications for the physical environment and the social, cultural and economic lives of Indigenous Peoples (Inuit, Dene and Métis), who had several unresolved treaty disputes and land claims, and other inhabitants of the North. The project was the largest development in North American history, dwarfing the cost and impact of other projects such as the St. Lawrence Seaway, which when started in the 1950s was described as the "greatest construction show on Earth" (see Chapter 11).[61] This reality, coupled with the fluid situation with respect to historical treaties and emergent land claims by Indigenous Peoples, prompted the Canadian government to initiate a commission of inquiry – the Berger Commission (or Inquiry) – in 1974 to study the feasibility and potential impacts of what became known as the Mackenzie Valley Pipeline.[62] The inquiry was led by British Columbia Supreme Court Justice Thomas Berger, a former provincial and federal politician.

The Berger Inquiry:
A landmark consultation process for a river and its people

THE HISTORY of Canadian and US governments' formal negotiations and consultations with Indigenous Peoples regarding their rights with respect to the land is littered with examples of misunderstanding, suspicion, unfulfilled promises, manipulation and outright failure.[63] The Berger Inquiry, however, stands in marked contrast to such mediocre performance. Although not without some criticisms regarding the whole process and on specifics of the report,[64] it was widely hailed as an "innovative" approach to government decision-making.[65] Berger's 1977 report, *Northern Frontier, Northern Homeland: The Report of the Mackenzie Valley Pipeline Inquiry*, has been described as a "blockbuster," "visionary," "ahead of its time," "transformative" and an "international classic on indigenous-white relations."[66] The mandate of the inquiry was to investigate the environmental, social and economic impacts of a natural gas pipeline on the Mackenzie River valley.[67] Before formal hearings eventually started in the late winter of 1975, Berger set the tone for the inquiry; he spent the previous summer with his wife and family travelling 16,000 km through the valley by land, water and air visiting myriad communities talking and *listening* to people. Sometimes that listening included long pauses, sipping tea while "just looking at the river."[68] One of the critical lessons learned by Berger during that summer was that listening to Indigenous Peoples, and individuals, of the Mackenzie Valley would not be successful without patient, two-way conversations,[69] which may include long periods of reflection, across the fullest range of communities as possible. One of the signature features of the Berger Inquiry was revealed in his comment that "I will not diminish anyone's right to be heard" and that the inquiry would not be rushed despite the federal government's position that it might not wait for the end of the inquiry "for us to take action."[70] In fact, and much to the government's chagrin, Berger delayed beginning the inquiry for a year to allow one his counsels, University of British Columbia professor Michael Jackson and his family, to live in a Dene village and help organize community hearings to gather local perspective for the hearings, and to give all participants time to prepare materials. To further implement his philosophy, instead of restricting hearings to relatively large centres like Yellowknife or Inuvik, NT, or Whitehorse, YT, Berger took his inquiry and small group of key staff throughout the valley travelling widely to innumerable small communities. There is a wonderful and telling photograph on the back of Martin O'Malley's *The Past and Future Land. An Account of the Berger Inquiry into the Mackenzie Valley Pipeline*. In it, Justice Berger sits, alone, at a small, simple table

Justice Thomas Berger (seated at table) conducting a community meeting at Nahanni Butte, Northwest Territories.

in front of a small log cabin with the majestic Selwyn Mountains in the background. In front of him are 20 or so people from Nahanni Butte, at the confluence of the Nahanni and Mackenzie rivers, giving or listening to testimony. This would be no typical judicial inquiry!

Indeed, the inquiry was remarkable in several ways. First, as described above, it travelled *to* the people, visiting over 30 communities in the North, and provided simultaneous translation so that as many people as possible could be heard. The inquiry was also the first of its kind to fund the gathering and hearing of evidence from environmental and Indigenous groups about impacts of the proposed pipeline.[71] The inquiry also travelled to major southern cities (Vancouver, Winnipeg, Montreal, Toronto, Halifax) to promote the education of as broad a spectrum of people as possible about the North and the potential impacts of a huge energy corridor. The inquiry also had a strong media presence *and* strategy devised by a communications officer. Further, the Canadian Broadcasting Corporation created an Aboriginal news team that broadcast nightly summaries in six languages,[72] and a prominent *Globe and Mail* journalist, Martin O'Malley, followed the inquiry closely, which formed the foundation of his book.[73] The inquiry was comprehensive in that it considered the impacts of an "energy corridor," encompassing infrastructure associated with the pipeline such as roads, a possible oil pipeline, spur gas pipelines, compressor stations, gas refrigeration plants, power plants and other facilities, not just the gas pipeline itself (described rather optimistically by one energy proponent as "a thread running across a football field"!).[74] It resulted in a multi-volume, almost 50,000-page report, summarizing 1,717 witness statements, released in two parts in the summer and autumn of 1977. It became a bestseller with over 10,000 copies circulated in the first week alone.[75]

In the end, the Berger Inquiry's mandate did not include making an explicit recommendation for or against the general *idea* of a pipeline in the Mackenzie Valley, but its conclusions were not encouraging to proponents of an energy corridor or the specific routes proposed. The inquiry concluded that a pipeline would likely be too disruptive both to the environments of Mackenzie River Delta and the adjacent North Slope of the Yukon, particularly if the gas pipeline encouraged a subsequent oil pipeline, but also that south of these areas environmental impacts would be minimal and that any impacts there could likely be mitigated.[76] Economically, the inquiry concluded that positive impacts of a development, wage-based economy *for the North* would be minimal and short-term at best, and likely damaging to the existing land-based economy. Crucially, the inquiry concluded that negative impacts of *not* building the pipeline would be insignificant. Probably most impactful were Berger's conclusions about the social impacts of a Mackenzie Valley pipeline, which he described as likely to "not only be serious – they will be devastating."[77] In this way, the inquiry acted to "humanize"[78] the impacts of a pipeline. The inquiry's report also concluded that Indigenous culture and connection with the land were not taken seriously enough and that any development must include Indigenous Peoples' desires regarding if, and how, it should proceed. In the contemporary parlance of "consultation," Berger's inquiry indicated that a disconnect existed between the input from proponents on if and how any development should proceed and that of local peoples. This critical limitation, when coupled with several land claims under negotiation with the federal government, led to the key recommendation of the inquiry – that there should be a ten-year moratorium on any potential pipeline development until Indigenous land claims were settled and appropriate wildlife conservation areas were created (e.g., the current Ivvavik National Park on Yukon's North Slope).[79] Two changes of the federal government in rapid succession contributed to no formal actions being taken by these governments to further promote development. Thomas Berger himself suggested that Prime Minister Trudeau's camping trip to the Yukon's North Slope, at Berger's urging, in 1977, may have influenced government priorities for action.[80] This and less favourable market conditions for natural gas and oil acted to shelve the proposal for the past 44 years.[81]

The Mackenzie River, its water, land and people have thus had a profound impact on the North and its people, and in environmental assessment more generally. First and foremost, the inquiry resulted in the protection of the Yukon North Slope and the rejection of the idea of a pipeline from Alaska to Canada, while establishing the national and international profile of the region as a key wildlife area. A total of five national and territorial parks and four bird sanctuaries now dot the region. Second, the inquiry reinvigorated the land claims process by recommending no pipeline in the valley proper until these claims were settled. This eventually led to the Inuvialuit Final Agreement with the federal and territorial governments (1984), covering the Beaufort Sea, Mackenzie River Delta, Yukon North Slope, northwestern Northwest Territories and the islands of the western Canadian Arctic. The Gwich'in Comprehensive Land Claim Agreement followed in 1992 and covers a T-shaped area from Aklavick and Inuvik, NT, south for about 320 km to an area west of the Mackenzie River to the Yukon–NT border.[82] Next came the Sahtu,

Dene and Métis Comprehensive Land Claim Agreement (1994) to the south and east, and the Tlicho Agreement (2005) bordering it to the east in the central NT. Together, these land claims recognized ownership of some 193,509 km^2 by Indigenous groups of the Mackenzie River area, provided cash payments, protection of traditional ways of life, resource development opportunities, co-management of lands and resources, participation in the resource use decision-making process and, in many cases, provision of self-government rights.[83] While some aspects of these agreements are not without operational flaws,[84] more than 100 land claims are presently in various stages of negotiation across Canada and are a vital component of the Canadian government's commitment to reconciling pre-existing Indigenous land rights with the Crown's assertion of sovereignty – a key societal issue facing Canada.[85]

While the first land claim, the James Bay and Northern Quebec Agreement (1975), predated the Mackenzie River area claims by at least nine years, the Berger Inquiry, as reflected in its title *Northern Frontier, Northern Homeland,* confronted decision-makers and other Canadians with the fundamental duality of the North; it represents both a frontier with innumerable development opportunities *and,* for thousands of years, a homeland for people who have the right to have a say in whether, and how, such development proceeds. Conflicting visions of resource development in the Mackenzie River valley exposed during the inquiry acted as a "prism"[86] to help Canadian society better understand the North as a complex social environment, and not just a storehouse of resources, and helped to frame conflicting views on land use in terms of Indigenous land rights.[87] In 1982, these rights were enshrined in section 35(1) of the Canadian Constitution Act, which states that "Aboriginal rights are recognized and affirmed." While it would take subsequent court decisions to define the specifics of these rights, the principle was a major legacy of the Berger Inquiry that left "an indelible mark on Canadian history."[88]

The expression "to gain social licence" in order for contemporary resource development proposals to proceed (e.g., the currently contentious Trans Mountain Pipeline expansion in British Columbia and Alberta) stems in no small part from the "gold standard"[89] of consultation set by the Berger Inquiry, a model employed in subsequent territory-wide consultations via the Northwest Territories Constitutional Alliance of the 1980s on developing a constitution for the territory. This social licence also applies to environmental concerns, and the Berger Inquiry was the first to seek and provide funding for environmental groups, because Berger considered "equivalence of funding in an adversarial process"[90] critical to the inquiry being fair and, ultimately, its report being accepted by as broad a range of society as possible, particularly in the context of growing societal awareness of environmental issues.[91] The Berger Inquiry also recognized the value of Indigenous traditional ecological knowledge (TEK, as opposed to ecological knowledge viewed solely through the lens of Western science) in assessing impacts of a pipeline in the river valley. Arguably, Berger's valuing of TEK laid the partial groundwork for the subsequent widespread use of TEK in environmental assessments as certified by the United Nations' Brundtland Commission on Environment and Development and its report, *Our Common Future*, in 1987.[92] The Berger Inquiry's focus on Indigenous perspectives on the land and resource development is also considered to have contributed, in part, to international acceptance of the importance of such perspectives even more broadly, resulting in developments such as the UN Declaration on the Rights of Indigenous Peoples adopted in 2007 after decades of work (although, ironically, Canada did not abandon its "objector" status until 2016).[93] Finally, the Berger Inquiry into the impacts of an energy corridor on the Mackenzie River and its people was a key development in the North finding a collective voice and resulted in a rebalancing of national politics in Canada to better include the North and, in particular, its Indigenous Peoples. It acted to empower many Indigenous people, and that experience arguably helped some to develop into leaders on the national stage, such as individuals who later served as a premier of the Northwest Territories and as National Chief of the Assembly of First Nations.

The different perspectives on the Mackenzie River valley both as a frontier and an ancient and current homeland and its impacts on resource development re-emerged with renewed interest in a gas pipeline in 2004 when the C$16.2 billion Mackenzie Gas Pipeline was proposed.[94] This proposal included a one-third ownership held by the Aboriginal Pipeline Group, which consisted of Inuvialuit, Gwich'in and Sahtu members.[95] The social and environmental assessment process for this project (approved by the federal government in 2010) did not, however, achieve the standard set by the Berger Inquiry and the project was cancelled in 2017 owing to declining market conditions.[96] Nearly 50 years after a gas pipeline along the Mackenzie River valley was first proposed, no such development has come to fruition. The potential for such developments and the investigations into their potential social, economic and environmental impacts, however, provide compelling examples of how great rivers, the resources within their drainages, and the history of human interactions with rivers and the surrounding landscape have helped shape national conversations of profound importance and impact.

— THREE —

The Yukon River
The Lure and Legacy of Gold

I wanted the gold, and I sought it;
I scrabbled and mucked like a slave.
Was it famine or scurvy—I fought it;
I hurled my youth into a grave.
I wanted the gold, and I got it—
Came out with a fortune last fall,—
Yet somehow life's not what I thought it,
And somehow the gold isn't all.

—ROBERT SERVICE, "The Spell of the Yukon," 1907

Gold – number 79 and denoted "Au" in the periodic table of the elements, just before Mercury and just after Platinum. Owing to its rarity (1–3 parts per billion of the Earth's crust; iron is more than 14 million times more abundant), "rich, seductive"[1] colour, malleability, durability, and diversity of uses in jewellery, investment, monetary exchange, industry and even as a decorative food additive, no other precious metal excites the human imagination as much as gold – "the king of metals."[2] Humans have valued gold for millennia for the inherent properties of its appearance and feel, from divine ordination, as a measure of the labour required to find and extract it, or even as the pinnacle of Darwinian natural selection applied to economics. The value of gold was considered by one US senator "as immutable as the law of gravitation."[3]

The oldest gold artifacts date to the fourth millennium BC,[4] and many texts from ancient Asian, middle Eastern and European societies are replete with references to gold in culture, industry and mythology. More recently, much of the exploration of the Americas, particularly by the Spanish, was driven by the quest for gold (see Chapters 7 and 8), especially after viewing ornamental gold displayed by Indigenous Peoples that they encountered. Throughout history, it is estimated that a total of about 6.4 billion troy ounces of gold have been extracted by humans – a total value of US$11.1 *trillion* at mid-2021 prices – an amount that if formed into a single ingot would measure 21 cubic metres.[5]

Although a considerable amount of gold was locked up within the Earth's core as the molten proto-Earth cooled, much of the gold coveted and exploited by humans probably originated about 3.9 billion ya from asteroid bombardments onto the mantle and crust of the Earth's outer margins – the so-called "veneer hypothesis."[6] The term "El Dorado" was originally coined by Europeans to describe an ancient Colombian king who covered himself in gold in an initiation ritual. Geographically, it describes any place where large gold deposits are rumoured to be found. The Earth's single most productive gold-producing area (accounting for almost 50% of all gold mined on Earth) is the Witwatersrand deposit near Johannesburg, South Africa, which is thought to have been brought to its current "erosion surface" by a massive meteor impact some 2.2 billion ya and concentrated by the actions of ancient rivers or by hydrothermal injections from the Earth's crust.[7] The discovery of the Witwatersrand deposit in 1886 was an "El Dorado" moment that instigated one of the many "gold rushes" of history – a sudden, often chaotic dash of humanity to exploit the new-found gold – and led to the establishment of Johannesburg.

Most gold is found in ore deposits as a native metal, often in combination with silver as a gold-silver alloy or embedded in rock fissures with quartz as a "lode" deposit. Gold can also be found as "free" flakes that have been eroded from rock by water. These flakes may become amalgamated into larger "grains" or "nuggets" by the action of water. Erosion by water and the high density of gold (19 times denser than water) results in the loose deposition of these flakes or nuggets as "alluvium" in creeks and rivers downstream of the source of the erosive water. The deposits of gold associated with rivers and creeks in this manner are called "placer" deposits, placer stemming from the Spanish word meaning "alluvial sand." Creeks and rivers, therefore, are important sources of concentrations of gold, and wherever there is gold, history has shown that humans are sure to follow.

This chapter explores gold and rivers, specifically the collective "lunacy"[8] associated with the gold rush in the Klondike River (1896–1899), a tributary of the Yukon River in Yukon Territory, Canada. While there have been several gold rushes in North America, including in other areas of western North America and even the Yukon River itself, the Klondike gold rush was the last of the great gold rushes and the most flamboyant.[9] It is perhaps the most celebrated gold rush in books, poems and film, and gold mining is still productive in the Klondike. Further, although it occurred in Canada, the Klondike gold rush had a tremendous impact on the development of Alaska, which was only acquired by the US from Russia in 1867. As will be discussed below, the evolutionary history of a river, at multiple scales of time and space, is critical to the accumulation of gold and all that follows.[10]

The geography and origin of the Yukon River

THE NAME "Yukon River" stems from the Loucheaux (now Gwich'in) Indigenous word "Yuchoo" meaning "the greatest river" or "big river." The English name was coined by a Hudson's Bay Company trader, John Bell, in 1846 after he encountered Indigenous people at the confluence of the Yukon and Porcupine rivers who called it "youcon."[11] What is now the lower portion of the river was named earlier in 1835 by a Russian explorer, Andrei Glasunov, who called it the "Kwikhpak River," from an Aleut word meaning "great river."

The Yukon River originates from the Llewellyn Glacier field at the southern end of Atlin Lake, in northwestern British Columbia, and the river flows for 3190 km to the Bering Sea. From its head-waters,

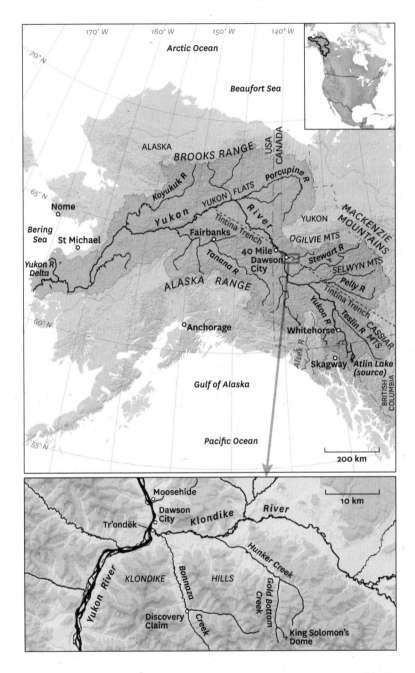

The Yukon River Basin. Inset shows the Klondike River with some major gold-bearing creeks: Bonanza (Rabbit) Creek and Hunker Creek.

the Yukon River first flows in a northwesterly direction through Yukon Territory, crossing the US border near Eagle, Alaska, where it continues northwest until turning sharply southwest before emptying into the Bering Sea at Norton Sound. Its total drainage area is about 832,700 km^2 (40% of which occurs in Canada). The Yukon River is the third longest in North America (21st in the world), and it is the fifth largest in drainage area (33rd in the world). Perhaps 140,000 people live within the Yukon River basin, with more than 75% of those living in Alaska.[12]

The Yukon River is a good example of a "transboundary" river system, meaning that it passes through two or more political jurisdictions: two within Canada (British Columbia and Yukon Territory), and two national ones (Canada and the United States). Upon second glance, the course of the Yukon River is an odd one, especially in the upper river. First, its headwaters in northwestern British Columbia are only 50 km from the Gulf of Alaska, yet it does not reach the sea until it flows thousands of kilometres north and west to the Bering Sea. Second, it crosses a northeastern drainage divide formed by the Dawson Range as it flows northwest through Yukon Territory, crosscutting the underlying geology, before entering the US.[13] This somewhat anomalous present-day course of the river suggests that its length, drainage area and flow direction have changed greatly since the formation of its present configuration during the early Pliocene (5–3 million ya).

The Yukon River is contained within the structural framework of the Northern Cordillera and the slices of the Earth's crust ("terranes") that broke off from oceanic tectonic plates and that were subsequently sutured, or "accreted," to the North American continental plate. The rock types that dominate these mountain and terrane features range in age from over 2 billion years to about 2 million years.[14] These formations and their antiquity are the dominant organizing features of the topography of Yukon Territory and its rivers, which tend to flow in northwest or northeast directions as dictated by divides along the Northern Cordillera and the associated terranes. The Tintina Trench in central Yukon, a northern extension of the Rocky Mountain Trench, contains the flow of a major Yukon River tributary, the Pelly River, as well as parts of the Yukon itself. Studying patterns in the layers of rocks (stratigraphy) along the Tintina Trench indicates that several paleo-drainages around the contemporary upper Yukon River ran south from the Ogilvie Mountains of central Yukon and merged just downstream of the present location of Dawson City, Yukon. These drainages followed the Tintina Trench in a *southeasterly* direction to join with the southwesterly flowing paleo-Yukon River drainage that eventually emptied into the Gulf of Alaska between the Alaska Range and the Cassiar Mountains of British Columbia (i.e., opposite to the direction of contemporary flows). Also, at this time the lower two-thirds of the current Yukon River system constituted the ancient Kwikhpak River. Thus, the Yukon River system as we now know it was at one time *two* independent rivers: one, the Kwikhpak River, flowed to the Bering Sea; and a second, the paleo-Yukon River, flowed to the Gulf of Alaska.[15]

This ancient orientation of the Yukon River existed for at least 2 million years until near the mid-Pliocene, when the climate cooled and the area experienced its first major glaciation. Glaciers of the Cordilleran Ice Sheet, advancing north and west from the Ogilvie Mountains and north and east from the St. Elias Mountains in southeastern Alaska, pinched off the southward flow of the paleo-Yukon River and created a large proglacial lake whose outflow formed just west of the present location of the Fifteenmile River northwest of Dawson City. These events, and uplift of the St. Elias Mountains, precipitated a new, northwestward flow of the upper Yukon River and resulted in its merging with the much larger Kwikhpak River. The Kwikhpak River had formed most of the current extent of the Yukon River in Alaska until this point in the mid-Pliocene (2.5 to 3 million ya). This tectonically and glacially inspired capture of the paleo-Yukon River by the Kwikhpak River was repeated farther west and resulted in the Tanana River, the major tributary of the Yukon River in Alaska today, also joining the nascent Yukon River drainage.[16]

The historical changes in the Yukon River's flow had major implications for the concentration of placer gold deposits. The streams of the paleo-Yukon River were critical to the concentration of thick layers of gravels and the aggregation of gold in placer deposits in the

Dawson Range–Klondike Plateau area. Massive shifts in the Tintina Trench (via movements in the underlying fault) caused rivers that flowed through it, such as the Klondike River and its various tributaries, to accumulate thick layers of gravels and associated placer gold. Glaciation in the area and reversal of Yukon River flow to the northwest resulted in the cutting of new channels and the formation and concentration of further placer deposits. The Klondike River area deposits are particularly rich owing to the repeated glaciations and associated "outwash" floods that occurred in the area.

The various geological, geomorphological and climatic events over the last 5 million years resulted in three layers of placer deposits: "high-level" occurring in bench deposits 10–200 m above contemporary river and creek beds that accumulated some 3 to 4 million ya; "intermediate-level" deposits 1–50 m above current river and creek levels that accumulated some 0.8 to 1.6 million ya; and "low-level" deposits exposed as alluvium along contemporary river and creek beds that accumulated 26,000–38,000 ya during and after the most recent glaciation.[17] These levels of gold deposits are underlain by bedrock that dates back to the Paleozoic Era (at least 0.5 billion ya). Consequently, the multiple layers of placer deposits owe their origin to erosional and depositional processes that "worked" the gold-bearing quartz veins housed within the terranes accreted to the continental bedrock of the ancient margin of northwestern North America.[18] Historically, the low-level deposits were the most important owing to their relative accessibility, but the high-level, and to a lesser extent, the intermediate-level deposits are the most important to the current mining industry.[19] Consequently, the geological "theatre" of the Yukon River valley, in an act playing over millions of years, set the stage for one of the greatest gold rushes in history.

Early human history of the Yukon River basin

ESTIMATES for the first arrival of humans across the Bering Land Bridge to the Americas via the lower Yukon River area of Beringia (see Chapter 2) range from 14,000–18,000 ya (i.e., postglacially), inferred from ages of the first widely accepted human artifacts in

North America, to perhaps as long ago as 25,000 ya inferred from genetic analyses.[20] Notwithstanding some continuing uncertainty about the exact date of first arrival of humans in North America and whether they may have first arrived by coastal or marine routes (thus bypassing the lower Yukon River area), there is general agreement that the unglaciated Yukon River was probably one of the important gateways to North America. Recent genetic analyses indicate that the oldest remains of humans in North American Beringia (~11,500 cal ya) were found in the Tanana River valley of the central Yukon River valley.[21] The three major Indigenous language family groups of the Yukon River valley are the Yupik-Inuit, the Tlingit and the geographically more extensive Athabascan (Na-Dene) group.[22] There are more than 15 First Nations (in Canada) or Tribes (in the US) that include the Yukon River valley as part of their traditional lands. The territory of one of these First Nations, the Hän ("people of the river") encompasses the Klondike River drainage and adjacent areas of the Yukon River to about 80 km downstream of Eagle, Alaska.

The Indigenous Peoples of the Yukon River first encountered Europeans and Russians exploring the area for furs, not gold. Russians began trading with Indigenous Peoples in coastal Alaska, including the lower Yukon River area, in the early 1800s, although they had first explored coastal Alaska some 100 years earlier.[23] As part of the Russian-American Company, Russians explored and mapped more than 800 km of the Yukon River upstream from the Bering Sea by 1867. Feeling geographically stretched and not profiting as much from gold, furs or whaling as had been anticipated, however, the Russians eventually decided to concentrate their commercial interests in Asia and sold Alaska to the US in 1867 for US$7 million. While the Russians were exploring and charting the lower river, several groups of Euro–North Americans were probing the upper reaches, including the traditional area of the Hän. In the 1840s, Robert Campbell of the Hudson's Bay Company explored a major upper Yukon River tributary, the Pelly River, and established an outpost, Fort Selkirk, at the confluence of the two rivers in 1848. He was the first to designate "Yukon" as the name for the river.[24] During his explorations of the Porcupine River, John Bell established Fort

Yukon, Alaska, in 1844 near the confluence of the Yukon and Porcupine rivers where the Yukon River begins its sweeping turn to the
southwest. During the 1870s, three traders, Leroy McQuesten, Arthur
Harper and Alfred Mayo, working under the auspices of the Alaska
Commercial Company, founded several trading posts. These three
also spent considerable time, when they were not engaged in the fur
trade, prospecting for gold and other minerals. Eventually, the three
invested in supplies for mining and engaged many other traders in
prospecting. To enhance mapping of the geography and resources of
the river, American general Nelson A. Miles, a veteran of the Civil
and Indian wars and commander of the Department of the Columbia (under which Alaska was administered), sent soldiers upstream
to explore the upper Yukon River beginning in the 1880s. Perhaps
the most famous mission was that led by Lt. Frederick Schwatka of
the US Army. Schwatka's party crossed the Chilkoot Pass between
southeast Alaska and Yukon, and after building rafts, they travelled
down to the Yukon River and along its length to the mouth – some
2092 km – the longest voyage by raft at the time (Schwatka had also
made an earlier 4360-km sledge journey in the Canadian Arctic).
Schwatka's epic trip resulted in the naming of many features along
the river, and an account of his trip, the river and its flora and fauna,
Along Alaska's Great River, was published in 1885. Schwatka's exploits
so agitated the Canadian government that it sent George M. Dawson,
a Canadian scientist and noted surveyor of western Canada and after
whom Dawson City was named, on an exploration mission in 1887.

  With all this activity and with memories of recent gold rushes
in California, British Columbia and south-central Alaska from the
1840s through the 1890s, activity in the Yukon River basin intensified and discoveries of gold began to trickle in. Ed Schieffelin,
an Arizona prospector with large discoveries of silver under his
belt, studied maps of mineral deposits and concluded that a great
arc of minerals running from South America to Asia through the
continental divides must exist and that, somewhere, this "golden
highway"[25] should cross the Yukon River in Alaska. Schieffelin did
discover small deposits in the Yukon River in the early 1880s, but
nothing of the magnitude to keep him in Alaska longer than a few

years. Placer gold was discovered in the Stewart River in 1885, in the Fortymile River, just downstream of Dawson City, in 1886, and near Circle, Alaska, just across the Canada–US border, in 1893. The discovery at Circle resulted in the small river-based supply post (run by McQuesten) growing to over 1,200 people, and it became known, perhaps somewhat generously, as "the Paris of Alaska"[26] owing to the relative richness of its amenities. It is estimated that when the Klondike River discovery was made in 1896 (resulting in the virtual desertion of Circle), some 1,600 people were in the upper Yukon River basin, in whole or in part on the search for gold.

Gold discovery on the Klondike River

THE KLONDIKE RIVER is a 160 km long river draining the Ogilvie Mountains that empties into the upper Yukon River at the southern margin of Dawson City. Just upstream of the confluence of the two rivers is a feature known as "King Solomon's Dome," a 1234 m high elevation comprising part of the divide between the Yukon and Mackenzie river drainages. Several creeks and rivers flow off this peak and eventually empty into the Yukon, Indian and Klondike rivers. In mid-August of 1896, George Carmack, a California-born prospector, his wife Kate (a member of the local Tagish First Nation), her brother, "Skookum Jim" Mason, and their nephew, Dawson (Tagish) Charlie, were travelling and fishing near the mouth of the Klondike River. Apparently acting on a tip from a fellow prospector, George Henderson, the trio began searching for gold on Bonanza Creek (then known as Rabbit Creek), which runs from its source on King Solomon's Dome for about 30 km north to its confluence with the Klondike River. The tip was a solid one as Henderson had only a few months before discovered gold on Gold Bottom Creek, a small tributary of Hunker Creek located just east of Bonanza Creek. There remains some uncertainty as to who made the Bonanza Creek discovery. Skookum Jim is thought to have noticed a twinkling of yellow colour in the water while washing a pan, but it was clear that huge amounts of gold were present and easily accessible along the creek. Carmack measured out four claims on August 17 (two for himself, one being the famous "Discovery Claim," and one each for Skookum Jim and Dawson Charlie), each measuring 150 m along the creek. The three prospectors decided to register Carmack as the original discoverer lest mining authorities fail to recognize a claim originated by an Indigenous person. After the claims were registered at the Yukon village of Forty Mile in late September, news of the find spread so quickly that all the creek bed of Bonanza Creek had been claimed by miners by the end of August. As prospectors began spreading to nearby creeks, one of them found an even bigger deposit on a small tributary of Bonanza Creek, subsequently named Eldorado Creek. Owing to slow communication and transportation imposed by the impending winter months, the impacts of these finds and the selling of claims among miners were largely restricted to local areas. Still, a few determined miners travelled to the Klondike from surrounding areas by dogsled. It was not until June of the following year, 1897, when the first boats left the upper Yukon River with accumulations of mined gold, however, that the real rush began.[27]

The Klondike gold rush

AT THE TIME of the news of the Klondike gold finds, interest in gold was especially intense. There had been a series of bank failures and depressions in the US. Debate on the continued use of the "gold standard" was at a fever pitch in that country. Gold was valuable because of its beauty as well as its constancy; its supply directly determined the value of paper money. Given this "culture of gold"[28] that had existed for millennia and the economic conditions at the time, it is understandable why the "most frenzied of the great international gold rushes"[29] occurred after the word got out about the Klondike gold discovery – a rush that spread across a continent that had gone "Klondike crazy."[30] The steamer *Excelsior* docked at San Francisco on July 17, 1897, with an estimated US$500,000 (~$42,275,000 in 2021) worth of Klondike River gold and caused a huge stir. The *Portland* docked on July 20 in Seattle with more than US$1 million (~$83,800,000 in 2021) of gold on board and was, predictably, met by a massive crowd.[31]

By the end of July 1897, huge numbers of people had booked passage on ships or otherwise collected themselves at Dyea and Skagway, Alaska, to make their way overland via the famous White Pass and Chilkoot trails to the Klondike goldfields in a "solid stream of unsatisfied restless humanity."[32] The overland route via the Chilkoot Pass generated many of the iconic photographs of the gold rush by Eric Hegg and was the most popular route, with an estimated 22,000 prospectors using it. It included a very arduous 300 m final climb to the 1067 m summit and it could be treacherous; over 60 people died in a snow slide in April 1898. Just to the west, the White Pass Trail was less arduous, but less reliable in terms of passage, and an estimated 3,000 horses died working that trail, which led to its unofficial name "Dead Horse Trail."[33] As if trudging across the passes were not enough, those who made these trips assembled at Bennett and Lindeman lakes, where they still faced a treacherous 1000 km passage downstream on the Yukon River to Dawson City. During the river voyage, the loss of human lives to a combination of cold water, rapids and boats of dubious structural integrity steadily mounted. The Canadian government was so concerned that it eventually stationed North-West Mounted Police, including the legendary Sam Steele, at one site to inspect boats and instruct women and children to walk around the rapids. Alternative routes to the Klondike involved sea and river passage via the Yukon River at St. Michael, Alaska (slower and more expensive, but less arduous) to overland "all-Canadian" and brutal routes through British Columbia and northwest Alberta that could take as long as 18 months to traverse.[34]

West coast port towns like Seattle, Tacoma, San Francisco, Vancouver and Victoria prospered immensely as supply and transportation hubs, all driven by the quest to reach the goldfields. By the summer of 1898, Skagway was the largest city in Alaska. Dawson City exploded from a rough settlement of a few hundred people in 1896 to over 30,000 by 1898. The town site was established by two locals who saw easier riches to be made in land than mining when single lots sold for as much as C$8,000 (about $250,000 in 2021).[35]

In all, the Klondike gold rush saw an estimated 100,000 people (including the mayor of Seattle, author Jack London, theatre and

A crowd watching foot races as part of July 4, 1899, celebrations, Dawson City, Yukon.

movie mogul Alexander Pantages and several future politicians and business leaders) make a dash for the goldfields. The rate of attrition was high. Only between 30,000 and 40,000 made it, and of those, perhaps 20,000 actually prospected, only about 4,000 found any gold, and a few hundred became rich. Further, many of those who made fortunes also lost them. "Big" Alex McDonald, a Nova Scotia–born prospector, was known as "King of the Klondike" for amassing 28 claims and interests in 75 mines, some yielding up to C$20,000 in a single day, worth up to C$27 million.[36] He lost most of his worth on less productive purchases after the gold rush and died in 1909 – alone, in a simple cabin, and in debt.[37] Of the three original discovers of gold, George Carmack was reported to have lived out his life in relative wealth although he and his wife Kate separated and she returned to her people, Skookum Jim continued to prospect until his death in 1916 searching in vain for another big find, and Dawson Charlie had died in an accident eight years earlier.[38]

By 1899 the rush, however, was over. The best claims had all been staked; many new miners left as soon as they arrived, discouraged by the lack of opportunity, depressed wages from the oversupply of labour and the increasing civilization of towns like Dawson City and Skagway that were becoming, in a relative way, "respectable."[39] In addition, new finds of gold, especially north of the mouth of the Yukon River near Nome, Alaska, turned peoples' attention elsewhere; they left in droves, and the Klondike gold rush was over. By 1902, Dawson City's population had dwindled to under 5,000 people just as it was incorporated as a city; by 1972 it was hovering around 500 and has grown in the ensuing years to be 2,300 in 2020.[40]

Legacy of the Klondike gold rush

BETWEEN 1896 AND 1900 at least US$68 million (almost $5.7 billion at 2021 prices) worth of gold had been pulled, dug, dredged, scratched and blasted from the creeks of the Klondike, and tens of millions more made and lost in related businesses.[41] One aspect of the legacy of the Klondike gold rush obviously involves the making and losing of considerable sums of money through an intense, colourful but relatively brief period of human history, itself the product of millions of years of geological history of the Yukon River. Charlotte Gray in her terrific book *Gold Diggers: Striking it Rich in the Klondike*, suggested that the Klondike gold rush was a "flash in the pan" and has left "little lasting impact on the Yukon."[42] While this is perhaps accurate in terms of the meteoric rise in the population of Dawson City followed by its precipitous decline following the discovery of gold in Nome, a broader view indicates a profound and enduring legacy of what that August day on Bonanza Creek started.

The Klondike gold rush was instrumental in the development of Yukon and Alaska. Before the gold rush, Yukon was an administrative district of the Northwest Territories, and its capital was more than 3200 km away in Regina, Saskatchewan. Its borders with Alaska were the subject of dispute with the US, a dispute inherited from previous Russian ownership of Alaska. It is no coincidence that Yukon was split off from the Northwest Territories and made its own territory in 1898,[43] or that four gold coins and symbols for rivers form part of the Yukon coat of arms. An international boundary was established in 1903, with not altogether favourable results for Canada because of somewhat meek negotiations led by Britain (see also Chapters 4 and 5). While the Klondike gold rush ended in 1899, gold mining and production entered a more sustained period of wealth generation in the area. The White Pass and Yukon Railway from Skagway to Whitehorse, Yukon, completed in 1900, allowed heavy equipment to be moved to the upper Yukon River and barged to the goldfields. This promoted an intensive period of dredge and hydraulic mining in creek and river beds, and "professional" mining for other minerals. In fact, following the mass exodus of most miners in 1899, recovery of gold increased until 1903, with 1900 being the single greatest year with C$22 million produced. Estimates vary, but as of 2020 over 20 million troy oz. (622,000 kg), worth over US$30 billion at the average 2021 price, have been recovered from the Klondike goldfields and hundreds of new claims are staked every year.[44]

The Klondike gold rush was one of several in Alaska and involving the Yukon River. Alaska, previously administered as a district, was incorporated as a territory following the most intensive period of gold finds in 1912 and admitted as a state in 1959. Amazingly, after Alaska was purchased from Russia by the United States in 1867 for US$7 million, some considered the purchase "folly."[45] The New York World proclaimed Alaska "a frozen wilderness" that contained nothing of value "but fur-bearing animals ... hunted until they were nearly extinct." The editors, perhaps prophetically, further opined that "unless gold were found in the country much time would elapse before it would be blessed with Hoe printing presses, Methodist chapels and a metropolitan police."[46] In 2019, and after the Klondike and other gold rushes of the Yukon River valley, Alaska ranks 14th in terms of per capita personal income in the United States, and 7th in per capita gross domestic product (GDP)[47] with an economy whose export values are dominated by seafood and mining, with gold accounting for 5.3% of all export value in 2019.[48] The Klondike gold rush greatly stimulated the development of Alaska as it was the major gateway to the goldfields (Skagway's nickname is "Gateway to the Klondike"). The state seal features a smelter, and the state mineral is gold – a reflection of the importance of gold mining to Alaska.

One of the enduring legacies of the Klondike gold rush is a cultural one. Famous novelists and books emerged from this period, the most notable being American writer Jack London (1876–1916). London was one of many who developed scurvy in the Klondike owing to the harsh conditions and poor food supply. The malady forced him to give up on mining, but his experiences in the Klondike, particularly the harsh cabin-bound winters, the dance halls and saloons, inspired critically acclaimed writings such as the short story "To Build a Fire" (1902) and the better-known Yukon-related novels *Call of the Wild* (1903) and *White Fang* (1906).[49] The popularity of the poems "The Cremation of Sam McGee," "The Shooting of Dan McGrew" and "The Spell of the Yukon" (all published in 1907) earned the British-born Robert Service (1874–1958) the title of "The Bard of the Yukon."[50] Service composed these works after he arrived as a bank clerk in Whitehorse, Yukon, in 1904, well after the gold rush, but he was inspired by the stories he had heard. His compilation *Songs of a Sourdough* (1907) was a popular and commercial success before he ever set foot in Dawson City in 1908. Service became a full-time writer and wrote extensively over the next four years in Dawson City and after he left. His work remains very popular today and his two-room Dawson City cabin is now preserved by Parks Canada and serves as an important tourist attraction. Some notable films have also been produced that were inspired by the Klondike gold rush: Charlie Chaplin's *Gold Rush* (1925), the highest-grossing silent movie comedy of all time, was inspired by his viewing of photographs of the Chilkoot Trail.[51] *The Far Country* (1955, with Jimmy Stewart), *The Trail of '98* (1928, based on a Service novel of the same name) and *Klondike Annie* (1936, with Mae West) all were gold rush–inspired films.

Much of the legacy of the Klondike gold rush is less inspiring. The Fortymile River area lay within the traditional territory of the Hän people, a member of the Athapaskan language group whose name in Gwich'in means "people of the river." The Hän had a seasonal chum

(*Oncorhynchus keta*) and chinook (*O. tshawytscha*) salmon fishing camp at the mouth of the Klondike River – just opposite the future site of Dawson City – known as Tr'ondëk. The Hän had interacted with earlier fur traders and prospectors for years, but the gold rush changed everything for them. First, their ancestral camp was moved about 5 km downstream on the Yukon River, to a site known as Moosehide, because of the disruption caused by the massive influx of miners. Their population dropped greatly after this move; disease (smallpox, typhoid) and contamination of the water supply from sewage, mining and related activities, as well as from degradation and loss of use of traditional fishing areas, all contributed to the decline.[52] By 1904, a once-independent community required help from the North-West Mounted Police to avoid starvation. By the 1960s, Moosehide had been largely abandoned; the descendants of the Hän, the Tr'ondëk Hwëch'in, began resettling Tr'ondëk, and land claim negotiations began in the 1970s.[53] Mining activity on Tr'ondëk beginning in 1991 precipitated a lawsuit by the Tr'ondëk Hwëch'in that challenged the issuance of mining rights on Indigenous, unceded land. A final land claim agreement was reached in 1998 and the Tr'ondëk Hwëch'in designated it as a heritage site.[54] Tr'ondëk was subsequently recognized as a National Historic Site of Canada in 2002.[55] The Tr'ondëk Hwëch'in and Parks Canada are considering making a 2020 application to the United Nations (UN) to have Tr'ondëk, Dawson City and adjacent Klondike goldfields ("Tr'ondëk-Klondike") designated as a UNESCO World Heritage Site (an earlier application made in 2004 was withdrawn).[56]

A Google Earth image of the Klondike River for 10 km upstream from Dawson City at an eye elevation of 10 km reveals a remarkable set of features – long "worm-like" formations all along the south margin of the river, acting almost as sentinels along both sides of the Klondike Highway. These are mine tailings, the result of eviscerations of the Klondike River by massive dredges, or "Monsters on the Klondike,"[57] that created huge piles of river boulders and gravel. These piles of rock are still reworked and yield gold. Standing next to these tailings, with the interspersed pools of water formerly part of the Klondike River, is fascinating in an eerie kind of way. To

The worm-like piles of mine tailings bordering the south bank of the Klondike River (near top of image) a few kilometres east of Dawson City, Yukon, viewed from an elevation of 10 km. The thin white line running horizontally across the middle of the image is the Klondike Highway (Yukon Highway 2).

think that a river could be worked so extensively, and its boulder "flooring" discarded as so much refuse is disturbing, but the tailings are strangely intriguing. They are amazingly consistent in size and shape, smooth to the touch, and one cannot but marvel at the immense effort and desire that resulted in their creation. The tailings resemble a kind of "moonscape"; little vegetation grows among them, and the tailings ponds are largely devoid of fish life.[58] These tailings are part of the environmental legacy of the Klondike gold rush and all that followed. To say that long-term thinking on the environment and effects of resource extraction in Yukon circa 1896 was poorly developed is a colossal understatement. The minister responsible for Indian affairs at the time, Clifford Sifton, considered Yukon to be "good for nothing except mining."[59] Plus, it all happened, and was over, so fast – in three years. The laissez-faire environmental attitude of the Canadian government, its active promotion of mining and use of water and forests for mining, plus the speed and intensity of events was a situation bound not to end well for the environment.

The impacts of the gold rush on the environment can be classified as indirect and direct ones. Indirect effects involve those that relate to ancillary activities of mining per se. For instance, the huge influx of miners resulted in a spike in demand for wood (for cooking, heating, boats, mining infrastructure, housing and other buildings, fuel for steamships); increased the frequency of forest fires (from the influx of miners and camping); caused soil erosion, habitat loss and poaching of fish and wildlife; and changed the hydrology and distribution of permafrost from road, railway and dam construction and forestry – all of which led to drastic changes in the landscape. While some wildlife regulations were in place, enforcement by the small contingent of police was insufficient. In some cases, protection was non-existent. The chum and chinook salmon of the area, the latter noted for having the longest migrations in North America, received no protection at all. In the words of the minister of marine and fisheries and referring to the effects of fisheries downstream in Alaska: "There is no object in protecting [the salmon species] in the upper waters when every effort is made to exterminate them before they reach Canadian territory."[60] The lack of regulation and enforcement led to catastrophic overexploitation of fish and wildlife, already negatively affected by habitat loss and degradation, and the collapse of many populations.

The changes to landscape, fish and wildlife during the gold rush years have been described as "harrowing," and the developments that led to these changes were opposed by some government officials, such as Yukon commissioner William Ogilvie.[61] Once the rush was over, however, some changes were reversible and recovery took place, albeit over many decades. More enduring changes came about from direct impacts of placer mining and the dredge and hydraulic mining that supplanted small-scale placer mining after 1900, especially in the Klondike River and its tributaries. Placer mining by individuals or small groups of men who used hand tools and small water diversions to work the overburden resulted in permanent physical alterations to the land and waterscape. The sheer number of mining claims, extended to a width of 83 m in 1898, totalled about 31,000 in 1900, and their concentration in the Dawson City area speaks to the havoc wrought on the local rivers, streams and creeks. Hand-mining of placer deposits involved the thawing, by fire, of permafrost and the lugging of buckets of overburden to be dumped as tailings on land or in water bodies. Mercury, known since the days of ancient Rome to be highly toxic to human and environmental health,[62] was used to amalgamate gold during the sluicing process. Samples of fish and gold from the Klondike River assayed as late as the 1980s show levels of methyl mercury contamination above levels recommended for subsistence consumption.[63]

Once the more easily accessible near-surface placer deposits were exhausted (by 1900), hydraulic mining was instituted. Hydraulic mining was used extensively in the earlier California gold rush (see Chapter 6) and aids in "stripping" the vegetation and overburden from gold-bearing deposits. All that was required was massive diversion of water from the Klondike River and other water courses using a series of flumes and dams. Such concessions for water diversion were eagerly promoted by the Canadian minister of the interior and approved by the federal government; by 1902 over 1000 km of such concessions had been granted. Government control of these concessions was explicitly discouraged, as was "hyper-criticism of details"[64] of mining, as being inhibitory to the development of the Yukon's mineral riches.

Next, the innovation of dredge mining arrived in the Klondike River valley after about 1898.[65] A dredge is basically a movable mine that floats. As it moves forward in a river or stream, the dredge's conveyer belt series of buckets, which can work down to 18 m into the stream bed, removes vegetation and rocks that are then fed into sluice boxes within the giant "gut" of the dredge. Physical separation retained the gold while the gravel and rock are moved to the back of the dredge to be dumped along the path of movement of the dredge by a second, rear-facing conveyer belt. Seeking out a veritable movable feast of gold, these dredges eviscerated creeks and destroyed the original topography, leaving the sculpted, winding trails of tailings described above. Some dredges had the capacity to process 80,000 m³ or more of river bed per month (a volume equal to 32 Olympic-sized swimming pools). Further, as in hand mining, mercury was used to concentrate gold within the dredges' sluice boxes – mercury that was later discarded on the land and in water. The Klondike gold rush only saw the birth of dredge mining in the Yukon River – it continued until 1966, a period that saw "the greatest amount of environmental destruction for both sides of the Klondike River and many of the creeks of the Klondike Valley."[66] Sometimes, however, the watershed got its revenge on the dredges. In 1902, a tree stump became lodged in the machinery of one dredge necessitating a shut down and repair with the loss of valuable dredging time.[67]

Historical and contemporary eras of gold mining in the Klondike River area are considered significant contributors to the persistent (to 2012, see also Chapter 12) rating of water quality of the river above Bonanza Creek as only "fair," which is defined as: "Aquatic life is protected, but at times may be threatened or impaired. Measurements sometimes exceed water quality guidelines and, possibly, by a wide margin."[68] Awareness and efforts to minimize or reverse such impacts have increased since the peak of the gold rush, but highly intrusive placer mining persists to this day.[69] These environmental changes, some reversible to a degree, others not, are, in addition to the effects on the Hän people, a darker legacy of the Klondike gold rush – a debt to nature that has yet to be repaid.

And what of Dawson City, which at its peak in 1898 was larger than Vancouver and the 7th or 8th largest city in Canada, yet by the 1970s had dwindled to about 500 souls? The population size has rallied, up to 2,300 people as of 2020. Gold mining is still important to the area, especially with the sustained high price of gold. New claims staked in the Dawson area of Yukon have almost tripled since 2000 to 1,331 in 2019, with the Klondike River and nearby Indian River being the top producers of gold, about 69,364 troy ounces in 2019/2020 worth C$120 million[70] at mid-2021 prices.[71] Mining, coupled with a tourist industry that exploits romantic visions of Klondike gold in another way, forms the basis of the local economy. The famous "Dredge No. 4" located on Bonanza Creek is a sight to see. It is the largest wooden, bucket-line dredge in North America (eight storeys high and 72 m in length) and, along with the adjacent Discovery Claim site, is a National Historic Site of Canada. Dawson City also has a thriving arts community with the Yukon School of Visual Arts and annual music and short film festivals. I have been lucky enough to visit Dawson City on several occasions, and from its simple origins, "Dawson" underwent tumultuous changes during the gold rush, but it has settled into what is hopefully a more sustainable, albeit perhaps less colourful, future. Hopefully, the same future will unfold for the nearby creeks and rivers of the upper Yukon River's Klondike River drainage, which have contributed so much to the history and development of contemporary Yukon and Alaska.

— FOUR —

The Fraser River
Sculptor of Biodiversity

Essentially the story of the river, by length of occupancy, by the test of endurance, and by the ordeal of adventure, belongs to the salmon, not to man.

—BRUCE HUTCHISON, *The Fraser* (1950)

"Biodiversity" – the variety of life. It is a simple concept, but our understanding of how it develops, how it persists and what it means to humans is endlessly complex. The variation in DNA, the variety of cells and organs, differences among individuals, populations, species and assemblages of species in different areas of the world are all components of biodiversity. We do know that biodiversity arises in a variety of ways. Some involve random changes in the genome from mutation of DNA during its replication. Other changes may occur by "genetic drift" across generations. Here the characteristics of offspring are only a random subset of those in a population of breeding parents, because some of these parents have better luck at reproducing than others. Biodiversity also arises by natural selection. Natural selection is the greater survival and/or reproductive performance of some individuals compared to others living in a common environment owing to differences in their traits.[1] These traits may be things like body size, body shape or behaviour, or traits related to physiology, like flying or swimming ability. Differences arising by natural selection are not random because they are driven by the interaction between *particular* traits and *particular* environments – environments like rivers. These interactions are what determine survival or reproductive success of individuals. The existence of different river systems and the variety of environments that they represent, therefore, may promote biological diversity via so-called divergent natural selection. Here, natural selection acting within a population in one river may, for instance, favour individuals returning to their rivers as adults in the summer because this timing enhances survival or reproduction in that river, while in another river natural selection may favour individuals returning in the fall. If there is genetic control of adult migration timing, then the populations in the different rivers diverge in migration timing across generations. Divergent natural selection may occur across different spatial scales, from differences among rivers separated by thousands of kilometres (e.g., the Fraser and Yukon rivers), to differences between tributaries of a single major river (e.g., tributaries separated by only a few tens of kilometres), to differences between river sections of the same tributary (upstream and downstream sections separated by a few kilometres only).

One of the most spectacular, well-known, and best-loved examples of these phenomena is the variety of different species and populations of salmon and trout, particularly those observed in the many lakes, rivers, streams and marine environments of the Pacific Basin.[2] Think of sockeye salmon appearing as a sea of red in the tens to hundreds of thousands as they migrate upstream from the sea, some in early summer, some in the fall, to spawn in the streams where they were born – a sight that I witnessed first in 1986 in British Columbia's famous Adams River and which cemented in my mind the notion that I wanted to spend my life on the west coast. Or, consider chinook salmon, which may weigh 35 kg or more in some rivers, and "muscle" their way more than 3000 km upstream to spawning grounds in the upper Yukon River in the late summer. Other populations of chinook salmon may migrate only a few tens of kilometres and spawn in the fall. These are but two examples of this spectacular biodiversity within and between Pacific salmon species. Altogether, tens of millions of salmon return annually to their spawning grounds around the north Pacific Basin in arguably the most spectacular annual migration on Earth.

The Pacific salmon and trout are so-called "soft-rayed" fishes of the genus *Oncorhynchus* (meaning "hooked-snout"). There are 12 species of Pacific salmon and trout native to the Pacific Basin, from the mountains of western Mexico, north and west to Alaska, the Russian Far East and south to Japan and the Korean Peninsula. The origin of these species is thought to have been driven, in large part, by the many geological changes in the Pacific Rim that resulted in isolation of distinct populations once part of the same ancestral species in different geographic areas, particularly during the Miocene (24–5 million ya).[3] Many great rivers around the Pacific Rim, from the Amur River in eastern Siberia to the Yukon River in western Alaska and Yukon, to the Sacramento–San Joaquin in central California, to rivers of the central Sierra Madre Occidental in Mexico, contain populations of Pacific salmon and/or trout.[4] The Fraser River, in British Columbia, Canada, is one of these rivers. In addition to having several species of Pacific salmon and trout, the Fraser River (as well as most rivers) contains an incredible diversity of distinct populations *within* each species. These distinct populations may comprise fish with distinct seasonal migration timing, body sizes, behaviour, physiology, colouration and body form. This diversity is, in large part, the direct result of the geographic history and complexity of the Fraser River. While the geography of the river has influenced salmon, the salmon have likely had a reciprocal impact on the Fraser River. The spawning of Pacific salmon can be a potent force acting to influence the flow and biology of rivers by disturbing gravel during spawning and through nutrient enrichment from their decaying bodies.[5]

Pacific salmon have been of critical importance to humans since we first crossed the Bering Land Bridge (and for much longer to Indigenous Peoples in Siberia) to colonize North America at least 11,500 cal ya and perhaps much earlier.[6] In fact, it has been suggested that sea-run salmon and trout were not just an important food item, but that they may have *drawn* humans to cross the Bering Land Bridge and colonize North America as the ice sheets retreated.[7] This chapter explores the nexus between the biodiversity of Pacific salmon and trout, its geographic underpinnings and the significance of this interaction to the humans within the Fraser River basin.

The geography and origin of the Fraser River

THE FRASER RIVER is 1375 km in length and is the 16th longest river in North America, but the river is the longest on the west coast of North America having no dam on its main stem. The Fraser River's drainage basin is 223,000 km², making it the largest drainage basin wholly contained within British Columbia. The river begins in a tiny spring at Fraser Pass in the Canadian Rocky Mountains and takes on a giant "S" shape as it flows northwest from its source before making a sweeping turn almost due south just northeast of Prince George, BC. The river flows farther south for some 560 km before a final, abrupt shift westward to flow another 150 km before meeting the sea at Vancouver.

The S-shaped path separates the river into three major units organized by great clefts in mountain ranges. The upper river (from the source to just before it turns south near Prince George) is contained within the Rocky Mountain Trench, which separates the Rocky Mountains from the Columbia Mountains. The middle river runs through the broad Interior Plateau between the Coast Mountain range (to the west) and the Columbia Mountains (to the east). The lower river encompasses the last 150 km after it turns west and punches it way through the seam between the Coast and Cascade mountain ranges to reach the sea at Vancouver. Approximately 3.2 million people live in the Fraser River basin, about 63% of British Columbia's population.[8]

The Fraser River has a deep geological history as even today the river uses ancestral drainages that date back well into the Cretaceous Period (145–66 million ya).[9] Throughout the last 100 million years or so, there have been numerous periods of geological uplift driven largely by ongoing movements of continental and oceanic tectonic

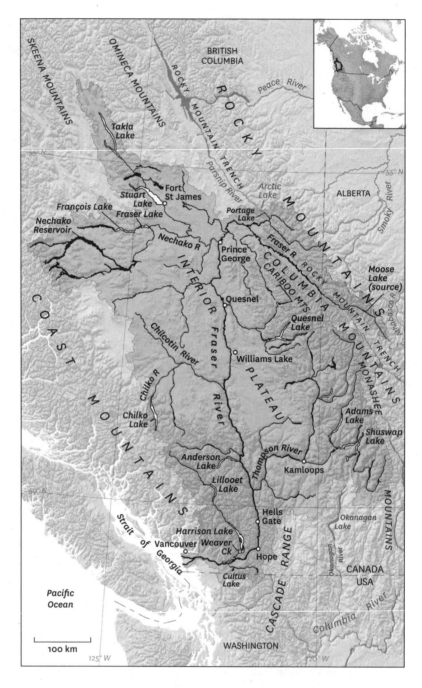

The Fraser River Basin. The lakes shaded white are major sockeye salmon nursery lakes.

plates that constitute the landform of British Columbia and the adjacent marine areas. Such uplifts, and subsequent subsidence, mean that the "base level," the level beneath which a river cannot erode, of the Fraser River has fluctuated over time to a remarkable degree. For instance, around the mid-Cretaceous (95 million ya) the base level of the Fraser River was 1700 m *higher* than the contemporary river level. It subsided to near current levels in the Eocene (56–34 million ya) yet uplifted again during the Pliocene-Pleistocene (< 5 million ya). These shifting periods of uplift and subsidence meant that the Fraser River changed its flow pattern markedly. From at least the Eocene, the pattern of sediments deposited by the river indicate that the Fraser River flowed *north*, with the Coast Mountains serving as an effective drainage divide. A subsequent uplift in the Coast Mountains saw the lower "proto-Fraser" (from modern day Hope, BC, to Vancouver), which flowed south and west, cut northward to link with the northward-draining, but southward-eroding, middle proto-Fraser River near the former drainage divide at Hells Gate in the Fraser Canyon. This flow reversal to the modern, southward, flow pattern is thought to have taken place somewhere between 15 and 1 million ya, possibly aided by glacial erosion and meltwater during the last 2 my. Interestingly, a major tributary of the middle Fraser River, the Chilko River, originates in the Coast Mountain and maintains its historical northward flow even today.

Other examples of flow reversals in the Fraser River have implications for salmon biodiversity in the drainage and involve connections between watersheds driven by glacial ice retreat, ice-dam blockages and subsequent merging of watersheds. The Pleistocene Glaciations comprised up to 20 cycles of ice advance and retreat of the Cordilleran Ice Sheet, which covered British Columbia with up to 3 km thick sheets of ice over the last 2 million years. The most recent, Wisconsinan, glaciation lasted from about 110,000 to 12,000 ya. At the margins of ice sheets, huge proglacial lakes formed. In addition, ice dams often formed and blocked the outflow of such lakes in one direction and forced the flow of rivers to reverse direction. One such ice blockage occurred downstream of present-day Prince George, BC and reversed the flow of the Fraser River north from around present-day Portage Lake into the upper portion of the Parsnip River via Arctic Lake, which eventually flows to the Peace and Mackenzie rivers and ultimately to the Arctic Ocean. Another blockage resulted in a transcontinental divide connection between the Fraser River upstream of Prince George and the Athabasca River (also flowing to the Arctic) near where Moose Lake (Fraser drainage) and the Miette River (Athabasca drainage) approach one another.[10] A third ice blockage caused an outflow of the middle Fraser and the Thompson River, a major tributary, into the Columbia River to the southeast via glacial Lake Penticton. The directional flow of the Fraser River, therefore, has been modified extensively over time by the dynamic nature of the surrounding landscape. These changes to the river's flow have had significant impacts on its biodiversity of salmon and trout, with consequences for humans.[11]

Early human history on the Fraser River basin

THE EARLIEST HUMAN HABITATION on the Fraser River by Indigenous Peoples of the Coast Salish cultural and linguistic group dates to 8,000 to 10,000 ya as inferred from archaeological finds in the lower and middle Fraser River.[12] These settlements were inhabited by the Stó:lō People ("the river people"), who ranged from the lower Fraser Canyon to just upstream of the estuary. The discovery of the Great Marpole (or Great Fraser) Midden in 1884 established residence of the Musqueam peoples in the Fraser River estuary and adjacent areas perhaps as long as 4,000 ya.[13] As might be expected from the later glacial retreat from the interior portions of the Fraser River, evidence of Indigenous settlements there are younger, but still date back thousands of years, and include the St'at'imc, Secwepemc and Nlaka'pamux peoples.[14]

In 1791, a Spanish explorer, José María Narváez (1768–1840) sailed through the Fraser River freshwater plume as he probed the southern Strait of Georgia (part of what is now known as the Salish Sea) to see if the strait formed part of a vast inland sea and could serve as a possible route to the Mississippi River. He noted that the water tasted sweet rather than salty, but he did not enter or see the Fraser

River itself. A year later, two other Spanish explorers, Dionisio Alcalá Galiano (1760–1805) and Cayetano Valdés (1767–1835), were the first Europeans to encounter the Fraser River proper when they entered its mouth from the sea in June 1792.[15]

The explorations of the upper river and the first descent of the entire river are further examples of the epic nature of travels associated with the fur trade in Canada. The first European to travel on the upper river was Alexander Mackenzie (1764–1820), the Scottish explorer employed by the North West Company and the first European to descend the Mackenzie River to the Arctic Ocean (see Chapter 2). After his exploration of the Mackenzie River, Mackenzie spent some time back in England refining his navigation skills and reading accounts of explorers.[16] He returned to Canada in the spring of 1792 and set out again from Montreal for Fort Chipewyan on Lake Athabasca in what is now northern Alberta and Saskatchewan. In October of the same year he left the fort to search for a route to the Pacific from Lake Athabasca. On this trip, Mackenzie entered the Peace River from the east, wintering at the confluence of the Peace's great southern- and northern-flowing tributaries, the Finlay and Parsnip rivers. In the spring of 1793, Mackenzie travelled upstream on the Parsnip River and entered the upper Fraser River by using a portage known to Indigenous people that passed between Arctic Lake (tributary to the Parsnip River) and Portage and Pacific lakes (tributaries of the Fraser River via the McGregor River), all of which straddle the Continental Divide across less than 10 km of a narrow, steep-sided valley. From here, Mackenzie was warned by Indigenous people that the Fraser River, and the canyon in particular, was too dangerous to descend owing to the violent flows and the hostile local natives. Accordingly, and after having some canoes destroyed and almost drowning in one Fraser River canyon, Mackenzie left the Fraser River by ascending one of its tributaries, the West Road River (or Blackwater River), about 170 km downstream from where he first entered the upper Fraser River. From the West Road River, Mackenzie crossed the Coast Mountains crest and entered and descended the Bella Coola River, which empties into West Bentinck Arm, an inlet to the Pacific Coast. By doing so, on July 20, 1793, Mackenzie became the first European to cross North America (north of Mexico – some 10 years before Lewis and Clark accomplished this feat via the Missouri and Columbia rivers in the United States.[17] Mackenzie was knighted in 1802 by King George III for these and other epic efforts (see Chapter 2).

While Mackenzie's exploits opened considerable new territory for exploitation of furs, the route to the Pacific that he charted proved impractical for commercial use. Consequently, Simon Fraser (1776–1862), born in New York, but of Scottish descent and in the employ of the North West Company, was assigned the task of establishing trading posts west of the Rocky Mountains and developing a practical route to the Pacific Ocean. In 1803, from his base in the Athabasca Department of the North West Company, Fraser retraced Mackenzie's steps up the Peace River, but crossed into the upper Fraser further west at a portage between the Parsnip River and the Pack (Crooked) River. Here he established the first permanent European settlement west of the Rocky Mountains in Canada (Fort McLeod) at what is now McLeod Lake, and named the area "New Caledonia." Fraser and assistants established other forts, including Fort St. James (on Stuart Lake) and Fort Fraser (near Fraser Lake). From Stuart Lake, Fraser learned from local Indigenous people that one could reach the Fraser River via downstream passage of the Stuart River and then the Nechako River. Fraser explored the area while waiting for resupply and in 1807 founded Fort George (now Prince George) near the confluence of the Nechako and Fraser rivers. From here, Fraser began his epic voyage down what he thought was the Columbia River (the mouth of which had been explored by 1792 – see Chapter 5) to find a practical route to the Pacific.

Fraser's trip down the river named after him has been called the "climax" and the "most terrible and wonderful" inland voyage of the various fur-trading adventures in North America, a voyage down what Hugh MacLennan in *Seven Rivers of Canada* described as "the savagest of all the major rivers of America. It is probably the savagest in the world."[18] The voyage consisted of four canoes and 23 fur traders and began in May 1808. Passing the point where Mackenzie left the Fraser at West Road River, Fraser and his party entered the

"Black Canyon" near the confluence of the Chilcotin and Fraser rivers. Fraser was confronted by surging waters enclosed by massive cliffs where the river was considered completely impassable. Caching canoes and some supplies, the party set off on foot along treacherous riverside paths. Upon reaching an area near the present-day town of Lillooet, BC, and later a point near the confluence of the Thompson and Fraser rivers, Fraser traded for enough canoes for his party to continue the river voyage. Again, however, some 60 km downstream after more portages and rapids Fraser had to abandon the canoes for another overland route owing to the extreme violence of the river's flow. Faced with starvation or potential plunges to death from cliffs thousands of feet above the river, Fraser had no choice but to press on. Eventually, and remarkably, Fraser emerged from the canyon near Yale, BC, where the river became navigable again. Here, supplied with salmon and purchasing canoes from local Indigenous people, Fraser's party reached the Pacific Ocean near Vancouver, BC, in July 1808.[19]

Reminiscent of how Mackenzie felt after his voyage down the Mackenzie River, Fraser evinced "great disappointment"[20] with his effort when he realized that his estimation of latitude at the mouth of the Fraser River (49°N) was too far north for it to be the Columbia River (46°N), and because of the obvious problems with navigating the Fraser River; navigation was "absolutely impracticable.... We had to pass where no human being should venture."[21] He was not alone in his opinion. After his own inspection of the Fraser River in 1828, Sir George Simpson, a governor of the Hudson's Bay Company, declared: "I should consider the passage down, to be certain Death, in nine attempts out of Ten. I shall therefore no longer talk about it as a navigable stream."[22] Worse still, Fraser now needed to return upstream, back to Fort George, necessitating a second passage of the Fraser River and its "innumerable perils."[23] Further, Indigenous people at the mouth of the Fraser River proved to be somewhat less welcoming and Fraser needed to move upstream perhaps more hastily than he had wished. Bad feelings between Fraser's party and Indigenous people seemed to spread upstream. Bombarded by rocks from above by the now hostile local people en route, low on food, understandably physically and mentally exhausted, and with a mutiny brewing, Fraser's voyage reached its nadir. Displaying great leadership, Fraser sensed impending doom. Consequently, he assembled his men and all took the following oath: "I solemnly swear before Almighty God that I shall sooner perish than forsake any of our crew during the present voyage."[24]

Pressing on, Fraser's party found their cached canoes and supplies above Hells Gate and eventually crawled, dragged canoes and powered their way upstream to arrive back at Fort George in early August 1808 after 37 days of travel. While failing to establish a viable transportation route from the Athabasca country to the Pacific Ocean by canoe, Fraser's exploits were key to helping British claims to sovereignty over the area and to the establishment of the 49th parallel boundary between the US and what is now Canada after the War of 1812. Fraser's information about the Fraser River was key to establishing Fort Langley on the south side of the river in 1827, and hence extending the 49th parallel to the west coast (and securing all the Fraser River basin for Canada) with the Treaty of Oregon in 1846.[25]

Pacific salmon: Iconic biodiversity of the Fraser River

ONE OF THE KEY ELEMENTS for the survival of Fraser's party was the timely provision of food in the form of salmon traded for, or given as gifts from, local Indigenous Peoples. In fact, Fraser's May–August return trip overlapped with the movement of many runs of adult salmon returning from the ocean to spawn in fresh water. There are five species of Pacific salmon native to the Fraser River: pink salmon (*Oncorhynchus gorbuscha*), chum salmon (*O. keta*), sockeye salmon (*O. nerka*), coho salmon (*O. kisutch*), and chinook salmon (*O. tshawytscha*). Two species of Pacific trout, the rainbow/steelhead trout (*O. mykiss*) and the cutthroat trout (*O. clarkii*), and several species of char and whitefishes (all members of the family Salmonidae), also inhabit the river.

Listing of the 20 or so species of salmon, trout, char and whitefishes that inhabit the Fraser River is, however, a meagre summation of the incredible diversity of this group of fishes, and of Pacific salmon in particular. This is because each species consists of myriad subgroups defined by areas in which they breed and by distinctions in their physical attributes.[26] These subgroups can range from collections of populations ranging over various watersheds to individual local populations that may be restricted to a small tributary or a portion of a tributary (e.g., above a waterfall that is passable only during certain times of the year). This propensity to differentiate into local populations or varieties is characteristic of salmon and trout worldwide and stems from three principal factors: (i) the geographic history of each area inhabited by salmon, particularly in terms of glacier history, (ii) differences in environmental factors among rivers, and (iii) the uncanny ability of adult salmon to "home" or return to their natal stream or lake to reproduce. Geographic history and salmon homing tend to promote isolation among spawning populations of salmon. The occurrence within the Fraser River basin of each of the various Pacific salmon species in multiple rivers which differ in a host of ways (e.g., water temperature, distance of spawning areas from feeding areas, water velocity, kinds of predators), raises the possibility that natural selection may promote differentiation among populations of Fraser River salmon in particular ways. Of course, other major rivers of the Pacific Coast (e.g., the Yukon, Columbia and Sacramento-San Joaquin rivers) also contain various populations of one or more Pacific salmon species spread across different rivers, lakes and streams within their basins. With the evolutionary forces of drift and natural selection operating across such a vast range of geography and environmental conditions, it is easy to see how the spectacular diversity of species and population of Pacific salmon has developed.

Natural selection, first articulated by Charles Darwin and Alfred Russell Wallace in the mid-19th century, can act to favour local attributes of fish from specific rivers, attributes that are associated with higher survival or reproductive success in those rivers. If such natural selection on attributes produces changes that are inherited by offspring from their parents, then the frequency of a favoured attribute may increase over multiple generations within a population. This is evolution by "local adaptation" – a phenomenon for which salmon and trout are among the most famous examples.

Further, if a trait (e.g., upstream migration of adult salmon during the summer months) enhances survival in one river compared to another river (e.g., where migration in the autumn is advantageous) local adaptation *within* each population drives differentiation *between* salmon populations from these two rivers within the Fraser River basin.[27] This differentiation will be enhanced because the salmon are in different rivers, which reduces the potential for interbreeding between the two populations (interbreeding acts to constrain differentiation). Hence, three factors: geographic history, salmon homing, and environmental differences among rivers, have interacted over the history of populations to produce what is a striking degree of biodiversity within each species of Pacific salmon via local adaptation.

Good examples of local adaptation are the many and varied instances of microscale specialization of populations to their specific stream/lake habitats in the Fraser River. For instance, the migration life history of juvenile sockeye salmon can vary among populations. In the most common pattern, however, juveniles live and feed in lakes for 1–2 years after they emerge from their gravel nests, which are typically found in streams tributary to these "nursery lakes" (see Map 6). These tributary streams can be lake inlets (in which case the young fish, known as "fry," must move *downstream* to the nursery lake), lake outlets (in which case the fry must swim *upstream* to the lake) or sometimes the spawning tributaries may be smaller streams that flow into inlets or outlets. These different stream orientations relative to the nursery lake result in fish from different populations becoming specialized for different behaviours. One striking example of local adaptation at a small spatial scale is provided by the fish from Weaver Creek, a small tributary of the Harrison River that forms the outlet for Harrison Lake and eventually empties into the Fraser River about 80 km upstream of Vancouver. The physical relationship between Weaver Creek, the Harrison River and Harrison Lake means that sockeye salmon fry from Weaver Creek must first move downstream to reach the Harrison River, and then *reverse* their movement and swim upstream in the Harrison River to reach the nursery lake, Harrison Lake. That the fish do this reflects incredible specialization to their physical environments. Weaver Creek fry, for instance, have an innate tendency to orient in a northeast direction, and Harrison Lake is located northeast of the Weaver Creek spawning areas. Such directional orientation is not altered when magnetic fields are experimentally reversed (adult salmon can orient using magnetic fields during their oceanic migrations), and the innate directional preference of juveniles gets stronger over time, when the moon is visible, and upon exposure to Harrison River water. These observations suggest that the innate directional orientation of Weaver Creek sockeye salmon fry is a result of local adaptation to the orientation of the spawning, migratory and nursery habitats and that its expression is facilitated by temporal and environmental cues (water flow, position of the moon).[28]

Not all intraspecies biodiversity of Pacific salmon is, however, a result of local adaptation; some large-scale patterns in biodiversity have been driven by changes in the genome that are not the action of selection – so-called "neutral" traits – that have occurred independently in assemblages of populations isolated by historical changes in their geographic distributions.[29] For instance, during the multiple episodes of Pleistocene glaciation, during which the Fraser River drainage was completely covered by ice, Pacific salmon persisted in freshwater habitats south (e.g., in the lower Columbia River) or north (e.g., in unglaciated portions of the Yukon River or adjacent areas of the coast) of the Cordilleran Ice Sheet. These "glacial refugia" were sufficiently isolated from one another for thousands of salmon generations that populations within them accumulated neutral genetic differences. As the ice sheets retreated, salmon from these different refugia sometimes colonized the same watersheds, and the differences that accumulated through isolation in distinct refugia can still be observed through genetic analysis of today's populations. In the Fraser River, two major genetic groups or lineages of coho salmon have been identified: one composed of spawning populations located below Hells Gate (near the downstream end of the Fraser Canyon) and the other from populations spawning in streams tributary to the upper Fraser River and a major tributary above Hells Gate, the Thompson River.[30] These two groups appear to have resulted from the postglacial colonization of the Fraser River by one group of coho salmon that survived in coastal refugia in and around Puget Sound and the lower Columbia River (these fish colonized the lower Fraser River), and a second group from an inland refuge in the unglaciated Columbia River (these fish colonized the upper Fraser River and Thompson River). This "double colonization" may have occurred because early during deglaciation, the lower Fraser River was blocked by an ice dam, so that the upper Fraser River, which was ice free, flowed to the sea via the upper Columbia River, which was connected to the upper Fraser River through glacial lakes, Merritt (now part of the Thompson River drainage) and Penticton (now part of the Okanagan River).[31] The upper Fraser-Thompson River group of coho salmon colonized the Fraser through this interior route, whereas the coastal salmon colonized the lower Fraser directly from the sea after the ice dam melted. These two lineages of coho salmon in the Fraser River are, therefore, signatures of the geological history of the basin and part of the evolutionary legacy of the species. The unique geographic history of the Thompson River coho salmon is, in large part, the reason why their conservation status is determined separately from all other coho salmon populations in the basin under Canada's Species at Risk Act. Hence, large temporal and spatial scale aspects of the Fraser River's geomorphology have impacted the biodiversity of a single species, with consequences for humans and salmon conservation.[32]

These different forms of biodiversity among populations of coho salmon and sockeye salmon of the Fraser River are but two examples of what are literally probably hundreds of divergent populations driven by the combined actions of historical and contemporary physical isolation, variable environments and natural selection adapting populations to different conditions within this river system. Such diversity is the joyful playground of fish watchers and professional ecologists and evolutionary biologists. Indeed, much of my own career has been occupied with travelling portions of the Fraser River and its tributaries studying the diversity of salmon and trout and the processes that generate and sustain it.

Salmon and trout biodiversity also has very practical value. Biologists interested in the consequences of biodiversity refer to the "portfolio effect" provided by diverse populations within a species distributed across a landscape. This analogy to the economic concept of an investment portfolio provides a species with a "buffering" effect against population declines in the presence of environmental variation. Having a diversity of salmon population types means that when environmental conditions that prevail in some years (say, low water levels) depress some populations, other populations that are adapted to these same environmental conditions may do better. Spread across a complex of populations experiencing environmental variation across space and time, this diversity means that the species *as a whole* is less subject to the ups and downs of the environment and the species' overall productivity can be relatively stable in the face of such environmental "noise" (much as having a diversified investment portfolio means that the investor is less exposed to downturns in one particular aspect of the economy). A striking example of the portfolio effect occurs in Bristol Bay, southwestern Alaska. Here, sockeye salmon consist of a complex of hundreds of distinct populations inhabiting different watersheds. The sockeye salmon are caught in fisheries in Bristol Bay (North America's largest), and the performance of the fishery, in terms of total catch averaged over years, appears to benefit from the portfolio effect. Observations of fishery catches and population size show that the biodiverse Bristol Bay sockeye salmon assemblage of populations exhibits a relatively stable overall population size in the face of year-to-year environmental variation, resulting in fewer fishery closures (fewer than four per century) and much greater and more sustainable economic gains. By contrast, under scenarios where the species is composed of a single homogenous population, abundance is predicted to be much more variable as environments change, and this results in more fishery closures (every 2–3 years).[33] Consequently, conserving habitats and processes that generate diversity like that displayed by Bristol Bay sockeye salmon is of tremendous importance not only for sustaining natural biodiversity but also for sustaining the livelihoods of those who depend on the fishery.

Importance of salmon to humans along the Fraser River

SALMON have undoubtedly been supporting other wildlife and ecosystems since they first colonized the proto-Fraser River perhaps
10–15 million ya, whether as prey or from nutrient enrichment provided by their post-spawning, decomposing bodies. To humans,
Fraser River salmon are of tremendous aesthetic, cultural, recreational and commercial importance. This multifaceted significance
is reflected, in part, by the recent recognition of Pacific salmon as the
official fish(es) of British Columbia. One aspect of the importance of
Fraser River salmon is the fishery that exploits them. The fishery for
Pacific salmon has developed to comprise three components: Indigenous communal, recreational and commercial.

The importance of Pacific salmon culturally and as sources of
food to Indigenous Peoples of the Pacific Rim is reflected in their
specific names (e.g., *nerka*), which stem from the local names given
to each species by native inhabitants of Kamchatka.[34] Many kinds of
fishes have been important to humans along the Fraser River (e.g.,
eulachon, sturgeon), but it is the Pacific salmon that have had the
greatest impact given their generally large size (from 2 to more than
40 kg), huge abundances (sockeye salmon and pink salmon runs
can number in the millions to tens of millions annually), high nu-
tritional value and seasonal predictability of return to fresh water.
Archaeological evidence suggests that salmon were exploited at canyon sites on the Thompson River (a tributary of the Fraser River) at
least 7,500 ya,[35] and were critical aspects of human diets that promoted settlement and, during shortages, precipitated periodic cultural
collapse.[36] More sophisticated use of traps began at least 4,600 ya and
gillnet technology was in use by 3,000 ya.[37] At least in the lower river, salmon as part of a general Northwest Coast Fishery subsistence
economy likely contributed to the development of societies with a
level of spatial permanence, cultural development, status, specialization and population size not normally associated with exploitation of
wild food, particularly as river levels stabilized after about 5,000 ya.[38]

The historical and current importance[39] of salmon to Indigenous
Peoples of the Fraser River is reflected in ceremonies such as the

First Salmon Ceremony of the Stó:lō. Here, the first salmon of the season are brought back and shared with the community. The bones are then returned to the river to ensure good luck in fishing and a strong run of salmon. Salmon were also a critical aspect of trade, especially after contact began with Europeans; one exchange involved over 7,000 salmon traded with the Hudson's Bay Company at Fort Langley.[40] The long-standing traditional importance of salmon to Indigenous Peoples in the Fraser River basin is also reflected in the fact that the right to fish for salmon (or other food fishes) is a legal one, recognized in the Canadian Constitution Act (1982) and is subject to forfeiture only in the name of conservation.[41] Today, the Indigenous fishery in the Fraser River involves use of, and priority access to, salmon for food, cultural and ceremonial purposes and occasionally for commercial sale. The continued viability of the Indigenous fishery for Fraser River salmon is considered a "vital"[42] aspect of the cultural, physical and spiritual well-being of many First Nations.

The recreational fishery for Fraser River salmon has been carried on for well over 100 years and is firmly established as an "icon of west coast lifestyle."[43] The recreational fishery provides a healthy leisure and social activity that helps connect people to their natural environments, and it also is the source of enormous economic benefits. As part of the general west coast recreational fishery engaged in by locals and tourists, fishing for Fraser River salmon, whether while they are at sea or in the river proper, contributes to thousands of jobs in British Columbia and millions of dollars of revenue (from expenditures on fishing gear, boats, fuel, and licence and retention fees) annually; up to 40% of the total value of fisheries resources in British Columbia is derived from recreational fishing.[44]

From the first trading of salmon between Indigenous Peoples and European explorers and fur traders, the commercial exploitation of Fraser River salmon has played a critical role in the industrial development of British Columbia. The fishery has provided a livelihood for families of diverse backgrounds across multiple generations, provided export products to 63 countries of the world and, at its peak in the mid-1990s, generated a landed value of up to almost $200 million dollars annually.

While the multifaceted importance of Fraser River salmon highlights their significance to British Columbia, it also greatly complicates their successful management by fisheries authorities. This complexity stems from the biological complexity inherent in a group of fishes with multiple species and hundreds of different populations, but is also a function of the legal developments pertaining to entitlements to Indigenous fishing, Canada's Species at Risk Act (2003, SARA) and the overlapping claims to the resource by First Nations and other users. The multiple species of salmon from different areas of British Columbia contribute in variable degrees to the combined value of Indigenous, recreational and commercial fisheries. The sockeye salmon fishery of the Fraser River, however, has been the most notable since Confederation owing to, on average, the higher market value and abundance of this species. Even the recreational fishery for Fraser River sockeye salmon, traditionally more focused on larger and more "robust" species such as chinook salmon and coho salmon, has become more important given the declines in catches and more restrictive conservation measures placed on chinook and coho salmon since the 1990s.

Since the early 1890s, total estimated annual returns of Fraser River sockeye salmon have ranged from fewer than 1 million to over 40 million. In 2010 alone, the estimated total return was just under 30 million fish. Unfortunately, the volatility of the total return is also notable and, in fact, in 2009, just one year before the boom year of 2010, the Fraser River recorded the lowest estimated return in over 50 years, just slightly over 1 million fish. This small return, the third in a row, resulted in a third consecutive year of fishery closures. The small returns were accompanied by evidence that Fraser River sockeye salmon were experiencing a persistent drop in productivity, i.e., the number of spawning fish ("recruits") in a river that result from spawning four years earlier (sockeye salmon in the Fraser River mature, predominantly, at four years of age). This decline in productivity occurred over several decades and has resulted in maximum consternation among users of the resource.

These negative developments in the Fraser River sockeye salmon fishery led the Canadian government to establish a judicial

Sockeye salmon holding before spawning, Adams River, South Thompson River, Fraser River drainage.

commission (i.e., one with the power of subpoena), led by Mr. Justice Bruce Cohen, under the Inquiries Act to investigate, broadly, the causes of the decline and the current and long-term status of the populations, and to develop recommendations to improve the long-term sustainability of the Fraser River sockeye salmon fishery. The critical interaction between the Fraser River sockeye salmon and humans is reflected in the fact this was the first ever inquiry into a fishery for a specific species in a single river (e.g., a Royal Commission 30 years previously had a broader mandate to investigate several Pacific Coast fisheries – The Pearse Commission on Pacific Fisheries Policy, 1982).

The Cohen Commission held 133 days of evidentiary hearings, heard from 179 witnesses, commissioned 15 technical reports, received over 900 submissions of comment from the public, received

2,145 documents as evidence and produced 14,166 pages of transcripts over its three years of activity. The final report, delivered in October 2012, was a three-volume 1,129-page document. In total, the commission cost the Canadian taxpayer at least $26 million and made 75 specific recommendations, many with associated benchmarks and timelines, ranging from a moratorium on further salmon aquaculture developments in certain areas to full implementation of the Canadian Department of Fisheries and Oceans' (DFO's) Wild Salmon Policy that had been stalled since its release in 2005.

With a respected commission of such scope completed at enormous cost in terms of time, effort and money, on a subject of clear and present importance to the people of British Columbia and Canada, it would normally be expected that timely action stemming from these recommendations by the Canadian federal government, which has legislative authority to manage salmon in Canada, would follow. Sadly, and perhaps somewhat predictably, this has not been so. Watershed Watch Salmon Society, a British Columbia–based, non-governmental organization whose mandate is to encourage and "catalyze efforts to protect and restore BC's precious wild salmon" produced a "Cohen Report Card" that evaluated the degree of action taken by the government on the 75 recommendations. Of 20 recommendations with initial or final deadlines for action of September 30, 2015, only one received a grade of "Complete"; all others were either "Incomplete" (14 recommendations) or there has been "No public response" from the federal minister of fisheries and oceans when queried on the status of a recommendation (5 recommendations).[45] Subsequently, DFO presented its final update on implementation of the commission's findings in 2018 and concluded that 100% of the recommendations have now been successfully implemented.[46] Conversely, Watershed Watch Salmon Society considered the self-evaluation of implementations by DFO to be "biased" and that many instances of implementation were "dressed-up" as action.[47] In principle, a self-evaluation by DFO in the absence of any external review is clearly problematic. In fact, perhaps the most important recommendation given by Justice Cohen appeared in the last paragraph of the commission's three volumes: that an "independent body such as the office of the Commissioner of the Environment and Sustainable Development should report to the Standing Committee on Fisheries and Oceans and the public ... on the extent to which and the manner in which this Commission's recommendations have been implemented."[48] Regrettably, no such high-level independent review has been completed.

Furthermore, the federal government has consistently refused to legally list salmon populations as Endangered, Threatened or Special Concern under SARA despite the recommendations of an independent science panel, the Committee on the Status of Endangered Wildlife in Canada (COSEWIC), that is charged with providing such advice to the government under the Act.[49] I was a member of COSEWIC for ten years and its chair from 2015 to 2018 and I felt, and still do, that this pattern of delayed action or inaction and the general modus operandi of DFO is inconsistent with protecting and restoring the diversity of wild salmon in the Fraser River basin.[50] Since the Cohen Commission finished its work, the fishery for sockeye salmon has been limping along; despite the largest run in 100 years in 2010 (just under 30 million fish), returns in 2011–2020 have been similarly variable, with some good years (~20 million in 2014) to disappointing years (about 2–3 million in 2013) to dismal; 2020 saw the lowest return in recorded history, fewer than 300,000 sockeye salmon (2019 was the previous low), and no commercial harvest was allowed. By way of comparison, the annual sockeye salmon run in the Bristol Bay, Alaska, fishery (with a combined drainage area of less than one-half of the Fraser River), has averaged 25.5 million fish during 1991–2010, over 29 million fish (range 23–39 million) during 2012–2014, and was 57.8 million in 2020 (with over 39 million retained by the fishery)![51] While there are important differences between the two areas and their sockeye salmon that defy direct comparisons, the uncertainty about the extent and effectiveness of the Cohen Commission recommendations in light of ongoing variability of the Fraser River sockeye salmon run sizes continues to place these populations at risk and does not bode well for the sustainability of the fishery for Pacific salmon. The deteriorating situation is also reflected by assessments by COSEWIC since 2016 that have led to recommendations for at-risk status for 15 populations of sockeye salmon, 13 populations of chinook salmon, and the Thompson River assemblage of at least five subpopulations of coho salmon in the Fraser basin. No Pacific salmon have yet been listed under SARA, and while several listing decisions are still pending, based on past experience the likelihood of decisions to list is extremely low.

The future of salmon in the Fraser River

WHILE THE SOCKEYE SALMON and its fishery continue to struggle in the Fraser River, there are signs of recovery and occasional "super abundances" of other species such as pink salmon. It is not well understood why certain species are apparently doing well, at least in recent times, while others struggle, but one idea is that changes in ocean conditions, primarily changing water temperatures and their influences on salmon feed production and survival, are of paramount importance. Given that salmon species differ in behaviour, physiology and ocean distribution, it is not surprising that species of Pacific salmon exhibit some asynchrony in population trends.[52] For the Fraser River, the two most important factors likely to impact the long-term persistence of salmon biodiversity are climate change and increasing human development in and around the lower Fraser River, and the multifarious stressors associated with such development. These two factors are not independent of one another.

First, consider climate change. Arguably, the Fraser River is near the southern limit of the optimal environmental range for sea-run *Oncorhynchus*. For instance, the total pre-development run size for *all* species of Pacific salmon and steelhead trout in the Columbia River has been estimated at just under 8 million to perhaps as many as 16 million annually.[53] Although Pacific salmon exist well south of the Fraser River and large historical runs of chinook salmon have occurred in the Sacramento–San Joaquin River system (probably 1–2 million fish),[54] the Fraser River has been characterized as the greatest single river producer of Pacific salmon on the west coast.[55] Many factors (e.g., presence of large lake systems) clearly influence the distribution of salmon and their abundance across areas, but climatological factors in both fresh and marine waters likely also play an important role. Comparatively lower total run sizes in major rivers south of the Fraser River suggest that the Fraser River approaches both upper critical and optimal temperature conditions for salmon.[56] Consequently, changing (i.e., warming) climate is unlikely to enhance the survival of Pacific salmon of the Fraser River.

Water temperature can have direct and indirect effects on salmon survival during various life stages and in both marine and freshwater environments. Direct effects include mortality from heat stress; indirect effects include things like declines or other changes in food supply and increased susceptibility to diseases or pathogens. The Cohen Commission concluded that, although there was no single "smoking gun"[57] that could explain the declines in productivity of Fraser River sockeye salmon or very low returns, fluctuations in water temperature and their effects on salmon food production, and perhaps presence of predators in the marine environment, were probably very important factors. Furthermore, projections by the Intergovernmental Panel on Climate Change (IPCC) of a 2–4°C rise in North Pacific Ocean sea surface temperatures under the "business as usual" scenario suggest that conditions potentially unsuitable for feeding sockeye salmon could become the norm (i.e., July water temperatures of 12°C or less will not be a "significant" part of the North Pacific).[58] The water temperature of the Fraser River when adult fish return to spawn has increased by about 2.5°C in the last 60 years and a further 2°C increase is projected to occur over the next 75 years under some IPCC climate models. Episodic increases in water temperatures during the summer and early autumn upstream migration periods have been associated with significant increases in pre-spawning mortality in salmon. Even with only a modest increase in average summertime water temperatures of 1°C, salmon may experience a tripling of the number of days where temperatures exceed the upper critical thermal thresholds of 19°C. These conditions may decrease survival during migration by as much as 16% – estimates that are considered "optimistic."[59]

The biodiversity within each species described earlier in the chapter means that some species and populations may be able to cope better than others and that there is some evolutionary potential for salmon to adapt to climate change. Predicting what will actually transpire is, however, fraught with uncertainty. Further, Pacific salmon have clearly demonstrated resiliency to environmental change throughout a history accompanied by tectonic changes and glaciation. In addition to the fact that such resiliency to changes has occurred over much longer time frames than current climate change, the resiliency of Pacific salmon depends, critically, on a number of biological attributes that have been compromised by human exploitation and mismanagement of the species.[60] For instance, habitat loss may preclude the opportunistic use of alternative habitats by salmon. Hatchery practices can reduce genetic diversity within and among populations, or may transfer traits of hatchery salmon that are not optimal for survival in nature to wild fish through the interbreeding between hatchery and wild fish. Finally, managing fisheries for maximum yield can favour large, productive runs of salmon at the expense of smaller, less productive runs and reduce overall biodiversity. These factors all work against the "portfolio effect" described earlier and therefore degrade the inherent resilience of Pacific salmon.[61] The potential for the portfolio effect to operate in the Fraser River is suggested by the recognition of 24 "conservation units" (CUs) of sockeye salmon in the Fraser River by DFO.[62] These CUs are single populations, or groups of populations, that are sufficiently distinct from one another (usually in terms of location and/or a specialized trait) such that if any CU is lost it is probably irreplaceable over some agreed-upon timeframe such as a human lifespan or a particular number of salmon generations. The concept of conservation units was developed to promote population assessment and conservation. In his own words, Justice Cohen described the prognosis, at least for sockeye salmon in the Fraser River under climate change, as "bleak,"[63] saying that reduced productivity is to be expected. The commission also concluded that it was "likely"[64] that the number of these conservation units of sockeye salmon that are at risk and that will be lost will increase. The possibility that Pacific salmon as a group may respond to climate warming by shifting their distributions northward and perhaps making greater use of Arctic watersheds is cold comfort to those who value thriving populations within the Fraser River.[65]

The other major factor working against salmon biodiversity in the Fraser River (and all the benefits to humanity that flow from it) is increasing human encroachment on the river, especially the lower river. This effect is not wholly independent from climate change, because deteriorating conditions in habitat and water quality in the lower Fraser River may compromise responses of Pacific salmon to warmer water. One of the most critical habitats for Pacific salmon in the lower Fraser River (i.e., the last 150 km) is the Fraser River Estuary. The estuary itself is at least 300 km^2 in area and forms the outflow of a drainage basin of about 233,000 km^2. The estuary is one of the largest on the Pacific coast and is home to over 400 vertebrate species[66] and thousands of invertebrate and plant species. The Fraser River Estuary is also an integral component of the Pacific Flyway, the series of staging and feeding areas along the west coast for migratory birds originating from 20 countries and three continents. The estuary is also vital habitat for Pacific salmon. It provides an exceptionally productive feeding area for young salmon as they move from the freshwater habitats to the ocean. The estuary also allows the young salmon to "transition" physiologically to ocean life; the estuary has salinity levels higher than fresh water but lower than sea water and, therefore, provides an area where they can adjust to the higher salinity of marine habitats. The estuary and lower river are also the point of re-contact with fresh water for adults on the spawning migration. Consequently, the quality of habitat in the lower river and estuary is a critical factor influencing survival of salmon at the beginning and later portions of their remarkable lives.

The areas encompassing the lower Fraser River and estuary are also home to over just over 2.7 million people and Canada's third largest and fastest-growing major city, Vancouver.[67] The city of Vancouver lies mostly north of the estuary, but the Greater Vancouver Regional District comprises other municipalities (e.g., Richmond, Delta, Surrey etc.) which, together with Vancouver, completely surround the lower river and estuary. The Greater Vancouver area has attracted over 100,000 new residents since 2011 and has been projected to grow to over 4.1 million by 2041.[68] The middle and upper portions of the Fraser River are, by contrast, much less densely populated (the Fraser–Fort George Regional District is the largest, with a projected population of about 97,000 in 2041), but that does not provide immunity from human encroachment. The Mount Polley Mine disaster in August 2014 spilled 24 million m³ of mine tailings slurry into Quesnel Lake, a major producer of sockeye salmon, in central British Columbia, resulting in a persistent toxic plume circulating in the lake. Although its full effects are still being quantified,[69] the release of the toxic slurry into a formerly relatively pristine major salmon-producing system of the Fraser Basin is Canada's single worst mining spill and one of the severest human-caused environmental disasters in Canadian history.[70] Still, by any reasonable approximation, salmon will be sharing their habitat with an increasing number and concentration of humans at a focal spot for salmon biology – the lower Fraser River.

Human numbers (the number of people, their density, and increases in these demographic factors) have been described as the "alpha factor" – the key societal factor – affecting the future persistence of Pacific salmon.[71] Because increasing human population size is a key driver of demand for resources, whether it be space for housing or demand for fossil fuels, and associated economic policies, human demographic trends cannot be considered independent from anthropogenically driven changes in habitat quality like climate change. The Cohen Commission exhaustively reviewed the evidence for the roles of habitat loss, reduced water quality, contaminants, pollutants, pathogens etc. in the Fraser River, its estuary and adjacent areas of the Strait of Georgia (all of which experienced increases in human population size over the last 100 years) as causes of declining productivity and run sizes of sockeye salmon. The commission concluded that habitat loss and other "stressors" in salmon habitats have plausible mechanisms to negatively impact salmon and that none could be ruled out as factors contributing significantly to recent declines. The key limitation is research into the exact magnitude of these effects, either singly or cumulatively.

The "Salmon 2100 Project" was a collaborative effort with the stated goal to "improve the quality and utility of assessments of the ecological consequences of options to restore wild salmon to California, Oregon, Washington, Idaho, and southern British Columbia."[72] As part of this initiative, a basic question was posed: What does society have to do, specifically, in order to have sustainable runs of wild salmon at the end of the century? In developing strategies, policies and approaches for salmon to recover, the project acknowledged that people must be *willing* to act on the solutions proposed and accept the associated changes to their lifestyles. There has been a long and close relationship between Fraser River salmon and humans, and untold benefits have accrued to the latter from this relationship. Despite this history, the current perilous state of Fraser River salmon suggests that any assumption that society will say "yes" when asked if we are willing to make the necessary changes to our lifestyles to recover Pacific salmon is, sadly, not a safe one.

— FIVE —

The Columbia River
Empire Builder

On up the river at Grand Coulee Dam,
Mightiest thing ever built by a man,
To run these great factories and water the land,
It's roll on, Columbia Roll on.
Roll on, Columbia roll on
Roll on, Columbia roll on
Your power is turning our darkness to dawn,
Roll on Columbia roll on.

—From "Roll On Columbia" by Woody Guthrie, 1941

"Cascadia" is an informal geographical term denoting that region of northwestern North America encompassing southern British Columbia, Washington, Oregon and northern California. The name stems from the Cascade Mountain Range that runs from the southeastern edge of the middle and lower Fraser River in British Columbia to Lassen Peak in northern California. Many rivers flow to the Pacific Ocean from and through the Cascade Mountains, but the greatest of them all – the "master river"[1] of Cascadia – is the Columbia River. The Columbia River extends well inland from Cascadia and dominates the region owing to its size, the fact that the lower two-thirds of the river was unglaciated during the Pleistocene, and because some other great rivers of the area, like the Fraser River, were once tributaries of the Columbia River (see Chapter 4).

In 1807, David Thompson reached the source of the Columbia River, Columbia Lake, in southeastern British Columbia, where he noted chinook salmon spawning on the shores of the lake along the western slopes of the Rocky Mountains.[2] These salmon had surged over 1950 km to Columbia Lake from the ocean, a path with an elevation increase of over 800 m from the sea. In 1807, the chinook and other salmon of the Columbia River were a rich resource, with an estimated 8–16 million returning to spawn annually. Another resource so bountiful in the Columbia River was the water itself and the potential for that water to spur economic development through irrigation, barge transportation and power generation. These two fundamentally different products of the physicality of the Columbia River, salmon biodiversity and economic potential, would collide dramatically in 1942 with the completion of the Grand Coulee Dam 960 km upstream from the sea in central Washington. Without a fishway for the fish to use to move upstream, the Grand Coulee Dam sealed off almost 1000 km of river habitat to salmon and extinguished innumerable self-sustaining populations upstream of the dam, including *all* of those in Canada spawning as far upstream as Thompson observed – at the very western edge of the Rocky Mountains. In his 1985 book *Rivers of Empire: Water, Aridity, and the Growth of the American West*, Donald Worster coined the phrase the "hydraulic society of the West,"[3] a concept referring to the massive economic and social motivations and implications that stemmed from the spurt of dam building in the western US beginning in the 1930s, activity that was, to many, a necessary precondition to development of the American West. Hydropower was, in fact, central to the industrialization of the US more generally. As Martin Doyle described in *The Source: How Rivers Made America and America Remade Its Rivers*, if Britain's industrial revolution was powered by coal and steam, "America's ran on dams,"[4] from gristmills powered by coastal plains rivers of the Thirteen Colonies to rivers providing massive power and irrigation opportunities in the West.

The concept of the hydraulic West (also integral to this book's Chapters 6 and 7) built on the idea of the "hydraulic society"[5] and its socio-political implications such as the "Oriental despotism"[6] of Imperial China that developed, in part, through the growth of large state bureaucracies necessary to build, manage and control hydrological infrastructure for irrigation and flood control.[7] While perhaps not resulting in a society that could be called the "despotic West," the intensive period of dam construction on the Columbia River had, and continues to have, profound impacts on the environment and the societies that interact with the river. Like the river itself, the interactions between humans and the Columbia River are dynamic and reflect a continuum of effects that, in some cases, have come full circle – the *removal* of dams and attempts to restore ecosystems to pre-dam conditions. This chapter tells the story of the Columbia River and dams, and the social and economic motivations that drove the remaking of the river as a critical component of the hydraulic West.

The geography and origin of the Columbia River

THE COLUMBIA RIVER originates at Columbia Lake in the Rocky Mountain Trench in southeastern British Columbia. From Columbia Lake it flows northwest for 300 km before making a sweeping turn to the south just upstream of the Mica Dam. From there, the Columbia River travels generally south and southwest for 930 km before making a final turn west and northwest just south of Richland, Washington. It enters the Pacific Ocean at Astoria, Oregon, after a further 470 km. The Columbia River is the ninth longest in North America (52nd in the world), and seventh in terms of drainage area (657,490 km², 43rd in the world); 60% of its length and 85% of its drainage area occur in the United States, but up to 40% of the annual flow originates in Canada.[8] The Columbia River is, however, the largest in western North America in terms of discharge into the Pacific

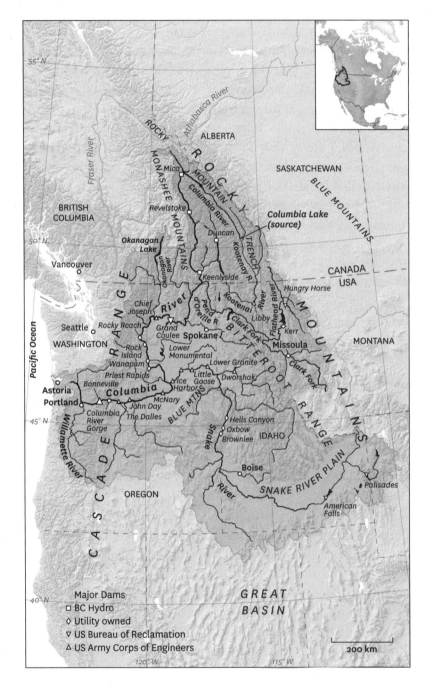

The Columbia River Basin. Major dams are shown as white squares, diamonds and/or triangles.

Ocean (average annual discharge of 7500 m³ – more than twice that of the Fraser River). As Blaine Harden stated in *A River Lost: Life and Death of the Columbia*, perhaps no other river in North America can match the Columbia River for "muscle";[9] the river drops in elevation at a rate per kilometre that is three times more than that of the Mississippi River across only slightly more than one-third the distance.[10] The Columbia River's major tributaries in terms of watershed area and discharge are the Snake River, Pend d'Oreille River (spelled Pend Oreille in the US), Kootenay (spelled Kootenai in the US) and Willamette River. As of 2010, the population size of the drainage was estimated at 8 million people across seven states and British Columbia, with about 98% of those living in the US. The basin in general shows strongly positive population growth trends and may well exceed 10 million by 2030.[11]

The origin of the current Columbia River, like that of many other west coast rivers, dates back at least 150 million years when the North American continent was drifting westward and terranes associated with oceanic plates joined with the western margins of the continental plate. These terranes were subsequently heavily modified by mountain building and volcanic activity and formed the structural framework for the modern Columbia River drainage. Through much of the Cretaceous Period (150–65 million ya), the proto-Columbia River was under shallow seas at the active western margin of North America. The last major period of mountain building in the Rocky Mountains, the Laramide Orogeny, occurred as a series of pulses lasting from about 85–50 million ya and may have been driven by the interaction between oceanic and continental plates and associated igneous activity (i.e., rocks formed by the extrusion and cooling of molten material from deep within the Earth).[12] These uplifts caused draining of the marginal Pacific seas, tectonically driven "warping" of the land and the resulting formation of folded mountain ranges and intervening intermontane basins. These processes set the basic drainage patterns for much of the northwest Pacific basin. More localized uplifting to current elevations occurred more recently in Oligocene to early Pliocene times (~33–5 million ya) and the Neogene. Much of the current waterscape and adjacent topography of the

Columbia River was formed subsequently during periods of tremendous volcanic activity in the Miocene and Pliocene (23–2.5 million ya) that created the Columbia River Basalt Group (CRBG) and the resulting Columbia Plateau.

The CRBG consists of a "stack-like" formation of multiple layers of basalt between the mouth of the Columbia River, through the Cascade Mountains and east to the Rocky Mountains. The CRBG stems from the eruption and massive flooding of basalt-forming magma (molten rock) that originated from volcanic plumes within the Earth's mantle.[13] These plumes of magma covered an area of over 200,000 km², largely in southeastern Washington State, northeastern Oregon and adjacent regions of western Idaho. There were hundreds of distinct plumes that erupted, running in various directions for up to hundreds of kilometres. An estimated 98% of these plumes erupted between 16.6 and 14.5 million ya, but the most recent occurred about 6 million ya. These plumes, owing to their power and weight, caused depressions in the landscape and formed or reinforced much of the current Columbia River drainage pattern through central Washington, punching through the rising Cascade Mountains to the Pacific Ocean. The northwesterly flow of the upper river was facilitated by continual uplifting along the western edge of the Rocky Mountains, depressions within the central Columbia basin (e.g., the Pasco Basin) and the earlier formation of numerous "dikes" of rock that channelled the flow. The layers of basaltic rock that formed during these floods were up to 4 km thick and, combined with sinking of the landscape, created the vast Columbia River Plateau, stretching from the eastern margin of the Cascade Mountains to the Rocky Mountains.[14]

The next major series of events that influenced the evolution of the Columbia River was the Pleistocene glaciations and resulting flood waters. The most recent of the multiple Pleistocene glaciations (see Chapter 1) was the Wisconsinan, which reached its peak about 18,000 ya. Here, the southern margin of the Cordilleran Ice Sheet (that ice sheet west of the Continental Divide) consisted of three prominent lobes that projected south of the main ice margin: the Puget Ice Lobe extending down through, and just south of, present-day Puget

Sound, WA; the Okanagan Ice Lobe, which extended south to just past Lake Chelan, in central Washington; and the Flathead Ice Lobe, which extended to the current southern edge of Flathead Lake, MT.[15] Consequently, most of the lower two-thirds of the Columbia River was not covered by the Cordilleran Ice Sheet.

These ice lobes or tongues created huge lakes when they crossed and blocked rivers. One such lake was Glacial Lake Columbia, formed by the Okanagan Ice Lobe as it crossed the Columbia River about 150 km west of a location near present-day Spokane, WA, which would have been submerged. The lake was over 1300 km² (the largest natural lake in Washington currently is Lake Chelan at 135 km²). Farther upstream, the Flathead Ice Lobe blocked the Clark Fork River (a tributary of the Pend d'Oreille River, itself a tributary of the Columbia River), creating the even larger Glacial Lake Missoula in western Montana. This lake was about 7700 km² in area and is estimated to have contained about 50% of the volume of water in today's Lake Michigan.[16] Several times during Wisconsinan deglaciation, the ice dam holding back Glacial Lake Missoula collapsed, resulting in perhaps 100 or more massive and separate floods of water over a 3,000–4,000 year period between 20,000 and 14,000 ya.[17] Because the outlet of Glacial Lake Columbia was still blocked by ice, these floods punched through the landscape in what is now Grand Coulee (a "coulee" is a very deep ravine). The floods released, in as little as 48 hours, as much as 13 times the current flow of the Amazon River (~10 cubic *kilometres* per hour at a minimum) at speeds of up to 130 kilometres per hour and carried more flow than many times that of all today's rivers in the world combined.[18] These periodic floods through central Washington, down through the Columbia River Gorge and even up the Willamette River valley created the Channelled Scablands of eastern Washington and exposed many of the previously formed basaltic layers of the CRBG, resulting in the area's striking geological landscape of today. These massive floods also deposited rich glacial lake deposits and soils from the scablands (an estimated 210 km³) downstream along the Columbia River and up the Willamette River valley.[19] Such features are prime examples of "cataclysmic,"[20] rather than gradual, erosional processes of the Missoula Floods.

Ecological regions (or ecoregions) are geographic areas that can be defined as having generally similar ecosystems and environments, and there have been 15 such ecoregions defined for North America.[21] The historical phenomena acting across the Columbia River basin – mountain building to the east and the west, massive basaltic and hydrologic floods, erosion and deposition, and glaciation – all interacted to create the three major ecoregions of the Columbia River basin that are recognized today: Marine West Coast Forest (west of the Columbia River Gorge); Northwestern Forested Mountain (along the Cascade, Columbia and Rocky Mountains) and North American Desert (central Washington, Oregon and south-central British Columbia).[22] In particular, the North American Desert ecoregion, located east of the rain shadow cast by the Cascade and Coast Mountains, has many areas that receive much less than 600 mm of precipitation per year (compared to well over 2500 mm throughout much of southwestern British Columbia, western Washington and Oregon).[23] Consequently, and as a legacy from the past, the early postglacial central Columbia River basin comprised a large, powerful river running smack through a desert underlain by fertile soils – a landscape rich in hydroelectric and agricultural potential[24] – but there was one problem. Virtually all of the water flowed through a river valley far below the fertile lands.

Early human history of the Columbia River basin

HUMANS MAY HAVE BEEN witness to, and indeed, victims of the Missoula Floods.[25] The earliest archaeological evidence of Indigenous Peoples inhabiting the Columbia River drainage are Clovis-style artifacts dated to about 13,600 ya, near East Wenatchee, WA, in the mid-Columbia River.[26] Other finds near the confluence of the Snake and Columbia rivers date to similar times.[27] In a bank of the Columbia River, near Kennewick, WA, a nearly complete human skeleton dated at about 9,000 cal ya was found in 1996 and dubbed "Kennewick Man."[28] A pre-Clovis site on the Olympic Peninsula, WA, albeit northwest of the Columbia River, has been dated to a slightly earlier time of 13,800 ya.[29] Large archaeological finds of salmon bones near

The Dalles, OR, about 280 km upstream from the ocean, suggest that humans were heavily invested in localized salmon harvest on the Columbia River at least 9,200 ya,[30] and with large settlements of several thousands of individuals established by at least 3,500 ya.[31] Some 26 Tribal Nations/First Nations have ancestry within the Columbia River basin in the US and Canada.[32]

The first Europeans to see the Columbia River were explorers and traders seeking new sources of gold and furs, and the elusive Northwest Passage from the interior and Atlantic basins to the Pacific coast. As with early explorations of the Fraser River (see Chapter 4), they were chiefly Spanish and British. The first to document viewing the mouth of the Columbia River was Bruno de Heceta (1743–1807), who was sent by the viceroy of Spain's colonies in Mexico and Central America to explore north of California in response to rumoured Russian incursions in the area.[33] In 1775, Heceta discovered a large bay that is the mouth of the Columbia River (the Columbia Bar area), but his ship, the *Santiago*, could progress no further inland owing to strong waves and currents caused by the mixing of Columbia's strong flow with the ocean. John Meares (1756–1809) was a British fur trader based on northwestern Vancouver Island who, during the summer of 1788, followed up on Heceta's reports, yet failed to find the Columbia. Meares named the northern terminus of the Columbia Bar "Cape Disappointment" as an expression of his frustration. Four years later, Captain George Vancouver of the Royal Navy sailed north past the mouth of the Columbia River and noticed a change in water colour from the mixing of fresh and sea water but, believing Meares' negative report, did not carry on with exploring any further for the river itself. In May, 1792, an American merchant ship captain, Robert Gray, deployed a smaller craft, found a small passage across the Columbia Bar and entered the estuary in the *Columbia Rediviva* for the first time. Gray had spotted the river mouth a month or so earlier but was unable to cross into the estuary. Gray named the river after his ship, and the local Chinook peoples referred to it as "Whimal," meaning "Big River." Gray sailed as far as 24 km upstream, trading with Indigenous people and charting the river for nine days. In the autumn of that same year, William Broughton

(1762–1821), a lieutenant of George Vancouver, was sent to explore the river after Vancouver obtained a copy of Gray's charts. Broughton penetrated about 160 km upstream and laid claim to the river in the name of Britain. Gray, who had left the area, had earlier claimed the river for the US, but as a merchant had not registered the claim formally.[34]

These explorations of the lower Columbia River fed speculation that it was linked with the Missouri River and formed part of the long sought-after Northwest Passage. This notion was dispelled with the epic voyage of Meriwether Lewis (1774–1809) and William Clark (1770–1838). The Lewis and Clark Expedition (1804–1806), or The Corps of Discovery, is perhaps the most famous exploration of the American West. The expedition was initiated by then President Thomas Jefferson to help explore the lands newly acquired in the Louisiana Purchase (from France, 1803), principally to the head-waters of the Missouri River and the unknown Pacific basin. The effort's focus was to find a practical route from the midwest to the Pacific Ocean, and to lay claim to these areas in the face of competition from Britain and Spain. Jefferson had been inspired to explore the northwest after reading Alexander Mackenzie's account of his travels to the Canadian Pacific in 1793 (see Chapters 2 and 4).[35]

Departing from a camp just east of St. Louis in the spring of 1804, the expedition followed the Missouri River to its headwaters, crossing the Continental Divide in what is now Idaho through the Bitterroot Mountains and into the Clearwater River system (a tributary of the upper Snake River), through the summer and autumn of 1805. The group eventually entered the Snake River, and finally the Columbia River. William Broughton's notes were used to negotiate the lower Columbia River, and the expedition reached the Pacific Ocean in late November 1805. Lewis and Clark established Fort Clatsop on the south side of the river mouth to spend the winter and as a mark of official claim as US territory. After spending the winter at Fort Clatsop, the expedition began a return trip to St. Louis in March 1806 and returned in September, again, via the Missouri River. The Lewis and Clark expedition represented the first American crossing of the Continental Divide to reach the Pacific

Ocean from the Mississippi River (Alexander Mackenzie had done it via the Peace–Fraser–Bella Coola rivers in Canada in 1793), produced a prodigious amount of scientific information on the flora and fauna of the regions, more than 140 maps, and established much of the basis for US legal claims to the area. They also met and established relationships with at least 70 groups of Indigenous Peoples without whose help, particularly from a 16-year-old Lemhi Shoshone woman – the famous Sacagawea – the expedition would surely have failed.[36] The expedition, epic as it was, could not make up for the lack of a continuous freshwater route from the Mississippi River to the Pacific Ocean, after firmly establishing that the upper Missouri and upper Columbia rivers were not connected to each other as earlier explorers had speculated.

By far the greatest explorer and detailer of the intricacies of the Columbia River drainage was David Thompson (1770–1857) or the "Star Looker" as he was known to many Indigenous Peoples.[37] Thompson was a British-born, Canadian-matured fur trader and explorer, and perhaps the "greatest practical land geographer that the world has ever produced."[38] He travelled over 88,000 km and charted over 3.9 million km² of territory in Canada and the US, all by the time he was 42. It is difficult to resist hyperbole when attempting to summarize the remarkable achievements of David Thompson. No less a heroic explorer than Sir Alexander Mackenzie considered that Thompson had achieved more in ten months than would anyone else, presumably himself included, over two years.[39] Thompson became an apprentice of the Hudson's Bay Company and found himself on the desolate shores of Hudson Bay near Churchill, Manitoba, in the spring of 1784 – at the age of 14! Thompson eventually left the Hudson's Bay Company and joined the rival North West Company in 1797, where he became a full partner in 1804. During this time, Thompson travelled and mapped much of the Athabasca River, the corridor between Lake Superior and Lake of the Woods, the region between Lake Superior and the headwaters of the Mississippi River, and the Lake Superior shorelines. In 1806, he was instructed to travel back to the northwest to chart the Columbia River to the ocean, likely as a response to the successful completion of the Lewis and Clark expedition that same year.

Thompson spent the summer of 1807 and several subsequent seasons exploring/mapping the upper Columbia River basin and establishing North West Company trading posts (Kootenae House, Kullyspell House, Saleesh House) in western Canada and northwestern Montana, Idaho and Washington. Thompson became known for the high quality and detail of his maps, which were considered authoritative for well over 100 years. In 1811, Thompson accomplished the first complete trip down the mainstem Columbia River by a European. He was instructed to travel to the mouth of the river and establish a trading post to counter the moves by American John Jacob Astor of the Pacific Fur Company in the area. Thompson camped at the confluence of the Snake and Columbia rivers on July 9, 1811, leading to the North West Company's establishment of Fort Nez Percés in 1818, but arrived at the mouth of the Columbia on July 14, 1811, only to find Fort Astoria already under construction.

Thompson returned upriver and wintered at Saleesh House, Montana, before eventually returning to Montreal and retiring from his travels in 1812. In Montreal, and after later moving to Ontario, Thompson completed mapping work for the North West Company, including a huge map (2 m × 3 m) showing the northwest from Hudson Bay to the Pacific Ocean and all the North West Company's trading posts (this map now hangs in the Archives of Ontario in Toronto). Thompson worked for the International Boundary Commission to survey land and establish the British North America–US border from Lake of the Woods to Quebec in 1817. Unfortunately, Thompson and his work were treated with little regard by the Hudson's Bay Company (his former employer) after its merger with the North West Company in 1821. Tragically, Thompson lost most of his sight in 1846, the result of intense note and map making by candlelight over a 28-year career, and suffered a series of financial misfortunes. He died, relatively uncelebrated (compared to, say, Sir Alexander Mackenzie, to whom his accomplishments are often compared) in 1857 without completing his book based on the 77 notebooks of his travels (the manuscript was later resurrected by the geologist J.B. Tyrrell and published as *David Thompson's Narrative* in 1916).

Fort Vancouver, near present-day Vancouver, WA, was established as the headquarters of the Hudson's Bay Company's Columbia District in 1825. Although the US and Britain signed a treaty in 1818 (renewed for an indefinite period in 1825) that was supposed to allow both countries to equally exploit the riches of the Oregon territory, the Hudson's Bay Company basically monopolized the region. The stranglehold of the company was maintained until around 1840 when significant numbers of Americans used the Oregon Trail to settle the area. The immigration of Americans into the Oregon Territory intensified the ongoing debate about where the boundary between British North America and the US should be located. The Hudson's Bay Company, via the British government, pressed for the boundary to be along the lower reaches of the Columbia River, but the Oregon Treaty of 1846 established the 49th parallel as the border (see also Chapter 4), resulting in 85% of the Columbia River watershed being ceded to the US. The border between the Oregon Territory (statehood granted in 1859) and the Washington Territory (which became a state in 1889) was, however, established along the lower Columbia River.

When the Oregon Treaty of 1846 was signed, the Columbia River was a free-flowing, powerful giant of a river, running unchecked to the sea for almost 2000 km. The river was a prodigious producer of all five species of Pacific salmon and steelhead trout; an estimated 8–16 million fish returned to spawn in the basin every year. Currently there are 56 hydroelectric dams on the mainstem Columbia or its major tributaries, including the Kootenay, Snake, Pend d'Oreille, Flathead and Willamette rivers, and a total of 400 multi-purpose dams across the entire watershed, generating more power than any other river system in North America (and about 40% of all hydropower in the US),[40] but dramatically altering the nature of the river.[41] Salmon populations have dwindled to perhaps 10% of historical run sizes and are now heavily dependent on hatchery production. In some years, run sizes of the American shad (*Alosa sapidissima*), a fish native to the Atlantic coast but which was introduced to the Sacramento–San Joaquin River in California in 1871 and spread to the Columbia River, outnumber runs of native salmon by several times.[42] Astoundingly, some now consider the American shad the "signature fish of the modern Columbia River."[43] It has been estimated that more than 55% of the drainage area and 31% of the stream distance available to salmon historically (over 14,000 km) has been eliminated by dam construction and associated reservoir development.[44] Many populations are considered Endangered or Threatened under the US Endangered Species Act (1973) or have been assessed as at risk of extinction by Canada's Committee on the Status of Endangered Wildlife in Canada (COSEWIC). All sea-run salmon and trout populations native to the Canadian portion of the Columbia River, except a small area of the Okanagan River, but including those salmon noted by David Thompson spawning at the western edge of the Rocky Mountains in 1807, are extinct. What social, economic and political forces could have motivated such a dramatic change in the character of the Columbia River and its salmon?

Remaking of the Columbia River

THE SO-CALLED "Inland Empire" of the US, a term coined in 1902,[45] is that region of central and eastern Washington and adjacent northwestern Idaho bordered by three mountain ranges to the west (Cascade Mountains), east (Rocky Mountains) and south (Blue Mountains) and is a semi-arid steppe environment. Although the region classically refers to geopolitical regions of the US Columbia Plateau area, its natural counterpart in Canada is the southern portion of the West Kootenays, especially in and around Castlegar, BC, west to the southern Okanagan River valley of BC. The region, early in the 20th century, was considered to have great potential for development (one writer of the time gushed that "its possibilities are beyond the mind of man to comprehend"[46]), especially in terms of water-borne transportation benefits that would exceed those of the Mississippi River.[47] The first explorers of the lower and upper Columbia River had noted that although it was navigable in small craft, it was not an easy passage either through the rough waters of the Columbia Bar or the tumultuous rapids and cascades in the interior for larger steamships and barges laden with commercial goods. Improved and safer navigation of the Columbia River from the US–Canada border to the sea was seen by the Republican Speaker of the Oregon House of Representatives, L.B. Reeder, as imperative to "the further successful development of this western country."[48] Consequently, a series of locks, small dams, jetties, canals and dredging operations were completed before 1920. By 1975, channel and dam construction (see below) opened commercial barge passage on the Columbia River from the ocean to Lewiston, Idaho – 750 km upstream.

More reliable and efficient water-borne transportation along the Columbia River was, however, only one of the major issues seen as constraining the potential of the Inland Empire. A lack of water for irrigation, or more accurately, a lack of an effective collection and distribution system for the abundant water in the Columbia River basin, was the issue, especially given that the most fertile land was hundreds of metres above the river.[49] Native Americans and individuals settling the Inland Empire area engaged in localized irrigation, but by 1889 the US secretary of the interior proclaimed that "it is hoped that within a few years the National Government will have devised and carried into effect a comprehensive system of water supply for this and other arid regions of the West, and thus solve the problem of providing homes for the homeless."[50] The social engineering aspect of irrigation was not a new theme, given the great settling of the west after the Civil War and would be a common theme in later years as well (see Chapters 6–8).[51]

The US Reclamation Service (now the Bureau of Reclamation), created in 1902, is a federal agency within the Department of the Interior. Its mandate is the management of water resources, particularly as it relates to the diversion, storage and delivery of water via projects that it constructs primarily throughout the western US. Given the abundance of water within the Columbia River and the rich soils in the valley, the Columbia Basin was a natural focus for the bureau. John Wesley Powell, the famous Director of the US Geological Survey and author of the *Report on the Lands of the Arid Regions of the United States* (1879), and Richard J. Hinton, author of *Irrigation in the United States* (1887), written for the US Department of

Agriculture, are seen as founders of the western US irrigation-based reclamation movement and projects.[52] The first major dam on the Columbia River or its chief tributaries, however, preceded the formation of the Bureau of Reclamation. The Swan Falls Dam on the mainstem Snake River, about 670 km upstream from its confluence with the Columbia River, was completed in 1901 by the Idaho Power Company to generate electricity. This dam had a poorly functioning fish ladder for salmon, so poor that later dams built upstream (C.J. Strike Dam, 1952) and downstream (Hells Canyon Dam, 1967) were built without fish passage facilities. The earliest dam on the Canadian portion of the Columbia River basin was the Lower Bonnington Falls Dam on the Kootenay River just above its confluence with the Columbia River, which began generating power for nearby mines in 1898.[53] In 1910, the Bureau of Reclamation demonstrated its potential by assisting in the building of, at the time, the world's tallest dam, the 99 m high Shoshone (now Buffalo Bill) Dam on the Shoshone River, a tributary of the upper Snake River, in Wyoming. The Shoshone Dam was promoted for its irrigation potential by "Buffalo Bill" Cody, American scout and bison hunter of the old west and founder of the famous *Buffalo Bill's Wild West* show. By 1922, however, it was perhaps the first multi-purpose dam in the basin, with its ability to provide irrigation, flood control and power, a major innovation of the Bureau.[54]

The major push for irrigation-based dam building on the Columbia River came in 1933 with the initiation of the Columbia Basin Project and its centrepiece, Grand Coulee Dam. In the 1920s, there was a vigorous debate between parties competing for a major irrigation project for the Inland Empire area; one wanted a gravity-fed canal from the Pend d'Oreille River, the other a dam on the mainstem Columbia River to flood the Grand Coulee area. As is common in large countries like Canada or the US, the rest of the country did not seem to care for grand schemes in the West; the Grand Coulee option was considered a giant, politically motivated "pork barrel" by many.[55] In the early 1930s, the US was still recovering from the Great Depression. In 1932's presidential election campaign, Democratic candidate Franklin Delano Roosevelt had promised the American people "a new deal" wherein the federal government would actively engage in infrastructure and social programs to get the country out of the Depression. In 1934, and in response to criticisms that public works projects were a waste of money, Roosevelt declared that: "No country, however rich, can afford the waste of its human resources. Demoralization caused by vast unemployment is our greatest extravagance. Morally, it is the greatest menace to our social order."[56] The potential of the Columbia River as a job creation project had been brewing in Roosevelt's mind for some time; 14 years earlier, during his run for vice-president, Roosevelt had travelled down the Columbia River and noted that it was "practically unused" and it needed to be developed "by the Nation and for the Nation."[57]

The Columbia Basin Project and Grand Coulee Dam were the "crown jewel" of Roosevelt's New Deal–inspired public works projects in the northwestern US. It promised thousands of construction jobs when unemployment was at 25%, and it would be a major asset for the region. Consequently, and following 13 years of debate, President Roosevelt approved the dam project in 1933 (under the National Industrial Recovery Act) and its initial expenditure of US$63 million.[58] Still, the harsh economics of the time led Roosevelt to be conservative and approve a lower-height dam for electricity generation only.[59] The extra infrastructure for irrigation would need to wait, but not for long. Roosevelt visited the dam site several times, and after a visit in the summer of 1934, favoured a higher dam design so that enough power could be produced to support irrigation works, an idea that was approved by the US Congress in 1935. Also, in 1934, construction of a second mainstem Columbia River dam began: the Bonneville Dam, located 725 km downstream of Grand Coulee Dam, which began producing power in 1937.

Roosevelt's goals of powering employment and economic opportunity during a time of great need were amply achieved. It is estimated that at least 8,800 direct and indirect support jobs were generated or sustained by the project and produced salaries of at least US$34 million during 1933–39 alone. This level of employment, coupled with the 5,000 or so employed in construction of Hoover Dam on the Colorado River during 1931–35 (see Chapter 7) and the

Grand Coulee Dam on the Columbia River. Lake Roosevelt is an upstream reservoir created by the dam (left portion of image).

Bonneville Dam's 3,000 or so workers, certainly provided major relief for many. The employment benefits were especially welcome in the 1930s as the Dust Bowl crises of the 1934–40 period (aka the "Dirty Thirties") ruined the farming prospects of thousands of people in the US prairies who now needed alternatives. While the federal Bureau of Reclamation was busy with Columbia Basin Project, state agencies in Washington and Oregon were engaged in building their own projects. To gain support for federal control of hydroelectric development on the Columbia River, the Bonneville Power Administration (the federal agency responsible for selling and distributing power from federal facilities) hired Oklahoma folk singer Woody Guthrie to pen his now famous *Columbia River Ballads* – including the state folk song of Washington, "Roll On Columbia" (1941) – all extolling the virtues of hydroelectricity, especially of the federal, New Deal–inspired variety.

The first part of Grand Coulee Dam and the generating station were completed in 1942, creating the massive, 242 km long Franklin

Delano Roosevelt Reservoir behind it – and just in time. The US was in the second year of its direct involvement in the Second World War, and power generation took precedence over irrigation. In 1940, the northwest Pacific of the US had no aluminum-generating capacity, but by 1946 it was producing 36% of the nation's output – a critical ingredient of the production of warplanes at the Boeing plant in Seattle. An estimated 33% of all Allied warplanes were constructed with aluminum produced with power provided by Grand Coulee Dam. Power from Grand Coulee Dam also help to produce plutonium at the Hanford, Washington, facility for use in one of the atom bombs dropped on Japan in 1945. After the war, President Harry S. Truman summarized the role of Columbia River dams in the war effort succinctly: "Without Grand Coulee and Bonneville dams [downstream on the Columbia River] it would have been impossible to win this war."[60]

Post-war developments on the Columbia River

AFTER THE SECOND WORLD WAR, irrigation became a higher priority for the Columbia Basin Project, and water for irrigation started flowing beginning in 1948 with the completion of a plant to pump water from Roosevelt Reservoir to Grand Coulee to create Banks Lake. In total there are now 8300 km of main and subsidiary canals and drains that have brought 2700 km^2 under irrigation (about 65% of the total potential). The Columbia Basin Project distributes more water over the Columbia Plateau area through irrigation than is contained in the entire annual flow of the Colorado River.[61] The project has effectively transformed a huge area, encompassing all or part of six counties, which normally receives 250 mm or less of rainfall a year, into one that receives (via irrigation) more than five times that: the equivalent of 1300 mm annually. This region of central Washington is now an "agricultural empire"[62] producing over US$1.4 billion dollars of agricultural crops per year, with an estimated cumulative annual economic impact, exclusive of hydropower generation, of US$4 billion. [63]

In 1948, a massive flood caused extensive damage along a wide swath of the Columbia River basin from Trail, BC, to Astoria, Oregon. This flood, which destroyed the town of Vanport, Oregon, home to 40,000 people, encouraged international development of dams on the Columbia River and led to the signing and ratification of the 1964 Columbia River Treaty between Canada and the US. In Canada, the treaty was part of then BC premier W.A.C. Bennett's "Two Rivers Policy," in which he promoted development of dams on the Peace River (see Chapter 2) and the Columbia River. Essentially, the treaty required Canada to build three dams primarily for flood control and storage to allow for more efficient power generation at US dams downstream. The three dams that Canada built were: the Duncan Dam (1967, on the Duncan River, which flows into the north end of Kootenay Lake); the Arrow Dam (1968, now Hugh Keenleyside Dam) on the Columbia River just upstream of Castlegar, BC; and the Mica Dam (1973) located near where the Columbia River takes its first turn to the south, 160 km north of Revelstoke, BC. In exchange, Canada would get payments derived from the sale of downstream US power ("The Canadian Entitlement") and benefit from flood control and development of Canadian sites for secondary use as power generation facilities (subsequently completed at Mica and Hugh Keenleyside dams). The US also built a storage and power facility at Libby Dam, on the US portion of the Kootenai River, and in 1984 Canada completed the Revelstoke Dam on the mainstem Columbia River as a hydroelectric facility (upgraded in 2010). The treaty was designed to be open to termination after 2024 by either country given a ten-year period of notice, but negotiations are under way to renew the treaty (see Chapter 12).[64] There are more than 400 dams scattered throughout the Columbia River basin, including the 11 mainstem dams in the US portion, generating more than a third of all hydroelectric power in the US, and the three in Canada, two of which are the fifth and ninth largest in Canada in terms of generating capacity.[65]

With the completion of the last dam on the mainstem Columbia, the Revelstoke Dam in 1984, the remaking of the Columbia River into what Richard White described as an irrigation–hydroelectric–flood control "organic machine,"[66] a major component of the hydraulic West, was complete. On the surface, this remaking of the river has been a huge economic success, helping to transform the region into one with a gross domestic product that ranks within the top ten worldwide, and one where high-tech firms like Google are moving a new type of farm, server farms, to take advantage of abundant space and still relatively inexpensive power.[67] The annual value of the Columbia Basin Project alone has been estimated at US$1.65 billion from agriculture, power generation, flood control and recreation, although claims of up to greater than US$4 billion in benefits have been made.[68] The social engineering aspects, at least as envisioned by Roosevelt, have been less successful as the goal of thousands of small, family-owned farms has gradually given way to larger, amalgamated agribusinesses.[69] There are many, therefore, who see the Columbia Basin Project as a textbook example of public money subsidizing private interests.[70]

On the negative side, remaking the Columbia River has resulted in several social and environmental consequences that should be considered as costs in addition to the "simple" analyses of trying to balance the costs of construction and operations against the financial gains from power generation and agriculture. The following have all been cited as negative consequences of building the "organic machine": pollution from irrigation runoff, soil and water contamination, excessive groundwater recharge from unused irrigation waters in reservoirs, potential climate changes from large-scale irrigation, opportunity costs from flooding of lands, cost overruns, the reduction and loss of migratory fish populations (e.g., salmon, sturgeon) due to dams and altered river conditions, the resultant impacts on Indigenous Peoples' way of life from the loss of salmon, and the costs incurred trying to mitigate such losses.

Leaving aside the unassailable contribution of the remaking of the Columbia River and resultant power production to the defeat of totalitarianism in the Second World War, and the economic benefits that have been characterized as "undisputed,"[71] how does one weigh the costs and benefits of such a massive change to the water/landscape to ask, Was it worth it and is it still worth it, in a larger sense?

Answers to such questions are made even more difficult because they apply to a region that has been characterized as containing two competing "major religions: irrigation and salmon."[72] These two religions are part of a larger split of opinion in much of the developed world into two competing "traditions": one promoting economic opportunity and growth through the exploitation of natural resources, the other focused on conservation, sustainable use of resources and an expectation of public access to wild places in nature.[73]

The religion of salmon dates back millennia; Indigenous Peoples depended on salmon as a major food supply, as objects of trade, and for spiritual and ceremonial reasons. The religion of salmon spread to European settlers due to their commercial and recreational exploitation and from the observation of the majestic life cycles of salmon, culminating in their "heroic"[74] spawning migrations. As described earlier, in the early 20th century irrigation was pursued with almost religious fervour, and projects of "biblical" proportions were promoted with the hymn-like creations of Woody Guthrie. Even the name Bureau of "Reclamation" has saviour-like connotations – remaking the land from its presumably unacceptable natural state.[75] In *A River Lost: The Life and Death of the Columbia*, Blaine Harden explains how little, apparently, these religions mixed. Harden cites his experiences as the son of a man employed by the Columbia Basin or related projects, when he recounts that "in twelve years of public school and four years of private college in the Northwest, the issue of salmon dying for cheap power never came up. I dimly remember hearing that dams killed salmon, but it seemed unimportant, especially compared to the mystery of having enough water to live in the desert."[76] Disputes between religions are typically intractable. The salmon–development contest is no different and will not be settled here. The decline of Columbia River salmon is certainly attributable to several reasons in addition to hydrological developments: overfishing, mining, pollution, changes in ocean conditions and, ironically, in many cases hatchery programs. There is no doubt, however, that projects like Grand Coulee Dam, built without a fishway, caused the extinction of many populations of salmon and sea-run trout, including all those upstream of the dam in Canada. W.E. Ricker, in his seminal work *The Stock Concept in Pacific Salmon*, which describes the magnificent behavioural, morphological and physiological diversity of salmon populations ("stocks"), wondered if "Canadian authorities at the time raised even the slightest of objections"[77] to the construction of Grand Coulee Dam. The answer appears to be that Canadian fisheries officials did not seem to care much. In 1934, Canadian diplomats in Washington, DC, noted that completion of the high dam at Grand Coulee with no fish passage facilities meant "ruin for Canadian Columbia River salmon."[78] In response to these concerns, the deputy minister of fisheries, W.A. Found, wrote what in 2021 seems as an incredibly myopic perspective: "The assumption that there is no commercial salmon fishery on the Columbia River in Canada is correct, and hence Canadian interests in that respect will not be affected if the dam at Grand Coulee is not equipped with fishway facilities."[79] The US-based Northwest Power and Conservation Council concluded: "Remarkably, the Canadian government wrote off Columbia River salmon because there would be no adverse economic impact from their loss."[80]

To the cost of the loss of such populations must be added the massive expenditures of time and money that have gone into the hundreds of mitigation projects to try and reverse or reduce the effects of the loss of salmon biodiversity owing to hydrological developments. Hatcheries, monitoring projects, "truck and haul" operations (where upstream migrating adult salmon are captured and transported by truck above dams), barging operations (where downstream migrating juveniles are captured and barged through reservoirs and then trucked below dams to avoid their bone-crunching turbines), habitat restoration, salmon reintroduction programs, Species at Risk Act (Canada) and Endangered Species Act (US)–related costs for listed species, and the monitoring of these operations, are all involved in such mitigation. The Bonneville Power Administration spent an average of US$673 million annually over the 11 years from 2009 to 2019 and a total of US$17.6 billion to 2019.[81] These costs alone certainly enforce a sobering perspective on the Bureau of Reclamation's estimates that the annual value of the Columbia Basin Project amounts to a minimum of $1.6 billion. Further, in

British Columbia, the Fish and Wildlife Compensation Program (a partnership among BC Hydro, the BC Ministry of Environment and Fisheries and Oceans Canada) planned to spend about C$5.5 million in the Columbia Basin during fiscal year 2020–2021 as a condition of water licences awarded to BC Hydro.[82]

A review of the performance and consequences (intended and otherwise) of the Columbia River Project in terms of irrigation, power generation and economic and social development by Gina Bloodworth and James White in 2008 outlined the myriad complexities of weighing the costs and benefits of such intensive hydrological developments. When such complexities are expanded to include *all* developments on the Columbia River across three states and one Canadian province in times when social and environmental perspectives are constantly shifting, it is easy to understand why an economic/social/environmental consensus on the value, in the broadest of sense, of developments on the Columbia River, let alone smaller components of it like the Columbia Basin Project, remains elusive.[83] At a minimum, however, is the fact that real costs to the environment and peoples' connections to the environment are acknowledged by, for example, the ongoing commitment to fish and wildlife mitigation programs discussed above. As another sign of the explicit acknowledgement of these costs is the increasing interest in dam removal projects, particularly since the mid-1990s.[84] Dams may be removed owing to safety concerns; the costs of retrofitting them to comply with new water licences becoming prohibitive, especially considering new social and environmental ethics; excessive sedimentation within reservoirs; and/or compliance with treaty rights. Economic, societal and ecological cost-benefit analyses of dam removals have been stimulated by the increasing interest in these proposals.[85] In fact, several smaller dams within the Columbia River basin have already been removed, and the largest dam removal–salmon restoration project in the world, on the Elwha River located on Washington State's Olympic Peninsula, is well under way.[86] The most notable and contentious proposals are for the removal of four dams located on the lower Snake River originally constructed by the US Army Corps of Engineers for water storage, hydroelectric generation and to facilitate barge traffic to Lewiston, Idaho. Opponents of the proposed removals suggested that jobs would be lost in favour of salmon restoration and would constitute an "unmitigated disaster and economic nightmare" and act like "taking a sledgehammer to the Northwest economy."[87] A comprehensive cost-benefit analysis demonstrates that these disaster scenarios are highly simplistic notions in the case of the Snake River dams and that a framework for truly inclusive general assessment of the impacts of dam removals includes benefits that extend beyond salmon conservation. In 2015, removal of these dams was characterized as "gaining support, but remains a long way away,"[88] yet in 2021 a detailed proposal was articulated by an Idaho congressman.[89] When or if these four dams are removed, many more remain, and it is unlikely that Grand Coulee Dam will ever be removed. Consequently, the Columbia River will remain an organic machine for the foreseeable future.[90]

In their introduction to *Rivers in History*, Mauch and Zeller discuss an apparent conflict in river historiography between those who see phenomena like the remaking of the Columbia River as part of Worster's "hydraulic West" as an example of environmental "despoliation,"[91] and those like Richard White in *The Organic Machine*, who see such developments as part of the continuum between human and natural history. In White's view, the evolution of a river, such as the Columbia River in the 20th century, is a combination of recent human creations (dams and reservoirs) and its own natural history which simply cannot, and should not, be separated. The "despoliation" and "continuum" views, however, are not themselves separable. The latter is an inevitable consequence of the existence and dependence of humans on riverscapes like the Columbia River. The former speaks to the necessity of our *collective* responsibility to sustain the form and function of such rivers, and the biodiversity they sustain, and the importance of marshalling the social and political will to fulfill that responsibility.

— SIX —

The Sacramento– San Joaquin River
A David vs. Goliath Water War

When we are diverting our water to save a couple of pinky-sized fish and leaving hundreds of thousands of acres to lie fallow, there's something wrong with our priorities.
> —TRAVIS ALLEN, California Republican Assemblyman, 2015
> (as reported by FoxNews.com)

Trying to blame the fish for a shortage of water is not right, and it's just not even true.
> —PETER B. MOYLE, Professor, U. California–Davis,
> April 2015 (as reported by FoxNews.com)

walked to a medium-sized grocery store in Vancouver, BC, on a quest for walnuts. The walnuts were an ingredient for one of my favourite fall salads that my wife makes. The walnuts, a product of California, were easily found, somewhat grudgingly paid for at a price of $4/100 g ($18/lb!), yet eagerly consumed later. Walnuts are small; the "meat" just a few centimetres in length. About 1300 km due south of the store where I bought those walnuts, in Suisun Bay, the inner basin of the larger San Francisco Bay, lives a similarly diminutive fish – the "delta smelt" (usually only between 5 and 7 cm in total length) which is scientifically known as *Hypomesus transpacificus*. Although small in size, the delta smelt is a biodiversity big deal – it is endemic to the Sacramento–San Joaquin Delta, meaning that this delta is the *only* place on Earth where this smelt is known to occur. The endemic distribution of the delta smelt is especially important because, by definition, the global distribution of the species is restricted to a single region that is very small in area. Consequently, the US, and California in particular, have a global responsibility for the conservation of the delta smelt and, therefore, of the river ecosystem on which it depends. These two seemingly completely disconnected things – walnuts and smelts – not only share a small size, but also share a critical dependence on water, the *same* water, from the Sacramento–San Joaquin river system in California's Central Valley.

The United States Endangered Species Act (ESA) was signed into law by US president Richard Nixon in 1973. The Act expanded on numerous earlier pieces of biodiversity-related environmental legislation that dealt mostly with restrictions on commercial marketing and hunting of animals that were at risk of extinction, e.g., the Lacey Act (1900) and the Bald Eagle Protection Act (1940). Later, the Endangered Species Preservation Act (1966) and the Endangered Species Conservation Act (1969) were the first to deal specifically with the protection of habitat of native species at risk of extinction. The ESA incorporated new principles in conservation biology, such as the listing and recovery of "distinct population segments" (DPS)[1] within species like distinct runs of salmon, and the protection and recovery of species *and* the ecosystems on which they depend. Among the Act's stated goals are the removal or lessening of threats to the persistence of a species or a DPS.

The critical codependence of walnuts (and many other agricultural products) and the delta smelt on water from the Sacramento–San Joaquin river system has exposed a clash of values and a ferocious fight for access to that water. The conflicts for water are especially pronounced during years of drought, of which the period between 2010 and 2021 has been particularly intense in California.[2] For proponents of the delta smelt, much of the battle for this water is fought using the legal arsenal provided by the ESA and especially its habitat protection provisions. By contrast, those who favour using water for agriculture employ arguments based on the economic and social costs of *not* allocating water for agriculture, and launch appeals based on interpretations of aspects of the ESA's wording. This chapter describes the Sacramento–San Joaquin river system and the battle for the "hearts and minds" of citizens and legislators in resolving conflicts for its water as a further example of important debates resulting from the development of the hydraulic West.

The geography and origin of the Sacramento–San Joaquin Rivers

THE SACRAMENTO–SAN JOAQUIN RIVER SYSTEM differs from the other rivers discussed in a few interesting ways. First, the system has a wishbone shape and consists of two almost symmetrically opposed drainage basins: the Sacramento River, flowing from the north-northwest, and the San Joaquin River flowing from the southeast. Both meet to create a common delta at Suisun (inner) and San Francisco (outer) bays to form what is, at 4143 km², the largest estuary on the Pacific Coast of North America.[3] The two rivers are similar in size: the Sacramento River is 719 km long (71,000 km² in drainage area) and the San Joaquin is 589 km long (82,362 km²), and both are fed primarily by the western slope of the Sierra Nevada Mountains, with contributions from the Cascade, Coast and Klamath ranges. Second, the Sacramento–San Joaquin system does not penetrate deeply inland; the main stem of both rivers extends no farther than about 200–300 km from the Pacific Ocean (by contrast the Yukon and Mississippi rivers both extend more than 10–15 times that length inland). Third, the Pit River is a major tributary of the Sacramento River that originates at Goose Lake some 300 km to the northeast on the Oregon–California border.[4] Goose Lake, however, is usually an endorheic (internal-flowing) basin such that its outlet only occasionally connects to the northeast fork of the Pit River, and

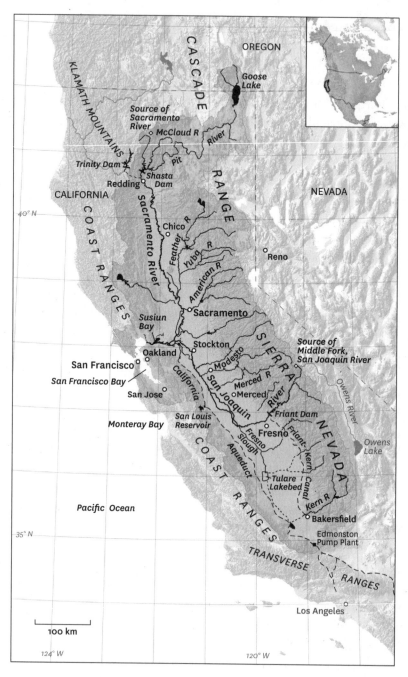

The Sacramento–San Joaquin Rivers Basin. The Central Valley is the light grey shaded area centred around Stockton, California.

hence to the Sacramento River. Fourth, the Sacramento–San Joaquin system is one of the younger rivers to be explored in this book, perhaps as young as 4 million years (see below). Finally, both rivers run straight through the Central Valley of California, a large, flat area of some 58,000 km² enclosed on all sides by mountains. Although the two rivers are relatively small in terms of length or drainage area compared to rivers like the Columbia or Yukon (individually they are not in the top 50 in North America by either measure), the shared valley and estuary mean that, in many ways, the Sacramento–San Joaquin rivers function, and have been exploited, as a single river. Approximately 7–8 million people live within the Sacramento–San Joaquin river system including the delta area, but its impact is much broader. It is estimated that these rivers (via the Central Valley and State Water Projects) supply drinking water to over 27 million people in California.[5]

The relative youth of the Sacramento–San Joaquin system rests in the fact that it is bordered by the Cascade and Sierra Nevada mountains to the east and the Coast and Klamath mountains to the west and north. In northern California, the Cascade Mountains take a bend to the east and eventually merge with the Sierra Nevada Mountains. The eastward bend of the southern Cascades results in the Pit River cutting through these mountains, while the Sacramento River proper is wholly contained west of the Cascades and the Sierra Nevada but east of the Coast Mountains. As with the other west coast rivers discussed so far, the underlying rocks of the Sierra Nevada consist of terranes that broke off from oceanic plates that were being subducted under the adjacent west coast of the North American continental plate. Over the past 110 million to 15–20 million ya these terranes were sutured or accreted to the continental plate. The subduction of the oceanic ("Farallon") plate underneath the continental plate resulted in considerable volcanic activity and igneous rock formation in what is now California.[6] Much of contemporary California, however, was under the sea and located within the subduction zone. The volcanic activity and associated intrusions of magma associated with plate subduction created much of the core "batholith" (a large mass of igneous rock) of the Sierra

Nevada and its characteristic features, such as Mount Whitney or Half Dome of the High Sierra, revealed by tectonic activity and subsequent erosion. During the time period between 75–50 million ya, the continental inland sea east of the Sierra Nevada withdrew, and the Laramide Orogeny began (see Chapter 1), resulting in a major uplift of the Rocky Mountains and formation of much of the western spine of North America east of the Sierra Nevada.[7] The Central Valley of California, however, remained an inland sea even after the northern portion of the Farallon oceanic plate disappeared and the North American continental plate and the Pacific oceanic plate came into contact ~15 million ya. The formation of the high relief of the Sierra Nevada, resulting from the placement of terranes and batholith formation, represents one end of the debate about the age of the current mountains and suggests that the contemporary relief is as old as the Cretaceous. At the other extreme is the idea that the initial relief built by terrane accretion and batholith formation was followed by a long period of erosion lasting until about 5 million ya. This erosion considerably reduced the relief of the Sierra Nevada and contributed much to the sedimentary deposits of the Central Valley.[8] Subsequently, a period of more recent uplift between 5 and 2 million ya, inferred from increased rates at which rivers incised (cut into) their landscape, created the current relief and topography of the Sierra Nevada.[9] Different kinds of geological data support both scenarios, and the debate continues; the Sierra Nevada Mountains may be much older than the Pliocene-Pleistocene age that is commonly assumed,[10] or perhaps the Sierra Nevada represents a composite of different-aged formations.[11]

Notwithstanding remaining uncertainty about the exact age of the current Sierra Nevada topography, the Sacramento–San Joaquin system did not come into existence until after the uplift of the Coast and Klamath mountains beginning some 5 million ya. This uplift enclosed the Central Valley at its northern end, drained most the inland sea, and caused the rivers to drain south from the Sacramento basin and north from the San Joaquin basin. The uplift contributed to the buildup of the valley floor from erosion by rivers now draining the eastern slopes of the Coast Mountains and later still from the

Sierra Nevada when the southern portion of the inland sea dried out by 2 million ya.[12]

The original outlet of the Sacramento–San Joaquin system is thought to have been farther north, through Monterey Bay,[13] than its current location. The outwash of the river occurred over a coastal plain that was up to 85 km farther offshore than under contemporary conditions owing to depressed sea levels during the Pleistocene glaciations. The Monterey Bay outlet resulted in the 480 km long Monterey Submarine Canyon, which has a profile remarkably like that of the Grand Canyon. The Monterey Bay outlet, however, was blocked about 2 million ya by movements along the San Andreas Fault. Further, the Pleistocene glaciations were muted in the Sacramento–San Joaquin system relative to more northern North American rivers, because the main Laurentide and Cordilleran ice sheets did not penetrate farther south than about 47°N, while the headwaters of the Sacramento River extend only to 41°N. Still, localized glaciers in the Sierra Nevada expanded and contracted with roughly the same periodicity as the main ice sheets. In addition to the sculpting of many of the landforms associated with the current Sierra Nevada, the Pleistocene glaciations were associated with increased precipitation in the Central Valley area, resulting in large "pluvial" lakes, particularly east of the Sierra Nevada (e.g., Lake Lahontan, Pyramid Lake, Mono Lake).[14] This pluvial period in combination with the blockage of the outlet of the Sacramento–San Joaquin at Monterey Bay, led to the flooding of the southern half of the Central Valley and the formation of the massive, 800 km long, and up to 300 m deep, Lake Corcoran (also known as Lake Clyde).

The current outlet of the Sacramento–San Joaquin system at San Francisco Bay formed about 650,000 ya from a collapse of a part of the shoreline of Lake Corcoran near San Francisco Bay, which formed the current narrow outlet at Carquinez Strait.[15] The combination of much of the Central Valley being an inland sea for millions of years, the formation of Lake Corcoran, and erosion caused by the ancestral Sacramento–San Joaquin system, has resulted in huge sediment deposits in the valley, some up to 15 km deep.[16]

Early human history of the Sacramento–San Joaquin River system

THE BEGINNINGS of human occupation of the Sacramento–San Joaquin system play into the general debate about timing, geographic origins and specific routes taken by ancestral North Americans, as described in earlier chapters. What is clear, however, is that numerous groups of Indigenous Peoples were living in central California by about 12,000 ya. Many established communities are evident from archaeological finds, particularly around ancient lake shores within the valley, by 8,000 ya.[17] The Sacramento–San Joaquin Valley may have supported most of the up to 300,000 culturally very diverse Native Americans estimated to have existed in California before European contact.[18] In the San Joaquin River valley, a population of at least 80,000 has been estimated consisting of the Sierra Mowik, Yokuts, the Plains, Western Mono and Tübatulabal. The Sacramento River valley housed a population of at least 50,000 individuals pre-Contact and consisted of Wintun, Maido, Yahi and Yana peoples.[19] Undoubtedly, the chinook salmon runs of the Sacramento–San Joaquin system, which numbered at least 1–2 million annually, provided a considerable food and trade resource that led to many settlements in the valley.[20]

European settlement of California was initiated by Spain as part of New Spain (Mexico) during the mid-1700s and consisted of two provinces: Baja California (or lower California) and Alta California (higher California). Alta California starts around present-day San Diego, and settlement began in 1769 with the Portolà expedition led by Gaspar de Portolà (1716–1786). The idea was to establish missions, like the military and religious missions in Baja California, to offset British and Russian interests on the west coast of North America. Portolà reached San Francisco Bay in October 1769 but did not see or establish the existence of the Sacramento–San Joaquin River. That distinction belongs to Gabriel Moraga (1765–1843), who, seeking to build more missions, encountered the river system as he explored eastward from the Presidio of San Francisco Bay (a military garrison) and named the two rivers as the Rio de los Sacramentos (River of the Blessed Sacrament) and the Rio San Joaquin, after Saint

Joaquin. Alta California remained in Spanish hands until Mexico achieved independence from Spain in 1821, and it then became part of the new Mexican Empire along with Texas and much of the southwestern US. During this time, the ever-active Hudson's Bay Company explored northern California from the Oregon Territory. By 1826, the company probed southward along a Native American trade route between the Willamette River Valley (lower Columbia River basin) and the upper Sacramento River and farther south, establishing what would be known as the Siskiyou Trail.

A key historical event that led to increased settlement and development of the Sacramento–San Joaquin system was, of course, the annexation of California by the US following the Mexican-American War of 1846–1848. The signing of the Treaty of Guadalupe Hidalgo in February 1848 ended the war and ceded California to the US. Soon thereafter, many more American settlers joined the ranks of native-born Spanish ancestry 'Californios.' An earlier German-born settler from the midwestern United States, John Sutter, had established a 198 km² settlement near present-day Sacramento in 1841 in the hopes of establishing an agricultural empire in the Central Valley. While constructing a sawmill on the American River, which enters the Sacramento River near Sacramento, one of Sutter's employees discovered gold in the headrace delivering water to the mill. This discovery of gold set off the California Gold Rush of 1848–1855, the first of several North American gold rushes, which saw some 300,000 people flock to California in search of fortunes of gold or to provide mining services (see also Chapter 3). Finds of gold also occurred in the northern portions of the Sacramento River and in the Klamath River and south along the eastern tributaries of the San Joaquin River. These finds swelled the population of non-native Californians from a few thousand to hundreds of thousands; San Francisco alone expanded from about 1,000 inhabitants in 1848 to over 30,000 in 1860.[21]

Of the many effects of the California Gold Rush, three stand out within the context of rivers. First, mining activity followed the trajectory described in Chapter 3; it began as relatively low-tech single to few-operator placer mining, but subsequently was transformed into mining by larger teams of people employing hydraulic methods. The hydraulic mining used water pressure from diverted streams and rivers that fed into pressure hoses used to remove massive amounts of overburden to feed into sluices where the gold could be separated. Later still, dredging and hard-rock mining of gold took over. From the early days of the gold rush to contemporary times, some 110 million ounces of gold have been removed from this area of California. In particular, the hydraulic mining period saw tons of sediment wash down and infill downstream areas of the Sacramento River and the Central Valley. Large floods, such as the Great Flood of 1862, which all but destroyed Sacramento and other towns in its path, were made worse by such infilling and led to calls for the engineering of the river to control it.

Second, California was admitted into the Union in 1850, no doubt in large part as a function of its rich resources, no more powerfully displayed than in the form of gold. Huge amounts of gold (perhaps $19 billion at 2021 prices)[22] were recovered between 1848 and 1853 alone. Thus, gold from one river system (the Sacramento–San Joaquin) would be a huge factor in financing the Union's efforts in a Civil War with a key battleground involving control of another river (the Mississippi River, see Chapter 9).

Third, the gold rush, with its massive influx of people, created a ready demand for food, especially meat. There were good profits to be made in cattle and sheep ranching.[23] Further, with the end of the gold rush, those who did not make a fortune (the majority) needed other ways to make a living, as did those who continued to move into California. Land was plentiful, there was a long growing season, the Central Valley was a huge, flat and fertile environment, and there was plenty of sunshine – all favourable for agriculture. Two problems, however, were apparent. First, the warmest months with the most sunshine (June to September) were also the driest. Second, most of the water that falls as rain or snow and is collected by rivers as runoff in California occurs north of San Francisco Bay, but most of the population was, and is, in the lower half of the state. Northern rivers such as the Klamath, Trinity and Sacramento provide almost 60% of the annual runoff. The San Joaquin River valley, however, contains most of the irrigated land, yet it contributes only about 9% of the surface-water runoff.[24] Even worse, because most precipitation in California falls as rain in the winter months, the majority of run-off occurs by the end of March, well before the height of the growing season. Rainfall also shows very high interannual variability in Cal-ifornia, which has resulted in spasms of drought and floods from the gold rush days until today. Finally, California rivers provide only about 36% of the runoff per square kilometre of that provided by the Ohio River basin and only 51% of the average for New England rivers. In summary, California's natural system of water supply was highly variable both spatially and temporally, and some rationaliza-tion seemed necessary. While groundwater supply was also rich (it can contribute up to 46% of state water use in drought years), it too is variable in distribution and quality, and its recharge is ultimately based on runoff.[25] Somehow, therefore, supplying water to where the people and farms were concentrated would need to occur for Cali-fornia's agricultural potential to be reached.[26]

Agricultural development in the Central Valley

THE FIRST MAJOR ACTIVITY in California agriculture after the gold rush was wheat farming, which produced more than was needed within the state by 1855.[27] Consequently, exports to European mar-kets flourished and agriculture tended to be rather more advanced technologically, with larger-scale, more extensive farms than char-acterized farms of the midwest and east. Wheat production peaked between 1890 and 1900 with almost 1.2 million hectares under cul-tivation, but dropped to less than a sixth of that by 1910 and never recovered. The main reasons for the decline in wheat production were lack of investment in improving cultivars and techniques, which led to soil exhaustion, and poor yields and quality of product. What followed was a reinvention of agriculture into smaller, more intensive fruit farms producing grapes and citrus and deciduous fruits. With the development of such "specialty crops," California hit the agricultural "sweet spot" and growth was rapid. Between 1869 and 1929 the number of farms increased by 560% (to 136,000), the

Patchwork-like pattern of intensive agricultural development south of Fresno in California's Central Valley.

average farm size dropped by more than 50%, and the share of total value of output represented by specialty crops grew to almost 80%. From a share of less than 4% of total value of California-grown crops in 1879, California produced 57% of the oranges, 70% of the prunes and plums, more than 80% of the grapes and figs, and the vast majority of apricots, walnuts, almonds, lemons and olives grown in the United States. In addition, California agriculture developed significant production of cotton (where yields were typically twice those in the US South) and livestock, particularly dairy products and poultry. In 1993, California displaced Wisconsin as the largest milk producer in the United States.

Today, California is an agricultural behemoth. The total value of agricultural products in California in 2019 (the last year for which statistics are available) was US$50.1 billion spread over more than 400 commodities. Leading the way was milk production ($7.3 billion), almonds ($6.9 billion), grapes ($5.4 billion) and cattle ($3.1 billion).[28] California produces almost half of the US-grown fruits, nuts and vegetables, and 14.7% of all US agricultural exports. Some products are dominated, on a global and local scale, by California production. According to the Almond Board of California, in 2019 California produced about 80% of the world supply of almonds, and virtually all the US supply, from about 7,600 almond farms clustered tightly along the Central Valley.[29] In total, California ranks at the top of US agricultural production; according to the most recent US Department of Agriculture Census of Agriculture (2017) it produced 11.6% of the total US agricultural cash value of $388 billion (Iowa was second at 7.5%) a complete reversal from its rank as the lowest in the country upon statehood in 1850 (total value = $3.9 million).[30] None of this staggering level of growth and total production would have been, or is, possible without irrigation supplied by water from the Sacramento–San Joaquin system.

Irrigation in California was variously viewed as either a "panacea or curse"[31] in farmers' attempts to adapt to the arid West. Many commentators and farmers from the eastern US viewed irrigation, with which they had little previous experience, with suspicion or outright hostility. It was considered unnecessary, too costly, fuel for land speculation and the spread of diseases like malaria, damaging to the land and soil, and a primitive and inefficient technique used only by Mexican Californians. Farming, therefore, appeared to have little potential, particularly in the Central Valley. Explorer Charles Wilkes intoned that based on his experience in a "barren and unproductive" California in the 1840s, "it will be doubted whether our countrymen would look upon it in the light of an agricultural country, or one so entitled to be considered as such, and so different from these United States."[32] Somewhat fanciful notions, such as the idea that increases in rainfall naturally occurred after land was cultivated ("rain follows the plough"), or that setting large fires, or the planting of trees caused increases in rainfall, were floated. Others thought that irrigation was a kind of "artificial rain" and would be a saviour, and that agriculture was a "farmer's gold mine"[33] that would diversify crops and lead to greater productivity. Stories were told of giant turnips, pumpkins and strawberries, and of apple trees that grew 3–4 m in a single season. Such productivity would stimulate innovation and lead to positive social reform by promoting more intensive, smaller, clustered family farms.[34] The resulting crusade-like enthusiasm for irrigation included grand visions such as the diversion of the flow of the Colorado River into the Imperial Valley in southeast California, first undertaken in the 1870s.

The first irrigation projects in California were relatively small scale and were related to draining land for agricultural reclamation, flood irrigation (soaking whole tracts of land surrounded by embankments) or to protect land from flooding through constructing hundreds of ditches, canals and levees. Irrigation by ditches and canals had been practised by Native Americans in the southwest for centuries and in and around California missions, but there was little headway made in the scientific approach to determining the optimal conditions (timing, extent) of irrigation for particular crops in specific areas until well into the 20th century. In the 1870s a maximum of 40,000 hectares (ha) of land was irrigated (in 2017 the total was at least 3.2 million ha or almost 9% of California's total land area).

During the mid-1800s, smallish enterprises in the hands of private water companies and settlement projects in and around Los Angeles County grew to larger plans for canals designed to take water from the now dry Tulare Lake (once the second largest lake in the lower 48 states west of the Mississippi River) to the San Joaquin River, and diversions of the Colorado (which were not completed until much later) and lower Sacramento rivers. These grand plans all failed for various reasons, and irrigation did not really take off until the 1870s when mining declined, more droughts occurred which devastated cattle ranching, and railroad infrastructure improved.[35] During this decade, the extent of irrigated land tripled, and a federal commission recommended a central plan to better organize irrigation throughout the Central Valley. The commission proposed a series of canals, the notion of "irrigation districts," the basic public administrative unit to obtain and distribute water for irrigation, began to take hold, and a state water engineer position was created. The 1870s also saw a surge in the number of court cases about water rights, particularly in the southern San Joaquin River valley, between cattlemen and farming/irrigation interests and between competing claims to water rights – the genesis, at least in terms of legal manoeuvring, of the so-called "California water wars."

California water laws, which have been described as "unequalled" in terms of their technical complexity and scope by the California Supreme Court itself, have led to legal battles over water that have burned "white hot" at various times.[36] This complexity is due, in large part, to what Donald Pisani described in *From the Family Farm to Agribusiness: The Irrigation Crusade in California and the West 1850–1931* as a patchwork-like construction of laws based on individual cases, "piled layer upon layer" and where decisions often "ignored the dictates of logic and consistency."[37] Eventually five basic types of surface-water rights emerged: prior appropriation rights, riparian rights, settlement or "pueblo" rights, rights reserved for use by the US government and area of watershed origin rights. Prior appropriation rights originated in the gold rush days and essentially recognized the right to use water for "beneficial use" (initially for industry, agriculture or urban use) to those who first exploited the water, the so-called "first in time, first in right" idea. Riparian rights involve the right of use of water by the owner of the land through which a source of surface water runs through or next to. Settlement or pueblo rights stem from Spanish and Mexican land grants that afforded rights to use of surface waters by settlements or pueblos. The city of Los Angeles is an example of a community that exercises settlement rights originally granted to it as a pueblo founded in 1781 under Mexican law. Water rights reserved for use by the US government involve situations where water may be used to fulfill the purpose(s) of lands reserved for use by the government such as Indian reservations, national forests, parks or monuments. Finally, area of origin watershed rights are like community/pueblo rights, but act to protect the *future* interests of areas, counties and watersheds in which water originates from loss of that water supply due to the operations and prior appropriations of water by enterprises (industry, agriculture) outside the watershed. Area of origin water rights developed following the virtual disappearance of Owens Lake, and resulting increased desertification of the Owens Valley, caused by the appropriation of its water by the city of Los Angeles some 250 km to the southwest in the 1920s, a key event in California's water wars.[38]

The myriad California water laws arguably owe their origin to the landmark court decisions of the famous *Lux vs. Haggin* case in the 1880s.[39] Essentially, the case, and the subsequent appeal, pitted riparian rights against prior appropriation rights. The former was the position of Henry Miller and Charles Lux, who had large cattle holdings on riparian lands, while the latter was championed by James Ben-Ali Haggin, who diverted large amounts of water upstream of the Miller-Lux lands for irrigation. The end result (1886) was that Miller-Lux won on appeal, but the California Supreme Court also recognized that both uses of water were legitimate, that appropriation rights were secondary to riparian rights, and that non-riparian uses of water could be sanctioned with compensation. This landmark "nesting" of water rights, coupled with the existence of settlement, area of origin and community water rights, provided a recipe for litigation during disagreements concerning the allocation of a scarce resource like water in California. In 1887, the Wright Act created irrigation districts to redistribute water, and the costs and benefits of same, equitably. By 1895, 49 irrigation districts had been formed covering over 800,000 ha, but the creation and operation of irrigation districts often also became the focus of court challenges. Some thought the Wright Act was unconstitutional, others focused on provisions of the Act that were unfulfilled, while still others questioned the boundaries of irrigation districts. The growth of irrigation stalled in California for this and other reasons until 1902 when the federal Reclamation Act and the creation of the Reclamation Service made it a national priority.

The first large-scale federal projects, pursued through 1916, focused on the section of the Colorado River that occurs in southern California, the Klamath river basin in northern California and Oregon and the middle Sacramento River. These projects produced middling results in terms of increases in irrigated land, settlement and increased value of farmed products. Subsequent new state laws like the Water Commission Act (1913) and the creation of the Water

Commission to oversee permitting led to some rationalization of water allotment and dispute resolution. These reforms led to huge increases in irrigation, with more than 1 million ha irrigated by 1910 and more than 1.7 million ha by the end of the First World War. More than 75% of irrigated land was within the San Joaquin River valley, compared to only 8% in the Sacramento River valley. Population increases mirrored increases in irrigation as southern California continued to outgrow northern California.[40]

Several major droughts during the 1920s and early 1930s, coupled with increased use of irrigated water withdrawn from the Sacramento–San Joaquin system, saw the first major instances of intrusion of saltwater from San Francisco Bay. The intrusion of seawater caused problems for domestic and agricultural use of water within the Sacramento–San Joaquin Delta region, and several lawsuits resulted. Conflicts also mounted between water-based transportation (which required minimum flow levels) and irrigation interests within the Sacramento River valley. In the San Joaquin River valley, it was the declining water table and resulting stresses on irrigation caused by pumping water from groundwater aquifers that generated increasing angst. All these conditions contributed to the creation of California's first comprehensive water plan with the 1919 publication of the "Marshall Plan" authored by R.B. Marshall, a geographer who had worked for the US Geological Survey when he first conceived the need for better planning. The Marshall Plan, at its core, envisioned a major dam on the main stem Sacramento River just upstream of Redding, CA; two diversion canals, one on the west side and one on the east side of the Central Valley running down to the San Joaquin River; and several smaller canals within the San Joaquin valley itself and in and around San Francisco and Los Angeles. Marshall's monumental plan could have provided 4.8 million ha of irrigated land and solved many problems with flood control, transportation, domestic water supply, and would also be used to generate power so that California's water would not otherwise "pour unused into the sea."[41] The plan was, however, also criticized by local irrigation districts, private power companies and some professional engineers. The Marshall Plan was never adopted, and an alternative plan developed by the

Department of Engineering and Irrigation proposed irrigating up to 7.3 million ha. Its key feature was a dam across Carquinez Strait in San Francisco Bay and diversion of fresh water impounded behind it to the San Joaquin River valley. Several other diversions from northern rivers into the Sacramento River and from the Colorado River into the Imperial Valley were also discussed in this plan and its subsequent revisions. Legal implications of these various plans and the daunting financial resources required to implement them stimulated state officials to re-engage with the federal government as partners in the ultimate solution to California's water problems. President Herbert Hoover was sympathetic; he had an engineering background and saw large irrigation projects as part of a "new federalism" that could help renew co-operation among state and federal agencies to solve economic and social problems. Two major dam sites, one on the Sacramento River and one on the San Joaquin River, were the core of the newest plan and would generate reservoirs with enough storage to provide minimum year-round flows to ward off saltwater intrusions and provide irrigation. Eventually, this kernel of a statewide water plan, coupled with the increasing need for economic recovery initiatives following the Great Depression, led the federal government to authorize initial funding for the Bureau of Reclamation (formerly the Reclamation Service) to begin what was to become known as the Central Valley Project in 1935.

The Central Valley and State water projects

THE CENTRAL VALLEY PROJECT was one of several large water storage, irrigation, flood control and power generation projects initiated by the Bureau of Reclamation in the 1930s as a component of President Franklin Delano Roosevelt's "New Deal." The Columbia Basin Project (Chapter 5) and the Hoover Dam Project (Chapter 7) were other large hydraulic infrastructure components of the federal government's initiative to mitigate the effects of the Great Depression and the Dust Bowl through economic and social development. At its core, the Central Valley Project consists of 20 reservoirs along the base of the Coast, Sierra Nevada and Klamath mountains. The two largest in the Sacramento River drainage, the Trinity and Shasta reservoirs, are at the north end, and Millerton Reservoir is impounded behind Friant Dam on the San Joaquin River. These and many other dams in the system store some 16 billion m³ (~13 million acre feet,[42] or 6.5 *million* Olympic-sized swimming pools) of water. Of this volume, about 9.1 billion m³ pass annually along its canals, 68% of which is used for irrigation, 8% for municipal uses and 10% to maintain minimum flows in its component rivers and the delta. The system also provides flood control and 2.25 gigawatts of power generation capacity. The important facilities of the Central Valley Project include export water pumps and a pair of diversion canals within the Sacramento–San Joaquin Delta itself that intercept water headed for San Francisco Bay and divert it south to farms and municipalities of the San Joaquin River valley. The initiation of the Central Valley Project also marked a transition in the history of California in that it signalled the end of the dream of using irrigation to help small family farms proliferate and create a utopian, rural-based California. In its place, irrigation became the "ally of the agricultural establishment" – large agribusinesses.[43]

In addition to the Central Valley Project, the state in 1960 initiated the State Water Project, which also consists of a series of dams, reservoirs, southern delta export pumps and canals. It has a storage capacity of 7 billion m³ of water, which it collects from rivers along the northwestern Sacramento River valley. The project sends about 2.9 billion m³ of water to areas in the south, principally (~70%) for municipal use and less so (~30%) for irrigation of Central Valley farms. The State Water Project also generates power with a capacity of about 2.99 gigawatts. The Central Valley and State Water projects are integrated so that water can be exchanged between them to meet fluctuations in supply and demand for water. Both water projects remain crucial to the development of California. It has been estimated that the Central Valley Project contributes water to enable about half of California's agricultural production, thus contributing 7% to the state's gross economic product, while the State Water Project provides drinking water to a minimum 23 million people and contributes $440 billion to the California economy annually.

While a narrow interpretation of economic benefits clearly finds substantial gains to the California economy and society from the irrigation and resultant agricultural boom, those gains have not come without substantial ecological costs. The various water projects involve dams, diversion of water, reservoir formation, and recharge of watersheds with agricultural runoff, changes to the physical structure of rivers, sedimentation, altered patterns of seasonal flow, loss of connectivity among habitats for migratory fishes, flooding of spawning grounds, pollution of surface and groundwater and changed aquatic thermal regimes, and has resulted in negative effects on aquatic biodiversity within the Sacramento–San Joaquin system. The river system once contained abundant runs of chinook salmon – perhaps as many as 2 million returned to spawn annually – as well as steelhead trout.[44] The run sizes now are a fraction of those historical numbers; the Central Valley Spring Run chinook salmon is listed as Threatened and the Sacramento River Winter Run chinook salmon as Endangered under the US Endangered Species Act.[45] While several factors have contributed to the declines in these fish, including overfishing and habitat degradation from mining, the irrigation-related changes the river system listed above are considered especially important contributors.[46] In recognition of these effects on salmon and other fishes and on wildlife, the US Congress passed the Central Valley Project Improvement Act (1992), which requires changes to the management of the project to ensure the protection and recovery of fish and wildlife in the basin. One of its main aspects is the requirement for the annual provision of 987 million m³ of water flow for the persistence of fish and wildlife.[47] This Act and the ESA with its critical habitat provision are the main legal mechanisms that are used to force provision of a minimum amount of water for fish and wildlife in the Central Valley area. Any water used for protecting wildlife and their habitats, however, is water that cannot be used for irrigation and growing of valuable crops like almonds and grapes. This conflict of competing demands is the basis for the legal tug-of-war for the state's increasingly limited water supply. For no animal more than the diminutive delta smelt has the legal battle for California's water been so intense.

The delta smelt: Icon of California water wars

"SMELTS" are a group of soft-rayed, silvery, small-bodied (rarely > 25 cm in length) fishes that are "trout-like" in general appearance. The delta smelt belongs to the family Osmeridae, which contains 14 species, all native to temperate marine and coastal freshwater habitats of the Northern Hemisphere. The North Pacific basin has the greatest diversity of smelts, with 12 of the 14 species. One genus, *Hypomesus*, contains five species: two in the northwestern Pacific, one in the Arctic basin bordering the Pacific and two in the eastern North Pacific. The delta smelt's closest relative is the surf smelt (*H. pretiosus*); the delta smelt and the surf smelt are thought to have diverged from a common ancestral smelt about 4 million ya and are so-called "sister species." The two species, however, have very different distributions; the delta smelt is endemic to the Sacramento–San Joaquin Delta and its distribution is wholly contained within that of the surf smelt, which is more broadly distributed from Prince William Sound, AK, to Long Beach, CA, including the San Francisco Bay area. The ranges of the two fish, at least in the San Francisco Bay/Sacramento–San Joaquin Delta area are, therefore, "parapatric" – they abut one another. A further difference between the species is that the delta smelt is an estuarine species found in the saltwater-freshwater transition zone of the Sacramento–San Joaquin Delta, and spawns farther upstream in fresh water. By contrast, the surf smelt is a wholly marine species.

The close evolutionary relationship between the delta and surf smelts and their respective life histories and geographic distributions suggest a possible scenario for their origins, one with an intimate role for the Sacramento–San Joaquin River. It is plausible that a broadly distributed ancestor of these two species existed in coastal central California within the large embayment in what is now the San Francisco Bay/Sacramento–San Joaquin Delta/Central Valley area before the uplift of the Coast Mountains. When the Sacramento–San Joaquin system formed after the uplift of the Coast Mountains the ancestral population may have been split across two contrasting habitats, the San Francisco Bay area and the emerging

Sacramento–San Joaquin Delta. This semi-isolation between smelt inhabiting the two areas coupled with adaptation to contrasting marine and brackish conditions may have driven the emergence of two new species: fully marine surf smelt, and the estuarine delta smelt. Geographic isolation, even if it is incomplete, and adaptation to alternative environments, are considered powerful phenomena in the origin of species (see Chapter 4).

The life history of the delta smelt is critical to understanding the Sacramento–San Joaquin water battle. As a likely result of its evolutionary history, the delta smelt is found across a range of salinities, typically 0–18 parts per thousand (ppt), with larval and juvenile fishes concentrated in a "low salinity zone" of 1–6 ppt. Averaged across all life stages, the delta smelt tends to prefer waters of about 2 ppt, and their distribution shifts as salinity varies with changes in freshwater outflow. Consequently, the extent of habitat available for delta smelt depends crucially on the relative strengths of saltwater inflow (which will increase salinity) from San Francisco Bay and freshwater outflow from the Sacramento–San Joaquin river system (which will reduce salinity). Under natural conditions, high saltwater inflow results in a compression of habitat preferred by delta smelt (i.e., the low salinity zone) eastward into the delta. By contrast, higher freshwater flows result in an expansion of preferred habitat westward towards San Francisco Bay. An index of available preferred, low salinity zone habitat is expressed as what is known as "X2" – the distance in kilometres eastward from the Golden Gate Bridge to the near centre of the 2 ppt zone.[48] The greatest areas and volumes, but shallowest depths of low salinity habitat, are associated with X2 values of 50 km and 60–75 km, respectively, with high freshwater flow. (Values of X2 can also be influenced by the topography of the delta and the distribution of 2 ppt waters in relation to topography.) By contrast, the smallest areas and volumes, but greatest depths of low salinity habitat, occur at X2 values of 50–60 km and at 80–85 km, respectively, under low freshwater flow and depending on the exact distribution of 2 ppt waters. Herein lies the basis of the water conflict – the most significant influence on the value and variability of X2, and hence on the habitat available for the delta smelt, is the degree of interannual variation in freshwater runoff between "wet" and "dry" years. Diversion of fresh water from the river system for irrigation and other human uses, particularly from the State Water Project and Central Valley Project export pumping stations in the southern portion of the delta, can, therefore, reduce the low salinity zone (the delta smelt's preferred habitat) especially during dry years. In essence, the fish and humans are competing for the same water.

The delta smelt was once one of the most common pelagic fish in the delta, so common that it was fished commercially. Its historical distribution extended from the eastern margins of San Pablo Bay upstream through the delta in Contra Costa, Sacramento, San Joaquin, Solano and Yolo counties. Unfortunately, the population sizes of the delta smelt have dropped precipitously since the 1980s, and they have virtually disappeared from the southern portion of the delta. Most recently, a total of only 108 delta smelt were captured in ten surveys throughout the delta between January and June 2015, while only two females (and no males) have been collected across three surveys in 2020.[49] By contrast, thousands of adult smelt were collected in surveys from the late 1960s to the early 1990s. The drastic and continuing decline in indices of abundance of the delta smelt led to their listing as Threatened under the ESA in 1993. In fact, the situation is even worse, as the US Fish and Wildlife Service has subsequently determined that the delta smelt actually warrants an ESA listing of Endangered, but that such a listing is "precluded" by higher-priority species (it was also listed as Threatened under California's Endangered Species Act in 1993 and up-listed to Endangered in 2010).[50]

Among the factors leading to the demise of the delta smelt are pollution and predation by, and competition with, invasive species. By far, however, the greatest threats to the species are indirect or direct effects of upstream water diversions or export of water directly from the delta and the facilities used for such export, associated with supplying water for irrigation of the Central Valley. State and federal water diversions/export impact the extent of low-salinity-zone critical habitat for delta smelt as discussed above. Water diversions from the delta also tend to increase water clarity (as sediment is deposited under reduced flows), which may make the delta smelt more susceptible to visual predators or reduce their feeding efficiency. In addition, water export facilities within the delta itself entrain (trap) smelt as they withdraw water. Declines in the abundance of the delta smelt are strongly associated with increases in export of water from the delta beginning in the early 2000s. The extent of entrainment varies seasonally and with smelt distribution relative to the intake ports, but it has been estimated that between 50% of the adult population and 60% of the juvenile population of delta smelt are entrained annually.[51] A large fraction of the reproductive potential of the delta smelt is literally "sucked out" of the delta every year.

Fish, farms and drought: The current battles for water

DEMANDS FOR AGRICULTURAL USE of Sacramento–San Joaquin water, the delta smelt's declining status and its dependence on the delta crashed into one another when various environmental groups sued the US Fish and Wildlife Service (USFWS) in 2006 for failing to protect the delta smelt under the ESA and for its conclusion in a "Biological Opinion" (BiOp) that water exports do not harm the fish. This action precipitated the "continuing war over protection of the delta smelt."[52] In 2007, a federal court threw out the USFWS's BiOp as a result of the suit and the agency wrote a new, 400-page opinion in 2008 that concluded that export of water from the delta *was* harming the delta smelt.[53] The new BiOp also suggested that reductions in export of water from the delta would be "reasonable and prudent" actions to help protect the smelt, actions that the Bureau of Reclamation and California Department of Water Resources intended to implement. The *Wall Street Journal* railed against the decision, citing large job losses in agriculture and that it constituted a "green war against San Joaquin Valley farmers."[54] A countersuit challenging these restrictions, however, was filed in 2009 by a group consisting of irrigation districts, water provision contractors and the municipal water districts. The group argued that the export restrictions were "arbitrary and capricious," i.e., that the ruling enforcing the restrictions should be invalidated because it was made on unreasonable grounds or without any proper consideration of circumstances, including estimates of losses of five thousand to tens of thousands of jobs.[55] Perhaps as a direct consequence of the complexity of the situation, a district court ruled partially in favour of the plaintiffs and partially in favour of the defendants, finding that although the export operations were likely detrimental to the delta smelt and its critical habitat, the specific export reduction amounts were not well justified. The court also ruled that yet another BiOp was required.[56] Next, an appeals court in San Francisco overturned this ruling in March 2014 and the restrictions of water exports to protect the delta smelt were upheld.[57] Finally, the case made it to the US Supreme Court, which in early 2015 refused to hear the case for no stated reason.[58] Public opinion remains deeply divided on the issue. The *National Review* viewed the delta smelt dismissively; it was "undistinguished" and "inedible."[59] The water export restrictions amounted to a "green drought" brought on by "an activist government run amok."[60] The water allowed to flow freely to the Pacific to protect the delta smelt's habitat, and not exported to farms, was "wasted forever, to the raucous applause of Luddites, misanthropes, and their powerful enablers."[61] By contrast, a lawyer for the Natural Resources Defense Council stated that the Supreme Court's de facto siding with the delta smelt (by its refusal to hear the case) was "good news for the thousands of fishermen, Delta farmers, and everyone who depends on the health of California's Bay-Delta estuary and its native fisheries and wildlife."[62]

The conflict between water for smelt and water for almonds, walnuts, lettuce etc., is made even worse by drought, and not the kind of "green drought" the *National Review* was referring to. The US Geological Society (USGS) defines a "drought" as a period of drier than normal conditions that results in water-related problems.[63] Droughts can result from lack of precipitation, lack of soil moisture or lack of stream flow or reduced groundwater. Tree ring records indicate that central California has experienced droughts for over 2000 years and that the frequency of droughts may change dramatically through time.[64] Some pre-Columbian droughts in the western US have lasted decades to hundreds of years. Since rainfall records began to be taken in the mid-1800s and the growth of the agricultural industry, serious droughts have occurred in California multiple times, most notably in the 1860s, 1890s, 1924, early 1930s and several years in the 1960s and 1970s. Since 1985, the severity and frequency of droughts has been increasing. On January 17, 2014, about one year before the Supreme Court decision not to hear the delta smelt case, California Governor Jerry Brown declared a drought state of emergency, calling on all Californians to reduce their use of water by 20%.[65] In 2015, the fourth consecutive year of drought, Brown declared another drought state of emergency, and in April of that year he instituted mandatory reductions in urban, but not agricultural, water use of 25%.[66] While the current situation is tense, the future does not look much better (see Chapter 12). Continuing trends towards a drier California and increasing agricultural vulnerability to climate change in the Central Valley are sure to lessen the prospects for peace in the water wars in the Sacramento–San Joaquin system.[67]

— SEVEN —

The Colorado River
Sacrificed

Either you bring the water to L.A., or you bring L.A. to the water.
—NOAH CROSS (played by John Huston), *Chinatown* (1974)

The Imperial Valley of southeastern California, the adjacent Salton Sea to the west, and the northern Gulf of California (Sea of Cortez) to the south represent one of the most startling landscapes in North America. The area is startling not because of majestic mountain peaks, broad seascapes or even the harsh beauty of the desert. Rather, it is the presence of vast, green vistas in one the hottest and driest regions of North America – an "accidental"[1] inland sea saltier than the Pacific Ocean that sprang from mistakes in water engineering – and the parched remnants of what was once the largest delta on the Pacific Coast – some 7770 km^2, or almost twice the size of the San Francisco Bay/Sacramento–San Joaquin Delta, – the Colorado River Delta. These features stem from the human re-making of arguably the most dramatic and wild, great river of North America – the Colorado River.

Several aspects of the post-1900 history of the Colorado River make its story a disturbing one, at least relative to those told of the other great rivers of North America. Disturbing, because the very

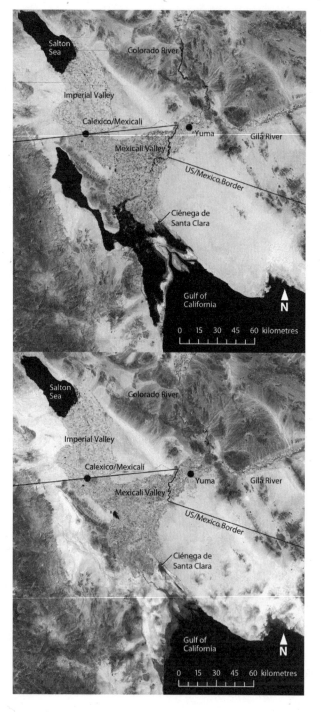

The Colorado River Delta (south and west of the Ciénega de Santa Clara) under high water flow (upper, 1984) and low flow (lower, 1990) conditions. Black shading represents flowing and standing surface water. The Imperial and Mexicali valleys are major agricultural areas supported by irrigation, as are the regions around Yuma and the Gila River. LANDSAT image courtesy of Alejandro Hinojosa-Corona (CICESE, Ensenada, México).

climax of the natural course of a great river – its final collision with the sea and all the life so created and sustained – no longer occurs, at least not without occasional assistance from humans. Except during particularly wet years, the water of the Colorado River is *completely* diverted for agricultural, industrial and municipal use before it reaches the Gulf of California.[2] For much of the year, the river is reduced to a drainage ditch with a meagre flow consisting of highly saline agricultural runoff. Denied the water that originates high in the Rocky Mountains of Colorado over 2000 km upstream from the sea, the delta is now less than one-tenth its historical size and a fragment of its former splendour.[3]

Not only has the terminal flow of the river been strangled, but upstream the river has been very much pacified. In his book *Colossus: Hoover Dam and the Making of the American Century*, Michael Hiltzik writes: "Throughout history, what has set the Colorado River apart from all other waterways of the Western Hemisphere is its violent personality.... No river matched its schizophrenic moods which could swing in the course of a few hours from that of a meandering country stream to an insane torrent."[4] That violent but creative energy scoured geological wonders such as the Grand Canyon, but has now been all but muted by dams, reservoirs and diversion canals. Given that the course of the Colorado River runs through what has been for several decades the fastest-growing region of the US[5] and that the river serves large communities such as Los Angeles, San Diego, Las Vegas, Phoenix, Tucson, Denver, Tijuana and Mexicali, it is unusual that no major metropolis lies on the banks of the river itself.[6] Further, it has, much like the Sacramento–San Joaquin system, no major tributaries that rival its own size and thus does not grow substantially as one proceeds downstream.[7] In fact, the Colorado River is a relatively small river compared to the others discussed in this book. It flows, however, through some of the hottest and driest regions of North America, so its importance is magnified well beyond its size, alone. Finally, the Colorado River is the only one of the rivers of North America of which it can be argued that a great river has been almost completely sacrificed to human ambitions. It has been said that for no other river has so much been asked as has been asked of the Colorado River.[8] Further, this sacrifice seems unfairly apportioned across the jurisdictions (seven US states, many Native American communities and two Mexican states) through which it flows, as are the benefits generated from its remaking. The uneven benefits of the development of the Colorado River, coupled with the uneven costs incurred across the watershed, are a recipe for conflict. This chapter recounts the story of the development of the Colorado River, "one of the most litigated, regulated, and argued-about rivers in the world,"[9] the life support system of major cities such as Los Angeles, Las Vegas and Phoenix, and home to some of the most remarkable landscapes and biodiversity in North America.

The geography and origin of the Colorado River

THE COLORADO RIVER runs for some 2333 km and drains an area of 637,137 km^2, making it the ninth largest river in both respects in North America (46th and 50th global ranks, respectively). Most of the river flows through the US; only about 6% of its length and 3% of its drainage area occur in Mexico.[10] In *A River No More: The Colorado River and the West*, Philip Fradkin described the form of the Colorado River drainage as a "splayed left hand, palm facing away and the thumb pointing down,"[11] with the major rivers of the drainage constituting the various digits. Offering a slight modification of Fradkin's description, the Green River is the pinky (in the 1 o'clock position), followed by the upper Colorado River (formerly known as the Grand River) as the ring finger; the San Juan River is the middle finger, the Little Colorado River is the forefinger (at 4 o'clock) and the Gila River is the thumb. The lower mainstem Colorado River takes a sharp turn south from the base of the ring finger to run south to the Gulf of California.

The source of the Colorado River is officially considered to be in the headwaters of the upper Colorado River at La Poudre Pass on the Continental Divide within the southern Rocky Mountains in north-central Colorado. Ironically, right at the source of this magnificent river is also the first diversion of its water out of the basin – the Grand Ditch Diversion – across the Continental Divide into the South Platte River

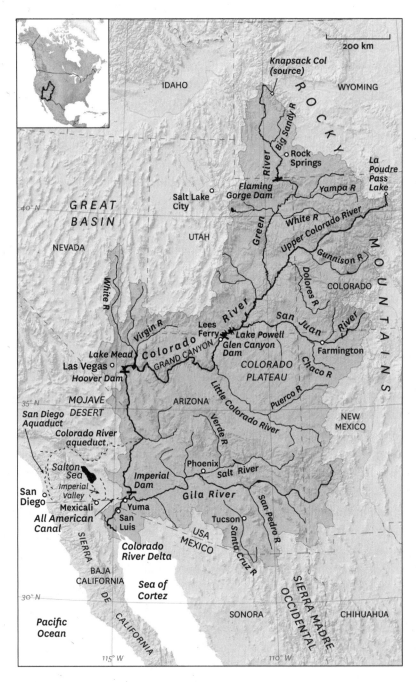

The Colorado River Basin. The river is divided into lower and upper basins at Lees Ferry, Arizona.

system (Mississippi River drainage).[12] It is, however, the headwaters of the Green River, which originates from ice high in Knapsack Col in central-west Wyoming, penetrates 300 km deeper inland and drains a larger area than the upper Colorado River, that many argue is the hydrologically correct source of the Colorado River.[13]

The hand-like form of the Colorado River is splayed almost evenly across portions of two major physiographic regions of the US: the Intermontane Plateaus and the Pacific Mountains. The upper Colorado River Basin drains about 90% of the Colorado Plateau Province (of the Intermontane Plateaus Region) to the Utah–Arizona border. The lower Colorado River Basin is encompassed largely within the Basin and Range Province, with the terminal portion of the river contained within the Pacific Border Province (of the Pacific Mountains Region). The Colorado River has two other notable distinctions. First, its source (whether it be in the Green River or the upper Colorado River) has the highest elevation, over 3000 m, of any of the rivers discussed in this book (the source of the San Joaquin River is second at a shade under 3000 m in the Sierra Nevada). Second, in its natural state and for its size, it carried by far the greatest silt load. Each year the Colorado River discharged up to an estimated 177 million tonnes[14] of sediment through the Grand Canyon and as much as 123 million cubic metres of sediment to the delta. The Mississippi River, which has a drainage basin more than five times the size of the Colorado River, is estimated to discharge only about 8% more silt – 191 million tonnes annually.[15] Ergo, one understands the origin of the infamous description of the Colorado River's water by early settlers – "Too thick to drink, too thin to plow,"[16] as well as its name, which stems from the original *Rio Colorado*, Spanish for "the red river." The Colorado River system is home to about 12.7 million people but provides water for over 30 million across seven US states and two states of Mexico.[17] The Colorado River supplies water to a vast web of communities, many outside the watershed itself, and its various uses contribute to more than one-quarter of the US economy.[18]

The origin of the Colorado River constitutes a "classic mystery in geology"[19] and is the subject of some debate, falling into two schools of thought. The allure of this mystery stems from a desire to better understand the erosional history of one of the Earth's most dramatic landscapes – the Grand Canyon, a 446 km long and up to 1.6 km deep gouge in the Colorado Plateau. One idea maintains that the river has had a continuous history as a single unit and emerged following uplift during the major recent period of mountain building in western North America, the Laramide Orogeny, between 85 and 50 million ya. Alternatively, the other and most widely accepted idea is that the contemporary Colorado River is an "integration" of different ancestral components with very different histories, some very young, and that the present river came into existence perhaps only 5–6 million ya.[20]

The idea of an integrated river system begins with the origin of the Colorado Plateau. While some rocks of the Grand Canyon within the plateau originated 1.7 billion ya, the plateau is an amalgam of layers of older and younger rocks derived from a variety of igneous and sedimentary rock-forming processes. The oldest rocks formed into great fault-block mountains (large broken-up pieces of bedrock) that were subsequently eroded and overlain by igneous rock intrusions. Marine-derived sedimentary rocks were deposited when the area formed the coastal margins of the North American continent and later still when the Cretaceous Seaway existed. The Laramide Orogeny initiated a major uplift of the Rocky Mountains but caused less extreme uplifting and deformation of the adjacent Colorado Plateau. Through much of this time, the upper portion of the ancestral Colorado River is thought to have drained off the plateau in a northern or northeastern direction.[21] The present-day courses of streams on the Colorado Plateau were established about 5–6 million ya following a major uplift (1000–3000 m) of the Rocky Mountains and the Colorado Plateau that caused a drainage reversal of the Colorado River to the southwest. Both these periods of uplift caused stream gradients to increase, resulting in erosion and major down-cutting of stream bottoms. This down-cutting likely contributed to the formation of the Grand Canyon, perhaps by the integration of a series of older canyons, by the ancestral Colorado River.[22] Notwithstanding the drainage reversal to the southwest, the Colorado River was not running to the sea. Its terminus at this time remains uncertain, but it may have been strictly an interior drainage dissipating into subterranean limestone caverns in and around the central-west Grand Canyon.[23]

To the south and west, what is now the lower Colorado River below the Grand Canyon rested within alternating canyons and alluvial plains bordered by mountains within the Basin and Range Province (the second of the three Intermontane Plateaus) running in a general north–south direction.[24] Until about 6 million ya, marine sediments dominated the Salton Trough (a basin extending from an area near the US–Mexican border north to the Salton Sea) within the Basin and Range Province. The present-day course of the lowest portions of the Colorado River and the delta is contained within the Salton Trough. The presence of marine sediments here and dated to 6 million ya indicates that the Colorado River did not enter the Gulf of California at this time. The presence of Colorado River sediments similar to contemporary material at the head of the Gulf of California by 5.3 million ya, however, indicates that integration of the river system running through this area with the upper Colorado River running across the Colorado Plateau occurred by this time.[25] The integration of the river system running through the Salton Trough with the ancestral Colorado River to form the contemporary system occurred, therefore, sometime between 5.3 and 6 million ya, either by headward erosion of the lower river to capture the ancestral Colorado River, by a "top down" series of spillovers of large lakes that formed on the Colorado Plateau, or by groundwater-aided erosion and collapse of barriers between the two once-isolated parts of the Colorado River (or perhaps by a combinations of these processes).[26] Over the subsequent millennia, the terminal course of the river has shifted between the eastern and western sides of the delta as well as north towards the Salton Sea and south towards the Gulf of California.[27]

Early human history in the Colorado River

THE FIRST HUMAN INHABITANTS of the Colorado River basin are thought to have been people of the Clovis or Folsom point cultures living in scattered groups on the Colorado Plateau as much as 12,000 ya (see also Chapter 8). During the period of 8,000 to 2,000 ya the so-called Desert Archaic Culture developed in the area, a largely nomadic cultural group that eventually gave rise to the ancient Puebloan Anasazi peoples, who thrived from around 600 to 1200 AD.[28] The Anasazi developed relatively large, interconnected population centres and were notable for extensive irrigation systems, particularly near Chaco Canyon in the headwaters of the San Juan River, in northwestern New Mexico. The decline of the Anasazi is attributed in part to mismanagement of natural resources, including water and soil, during a period of increasing aridity.[29] Farther south along the Gila River and near present-day Phoenix, the Hohokam peoples built extensive irrigation canals extending for distances of up to 400 km along the Salt and Gila rivers. The collapse of this culture around 1450 has also been attributed to failed water management in a dry climate.[30] Hohokam irrigation was relatively inefficient, and evaporation tended to concentrate salts in the soil that then contaminated surface and groundwater. Slow-running, salty irrigation water also infiltrated the soil and contaminated and raised the water table. Such salt-contaminated surface or groundwater is toxic to most plants and contributed to the decline of these civilizations. Ironically, the mismanagement of water stemmed from the application of too much irrigation water in an area with too little rainfall – a mistake that would be oft repeated. Subsequently, the Navajo, Apache, Mohave, Maricopa, Pima, Havasupai and Hualapai peoples inhabited areas within the Colorado River drainage beginning in the 11th century. Notable were the Mohave, who lived along the lower Colorado River and were known to be fishers as well as farmers along the river, exploiting, among other species, the endemic Colorado pikeminnow (*Ptychocheilus lucius*), which grew to over 40 kg.[31]

As with many of the rivers of western North America, initial explorations of the Colorado River by Europeans involved searches for the fabled Northwest Passage or for gold. Francisco de Ulloa (? – 1540), a Spanish conquistador, explored the Gulf of California to its head and sailed into the Colorado River delta in 1539 as he searched for one possible terminus of the Northwest Passage. In New Spain (now Mexico), the legend of the Seven Cities of Gold ("Cíbola") that were built by Native Americans in the deserts of the southwestern US fuelled the first major overland expedition from Guadalajara, Mexico, into the basin by Francisco Vázquez de Coronado (1510–1554) and 200 men between 1540 and 1542. From a base camp in western New Mexico, three units from the Coronado expedition probed different parts of the Colorado River.[32] Hernando de Alarcón entered the river from the Gulf of California to resupply Coronado but could not cover the vast distance to Coronado's camp and cached the supplies somewhere downstream of the lower half of the Grand Canyon. Melchior Díaz was dispatched from Coronado's camp to try and locate Alarcón, which he failed to do, but he did locate his supplies and explored the area around the confluence of the Gila and Colorado rivers.[33] Díaz was the first European to cross the Colorado River, which he named Rio del Tizon. Finally, Garcia López de Cárdenas was sent by Coronado to investigate rumours of a great river to the west reported by Native Americans living near Coronado's camp. Eventually, Cárdenas's group reached the south rim of the Grand Canyon and observed what they thought was a small river, thousands of feet below. Some of Cárdenas's men tried to make their way down to the river bottom but were defeated by sheer terror and the immensity of the canyon. Cárdenas declared that the great obstacle of the Grand Canyon and the foreboding landscape was a "useless piece of country."[34] Exploration and settlement by Europeans did not progress for the next 200 years. Missionaries seeking routes to Californian missions travelled along the Colorado River, and in 1776 one, Francisco Tomás Garcés, described the river in his writings as the Rio Colorado, or the Red River, although the name had been previously applied on some maps for several decades.[35]

After the Colorado River basin was transferred to the US as part of the Treaty of Guadalupe Hidalgo (1846), which ended the Mexican–American war, the Colorado River received more bad reviews from expeditions in the mid-1800s by Americans. Lieutenant Joseph C. Ives (1829–1868) led an exploration and mapping trip of the Colorado River from the delta upstream in 1857, reaching as far as the lower Grand Canyon before abandoning his shallow-draft ship and declaring, "Ours was the first and will doubtless be the last party of whites to visit this profitless locale."[36] In May 1869, John Wesley Powell, a retired Union Army major who had lost his right arm during the Civil War's Battle of Shiloh, set out to run the Green and Colorado rivers to the latter's confluence with the Virgin River as part of a scientific and mapping expedition. Powell was a geologist and naturalist, but he and his nine companions, while experienced outdoorsmen and adventurers, had no whitewater experience. Remarkably, in late August 1869 the party reached the Virgin River after traversing many cataracts, rapids and the Grand Canyon in an epic journey of one of the last unexplored areas of the American West.[37] Powell led a second expedition between 1871 and 1872 and published *Report on the Lands of the Arid Regions of the United States* in 1878. This report was very influential and incurred the wrath of western water interests because it helped promote the development of the irrigation district – the basic governing unit of western agricultural areas. Powell saw the West, including the Colorado Basin, as being inadequate for massive farming without organized, equitable water distribution through irrigation, much to the disappointment of more individualist immigration and farming boosters and land speculators. At an 1893 conference on irrigation in Los Angeles, Powell stated: "I tell you, gentlemen, you are piling up a heritage of conflict and litigation of water rights, for there is not sufficient water to supply the land."[38] Powell also advocated that the Colorado River, as well as other major rivers, should be managed on a watershed-by-watershed basis, i.e., irrigation and farming planning should be based on the limitations and potential of each watershed rather than by the potential for interbasin transfers. Unfortunately, and as will become apparent below, the American West's watersheds have suffered dearly for not adopting Powell's philosophy.

The first Americans of European descent to erect large-scale agricultural settlements with extensive irrigation works in the Colorado River basin were the Mormons (members of the Church of Jesus Christ of Latter-day Saints). Under original leader Brigham Young's vision of a desert empire (an unrecognized state called Deseret was envisioned and centred on Nevada, Utah, northern Arizona, southeastern California and parts of Colorado, Wyoming and New Mexico), Mormon settlers built towns near the confluence of the Virgin and Colorado rivers and along the Gila River and Little Colorado River in the 1860s–1870s. The historical agricultural development of much of the Colorado River basin by the Mormons, especially in Utah and Arizona, coupled with their disciplined and unified social structure, would ensure them a prominent place in the subsequent battles that carved up the basin and its water. Very much less involved were the Native Americans, who had much deeper roots in agriculture and irrigation of the Colorado River basin. Similarly, Mexico was essentially shut out of the initial major negotiations to apportion Colorado River water and was only reluctantly given water of minimal quality. The history of Colorado River water developments indicates that, indeed, "water flows toward the powerful and rich."[39] There is no better river to illustrate Worster's concept of a hydraulic West than the Colorado River.

Water developments and politics within the Colorado River Basin

THE COLORADO RIVER has been described as "an American Nile" because, like the great river of Egypt, it flows through an area where "so many people are so helplessly dependent on one river's flow."[40] The Colorado River's dams, reservoirs, irrigation canals and electrical generating stations provide water for almost 40 million people for agriculture, industry and municipal use in the US and Mexico. Approximately 1.8 million ha of land are irrigated by Colorado River water, and its dams generate over 12 billion kWh of electricity. The equivalent of four years of the river's flow are stored in its reservoirs, and if that supply ran out it is likely that most of southern California and Arizona and much of Colorado, Wyoming, Utah and New Mexico would be doomed. The Colorado River, for instance, supplies over 50% of the water for Los Angeles, San Diego and Phoenix. The importance of out-of-basin water delivery to Los Angeles as a key focus of California water wars was immortalized in the 1974 film Chinatown (see the quotation at this chapter's beginning) starring Jack Nicholson, Faye Dunaway and John Huston. The film, nominated for 11 Academy Awards and preserved in the US National Film Registry as selected by the Library of Congress, tells the story of a private investigator, played by Nicholson, who uncovers a plot to reduce water delivery to drought-stricken lands surrounding Los Angeles so that a group of conspirators can obtain the land at much reduced prices. Even more pointedly, the city of Las Vegas is utterly dependent on water from Lake Mead, the largest reservoir in the US, on the Colorado River, from which it gets 90% of its supply. The Imperial and Coachella valleys in southeastern California are desert lands that have been turned into agricultural powerhouses by irrigation using Colorado River water, generating over US$1.5 billion of winter crops annually for the US and international markets.

The critical role of the Colorado River and its water in the development and persistence of the modern southwestern US, coupled with the fact that the basin flows through dramatic and unique landscapes across seven US states, many Native American lands and two states in Mexico, explains why the Colorado River represents the peak of legal battles over water. Notwithstanding the severity of the "California water wars" (see Chapter 6), those are intrastate battles, but the confrontations over water across the Colorado basin involve a much greater diversity of players and interests.

The first transfers of water from the Colorado River to California took place in June 1901 with the construction of a canal through Mexico to drain water into the Alamo River, which drained north into the newly named Imperial Valley (a much more appealing moniker than the original Valley of the Dead) along the Salton Trough.[41] Development and settlement of the valley grew following irrigation. In 1905, however, violent floods on the Colorado River overwhelmed the canal intake, resulting in the entire flow of the mighty Colorado River being directed into the Imperial Valley to settle in an ancient former lake bed, the Salton Sea, formed when the growing Colorado River Delta isolated an embayment of the Gulf of California during the Pleistocene. The Salton Sea had intermittently dried up and refilled depending on the vagaries of the natural flow direction of the Colorado River throughout the Pleistocene. It took almost two years to repair the breach in the river bank and get the Colorado River to resume its course to the gulf, and in the meantime the "accidental" Salton Sea formed the largest lake in California at about 56 km long and 24 km at its widest point with a surface area of about 975 km². The marginal and saline (from agricultural runoff) inlets to the sea, coupled with the lack of an outlet and high evaporation, mean that the lake is gradually shrinking and increasing in salinity (currently at 44 ppt; adjacent parts of the Pacific Ocean are 35 ppt).

The Salton Sea mishap did not slake California's thirst for more water, but better control of the Colorado River was clearly needed. The state was growing much faster than the other Colorado River basin jurisdictions, yet its attempts to appropriate more water for the Imperial Valley and elsewhere via a dam and canal (within US jurisdiction) were unsuccessful, especially because California contributes virtually nothing to the flow of the river itself. Eventually, a negotiated settlement, the Colorado River Compact, was signed by all seven basin states in 1922. The compact divided the basin into upper (Colorado, Wyoming, Utah and New Mexico) and lower basins (California, Arizona and Nevada) at Lees Ferry, Arizona, and assigned 9.3 billion m³ of water annually to each basin and a bonus to the lower basin states of 1.35 billion m³ in years of surplus. The bickering among states, however, began during the ratification process. Eventually, the state-specific allotments in the lower basin were agreed to and the compact was ratified in 1928 (Arizona held out until 1944), and Mexico was assigned 1.85 billion m³ annually via a 1944 international treaty. The allotments among upper basin states were determined in a second compact signed in 1948. These and several other agreements together constitute what is known as the Law of the River.[42] Part of the solution to the lower basin allotment disagreements was the authorization of the Boulder Canyon Dam Project (renamed Hoover Dam) by the US Congress in 1928 to supply California with a reliable source of water if that state agreed to a maximum annual diversion limit. Unfortunately, the US Bureau of Reclamation's estimate of the annual flow of the Colorado River that formed the basis of the compacts' water allotments was based on unusually wet years and was, therefore, too optimistic. Subsequent flows have been nowhere near the estimated total average of 21.6 billion m³ annually. This has led to many disputes, especially in drought years, which have become increasingly common especially since 2000.[43] Consequently, the Colorado River is often referred to as a "deficit river" – its allocations for diversion exceed its annual supply from runoff, particularly in the lower basin.[44]

There are now at least 29 dams within the Colorado River basin, but the building of Hoover Dam on the river's main stem, is of course, a seminal event in the history of the basin. It is, however, much more than that – a project that transcends the basin itself given the enormity of the engineering challenges, the financial and labour resources required, plus its role as part of a broader, grand strategy for national renewal, and as a global symbol of the ecological consequences of major hydrological projects. As for the development of the southwest US as a hydraulic society, Hoover Dam started it all.[45] The dam was approved in 1928 and construction began at the Black Canyon site about 48 km southeast of Las Vegas in 1931. The dam fulfilled more than the desires of a thirsty California. Although approved by then President Herbert Hoover, the dam construction fit nicely within the national economic recovery strategy of President Franklin Delano Roosevelt (first elected in 1932) during a time of depression, high unemployment and mass movements of people westward as a result of the Dust Bowl in the Midwest (see Chapter 5 and 6).[46] In fact, it could be argued that Roosevelt saw the economic and social benefits of Hoover Dam (which in construction alone employed more than 5,200 people at its peak) as a model for subsequent involvement in, and development of, the Central Valley Project of California and the Columbia Basin Project (in Washington).[47] Regardless, Hoover Dam, at the time the largest dam in the world, was completed in 1935, cost $49 million to construct and used 2.48 million m^3 of concrete. It towers over 221 m in height, backs up the river to form 180 km long Lake Mead with a surface area of 640 km^2, can store up to almost two years of flow of the Colorado River, generates 4.2 billion kWh of electricity annually, supplies 400,000–800,000 ha of land with irrigation water and provides domestic water for more than 25 million people from Lake Mead alone.[48] A total of 112 people are officially recorded as having died during the surveying, planning and construction of Hoover Dam, and in one of those odd twists of fate, a father and son were the first and last to die, respectively, on the same day, December 20th, 13 years apart.[49]

As part of the Boulder Canyon Project Act that authorized the dam, two other projects were also built: the Imperial Dam (1938) located downstream near the US–Mexican border and, to take water from the Imperial Dam reservoir to the Imperial Valley, the All-American Canal (1942). Still other dams followed throughout the watershed: Parker Dam (1938), Davis Dam (1951), Morelos Dam (1950), Glen Canyon Dam (1963) and Flaming Gorge Dam (1964).

The water projects of the 20th century constructed within the Colorado Basin have been described as taking place in four basic phases following the formation of the federal Reclamation Service in 1902. The first phase involved relatively small and "non-controversial" projects, typically on tributary streams (e.g., the Roosevelt Dam on the Salt River in Arizona, the Strawberry Valley Project in Utah) as the service cut its teeth in the basin.[50] The next phase was the great dam-building period of the 1930s–1960s, the "Go-Go" years,[51] which began with Hoover Dam and ended with Glen Canyon Dam, both on the mainstem Colorado River. The third phase involved mostly a "conveyance phase" where efforts were concentrated on large canal and aqueduct systems to move water from one area to another from the late 1950s to the 2000s (e.g., the Central Utah and Central Arizona projects). The final phase began in 1974 and continues to this day – to "clean up the mess caused by the preceding phases."[52] Not all of those with rights of use of the Colorado River water resources, however, have participated equally in the first three phases and, some were disproportionately affected by the problems that the last phase was designed to address.

Native American water rights in the Colorado River: "Paper" versus "wet" water

NOTWITHSTANDING hundreds of years of history of irrigation of Colorado River waters, Native American rights to water in the basin were only somewhat vaguely recognized in the 1908 Winters Doctrine, named after one of the plaintiffs in a US Supreme Court decision.

In a case involving Montana's Milk River system the court found that the Fort Belknap Indian Reservation had "reserved" rights to water upon creation of the reservation (in 1888) and that a subsequent claim to rights was not necessary when inhabitants of the reserve wanted to use the water at a later date. The rights to water were implied upon creation of the reserve. Despite the promise of the Winters Doctrine, Native American rights to water in the Colorado Basin were either ignored, side-stepped or severely underrepresented in the subsequent decades. For instance, Native American groups were not invited to, nor did they participate in, the extensive negotiations between 1920 and 1950 leading to the Colorado River compacts and treaties where water allotments were made to the seven basin states and Mexico. The US government made only vague references to maintaining their "obligation" to Native American groups' water interests, obligations that were not specifically defined and that were subject to intense counter-lobbying by state interests.[53] Specific rights and water allocations were eventually made to only five of at least 25 lower basin Native American tribes as the result of an Arizona vs. California Supreme Court decision in 1964, but those allocations did not include the Navajo Nation – the largest nation in the basin.

The Navajo Nation includes lands in Arizona, New Mexico and Utah covering a territory of 71,000 km^2, the largest Native American territory in the US, which was formed under the 1868 Navajo Treaty. It has been estimated that if only 202,000 ha were irrigated on Navajo lands (only 4% of the land base), approximately 2.5 billion m^3 would be due the Navajo annually. Other estimates include claims up to 6.2 billion m^3 annually.[54] Arizona, however, has the largest allotment of Colorado River water among the three states spanning the Navajo Nation, but its total allotment is only 3.5 billion m^3.[55] Clearly, specific definition and allotments of Colorado River water to the Navajo Nation alone were not in the narrow interests of basin states and private water users. One analysis of Navajo water rights concluded that "early priority dates stemming from the 1868 treaty, acts of Congress, and executive orders creating the Navajo reservation place the Navajo claim at the forefront of almost all claims to water in the arid Colorado River Basin. Most of the relevant legislation, including the *Colorado River Compact* (1922), the *Boulder Canyon Project Act* (1928), the *Upper Colorado River Basin Compact* (1948), the *Colorado River Storage Project Act* (1956), and the *Colorado River Basin Project Act* (1968), either disclaim any intent to affect, or do not discuss, Indian water rights."[56] Another treatment offered that "the stark truth of the matter is that, beginning at the turn of the century, the offices and powers of national government were marshalled to plan, construct, and finance non-Indian agricultural development in the West, and nothing comparable was done for the Native American."[57] Although these conclusions were made decades ago and progress has been made in turning theoretical "paper" rights into actual "wet" water, much work remains to settle Native water claims so long neglected in the basin.[58] Between 10 and 20 Native American tribes have achieved priority water rights through settlements in the basin since the 1980s.[59] The Navajo Nation has a Water Rights Commission[60] and a Water Rights Unit within their Department of Justice. That unit is working to implement settlements as they arise (e.g., San Juan River claim in New Mexico, 2010) and continues working to settle claims made by the Navajo Nation in the main stem of the lower Colorado River, the Little Colorado River and in that portion of the San Juan River in Utah.[61] As the US Southwest continues to grow and some climate change analyses suggest flow reductions of between 7% and 30% by 2050, pressure mounts for Native American rights including the right to sell their water allocations out of state. Indeed, who wields "water power" within much of the Colorado River Basin may yet fully reverse the historical disadvantages of Native American groups.[62]

Turning on the tap:
Evolution of Mexican entitlements to the Colorado River

THE COLORADO RIVER IS, of course, a transboundary river flowing through seven US states and the territories of several Native American tribes. The river is, however, also an international transboundary system; about 100 km of river and the entire delta region are found in Mexico. The river was first seen and travelled upon by Europeans from what is now the Mexican side. Like many Native American groups, Mexico has struggled for recognition of its rights to water from the Colorado River and for fair allocations of water of enough quantity *and* quality since most of the basin was ceded to the US after the Mexican-American War. Although Mexico contributes virtually nothing to the natural flow of the river, neither does California, yet that US state is the greatest single user of Colorado River water. In *A River No More,* Philip Fradkin argued that the "desert meeting"[63] of the US and Mexico on the Colorado River and the disparities in quantity and quality of water crossing south across the border reflect the relative political, socio-economic and technical power of the two countries, and that the US has pressed its advantages in all areas over the decades to only grudgingly allocate enough of this critical resource to Mexico.

Mexicali is the capital of the Mexican state of Baja California and has a metropolitan area population of just over one million people. It is located right across the US–Mexican border and is the focus of the agricultural industry of the Mexicali Valley. The agricultural industry of the Mexicali Valley included 211,000 ha of irrigated land, employed more than 15,000 people and generated US $192 million in revenue in 2008.[64] It is the most productive agricultural region in Mexico. American interests in the area began early in the 1900s when the California Development Company received permission from the Mexican government to cut a canal from the Colorado River in the US and run it west through Mexico to the Alamo River and eventually to what became the Imperial Valley, CA. While some of this water was apportioned to Mexico, American influence in the area increased when a business syndicate, the Colorado River Land Company, purchased 340,000 ha – most of the valley. A huge agricultural enterprise developed that leased land to thousands of Mexican and imported Chinese workers and was based on the water allocated to Mexico from the Alamo Canal. The Mexican government of President Díaz was conflicted about such encroachment and protested only mildly. On the one hand, the Mexicans wanted foreign investment to encourage development. On the other hand, they did not want to lose sovereignty over the area or the larger region of

Baja California itself (in which the US government had shown much interest earlier).[65]

The beginnings of the Mexican Revolution in 1910 caused consternation among American landowners concerned about potential nationalization of the Mexicali Valley. In fact, Mexican soldiers were sent to the area to protect the US holdings rather than submit to US troops being sent. Members of the US–Mexicali agricultural syndicate were charged by a US grand jury, and eventually acquitted, of trying to promote revolution against the Baja California government. Such was the intensity of interest and conflict between the two countries for agriculture in the valley supported by the Colorado River. Eventually, the US holdings were expropriated by the Mexican government in the mid-1930s under new president Cárdenas's "Mexicanization"[66] program, although not before the US agricultural syndicate profited immensely from the operations in the valley and its transfer to Mexico.

On another front, control of the water that permitted the agriculture in the Mexicali Valley was being negotiated by the Colorado River Basin states, which resulted in the first (1922) Colorado River Compact. As with Native American groups, however, the Mexicans were neither invited to nor attended the negotiations and had no say in the compact's provisions. The US, if not explicitly admitting as much, appeared to rely on the Harmon Doctrine, the result of an opinion by US Attorney General Judson Harmon. In considering a protest by Mexico about water shortages in Mexican border areas with Texas owing to US diversions of the Rio Grande, Harmon decreed in 1895 that because the source of the water in the Rio Grande was in the US, the US had "absolute territorial sovereignty"[67] over the water and, therefore, no obligation to consider users of that water in Mexico. Consequently, Mexico received only a brief mention and no specific allocations in the Colorado River Compact and simply received whatever surplus water was (rarely) available. The original canal to the Imperial Valley through Mexico became irrelevant to US interests with the completion of the All-American Canal just north of the border in 1942. The lack of a formal agreement between the two countries deprived Mexican farmers of water during dry years, but also caused flooding and damage to crops during wet years, maintaining tension between the two countries into the 1940s.[68] This tension, exacerbated by continuing disputes over the Rio Grande (see Chapter 8), the potential for the US to lose a case before the World Court or other international tribunal, and the need to foster good relations during the years of the Second World War and the emerging Cold War, prompted an agreement reached in 1944. Mexico was awarded a *quantity* of 1.85 billion m³ of water annually from the Colorado River. This flow, however, could only come from so-called return flows, runoff water from irrigated fields, because no US state relinquished *any* water to meet this new commitment. Further, the *quality* of the water to be supplied to Mexico in terms of salinity was left ambiguous, perhaps deliberately so that the agreement could be sold to each country's respective constituents and governments.[69] Morelos Dam just below the border was completed on the Colorado in 1950 to ensure a ready supply of water to Mexicali farmers.

The issue of water quality (i.e., salinity) delivered to Mexico became crucial in the 1960s owing to two developments. First, the Wellton-Mohawk area of southwest Arizona just above the Mexican border was irrigated by water from the Gila River and twice in earlier history had failed to achieve sustainable agriculture.[70] History repeated itself in the mid-1900s as irrigation became problematic owing to declines in water supply from the Gila River of southwest Arizona and increasing salinity of pumped groundwater. The high salinity water was drained from fields, discharged into the Colorado River, and soon entered Mexico, where salinities reached between 1500 mg/l and 2700 mg/l, compared to values one-half to one-third just above the border, causing the elimination of over 40,000 ha of irrigated land in the Mexicali Valley. The natural salt load at Lees Ferry before any irrigation began in the Colorado Basin was estimated as 250 mg/l; it had reached 606 mg/l by 1972 owing to irrigation developments. The completion of the Glen Canyon Dam in 1963 in the upper basin resulted in surplus flows to Mexico being all but eliminated as the Lake Powell reservoir filled and further exacerbated the salinity problem.[71] Mexican farmers understandably protested, and demonstrations occurred at the US consulate in Mexicali. Clinging to the Harmon Doctrine, the US resisted any formal redress for the salinity issue, attempted engineering solutions failed, and the salinity problem and the anger of the Mexican Government persisted into the 1970s. The then Mexican president Luís Echeverría Alvarez used the salinity issue to reignite nationalist zeal in Mexico. The "big/rich country – little/poor country" conflict may have favoured Mexico internationally. It was a time of heightened concerns about US involvement in Vietnam, and the US probably did not want to further isolate a neighbouring country during the simmering Cold War. The Nixon Administration, however, also had to balance the protests and demands of Mexico with those of the seven Colorado Basin states, which balked at any agreement that only benefited Mexico, especially if those states alone had to pay for any solution. The idea that the US federal government would meet the costs of salinity control measures beyond the basin states that would benefit Mexico *and* western states, which lose between $500 and $750 million per year owing to salt damage to crops, helped calm the waters. After three years of study and negotiation, the Colorado River Salinity Control Act was signed by President Nixon in June 1974.[72] The agreement involved the building of the world's largest desalinization plant, retirement of some irrigated lands in the Wellton-Mohawk area, canal lining to reduce seepage loss of water, and construction of a bypass canal to discharge high-salinity water directly to the Gulf of California. The salinity control program is an ongoing one implemented by the Bureau of Reclamation and overseen by the International Boundary and Water Commission of the US and Mexico. The desalinization plant is the most straightforward technical solution to the salinity problem, but its construction was delayed, its costs escalated, it has required repairs, and it has been in operation only intermittently since it was completed in 1992.[73] Still, all of the steps initiated have resulted in the salinity of water delivered to Mexico just upstream of Morelos Dam declining considerably to no more than 868 mg/l between 2002 and 2018.[74]

Despite this progress, there is disagreement between the two counties on the issue of canal lining because, while it reduces loss via seepage and thus benefits the jurisdiction that the canals service (largely California for the All-American and Coachella canals), seepage acts to recharge groundwater throughout the affected area as well as provide flows to sustain the delta wetlands.[75] The canal issues also involve human safety because of the 550 recorded drownings that have occurred in the canals from illegal border crossing attempts into the US, leading the canals to be branded as a "death trap." The border service has installed signage, life buoys and climb-out ladders to help reduce the death toll.[76]

Since the early 1960s, the Colorado River has rarely reached its natural terminus in the Gulf of California. The extensive dam, reservoir and canal infrastructure in the US alone allows diversion of almost 90% of the river's flow. The Morelos Dam completed in 1950 diverts most of what remained of the flow in the lower Colorado River to irrigate the Mexicali Valley. Except in years of exceptional natural runoff, discharge to the delta consists only of agricultural return flows through shifting channels in the delta or via the Wellton-Mohawk bypass canal. Thus, what was once the most extensive estuary on the Pacific coast with an abundance of plant life and wildlife,[77] and what Aldo Leopold called a "milk and honey wilderness,"[78] was largely turned into a "barren, Mexican mudflat."[79] Development of irrigated land in the delta area has reduced the potential amount of area available for a resurgence of wetlands to between 170,000 and 250,000 ha, but episodic natural discharge and canal agricultural outflows have resulted in a partial re-vegetation and a remnant wetland, known as the Ciénega de Santa Clara. This area of about 16,000 ha, located just east of what is left of the main river channel, underwent a resurgence over about eight years and is now a lush wetland/marshland that is an important component of the interconnected series of habitats along the Pacific flyway migratory corridor for birds.[80] The wetland has more than 260 species of resident and migratory birds, including the endangered Yuma clapper rail and several other species at risk.[81] Unfortunately, the Ciénega de Santa Clara is dependent on outflow of water from the Wellton-Mohawk bypass canal, flow that would cease with the operation of the desalinization plant, and strategies (such as the use of groundwater flow) are actively being developed to sustain these resurgent wetlands.

The potential larger-scale restoration of the delta contributed to its entirety being declared part of a UN biosphere reserve, the 9.3 million ha Alto Golfo de California y Delta del Rio Colorado, in 1993 by the Mexican government.[82] Since this time, negotiations have continued between the two countries to further restoration of, at the very least, the central core of the delta, which most felt could be revitalized with minimal annual flows of water or larger amounts of intermittent flows.[83] These negotiations led in 2012 to the so-called "Minute 319" agreement, which was an addendum to the 1944 water treaty between the US and Mexico. Part of this agreement was the provision for a one-time "pulse flow" of 130 million m³ of water from the US portion of the river at Lake Mead to then be released at Morelos Dam to the main channel of the river over an eight-week period that began in March 2014. The goal of the manipulation was to mimic the natural spring pulse of water from the Rocky Mountains and to observe the effects on biodiversity within the delta in an effort to better understand how restoration can be effected in the longer term and in future agreements (Minute 319 ended in 2017).[84] This experimental release represents less than 1% of the annual pre-dam flow of the river and is the first binational agreement between the US and Mexico where the allocation of water was primarily intended for environmental benefits to Mexico. Initial indications are that the pulse-flow was a success, with water reaching the Gulf of California in mid-May 2014. Seeds were dispersed and germinated resulting in elevated "greenness" of the delta, particularly in the upper reaches, but the flow release largely benefited non-native *Tamarix*.[85] Given the short time frame of the manipulation, major changes in bird density were not expected, but several species altered their feeding behaviour in response to the pulse flow in ways that should increase migrant bird abundances.[86]

With examples like Minute 319, there is no question that US–Mexico relations over the Colorado River and its water have vastly improved from ones governed by crisis management to those more characterized by proactive, co-operative initiatives. Notwithstanding such improvement, full restoration of the delta is unlikely owing to the level of degradation and the longstanding development of the river. The river water upstream of the delta is simply too critical for so many people, an importance that will only become more acute with climate change and increasing water shortages in the basin even *if* human population pressures remained stable. In addition, most of the water needed to fully establish the delta would need to come from the US while the benefits, at least in the narrow sense, would go almost exclusively to Mexico.[87] Still, even a partial recovery of the delta would be a huge victory for the environment, which is perhaps the more reasonable expectation. In a larger sense, the true victory is that the environmental costs of the preceding century of developments along the Colorado River on the delta, an area that is far removed from where the benefits of such development accrue, have been acknowledged and some small steps taken to better mitigate them.

Ironically, the people most affected by the extinguishing of water flow to the Colorado River delta, the Cucapá people, or "the River People" in the Yuman language, have had little to no involvement in its restoration. The Cucapá lived along the Rio Hardy, a delta tributary of the lower Colorado River, for thousands of years. Here, they practised flood-plain agriculture as well as hunting, gathering and especially fishing. Some estimate that the Indigenous population of the area reached as high as 5,000 people, but now it is barely 300 souls living in a few communities such as El Mayor, a settlement upland from the river. Forced to move away from the river owing to declining productivity of the delta's streams as well as massive flooding when water was released from reservoirs during years of high flow, the Cucapá in the delta have "no fertile land, no rights, and little chance of sustainable livelihoods."[88] Historical fishing activities are further limited by the formation of the delta biosphere reserve itself. Perhaps more than any other benefit of delta restoration, the even partial return of the delta is a chance for the Cucapá to regain the river that is their heritage, and much like the Navajo before them, their voice is growing through collaborations with local NGOs like the Sonoran Institute and Pronatura Noroeste.[89]

In 1949, *A Sand County Almanac*, written by the American ecologist and environmentalist Aldo Leopold, was published posthumously. In the book, Leopold developed the idea of a "land ethic," i.e., guidance on how humans should treat and use natural resources so that any activities "preserve the integrity, stability, and beauty of the biotic community."[90] He also wrote that "a land ethic of course cannot prevent the alteration, management, and use of these 'resources' [the water, plants and animals], but it does affirm their right to continued existence, and, at least in spots, their continued existence in a natural state."[91] At least some of the motivation for this philosophy was inspired by Leopold's travels in the Colorado River delta area. With the pulse-flow experiment and continued collaborative efforts of the US and Mexico, perhaps this ideal can be realized for the delta, arguably the most heavily sacrificed region of the Colorado River.

EIGHT

The Rio Grande River/ Río Bravo
Life on the Other Side

The lights of Laredo dance on the water
And shine in a young man's eyes.
Who stands on the border and dreams of paradise.
He's heard crazy stories of how people live over
in the promised land.
He heard they eat three meals a day, just across the Rio Grande.

—DON COOK AND CHICK RAINS (songwriters),
"Just Across the Rio Grande"

There are at least 140 rivers on Earth that form all or part of an international boundary between two or more countries. An analysis by Laurence C. Smith in *Rivers of Power* estimated that at least 219 country-pairs are demarked by a river border.[1] Examples include the Danube River forming the boundary between ten countries of central Europe, the Mekong River forming the boundary between six countries in southeast Asia, and the Jordan River between Israel and Jordan. In North America there are 15 rivers forming parts of international boundaries between Canada and the US (12 rivers) and between the US and Mexico (3 rivers). Between the US and Mexico, it is the Rio Grande River than forms the longest international boundary – 2019 km, more than two-thirds of the total border distance between these two countries (the Colorado River also forms a very small 38 km portion of the border).

Rivers provide natural international borders owing to the physical separation between the lands that they flow through. In addition, using a river as an international boundary provides bordering nations with access to natural aquatic resources for recreation, transportation, fisheries, domestic use and hydroelectric potential that minimizes disputes over access to these resources if sharing agreements can be reached. Rivers also provide natural means to control access to border countries by people and goods because they provide physical "choke points" that can only be safely crossed via bridges, tunnels or ferries. These same attributes of rivers as natural borders, however, are also often the source of great conflicts.[2]

In mid-2021, the population of the United States was an estimated 330 million people, while that of Mexico was estimated at just over 130 million.[3] In 2019, the gross national income per capita for the US was $65,850 while that of Mexico was $9,480 (both figures in USD).[4] A Mexican immigrating to the US can expect their wage to be 2.5 times higher than in Mexico.[5] The United Nations uses the Human Development Index (HDI), a composite measure of the quality of life in a country as measured by "a long and healthy life, knowledge and a decent standard of living." As of 2019, the US ranked 15th of 189 countries in global HDI at 0.920, indicating "very high human development." While Mexico also fell above the threshold for "very high human development," it ranked only 76th at 0.767.[6]

The US–Mexican border has been described as "an open wound, where the Third World grates against the First and bleeds."[7] The sizable population of Mexico, coupled with the potential for higher incomes and other measures of standard of living in the US as well as the extensive border between the two countries, undoubtedly explains why immigration, legal and illegal, to the US from Mexico dwarfs that between any other two countries. Since the 1980s, immigration from Mexico has risen from about 5% of all immigrants to about 25%.[8] In the 1980s alone, a staggering three million people immigrated to the US from Mexico.[9] In 2017 there were an estimated 11.6 million immigrants in the US from Mexico, of which 43% are thought to be illegal.[10] The US–Mexican border is the world's busiest in terms of annual binational movement of people; there were at least 275 million legal crossings into the US in 2019 and up to 350 million total crossings in some years.[11] The Rio Grande River constitutes about two-thirds of the border between the US and Mexico, and river crossings of the Rio Grande comprise a key locus of illegal immigration from Mexico to the US. Further, although apprehensions of Mexican citizens illegally immigrating to the US have declined since a peak of 1.6 million in 2000 to about 166,000 in 2019, apprehensions of illegal non-Mexican immigrants, mostly from countries in Central America, have risen across the same time frame (685,000 in 2019).[12] In fact, the US border is divided into nine Border Control Sectors, five of which occur in Texas, with their southern margins meeting the Rio Grande. This chapter explores the history of the Rio Grande, a river with a history of shifting control, first by Native North Americans, then by Spain, Mexico, the Republic of Texas and now Mexico–US, and its role and impact in US–Mexican relations in terms of immigration.

The geography and origin of the Rio Grande

THE RIO GRANDE is the fifth longest river in North America (2nd in the US and 27th in the world) and flows 3035 km, from its source in a concave pocket on the eastern slopes of the Rocky Mountains in southwestern Colorado to the south-central tip of Texas, before discharging into the Gulf of Mexico. The river begins at the confluence of several smaller streams surrounding the base of Canby Mountain and grows to a drainage area of some 570,000 km^2 (not including several endorheic basins), the sixth largest in North America (and 35th worldwide). Despite its relatively large size, the Rio Grande is characterized by very low flows; at an average discharge of only 82 m^3/s, the flow of the Rio Grande is only 0.5% that of the Mississippi

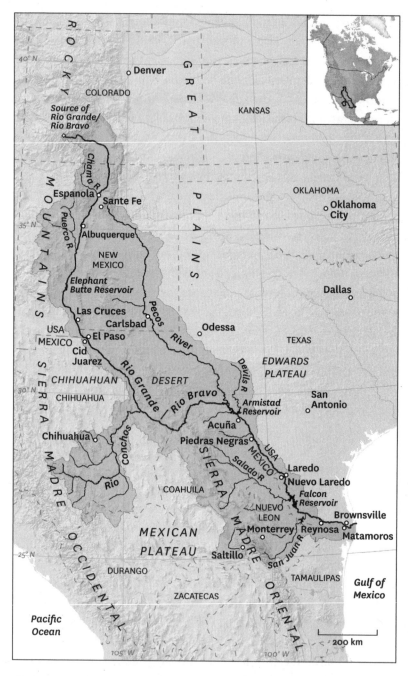

The Rio Grande Basin. The portion of the river forming a part of the US–Mexican border runs from Brownsville/Matamoros to El Paso/Cid Juarez.

River. The basin, however, supplies water to at least six million people across three US states and four Mexican states.

The Rio Grande owes its birth to the origin of the Rio Grande Rift, the easternmost result of the great disturbances of the Earth's crust that occurred in the western US over the last 35 million years. Here the Earth's crust and other parts of the lithosphere were pulled apart as the Colorado Plateau separated from the central North American craton – the stable block of the Earth's crust that forms the core of the continent. The Rio Grande Rift has been called a "classic" example of what is known as a continental rift and is located within the Basin and Range Physiographic Province, which also contains much of the lower Colorado River (see Chapter 7).[13] This rifting in the Rio Grande area began about 10 million ya and was a consequence of previous direct contact between the Pacific and North American tectonic plates and subsequent volcanism that likely acted to weaken the underlying lithosphere.[14] The result has been a series of north–south oriented interconnected "grabens" (sunken blocks of land bordered by faults). The depths of these grabens, if overlying rocks could be removed, would dwarf that of the Grand Canyon.[15]

During the most recent 5 million years, the Rio Grande has been dominated by tectonically driven tilt and growth of the basin floor, which has resulted in deposition of river-borne sediments of up to 100 m in depth. By contrast, the last 800,000 years or so has been dominated by climate-driven erosion and incision of the basin floor as the discharge of the river fluctuated during the growth and recession of Pleistocene glaciers.[16] Given its southern location running though desert-like landscapes, and its lack of large tributaries, the Rio Grande is unusual in that, unlike most rivers, it loses so much water from evaporation as it moves downstream that it is shallowest near its mouth.[17]

Early human history of the Rio Grande

THE RIO GRANDE has long been of significance to humans in North America because of its north–south orientation through a great rift valley. The upper Rio Grande River valley is also one of the most important sites of archaeological finds of the Clovis Culture once thought to be evidence of the earliest inhabitants of North America, which date to about 11,500 cal ya.[18] These Clovis peoples were Paleoindians who had moved south from Beringia as the most recent Pleistocene glaciers retreated. Their culture is largely defined by their characteristic fluted spear points and named for the first discovery of such artifacts near Clovis, New Mexico, in the early 1930s. Whether the Clovis peoples were the first inhabitants of the Americas south of Beringia is still a matter of some dispute (earlier sites in New Mexico, eastern North America and South America have been proposed), but the culture spread widely in North and Central America within a few hundred years of their first arrival.[19] The Clovis peoples, and others that followed, such as the Folsom and Cody traditions, were nomadic hunters and gatherers who established small hunting centres but no large settlements.[20] Driven by a warming climate and perhaps overhunting of large grazing mammals, the Paleoindian cultures gave way to the Archaic peoples (8,000 ya to ~2,000 ya), whose traditions including hunting of smaller game, gathering of plants and, late in this period, the planting of corn and squash as a subsistence strategy that filtered up from the south.[21] This cultural transition established the roots of agriculture, and at least seasonally occupied settlements, in the Rio Grande valley.

The earliest Archaic peoples eventually gave rise to three traditions: the Ancestral Puebloans (formally denoted as the Anasazi), Hohokam and Mogollon, centred on the San Juan and the Gila/Salt rivers (Colorado River) to the west and north of the Rio Grande. Especially significant within the Hohokam tradition was the development of irrigation in agriculture (see also Chapter 7). The Ancestral Puebloan tradition is famous for the development by 1000 AD of multi-room, multi-storey apartment-like stone and adobe mud dwellings with planned community spaces along rock walls. Such architectural developments, first called "pueblos" by the Spanish, and with prime examples at Mesa Verde, Colorado and Chaco Canyon, New Mexico, facilitated the development of settlements with hundreds to thousands of individuals.[22] Acoma Pueblo, located 80 km west of the Rio Grande in central New Mexico, is considered to be the oldest continuously occupied town in North America.[23] By 1492, the Rio Grande valley, with its productive lowlands and irrigation potential, was home to Pueblo Indians living in numerous towns and villages in what Carroll Riley described in *Rio del Norte* as a "golden-age New Mexico."[24]

The Spanish "River Kingdom" on the Rio Grande

THE MOUTH OF THE RIO GRANDE was first discovered by Europeans in 1519 when Alonso Álverez de Pineda led a Spanish exploration along the northern Gulf of Mexico. Lines of palm trees advertised the initial course inland, earning the river the name "Rio de las Palmas."[25] The first Spanish *entrada* into the Rio Grande valley, however, was a consequence of movements to the north from Spain's New World base in central Mexico (New Spain) following the conquest of the Aztecs. As discussed in Chapter 7, legends of "seven cities of gold" motivated several Spanish initial explorations of the northwest coast of Mexico and adjacent areas of the American southwest in the 1530s. The first to reach the Rio Grande was a remnant party of four men, including Alvar Núñez Cabeza de Vaca, who travelled to the confluence of the Conchos and Rio Grande rivers in 1535 after being part of a larger group making what turned out to be a disastrous trek from Florida to New Spain.[26] Cabeza de Vaca eventually returned to Sonora in Mexico and en route heard stories of people living to the north in large, multi-storey houses (pueblos) who traded turquoise, among other items, and perhaps had information on the seven cities of gold.

Francisco Vázquez de Coronado (1510–1554) was governor of Nueva Galicia in New Spain and moved north from Guadalajara with 200 men to explore the Colorado River basin between 1540 and 1542.[27] While at a base camp, Coronado received "exciting news of the region to the east"[28] from a trading party travelling west to the Zuni River (part of the Colorado River drainage). Hearing of the vast region of the Great Plains and its immense herds of Plains Bison, Coronado decided to extend his explorations to the east, sending his young lieutenant Hernando de Alvarado off towards the Rio Grande in August 1540. The party of 20 or so reached the Rio Grande somewhere just north of present-day Albuquerque, naming the river Nuestra Señora.[29] Alvarado explored north and south along the Rio Grande for some 600 km noting the existence of many towns and pueblos of the Tiwa people. As Coronado moved his entire army to the Rio Grande, commandeered pueblos and demanded supplies, tensions flared with the local Tiwa people resulting in the "Tiguex War" (the Spanish named the area Tiguex Province), which has the ignominious distinction of being the first named war between Native North Americans and Europeans on what is now American soil. This war, over the winter of 1540–41, resulted in many atrocities against the Tiwa, the conquest of the Arenal pueblo, a siege of a final mesa-top redoubt known as Moho, and the retreat of the Tiwa to mountain holdouts.

In the spring of 1541, Coronado continued explorations to the east onto the Great Plains in search of a great civilization known as "Quivira" that was described to him by a native, perhaps in an attempt to lure him away from the Rio Grande valley.[30] After several months of travel Coronado, disappointed with the lack of discovery of a grand civilization, returned to Tiguex Province in the Kingdom of Neuvo Mexico (New Mexico) in the spring of 1542 and soon thereafter decided to return to Mexico City in New Spain. Coronado's army was sick of the Southwest and his expedition had been a failure. He remained governor of Nueva Galicia until 1544, but his travels resulted in his bankruptcy and in charges of war crimes being brought against him, of which he was eventually cleared. Further, there is little evidence of a lasting cultural or technological legacy in subsequent Indigenous settlements because of Coronado's expedition.[31]

Although Coronado retreated from New Mexico, the Spanish were consolidating control of northern Mexico, especially areas with silver mines. The Spanish returned to the Rio Grande drainage in the 1580s via the Rio Conchos, a tributary of the Rio Grande in Chihuahua State. Numerous forays took place into New Mexico in a quest for silver mines and/or to enslave Indigenous people to work in the mines of northern Mexico, perhaps the most notable being that of Gaspar Castaño de Sosa. Castaño de Sosa, head of Nuevo León province, wished to move a settlement there to New Mexico, eventually establishing a base near the confluence of the Pecos and Gallinas rivers, just east of the Rio Grande, in 1591. Castaño was eventually forced to return to Mexico and was exiled to the Philippines for abandoning Nuevo León. While in New Mexico, however, he took over several pueblos in the name of the King of Spain and set up an administrative structure with Indigenous governors and a police force of sorts. This attempted settlement, while largely also a failure, did seem to impress upon the Pueblo peoples that, in the longer term, the Spanish were in New Mexico to stay. Essentially, even without lucrative new silver mines, the attraction of the Rio Grande area lay in entrepreneurial opportunities in the borderlands in the form of the products of Indigenous agricultural labour, land grants, trade with Plains peoples and Franciscan mission establishment. In 1595, a new governor was named for New Mexico, Juan de Oñate. He reached the Rio Grande in 1598 and had established effective control of many pueblos and obtained declarations of obedience from the bulk of the Indigenous peoples by the summer of that year. While Oñate eventually resigned his governorship in 1607, the Franciscan missions had baptized thousands of Indigenous people, which convinced Spanish authorities to continue in New Mexico and establish ranches and settlements along the Rio Grande. By 1680, perhaps 3,000 non-natives lived in the Rio Grande valley north to what is now the New Mexico–Colorado border.[32]

Despite the growing influence of Spanish missionaries and settlers, relations between them and the Indigenous people deteriorated owing, in large part, to the "harsh and generally uncompromising"[33] treatment of the latter by the former, which included the destruction of Pueblo religion and the discouragement of native languages. Brutal repression of some minor revolts, the effects of a drought between 1667 and 1672, and a steep decline in Pueblo population from around 40,000 to 15,000 from diseases introduced by the Spanish led to the so-called Pueblo Revolt of 1680. This revolt involved an alliance of native peoples, including Apache and Najavos, and was directed most fiercely towards the Franciscan missionaries. Twenty-one of thirty-three missionaries living in New Mexico in 1680 were killed. Most of the remaining colonists retreated to the mission at El Paso.

In 1692, however, the Spanish returned. Fearing encroachment by the French from the east, in the lower Mississippi River valley, the Spanish crown decided to reinvest in the American southwest under the leadership of Diego de Vargas. The Rio Grande pueblos were recolonized by the early 1700s and have remained under foreign control ever since. What is now Mexico remained the Viceroy of New Spain (which included areas from Florida to the Philippines) until 1821.

During this time, New Spain was considered a hinterland with resources that funded the operation of the larger Spanish Empire, supplying most of the tax income and the administrative support system for Spanish interests in North and Central America. Further, suppression of some economic activities that might compete with established operations in Spain, such as the cultivation of grapes and olives, likely bred resentment among many of the estimated five million people of New Spain. These conditions led to a series of revolts against the vice-regal government between 1810 and 1820. Known more broadly as the Mexican War of Independence, the conflicts culminated in the signing of the Treaty of Córdoba in August 1821, which established the independence of Mexico from Spain. At this point, Mexico reached well east of the Rio Grande to the Red River (at about 96 degrees longitude) in east Texas, west to the Pacific coast, north to the Oregon Territory (42 degrees latitude) and south to present-day Costa Rica.[34]

Birth of the border

DESPITE MEXICO'S territorial claim to its easternmost boundary as a vestige of the Adams-Onís Treaty (1819) between the United States and Spain, where the boundary might *eventually* be fixed was much more fluid, especially for a young but vibrant US, which had more than doubled its size in the 50 years since 1776. The US and Mexico were on a collision course for western and northern spaces claimed by Mexico. On the one hand, Mexicans considered areas like Alta California, Baja California, New Mexico and Texas (then part of the state of Coahila y Tejas) as not only economically and strategically important but as part of their natural inheritance from the Kingdom of Spain. Alternatively, the idea of an American "manifest destiny" was taking hold. Here, territorial expansion was justified for, and in fact essential to, the survival of a republic that depended on the ready supply of land where individual farms could be established, and hence peoples' liberty maintained.[35] The annexations of Louisiana and Florida were early manifestations of this philosophy. These territorial gains to the south and west, the migration of Americans westward into Texas, and the administrative weakness of Mexico in controlling its sparsely populated northern regions, motivated three US presidents (John Quincy Adams in 1825, Andrew Jackson in 1835 and James Polk in 1846) to make requests of Mexico to redraw the border to incorporate vast areas of Mexico into the US – all of which were rebuffed.[36]

The frustration of the US in its failure to acquire territory from Mexico did not stop increasing numbers of Americans from migrating to Mexico. In fact, in 1830 Mexican president Anastasio Bustamante established a law to close the Texas frontier to "Anglo-American settlers" as the Mexican government "took alarm at the swelling immigration in Texas, and the growing establishment there of a society made in the likeness of the United States." This poorly enforced law was easy to ignore; thus, Anglo-Texans outnumbered Mexican-born Texans by more than four to one by 1834.[37] The tenuous grip of the Mexican government on its states led to the overthrow of Bustamante by Antonio López de Santa Anna in 1832, at which time Texians (or English-speaking Texans) also took up arms and expelled all Mexican forces from east Texas. With Santa Anna as the new Mexican president, some of the grievances of Texians towards the Mexican government were alleviated, but tensions continued until the Texas Revolution began in 1835. Santa Anna led the Mexican army to suppress the revolt, which reached a nadir for Texians with the loss of the epic Battle of the Alamo in 1836. Notwithstanding this loss, Texians declared independence on March 2, 1836, and later its army under General Sam Houston defeated Santa Anna at the Battle of Jacinto. Santa Anna was captured during the battle and was forced to sign the Treaties of Velasco (1836), which ended the war. Mexico, claiming that Santa Anna had signed the treaties under duress, did not recognize the Republic of Texas.

Neither Texas nor Mexico had the resources to continue the war and defend their territorial boundaries, which remained in dispute.

In 1845, the US admitted Texas into the union under the presidency of James C. Polk. Not surprisingly, Mexico was furious and broke off diplomatic relations. Further, the US claimed that the southern border between Mexico and Texas was the Rio Grande River, but Mexico countered that the border was the Nueces River some 200 km farther north along the Gulf Coast. To enforce the US claim, Polk dispatched General Zachary Taylor to the Rio Grande in January 1846. In May of that same year, the Mexican army inflicted 16 casualties on a US patrol in the disputed area between the Rio Grande and Nueces rivers, which precipitated a declaration of war by the US – the beginning of the Mexican–American War.

The Mexican–American War (1846–1848) was a war of US conquest, waged by an expansionist President Polk.[38] The war was not much of a contest owing to the weakened state of the Mexican army, sapped by ongoing battles with native raiders along the border. In addition, growing US military prowess resulted in it making substantial gains in New Mexico, California and into Mexico proper, including the capture of Mexico City by General Winfield Scott. Consequently, peace negotiations, begun in the summer of 1847, focused on the only real question – where would the new border be? Proposals varied from that positioning the western boundary just south of San Francisco Bay (37 degrees latitude) to one that cut through central Mexico, including most of Baja California, from near the mouth of the Rio Grande (26 degrees latitude). Eventually, the Treaty of Guadalupe Hidalgo was signed in February 1948, and the boundary line was established as beginning in the east at the mouth of the Rio Grande and following its course northwest for 2018 km, then due west along the southern boundary of New Mexico to the Gila River, along the Gila until its confluence with the Colorado River, then west along the Colorado River (for 38 km) and then along the 32nd parallel to the Pacific Ocean. Turning this "negotiated border" into a real border in the absence of detailed knowledge of much of the landscape would prove a huge challenge for the appointed Joint United States and Mexico Boundary Commission.[39]

Between 1849 and 1855, extensive field work to survey the border, further negotiations, the Gadsden Purchase by the US (for $10 million) of land in Sonora and Chihuahua where the border turned west from the Rio Grande, and the appointment of a second commission (1854), resulted in a border that largely reflects that of today. Despite one commissioner's claim that the border had "been fixed in all its length"[40] it is, in fact, somewhat fluid along the Rio Grande (which comprises two-thirds of its length) given the constantly shifting course of the river.[41] One of the most persistent issues has been that of "bancos" or intrusions, horseshoe-shaped or oxbow curves in the river that resulted in large tracts of land (that might be on one side of the border) becoming isolated by erosion of new river channels (and hence becoming situated on a new side of the border). The International Boundary and Water Commission was established (1889), in part, to assign land ownership when river border changes influenced the position of bancos. Between 1910 and 1976, 245 land transfers involving bancos have occurred; a total of about 7200 ha has been transferred to the US and about 4700 ha to Mexico.[42] Issues involving larger tracts of land (e.g., any banco greater than 630 ha) or large populations have been settled with individual agreements. For example, the "El Chazimal Dispute" between El Paso and Ciudad Juárez dating from 1873 involved 243 ha that had been cut off from Mexico and settled by El Pasoans. This dispute was settled in 1963 with the signing of the Chamizal Convention, which transferred a total of about 180 ha to Mexico and 78 ha to the US.[43]

Immigration between the United States and Mexico

ONE OF THE RECURRENT THEMES of the 2016 US presidential election campaign was the promise by then candidate Donald Trump to "build the wall" along the US–Mexican border to prevent illegal immigration into the United States. Back in the early 1800s, however, it was a *Mexican* president who agonized over the stream of *Americans* moving into the then Mexican state of Texas, so much so that he passed (ineffective) legislation theoretically banning it. For most of its existence, however, crossing the border between the US and Mexico was a generally uncomplicated affair for those living in the borderlands given the long-standing economic relationship between citizens of the two countries living there. Further, the first federal legislation passed in the United States relevant to immigration across the US–Mexican border, the Page Act, was in 1875, and it was to prevent "undesirable" immigrants, such as ex-convicts and prostitutes, from entering the US, but these restrictions were largely directed towards Chinese and Europeans who might cross into the US from Mexico rather than through US ports, where control was easier.[44] In fact, it was not until the stream of refugees from the Mexican Revolution (1910–1920) began crossing the border that new federal laws placed restrictions on Mexican immigration into the US, restrictions that were typically only loosely observed by officials in response to continued demand for Mexican labourers in the US. Up to 1.5 million Mexicans are estimated to have moved to the US during 1910–1920, displaced by the revolution within the context of a global trend of increased migration. This increased migration, coupled with the outbreak of the First World War, prompted passage of the Immigration Act of 1917 and the Travel Control Act of 1918, both of which severely limited subsequent Mexican immigration into the US but still allowed passage for migrant labourers; almost 500,000 Mexicans migrated to the US between 1920 and 1928.[45] These migrants, however, were increasingly subjected to delays, inspections, visa fees and head taxes – all of which helped to spur interest in illegal entry, including use of human smugglers.

A major decline of immigration into the US and its eventual reversal (repatriation to Mexico) began with the onset of the Great Depression in 1929. First, the demand for Mexican labourers completely dried up, and second, resentment by Americans against Mexicans for taking what few jobs there were, increased. Immigration officials in the US began to strictly enforce existing regulations, and Mexicans sensed declining opportunities in the US; only 2,600 Mexicans immigrated to the US in 1932. Illegal Mexican aliens were increasingly subject to deportation – 18,412 in 1931 – and several hundred thousand ethnic Mexicans were deported or repatriated to Mexico between 1929 and 1939. At the same time, Mexico established immigration controls for foreigners competing for jobs with native and repatriated Mexicans. As Rachel St. John described in her history of the western portion of the border, *Line in the Sand: A History of the Western U.S.–Mexico Border*, by the late 1930s the border between the US and Mexico had been transformed from its initial role as merely a geographic separation between countries to one that "served new state priorities, including the regulation of American morality and the restriction of Mexican immigration."[46]

Following the Depression, immigration control into the US from Mexico liberalized somewhat in response to labour demands imposed, in part, by the Second World War. Programs to bring Mexican contract labourers into the US, such as the Bracero Program, were established, but restrictions imposed on such workers, long waits for visas and increasing economic disparity between Mexico and the US again increased the motivation to enter the latter illegally. The termination of the Bracero Program in 1964 and a new immigration act in 1965 that established a quota system for immigration to the US from all Western Hemisphere countries resulted in a surge of illegal entry; over a million US–Mexican border apprehensions occurred in 1979. Anxiety over illegal immigration into the US across the Mexican–US border contributed significantly to myriad initiatives (including spates of fence-building that began in the 1940s) with names such as operation "Gatekeeper," "Hold-the-Line," and "Safeguard" (all during the 1990s) and the Secure Fence Act of 2006. Gradually, immigration to the US from Mexico and apprehensions of illegal migrants have steadily dropped in the 2000s, from over 1.1 million in 2005 to 463,000 in 2010. While apprehensions of illegal immigrants increased in 2019, they are still well below historical highs.[47] In fact, a reversal of the flow of migrants has occurred since the recession of 2008–2009. Between 2009 and 2014, over 870,000 Mexicans left Mexico for the US, a dramatic decline from the 2.9 million who left Mexico for the US between 1995 and 2000. Further, nearly one million Mexican immigrants and their US-born children moved from the US to Mexico between 2009 and 2014, many citing family ties as reasons for returning. Consequently, net migration to the US has become negative and is predicted to continue.[48] Despite these trends, increasing numbers of Central Americans, including many unaccompanied minors, are attempting to enter the US through Mexico.[49]

An uncertain future in the US or apprehension and deportation back to their native countries are not, however, the worst fate for illegal immigrants – death is the outcome of many attempts. Murder by smugglers, suffocation in poorly ventilated trucks, dehydration in the desert and drowning in canals and the Rio Grande itself are common causes of death while attempting illegal crossing to the US. A total of 7,805 people died crossing the US–Mexican border between 1998 and 2019.[50] This figure, however, may underestimate the actual death toll as many bodies are never found, which has invoked the term "los desaparecidos" ("the disappeared").[51] About 35% of deaths between 1993 and 1997 (1,600) were caused by drowning in the Rio Grande and associated canals as reported by Mexican officials, a similar proportion to that reported by the International Organization for Migration so far to June 2020 (63 of 226 deaths).[52] Undercurrents, sudden changes in water velocity and depth, ensnaring vegetation, falls along steep banks, quicksand and covered drainage canals all make the water crossings hazardous ones.[53] Many other drownings are prevented by agents of the US Border Patrol, who regularly rescue people trying to cross the Rio Grande.[54]

Increased enforcement at more urban and controllable border crossing points (e.g., land checkpoints, bridges at major centres such as San Diego/Tijuana, Nogales, Arizona/Sonora, El Paso/Juarez) is considered to be a factor driving increased attempts to cross illegally via the Rio Grande along the eastern section of the US–Mexican border – the so-called "rechannelling effect" – and associated increases in migrant deaths.[55] In fact, "Operation Gatekeeper," while focused on California, has been considered by many to be directly and intentionally responsible for an increase in migrant deaths along other portions of the US–Mexican border. This is because natural barriers like the Rio Grande (and inhospitable stretches of desert) were used by policy makers in a strategy known as "prevention and deterrence"; an increase in deaths by drownings would deter future crossings.[56] After much criticism of this strategy, both Mexican and US immigration officials established programs, such as border agent

US National Guard personnel monitor the Rio Grande from a helicopter.

rescue teams, to try and prevent migrant deaths. Further, civilian humanitarian groups have established programs to prevent deaths, including the provision of "climb-out" ladders and life-rings along waterways, but scores to hundreds of drownings still occur every year.[57] Sadder still is that many of the dead are not or cannot be identified and these "ghosts of the Rio Grande" often end up in poorly marked graves.

The Rio Grande, owing to its nature as a meeting place between people of different cultures – the Spanish and Paleoindians, Mexicans and Texians, Mexicans and Americans, Mexicans/Americans and the Apache Indians – has a long history of conflict, violence and death.[58] Its establishment as part of a border between two countries with entwined, but unequal economies, and the migrant "diffusion" this causes, has sustained this legacy in a form of violence against illegal migrants. This violence, in what some have called a humanitarian crisis, raises some difficult questions.[59] Is it right to establish policies that knowingly place people in harm's way? Is there an "acceptable" level of migrant deaths when establishing policies to address illegal immigration? How does one fairly weigh the negative impacts on citizens of one country of polices designed to improve the life of those in another country? Given the billions of dollars spent on trying to prevent illegal immigration along the border, the limited success of these programs and the deaths of thousands of migrants since such attempted control began, is the cost justifiable given the demands of other social issues? The Rio Grande as a border, therefore, provides a compelling example of a river motivating larger questions of morality in society.

— NINE —

The Mississippi River
The Body of the Nation

But the basin of the Mississippi is the Body of the Nation.
—Editor's Table, *Harper's Magazine*, February 1863
(from Mark Twain's *Life on the Mississippi*, 1961).

Conditions on the ground dictate the actions you can take
—SUN TZU, *The Art of War* (5th century BC)

M ilitary geography is a term used to describe the understanding of the role of geography, human and physical, in warfare. Physical and/or human geography may influence warfare in the sense of being a source of conflict, e.g., about the location of a border, territorial expansion, control of resources that are geographically restricted, religion, ethnicity, economics or ideology. Physical geographical attributes have long been recognized as playing a key role in defining military strategy and tactics – a tool to achieve political objectives. The physical geography of an area, its "warscape," has been employed over centuries by tacticians to gain maximum advantage over the opponent's forces. Climate, terrain and landscape are key determinants of who wins battles.[1] In *The*

Art of War, the Chinese general Sun Tzu's classic 5th-century BC treatise on warfare, the author stated: "Not knowing the form of mountains and forests, defiles and gorges, marshes and swamps, one cannot move the army. Not employing local guides, one cannot take advantage of the ground." Second World War British field marshal Bernard Montgomery ("Monty") observed that advantages in "transportation, administration and geography" were essential to military victory.[2] For instance, in the Battle of Thermopylae in 480 BC, a few thousand Spartans and Greeks held back at least ten times as many Persians for many days using two high walls that formed "The Hot Gates" as a natural choke point to defend against the invading army of Xerxes. The Battle of Hastings (1066), which initiated the Norman conquest of England, is thought to have been lost by the defending King Harold when his troops descended from the high ground where they initially held advantage over William the Conqueror's army, positioned below.[3] The First World War was described as a "war of positions" where "the topographic situation of each town was important."[4] The failure of US forces to disable the Ho Chi Minh Trail during the Vietnam War despite one of the most intensive bombing campaigns in history was in large part due to its geographic complexity: its length, and its winding path with myriad branches through dense forests, which incorporated tunnels and streams. By contrast, swift victory by coalition forces in the first Gulf War (1991–1992) was surely aided, in part, by the flat, almost treeless "open terrain" of Kuwait and southern Iraq, which allowed rapid invasion during the ground phase.[5]

The year 2021 marks the 156th anniversary of the end of the US Civil War (1861–1865). The quotation at the beginning of this chapter reminds us that the Civil War years saw a ripping apart of the heart of the US. It has been estimated that more than 70,000 books have been published on the Civil War, more than 1.2 *per day* since the end of the conflict.[6] That conflict still resonates deeply within the consciousness of the US, and this chapter will explore how the Mississippi River – the body of the Nation at the time – influenced the motivation, prosecution and outcome of the war between the states.

The geography and origin of the Mississippi River

THE MISSISSIPPI RIVER, which drains some 41% of the continental United States, ultimately owes its name to the Ojibwe word *mi-si-ziibi*, which means "great river," or perhaps *gichi-ziibi*, meaning "big river."[7] The source of the Mississippi River is Lake Itasca, a "T-bone"– shaped lake in northwestern Minnesota. From there, the river travels some 3730 km to the Mississippi Delta in the Gulf of Mexico. The *current* terminus of the river, if such an exact spot can be determined in a highly branching delta, is considered to be Pilottown, Louisiana. From the western extreme of its drainage, the upper Missouri River, the Mississippi River is the longest and largest river in North America (6027 km), the fourth longest river and tenth largest in drainage area (2.98 million km^2) in the world and drains two Canadian provinces and 31 U.S. states. Some 72 million people live within the drainage basin. The two major tributaries of the Mississippi River, and great rivers in their own account, are the Missouri River, draining eastward from the Rocky Mountains (length = 3767 km, drainage area = 1,331,810 km^2) and the Ohio River, draining westward from the Appalachian Mountains (length = 1579 km, drainage area = 490,603 km^2). These two major tributaries are used to demark the river basin into three sections: the upper Mississippi River, from its source to the confluence with the Missouri River; the middle Mississippi River, that section between the confluences of the Mississippi with the Missouri and Ohio rivers; and the lower Mississippi River, from the confluence of the Ohio River to the Mississippi Delta. The Mississippi River is, by any measure, the "master river" of the southern half of North America. Still, while it flows almost wholly within the US, few perhaps recognize that the discovery and first traversing of the Mississippi River by North Americans of European descent was by Spaniards and Canadians. In fact, the name Mississippi stems most recently from a French rendering, *Messipi*, of the aforementioned Ojibwe name *misi-ziibi*.

As implied in the song "Ol' Man River," made famous by the 1927 musical *Show Boat* and later by the singer Paul Robeson, the Mississippi River is an ancient river, perhaps as old as 250 million years of

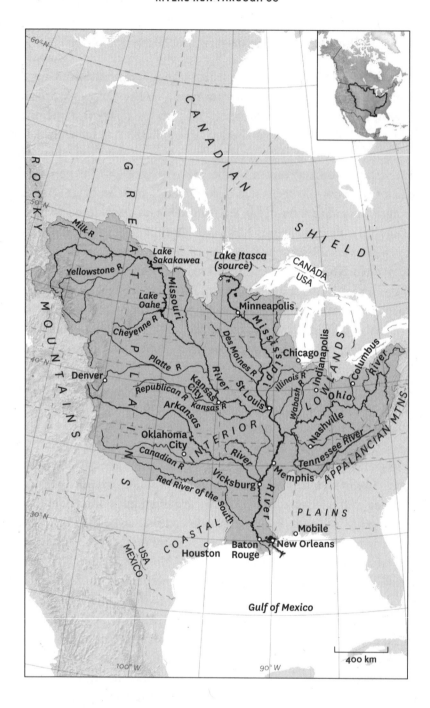

The Mississippi River Basin.

age, and thus one of the world's oldest rivers. The Mississippi River is the descendant of a much older river, the Michigan River, whose origin dates back to at least the Cretaceous.[8] The antiquity of the Michigan/Mississippi River is due to the fact that it rests within a "craton," an area of continental crust that is typically located in interior regions of continents and that is much older and more stable than other regions of continental or oceanic tectonic plates. Cratons are less susceptible to upheavals from volcanic activity, earthquakes or submergence of one plate under another, resulting in the Mississippi River being a very long-lived, stable drainage pattern (although the delta of the Mississippi may have migrated as much as 1000 km southwest to its current position).

Notwithstanding its great antiquity, the current form of the Mississippi River is a legacy of the more recent uplift of mountains and glaciations within the Pleistocene, particularly the Wisconsinan Ice Age, which ended about 11,000 ya. Pleistocene mountain building, particularly in western margins of the Great Plains, caused a great tilting of drainage systems towards the east, more than a thousand kilometres from their headwaters (e.g., the Platte and Red rivers).[9] Pleistocene ice sheets created drainage patterns along their margins that flowed south, away from the ice sheets, creating the modern Missouri and Ohio river systems and shifting the east–west drainage divide much farther north in North America. The repeated advances and retreats of the ice sheets permanently entrenched the Mississippi drainage, trapping tributaries like the Red, Arkansas and Tennessee rivers and causing a great coalescence of systems into the Mississippi River system. Beginning some 11,700 ya, melting of the Laurentide Ice Sheet at the end of the Wisconsinan, the resulting formation of glacial Lake Agassiz, and the intersection of continental divides all combined to force a great temporary outflow of Lake Agassiz via the extant Minnesota River to the Gulf of Mexico between the Rocky Mountains and the Appalachian Mountains. This southern outlet of Lake Agassiz was sealed off about 10,600 ya, but the drainage template, collecting waters from the Rockies to the Appalachians, had been set by Lake Agassiz's southern outflow. Still, the constituent tributaries of the contemporary Mississippi River were not always so.

Shifting drainage patterns meant that rivers such as the Minnesota, James and Milk rivers (now all current tributaries of the Mississippi or Missouri rivers) at some time flowed to the Hudson Bay drainage, and later found or re-established paths to the Mississippi River. Others, such as the Red River of the South, were independent drainages until being repeatedly captured during the Pleistocene and Holocene (and as recently as the 18th century).[10]

Early human history of the Mississippi River

THE MISSISSIPPI RIVER BASIN is considered one of a few independent centres of plant domestication by humans, and plant cultivation by Indigenous North Americans in the Mississippi basin dates to about 6,000 ya, a time period associated with the Bronze Age and the growth of Sumerian and Egyptian cultures.[11] Eventually, agricultural practices centred around growing beans, maize and squash introduced from Mesoamerica led to the so-called Mississippian culture, one characterized by mound building and complex trading networks of large population centres (some numbering up to 40,000) by the year 1200. The bulk of the Mississippian culture, however, had dissipated before first contact with Europeans. Given the vast size of the Mississippi River drainage and its overlap with three major Indigenous cultural divisions (Great Plains, Northeast and Southeast) and multiple language groups, there are literally scores of distinct groups of Indigenous Peoples throughout the basin, including the Choctaw, Illinois, Winnebago, Natchez, Missouria and Sioux.[12]

On a quest from the Spanish king to find gold, silver and, most of all, a route to China, Hernando de Soto (1496–1542) is credited with being the first European to discover and cross the Mississippi River after landing in Florida and travelling west.[13] De Soto named the river *Río del Espíritu Santo* (River of the Holy Spirit) and died on the banks of the lower Mississippi River. Despite de Soto's precedence, it was French-Canadian explorers, driven by their developing mastery of rivers as canoe routes for the fur trade as the famed *coureurs de bois*, who explored the full length of the Mississippi River and firmly established its significance as a transportation and trade route. The first of these explorers was Étienne Brûlé (1592–1633), who, although not finding the upper Mississippi River itself, was the first European to explore west of the St. Lawrence River, reaching Lake Superior in 1612. Brûlé's explorations were significant because he lived among the Huron peoples, learning their language and customs, especially those ways of living in the woods that greatly facilitated further exploration. Two French-Canadian cousins, Médard des Groseilliers (1618–1696) and Pierre-Esprit Radisson (1636–1710), explored west of Lake Michigan and the northern headwaters of the Mississippi, although they did not descend it.

The first notable descent of the river was by a French-Canadian Jesuit missionary, Father Jacques Marquette (1637–1675) and his explorer companion Louis Jolliet (1645– ~1700). Marquette had established a mission near present-day Ashland, Wisconsin, and heard stories of an inland trade route by river from the Illinois peoples. Receiving permission to explore the river, Marquette and Jolliet, after about a month's travel by canoe, entered the Wisconsin River using a portage near the present-day city of Portage, Wisconsin, and eventually entered the upper Mississippi River. The two explorers ventured to within about 700 km of the Gulf of Mexico and encountered several Indigenous groups that had goods and trinkets of European origin. Perhaps fearing an encounter with the Spanish, the likely source of the trinkets, Marquette and Jolliet turned back at the Arkansas River, but their voyage firmly established the Mississippi River as a viable water route from the centre of North America to the Gulf of Mexico.

Finally, perhaps the most famous of the early explorers of the Mississippi River, and one with certainly the most impressive name, was Réne-Robert Cavelier, Sieur de La Salle (1643–1687). It was La Salle who, among other exploring and entrepreneurial achievements, first explored the Mississippi River down to the Gulf of Mexico and in April 1682 claimed the entire region for the King of France as *La Louisiane* in honour of Louis XIV. With this act, La Salle had laid the foundation for a great arc of French forts and commercial enterprise that stretched from the Great Lakes across the Illinois, Ohio and Mississippi rivers, and down to the Gulf of Mexico. This feat would be the basis for French control of the area until the Treaty of Paris (1763) ended the Seven Years' War (which was known as the French and Indian War in North America) and ceded most of New France, including the area east of the Mississippi River in the Louisiana Territory – Spain retained control of the western side – to Great Britain in 1763.

Following a series of land transfers among Spain, France and the emergent US, the latter acquired ever greater control of the Mississippi River. This was first accomplished by obtaining free passage through it from an article in the second Treaty of Paris in 1783, which ended the American Revolutionary War. Further, British negotiators, acting on behalf of Canada, ceded access to the great river by agreeing to an international boundary that excluded British North Americans from the Ohio territory and the upper Mississippi River Valley.[14] Next, the US obtained the western side of the river from the French (who had recently reacquired it from Spain) as part of the Louisiana Purchase of 1803. Finally, the American victory against the British in the Battle of New Orleans (1815) forever gave the US political control of the entire Mississippi River. From this point on, a great migration and settlement occurred in the West, including the Mississippi River basin. So great was the movement that it inspired perhaps the first North American popular travel guide book: Zadok Cramer's *The Navigator* (1801), which went through 12 editions over 25 years (including an Appendix dealing with Lewis and Clark's voyage up the Missouri River to the Pacific Ocean and back). The guide book contained essential details for navigating the "much admired waters"[15] of the Ohio, Allegheny and Mississippi rivers.

The control of the entire Mississippi River by the US provided a key transportation link for more than a dozen states and territories and was likely instrumental in breaking down the division of the river into a largely frontier-exchange economy in the lower river and a Great Lakes–centred, more mercantile economy in the upper basin.[16] This and the subsequent development of cotton and sugar-based commercial activity, which relied heavily on slave labour, coupled with a revolution in transportation provided by the steamboat era, were key developments that led to the establishment, first informally and then by secession, of the Confederate States of

America (the Confederacy). Even the president of the Confederacy, Jefferson Davis, had a plantation on the banks of the Mississippi River – *Brierfield*.[17]

Just before the outbreak of the American Civil War, the 11 secessionist states that eventually made up the Confederacy had an economy based largely on small family farms that exported agricultural goods like cotton (at its peak accounting for two-thirds of the world's supply) and sugar that were produced on plantations with slave labour.[18] There was, by contrast, little manufacturing, forestry or mining. Transportation was heavily based on intracoastal routes, canals and rivers such as the Mississippi and the Red, rather than an interconnected network of railways. Those railways that did exist in the Confederate states appear to have been poorly designed and built as a *supplement* to river-based transportation. The Southern economy, therefore, has been described as a "pre-capitalist" one because it had a top-heavy income distribution (i.e., largely to the plantation owners) and because of the lack of a free labour market among the almost four million black slaves. These conditions severely limited the development of the sort of mass market that was burgeoning in the North, which, although also primarily agrarian, was more mechanized and had a free labour market.

The nature of the era of steamboat travel on the Mississippi River and tributaries between 1830 and 1870, and the mythical recounting of the navigation feats of its storied captains, is delightfully described in Mark Twain's *Life on the Mississippi* (1883). The first trip from the Ohio River to New Orleans took place in late 1811 and steamboat travel peaked in the late 1800s, after which the railway and modern ships become dominant. Steamboat transportation was commercially viable until about 1930. Even with the passing of the commercial steamboat era on the Mississippi, the river is a vitally important national and international transportation link in the contemporary US; the current barge system transports more than 454 million tonnes of goods annually.[19] For the South of the mid-1800s, however, the pre-capitalistic state of its economy and poor transportation infrastructure meant that it was critical to maintain access to relatively inexpensive river (and coastal) transportation routes – like the Mississippi River and its tributaries – and the Union leaders in the North knew it. At the beginning of the Civil War, President Abraham Lincoln (1861) stated that "the Mississippi is the backbone of the Rebellion."[20]

Strategic importance of the Mississippi River in the Civil War

CONTROL OF THE MISSISSIPPI RIVER, or more specifically the lower two-thirds of the river, was critical to the Confederacy. First, as discussed above, the Mississippi and the major eastern tributaries of the Ohio, Tennessee and Cumberland rivers provided crucial transportation links both upstream and downstream, but also across the river. Trans-Confederacy transport via the Mississippi River was particularly important because the most crucial railways of the Confederate states all ended on the east side of the river, whereas several railways in the North had connections across the river (e.g., at St. Louis).[21] The Mississippi River also divided the Confederacy in two, with Texas, Arkansas and much of Louisiana west of the river, and the remaining Confederate states east of the river. Loss of the river would clearly isolate the two parts of the Confederacy, with disastrous economic results, including lack of access to resources of each river valley and disruption of the considerable international trade that occurred between Europe and the Confederacy via Texas and Matamoros, Mexico.[22]

Second, loss of river-based transportation would have severe logistical consequences, especially in waging war. The Mississippi River was also critical to the North, as unfettered access to downstream ports (e.g., New Orleans) provided more efficient access to markets for resources of the upper Mississippi and the developing West (which the North controlled), compared to west–east transport by train and canal to the Atlantic. The Union's famous General William Tecumseh Sherman even proclaimed: "To secure the safety of the navigation of the Mississippi I would slay millions. On that point, I am not only insane, but mad."[23]

Third, the Mississippi River was fundamental to the geographic coherence of the Confederacy and a source of considerable "national" pride, morale and international prestige.[24]

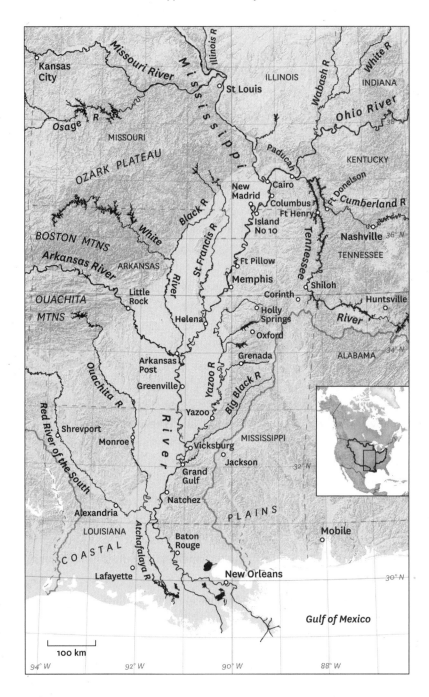

The central Mississippi River Valley.

Fourth, the Mississippi River obviously provided a wide invasion route for the Union Army into the heart of the Confederacy, both, as would eventually be realized, from upstream and downstream. In fact, the north–south flow of the Mississippi River and other rivers of the "western theatre" (e.g., the Red River of the South and the Tennessee rivers) invited such invasion and they would prove difficult to defend. By contrast, the rivers of the "eastern theatre" (e.g., in Virginia, Maryland, the Carolinas) run mostly west–east and provide natural obstacles to an army invading from the north (or the south).[25]

Fifth, the Mississippi River had many great confederate cities and towns along its banks (New Orleans, Memphis, Nashville). One of the jewels was Vicksburg, the second largest city in Mississippi (~4,600 in 1860) nicknamed the "Gibraltar of the Mississippi"[26] for its strategic and fortified position between Memphis and New Orleans and for the 80 m high banks along the east side of the river upon which it is situated.

Vicksburg was a key transportation centre for goods from the Arkansas and Red River of the South, both west of the Mississippi River, to the rest of the Confederacy east of the river via a critical ferry-rail system. Lincoln noted that "Vicksburg is the key…. The war can never be brought to a close until that key is in our pocket."[27] Jefferson Davis was similarly motivated to keep Vicksburg, remarking that it was "the nailhead that held the South's two halves together."[28] Finally, because Kentucky established a neutral position at the beginning of the Civil War, and because the Confederacy lacked a functional navy, it established defensive positions in Tennessee at Fort Henry and Fort Donelson on the banks of the Tennessee and Cumberland rivers, respectively, to protect these waterways from Union incursion. Such fortifications, and the later siege of Vicksburg, on the Mississippi River, exemplified what was, essentially, the defensive strategy of the Confederacy versus the more mobile, offensive strategy of the North.[29] Battles for these two forts would prove to be key Union strategic victories, but were also important in helping to hone the military and leadership skills of the Union's eventual overall military leader, General Ulysses S. Grant, the most celebrated military personality of the Civil War and future two-term president.

The Mississippi River campaigns

AN ANACONDA is a large-bodied, aquatic snake native to South America, best known for its ability to constrict, subdue and kill its prey. The so-called "Anaconda Plan" was the unofficial name given by critics of a strategy devised by the aging General Winfield Scott of the Union Army to constrict the Confederate states into submission. The plan consisted of two components: first, an invasion down the Mississippi River to slice the Confederacy in two, and second, a blockade of the Confederacy's seaports. With a demoralized South split in two and isolated through blockades, it was hoped, perhaps naively, that this strategy would soon result in capitulation of the South and the end of secession. Notwithstanding the critics, and while never adopting the plan formally, President Lincoln established a military blockade of 12 southern ports in 1861 (e.g., Wilmington, New Orleans, Charleston, Mobile) and began planning for invasions of the Mississippi River.[30]

The struggle for control of the Mississippi River by the Union Army had two basic components: (i) sealing off areas and establishing control near the confluence of the Ohio and Mississippi rivers and in and around New Orleans, which were strategic positions controlling access to upper and lower portals of transportation and keys areas of the Confederacy; and (ii) the battle for control of Vicksburg. The upper Mississippi and Ohio rivers were already in control of the North by 1862 or earlier, and Brig. Gen. U.S. Grant established a base of operations in Cairo, Illinois. After an initial failed attempt to take Columbus, Kentucky (the northernmost Confederate bulwark against invasion by the North on the Mississippi) via a water-borne attack from upstream during the Battle of Belmont (Missouri), Grant concentrated on obtaining control of the Tennessee River, which would give the North control of much of Tennessee and provide an invasion route to northern Alabama. The North had amassed several new and refitted ships, including the first appearance of the fearsome-looking, but somewhat awkward "ironclads," into what was known as the Western Gunboat Flotilla.[31] The Confederacy, however, lacked a formal navy or the industrial base to produce one (although, ironically, it did produce the first submarine – the *H.L. Hunley* – which successfully sank an enemy ship [and then, itself, sank!]), so it relied largely on the river itself and fortifications for defence. In February, 1862, Grant steamed up the Tennessee River and, provided with naval support by the flotilla commanded by Flag Officer Andrew H. Foote, took Fort Henry after a short engagement. While Foote continued to wreak havoc further upstream on the Tennessee River, Grant took his army northeastward to cross into the Cumberland River valley and surrounded Fort Donelson. Although the 14 ships of the flotilla suffered considerable damage and two assaults were necessary, by the middle of February, Fort Donelson also surrendered to General Grant. As well as losing more than 14,000 men and many supplies in these battles, the loss of these two river forts was a strategic disaster for the Confederacy. First, it now opened the Cumberland River all the way upstream to Nashville, Tennessee. Second, the Tennessee River in its lower 160 km runs north to south in parallel with the Mississippi River, which meant that the position held by the Confederates at Columbus, Kentucky, 160 km to the west, was essentially surrounded by the North. These developments led Gen. Albert S. Johnston, commander of the Confederate army in the western theatre, to abandon Kentucky and central Tennessee (including Nashville) altogether and retreat to northern Alabama, while his subordinate, Maj. Gen. Leonidas Polk, retreated from Columbus to Island No. 10 on the Mississippi River just south of the Missouri–Tennessee border.[32]

The victories by U.S. Grant's combined army-navy force gave the North a huge morale boost; they were the first major victories by the Union Army in the Civil War. Grant became a national sensation (and earned the nickname "Unconditional Surrender" Grant).[33] Grant's next ambition was to capture the town of Corinth, Mississippi, an important railway link in the South, and he based his troops near Pittsburg Landing on the west side of the Tennessee River. Meanwhile, Island No 10. eventually fell to Foote's naval force on April 8. The next downstream fortification of the Confederacy was Fort Pillow; if it fell that would leave Memphis vulnerable to attack from the north. The advance of the Union Army downstream on the Mississippi River, however, was stalled by the shifting of the army forces upstream to support Grant after the disastrous, for the Union, first day of the Battle of Shiloh just upstream of Pittsburg Landing on the Tennessee River. The Western Flotilla, lacking such support, was effectively stalled on the Mississippi, at Fort Pillow, especially after the appearance of the Confederate River Defence Fleet.[34] Meanwhile, the Union Army, reinforced by the Army of the Ohio arriving from Nashville, rallied on the second day of the Battle of Shiloh, won the field, and by the end of May, Corinth was in Union hands and Memphis was essentially cut off from rail supply (making river connections ever more critical). Thus, with the costly victory at Shiloh, both Fort Pillow and Memphis had become isolated from sustaining Confederate forces owing to the control of areas east of them by the North. Fort Pillow was abandoned in June 1862, and a new commander of the Western Flotilla, Flag Officer Charles H. Davis, moved down to Memphis. Here, the innovative use of more manoeuvrable "ramming" boats by the Union, in one of the few purely naval engagements of the Civil War, resulted in the loss, crippling or escape downstream of most of the Confederate gunboats. Memphis was lost by the end of the first week of June. Therefore, in the first six months of 1862 the Union had made a rapid, albeit costly, advance, taking control of the Cumberland and Tennessee rivers, and (somewhat later) of the Mississippi River down to Memphis. In addition to the loss of territory around the middle Mississippi River, a major cost to the Confederacy of the defence of these areas was that resources were drained from the defence of New Orleans – the largest (170,000 people) and most important commercial city of the Confederacy.

The opposing forces in the struggle for New Orleans were Major General Mansfield Lovell of the Confederacy and Flag Officer David G. Farragut, of the Union. New Orleans was defended by river obstructions (e.g., chains, log booms, assorted debris) and two downstream fortifications, forts Jackson and St. Philip. In mid-April, Farragut led 14 warships up to Fort Jackson and opened fire, beginning an attack that lasted one week. With little sustained damage to the fort, Farragut decided to run past the forts at night after Union advance troops had broken through some of the in-river barriers. In a fiery night engagement that saw deployment of drifting raft fires towards Union navy ships, Farragut's fleet managed to get through with the loss of only a single ship. All the outmatched Confederate ships, including the first ironclad built, the *Manassas*, were destroyed or captured. Steaming up to New Orleans, which had been reduced of Confederate soldiers by necessary redeployments further north, Farragut anchored off the New Orleans waterfront and demanded surrender of the city, which was duly given by Lovell on April 29, 1862, without a shot being fired. The loss of the so-called "First City of the Confederacy" with its resources and prestige was a crushing blow to the Confederacy and stemmed from the chronic under-capacity of the Confederate forces, stretched across a huge front on the Mississippi River, as well as the military daring of Union officers such as Farragut and Commander David Porter.

Farragut pressed on, and by May 18, he had steamed up the Mississippi River, capturing Baton Rouge (the Louisiana state capital) and Natchez along the way, to just downstream of Vicksburg – the last defensive position of the Confederacy on the vast Mississippi. Here, Farragut was to join forces with the Western Flotilla, stalled just upstream at Fort Pillow, and take the city. The struggle for Vicksburg would, however, prove to be an entirely different story from the almost effortless capture of New Orleans. The city was situated atop 80 m high cliffs that towered over the Mississippi River and was being commanded by an effective combination of a particularly skilled military engineer, Brig. Gen. Martin L. Smith, and an obstinate local military commander, Lt. Col. James L. Autry, who upon being called upon by Farragut to surrender the city, responded that Mississippians neither knew nor cared to learn how to surrender, but "if Commodore Farragut or Brigadier General Butler [Union officer commanding the newly captured New Orleans] can teach them, let them come and try."[35]

The Vicksburg Campaign

THE BATTLE for the city of Vicksburg and all the strategic advantage that would accrue to the victor had three essential stages: (i) attempts at a strictly naval assault led by Farragut and the Western Flotilla; (ii) a series of "experiments" led by Grant from the east, north and south of the city; and (iii) the eventual monotonous siege of the city

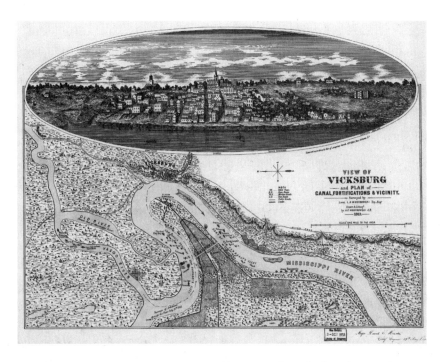

Vicksburg, Mississippi, situated above the Mississippi River. De Soto Point is the point of land on the west shore of the Mississippi River directly opposite Vicksburg.

and its inhabitants after the Union Army crossed the river from the west. During the first stage, Gen. Smith had built Vicksburg into a "Gibraltar on the Mississippi" by dispersing guns along the river and on top of the bluffs. This deployment was aided by the virtual 180-degree turn that ships running past Vicksburg had to run as the river bent around De Soto Point due west of Vicksburg.

After a brief return to New Orleans, Farragut and reinforcements returned to Vicksburg and began shelling the city, to little effect, on June 19, 1862. Later, Farragut successfully steamed upstream past Vicksburg under a hail of cannon shot to merge with the Western Flotilla above Vicksburg. At this point, Farragut began what turned out to be a series of "engineering" works to try and modify the flow of the Mississippi to isolate Vicksburg and create a canal through De Soto Point to avoid the guns of Vicksburg. Poor soil for digging, dropping river levels and malaria and dysentery among the soldiers and slave workers confounded the attempt, which was subsequently abandoned. Still, the eastern terminus of the railroad at De Soto Point was destroyed, which meant that the only way to transport goods to Vicksburg from the west was by the Mississippi River itself from downstream via the Red River of the South. At this point, Farragut and his superior, Secretary of the Navy Gideon Welles, had concluded that Vicksburg was too entrenched and posed too great a risk to the navy ships. The city could only be taken by a ground assault led by the army, and Farragut was instructed to return to New Orleans, which he did in late summer. Farragut was then appointed as the first admiral in the US Navy for his heroics at forts St. Philip and Jackson. The Western Gunboat Flotilla retreated to Helena, Arkansas, more than 350 km upstream of Vicksburg, to refit. For now, Vicksburg was safe from further Union water-borne assaults. After an unsuccessful attempt to dislodge the Union garrison from Baton Rouge to re-establish a "southern anchor" for the Confederacy on the Mississippi River, Maj. Gen. Earl Van Dorn, who had replaced Lovell as commander responsible for Vicksburg, established a defensive position at Port Hudson between Baton Rouge and the mouth of the all-important Red River of the South. For the time being, at least, this maintained river transport between Texas and Vicksburg and, thence by rail, to the rest of the Confederacy to the east.

By the autumn of 1862, U.S. Grant, recovered and restored from the shock of the Battle of Shiloh, was placed in command of the Army of Tennessee, which initially advanced westward via Jackson, Mississippi by rail to begin a land assault of Vicksburg. Here, Lt. Gen. John C. Pemberton was now in charge, and Brig. Gen. Smith and another engineer, Maj. Samuel H. Lockett, began constructing a semicircular set of earthworks 15 km in length, anchored north and south by the Mississippi River, to defend the eastern periphery of Vicksburg.[36] Eventually, and following a series of Confederate cavalry raids (one led by the famous Brig. Gen. Nathan Bedford Forrest) that harassed Union forces and destroyed forward supply posts, Grant abandoned the overland operation and instead settled on a solution to taking Vicksburg by the "Father of Waters" itself.

Grant's overall strategy involved dividing his army in two, with Maj. Gen. W.T. Sherman attacking Vicksburg from the northeast down the Mississippi River and Grant moving to downstream positions through central Mississippi to attack Vicksburg from the south. To accomplish this, Grant tried several approaches in a "series of experiments"[37] to take the city during the winter of 1862–63, all of which eventually failed but were critical in the development of Grant as a general and in terms of further developing the productive relationship between Sherman and Grant. These experiments were either forays by segments of the army (battles of Chickasaw Bayou and Arkansas Point) or more canal building attempts to get the Army of the Tennessee close enough to Vicksburg to avoid a long overland route or to avoid the guns guarding the Mississippi River approach ("Grant's Bayou Operations"), all of which had failed to result in the capture of the city by April 1863.

Eventually, Grant, his firm determination in full evidence, decided on a final strategy. His army would march west and south circling around Vicksburg, then east across Louisiana, cross the Mississippi River south of Vicksburg and attack from there. Admiral Porter, commanding the Western Flotilla, would need to move downstream past Vicksburg to transport Grant's army and supplies to the eastern side of the Mississippi, which he successfully did with 15 boats in late April. After crossing the river, Grant (along with Maj. Gen. Sherman, Maj. Gen. John A. McClernand, and Maj. Gen. James B. MacPherson) engaged in a series of seven battles across and inland in Mississippi from April to May 1863, most of which were successful, including the taking of the state capital, Jackson. These battles helped to draw the defender of Vicksburg, Lt. Gen. Pemberton, out into the field of battle and, by defeating him, to weaken and demoralize that force. By May 17, the ravaged Confederate forces were back in Vicksburg with the Union Army not far behind, just outside the various earthworks. From this position, Grant attempted two direct assaults on the city over the next week, both of which failed with heavy casualties (at least 3,000 on the Union side). Despondent, yet still determined, Grant settled on a siege of the city; he would "out-camp the enemy."[38] Food and supplies ran out for the citizens and Confederate defenders of Vicksburg over the next six weeks. Unable to escape and with reinforcements from Gen. Joseph E. Johnston unable or unwilling to reach the city, Pemberton surrendered the city, and his almost 30,000 troops, to Grant on July 4, 1863. Less than one week later, Port Hudson, lower on the Mississippi, surrendered on July 9 to Maj. Gen. Nathaniel P. Banks, who had laid siege to it since late May.

More than a year and a half since Grant had first steamed up the Tennessee River, more than a year after Farragut first demanded the surrender of Vicksburg, and at a cost of 20,000 soldiers killed and wounded, the Union was finally in control of the entire Mississippi River, which as Lincoln put it, "again goes unvexed to the sea,"[39] and the Confederacy was cut in two. The battle for control of the Mississippi River was the death knell for the Confederacy. Although it managed to limp on for another two years, the loss of the trans-Mississippi corridors put an end to the concept of the Confederacy as a viable state; the loss of the rich human and natural resources of the West and any way to get them to the East was simply too much. Coupled with Gen. Robert E. Lee's loss at Gettysburg, on July 3, 1863, a turning point in the war had been reached, and one Confederate colonel, Josiah Gorgas, remarked, "The Confederacy totters to its destruction."[40] Further, the Mississippi River campaigns placed U.S. Grant as the undisputed leader of the Union Army. He was promoted to Major General by a grateful (and relieved) Lincoln after Vicksburg, and eventually was the first American to hold the rank of General of the Regular Army.

The Mississippi River was the geographic pillar of the Confederacy, and the battle for its control has been described as the "longest and most complex campaign, or series of campaigns, in the Civil War."[41] It required close collaboration between army and navy, involved innovative naval vessels, extensive military engineering developments, the largest amphibious landing by a US army until Normandy in the Second World War, the largest surrender of American troops in the nation's history, and the two longest sieges in US military history[42] – all, in large part, owing to the complexity imposed on the combatants by the size, flow patterns and orientation of *misi-ziibi* and its surrounding landscape.

— TEN —

The Hudson River
Source of Inspiration

The painter of American scenery has indeed privileges superior to any other. All nature is here new to art.
—THOMAS COLE, earliest member of the Hudson River School of artists, 1836

Art sighs to carry her conquests into new realms.
—WILLIAM CULLEN BRYANT, *Picturesque America* (1872)

The natural world has been an inspiration for the arts for millennia. Beginning with cave paintings made a minimum of 44,000 ya,[1] humans have found inspiration in the depiction of animal and plant life, natural events, landscapes, seascapes and the evening and daytime skies. Such inspiration has taken varied forms: literature, music, dance, sculpture, theatre and film, architecture and all manner of engraving, drawing and painting.

When a specific art form introduces or promotes a particular theme, methodology or genre, usually over a defined time frame, such focus can be described as a "school" of art or an art "movement." Thus, one can speak of "Realism" within visual arts and literature that developed in mid-19th century France, or the early 20th century "Art Deco" movement with widespread effects in the visual arts, architecture and design. Such schools of art within a discipline may act as points of debate among alternative schools, each vying for influence or supremacy. Examples include the development of Realism as a reaction to "Romanticism," which emphasized emotion and individualistic artistic imagination and inspiration during its heyday between 1800 and 1850. Schisms may even appear within a singular school, as exemplified by the split of the "Naturalist School" from within Realism. Naturalists tended to express reality within a larger context by including the role of Nature in impacting the reality of people's social and political experiences. Such vigorous exchanges among alternative schools may signal a mature society, i.e., one wherein there has been enough time and affluence to promote the development of multiple schools of thought or artistic expression.

In newly colonized areas, the birth of an influential school of expression may mark the emergence of a country or region into an advanced stage of cultural development and as a new and significant source of influence.[2] The US of the mid-1800s was a nation not yet 100 years old, with a population concentrated east of the Mississippi River. Although notable writers and artists were establishing individual worldwide reputations (e.g., Washington Irving, Edgar Allan Poe, Harriet Beecher Stowe, Benjamin West, John Singleton Copley), no thematic school of art, at least in the visual arts and relative to established groups in Europe, had yet emerged. This all changed in the period 1800–1900 with the rise of the Hudson River School of landscape art and its painters. Landscape art has been described as a relative latecomer to American art, yet also as an essential aspect of the "emotional and spiritual development of the American ethos" of discovery and familiarization with American history.[3]

This chapter recounts the role of the Hudson River and its waterscapes and landscapes as the crucible within which the first visual artistic school in America developed and prospered. Within this development rests the story of the social and economic evolution of the Hudson River valley, and its central role in "the process of national self definition."[4] The importance of the Hudson River in the history of forming a national identity of the US is evident in descriptions of the Hudson as "America's River," "America's First River," "The Rhine of America" and "the most interesting river in America."[5]

The geography and origin of the Hudson River

BY THE GEOGRAPHIC STANDARDS set by the other rivers treated in this book, the Hudson River is unusual in several respects. First, at only 507 km in length and 36,260 km^2 in drainage area the Hudson River is a rather minor player geographically. In fact, it is only the fourth-longest river in New York State alone. Second, the Hudson River's course, except for two small deviations, flows in an almost entirely straight north–south direction. The source of the Hudson River is the exotically named Lake Tear of the Clouds, high in the Adirondack Mountains some 1320 m above sea level.[6] Other than a sharp turn to the east where the Hudson and Indian rivers meet some 40 km downstream from Lake Tear of the Clouds, and a second short jag to the east a further 70 km downstream, the Hudson River deviates less than 1° of longitude from its source to its terminus near the southwestern tip of Long Island. By contrast, the Columbia River traverses just over 9° of longitude from its source in southeastern British Columbia to Astoria, Oregon. Third, the Hudson River can be divided fairly equally into an upper basin (from Lake Tear of the Clouds to Troy, NY, ~ 190 km) and a lower basin (downstream of Troy to New York City and lower New York Bay ~240 km), with the start of the lower basin marking the beginning of tidal influence on the river. Consequently, about half the length of the Hudson River consists of an estuary! In fact, the Indigenous names for the Hudson River ("Muh-he-kun-ne-tuk" of the Mahicans or "Muhheakantuck" of the Lenape) roughly translates to "river that runs two ways." Finally, the Hudson River is a postglacial remnant of a formerly much longer river owing to it being a so-called "drowned river." Following the end of the Wisconsinan glaciation, rising sea levels on the east coast generated a marine incursion from the sea that submerged parts of the lower Hudson River that once flowed southeast from Lower New York Bay, across the continental shelf (that was exposed

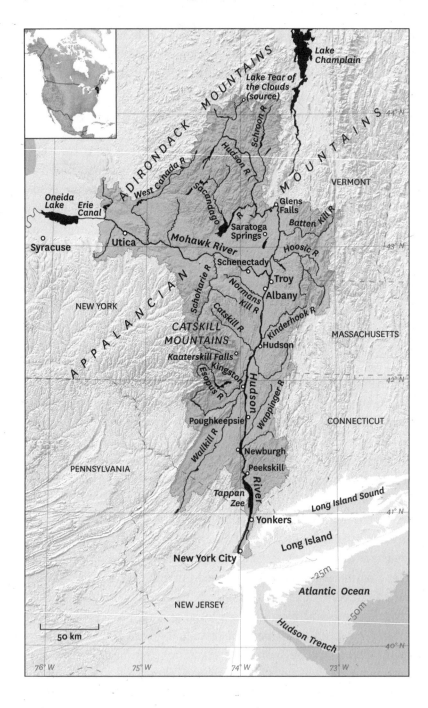

The Hudson River Basin.

when glaciation lowered sea levels) for over 160 km. This older outlet of the Hudson River discharged larger flows and sediment that helped to sculpt the massive Hudson River Canyon, a great scar carved in the sea floor to a depth of 1.2 km (the Grand Canyon maximum depth is ~1.8 km) and over a length of 640 km.[7]

Although the Hudson River might pale in comparison geographically to the other great rivers of North America, historically it punches above its weight. Tom Lewis, writing in *The Hudson: A History*, described the Hudson River as a "river of firsts" to Americans. It was the first river encountered by Europeans in the American New World along the east coast and was probably the nation's first "melting pot" where Indigenous Peoples mixed with colonizing Dutch, English, French Huguenots, German Palatines and slaves of African descent.[8] The Hudson was also the first wholly American river to provide access to the vast interior, the first line of defence in the American Revolution, the inspiration for America's first great writers and painters, the first river to greet legions of new immigrants to a young country, the river whose deepwater port promoted the development of America's first and still greatest financial centre – New York City; and finally, it was the inspiration for America's first great conservationists and the epicentre of some of the first environmental battles. Including New York City, the Hudson River runs through an area that is home to more than 11 million people.

The geological foundations of the Hudson River date back to over 1 billion ya during a major North American mountain-building stage known as the Grenville Orogeny. This episode was associated with tectonic changes within and among the great continental and oceanic plates that occurred repeatedly over hundreds of millions of years. When the ancient supercontinent, Rodina, formed from the merging of continental plates about 1 billion ya, it created a belt of rock along the eastern and southern margins of the North American craton – essentially the rock "basement" of North America. The resulting mountain belt stretches from southeastern Mexico, through Labrador and on to Scotland. The significance of this event to the formation of the Hudson River is the creation, during the earliest stages of the Grenville Orogeny, of a massive dome or "massif" of metamorphic rock which, while eroded down over the ensuing 400 million years, would eventually form the core of the Adirondack Mountains. Rifts running north–south in the present-day Hudson River valley area began to form when Rodina began to split apart about 750 million ya, creating the North American paleocontinent, Laurentia. The rifts so created set the north–south course of the Hudson River as seen today in the formation of systems like Indian Lake, Schroon Lake and Lake George, the former two of which drain into the Hudson River. Various other episodes of continental rafting and collisions and associated periods of mountain building culminated in the formation of the Pangaean supercontinent about 335 million ya. As Pangaea split apart beginning some 220 million ya, the Atlantic Ocean was born, and the eastern North American continental margin formed along the Appalachian Mountains, another product of the Grenville Orogeny. Massive rivers deposited materials along this margin, forming the continental shelf of today. Sometime during the final stage of Pangaean breakup, perhaps 65 million ya, a volcanic "hotspot" is thought to have formed under the ancient Adirondack area, causing heating and expansion of underlying rocks that "punched" the Adirondack rocks up into the dome-shaped formation of today. Streams flowing down from this newly created height of land gave birth to the Hudson River.

The final stage in the formation of the current Hudson River watershed involved the last of the Pleistocene glaciations, the Wisconsinan Glaciation (see Chapter 1), which existed from about 110,000 to 10,000 ya in the New York area. The Wisconsinan glaciers existed in New York as several ice streams or "lobes" of ice, e.g., the Hudson-Champlain lobe covered much of the current Hudson River valley to a depth of 1–2 km. Altogether, these ice lobes extended to the now southern margin of Long Island, itself formed by the ice piling up glacial rock debris ("till") at its terminal margin. As the ice retreated in New York State, large volumes of meltwater collected in lowland areas to form huge proglacial lakes. The largest of these was 260 km long Glacial Lake Albany, which formed about 15,000 ya in the Hudson River valley and persisted for 4,000 years. Glacial Lake Albany was connected to the much larger Glacial Lake Iroquois (the precursor to Lake Ontario, but about three times its size) to the north and west, and to the smaller Glacial Lake Hudson to the south. Glacial Lake Iroquois was formed by an ice dam on the St. Lawrence River and Glacial Lake Hudson by a westward extension of the Long Island moraine. About 13,400 ya, the ice dam on Lake Iroquois broke, sending massive floodwaters down along the Hudson River Valley punching though the blockage at the Narrows between Staten Island and Brooklyn to create the current outflow of the Hudson River to the Atlantic Ocean.[9]

The massive outflow from Glacial Lakes Iroquois, Albany and Hudson spread out over the exposed continental shelf (glacial advances were associated with drops in sea level of 120 m or so) to a length of some 160 km where the mouth of the Hudson River finally met the sea. Here, the erosive power of the ancient Hudson's outflow carved out the Hudson Canyon, one of the world's largest submarine canyons at over 640 km long, reaching depths as much as 3500 m below sea level and a maximum rim-to-rim span of 12.4 km – a "Pleistocene Grand Canyon" – where the influence of the Hudson River finally ends.[10] The Hudson River still "works" the canyon with some of its estimated annual flow to the sea of 300,000 to 1,000,000 tonnes of sediment.[11]

Early human history of the Hudson River

HUMANS HAVE INHABITED the Hudson River valley for at least 10,500 years. The first archaeological finds (Clovis-type fluted points) date to perhaps 11,000 ya and represent Paleoindians who spread up the east coast from initial concentrations centred in the Ohio, Cumberland and Tennessee river valleys, themselves formed by migration from the north and west following melting of the Wisconsinan glaciers.[12] The very nature of the drainage patterns of rivers east of the continental divide, such as the Missouri, Platte, Arkansas and Red rivers, likely acted to funnel early humans along the ice-free corridor from Beringia south and east to the central Mississippi River "staging areas" during deglaciation.[13] At least one major Paleoindian site, the West Athens Hill site, is known from the southwestern region of the Hudson River valley.

From these beginnings, four principal Indigenous Peoples established themselves and their cultures in the Hudson River valley, all part of the Algonquian and Iroquoian major language groups: the Mahican, Lenape (more broadly known as the Delaware people), Wappinger and Mohawk. The Lenape lived from western Long Island up the Hudson River to about the present location of Catskill, NY, as well as south and west to between Chesapeake and Delaware bays. The Wappinger were concentrated on the east bank of the Hudson River from Manhattan Island north to Roeliff Jansen Kill (a tributary of the Hudson) and east to the Connecticut River. At the confluence of Roeliff Jansen Kill and the Hudson River begins the traditional territory of the Mahican people, which extended north to southern Lake Champlain and the Green Mountains of Vermont, west along the Mohawk River and east to the Connecticut River. The Mohawk peoples were concentrated outside the Hudson River area proper along the lower Mohawk River, a major Hudson tributary entering from the west. Their territory extended over a much larger area: north to the St. Lawrence River and into Ontario and Quebec, northeast to the Green Mountains and west to the territory of the Oneida people, which began about midway along the Mohawk River. All groups of Indigenous Peoples lived in villages, many scattered along the Hudson and Mohawk rivers where the Algonquians grew maize, corn and squash, hunted, and exploited the Hudson River's rich bounty of fishes such as striped bass, sturgeon and American shad, as well as oysters. In addition to hunting and some agriculture, the Mohawk were lively traders, apparently supplying flint, essential for tool making, to other members of the Iroquois Confederacy to the west. The adjacent territories of the Mohawk and Mahican peoples often brought them into direct conflicts, conflicts that ultimately contributed heavily to the demise of the Mahicans. The eventual fate of each group depended on their interactions with each other as well as European colonizers. After military defeats inflicted by the Dutch and losses suffered in the American Revolutionary War, the Wappinger moved west to Ohio, where they joined with a newly formed Algonquian-speaking Stockbridge-Munsee tribe. That group was later moved to Wisconsin under various federal government

Indian removal policies. A similar fate befell the Lenape, Mahican and Mohawk, who now exist largely in Oklahoma, Wisconsin, southern Ontario (Lenape and Mohawk), southern Quebec (Mohawk) and northern New York (Mohawk).

A Dutch experiment in the New World

THE FIRST EUROPEAN to encounter the Hudson River was not its namesake, Henry Hudson, but the Italian mariner Giovanni da Verrazzano (1485–1528) exploring in the service of France. In 1524, da Verrazano was travelling up the eastern seaboard seeking new trade routes and entered lower New York Bay in his ship *La Dauphine*. Here, he briefly encountered the Lenape, and while declaring the area "a very agreeable place" with a "wide river, deep at its mouth," he did not explore the river proper and continued his trip north that same day.[14] Henry Hudson (1565–1611) was an Englishman in the employ of the Dutch East India Company, a firm desperate for a route to the Orient via the Arctic. The route around the Cape of Good Hope was controlled by the Spanish at the time, and rumour abounded regarding a route via the North Pole. In April 1609, Hudson, under strict orders *not* to proceed westward to North America to find "a way to reach Cathay,"[15] set sail in the *Halve Maen* (*Half Moon*). Foul weather and endless ice eventually prompted Hudson to turn southwest, where the *Halve Maen* anchored initially off the coast of Maine before encountering the mouth of the Hudson River in early September. Here, Hudson also encountered the Lenape, described by the sailors as "Wilden" (or wild men).[16] Initial encounters between the Lenape and Hudson's group were a mixture of distrust, fascination, marginal tolerance and outright hostility (at least one sailor and several Lenape were killed in various skirmishes). Hudson and his crew moved upstream on the Hudson, eventually anchoring off present-day Albany, where the river became narrower. Sending a scouting party farther upstream, the group was finally forced to admit that no passage to the Orient existed in the Hudson River and they eventually returned downstream to the *Halve Maen* in late September.

Hudson returned to England and later died in a final quest for a northwest passage after being abandoned by his crew in Hudson Bay. While the principals of the Dutch East India Company were disappointed in Hudson's failure to find a path to the Orient, they were encouraged to return, owing to reports of abundant populations of beaver, much prized in fashionable Europe. With the French controlling the beaver trade in Canada, areas to the south like the valley of the Hudson River provided tantalizing opportunities for the Dutch.[17] Variously called the Mauritius and Noort (North) River by the Dutch, the area became the focus of exportation of furs, especially beaver, by a consortium of Dutch merchants and then competition among several consortia. The activity on the river led to the establishment of a trading post, Fort Nassau, on Castle Island, near the site of present-day Albany in 1614 – the first attempt at permanent Dutch settlement in the New World. Eventually, in 1615, the consortia merged as the New Netherland Company which lasted for three years. In 1621, the Dutch West India Company was established, in part to organize trade in New Netherland (New York) with headquarters on Manhattan Island at New Amsterdam (today's New York City, population ~270 in 1628).[18] It is no accident that two beaver form part of the official seal of New York City.[19]

The first attempts at significant colonization by the Dutch involved 30 Walloonian (French-speaking Belgian) families, who arrived on the *Nieu Nederlandt* in 1624. Eighteen of these families established Fort Orange (later Albany, NY), just upstream of the flood-prone and by then abandoned Fort Nassau, with the other families establishing colonies on the Delaware and Connecticut rivers. The establishment of Fort Orange intensified the competition between the Mahicans and the Mohawks for trade with the new arrivals, culminating in the Mahican-Mohawk war of 1624–1628. The Mohawks were the victors in this conflict, driving the Mahican out of the Hudson River valley and leaving the Mohawk in control of trade with the Dutch. Fort Orange became an isolated, but still critical, trading outpost as most of its inhabitants repaired to New Amsterdam on Manhattan Island (infamously purchased from the Lenape in 1626 with goods worth about US$24).[20] In addition to Fort Orange, the Dutch experimented with a series of "patroonships," large manorial estates under the control of a "patroon" (master) who was obligated to establish a colony of at least 50 people. Each patroonship was a "perpetual fief of inheritance," with the largest, at 283,000 ha, and longest lasting being Rensselaerswyck, near Fort Orange. The axis of trade from the hinterlands of the New World down through Fort Orange and on to New Amsterdam clearly established the Hudson River as "the spine of New Netherland,"[21] upon which the fate of the Dutch experiment in North America would be determined.

Under the director-generalship of Peter Stuyvesant, the Dutch West India Company prospered in New Netherland. In 1664, about 40% of New Netherland's population was Dutch and centred in the Hudson River valley. Notwithstanding this success, tensions were increasing with Indigenous people along the Hudson as they were pushed progressively further inland by the Dutch and away from their traditional water highway, the Hudson River. Although the Dutch eventually prevailed after a series of deadly conflicts, a longer-lasting problem involved the English.

The English constituted only 15% of New Netherland's European population at the time, but they predominated southwest and northeast of the Hudson River valley and were slowly moving both north and west. Further, in England King Charles II gave his brother James, the Duke of York and Albany, control over New Netherland should the English be able to wrest control from the Dutch. Obtaining such control took little effort as New Amsterdam was poorly protected. Colonel Richard Nicolls, commanding four ships and 400 soldiers, entered New Amsterdam's harbour in 1664 and received Stuyvesant's surrender of the colony after only a few days of negotiations. New Amsterdam was promptly renamed New York and Fort Orange renamed Albany. While the Dutch briefly regained control of New York City (renamed New Orange in 1673) because of another English–Dutch conflict across the Atlantic, the Treaty of Westminster returned control of the Hudson River to the English in 1674. The Dutch era of control was forever ended, and although the English had referred to it as the Hudson River as early as 1619,[22] only now would the name stick, despite more changes to come.

The English Era and the American Revolutionary War

THE RETURN of the Hudson River to the English proved critical to their fortunes in North America for the next 100 years. The port city of New York and the Hudson River now gave the English unchallenged control of eastern North America from Virginia to Maine. The river itself provided a northern route to their main competitors, the French, concentrated in the St. Lawrence River valley. From the perspective of everyday life, the switch from Dutch to English government was a gradual one, with many accommodations made to Dutch residents (e.g., translation of legal proceedings into Dutch, renewal of land grants, religious tolerance).[23] The legacy of the Dutch period is still evident today in the many Dutch or Dutch-derived names that persist, e.g., Yonkers, Hoboken (in adjacent New Jersey), Tappan Zee Bridge, Patroon Island and Schuylerville. The English also continued the manorial land development system of the Dutch along the river and greatly expanded its agricultural production. The Hudson River valley, however, unavoidably became more closely tied to British foreign policy, especially towards the French and related conflicts such as Queen Anne's War and the French and Indian War during the period 1702–1763. The importance of Albany as a guard against French incursions and a collection point for the burgeoning fur trade grew, as did its population, which in 1737 exceeded New York City's (10,681 versus 10,664).[24]

The American Revolutionary War was a conflict between American Patriots and their British rulers within the more broadly defined American Revolution. The latter was a revolt by America's 13 colonies between 1765 and 1783, which essentially started as a series of protests against the levying of taxes by the British on colonists without those same colonists having representation in the British Parliament. Colonial lawyer James Otis's famous phrase "taxation without representation is tyranny" summarized the growing discontent against legislation such as the Stamp Act (1765, repealed 1766) and the Tea Act (1773, repealed 1861). These Acts and other related actions, such as revoking Massachusetts's right to self-government, led to the Patriots' establishment of an alternative government in

1774 and their declaration of independence in 1776. A series of conflicts such as the battles of Concord and Lexington eventually led to the establishment of the American Continental Army in 1775 under the leadership of George Washington.

Both the British and Washington recognized the importance of the Hudson River to the outcome of the war. In a letter to a fellow-general, Washington described it as "indisputably essential to preserve the communication between Eastern – Middle – and Southern States." The Hudson River valley was a "nexus of the conflict" for three fundamental reasons. First, controlling it meant that one controlled, via its tributary the Mohawk River, access to the Great Lakes and the Mississippi River. Second, its proximity to lakes George and Champlain in the north meant that the British could control the route via water between Montreal and New York City, the latter quickly becoming a major, global deepwater port. Third, and just as the Mississippi River cut the Confederacy in two during the Civil War (Chapter 9), the Hudson River could sunder the Patriots' stronghold in New England to the east from other states to the west and south. The British probably also reasoned that they had a good chance of consolidating Loyalist support in the south if they controlled the Hudson River valley.[25]

Although the war first flared up outside Boston and its finale occurred in Virginia, a series of critical campaigns took place in the Hudson River valley. These conflicts were set up after the British defeated the much smaller American Continental Army in the Battle of Long Island (summer 1776), which resulted in the latter's retreat across the East River, north to Manhattan, and eventually up to White Plains, NY. Moreover, back and forth battles pushed the Americans farther north, west across the Hudson River and back south and west into New Jersey and Pennsylvania. Washington's army sought to solidify positions on the lower Hudson River through the construction of forts Clinton and Montgomery near a narrowing of the river in the Hudson Highlands. This area also saw the construction of two iron chains as well as wooden barricades strung across the river to prevent the British from sailing upriver. A series of battles near Saratoga, upstream of Albany, proved to be decisive to the war. British general John Burgoyne marched south from Quebec along the Champlain River valley. At the same time General Barry St. Leger was marching east along the Mohawk River valley. Soon after General Burgoyne took Fort Ticonderoga, he continued south towards Albany. St. Leger's advance, however, was halted by Patriot general Benedict Arnold at the western edge of the Mohawk valley. Further, British general Henry Clinton's advance upstream from New York City was blunted in the Hudson Highlands, and he returned to shore up defences at New York City. Consequently, Burgoyne, denied resupply from the east and reinforcements from the west and south, lost a series of battles near Saratoga and surrendered in October 1777. Not only did Burgoyne's surrender blunt the British invasion from the north, but it was also crucial to the French decision to join the American side in the war in 1778. These battles, plus the collapse of the British "southern strategy"[26] following their defeat by a combined French-American force at Yorktown, Virginia, in 1781, and increasing military pressures on Britain in Europe, ultimately led to the Treaty of Paris, in 1783, whereby American sovereignty was recognized. The Hudson River, specifically West Point in the highlands, was also the site of general Benedict Arnold's treasonous act of planning to hand over the American Continental Army's West Point fortifications (Arnold was annoyed at having been passed over for various promotions and at having used much of his own money to prosecute the war). The plot was ultimately foiled by the capture of the British commander to whom Arnold was to surrender West Point, but Arnold escaped, was commissioned in, and fought for, the British army in the war's latter stages.

With the evacuation of British forces from New York in 1783, the colonial era ended in time for the new nation of America to take full advantage of the Industrial Revolution. A key aspect of realizing the benefits of industrialization was transportation. Notwithstanding their new-found freedom, Americans were still relatively "hemmed in" along the east coast by the Appalachian Mountains.[27] Transportation west was still most efficient by water, yet coastal areas and larger rivers were interconnected via relatively difficult and weight-limited overland routes. This all changed with the opening of the Erie Canal in 1825, connecting the Hudson River at Albany to Lake Erie at

Buffalo (584 km away) along a seam through the mountains provided by the Mohawk River.[28] The Erie Canal, largely the brainchild of New York Governor DeWitt Clinton, connected the frontier regions to New York City and allowed much higher-capacity barge traffic. The two great basins – the Great Lakes and the Atlantic Ocean – were joined in a "wedding of the waters,"[29] as Clinton stated. The marriage was symbolized with the dumping of a keg of Lake Erie water in the Atlantic Ocean, and vice versa, in the autumn of 1825. Here again, the Hudson River was transformative for the new nation. Nathaniel Hawthorne described it in 1835 as a "water highway, crowded with the commerce of two worlds, till then inaccessible to each other."[30] In joining the western and northern frontier regions to the great port city of New York, the canal promoted the colonization and development of the former and created the conditions that would define the industrial, political and cultural ascendancy of the latter. The canal also begat other canals between Lake Champlain and the Hudson River, between the Great Lakes and the Mississippi River, and between the Hudson and Delaware rivers. New York and the Hudson River valley prospered. Barge tolls were in the hundreds of thousands of dollars even before the entire canal was opened, towns and industrial centres sprang up along its route, agriculture increased, and wealth was generated for a greater diversity of individuals through business enterprises than for a relatively few via the antecedent manorial system.[31] The proliferation of steamboat and railway travel on the Hudson River in the early 1800s was followed by the mid-century consolidation of smaller rail lines into the Hudson River Railroad. The advent of eased transportation facilitated excursions into the Hudson River valley by Americans and an increasing number of visiting Europeans. Such visitors often recounted their "love of the Hudson" or "the gentle beauty of the banks ... the noble outlines of the Catskills" or that while on the river they felt "the immediate presence of God."[32] In *The Hudson*, Tom Lewis described the mid-to-late 1800s as a "halcyon time"[33] on the Hudson River. The intersection of the river's beauty with its emergent importance as an economic, social and cultural centre was the crucible for the development of the Hudson River School of landscape art.

Emergence of the Hudson River School of landscape art

IN THE EARLY 1800S, life in the eastern US had become comfortable enough for more and more people to regard the landscape as something that could be beautiful rather than always threatening or merely "useful" for providing a livelihood. Further, American intellectual leaders pined for art with a distinctive American character, especially when British critics held opinions as expressed by the Reverend Sydney Smith in 1820: "In the four corners of the globe, who reads an American book? Or goes to an American play? Or looks at an American picture or statue?"[34] The beauty of the Hudson River was thus primed to stimulate artistic works in art, music, writing and poetry. Carl Cramer, in his foreword to J.K. Howat's *The Hudson River and Its Painters*, contended that "landscape has a special influence on those that inhabit it ... in spiritual and psychic ways.... Perhaps because rivers in their courses offer poetic parallels to human life, people are inclined to attribute to them influences that strongly affect their lives."[35]

Into this mix, famous American writers such as James Fenimore Cooper and Washington Irving (the first American author to become well known in Europe) "extolled the virtues" of the rural and frontier life, particularly with their tales of the Hudson River and adjacent areas in classic works such as *The Last of the Mohicans* (Cooper), and *Rip Van Winkle* and *The Legend of Sleepy Hollow* (Irving). Other contemporary writers of a philosophical bent, such as Ralph Waldo Emerson and Henry David Thoreau, wrote of the human *need* for wilderness.[36] Up to this point, however, landscape painting held little appeal in Europe and even less in the US. Certainly, collections of engravings of landscapes such as William Henry Bartlett's *American Scenery* and the landscapes of Washington Allston and Thomas Doughty were known, but were not seen as serious art when compared to portraiture and historical paintings, engravings, wallpaper, sconces, looking glasses and inlaid chests and cabinets.[37] The emergence of the Hudson River School thus required more than the natural beauty of the river as subject matter (after all, the river already featured heavily in the engravings within *American*

Scenery). It required "a new milieu, a major change of taste, as well as an increase in the number of men with extra money to spend."[38]

Several factors are thought to have driven the emergence of the Hudson River School: (i) the Erie Canal increased the importance of the Hudson River and New York State as a major conduit between the east coast and the near west; (ii) the urge of an expanding nation to express itself, its natural wonders and history, particularly within the prevailing Romantic movement; (iii) a resumption of cultural and business ties with Europe, especially England; (iv) a growing number of young painters and engravers and their mixing with people of greater affluence as patrons who commissioned painters; and (v) the development of art schools and galleries where artists could learn their trade and display their work.[39]

This was the context within which a young Thomas Cole (1801–1848), an Englishman from Lancashire, found himself after moving to America with his family in 1820. Cole was trained originally as an engraver supporting the manufacture of calico fabrics, wallpaper and even carpets, and he travelled, mostly by walking, in the northeastern US in support of his trade. He met a portrait painter, John Stein, whose work fascinated him, and Cole decided to try portraiture, often being paid with bartered goods. His wanderings around the countryside provoked many sketches, and in Barbara Babcock Millhouse's history of the Hudson River School, *American Wilderness: The Story of the Hudson River School of Painting*, the author suggests that these wanderings provoked a kind of self-discovery in Cole concerning "whether he could transmit the feelings that nature aroused in him to his drawings."[40]

While Cole was wandering and wondering about his future, the work of Thomas Doughty, a Boston and New York City–based leading landscape painter of areas in the northeast US, caught Cole's eye while he was in Philadelphia visiting the Pennsylvania Academy of Fine Arts. Cole admired Doughty's work but thought he could do better. Cole thought that Doughty departed too much from the essence of Nature and painted too much "from himself."[41] Cole, by contrast, wanted to combine pure landscapes of his adopted country and imaginary compositions.

Kaaterskill Falls, Thomas Cole (1826).

Cole moved back to New York City, where later an owner of some of his early work encouraged and paid for a steamer trip up the Hudson River in 1825, to try and capture the beauty of New York State. After much rambling in the Catskills and sketching, Cole returned to New York City and convinced a Broadway bookshop owner to display three of his oil works in the front window. Here, they were eventually spotted by one Colonel John Trumbull, president of the American Academy of Fine Arts. Trumbull was a painter of historical scenes, particularly of the Revolutionary War, and was the first to realize Cole's work as "the answer to the call for a purely American subject and style."[42] Trumbull was particularly impressed, and purchased Cole's *Kaaterskill Falls* (1826), which he showed to two of his colleagues, art critic William Dunlap and Asher Durand, a young engraver.

Both Dunlap and Durand agreed that Trumbull had discovered a genius, and the two purchased the remaining paintings, *Lake with Dead Trees (Catskill)* (1826), and *A View of Fort Putnam* (1826). Trumbull was so impressed it is claimed that he said, "I am delighted, and at the same time mortified. This youth has done at once, and without instruction, what I cannot do after 50 years' practice."[43] Dunlap wrote rave reviews of Cole's work in the New York *Mirror* and his reputation as a landscape artist "spread like fire" according to Durand. This led to greatly increased sales of Cole's work (including a doubling of the offer price of *Lake with Dead Trees* (*Catskill*) – from $25 to $50!), introductions to patrons, and the birth of America's first indigenous art movement.

The Hudson River School did not become known as such until much later than Cole's discovery by Trumbull in 1825, and as many as 50 artists have been associated with the movement. Cole himself drifted from pure Hudson River valley–based landscapes after trips to Europe with more thematic works such as *The Course of Empire* series (1833–36) and *The Voyage of Life* series (1842) in which Cole combined morality with landscapes.[44] Cole eventually returned to the Hudson valley and created many more works, inspiring Asher Durand, the country's most accomplished engraver, to adopt landscape painting full time. After Cole's death in 1848, Durand became a central figure in the movement with works such as *Hudson River Looking Toward the Catskills* (1847). Durand's ascent increased the influence of Cole's work and further inspired younger artists such as John F. Kensett, Jasper Cropsey, and Sanford Gifford and, perhaps most famously, Cole's former student Frederic Church. Church completed many fine landscapes in the east e.g., *West Rock, New Haven* (1847) and *Niagara* (1857) but also created several famous works based on subjects in South America (e.g., *Heart of the Andes*, 1859) and the Middle East. Albert Bierstadt was another central figure who extended the Hudson-inspired landscape art to the American West, particularly scenes of the Sierra Nevada (*Sierra Nevada*, ca. 1871–73) and the Rocky Mountains (*The Rocky Mountains, Lander's Peak*, 1863). Thus, scenic aspects of the Hudson River sparked American landscape art in a much broader sense during its heyday from the mid-1820s until about 1870, depicting landscapes from the Arctic, to South America, to Asia.

The first reference to these artists and their art as the "Hudson River School" appeared in the 1870s, perhaps driven by an emerging struggle between the traditional, older and generally self-taught landscape artists and a new breed of younger, European-trained artists who embraced a more impressionist style with bolder strokes, focused on figural subjects.[45] Although the originator of the moniker remains obscure, it first appeared in print in 1879 in *Art Amateur,* and in a context that cannot be considered entirely positive. Critic Edward Strahan contrasted the "old and conventional" work of the "old men" of the Hudson River School with the "ideas sprouting in the minds of those who have been seeking a fuller education in Paris or Munich, are seen lending their fuller color to the wall."[46] Ironically, the coining and early use the term Hudson River School was associated with the period of its demise. Another critic in *Art Amateur* characterized European opinion of the American landscape painters as "the American savages in art."[47] The term was firmly established as a historical reference certainly by the mid-1880s.

Many reasons have been offered for the decline of the Hudson River School–style landscapes. Certainly, the carnage of the Civil War years (1861–1865) had dented much of the romantic notion of America. The age of exploration was rapidly being replaced by the age of industrialization, particularly in the east. As Barbara Millhouse noted in *American Wilderness,* "Faith in nature gave way to faith in the machine,"[48] and America was becoming more cosmopolitan in its artistic tastes.[49] This new era called less for what many considered to be brooding, repetitious "academic" landscapes. The less traditional, less romantic, impressionist style of the younger artists seemed a better fit to an era of bold innovations in industry and business. After all, the Hudson School was really defined not so much for a common artistic style as for a common reverence for nature and its members' "desire to portray its spiritual and moral value,"[50] particularly as exemplified by the Hudson River itself.[51] The next generation of landscape artists, including Albert Bierstadt, were also exploiting dramatic scenes in the more novel American West, which tended to blunt interest in more familiar scenes on the Hudson River.[52] Finally, the rise of lithography, and its ability to create prints by the thousands by the famous firm of Currier and Ives, and photography, the ultimate realist expression, contributed to the declining popularity of landscape art.[53] Clarence Cook, an influential art critic of the *New York Tribune*, sounded the death knell of the Hudson River School when, in describing the ascendancy of the new impressionists in 1883, he stated that "it was not possible to regret the change. Nothing more alien to what is recognized as art everywhere, outside England at least, has ever existed anywhere, than the now defunct or moribund school of landscape art once so much delighted in as the American school, but now so slightingly spoken of as the Hudson River School."[54] Critical decline was accompanied by financial decline when prices upwards of $25,000 for work by Church or Bierstadt's works in the 1860s dropped to $8,000 or less in the 1890s.[55] One of Cole's works, *The Cove* (1827) sold for as little as $70 in 1905. Ironically – and perhaps the ultimate sign of indignity – during the 300th anniversary of Henry Hudson's exploration of the Hudson River, celebrated in 1909, no paintings of Hudson River School artists were represented during a celebratory exhibition at the Metropolitan Museum of Art.[56]

Although its influence peaked in the 1860s, the Hudson River School left a significant bequest to American art: it established landscape art as the quintessential American genre. Eventually, figural painting faded among the younger painters and American impressionists came to embrace native landscapes as subjects. This resurgence of landscape art undoubtedly was built upon the foundation laid by the Hudson River School. The emergence of the Ashcan School in the early 1900s, focusing on gritty scenes of urban landscape realism in New York was a rebellion against American Impressionism and a recommitment to native subjects.[57] The Hudson River School formally re-emerged as an appreciated genre during an exhibition in 1917, *Paintings of the Hudson River School,* in the Metropolitan Museum of Art. The resurgence of the Hudson River school began with a scholarly phase in 1900, continued during a public and critical phase in the mid-1910s, and then peaked with a financial one beginning in the 1960s.[58] In particular, the financial resurgence is rather remarkable; Cole's *Portage Falls on the Genesee* (1839), once owned by Abraham Lincoln's secretary of state, William H. Seward, was appraised at $18 million in 2008.[59]

The beauty and history of the Hudson River and its role in the emergence of the Hudson River School was, undeniably, a seminal

Portage Falls on the Genesee, Thomas Cole (1839).

era in early American culture. As one European critic expressed it during an exhibition in Paris in 1867: "Every nation thinks it can paint landscape better than its neighbor; but it is not every nation that goes about the task in a way peculiar to itself. No one is likely to mistake an American landscape for the landscape of any other country. It bears its nationality on its face smilingly."[60] A more noble characterization can hardly be imagined.

— ELEVEN —

The St. Lawrence River
Gateway to a Continent

It has moved the ocean a thousand miles inland.
—*The Globe and Mail* (1959)

The old river rested in its broad reach unruffled at the decline of day, after ages of good service to the race that people its banks, spread out in tranquil dignity to a waterway leading to the uttermost parts of the earth.
—JOSEPH CONRAD, *Heart of Darkness* (1899)

Rivers, by definition, move and thus contain kinetic energy. This energy can be harnessed in the form of hydroelectric dams (see Chapters 5 and 7) or by moving people and things from one place to another. Transportation of people and things is facilitated by the buoyant properties of water; it can support weight. Given that the movement of people and commodities is fundamental to human commerce, rivers have played a central role in economic development.[1] Although early humans almost surely moved along rivers on foot, on single logs, or simple rafts, the earliest acknowledged "boat" is the "Pesse canoe," an almost 2 m long, 0.5 m wide dugout canoe made from a single Scots pine.[2] This canoe, which has been estimated to date to 9,000–10,000 ya, was discovered near the town of Pesse in northeastern Holland. Transportation along rivers was further aided by the advent of canals, the first of which were developed in Mesopotamia by at least 5,000 ya, extensively in China (one reached almost 1800 km by the year 620), and in Europe by the Middle Ages.

Employing a narrow definition of navigable waterways (characterized by minimum depths, widths and being free of rapids, or by having canals to circumvent rapids and permit unhindered navigation), the United States has about 41,000 km of inland navigable waterways (about 0.15% of all transportation infrastructure by length), and Canada has been estimated to have between 660 and 5500 km.[3] These waterways provide a tremendous economic benefit in terms of provision of transportation services. A 2014 study estimated that job and monetary losses would, within one year, exceed 540,000 jobs and US$29 billion (in 2012 dollars), respectively, if inland waterway navigation wholly within the US became unavailable and alternatives needed to be sought.[4] In Canada, inland waterway transportation supported more than 90,000 jobs, and more than US$25 billion in economic activity, wages, personal and business spending, and taxes in 2017.[5] In the US, inland transportation is dominated by the Mississippi/Missouri/Ohio River system, with smaller contributions from the Columbia River in the Pacific Northwest and the Gulf Intracoastal Waterway from northwest Florida to southeastern Texas. In Canada, inland commercial transportation is dominated even more so by the Great Lakes–St. Lawrence Seaway system, which also makes substantial contributions to the US economy.

The Great Lakes–St. Lawrence Seaway is the longest deep-draft navigation system in the world and is a modification of a river system that has supported vital transportation links for humans almost since ice from the last glaciation retreated some 15,000 ya. This chapter explores the St. Lawrence River, a transboundary river that literally opened up much of the North American continent to the European settlers who exploited river transportation links first established by Indigenous Peoples. Ray H. Whitbeck declared in a 1914 essay that the exceptional size of the river quickly led the

French to the heart of the continent and nominal control of a huge area from the mouth of the St. Lawrence River to the mouth of the Mississippi River. At the same time, the vast area made effective defence impossible and "it is doubtful if a better example of the beneficent and baneful influence of a great river upon history exists, certainly none in America."[6] In *Seven Rivers of Canada*, Hugh MacLennan stated of the St. Lawrence that "it has made nations,"[7] and this is particularly true for Canada, where the St. Lawrence River is widely acknowledged as "Canada's original highway."[8] While the crucible of American development lay to the east of the Appalachian Mountains along the Atlantic seaboard, that of Canada lay in the St. Lawrence River valley, from which issued "the river of Canada."[9] The geographic fact of these two foci of settlement and economic development would later contribute to the lengthy binational debates that would ultimately determine the fate of the river. Consequently, the story of the St. Lawrence River is largely the story of almost 100 years of international negotiation and, eventually, co-operation between Canada and the US that ultimately resulted in an inland seaway and hydroelectric complex created by what was to become known as "the greatest construction show on Earth."[10]

The geography and origin of the St. Lawrence River

THE ST. LAWRENCE RIVER forms as the outlet of Lake Ontario, one of the five Laurentian Great Lakes of North America. An unusual feature of the St. Lawrence River relative to the other rivers of this book is that it is the five massive Great Lakes, which constitute 21% of the Earth's surface fresh water and are the largest interconnected lake system in the world by area (244,106 km²), that together form the source of the St. Lawrence River.[11] The St. Lawrence River is unusual at its terminus as well – the St. Lawrence Estuary is the largest in the world, eventually yielding to the Atlantic Ocean at the western end of Anticosti Island in the Gulf of St. Lawrence. The size of the St. Lawrence River itself can be contentious given the unusual properties of its source and the size of the estuary. For instance, the river, including the estuary, flows some 1197 km from the outlet of Lake

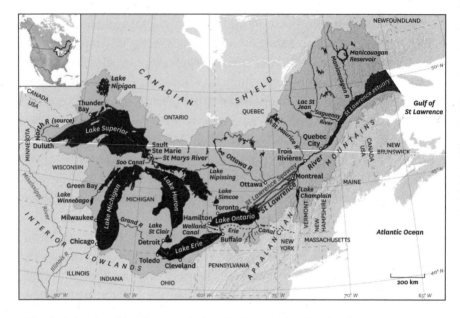

The St. Lawrence River Basin including the Great Lakes. The boxed area shows the location of the St. Lawrence Seaway.

Ontario to the Atlantic Ocean.[12] The US Geological Survey, somewhat arbitrarily, considers the ultimate source of the St. Lawrence River, however, to be the North River – a headwater stream tributary to western Lake Superior, the most upstream of the Great Lakes.[13] From here, the St. Lawrence River system flows some 3060 km to the sea, making it the fourth longest in North America (27th worldwide) with a drainage area of 1,030,000 km², also ranking fourth in North America (19th worldwide).[14] When including the estuary, however, the St. Lawrence drainage balloons to 2,374,000 km². The Great Lakes–St. Lawrence River basin provides the primary source of water for over 40 million people in Canada and the US.[15]

The St. Lawrence River system has a particularly complex origin both temporally and spatially. The river valley has the appearance of a flat, coastal, lowland plain, with a few elevational intrusions, underlain by flat Paleozoic rocks. Unusually, the valley also tends to narrow as one proceeds downstream from Montreal (where it is widest) to Quebec City before widening considerably at the estuary.

The estuary deepens to over 200 m and up to 550 m in depth and forms a submarine trough that extends southeast 1200 km to the margins of the continental shelf, with a minor branch running northeast towards the Strait of Belle Isle between the island of Newfoundland and mainland Labrador. These features of the river/submarine valley led to initial ideas that the valley was formed by a combination of river erosion and subsequent drowning, glacial scour and submarine turbidity currents. Assembling information on dimensions and form of the valley, distribution of fault line scarps (straight, abrupt escarpments comprising the "Laurentian Scarp") and fault lines, "tilting" of edges of the valley, distribution of earthquakes, strong association with alkaline rocks, and the presence of gravity "anomalies" has led to a different conclusion: that the St. Lawrence system originated as a rift valley, similar to those characterizing the basins of the East African Rift Lakes (Victoria, Malawi etc.), the Dead Sea, Lake Baikal and the Gulf of Suez.[16] This "St. Lawrence Rift System" is part of a branching network, perhaps 2200 km in length, that extends between Nova Scotia and Newfoundland, where it incises or cuts into the Appalachian formation. It also has branches northwest up the Ottawa River system to Lake Nipissing, along the Saguenay River system of Quebec, and along the aforementioned Strait of Belle Isle submarine trough. The rift system developed from the downward movement of land in response to faulting activity on the northeast side of the valley, the Laurentian Uplands (formed during the Grenville Orogeny – see Chapter 10). This faulting formed a half-graben bending to the southeast, and a resultant broad valley between the Laurentian Uplands and the Appalachian/Adirondack highlands, which form much of the eastern axis of North America.[17]

What drove these faulting pressures? Remarkably, it is thought that the initial fault lines in the St. Lawrence system date back over a billion years to the Precambrian Shield rocks of the Laurentian Uplands that formed part of the "nucleus" of the continent.[18,] This faulting was associated with the opening of the Iapetus Ocean, the precursor to the Atlantic Ocean.[19] These initial lines of weakness were the focus of subsequent faulting in the region that dates to the lower Cretaceous and as far back as the Silurian (140–440 mya). The St. Lawrence

Rift System is thought to have extensions west into the Lake Superior Trough and southwest into the Mississippi River valley. Such extensions are also observed in the East African Rift Valley (north to the gulfs and Suez and Aden) and may be part of the "world-girdling" system of ridges and rifts, such as the mid-Atlantic Ridge and the East Pacific Rise.[20] Thus, the lowlands of the St. Lawrence River valley that formed a water-channelling trough and created ancient rivers had an origin in the distant past from processes acting on a global scale.

The origin of the current St. Lawrence River system stems from changes to this ancient template by events that date to the action of the Wisconsinan glaciers that created the Great Lakes system. Although it has been proposed that the Great Lakes were formed by deposition of glacial-eroded material at the ends of pre-glacial depressions, by river erosion following pre-glacial uplift, or by "diastrophic" processes (those generating folds, faults and "twists" in the Earth's crust),[21] the current consensus is that the Great Lakes were created by Quaternary (Pleistocene) glacial "excavation."[22] Before the Pleistocene glaciations, the drainage system of the Great Lakes region consisted largely of two subaerial systems, i.e., on or near the Earth's surface: the Laurentian and the Teays-Mahomet valley systems. The Laurentian system at its maximum extent ranged from western tributaries of present-day lakes Superior and Michigan east to the head of the current St. Lawrence River valley.[23] The Teays-Mahomet valley system existed south of the Laurentian system and was tributary to the Mississippi River. The divide between these two ancient drainage systems ran along a southeast–southwest arc below the contemporary Great Lakes.

Glacial scour during the Pleistocene carved the present basins in pre-existing bedrock valleys consisting of relatively "weak" and erodible limestone and shale rock that lay above more resistant and older Precambrian rocks. As discussed in previous chapters, there were repeated glacial advances and retreats during the Pleistocene Epoch. The most recent, and most lasting in terms of its effect on the contemporary St. Lawrence River, was the Wisconsinan Glaciation that occurred between 110,000 and ~10,000 ya. The Laurentide Ice Sheet was thought to be up to 1750 m thinner over the Great Lakes relative to its height on the continent, and while it eventually covered the entire basin, there were periods when parts of the Great Lakes basin were not ice-covered and several glacial lakes existed, especially along the southern margins of the watershed.[24] After several minor ice retreats and re-advances, the massive ice sheet began its final retreat to the northeast about 10,000 ya, and the Great Lakes area was completely free of ice by 9,000 ya.

During these glacial retreats, several glacial and proglacial lakes existed with a series of outlets that drained the meltwater to the south, southwest and southeast. Prominent among these was proglacial Lake Algonquin (~13–12,000 ya), which had several outlets, one of which, the North Bay Outlet, drained southeast from an area encompassing contemporary eastern Lake Superior, Lake Michigan and Lake Huron/Georgian Bay into what is now the Ottawa River valley. During one of the many phases of Lake Algonquin, it also had an outlet that drained into the precursor to Lake Ontario (Lake Iroquois) and eventually into the Mohawk Valley of the Hudson River system.[25] Glacial Lake Iroquois had a second outlet at its eastern end via the developing upper St. Lawrence Valley.[26]

The weight of the massive ice sheet depressed the underlying land and when the ice retreated the land "rebounded" in processes known as "isostatic depression" and "isostatic rebound," respectively. Lake Superior, for instance, is thought to been depressed by up to 240 metres relative to sea level at the height of the last glaciation. The subsequent rebound occurs in two stages, one almost immediate, but incomplete, and a subsequent, slower and ongoing rebound that occurs at a rate of about 1 cm/yr or less. Further, the massive amounts of meltwater draining from the glaciers increase sea levels. The rise in sea levels, on the order of 120–140 m depending on the area, coupled with the delay in isostatic rebound, leads to invasion of the land by the rising seas during what are known as marine incursions. The spatial extent of a marine incursion will depend on the interaction among many factors such as tidal strength, local topography and volume of freshwater discharge. One such incursion up the St. Lawrence and Ottawa river valleys and the Lake Champlain valley created what is known as the Champlain Sea – the first "St. Lawrence Seaway" created without the aid of humans.

The Champlain Sea began to form about 13,000 ya.[27] As inferred from the presence of marine deposits, fossils of marine fishes and invertebrates, pollen records and the contemporary distribution of freshwater fishes that are intolerant of sea water, the Champlain Sea extended westward from the Atlantic Ocean to about 200 km up the Ottawa River valley, 150 km beyond the southern extent of Lake Champlain and to within about 30 km of the present-day eastern end of Lake Ontario. The sea had a surface area of some 55,000 km² and sea level was up to 150 m higher than the current elevation of the St. Lawrence River.[28] Eventually, by about 9,500 ya, isostatic rebound of about 135 m in the Champlain Sea basin drained the marine waters. Further, during the rebound process, the various glacial and proglacial lake outlets of the proto–Great Lakes were cut off, and the current connections between the Great Lakes and the terminal outlet of Lake Ontario, the beginning of the St. Lawrence River, were formed. The St. Lawrence River received its last direct inputs of glacial meltwater around 8,200 years ago, with the collapse of glacial Lake Ojibway, a derivative of Lake Algonquin, towards Hudson Bay, which had been draining south from the ice sheet margin in northern Ontario and northwestern Quebec.[29]

Early human history of the St. Lawrence River

THE EARLIEST HUMAN INHABITANTS of the St. Lawrence River valley arrived following northeastern movements of Paleoindians who dispersed from pre-Clovis sites perhaps 20,000 cal ya, centred east of the Appalachian Mountains and on the eastern US coastal plain. These movements were probably extensions of dispersal by humans to the south and west in the Hudson River valley (Chapter 10), and southern margins of lakes Erie and Ontario, respectively. The first Paleoindian sites occurred along the southeastern shoreline of the Champlain Sea in Vermont some 13–12,200 cal ya, and by the late Paleoindian period, 10,800–10,000 cal ya, there were numerous sites all along the south shore of the fading Champlain Sea and the St. Lawrence River valley itself (e.g., the Thompson Island site in Lake St. Francis).[30]

The Paleoindian stage was followed by the Archaic period, which lasted from about 9,000 to 3,000 ya[31] and was characterized by assemblages of distinctive projectile points with side and corner notches.[32] The St. Lawrence River valley Archaic people are recognized as a distinctive material culture subgroup relative to others found farther to the north and east: the Laurentian Archaic.[33] The Archaic period yielded to the Woodland cultural period, beginning about 3,000 ya and ending with European contact. It was characterized by a less nomadic lifestyle, the raising of corn, beans and squash, the creation of distinctive pottery styles and burial mounds, and a significant growth in population size.[34] The Woodland cultural period in the St. Lawrence River valley was dominated by two linguistic groups: the Algonquian, largely to the north and along western portions of the valley, and the Iroquoian in the valley itself and to the south. It was these two language groups that gave rise to the many Indigenous Peoples who contacted Europeans along the St. Lawrence River and adjacent areas: the Algonquin, Iroquois (the historical St. Lawrence Iroquois and contemporary Iroquois), Huron, Mohawk, Seneca, Onondaga and Oneida.[35]

Likely, the first Europeans who contacted the eastern margins of the St. Lawrence River were Basque whalers and fisherman who sailed from the Basque Country of northeastern Spain and adjacent parts of southwestern France throughout most of the 1500s. The Basques established settlements at least as far upstream as Île aux Basques, only about 200 km downstream from Quebec City.[36] It was Jacques Cartier (1491–1557), a French explorer from Brittany, who was the first to explore and map the St. Lawrence River as far upstream as Montreal. Cartier first skirted the area around Anticosti Island in 1534 in the oft-repeated quest to find a trade route to Asia. In 1535, Cartier returned to explore further upstream of what he considered a gateway to Asia, initially reaching the St. Lawrence Iroquoian settlement of Stadacona (near today's Quebec City). Further upstream, he reached Hochelaga (now Montreal), where he encountered rapids that stalled further exploration. Surely, Cartier reasoned, Asia lay just beyond the rapids, which he optimistically named "La Chine" – today's Lachine Rapids. Based on his explorations of the St. Lawrence River and its Iroquoian settlements, Cartier also named the new land that he claimed for France as "Canada," which stems from the Iroquoian word "Kanata," for settlement, "town" or "cluster of buildings." Iroquoians accompanying Cartier referred to the St. Lawrence River as "the way to Canada" and he, therefore, first referred to the river as "la rivière de Canada."[37] Ultimately, and because Cartier arrived during his second voyage on the day of the feast of St. Lawrence, he named the area of his first voyage the Gulf of St. Lawrence and the river draining into it became known as the St. Lawrence River in the 1600s.[38] Cartier was thus the first European to penetrate the eastern interior region of North America, and in a third voyage in 1542 he consolidated France's claim to Canada with the first attempt at European settlement with a fort at Charlesbough-Royal. While this settlement ultimately failed in 1543, this attempt, and Cartier's initial engagements with Indigenous Peoples, would prove vital to French colonization of North America and the subsequent emergence of New France.

The French hold on the St. Lawrence River valley was solidified by the arrival and explorations of Samuel de Champlain (1567–1635), a French explorer, geographer and cartographer. Champlain made many voyages to lands of the western Atlantic in the early 1600s, from the Caribbean to the Gulf of St. Lawrence. In 1608, he led an expedition to establish a fur-trading colony and established Quebec City as a fortified site on July 3. For the next ten years, Champlain explored the St. Lawrence River upstream of Quebec City and made several alliances with local First Nations, especially the Huron, Montagnais and Algonquin, and aided them in their battles with the Iroquois and Mohawk peoples. Owing to impassible rapids at La Chine on the St. Lawrence River, Champlain explored the upper reaches of the Ottawa River to lakes Nipissing and Huron. These explorations and the founding of the Compagnie des Marchands de Rouen et de Saint-Malo by Champlain laid the foundation for the expansion of the fur trade centred in New France in the Great Lakes–St. Lawrence River valley. This trade solidified with the formation of the Compagnie des Cents-Associés (Company of One Hundred Associates), with Champlain as its commander, in 1627.

Consequently, the St. Lawrence River and a major tributary – the Ottawa River - became a key route for exploration of the interior of eastern North America. Also, Donald Creighton, in his book *The Empire of the St. Lawrence: A Study of Commerce and Politics,* argued that the French-controlled northeast–southwest axis of the St. Lawrence River acted as an important counterpoint to the competing north–south axis along the Hudson River–Lake Champlain corridor controlled by the Dutch and then the English. It has been further argued that the St. Lawrence River valley was thus at the heart of the economic birth of Canada – "a great competitive east-west trading system, founded on the St. Lawrence River and the Great Lakes, one end of which lay in the metropolitan centres of western Europe and the other in the hinterland of North America. It was a transoceanic as well as a transcontinental system."[39] This geographical determinism was formalized as the "Laurentian thesis" – that the St. Lawrence watershed was fundamental in determining the developmental history of Canada, a thesis that, while no longer considered as a singular explanation, still provides a valid indication of the importance of the river to Canada.[40]

The importance of the St. Lawrence River valley as a key transportation and economic hub is also reflected by several attempts by the British to gain control of it. These attempts culminated in the Seven Years' War (1756–1763), a global conflict with battles occurring among all major European powers and in regions of Europe, the Americas and the Philippines (see Chapter 9). Within the North American context, the war was known as the French and Indian War, and after the British defeated the French during the Battle of the Plains of Abraham (1759), just west of Quebec City, the French ceded control of the St. Lawrence River valley to the British. The final division of the St. Lawrence River between British North America (now Canada) and the United States needed to await the outcomes of the American Revolutionary War (see Chapter 10) and the War of 1812 involving the British and Americans. After the 1783 Treaty of Paris ended the American Revolutionary War, the border was established from approximately the "northwest angle of Nova Scotia" (a somewhat ambiguous point in present-day New Brunswick around the 47th parallel) south to the northwestern limit of the Connecticut River and then along the 45th parallel to the southern margin of the St. Lawrence River and the Great Lakes.[41] The current border through roughly the middle of the St. Lawrence River beginning between Cornwall, Ontario, and Rooseveltown, New York, and the Great Lakes was established following surveying mandated by the Treaty of 1908 between the US and Great Britain.

That it required more than 100 years of negotiation, at least one war, and several treaties to finally establish the Canada–US border through the St. Lawrence River valley (and beyond) could perhaps have served as a harbinger of challenging days ahead for international planning regarding the use of the river and its resources. Indeed, the opening of the Lachine Canal in 1825 to bypass the rapids that frustrated Champlain and facilitate upstream navigation in the river, and the hydropower associated with the canal, illustrated the economic potential of modifications of the river. Construction of other notable canals such as the Welland Canal (to bypass Niagara Falls) and the canal and locks to bypass the St. Marys River rapids between lakes Superior and Huron provided the St. Lawrence–Great Lakes system with a chance to supplant the Erie Canal as the eastern commercial gateway to the Great Lakes and the fast-developing western regions of both Canada and the US. For this to be accomplished, however, the narrower, shallower canals in the St. Lawrence River proper would need to be enlarged to accommodate ocean-going vessels.[42] Despite the fact that the St. Lawrence River system was the only viable course for open ocean–sized vessels to enter the Great Lakes system, it would take 55 years of negotiation and the longest debate in US congressional history to make that "Golden Dream" a reality.[43]

Origins of "The Golden Dream"

THE ST. LAWRENCE RIVER and its major tributaries had been an important trade route for Indigenous Peoples for centuries before first contact with western Europeans.[44] For the latter, the concept of unfettered water transportation via the St. Lawrence River system as a "golden dream" began with Cartier and the quest for a western route to Cathay and the riches of China and India.[45] When the obvious limitation to the realization of that dream became apparent, the advantages of the St. Lawrence River for water transportation from the growing midwest to Europe became apparent; Montreal, Quebec City, and the mouth of the St. Lawrence are much closer to Europe than their rivals, New York and the Hudson River. Consequently, attempts to correct what Donald Creighton termed as "the problem of the St. Lawrence"[46] by improving river travel began well before the initiation of the seaway project, proper. The 1800s was the "age of canals" on the system, but the first one had been constructed at Lachine in 1689. Even with this first canal, the motivation was a dual purpose one: to circumvent the rapids and provide more water for grain mills in the area.[47] This attempt and a later one in 1700 failed owing to hostilities with Iroquois and engineering troubles. The first canal with locks was completed in 1781 and served to bypass most of the series of rapids upstream of Lachine, but even this canal and others associated with it usually required unloading of cargo and its conveyance by wagon while the "bateaux," flat-bottomed riverboats, were hauled through the canal and lock system. This laborious system, plus remaining obstacles at Lachine and Long Sault, meant that the upstream trip between Montreal and Lake Ontario took about two weeks and the downstream trip through the rough-and-tumble rapids often ended in disaster.[48] By 1820, the growing demand for cargo resulted in the common use of the so-called Durham boats, with a capacity of 18–27 tonnes, and the widening and deepening of canals to accommodate them. Still, while some canals lessened the burden of water transportation, there remained the 327-foot drop between lakes Erie and Ontario at Niagara Falls and the 20-foot drop at the St. Marys River rapids between lakes Huron and Superior. The latter precipitated the construction of a rudimentary canal by the North West Company – the first built explicitly to serve the western and central North American fur trade. This initial drive to more easily deliver resources of the North American interior would be replicated in demand for transportation of western grain and provide a major thrust to develop the St. Lawrence Seaway.[49] A seaway was also seen as an important development to help link the British colonies of Upper and Lower Canada, which, as commercial units "cut into two unequal fragments,"[50] were feeling increased competition with a more economically and politically integrated US.

Vibrant trade along the Lake Erie–Ontario–St. Lawrence River corridor spurred a boom in canal building – a "canal mania"[51] – in the first half of the 19th century, the most significant being the completion of the Erie Canal between the Mohawk/Hudson rivers and Lake Erie in 1825 (see Chapter 10). The Erie Canal–Hudson River route represented a competing trade route for the St. Lawrence River corridor and siphoned much of the agricultural production from that route. Another focus of canal building that drew attention away from the St. Lawrence River was the Ottawa and Rideau river systems. The rapids upstream of those at Lachine could be bypassed by using the Ottawa River route to Lake Nipissing and eventually Lake Huron. The Rideau Canal, completed in 1832, connected the Cataraqui River, which empties into Lake Ontario, with the Rideau River, which drains into the Ottawa River. Consequently, the triangular route between Lake Ontario, the Ottawa River (and hence the upper Great Lakes via Lake Huron) and the St. Lawrence River at Montreal, presented another challenge to an all–St. Lawrence River route.

In addition to being about 80 km shorter, however, a direct route between Lake Ontario and Montreal would involve many fewer locks than the St. Lawrence–Ottawa–Rideau route. Furthermore, to circumvent Niagara Falls the Welland Canal was completed in 1829, and an all–St. Lawrence River route to the interior became more appealing (the author's maternal great-great-grandfather, Samuel DeVeaux Woodruff, was a chief engineer of the canal between 1840 and 1869). By 1837 over 5000 km of canals had been completed, but competition for trade from the west remained, between the St. Lawrence, Ottawa–Rideau, and Erie Canal–Hudson River routes. At this point, the St. Lawrence was "in a state of war" commercially with the Atlantic seaboard and Hudson Bay through the latter half of the 1700s and the early 1800s.[52] Only improvement to canals along the often "tortuous"[53] St. Lawrence River route between Prescott, Ontario and Montreal could tilt the balance in favour of the St. Lawrence River. After "unremitting agitation for improvement"[54] by

St. Lawrence valley merchants, a series of canals and canal improvements at Welland, Lachine, Cornwall and Beauharnois resulted in a complete St. Lawrence River canal system to a minimum depth of almost 3 m, suitable for larger ships than the Erie Canal could accommodate, by 1850.[55] By the early 1900s, improvements to canals around the St. Marys River both in Canada and the US, completion of a fourth version of the Welland Canal, and improvements to more than 90 ports in the US and at Toronto and Montreal, had clearly positioned the St. Lawrence River route to take over the bulk of western trade. The Erie Canal had become largely obsolete by 1900 for anything other than barges, and more recent competitors such as the port at Churchill on Hudson Bay, completed in 1931, and the Chicago Sanitary and Ship Canal connecting the Chicago River (which naturally drained to Lake Michigan) with the Missouri/Mississippi system never lived up to their potential.[56] The remaining limitation to the Great Lakes–St. Lawrence system becoming the pre-eminent shipping route for ocean-going vessels and providing a more economical option than shipment by rail both in Canada and the US, was the capacity of the canals within the St. Lawrence River itself. Virtually all the canal work on the St. Lawrence River was, however, limited to the Canadian side. The 1854 Reciprocity Treaty ensured that US ships had full, toll-free access to Canadian canals, which American politicians considered reason enough not to invest in canals themselves.[57]

The promise of power

POLITICIANS in both countries had introduced motions for improvements to the existing seaway in the early 1890s. Furthermore, pressure for an efficient St. Lawrence River route increased from American interests at the western end of the Great Lakes (e.g., Minnesota, Wisconsin and Michigan), who desired better access to their ports for ocean-going vessels. In 1894, the International Deep Waters Commission (later to become the International Joint Commission, or IJC) was formed to study improved navigation along the St. Lawrence–Great Lakes route. Both countries issued a report in 1897, but each made different recommendations; the Americans favoured a Hudson River–based corridor, while the Canadian report favoured the St. Lawrence River. These proposals stalled owing to American wariness of a vital transportation corridor that would partially run through another country, and Canadians were likely uncomfortable with sharing the resources of what they popularly considered "Canada's river."

Two important factors drove renewed impetus for a binational project to develop a modernized, deeper seaway on the St. Lawrence in the early 1900s: the improvement of relations between Britain and the US and between the US and Canada, resulting, for instance, in the formation of the IJC, and the promise of hydroelectric benefits from developments on the St. Lawrence River. The latter optimism stemmed from hydropower developed with canals at Cornwall, ON, Massena, NY (associated with the Aluminium Company of America, Alcoa, plant at Massena), and at Niagara Falls. The need for power became more acute as part of the post–Second World War political and economic strategies both in Canada and the US. Consequently, development for navigation and hydroelectric power became intertwined in the St. Lawrence Seaway debate, with the latter eventually becoming the predominant motivation. Development of large-scale hydropower projects on the river, *compatible* with improved navigation, necessitated a binational approach because such large projects would cross the entire river and, hence, the Canada–US border.[58]

In 1913, President Woodrow Wilson was encouraged by the US Senate to begin formal negotiations with Canada to implement plans to improve boundary water navigation. The outbreak of war in 1914 and the continuing reticence of the Canadian government stalled the initiative. A seaway bill was later introduced into the House of Representatives by New York congressman Bertrand H. Snell in 1917. A series of hearings into the feasibility and logistics of a deep-water seaway by the IJC ended in 1921 and produced a recommendation to negotiate an international treaty to construct the seaway. The next year, President Warren G. Harding arranged for a formal request for negotiations to Prime Minister Mackenzie King, a leader who became known for taking bold action only when absolutely essential.[59] King was reticent owing to possible damage to the business of the national railways, and Ontario's premier remained firmly opposed.[60] Further positive recommendations by advisory boards in the US (1926) and Canada (1929) followed, but again, Canadian officials stalled, thinking that the risk to Canada was too high and that the US might proceed alone, yet allow access to the seaway and the purchase of its power by Canadian interests. The Power Authority of the State of New York (PASNY) was established in 1930 to oversee planning and development on the St. Lawrence River. In Ontario, Ontario Hydro had been created in 1906 with a similar mandate for the province, but more in terms of private power developments. The 1930s brought Franklin Delano Roosevelt to power in the US. He was enthusiastic about public power projects such as those initiated on the Columbia River (Grand Coulee Dam, Chapter 5) and the Colorado River (Hoover Dam, Chapter 7) and wanted the same for the St. Lawrence River. In fact, the first seaway treaty with Canada was signed under the previous administration of Herbert Hoover, and powerful business interests in Alcoa, Dupont and General Electric also drove interest in St. Lawrence River power. With a planned cost of almost $550 million to be incurred during the Great Depression, Canada's prime minister, Richard B. Bennett, and many in the US, demurred. Despite other setbacks in US legislative bodies, owing to the fears of opposing interests in railways and non–Great Lakes ports, Roosevelt presented the long-term view when he stated that the seaway would eventually be built "as sure as God made little green apples."[61]

Surely enough, political changes in Canada and Roosevelt's new attitude that the seaway constituted not just a commercial enterprise, but with war looming in Europe, one that was essential to war production and "the joint defense of the North American continent"[62] kept the dream alive in both countries. While some testing of potential construction sites was initiated, the seaway project was further stalled by the prioritization of workers and supplies for the prosecution of the Second World War. Following the end of the war in 1945, Canada was enjoying robust economic growth, and the demand for power as a component of a seaway project grew tremendously, especially for the growing population and industrialization of the lower

Great Lakes–St. Lawrence River area.[63] Existing electrical generation capacity could not keep up with the increasing demand for power in post-war Ontario, and mining interests in Quebec were keen on economical options (i.e., water shipping) to transport newly discovered iron ore deposits to Great Lakes–area steel mills. These developments led to passage of the St. Lawrence Seaway Authority Act in Canada's parliament in 1951, and Canada was prepared to go it alone as an "all-Canadian Seaway." In the US, the seaway bill was rejected by Congress in 1952, but arguments for the necessity of the project as a partnership in North American security continued, especially in the context of the 1950–1953 Korean War and the Cold War more generally. After further reports and hearings addressing concerns of eastern railroads and competing harbour interests, the US House of Representatives and the US Senate passed a bill (the Wiley-Dondero Act) authorizing construction of the seaway in 1954 and President Dwight D. Eisenhower signed the bill in May of the same year, ending the longest legislative debate in US history. Canada was to pay 70% of the $470 million cost, a reduction from earlier estimates owing to the imposition of tolls and the absorption of some of the costs by Ontario and New York State.

The build: The greatest construction show on Earth

THE CONSTRUCTION of the St. Lawrence Seaway was described by Ronald Stagg in his *The Golden Dream: A History of the St. Lawrence Seaway* as "one of the greatest logistical, engineering, and construction projects of the twentieth century."[64] A perhaps somewhat immodest description of it as "the greatest construction show on Earth" was offered by an administrator with the Seaway Development Corporation, Martin W. Oettershagen,[65] upon completion in 1959. It was even described as "the eighth wonder of the world"[66] in John Brior's *Taming of the Sault: A History of the St. Lawrence Power Development – Heart of the Seaway*. Such hyperbole reflected the complexity of the project. It was to be the largest inland waterway project in the world. It spanned 265 km; involved the construction of seven locks lifting ships a total of 180 m; many canals, and three massive storage and hydroelectric dams; bridge modifications; the flooding of 260 km² of land; and the expropriation of large areas of land involving the relocation of 6,500 people in Ontario, 1,500 in Quebec, 1,100 in New York, and the relocation of towns, homes and cemeteries.[67] More than 22,000 engineers, carpenters, cement workers and other labourers toiled on a project that involved two national governments, two provincial governments, a state government and their various agencies, including Ontario Hydro-Electric Power Commission (HEPCO), the PASNY and the US Army Corps of Engineers. The work involved the movement or removal of more than 160 million m³ of earth (more than twice that moved in constructing the Suez Canal), and almost 5 million m³ of concrete were poured (almost twice that used in constructing the Hoover Dam on the Colorado River).[68] The complexity was multiplied by unforeseen difficulties of dealing with varied substrates, and the fact that construction continued throughout the winter months, particularly on the Canadian side where workers had greater experience in construction in often frigid conditions.[69] Further, land expropriations occurred in areas at the heart of the 18th- and 19th-century Canadian "empire of the St. Lawrence" – long-settled towns and homes with families extending back generations.[70]

The project began in September 1954 and consisted of three major navigation sections and three storage/power dams. The Canadian portion included the 50 km long Lachine Rapids section, involving dredging, bridge, lock and the La Prairie Canal construction around the rapids along the river's south shore. Next came the 25 km Soulanges section to deal with the many sections of rapids between lakes St. Louis and Francis, which included the Beauharnois Canal and Power Dam, two locks and two water-level control dams. The final Canadian section involved dredging over 46 km between Lake St. Francis and Cornwall, ON. The 71 km long International Rapids section extended from the head of Lake St. Francis to Ogdensburg, NY, and included locks, canals, dykes, the massive transboundary Robert Moses–Robert H. Saunders Power Dam between Cornwall, ON, and Massena, NY, and the supporting Iroquois and Long Sault dams (upstream on the US side). Finally, the US contributed dredging and shoal removal within the 110 km Thousand Islands section.[71] Although not within the St. Lawrence River proper, improvements to the Welland Canal and the "Soo Locks" at Sault St. Marie over the years extended the reach of the project to the western edge of Lake Superior. Today, the "St. Lawrence Seaway" proper (the "Seaway") typically refers to the canal and lock–intensive section from Montreal to Lake Erie. The "Great Lakes–St. Lawrence Seaway System" includes the area from Montreal to Duluth at the western edge of Lake Superior, and the "Great Lakes–St. Lawrence River Waterway" encompasses all the Great Lakes, the Seaway and the lower St. Lawrence River to the Atlantic. Altogether there are 65 ports in the entire system from Duluth to Havre-Saint-Pierre, Quebec.[72]

The two main organizations that led the navigation aspects of the project were the St. Lawrence Seaway Authority (Canada) and the St. Lawrence Seaway Development Corporation (US), the latter of which engaged the US Army Corps of Engineers. Lionel Chevrier, a long-time advocate for the project and former politician, led the Canadian authority, and Lewis Castle, a leader within the similarly keen Great Lakes–St. Lawrence Association, headed the corporation. Overall supervision of the project was under the Joint Board of Engineers formed by the International Joint Commission. Construction of the major power dam of the project, the Moses-Saunders Dam, was led by two dynamic individuals: Robert H. Saunders on the Canadian side and Robert Moses on the American side. Saunders, a former lawyer and politician and outspoken head of HEPCO, never hid his feelings that the US needed to engage and help pay for the project; a Canadian-only funding scheme was "preposterous," and he was so confident that the US would eventually agree that he had HEPCO engineers working on the dam project well before the 1954 treaty was signed. Moses also had considerable experience in public works projects and has been described as even more forceful, even "dictatorial,"[73] as head of PASNY, especially when dealing with landowners. Despite their mutually forceful personalities, or perhaps because of them, the two men are reported to have approached the project in a remarkably compatible way.[74]

The task of taming the St. Lawrence River with the seaway construction had huge impacts on local towns and communities that remained in place, especially Cornwall and Massena, as men (mostly) and their families from across both countries flooded the region, along with equipment. Such rapid and extensive movement and settlement of people required similarly rapid development of infrastructure (schools, housing, hospital improvements, recreational facilities etc.), and inevitably, mismatches between the two occurred. This led to some conflicts between locals and new residents, exacerbated by their often very different educational and cultural backgrounds, rent speculation, an increase in traffic and rates of mostly minor crimes, stress on local community budgets, a proliferation of trailer parks, and related tensions. The social history of the project is well detailed with personal reflections of many workers of all types in Claire Parham's social history *The St. Lawrence Seaway and Power Project*. Despite the disruptions of imposing such a huge project on a relatively "sleepy" area, that influx of workers, many of whom eventually settled long-term in the St. Lawrence Valley, provided a vibrant boost to local communities by contributing to their growth in myriad ways, from forming local social, cultural and sports clubs to advocating for better educational institutions. The experiences of such a wide range of people involved in a huge project will always be mixed.

With such a large project, it was inevitable that there would be construction dilemmas as well. Some of the problems were political in nature, such as the characteristic resistance of Quebec premier Maurice Duplessis to a project led by Canada's federal government, or disputes with Indigenous groups whose land near Montreal would be impacted, a dispute that reached the World Court. Other issues involved strikes, companies abandoning contracts when conditions proved too tough, squabbles among the five agencies involved in the project, material shortages, a huge number of change orders, and the inevitable injuries or fatalities (remarkably there seems to be no official count of those who died, although at least three are acknowledged to have perished).[75] The more impactful problems, however, involved physical challenges presented by the river itself, a legacy of its past as well as its current features. First, the cofferdams, which are temporary structures built to hold back water so that an area can be pumped out and construction take place under dry conditions, were difficult to construct owing to the sheer volume of the St. Lawrence River. For instance, several cofferdams were required where the Iroquois Control Dam and control and power dams at Long Sault were to be constructed. A key problem was that a cofferdam built in one area restricts flow and thus increases water flow in the area to which the water is being diverted. For one area of Long Sault, the typical steel frame cofferdams could not be used owing to the force of the flow. A stone cofferdam was thus constructed by dumping 23 tonnes of stone at a time from an overhead cable-and-bucket apparatus strung across the river supplemented with loads of stone from trucks. At one point, however, the ever-constricting river fought back, so that stone was being washed downstream as fast as it was being dumped into the river.[76] It was not until engineers conceived of using six-legged steel "hexapedian" structures cabled to the shore to trap the rock that the cofferdam could be completed and the Long Sault Rapids subdued – four *months* later than anticipated. The other major material condition of the river that humbled construction workers and engineers was a legacy of the postglacial Champlain Sea and glacial meltwater. Marine clays, distributed much more extensively than expected, became sticky and incredibly viscous when wet (i.e., after they become exposed to the weather by excavation) so that they were not easily worked, and thus would not flow out from dump trucks – a problem that was compounded during cold weather – and equipment became trapped in the gooey bogs that developed. Glacial till, the mixed-size sediment created, moved and eventually deposited by glaciers, was the other villain. Harder than concrete when dry, it literally destroyed equipment used to excavate or move it owing to its abrasiveness. The till proved so tough that contractors found they needed to replace cutting or scraping teeth on excavators after *every shift*; some quit in despair. In a few localities, marine clays and glacial till combined to make construction conditions miserable.[77]

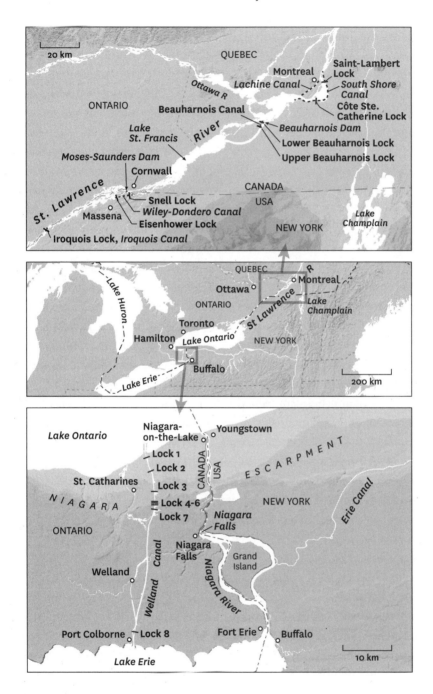

The St. Lawrence Seaway and the associated Welland Canal.

Despite the many challenges presented by the scope of the St. Lawrence Seaway and Power Project, the endeavour was essentially complete by July 1, 1958. The cofferdam holding back the St. Lawrence above the Moses-Saunders Power Dam was breached using dynamite at 8 o'clock in the morning before an excited crowd. Despite the initial disappointment of a less than cataclysmic explosion, over the next four days the flow generated by blasting the cofferdam slowly began to "swallow up the past" – old canals, gravesites, historic battlegrounds, roads and highways, now-abandoned town sites disappeared – as the new Lake St Lawrence formed. On the fifth day, the power switch on the dam was thrown to begin generating power and sending it to Ontarians, and 12 days later the American generators began their work. By December 1959 all generators were in action. The inaugural shipping season began in April 1959 when the icebreaker *D'Iberville* became the first ship to pass through the Seaway and all ships could use the entire 8 m (27 ft.) depth from Montreal to the western end of Lake Erie (and thus on to the western edge of Lake Superior at Duluth, Minnesota). The official opening occurred two months later when the royal yacht *Britannia* bearing Queen Elizabeth II entered the St. Lambert Lock near Montreal. Here, she and President Eisenhower officially opened the Seaway on June 26, 1959. A day later, a similar ceremony was held at Massena, NY, with US vice-president Richard Nixon accompanying the Queen at Eisenhower Lock. After all the dreaming, planning, negotiation, construction and the official openings, all that was left to do was to realize the promised benefits of a project that now made "every lakeport a seaport."[78]

The St. Lawrence Seaway at 62: A tarnished dream

THE YEAR 2021 marks the 62nd anniversary of the official opening of the St. Lawrence Seaway and Power Project, and, overall, the benefits of the Seaway by many measures of commercial success have been much lower than anticipated. In addition, several unintended consequences of the Seaway's opening and operation have been highly detrimental to the Great Lakes and St. Lawrence River ecosystem.

The Eisenhower Lock on the American side of the St. Lawrence Seaway looking west towards Massena, NY.

Naturally, there was heightened anticipation of benefits as construction wrapped up and during the early years after the Seaway opened. Ports in cites such as Montreal, Toronto, Hamilton, Buffalo, Chicago and Duluth expected to cash in on the Seaway and made improvements to best exploit the new opportunities. Even Mississippi drainage city ports such as St. Louis and Kansas City had aspirations of benefiting from Seaway shipping via canals that would connect the Mississippi River to Chicago and the Great Lakes system. The Seaway, however, experienced initial growing pains such that shipping by tonnage in the early years of operation was only 80% of that during the year immediately *preceding* opening.[79] Seagoing ships with crews inexperienced on the Great Lakes, low capacity and slow locks, and loading/offloading facilities at ports that were not necessarily interchangeable between seagoing and lake ships, all contributed to inefficiencies and to accidents. Carlton Mabee recounted in *The Seaway Story* that during the first few months of operation, Seaway shipping was "often in chaos" and that of all the accidents involving major marine casualties on a worldwide basis, about one-third occurred along the Seaway during its first opening weeks.[80] Notwithstanding lower than projected tonnage in the first year (about 18 million tonnes), most points in the system eventually saw significant increases in tonnage from years before the Seaway opened: the Welland Canal (+29%), the St. Lawrence River (+75%) trade increased by between 300% (Cleveland, Toronto) and 1,000% (Rochester). Grain shipments from Chicago increased by 2100% and from Duluth by a staggering 11,000%![81] Indeed, the next 20 years saw, with only a few exceptions, a steady increase in use of the Seaway so that by 1979, in excess of 74 million tonnes passed through the system.[82] Since those heady days, however, use of the Seaway as measured by tonnage has dropped by an average of about 45% to between 35 and 39 million tonnes between 2014 and 2020.[83] Reasons for the decline are varied and include: an increase in tolls, increasing competition from trains, completion of interstate and trans-Canadian highway systems that improved the efficiency of trucking, construction of oil pipelines, and "containerization" – the practice of packing goods in containers that could be efficiently stacked on larger ships and transported on trains and trucks. The efficiency of container packing meant that the larger ships could no longer use the Seaway – a system was built for the 1950–60s, not for the large ocean-going ships of the 2000s. In fact, by 2009 only 10–25% of all ships could enter the Seaway.[84] In current times, the vast majority of Seaway traffic transports bulk cargo: grain, coal, dry bulk (salt, coke and potash) and iron ore.[85] Further, the Act authorizing the Seaway contained a proviso that advertising to promote its use was banned, a proviso championed by opponents of the Seaway. It was not until the early 1970s that this ban was circumvented by public relations efforts and in 2004 the Seaway was rebranded as "HwyH$_2$o."[86] Ironically, the use of the Seaway has declined steadily as one of its major limitations, being icebound for much of the year, was being eased; in 2017 the Seaway set a new record for being open between March 20 and January 11 – 298 days.[87] In summary, Seaway usage after initial growth, and despite improvements to the system (e.g., retrofitting of the Welland Canal in 1986), has consistently not met expectations. Although it punches below its weight, the Seaway does enable trade with 50 overseas nations, has moved almost 2.7 billon tonnes of cargo since 1959, and serves the third largest economy in the world (the sums of the economies of two provinces and eight states). The Great Lakes–St. Lawrence Seaway system generated C$59 billion in economic activity and supported 330,000 direct and indirect jobs in the US and Canada as reported in 2020.[88] By connecting the upper Great Lakes to the Atlantic Ocean to create the Great Lakes-St. Lawrence River Waterway, the Seaway enables economic activity with totals at least three times greater than just within the Seaway system itself (i.e., between Montreal and the Welland Canal area.)[89] Part of the marketing campaign for HwyH$_2$o was to explain the environmental benefits of the Seaway – "a sustainable way to power economic growth."[90] Here, Seaway proponents explain the benefits of Seaway transportation in terms of reducing congestion on highways, using fuels more efficiently and lowering greenhouse gas emissions compared to rail and trucking. Against these potential benefits to Seaway usage, however, must be balanced the arguably catastrophic damage done to natural aquatic ecosystems within the St. Lawrence Seaway and adjacent Great Lakes.

The environmental damage to the Great Lakes–St. Lawrence system from the Seaway construction and operations has occurred in myriad forms. Dam construction and associated reservoir formation ("Lake" St. Lawrence) resulted in destroyed flood-plain wetlands, loss of important habitats for fishes and migratory birds, and elimination of fast-water spawning areas for fishes in and near rapids. The Moses-Saunders Dam disrupted nutrient-loading downstream into Lake St. Francis, impacting fish populations and the fisheries that depend on them. Further, the dam (as well as the Beauharnois Dam 80 km further downstream) created a migratory barrier for fishes moving upstream from Lake St. Francis and the Atlantic Ocean and impacted iconic species such as the American eel (*Anguilla rostrata*). Here, young eels used to be able to move upstream into tributaries of the St. Lawrence River and into Lake Ontario where they grew and matured. Adults, some over a metre long, would then migrate downstream, supporting fisheries, and then to the ocean where they spawned in the Sargasso Sea. While the creation and successful use of fish ladders has facilitated the movement of young fish up and over the dams,[91] adults migrating downstream suffer high mortality as they pass through the 32 propeller-type turbines in the power stations (then another 36 at the Beauharnois Dam) – an estimated 41% of all eels migrating downstream die after passing through both sets of turbines.[92] Although not the only cause, these hydroelectric facilities have been implicated as a factor contributing significantly to the estimated 98% decline of Upper St. Lawrence–Lake Ontario American eels, the largest and farthest-migrating across the species range, since the 1950s.[93] The flow regulation associated with dams and hydroelectric generation also eliminated the natural hydrographic pattern of seasonal flooding, which is important for river nutrient cycling, groundwater recharge, contaminant flushing and providing cues for the seasonal reproductive activities of some aquatic life. Flood control at dam sites in the river proper can also cause extreme flooding in upstream lakeshore habitats, a problem exacerbated by increased precipitation under climate change.[94] Pollution from industries, some that arrived to exploit the power generation at Cornwall and Massena, raised contaminant levels in aquatic and terrestrial environments. The pollution, including so-called "legacy pollutants" that existed before the Seaway was constructed, has been the focus of US "Superfund" cleanup actions, and the area around Cornwall and Massena is designated as an "Area of Concern" in both countries.[95] The use of icebreakers to extend the shipping season disrupted the natural ice cover pattern, altering its seasonal use by migratory animals. The wakes of large ships cause shoreline damage, and dredging channels disturbs contaminated sediments, destroys fish habitat and has permanently lowered water levels in some areas.[96] Notwithstanding the seriousness of these impacts, perhaps the

A pipe clogged with zebra mussels.

most dramatic change to the ecosystem wrought by the Seaway has been its facilitation of the colonization of the St. Lawrence–Great Lakes system by scores of invasive species introduced from ballast water of ocean-going ships. In *Pandora's Locks: The Opening of the Great Lakes–St. Lawrence Seaway,* Jeff Alexander describes the increase of invasive species owing to the opening of the Seaway as a "devastating, chronic illness called biological pollution"[97] resulting from transoceanic ships, each one a potential "Trojan horse."[98] Other vectors for introduction of invasive species are known (e.g., intentional releases, range expansions, recreational boating, aquaculture), but ballast water from shipping has been the major vector.[99]

Perhaps the most notorious of these species is the zebra mussel (*Dreissena polymorpha*), a small bivalve (2–5 cm) native to lakes of southern Russia and Ukraine, including the Black and Caspian seas. In 1988, the mussel was discovered in Lake St. Clair and has since spread from Montreal to Lake Superior (and to many other watersheds, particularly the Mississippi River, in the US). The zebra mussel has proven to be very prolific, which has caused a host of problems:

smothering and outcompeting native mussels; clogging water intake pipes used to supply municipalities and hydroelectric plants; being a source of avian botulism that has killed thousands of birds since the 1990s; altering ecosystem dynamics owing to their high densities and filter feeding, which reduce plankton densities as a food source for other aquatic life; and cluttering shorelines during die-offs.[100]

As if the zebra mussel were not enough, a close relative, the quagga mussel (*D. bugensis*), another Ponto-Caspian hitchhiker on Seaway freighters, was discovered in Lake Erie in 1989. With impacts similar to those of the zebra mussel, the quagga mussel has spread to some watersheds in the western US, including Lake Mead and Lake Powell (Colorado River), and most jurisdictions now have collaborative invasive dreissenid mussel monitoring programs (e.g., see invasivemusselcollaborative.net). Other invaders include fishes (the round goby, *Neogobius melanostomus*, and tubenose goby, *Proterorhinus marmoratus*), amphipods (the scud, *Echinogammarus ischnus*) and water fleas (e.g., the fishhook water flea, *Cercopagis pengoi*). Although in the US, ocean-going vessels have been required to exchange freshwater ballast with high salinity ocean water in the US (Canada did not require such treatment until 2006), this has not proven 100% effective, as even some freshwater species may have high tolerance to sea water. Further, some ships contain sediment in ballast tanks or residual fresh water elsewhere that may contain potentially invasive species.[101] In fact, the scud and fishhook water flea appeared after the 1993 regulations were created. Furthermore, even if ballast water exchange or treatment of ocean-going ships proves effective, interlake shipping may contribute to secondary invasions of established species.[102] Together, these invaders and the dreissenid mussels have been estimated to cost the Great Lakes economy at least US$200 million (and perhaps as much as $800 million) *per year*.[103]

George Santayana, an American 20th-century philosopher and writer, once wrote, "Those who cannot remember the past are condemned to repeat it."[104] This maxim applies to species invading the Great Lakes via the Seaway perhaps as much as it does to politics. Why? Because the earliest and most famous example of an invader into the Great Lakes is the sea lamprey (*Petromyzon marinus*), a parasite fish up to one metre in length that latches onto the sides of other fishes. The sea lamprey uses its circular mouth rimmed with sharp teeth and a bony, boring tongue to feed on the flesh and blood of its hosts, which typically, but not always, kills the latter. The sea lamprey is native to the Atlantic basin, including the St. Lawrence River, the Hudson River and the Finger Lakes area of New York. The sea lamprey may also have been native to eastern Lake Ontario, but was not observed in the lake until 1830. Niagara Falls, at 51 m in height, provided a complete natural migration barrier from Lake Ontario upstream to Lake Erie and the other Great Lakes. The first sea lamprey was observed, however, in Lake Erie in 1921 and may have entered the lake from the Finger Lakes or the Hudson River via the Erie Canal, which connected these areas with Lake Erie after it opened in 1825. Further, the Erie Canal could have allowed movement of sea lamprey into Lake Ontario at the western end, via a side channel of the Erie Canal. Still, it appears to have taken almost 100 years for the sea lamprey to appear in Lake Erie (1921) after the opening of the Erie Canal. Rather, it was the deepening of the Welland Canal, first built in 1829 to bypass Niagara Falls, in 1919 that is most closely associated in time with the appearance of the sea lamprey in Lake Erie.[105] From 1921, it took less than 20 years for the sea lamprey to spread throughout lakes Erie, Michigan, Huron and Superior.[106]

Parasitism by the sea lamprey is thought to have been responsible for the devastating collapse of lake trout (*Salvelinus namaycush*) and large-bodied whitefishes (various *Coregonus* species) that had been the mainstays of Great Lakes fisheries since the 1800s. It has been estimated that when the sea lamprey was at its height in the early 1950s, it killed 45 million kg of fishes annually – *five times* the weight of fishes taken yearly in the commercial fisheries in the upper Great Lakes.[107] Although the Sea Lamprey Control Program, a Canada-US effort run by the Great Lakes Fishery Commission begun in the late 1950s, has reduced sea lamprey abundance by more than 90% and initiated native fishes' restoration programs, sea lamprey control will be an ongoing program and costs at least US$20 million annually.[108] In *Pandora's Locks*, Jeff Alexander described the sea lamprey invasion as a "shot across the bow of all who dared tinker with the natural order of the lakes."[109] It was a lesson from history evidently unheeded, if even considered, by the principals who conceived and constructed the St. Lawrence Seaway, and the costs of that unlearned lesson mount every day. The Seaway project has been described as a classic example of "high modernism"[110] – the idea that scientific and technical knowledge drive progress, continual progress itself is a desired goal, and that nature can and should be controlled to achieve progress. Consequently, almost 500 years after Cartier first explored the St. Lawrence River as a portal to unknown worlds, the Seaway has literally and figuratively cemented the "Empire of the St. Lawrence" as an icon of the post-war North American industrial, social and environmental zeitgeist. The hubris of high modernism, however, has inflicted such huge social and environmental costs on the Great Lakes–St. Lawrence region that the ultimate future of Cartier's dream seems uncertain to all those who have studied the system.[111] Review of financial statements of the agencies that now run the Seaway (the St. Lawrence Seaway Management Corporation in Canada and the now Great Lakes Saint Lawrence Seaway Development Corporation in the US) shows that the Seaway's annual revenues do not always balance operating expenditures and any profits that do occur are dwarfed by "asset renewal expenses" (regular and "major" maintenance, capital expenditures).[112] Increases in global container traffic predicted in the 2007 Great Lakes–St. Lawrence Seaway Study,[113] which the Seaway could exploit, have proven to be optimistic, being about a third of projected,[114] and have trended consistently below expectations. Further, the total annual tonnage passed through the Seaway sections has dropped by about half since the heady days of the 70s (see above) and remained flat over the past ten years.[115] Still, it is undeniable that the Seaway has had major and positive impacts on the Canada–US economy, especially in the Great Lakes–St. Lawrence region,[116] so the real question is: Do these benefits justify the equally undeniable costs of the Seaway, particularly in terms of impacts on the Great Lakes–St. Lawrence ecosystem? Compelling as that question is, it is simply unanswerable, because so much of any answer depends on personal perspectives and values. Rather, solving Creighton's original "problem of the St. Lawrence" has only created other problems, and the future perception of the value of the Seaway will depend critically on striving to eliminate or mitigate its negative impacts on the Great Lakes–St. Lawrence River, an ecosystem encompassing the largest area of lakes on Earth.

— TWELVE —

The Future of North America's Great Rivers

Any river is really the summation of the whole valley. To think
of it as nothing but water is to ignore the greater part.
—HAL BORLAND, *This Hill, This Valley*, 1957

But thou, exulting and abounding river!
Making thy waves a blessing as they flow
Through banks whose beauty would endure for ever,
Could man but leave thy bright creation so
—LORD BYRON, "Childe Harold's Pilgrimage" 1812

Borland's quotation, which opens this chapter, illustrates the "watershed" approach to understanding rivers, which is a primary prerequisite to effecting ecosystem sustainability. The central idea of this approach is that while we often think of land and water as separate entities, rivers and the surrounding landscape are closely intertwined (see Chapter 1). Water flows across, through and within the land. The land supplies structure and nutrients to the flow of rivers. Hence, a watershed is a land area separated from other such areas, that contains flowing water and whose structure funnels and influences the nature of the flow of water (originating as rain, snow and melting ice) through streams, rivers, groundwater and lakes to its ultimate destination – usually the sea. That flow has a feedback effect on the land of a watershed through the processes of weathering and erosion. Consequently, a watershed is an integrated system of land and water that influence each other intimately. This book has argued, using examples from patterns of human migration and settlement, transportation and economic development, artistic expression, origins of biodiversity and its importance to humans, human rights and warfare, that the same reciprocal land–water connection encapsulated in the term *watershed* is applicable to the human experience in North America and the role of great rivers in shaping it. Roy MacGregor in his recent book *Original Highways: Travelling the Great Rivers of Canada*, suggested that the health of rivers was a metaphor for the health of Canadians, as their country is "so inextricably tied – historically, economically and psychologically – to its rivers,"[1] a condition that is clearly applicable to North Americans more generally.

The impacts of North America's great rivers on North Americans are ongoing and highly relevant today; even though the Klondike gold rush and the US Civil War both ended more than 100 years ago, the central role of rivers in these events and their impacts clearly still resonate today. Recall Laurence C. Smith's summary in *Rivers of Power* of the five fundamental benefits that rivers provide to humanity: access, natural capital, well-being, territory and a way to express power.[2] The St. Lawrence River provided access to the North American interior to early explorers. The natural capital of salmon provided by the Fraser River (and many others) has sustained humans for millennia. The Hudson River provided artistic inspiration, appreciation and feelings of well-being (and many readers of this book will have fond memories of finding relief on a hot summer's day in a local river's "swimming hole"). The Rio Grande provides the key territorial boundary between Mexico and the US. The battles for control of the Mississippi River constituted a key power struggle during the US Civil War. These relationships imply that it is not just our past or present experiences, but also our *future* ones, that are tied, inexorably, to North America's great rivers. This chapter explores the future of

North America's great rivers, their prospects for a sustainable future and the implications for North American society.

The current status of North America's great rivers

FROM THE EARLIEST irrigation canals of Indigenous North Americans, to the development of megacities like New York City, the influence of human settlement on rivers has obviously been dramatic. It has been argued that there has been a fundamental shift in the processes that "control" rivers, including rivers of North America, from those once dominated by the Earth's historical and contemporary "system processes" (e.g., climate, glaciation and tectonic processes) to ones dominated now by human impacts – an aspect of the more general concept of the Anthropocene.[3]

Human impacts can be thought of as a series of "syndromes": flow regulation; fragmentation; sedimentation imbalance; extreme flow reduction ('neo-arheism'); acidification; eutrophication; thermal regime regulation; and chemical, radionuclide and biological – including microbial – contamination.[4] These syndromes represent collections of impacts (river diversion, dam and reservoir construction, water quality changes) from a host of human activities (land use changes from agriculture and forestry, mining and energy production, urbanization, industrialization, water management – such as dredging, hydroelectric and storage dam construction – and irrigation), each with many impacts on the morphology, biology, hydrology, and nutrient cycling of rivers.[5] Water supply and quality is connected to environmental, societal and economic risks ranging from biodiversity loss and ecosystem collapse, to food crises and mass human migrations, failures in urban planning, and energy price shocks.[6] Consequently, concern about human impacts on river systems, both on local and global scales, is contained within a more general concern regarding the quantity and quality of global freshwater resources in response to increasing human demands and climate change. For instance, a recent story in *The Atlantic* reported the "loss" of 28,000 rivers in China owing largely to unregulated over-extraction for industry and agriculture.[7] Shrinking glaciers in the "third pole" – the Himalayas – are threatening the supply of water to major rivers and lakes in central and southeast Asia.[8] Past projections of future global water extraction and use that could quadruple may have moderated recently, but they still indicate a general increase to 2080. The increasing demand for fresh water has led to a call for a shift from "hard path" development of water infrastructure (e.g., large-scale dams, reservoirs and canals) to "soft path" development, i.e., development that increasingly relies on smaller-scale decentralized facilities, with the goal of increasing the *productivity* of per unit water use rather than just seeking greater supply.[9] Further, because hundreds of political jurisdictions share at least one transboundary river, concern over supply and development of water from rivers is a significant source of international and intranational conflicts.[10] Such rivers include the Mekong River, Nile River, Jordan River, Indus River and rivers of the Tibetan Plateau's "Water Tower" (mountain ranges that play critical roles in the supply of water for downstream use),[11] and create an urgent need for effective transboundary river governance[12] and "hydro-diplomacy."[13]

Of the great rivers discussed in this book, impacts on the fundamental flow of rivers range from slight to non-existent in the case of the Mackenzie, Yukon and Fraser rivers, which flow essentially unimpeded to the sea, to the virtual strangulation of flow to the sea in the Colorado River and the Rio Grande due to water extraction and the development of dams. These high-level differences are reflected in the relative vulnerability of the 13 major water tower units (mountain ranges and their associated river basins) in North America. There is a strong inverse relationship between the *demand* for water, by humans from irrigation, industry and domestic use, and by Nature from natural water demand – an estimate of the amount of water required to sustain ecosystems – and natural water *supply* by the associated water tower unit (from glaciers, precipitation, lakes and snowpack). Those rivers with the highest demand (Rio Grande, Colorado, Sacramento–San Joaquin, Columbia and Missouri–Mississippi) also tend to have the least supply and are, therefore, the most vulnerable.[14] By contrast, the Mackenzie, Fraser and Yukon basins currently have relatively low demand and relatively large supply. These latter rivers (in addition to the Columbia and the Colorado rivers) were, however, rated among the most susceptible to future vulnerability owing to climate change, increasing demands and governance issues.[15] Similarly, impacts on overall water quality range from slight and localized in vast drainages such as the Yukon and Mackenzie rivers, to widespread and continuing problems with chemical pollution from a legacy of polychlorinated biphenyl (PCB) dumping in the early 1900s in the much smaller Hudson River.[16]

A detailed assessment of the condition (biological, chemical and physical) of each of the rivers in this book is problematic given their vast geography, because large rivers are inherently difficult to study, and directly comparable national assessment schemes are underdeveloped. A general sense of the current state and key threats to North America's great rivers can, however, be gleaned from water quality reports from agencies such as Environment and Climate Change Canada, the US Environmental Protection Agency and the US Geological Survey,[17] and general assessments such as the World Wildlife Fund's (Canada) *Watershed Reports* and American Rivers' *America's Most Endangered Rivers* reports. Virtually all the great rivers are currently, or potentially, threatened by the factors discussed below, but I highlight only the most urgent or current issues in each case.

The St. Lawrence River was included in the number nine spot in American Rivers, 2016 list of the ten most endangered rivers.[18] American Rivers cited "harmful dam operations" based on rationales developed in the 1950s when the interests of coastal and riverine ecosystems "were not considered."[19] Key issues were operations of the Moses-Saunders and Long Sault hydroelectric dams that altered the natural hydrological regime in terms of seasonal changes in flow levels (see Chapter 11). Power level generation at the dams influences the outflow from Lake Ontario and thus the lake's water levels, as well as water levels downstream of the dam site on the river. In essence the hydrograph was compressed to reduce the range in water levels and thus produce a more consistent level of power, but also to facilitate transportation along the Seaway and to protect shoreline properties.[20] In 2006, the International Joint Commission concluded, in part, that the original and modified operations' plans had caused significant damage to wetland and coastal habitats.[21] After several years of study and consultation, a new operations plan, Plan 2014, was developed and approved by Canada and the US in 2016. Here, a greater range of water levels will be generated through planned water releases, following prescribed "release rules" to better simulate natural flow regimes, which should improve habitats for coastal and wetland fish and wildlife in the upper river and in Lake Ontario.[22] The best-laid aims of Plan 2014, however, are running into difficulties in trying to balance the needs of power generation, flow control for shipping and its economic implications, and flood management for the needs of biodiversity and shoreline property owners.[23]

With a current human population of about 30 million people[24] and its status as one of the two epicentres of early European colonization of the US and Canada (the other being the eastern seaboard), it comes as no surprise that although conditions have improved over the past 50 years with the growth of the environmental movement and initiatives such as the US Clean Water Act (1972) and the Canada Water Act (1985), the St. Lawrence River system (including the Great Lakes) continues to suffer from a number of abuses from industrialization and urbanization. Two stand out: pollution and invasive species. The WWF–Canada Watershed Report lists the St. Lawrence River as Fair in terms of Overall Health and Moderate in terms of Overall Threats, with pollution, habitat loss and habitat fragmentation being the greatest issues. The Great Lakes were Data Deficient in terms of Overall Health, but Very High in terms of Overall Threats (pollution, habitat fragmentation, habitat loss, overuse of water and invasive species were all rated as Very High). In the US, there are 22 environmental "Areas of Concern" (AOC), defined as geographic areas "where significant impairment of beneficial uses has occurred from human activities at the local level. An AOC is a location that has experienced environmental degradation."[25] Such degradation may be in the form of chemical, physical and/or biological impairments to the Great Lakes ecosystem.[26] Several AOCs have been delisted owing to recovery efforts. One AOC exists at Massena, NY, in the St. Lawrence River owing to significant pollution from various sources, and remedial actions that began in the early 1990s are ongoing.[27]

As introduced in Chapter 11, invasive species are a major legacy of the St. Lawrence Seaway project. More than 180 documented invasive species in the Great Lakes–St. Lawrence River have "severely damaged" their ecosystems[28] and cost the region billions of dollars in control, remediation and lost opportunities since the Seaway opened.[29] Although initiatives such as the Sea Lamprey Control Program of the Great Lakes Fishery Commission and changes to ballast water regulations have had some success, new threats are always at the doorstep. For instance, there is considerable angst throughout the watershed about the threat of invasion by "Asian carp" (an assemblage of four species native to Asia). All four species of carp can grow to over 45 kg. They are voracious predators on aquatic invertebrates or feed on aquatic plants. These fishes, originally imported to the southeastern US to control pests in aquacultural settings, escaped into the Mississippi River, which they have rapidly colonized. Two species, the bighead carp and silver carp, are found in the upper Illinois River, a tributary to the Mississippi River, and thus within 50 km of Lake Michigan. The Illinois River, once part of a drainage basin separate from the Great Lakes, is now connected to Lake Michigan after the Chicago Sanitary and Ship Canal was constructed in 1900 to reverse the flow of the Chicago River. Instead of flowing into Lake Michigan, the canal allowed the Chicago River to flow into the Des Plaines River, a tributary of the Illinois River, now a source of Asian carp. Should these Asian carp breach various barriers installed in the canal (e.g., electrical fences) and enter and colonize the Great Lakes, they would pose a major threat to the Great Lakes–St. Lawrence River ecosystem through competition with native fishes and/or habitat disruption.[30]

The Hudson River was ranked as the second most at risk in America in 2019 by American Rivers.[31] It has been the focus of environmental concerns since it first became channelized and dredged in the early 19th century. Industrial pollution in the mid-20th century, especially long-lasting PCBs, has resulted in restrictions on commercial and recreational fisheries throughout much of the river and the designation of part of the river as a US Federal Superfund cleanup site. While remediation continues, and water quality improves, the basis for the American Rivers designation concerned potential changes to the river wrought by efforts to mitigate extreme weather events and flooding caused by sea level rise induced by climate change. Proposed mitigation strategies by the US Army Corps of Engineers involve massive sea-based barriers to protect against storm surges (as experienced during 2012's Hurricane Sandy). These in-sea barriers may hinder fish migrations and tidal exchange essential for effective water, nutrient and oxygen flow and contaminant flushing in the 250 km estuary, reducing the capacity of the estuary to act as the "lungs" of the river system. Land-based barriers or flow directors may be a better option, especially as sea-level rise expected under climate change may eventually overwhelm the sea-based barriers.

A portion of the Mississippi River, the mainstem upstream of its confluence with the Ohio River, is ranked No. 1 on the list of America's ten most endangered rivers for 2020. The major risk to the Mississippi, and adjacent portions of the river, involves the raising of (unpermitted) flood control levees to deal with increasing threat from floods induced by extreme rain events. The levees sever the natural links between the river and the flood plain, which leads to habitat degradation (from the prevention of flood plain inundation in the levee area and increased surge flooding in downstream areas that receive the levee-shunted floodwaters).[32] American Rivers called for more coordinated "nature-based" flood control solutions such as increasing wetland area, flood plain restoration and increasing the distance that the levees are set back from the river to better absorb passing floodwaters.[33] The overreliance on levees is an example of the general problem of flood plain restoration in much of the Mississippi River Valley. The Mississippi River Alluvial Valley (from Cairo, Illinois, to the Gulf of Mexico) has lost about 72% of its original hardwood forest area since post-Contact settlement. Various voluntary programs for landowners to manage their lands for the benefit of forest and wetland recovery have been developed and have generated some successes; e.g., a wetlands reserve program (WRP) developed by the USDA recovered about 3% of these lost wetland areas and is now part of a more general land easements program of the USDA.[34] In 2010, the Mississippi River was found to be the second most polluted river in the US (one of its major tributaries, the Ohio River, ranked No. 1, and another, the Missouri River, ranked 7th) based on the total weight of various toxins released into the river.[35] In 2016, a "State of the River Report" co-sponsored by the US National Park Service found that while conditions in a portion of the river (805 km of the upper Mississippi River centred on the Twin Cities area) have improved over the last several decades, major water quality issues remain from agricultural runoff (nitrates and phosphorus), increasing water flow (leading to increased sedimentation and flooding) and increased bacterial loads.[36] The excessive nutrient loads in the Mississippi River have far-reaching impacts, such as being the major cause of the 20,277 km^2 hypoxic "dead zone" in the Gulf of Mexico.[37]

The Rio Grande faces that most existential threat to any river – a lack of water. In 2007, the World Wildlife Fund issued a report that listed the Rio Grande as one of the ten most threatened rivers in the world, citing water diversions, flood plain alteration, dams and pollution as the drivers of its poor status.[38] According to the Rio Grande International Study Center based in Laredo, Texas, the Rio Grande remains today as imperilled as cited in 2007.[39] Irrigation for agriculture uses about 80% of the water in the Rio Grande. Other uses for industry located along the Mexican side of the border (the "maquiladoras" or export assembly plants that proliferated after the 1994 North American Free Trade Agreement), energy extraction (fracking) and urbanization along both sides of the border result in the Rio Grande being an "over-allocated" river – the demand for water exceeds its supply. The over-allocation problem is exacerbated by the fact that the Rio Grande is susceptible to multi-year droughts and because invasive species such as salt cedar (various species of *Tamarix*) outcompete native plants and use more water than native plants.[40] Water supply stress is so bad that the river typically disappears downstream of Presidio, Texas (e.g., *zero* cubic metres per second on Oct. 20, 2020)[41] before the Rio Conchos flowing eastward from Mexico restores some flow. Further, pollution from industrial waste, salinity from agricultural runoff, and raw sewage remain major contributors to the very poor water quality of much of the Rio

Grande, a problem heightened by differing water quality standards and monitoring programs across several states and two countries.[42] Finally, American Rivers listed the lower Rio Grande as the fourth most endangered river in America in 2018, owing not to the usual suspects listed above but rather to an extension of the border wall being constructed between the US and Mexico. Here, the 50 km of new border wall approved by Congress will separate the river from its flood plain, compromising natural hydrological processes and the wildlife that depends on them. Further, border wall construction is immune from environmental regulations under the Homeland Security Act (2002).[43]

The Colorado River is perhaps the "poster child" for degradation and threats to the very existence of a river from dam and water diversion construction and the over-allocation of water.[44] More than 100 dams are found in the watershed and new ones are planned in the upper basin.[45] The river has been so transformed that 99.6% of the seasonal variability in surface-water storage is driven by reservoirs in the basin (compared to 19.7% for the Yukon River and 2% for the Mackenzie River).[46] The river also has the dubious distinction of running completely dry before it reaches its former delta in the Gulf of California. Drought conditions in the southwest US for much of the 2000s have resulted in further stress on water supply, so much so that Lake Mead, created by Hoover Dam, has not achieved its standard volume, "full pool," since the early 1980s. In May 2016, the lake reached only about 40% storage capacity,[47] and several new records for low water levels were set in the 2010–2016 period, threatening water supply to more than 20 million people across California, Arizona, Nevada and Mexico. Water levels rebounded to 88% of full pool in August 2020, but the threats to water supply are serious enough that US$1.5 billion was spent to construct a new, lower intake pipe (at 256 m, 61 m lower than the original intake level) – the so-called "third straw" – to ensure water supply for Las Vegas.[48] Any climate changes increasing the frequency or severity of drought conditions (see below) could create conditions of the dreaded "dead pool" – a water level so low that no water can be delivered from Lake Mead to California or Arizona.[49] One analysis projected that any climate change–induced increases in precipitation will not compensate for warming-based drying in the basin and concluded that "an increasing risk of severe water shortages is expected."[50] Demands for Colorado River water by California could increase and place further stress on the system should another major source of water for California, the Sacramento–San Joaquin system, become compromised by environmental changes in its delta (see below).[51] Poor water quality in portions of the basin from agricultural runoff–based salinity increases (especially in the lower river[52]) and contaminants (mercury in the Grand Canyon; radioactive waste in Lake Powell) are also significant concerns for the river.[53] Finally, invasive species threaten unique ecosystems in the Colorado River that have evolved as a function of the basin's isolation over millions of years and distinctive environmental conditions. For instance, although the Colorado River has a relatively low number of native species of freshwater fishes (32), compared to the 13 other freshwater provinces in North America, it has the largest percentage (69%) that are endemic (found nowhere else), e.g., the humpback chub (*Gila cypha*), bonytail chub (*G. elegans*) and razorback sucker (*Xyrauchen texanus*).[54] Invasive species, introduced for sport fishing opportunities facilitated by dam-related hydrological and water temperature changes, such as rainbow trout (*Oncorhynchus mykiss*) and brown trout (*Salmo trutta*), endanger these native fishes through predation and competitive displacement. Invasive quagga mussels (*Dreissena rostriformis "bugensis"*) native to Europe were discovered in Lake Mead in 2007. They form huge concentrations and there is an active program to combat their debilitating impacts on water delivery (e.g., by clogging intake pipes). Plants of the genus *Tamarix* pose similar threats to the Colorado River habitats and water supply as described for the Rio Grande.[55]

The Sacramento–San Joaquin River Delta is the largest estuary on the North American Pacific coast. The estuary is where the rivers' fresh water mixes with the saline water of San Francisco Bay. The distribution of the resultant "brackish" water in the estuary is a balance of the outward flow of fresh water and the inflow from the sea. When freshwater flows are low (owing to drought and/or high allocation for human use) the low-salinity area shrinks, and higher salinity saltwater intrudes into the delta. Such salt water intrusion compromises habitat for aquatic species with low salinity tolerance (e.g., the endangered delta smelt – see Chapter 7), and the quality of fresh water pumped from the southeastern end of the delta used for irrigation of crops.

As described in Chapter 7, the delta contributes to the massive agricultural output of California's Central Valley both in terms of agricultural lands within the delta and the fresh water that is supplied to areas farther south. These critical areas of the delta are protected from flooding by sea water by levees. The delta area faces significant threats to its very existence as a diverse habitat and as working land, owing to flaws in existing water management and proposals to address these flaws. For instance, owing to sinking of the land, many of these delta lands are 4.6 m below the levels of the rivers (which are at sea level). Any collapse of the levees (e.g., from storm surges or an earthquake) would inundate these lands with saline water, rendering them useless for agriculture. Further, two major freshwater pumping stations are located at the south end of the delta, and flooding of the delta area by the Sacramento–San Joaquin rivers would weaken the freshwater "push" against the sea and allow saline water to flood areas served by the pumps.[56] This issue has led to a plan to install two giant water tunnels at the north end of the delta just south of Sacramento and pump water underground some 49 km south to the existing pumping stations of the State Water Project and the Central Valley Project for use in the western San Joaquin River valley and southern California. This proposal has been estimated to cost US$23–$25 billion dollars and has been labelled as the "California WaterFix." Needless to say, the plan has met stiff opposition from those concerned about the costs[57] (it would be the most expensive water project in the history of California, with costs estimated at four times potential benefits). Others are concerned about construction-based habitat losses, potential huge removals of water from the delta and resultant impacts on habitat of several threatened species of Pacific salmon, white and green sturgeon (*Acipenser transmontanus* and *A. medirostris*), and smelt,[58] and reduced water quality supplied to agricultural and municipal water users (including the city of Stockton). The plan would also result in ancillary changes to the watershed far removed from the tunnels that impact water supply to the delta, e.g., a proposal to raise Shasta Dam by 5.5 m on the upper Sacramento River and the construction of a new dam (Temperance Flat Dam) on the upper San Joaquin River. The proposed Temperance Flat Dam would reduce flows further in the San Joaquin, a river that already typically dries up near Fresno, CA, and eliminate significant environmental and cultural values.[59] American Rivers listed the San Joaquin as the most endangered river in 2014 (and second most in 2016) owing to poor and outdated water management.[60] A new dam to store water for agricultural use is unlikely to improve matters. Elevated salinity from agricultural runoff, pollution from fertilizers, pesticides and municipal wastes, and mercury contamination in the Sacramento River as a legacy of the California Gold Rush, plague parts of the system. Water quality is generally considered to be poorest in the lower San Joaquin River.

The Columbia River Treaty (1961) between Canada and the US was an agreement on construction and operation of four dams (three in Canada, one in the US) on the upper Columba River to generate benefits related to water storage for hydropower generation and for flood control (see Chapter 5). The treaty terminates in 2024, but negotiations to update the treaty began in May 2018. There are two major changes to the negotiations compared to those that led to the original treaty. First, in 2015 the US announced that in addition to hydropower development and flood control, "ecosystem function" would be added as a third pillar of the treaty.[61] For instance, dam construction and operation have either completely blocked or impeded migrations of Pacific salmon and steelhead trout throughout the basin (and eliminated all runs upstream of Grand Coulee Dam – a pre-treaty dam). The impacts on salmon runs extend beyond the fish themselves; Indigenous Peoples of both countries revered, exploited and depended on many of these runs for centuries, and reduction or loss of spawning salmon has resulted in the reduction or loss of marine-derived nutrients to aquatic and terrestrial ecosystems.[62] While restoration and recovery of salmon runs is a key component of restoring ecosystem function, there are many other potential benefits of an explicit ecosystem perspective of dam operation: restoring natural hydrographs (seasonal flow patterns), water temperature management, restoring flood plain connectivity and wetlands, and managing the Columbia River plume to improve nearshore ocean conditions as a function of the plume.[63] Second, in April 2019 Canada announced that three First Nations (the Ktunaxa, Syilx/Okanagan and Secwepemc Nations) will officially participate in the negotiations as observers in addition to their key role in helping to frame Canada's positions during consultations outside the formal negotiations.[64] Canada's inclusion of First Nations as observers is an important acknowledgement of the rights of Indigenous title holders and the past and current impacts of the Columbia River Treaty on their communities and should promote implementation of ecosystem functionality as an important aspect of a renewed treaty as proposed by the US (including Indigenous groups). Given that Indigenous rights or perspectives and biodiversity values were absent from the original treaty, a successfully updated treaty will hopefully reflect a significant change from managing the Columbia River as simply a "hydraulic machine" to that of a still working, but better functioning *watershed* and serve as a "model of international water management."[65] More generally, there are also encouraging signs that the dams vs. the environment divisions are being bridged through *joint* efforts of industry and environmental groups to promote renewable hydropower while minimizing the negative ecological impacts of dams and removing dams that are no longer needed.[66]

The WWF-Canada *Watershed Reports* rates 25 of Canada's major watersheds in terms of "Overall Health" and the "Overall Threats" they face. Overall Health is based on data from a combination of four metrics measured at a series of sites: water flow, water quality, fish biodiversity and invertebrate biodiversity. Overall Threats are a compilation of seven factors: pollution, habitat loss, habitat fragmentation, overuse of water, invasive species, climate change and alteration of flows.[67] The Overall Health ratings range from Data Deficient, to Very Good, Good, Fair, and Poor to Very Poor. The Overall Threats ratings range from Unknown, to No Threat, Very

Low, Low, Moderate, High and Very High. The Canadian portion of the Columbia River received a rating of Very Good for Overall Health (but water quality was Data Deficient) and an Overall Threats rating of Very High (with invasive species, alteration of flow, habitat fragmentation and pollution all being High or Very High). Similar issues with contaminants and the impacts of impoundments and flow regulation from the Columbia River's 11 mainstem dams in the US characterize that portion of the river.[68]

The canyon, middle, and upper reaches of the Fraser River remain largely remote, relatively wild, and are unimpounded. Where the river undergoes a dramatic geographical change as it spills out from the narrow confines of the Fraser Canyon to the broad alluvial flood plain of the lower Fraser Valley, however, has been heavily impacted. From the exit of the canyon, the lower 150 km of the river consists of three major parts: a 50 km long multi-channel stretch of gravel-cobble beginning downstream of the canyon section, a subsequent single channel 65 km sand-bed section, and finally a 35 km long braided delta region.[69] The gravel-cobble section is known locally as "the gravel reach" and has been described as the signature portion of the Fraser River that defines it in the public eye, much as the confluence of the "blackwater" Rio Negro and the "whitewater" Amazon River does for the latter or as the Three Gorges, before being largely impounded, once did for the Yangtze River. Consequently, the gravel reach area of the Fraser River has been referred to as the "Heart of the Fraser" for its stunning beauty within a lush, expansive valley rimmed by mountains, but also for its rich geological, historical, biological and cultural value.[70]

One of the key drivers of the biological productivity of the area (and the rich history and Indigenous cultures that developed there, in large part based on this productivity) is the seasonal flooding during the late spring–early summer period that characterizes the annual hydrological cycle of the river. The seasonal flooding (which may raise water levels in the Fraser canyon by 20–30 m and in the lower valley by 3–4 m)[71] also provides the materials from erosion across the watershed (comprising about 25% by area of the province of British Columbia) and the power to deliver and redistribute these materials along the gravel reach. Consequently, the river's floods repeatedly create, destroy, re-create and reconfigure the varied habitats of islands, bars, channels and sloughs consisting of various sizes of substrates (gravels, cobbles, silt, clay, sand) within the reach. The diversity of habitats created in the flood plain and within the reach itself by these processes creates abundant opportunities for various plants and animals to thrive in the area.

As described in Chapter 4, the lower Fraser Valley attracted rapid colonization and development by Europeans after the mid-1800s. Diking and draining for agriculture and flood protection has isolated or eliminated much of the flood plain and perhaps as much as 85% of wetland areas have been lost to development.[72] Also, the lower Fraser Valley is adjacent to Metro Vancouver, with a population of 2.7 million people that has been projected to grow to 3.9 million (a 40% increase) by the early 2040s.[73] Thus, while the majority of degradation of the gravel reach area occurred by the mid-1900s, the pressures of seemingly unrelenting growth and development on what remains, continues. The lower river and its remaining ribbon of riparian habitat, however, is an important counterweight to the increasing urbanization of the area and still provides abundant aesthetic, biological and recreational value. Consequently, as Michael Church, professor emeritus of the UBC Department of Geography, has succinctly noted, the lower river is "caught in a classic problem posed by the opposition of social development and environmental stewardship."[74] These pressures have motivated initiatives such as "Defend the Heart of the Fraser" to oppose specific developments and to promote biodiversity values as the basis for inclusive management of the area.[75] Gravel and sand mining in and adjacent to the river bed, boat navigation and associated dredging, forestry on gravel reach islands, agriculture, flood control infrastructure and property development all continue to pressure habitat in the Heart of the Fraser.[76] The WWF-Canada *Watershed Reports* rates the Fraser River's Overall Health as Fair, with the upper Fraser rated as Good and the middle and lower Fraser as Fair; water flow and poor water quality were the largest issues. Overall Threats were rated as High throughout the basin, driven largely by pollution, habitat fragmentation and habitat loss. The Alexandria (?Esdilagh) First Nation in the BC interior has recently adopted its own historic Elhdaqox Dechen Ts'edilhtan (Sturgeon River Law), which will require "free, prior and informed consent"[77] for any future developments on the river to address what it feels are excessive problems with pollution.

The Yukon River is perhaps unique among all the great rivers of North America in that it currently experiences no major threat to its fundamental structure or function, or to any major section of the vast watershed (but see below).[78] Its Overall Heath status was assessed as Good and Overall Threats as Low for the Canadian portion of the river in the WWF-Canada report,[79] but there were some concerns in the headwater areas owing to habitat loss from forestry and mining operations (see Chapter 3).[80]

In the past, schemes such as large-scale water diversions to the southwest US, or massive dams, have been contemplated or planned for the Yukon River, but have died for various reasons. For instance, the Rampart Dam 169 km northwest of Fairbanks, Alaska, was proposed in the mid-1950s and would have created a reservoir almost as large as Lake Erie and virtually wiped out one of North America's largest wetland areas – the Yukon Flats – of great significance to myriad species of fish and wildlife.[81] Further, there are several more local environmental and land use issues in the Yukon River basin. For instance, there are disturbing reports of greater than expected (based on watershed size) mercury contamination speculated to result from permafrost melting owing to climate change and the Yukon River's placement as a catchment for pollution from Europe and Asia.[82] Finally, in a recent assessment of global major transboundary rivers, the Yukon River was assessed as being in the top risk category ("Very High") in terms of international governance. This high-risk status was owing to the absence of a legal framework based on the key principles of international water law, which compromises basinwide management.[83] By contrast, the Rio Grande, Mississippi, Colorado, St. Lawrence, Fraser and Columbia rivers were all ranked in the second lowest risk category ("Low") in terms of legal frameworks relevant to international governance.[84]

The Mackenzie River proper (i.e., that section beginning at the outlet of Great Slave Lake) has an Overall Heath rating of Data Deficient, and an Overall Threats rating of Low according to the WWF-Canada report, but ratings for some sub-watersheds (e.g., Laird River, Hay River, Peel River and Beaufort Sea, Peace-Athabasca rivers) ranged from Poor to Fair, Very Good and Data Deficient across both categories, indicating the complexity of assigning an overall rating to a vast watershed (20% of the area of Canada). Much like the Yukon River, the Mackenzie River at present faces no existential threat to its integrity as a functioning watershed (but impacts of a potential future energy corridor will always be present – see Chapter 2). That said, its two primary headwater drainages, the Peace and Athabasca rivers, face major issues in terms of dams and impoundments and industrial development and pollution.

In the Peace River, the "Site C" hydroelectric dam was approved for construction by the British Columbia government in 2014. The 60 m high dam will create a reservoir of 9330 ha, generate 5,1000 GWh of electricity annually, flood about 80 km of the Peace River Valley, and cost anywhere from C\$9 billion to at least C\$12 billion. The Site C Dam is the third dam on the mainstem Peace River in British Columbia; the W.A.C. Bennett Dam, 106 km upstream of Site C, was completed in 1968, and the Peace Canyon Dam, 83 km upstream of Site C, was completed in 1980. The Site C Dam remains controversial for several reasons. Three Canadian First Nations voiced concerns and launched lawsuits under the assertion that the dam violates established treaty rights and because such developments can have deleterious impacts on local First Nations, as is acknowledged widely for the W.A.C. Bennett Dam project. The high cost of the project has been criticized, especially when many felt that the case for increased electrical demand was poorly demonstrated and alternative sources for electricity were not adequately evaluated (e.g., geothermal, wind, potential gains from the renegotiated Columbia River Treaty). The project will result in the loss of some high-quality agricultural land that will be flooded. There are also impacts on fish and wildlife from conversion of the river to a reservoir, and cumulative impacts from the construction of a third dam and reservoir on the river. The two other dams on the Peace River have had substantial negative impacts on the Peace-Athabasca Delta (downstream of the dams where the Peace River merges with the Slave River at Lake Athabasca). The delta is a UN World Heritage Site and part of Canada's largest national park, Wood Buffalo National Park. The delta has massive ecological significance, with rich plant and animal biodiversity (including one of the largest herds of free-ranging bison) and is a critical staging ground for migratory birds on their way to and from the Arctic (some 400,000 to 1,000,000 annually).[85] Dams on the Peace River, however, have reduced flows into the delta by between 15% and 70%, resulting in subsidence of so-called "perched" wetlands, reduced flushing of toxins, and the loss of about 50% of all wetland areas, which dried out and were replaced by woody plants – with negative impacts on fish and wildlife dependent on aquatic habitat. Reservoir formation increased methyl mercury contamination in fish as the decaying vegetation and flooded soils promoted bacterial conversion of mercury (from natural and human sources) to methyl mercury.[86] The natural seasonal flow pattern of the Peace River (high in spring-summer, low in winter) has been reversed by dam operations, resulting in a series of changes to the ecosystem. These changes range from water drawdown in reservoirs and exposure of beaver lodges, increased dust storms from exposed muddy foreshores, to increased downstream winter flows that have decreased ice formation and ice jams, which were important drivers of flooding that replenished the flood plain and delta in the spring. How a third dam on the Peace River (Site C) might exacerbate these problems for the delta is unknown, but a Joint Review Panel appointed by the governments of Canada and British Columbia concluded that the project will have no "measurable" impacts on the delta.[87]

The delta's other major input comes from the outflow of the Athabasca River into Lake Athabasca just southeast of where the Peace/Slave rivers enter the lake. As detailed in Chapter 2, most of the lower half of the Athabasca River cuts right through the massive Athabasca Oil Sands deposit and its associated extraction and initial processing infrastructure. Such infrastructure includes 19 tailings ponds adjacent to the river consisting of "process affected water" containing myriad chemicals at elevated concentrations that can prove toxic. These chemicals include inorganic substances such as sodium, sulphates and ammonia, organics such as phenols, bitumen, benzene and toluene, and heavy metals such as cadmium, zinc, arsenic and lead, many at concentrations that are toxic to fishes and birds.[88] These contaminated waters cover an area up to 220 km²,[89] contain an estimated 1.18 trillion litres of material, and continue to grow. Although the Alberta government has stepped up regulations, and efforts to clean up and reclaim the ponds are ongoing, enforcement appears weak, and the tailing ponds leach up to millions of litres per day, contaminating lands, water, fish and wildlife (often consumed by humans) up to 200 km downstream at Lake Athabasca. A breach of barriers between the ponds and the river is a major potential threat to areas farther downstream in the Mackenzie River mainstem.[90] Further, 50 years of oil sands exploitation has resulted in atmospheric transport of chemicals from processing that have led to elevated levels of toxic chemicals such as polycyclic aromatic hydrocarbons in lake sediments up to 90 km from specific sources.[91] The WWF-Canada *Watershed Reports* rates water quality in these regions of the Athabasca River as only Fair. Further, habitat loss of flood plains and wetlands amounting to more than 65,000 ha has occurred as of 2008 from construction of tailings ponds, pits and infrastructure. Given that Canada's National Energy Board projects a 50% increase in oil sands production and a 30% increase in natural gas production to 2040 under a variety of scenarios, the environmental issues connected with such production and the drive for solutions will only become more pressing.[92]

Climate change as the common threat

AS SUMMARIZED ABOVE, each of our great rivers of North America faces a combination of threats shared to varying degrees in terms of scope, intensity and time frame driven by their unique geographies and histories. One overriding challenge broadly shared by all rivers, however, is climate change – specifically, global warming. By global warming, I refer to the well-documented increase in *globally averaged*, combined surface land and ocean temperature of the Earth since 1880 (average of about 0.85°C[93]) and associated changes in precipitation, ocean salinity and pH, sea-ice coverage, snowpack, drought frequency and magnitude, and glacier mass.[94] The principal supply of water for rivers is runoff from precipitation, rain and snow (snowfall and water from snowmelt). Thus, changes in precipitation associated with warming-driven climate changes will profoundly affect the magnitude and pattern of river flow. This is critical for all the rivers discussed in this book, because their water supply is dominated by melting snow and ice, and the greatest changes to the hydrological cycle from warming are predicted to be in snow-dominated regions of mid- and high latitudes.[95] Long-term records demonstrate that snowpack in the Western Cordillera has declined since at least the 1950s and is projected to decline further in the 21st century.[96] Further, precipitation that does occur is increasingly in the form of rain, which can drive snowmelt and associated runoff to occur earlier in the spring.[97] Earlier timing of runoff could threaten water supplies later in the summer and fall for rivers with inadequate storage capacity and create greater conflicts between competing demands for water in different seasons (e.g., hydropower, irrigation, fish habitat, shipping).

Climate change projections for different areas of North America are based on a set of so-called representative concentration pathway (RCP) scenarios that have been adopted by the Intergovernmental Panel on Climate Change (ICCP). The RCPs are projections based on a range of possible human-caused greenhouse gas emission levels that are themselves based on various socio-economic conditions.[98] These scenarios combine the impacts of physical Earth systems (oceans, atmosphere, land and ice) with human activities on climate.[99] Greenhouse gases are those such as carbon dioxide and methane that cause atmospheric warming. These scenarios represent the best summary of the potential range of effects of greenhouse gases, other human-origin pollutants, and land-use changes on the global climate and are based on the work of various research groups using specific protocols as described in various reports of the most recent 2014 IPCC Assessment.[100] Climate change projections and the levels of uncertainty based on these protocols have been developed by national agencies such as Natural Resources Canada, Environment and Climate Change Canada, the US Department of Agriculture, and the US Global Change Research Program (USGCRP).

The resulting four RCPs are: RCP2.6 – a global mean surface temperature increase of less than 2.0°C by 2100 (a low scenario); RCP4.5 – an increase of 2.0°C to 3.0°C by 2100 (an intermediate scenario); RCP6.0 – and increase of less than 3.5°C by 2100 (also an intermediate scenario); and RCP8.5 – an increase up to 5°C to 2100 (a high scenario).[101] The low emission RCP2.6 scenario requires that greenhouse gas emissions start to decline in 2020 and reach *zero* by 2080. The intermediate scenarios, RCP4.5 and RCP6.0, require that greenhouse gases start to decline by 2045 and 2080, respectively, and the RCP8.5 scenario assumes continued growth in greenhouse gas emissions that approach a plateau near 2100.[102] The resulting projections are expressed for time periods in the mid-21st century (e.g., 2031–2050 when results of the emission scenarios described above differ little) and late 21st century (e.g., 2081–2100 when emission scenarios diverge considerably) and represent changes relative to a reference period in the recent past (e.g., 1986–2005).

Before giving a basic description of projected climate changes based on RCPs, two caveats should be mentioned. First, there is variation among projections depending on the metric (annual vs. seasonal maximum or minimum temperature), the region investigated, and the inherent uncertainty of climate change modelling. Second, the rivers of this book encompass large areas, and model projections are generally presented on a grid scale (100–200 km) larger than relevant to regional climate projections (~10 km).[103] Consequently, there will be considerable spatial variation in climate and climate change within and across watersheds spanning tens of thousands to millions of square kilometres and with distinct topographies. There are, however, some broadly consistent trends that emerge from what might best be characterized as the "family" of global climate models. The trends below come from considering results from the US Global Change Research Program, Natural

Resources Canada's Changing Climate Program and the US Bureau of Reclamation's climate change assessments, each of which presents their results in slightly different ways. In general, scenario projections typically suggest that warming will be greatest in northern Canada and in Arctic/subarctic regions of Canada and the US. This includes areas encompassing much of the Mackenzie and Yukon river basins and suggests a range of a 1.0–4.0°C increase in average daily temperature during winter (December–February) for RCP2.6 to up to a 5°C increase for RCP8.5 by the mid-21st century. Average daily summer (June–August) temperature were projected to increase by 1.0–1.5°C for RCP2.6 and up to a 3°C increase for RCP8.5 by the mid-21st century.[104] For regions encompassing other rivers in this book, potential temperature increases were generally less pronounced and ranged from 0.5–2.0°C (RCP2.6) to 1.5–3.0°C (RCP8.5) in the winter and from 1.0–2.0°C (RCP2.6) to 1.5–3.0°C (RCP8.5) in the summer by the mid-21st century.

Projected changes during the mid-21st century to 2100 period remained similar for RCP2.6 for both seasons, but increased markedly in RCP8.5 to a 4–11°C increase in winter and 4–7°C in summer for large areas of the Mackenzie and Yukon basins.[105] Projected temperature increases during the mid-21st century to 2100 period for the areas encompassing the other rivers treated in this book ranged from 1.0–2.0°C (RCP2.6) to 4.0–7.0°C (RCP8.5) in the winter; and 1.0–1.5°C (RCP2.6) to 3.0–7.0°C (RCP8.5) in summer.[106]

Precipitation (expressed as percentage change) was projected to increase in most areas during the winter months, with greater increases in the northwest Arctic and subarctic and ranged from a 0–10% increase in most areas of North America under either RCP2.6 or RCP8.5 by the mid-21st century. The northwest Arctic and subarctic as well as the Great Lakes region, however, had a much higher area projected to increase between 10–20% under RCP8.5. By contrast, most regions encompassing rivers other than the Mackenzie and Yukon were projected to see a mix of increased (up to 10%) to decreased (as low as −10%) precipitation by the mid-21st century, with a greater extent of declining precipitation under RCP8.5, especially in the western and southwestern US.[107] During the summer months, annual

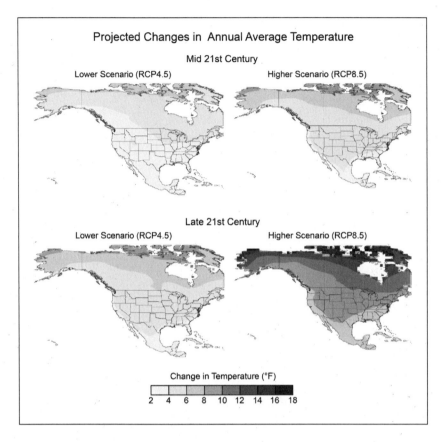

Projected changes in annual average temperatures (°F [=0.56°C]). Changes are the difference between the average for mid-century (2036–2065; top) or late-century (2070–2099, bottom) and the average for near-present (1976–2005) as a function of two representative concentration pathway scenarios (RCPs). Source: US Global Change Research Program (USGCRP) (2017).

precipitation was projected to increase for large areas of the north-west, subarctic and northeastern North America by the mid-21st century. By contrast, precipitation was projected to decrease by as much as 30% in areas of western and southwestern North America.

Projections suggested precipitation increases in large areas of the northwest Arctic and subarctic from a maximum of 20% (RCP2.6) to 40% (RCP8.5) in the winter months during the mid-21st century to 2100 period. Increases of up to 10% prevailed across much of the rest of North America except for far southwest portions of

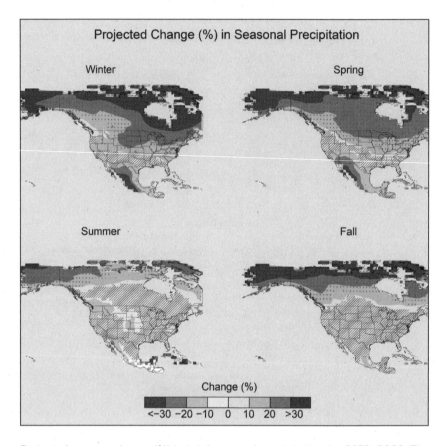

Projected average change (%) in total seasonal precipitation for 2070–2099. The values represent percentage change relative to the average for the period 1976–2005 under the representative concentration pathway (RCP) scenario 8.5. Large changes relative to natural variation are shown by stippling, those that are small compared to natural variation by hatching, and areas where no significant changes could be projected are shown as blank areas. Source: US Global Change Research Program (USGCRP) (2017).

the US (up to −10% decline) under RCP2.6. By contrast, increased precipitation to a maximum of 20–30% characterized much of North America east of the Rocky Mountains, with a 10–20% increase west of the mountains under RCP8.5. In the summer months, all areas were dominated by a projected increase in precipitation of up to 10% under RCP2.6. By contrast, under RCP8.5, the northwest Arctic and subarctic and much of northeastern North America was projected to see increases in precipitation of up to 10–30%, whereas much of western North America could see declines of 10–30%. The Great Lakes area was projected to see declines of up to 10% in the western basin, with the eastern basin and the Atlantic (Hudson River) basin seeing increases of up to 10% over the mid-21st century to 2100 period under RCP8.5.[108]

In the end, these climate change projections have been used to understand potential associated changes in the magnitude and seasonality of river discharge.[109] The value of such projections is heightened by the recent demonstration that fluctuations in the flows of the Earth's rivers between 1971 and 2010 can only be fully explained if human-driven climate change is incorporated into flow models – relying only on human-based changes in water and land management is not sufficient.[110] Furthermore, any changes in water supply to rivers driven by climate change will impact the relationship between streamflow and the refilling of groundwater aquifers. Many rivers in the US, especially in the southwest and the lower Mississippi River area, are especially susceptible to climate-driven decreases in water supply because they already lose water when recharging groundwater aquifers.[111] Any "business as usual" climate warming scenario (such as RCP6.0 or 8.5) generates hydrological models that predict substantial declines in total annual runoff in much of the western Cordillera, the western Mississippi (Missouri) and western Gulf of Mexico. By contrast, the central and eastern Mississippi, the northwestern Arctic and subarctic, and much of the Great Lakes–St. Lawrence River regions are predicted to experience increases in runoff, and the lower St. Lawrence and Atlantic basin to see relatively stable levels to the mid-21st century.[112] Declining annual and warm season (June–September) runoff is associated with predicted increases in "water stress" (where the ratio of water demand to water supply increases), with rivers like the Colorado, Sacramento–San Joaquin and Columbia, all already heavily impacted by dams and water extraction, expected to require intervention to try and mitigate increased water stress by the 2050s (e.g., through wetland restoration, modified dam operations, limiting evaporation from reservoirs).[113] Watersheds expected to gain discharge (Yukon,

River, Mackenzie River, parts of the Mississippi River) may suffer from increased flooding, weathering and erosion, potential dam failures, or reduced water quality from pollution and/or nutrient fluxes, impacts that will also require intervention.[114] Interventions to mitigate changes in river discharge owing to climate change are likely to be very complicated, expensive, and involve myriad social costs. Economic losses from floods in the US totalled $20 billion in 2019 alone.[115]

Finally, changes in river-water temperature, flow levels and their seasonality are likely to have substantial impacts on the biodiversity and functioning of river systems given that temperature and precipitation tend to be excellent predictors of species distributions in a variety of aquatic plants and animals. For instance, increases in water temperatures in many western US rivers are considered to be a major stressor for typically coldwater fish species like Pacific salmon and trout, a stressor that will be compounded by declines in discharge and climate change impacts on the surrounding landscape (e.g. wildfires and post-fire increases in sedimentation).[116] Myriad ecosystem impacts such as altered dispersal potential for various species (say from flooding), novel species interactions (as species change distributions) and changes in pathogen distributions may all impact river biota.[117] Water temperature changes can change basic processes in rivers such as nutrient cycling, primary and secondary productivity, microbial production and decomposition rates, while precipitation and discharge can impact sedimentation rates and patterns, nutrient loading and water quality.[118]

In summary, all of the great rivers of North America will be impacted by climate change, but the precise direction and magnitude of changes will depend on their individual characteristics (size, current discharge, topography, existing biota), how humans have impacted them notwithstanding climate change (degree of urbanization, existence of dams, current levels of water extraction) and the magnitude and rates of climate change in specific areas. The ultimate impacts on rivers will depend on their inherent resiliency as well as various proactive and reactive adaptation actions by humans.[119] The former are those actions taken now to maintain or increase river resilience to climate change (e.g., restoring wetlands and riparian habitat, levee setbacks, protection for at-risk species including research on susceptibility to climate change), while the latter are responses to climate change impacts as they arise (e.g., repairing flood damage to habitat, species translocation programs, dredging accumulated sediment, pollution abatement). Reactive measures, while clearly necessary at times, are sure to be more expensive in the long run and especially risky when human lives are at stake. Some of the constraints to effective climate change adaptation strategies may stem from outdated management regimes. For instance, much of the projected economic cost of climate change in the Colorado River basin is attributable to the rigid nature of the seven-state Colorado River Compact signed almost a century ago (1922).[120] Consequently, it has been argued that climate change impacts to river systems, in addition to the existing anthropogenic stressors, call for a new system of more flexible, co-operative, inter-interest-group coordinated planning at watershed-specific ("place-based") scales to effectively and adaptively manage rivers (see below).[121]

Back to the future: Large scale water diversions

POSSIBLY THE MOST existential threat to the future of our existing great river systems, although perhaps less likely now than in the not too distant past, is the recurring nightmare of massive interbasin water transfers. Here, infrastructure works (tunnels, pumps, canals) are used to divert water from one watershed to another. The principle has been referred to euphemistically as "augmentation"[122] of water-stressed basins with water from basins that proponents feel contain a "surplus"[123] of water that is, therefore, potentially running to "waste."[124] It may come as no surprise that the Colorado River holds the dubious distinction of being the site of the first trans–Continental Divide, interbasin transfer of water in North America. In 1890, construction began on an aqueduct, commonly known as the "Grand Ditch," that eventually fed water for 23 km from high elevation tributaries of the Colorado River in the mountains of northern Colorado through the Continental Divide at La Poudre Pass at 3101 m to Cache La Poudre River, a tributary of the South Platte River of the Missouri River (Mississippi River) drainage. This diversion was constructed to augment over-appropriated water from the South Platte River basin for eastern plains farmers and typically transfers 25,000,000 m³ annually from the Colorado River basin to the Mississippi River basin.[125]

From such humble beginnings, some truly massive augmentation schemes have been planned. The US Bureau of Reclamation hatched a plan in 1971 to divert 7.4 billion m³ from the lower Mississippi River to the plains of west Texas and eastern New Mexico (a scheme involving power generated by a proposed six nuclear plants!). In the 1960s, increasing demand for Colorado River water led the Bureau of Reclamation to commission the "United Western Investigation" to determine how best to proceed with augmentation of water delivery to California. One serious possibility was a plan to dam the Klamath River, which runs through southern Oregon and northern California, and divert much of its annual 14.8 billion m³ flow to the Sacramento River via a 97 km tunnel feeding into the State Water Project facilities. While this plan failed over concerns for the loss of prodigious salmon runs in the Klamath River, opposition by Native Americans and other supporters of the Klamath River in northern California, and the city of Los Angeles (who feared a diversion of the Klamath River would diminish their claim to Colorado River water), a smaller diversion of a Klamath River tributary, the Trinity River, does transfer 1.5 billion m³ annually to the Sacramento–San Joaquin basin. The Columbia River was also in the sights of water diverters in the 1960s; a plan to divert 9.3–18.6 billion m³ of water from the Columbia River to augment Colorado River supply was once under consideration. A fear of loss of hydroelectric potential in the Columbia River and dodgy economics killed this proposal (a 1600 km aqueduct and total costs as high as US$10 billion, out of a total federal budget of US$118 billion in 1965, would have been required).[126] The granddaddy of all interbasin transfer proposals, however, dwarfed these other plans and involved potential transfers from massive, untainted rivers far to the north in Alaska, Yukon and British Columbia. Water planners in the southwest US drooled at the prospect of tapping the water from huge, but relatively unknown (to the average citizen of the southwest US) rivers running though the rain-soaked mountains of Alaska, Yukon and British Columbia – the Fraser, Skeena, Stikine, Peace, Copper, Sustina, Tanana and upper Yukon rivers. The Fraser River *alone* produces almost twice as much runoff annually as *all* the rivers of California.[127] A Los Angeles engineer conceived the plan, dubbed the North American Water and Power Alliance (NAWAPA), in the 1950s. Described by Marc Reisner in *Cadillac Desert: The American West and its Disappearing Water* as "undoubtedly the grandest scheme ever concocted by man,"[128] the plan envisioned large dams on myriad northern rivers. The reservoirs created would have their contents pumped into the Rocky Mountain Trench (through which parts of the upper Fraser, Columbia and Peace rivers flow currently) to create a massive storage and distribution reservoir 800 km long, five times bigger than Lake Mead on the Colorado River. Here, the water (an estimated 148 billion m³ annually) would be shunted east along the "Canadian–Great Lakes Waterway" to the Great Lakes and the Mississippi River. The water would also flow south and be used to augment flows in the Columbia, Missouri/Mississippi, Colorado and Rio Grande rivers as well as stabilize water levels in the Ogallala Aquifer of the western Great Plains. Proposed benefits other than increased water supply in stressed areas included increased power generation capacity and improved transportation (e.g., by the Canadian–Great Lakes Waterway from Alberta to the Great Lakes). While initial consultations between the US and Canada occurred with the enthusiastic support of some politicians,[129] the rise of the environmental movement in the 1960s and 1970s, generally negative public sentiment in Canada, and an estimated project cost on the order of $100 billion in 1975 US dollars killed the plan. The environmental disruption of NAWAPA was described by some as involving "unprecedented destructiveness"[130] and "the kind of thing you think of when you're smoking pot"[131] in Reisner's *Cadillac Desert*. Luna Leopold, professor of hydrology at UC–Berkeley (and son of Aldo Leopold) stated that the project would "cause as much harm as all of the dam-building we have done in a hundred years."[132] General Andrew G.L. McNaughton, a

1. Susitna Reservoir
2. Yukon Reservoir
3. Copper Reservoir
4. Taku Lift
5. Canadian/Great-Lakes Waterway
6. Rocky Mountain Trench
7. Sawtooth Lifts
8. Dakota Waterway
9. Sawtooth Tunnel
10. Great Basin Waterway
11. Lake Nevada
12. Colorado Reservoir
13. Baja Aqueduct
14. Colorado Aqueduct
15. Sonora Aqueduct
16. Chihuahua Aqueduct
17. Rio-Grande Aqueduct
18. Hudson Bay Seaway
19. James Bay Seaway
20. Knob Lake Barge Canal

A series of massive inter-basin water transfers and associated reservoirs, lifts, and waterways (canals) as envisioned by the North American Water and Power Alliance XXI. Black arrows indicate water flow facilitated by such infrastructure, which would interconnect all of North America's seven major watershed basins by breaching all but the Eastern Divide (see Chapter 1).

well-known Canadian war figure, engineer and ex-politician/diplomat who participated in negotiation of the initial Columbia River Treaty, described NAWAPA as "a monstrous concept, a diabolical thesis."[133] The Peace River Reservoir would have flooded the central BC regional centre of Prince George, a city of 60,000 people in 1975. In short, the project died as "a victim of its own grandiosity."[134] The project has, however, occasionally twitched with life since its original incarnation and even now the project has supporters; one can view animations of an updated version, "NAWAPA XXI," on YouTube.[135]

A project like NAWAPA, an existential threat to the natural integrity of many of the great rivers of western North America, demonstrates how far some may go to augment supply in water-stressed areas. Although current proponents of projects like NAWAPA XXI may seem on the fringe, some massive projects are underway in other countries (e.g., China's 4.5 billion m³/yr South–North Water Transfer Project [SNWTP]).[136] It behooves all committed to the integrity of wild rivers not to be sanguine about the threat of projects like NAWAPA because, as Marc Reisner warned in *Cadillac Desert*, "Perhaps in some future haunted by scarcity, the unthinkable may be thinkable after all."[137]

Restoring and safeguarding our great river ecosystems: Progress towards a new model of river benefits and development

THE CURRENT STATE of our great rivers is largely a product of society's general perception of rivers as a resource to be exploited by humans to further economic development and prosperity – exploitation for hydroelectricity, irrigation, food sources, drinking water, transportation, industrial uses and even recreation. This perception has been the guiding principle of water "development" for North America's rivers certainly at least since European contact.[138] Consequently, because the health of river ecosystems is typically not an explicitly stated goal of river developments, the requirement for the needs of rivers to maintain natural functionality, including the role of ground water,[139] and the ecosystem services that such health provides to humans, have been "unrecognized and unspecified."[140] Rivers typically get what flows are "left over" after human use, and in cases like the Colorado River sometimes that flow level is zero, at least by the time the delta is reached.

In their 2003 book *Rivers for Life: Managing Water for People and Nature*, Sandra Postel and Brian Richter discussed this mindset and introduced the idea of a "sustainability boundary" for river ecosystem health and function. Here, the sustainability boundary is that threshold point of human use of water from a river, above which rivers cease to function properly and their ability to provide ecosystem services and sustain freshwater life becomes compromised. The essential problem with our past and most common current river development paradigm is that there has been no, or insufficient, consideration of how much water, given the seasonal pattern of water supply, is required to sustain natural river ecosystems *before* plans and decisions are made about how much river is taken for *human* uses. Postel and Richter proposed a new paradigm of river development, one that had at its core the idea of an "ecosystem support allocation" (or eco-support allocation), which they defined as "the quantity, quality, and timing of flows needed to safeguard the health and functioning of river systems themselves."[141] The limit to which society can alter a river's flow before its functional integrity is compromised is the aforementioned sustainability boundary. This paradigm represents a fundamental shift from an economic mindset for river development to an ecological mindset, one that need not, as Postel and Richter explain, compromise economic development. Rather, this shift rebalances the uses of rivers to maximize instream *and* extractive benefits of flows and is an explicit recognition that both have value and that rivers are both ecological and social systems at the same time.[142] In *River Republic: The Fall and Rise of America's Rivers*, Daniel McCool approached this idea when he wrote, in a rebuttal to traditional approaches to water development, that we err when we focus on single river attributes as resources (e.g., irrigation, power). In other words, when we focus on exploiting one aspect of a river as a resource (e.g., its water for irrigation or power) at the expense of another (fish production, wetland persistence) we misuse the river because in its totality, "the river *is* the resource."[143]

Methods do exist to determine how much water is required, and when, and to create limits to human uses of water to promote river ecosystem sustainability. Systems such as the "instream flow incremental methodology" (IFIM) focused on defining minimum flow levels to sustain specific aspects of river functionality (usually fish production), but neglected flow variation, particularly the importance of seasonal floods.[144] These simplistic beginnings eventually led to the current notion that the full range of natural flow levels was required to sustain river ecosystems; the natural flow regime is the "master variable"[145] influencing river functionality. Further work worldwide led to the idea that if a river's flow becomes modified it should still mimic the natural hydrograph (the seasonal pattern of flow variation) as much as possible, e.g., provision of suitable low flow conditions during the dry season, periodic high flow spikes during the wet season and retention of periodic natural flood periods. This has become known as the "holistic approach," as it considers benefits to the totality of river biodiversity (i.e., not single species) and considers the full spatial and temporal range of river flows as the guiding principle in identifying the potential limits to human use of flows. A so-called "benchmarking methodology" has been developed to identify the points at which human use of river flows start impacting river functionality. These are important developments for North America's great rivers because in cases of severe degradation of flows (e.g., the Colorado or Rio Grande rivers) river restoration can be guided by understanding how much flow must be restored (and when) to regain ecosystem health. Similarly, for rivers with currently limited impacts on flow (e.g., Fraser River, Yukon River), any potential future developments can be guided by understanding how much alteration of flow is too much, so that the sustainability boundary is not breached.

Postel and Richter outlined a few case studies in Australia and South Africa where these ideas have been put into effect to present explicit ecological implications of differing levels of river developments, and the economic costs of compromised river ecosystem services. The ecosystem perspective is considered in light of the proposed societal benefits of river developments in promoting of more inclusive, transparent and democratic decision-making. South Africa pioneered the idea of a water "Reserve," with its National Water Act (1998) by recognizing water resources as a public trust and allocating a sufficient quantity and quality water in two parts: an allocation to sustain the functioning of aquatic ecosystems upon which the second allocation, to guarantee peoples' essential uses of water for drinking, cooking, sanitation and other fundamental uses, ultimately depends. All other uses (e.g., irrigation, industry) are subsidiary to the Reserve. [146] Such thinking is in line with the idea of "river republics,"[147] where broad sectors of society (and not just large industrial or government interests) are deeply involved in river management to best serve the natural and societal functions of rivers through an open, democratic process. Further, Australian states, territories and the federal government initiated a "cap" on allocations of water to human uses if the primary ecological allocation to rivers is inadequate to sustain their ecosystems. The Brisbane Declaration (2007) summarized the findings of an international symposium, defining environmental flows as "the quantity, timing, and quality of water flows required to sustain freshwater and estuarine ecosystems and the human livelihoods and well-being that depend on these ecosystems."[148] An updated version (2018) strives to better integrate cultural and social values from diverse perspectives into the definition of environmental flows.[149]

Despite these principled initiatives, the US still has no "overarching vision or goal to secure flows to rivers needed to support the diversity of freshwater life and to sustain ecological functions" as Postel and Richter wrote back in 2003. Since that time, progress in the US has been "incremental" rather than profound, as represented by the eco-allocation model,[150] let alone any incorporation of social or cultural values. The US federal government typically defers to the states in matters related to water use and allocation, but there does exist a patchwork of federal laws (e.g., Endangered Species Act, Clean Water Act, National Environmental Policy Act, SECURE Water Act) and agencies that work to manage flows and plan for climate change under these laws (e.g., Fish and Wildlife Service, Bureau of Reclamation, Environmental Protection Agency, U.S. Geological Survey) that can influence individual aspects of river ecosystem sustainability. The Wild and Scenic Rivers Act (WSRA, 1968), which seeks to protect certain US rivers, or sections of rivers, with "outstandingly remarkable scenic, recreational, geologic, fish and wildlife, historic, cultural, or other similar values," is an Act created to offset, in part, alterations on other rivers such as dam construction and other habitat changes. For example, the Act covers two sections of the heavily impacted Rio Grande totalling 420 km in New Mexico and Texas. In all, 226 rivers or river sections have received a WSRA designation as of April 2019 (<0.5% of all rivers in the U.S.).[151]

Similarly, the Canadian federal government has jurisdiction over fisheries, navigation, international river relations and environmental pollution standards, but use and allocation of water is under provincial/territorial jurisdiction. The Canadian federal Water Act simply refers to "implementation of programs relating to the conservation, development and utilization of water *resources*" (emphasis added). The Act did help to shift thinking from one dominated by the infrastructure-based uses of water (dams, canals etc.) to a mindset that appreciates and tries to sustain all the beneficial "functions of freshwater environments" in a watershed, and thus often at the interjurisdictional level.[152]

It is perhaps naïve or simplistic to think that countries as vast and geographically and jurisdictionally complex as Canada and the US, and after two centuries of water developments under the "economic mindset," can adopt a national (or international) holistic approach to river restoration or future development. That said, the holistic approach is creeping into planning for individual watersheds. For instance, joint Canadian and US agencies, such as the International Joint Commission, are engaged in more ecologically focused flow management initiatives for the shared St. Lawrence River (see discussion of Plan 2014 above and the IJC's International Watershed Initiative in Chapter 11).[153] Further, the current Columbia River Treaty renegotiations have adopted "ecological function" as the third pillar (in addition to hydroelectric generation and flood control) for future operations on this heavily impacted river. At the jurisdictional level, British Columbia enacted the Water Sustainability Act in 2016, an Act that recognizes "environmental flow needs," which are defined as "the volume and timing of water flow required for the proper functioning of the aquatic ecosystem of the stream." The Act also introduced the concept of "critical environmental flow" as "the volume of water flow below which significant or irreversible harm to the aquatic ecosystem of the stream is likely to occur," although the Act only requires regulators to "consider" such ecosystem needs when making decisions that impact rivers.[154] Quebec also enacted legislation, the Sustainable Development Act (2006), that seeks to reconcile the requirements of ecosystems with economic activities and recognizes hydrological units as the basis for integrated water management.[155] Other opportunities for applying the holistic approach on a river-specific basis include modification of dam/reservoir operations to restore ecological function through the idea of "designer"[156] flows (e.g., periodic releases of water to resuscitate the Colorado River Delta; planned releases of Columbia River water to protect salmon runs), and imposing new requirements during dam relicensing applications.[157]

In the Epilogue to *Rivers for Life*, Postel and Richter articulated a prescription for the restoration of heavily degraded rivers (mostly in terms of flow regulation) and for more enlightened future management of lightly impacted rivers. Their words are as true and relevant today as in 2003 and generate some optimism when combined with the observation that rivers and their ecosystems, when given the chance, can often be restored. For instance, removal of two century-old dams on the Elwha River on Washington State's Olympic Peninsula saw Pacific salmon and trout swimming upstream of the old dam sites within a year of dam removal.[158] That said, Postel and Richter emphasized that some fundamental societal changes will be required for a new era of river sustainability to be achieved. First, the concept of eco-support allocations to the rivers themselves needs to be widely embraced and should not be subservient to human uses of water. Second, North American societies need to become better integrated with the limitations of Nature and its cycles. Instead of engineering away the constraints imposed by a river's natural cycles (e.g., building levees and cutting off a river from its flood plain), more efforts need to be made to live within these limits (e.g., constraining human developments within flood plains). Third, human pressures on river ecosystems need to be reduced by slower and smarter development and by increasing water productivity (e.g., limiting growth in water-stressed areas, more efficient irrigation systems, promotion of less water-intensive, plant-based diets).[159] This is perhaps the greatest challenge, given the continuing importance of rivers in promoting economic development.[160] Fourth, rivers and their water need to be broadly embraced as a public trust, or a "commons,"[161] and not simply a commodity to be traded in unregulated markets. Here, "in-place" water opportunities reflecting public values of recreation, aesthetics, climate impacts, scientific study, environmental and ecological services and water allocation must be considered alongside proposed commercial, industrial or other appropriative private uses, which themselves should serve a public interest as well.[162] For instance, there was concern in Canada that naturally occurring water could fall under the definition of a "tradable good," "service" or "investment" in the original North American Free Trade Agreement (NAFTA) and its predecessor the Free Trade Agreement (FTA). Canada is widely *perceived* to have a vast oversupply of water, yet 60% of Canada's *renewable* water supply flows north to where only 2% of the population resides.[163] Further, Canada and the US actually have similar percentages of the world's renewable water supply, ~7%, to service about the same landmass, both about 9.8 million km^2.[164] These trade agreements generally sought to remove restrictions on trade, and thus it was feared that "bulk" water exports (i.e., those other than water in bottles or tanks) to the US would be uncontrollable by Canada.[165] The Canadian federal government, however, has repeatedly insisted that "bulk" water exports are not covered by NAFTA and are "contrary to the 1987 federal water policy,"[166] which expressed opposition to large-scale exports of water from Canada. Owing to continuing debate on the issue, the recently renegotiated NAFTA (now known as the United States–Mexico–Canada Agreement, USMCA) contained a side letter on natural water sources stating that the "Agreement contains no rights to the natural water resources of a Party to the Agreement." It continued with, "Nothing in the Agreement would oblige a Party to exploit its water for commercial use, including its withdrawal, extraction or diversion for export in bulk."[167] Still, some feel that the side letter is ambiguous and water from natural sources should be explicitly excluded from the USMCA in an amendment.[168] Furthermore, there is considerable interest in expanding market-based approaches to water conservation and allocation, as presently exist in parts of the western US, to increasingly stressed watersheds such as the Colorado River.[169]

The Community Environmental Legal Defense Fund's International Center for the Rights of Nature (based in Pennsylvania) is "spearheading the advancement of the Rights of Nature around the world."[170] Certain legal rights before the courts have been assigned to one river in New Zealand, two in India and one in Colombia, as is not unprecedented for non-human entities such as businesses, non-profits and religious organizations and deities.[171] A similar effort to have legal rights assigned to the Colorado River, however, failed in 2017.[172] Rivers in the state of Victoria, Australia, fall under a slightly modified system whereby its rivers are under the corporate guardianship of the Victorian Environmental Water Holder, created as a legal person with rights of water holding and use, including the possible sale and purchase of water,[173] all in the service of achieving "the best environmental outcomes with the water that is available."[174] As the Rights for Nature initiative advances, I strongly echo Postel and Richter's recommendation that at the very least a fundamental "water ethic" needs to be embraced (a call repeated in Canadian water activist Maude Barlow's 2014 *Blue Future: Protecting Water for People and the Planet Forever* and Postel's 2017 *Replenish: The Virtuous Cycle of Water and Prosperity*). Rather than bending rivers to our will in unsustainable ways, the precautionary principle should be embraced. Here, we must learn to *share* water with the natural world and, if anything, err on the side of allocating too *much*, rather than too little, water to rivers to sustain their ecosystems. To achieve this shift, our societies will need to embrace what Luna Leopold called a "reverence for rivers"[175] and learn to live within the constraints imposed by the variable but "time-tested"[176] cycles of rivers. As we enter the UN International Decade on Ecosystem Restoration (2021–2030),[177] our great rivers, through whose waterscapes the history of North America has flowed, deserve no less.

Appendices

Appendix 1

Comparative statistics of rivers.

Statistics are approximate and meant to illustrate relative differences.

Gazetted name	Aboriginal names (language)*	Length (km, rank in world)	Drainage area (km², rank in world)	Annual discharge (m³/s, rank in world)	Source/outlet	Major tributaries	Human population (millions, approx.)	Major industries
Mackenzie River	Dehcho (South Slavey), Deho (North Slavey), Grande Rivière (Michif), Kuukpak (Inuvialuktun), Nagwichoonjik (Gwich'in)	4241 (13)	1,790,000 (13)	9125 (25)	Thutade Lake/Beaufort Sea	Peace, Liard, Peel, Athabasca	0.450	Oil and gas, fishing, trapping, transportation
Yukon River	Uug Han or Yuk Han (Gwich'in), Kuigpak (Yup'ik), Inupiaq: Kuukpak (Inupiaq), Chu Niikwän (Southern Tutchone)	3185 (23)	850,000 (26)	6428 (44)	Atlin Lake/Bering Sea	Tanana, Porcupine, Koyukuk, Teslin, Pelly, Stewart, White	0.126	Fishing, mining
Fraser River	Lhta Koh (Dakaleth), Stó:lō (Halq'eméylem); ʔElhdaqox (Tŝilhqot'in)	1368 (104)	220,000 (74)	3475 (75)	Moose Lake/Salish Sea	Thompson, Stuart, Chilcotin, McGregor, Harrison	1.2	Fishing, agriculture

River	Aboriginal names				Mouth	Major tributaries		Uses
Columbia River	Nch'i-Wana (Sahaptin)	2250 (53)	415,211 (48)	7500 (37)	Columbia Lake/Pacific Ocean	Snake, Willamette, Kootenay, Clark Fork	4.6	Hydropower, transport, fishing, agriculture
Sacramento–San Joaquin River	Bohema-Mem or Nom-Tee-Mem (Wintu); Typici h huu' (Mono)	640/589 (>200)	69,000/40,000 (>115)	665/145 (>150)	Pacific Ocean	Feather, McCloud, Pit rivers/Merced, Tuolumne, and Stanislaus	6.25	Agriculture, hydropower, fishing
Colorado River	Hakatai (Havasupai); Nah-un-kah-rea (Ute)	2333 (47)	390,000 (59)	500 (>150)	Sea of Cortez	Green, Gunnison, Gila, San Juan	30**	Hydropower, agriculture, municipal
Rio Grande/Rio Bravo	P'osoge (Tewa); Tšina (Cochiti); Ha'n'ap'akawa (Jemez)	3051 (28)	570,000 (36)	68 (>200)	Gulf of Mexico	Rio Conchos, Pecos River, Rio San Juan	6.0	Agriculture, hydropower, municipal
Mississippi River	Messipi or Mee-zee-see-bee (Anishinabe); Hahawakpa (Dakota)	6275 (4)	2,980,000 (5)	16,200 (15)	Gulf of Mexico	Ohio, Missouri, Arkansas, Illinois, and Red	30	Transport, agriculture
Hudson River	Mahicantuck (Lenape)	507 (>200)	36,000 (>200)	606 (>150)	Lake Tear of the Clouds/Atlantic Ocean	Mohawk, Wallkill	9.0	Transport
St. Lawrence River	Kaniatarowanenneh (Mohawk)	3058 (27)	1,030,000 (19)	16,800 (14)	Gulf of St. Lawrence	Ottawa, Saguenay	40.0	Transport, hydropower, fishing
World leader	NA	6650 (Nile River)	7,050,000 (Amazon River)	209,000 (Amazon River)	NA	NA	>400 (Ganges River)	NA

*List represents examples only. Most Aboriginal names refer to the word for river, river confluences, the large size, greatness, importance, or location of each river, or to peculiarities of flow (e.g., that the Hudson River flows in two directions owing to tidal influence)

**Includes population of parts of California that depend on Colorado River water supply

Appendix 2

A "rivers playlist": A sampling of songs with rivers as central themes.

Many selections were compiled with the help of Tim Falconer, Dawson City, YT, June 2012.

Song	Artist	Year	Album
Across the River (5:21)	Alejandro Escovedo	2001	*A Man under the Influence*

River theme: Based on a Mexican folk tale of tragedy following failed love between a peasant woman and a wealthy landowner in the land of the Rio Grande.

Up on Cripple Creek (4:33)	The Band	1969	*The Band*

River theme: A song with The Band's classic mix of Americana mythology dealing with the relationship between a trucker and his free-spirited girlfriend, "Bessie," who "mends me" up on Cripple Creek, which may be a metaphorical Shangri-La. Brief reference to the Mississippi River.

Meeting across the River (3:19)	Bruce Springsteen	1975	*Born To Run*

River theme: A sombre, but sympathetic, tribute to two petty criminals' "last chance" for a big score involving a meeting with another man across the river, presumably meaning travel between New Jersey and New York across the Hudson River.

Rivers of Gold (5:14)	Bry Webb	1978	*Provider*

River theme: The beauty of the Canadian wilderness. Inspired by Webb's travels in northwestern Canada, beginning in Dawson City, YT.

Green River (2:34)	Creedence Clearwater Revival	1969	*Green River*

River theme: Vacation reminiscences, of a stream in northern California, by John Fogerty, in the "swamp rock" genre.

Many Rivers To Cross (3:02)	Jimmy Cliff	1969	*Jimmy Cliff*

River theme: An immigrant songwriter's trials and tribulations while trying to build a musical career, using the metaphor of crossing many rivers during a journey.

Big River (2:33)	Johnny Cash	1958	N/A (single)

River theme: The river, in this case the Mississippi River, as a metaphor for a long journey in pursuit of the love of a woman who remains elusive at every turn of the river.

River (4:05)	Joni Mitchell	1971	*Blue*

River theme: More about a relationship than rivers per se, it is my personal favourite non-Christmas Christmas song. Still, the song's beauty stems much from the feeling of escape while skating on a frozen river in wintertime – wonderful!

Song	Artist	Year	Album
River of Fools (2:55)	Los Lobos	1987	*By the Light of the Moon*

River theme: A theme of immigration, troubled pasts and uncertain futures for those who travel "To a place they know not where."

The River (4:59)	Bruce Springsteen	1979	*The River*

River theme: The river as hope or dreams for the future in uncertain times.

When the Levee Breaks (7:08)	Led Zeppelin	1971	*Led Zeppelin IV*

River theme: Classic drum opening by John Bonham marks this urban blues song recounting the devastation that can result when the Mississippi River floods, as occurred in 1927, when over six million hectares of the delta was flooded killing hundreds of people, displacing thousands more and causing hardship for those battling the flood. Based on the original country blues by Kansas Joe McCoy and Memphis Minnie, recorded in 1929 when memory of the flood would have been recent.

Rivers of Babylon (4:20)	Melodians	1970	*Rivers of Babylon*

River theme: Heavy biblical themes based on Psalms 19 and 137 and the conquests of the Jewish people by the Babylonians. The rivers referred to are the present-day Tigris and Euphrates rivers in Iraq. Adapted in reggae genre to tell the story of repression of the Rastafarian faith by Jamaican authorities: "Babylon" is a term in Rastafarian faith for any oppressive or unjust system.

Down by the River (9:17)	Neil Young/ Crazy Horse	1969	*Everybody Knows This Is Nowhere*

River theme: Another song about a troubled relationship between a man and a woman. Long, "violent" guitar solos evoke the angst the man suffers after "blowing your thing with a chick." Apparently, the shooting is figurative and not to be taken literally.

Somewhere down the Crazy River (4:58)	Robbie Robertson	1987	*Robbie Robertson*

River theme: A song renowned for evoking vivid imagery in the listener. Recollections of life in the steaming Deep South, perhaps in the Mississippi valley.

Take Me to the River (5:04)	Talking Heads	1978	*More Songs about Buildings and Food*

River theme: A new take on an original Southern soul piece mixing religious conviction (e.g., baptism) with more secular interests.

River of Love (3:31)	T-Bone Burnett	1986	*T-Bone Burnett*

River theme: Rivers as a metaphor for love that "rolls on."

Song	Artist	Year	Album
Rivers and Roads (4:47)	The Head and the Heart	2011	*The Head and the Heart*

River theme: Rivers (and Roads) as representative of the distance, literal or emotional, that sometimes separates us from those we love.

The River of Dreams (4:05)	Billy Joel	1993	*The River of Dreams*

River theme: Borrowing the feel of black gospel and spiritual music, this song seems to invoke feelings of Joel's quest for life's meaning as he voyages along a metaphorical "river of dreams."

The Cool, Cool River (5:27)	Paul Simon	1990	*The Rhythm of the Saints*

River theme: A somewhat sobering commentary on the poor human condition for many with the "cool, cool river" perhaps referring to the slow pace of social progress.

Chattahochee (3:57)	Alan Jackson	1993	*A Lot about Livin' (And a Little 'bout Love)*

River theme: An upbeat, coming-of-age, seeking-love song about summer fun along the Chattahochee River, Georgia.

River of Light (3:48)	Gordon Lightfoot	2004	*Harmony*

River theme: From the songwriting legend's 20th album, this song meanders like a river. Perhaps inspired by his near-death illness two years before the record's release.

The End of All Rivers (5:53)	*Bruce Cockburn*	2005	*Speechless*

River theme: A guitar instrumental piece about rivers ending their journeys to the sea. It flows beautifully as a river should.

Roll On Columbia (3:10)	Woody Guthrie	1941	*Columbia River Ballads*

River theme: Commissioned by the Bonneville Power Administration as part of a compilation extolling the virtues of the Columbia River and hydropower and irrigation development within the context of the Great Depression's impacts and the Second World War. It is the official folk song of Washington State.

Notes

When multiple sources are listed for any single endnote, the first citation refers to either the source of a direct quotation or the primary source for the point that is being cited in the text. Any sources following the one associated with the numbered endnote are general sources for the point/idea or quotation.

Introduction

1 A. Sunil. 2018. Unruly Waters: How Rains, Rivers, Coasts, and Seas Have Shaped Asia's History. New York: Basic Books.
   P. Ball. 2016. The Water Kingdom: A Secret History of China. Chicago: University of Chicago Press.
   B. Campbell. 2012. Rivers and the Power of Ancient Rome. Chapel Hill: University of North Carolina Press.
2 M.W. Parkes et al. 2010. Towards integrated governance for water, health and social-ecological systems: The watershed governance prism. Global Environmental Change 20: 693–704.
3 C. Mauch and T. Zeller (eds.). 2008. Rivers in History: Perspectives on Waterways in Europe and North America. Pittsburgh: University of Pittsburgh Press.
4 This book cites many dates associated with geological and human events. For the most part, all dates preceding the common era, CE (i.e., before year 1 of the current Gregorian calendar also known as AD), are expressed as "years before present," ya, which, by convention, means calendar years before 1950 CE (around the time radiocarbon dating was invented). Up to approximately 50,000 ya, these dates refer to those estimated using radioactive carbon dating of organic materials. Ages of rocks and geological events are generally inferred from fossil remains and/or radioactive decay of other radionuclides with longer half-lives (e.g., the decay of Uranium^{235} to Lead^{207} will reach 50% in 700 million years). Unless stated otherwise as "cal ya" (calibrated years ago), all carbon-based dates are estimates that are uncalibrated for natural variability in the amount of carbon in the atmosphere. For simplicity, I have elected to express "years before present" as described above as "years ago, ya."
5 P. Brewitt. 2019. Same River Twice: The Politics of Dam Removal and River Restoration. Corvallis: Oregon State University Press, p. 2.
   G. Haidvogl. 2018. Historic milestones of human river uses and ecological impacts. In S. Schmutz and J. Sendzimir (eds.), Riverine Ecosystem Management: Science for Governing Towards a Sustainable Future, Aquatic Ecology Series 8, pp. 19–39. Cham, Switzerland: Springer.

6 I. Lucchitta. 1990. History of the Grand Canyon and of the Colorado River in Arizona. In S.S. Beus and M. Morales (eds.), *Grand Canyon Geology*. New York: Oxford University Press, pp. 311–32.

7 D. Worster. 1986. *Rivers of Empire: Water, Aridity, & the Growth of the American West*. New York: Pantheon, p. 320.

8 Businesswire.com. 2012. Importance of river basins in driving global economic growth to rocket: Top ten basins' GDP to set to exceed that of USA, Japan, and Germany combined by 2050. June 2012. https://www.businesswire.com/news/home/20120611006498/en/Importance-River-Basins-Driving-Global-Growth-Rocket. Accessed February 22, 2018.

9 R.G. Wetzel. 2001. *Limnology: Lake and River Ecosystems*. San Diego: Academic Press.

10 P. Horgan. 1954. *Great River: The Rio Grande in American History*, vol. 1, *Indians and Spain*. New York: Reinhart), p. 4.

11 S. Postel. 2020. *Replenish: The Virtuous Cycle of Water and Prosperity*. Washington, DC: Island Press.

12 A.S. Tribot, J. Deter, and N. Mouquet. 2018. Integrating the aesthetic value of landscapes and biological diversity. *Proceedings of the Royal Society B: Biological Sciences* 285: 20180971.

13 L.C. Smith. 2020. *Rivers of Power: How a Natural Force Raised Kingdoms, Destroyed Civilizations, and Shapes Our World*. New York: Little, Brown Spark, p. 290.

14 C. Mauch and T. Zeller (eds.). 2008. *Rivers in History: Perspectives on Waterways in Europe and North America*. Pittsburgh: University of Pittsburgh Press, p. 7.

15 E. O'Donnell and J. Talbot-Jones. 2017. Three rivers are now legally people – but that's just the start of looking after them. *The Conversation*. March 23. https://theconversation.com/three-rivers-are-now-legally-people-but-thats-just-the-start-of-looking-after-them-74983?utm_source=twitter&utm_medium=twitterbutton. Accessed August 12, 2019.

16 Z.L. Jiang, G.S. Kassab, and Y.C., Fung. 1994. Diameter-defined Strahler system and connectivity matrix of the pulmonary arterial tree. *Journal of Applied Physiology* 76: 882–92.

17 H. MacLennan. 1961. *Seven Rivers of Canada*. Toronto: Macmillan of Canada, p. 5.

18 C. Mauch and T. Zeller (eds.). 2008. *Rivers in History: Perspectives on Waterways in Europe and North America*. Pittsburgh: University of Pittsburgh Press, p. 1.
T.S. McMillin. 2011. The Meaning of Rivers: Flow and Reflection in American Literature. Iowa City: University of Iowa Press.

19 E. Wohl. 2004. *Disconnected Rivers: Linking Rivers to Landscapes*. New Haven, CT: Yale University Press, p. 271.
T.S. McMillin. 2011. *The Meaning of Rivers: Flow and Reflection in American Literature*. Iowa City: University of Iowa Press.

20 *The Economist*. 2013. Kumbh together: The world's biggest gatherings. Graphic detail. January 15. https://www.economist.com/graphic-detail/2013/01/15/kumbh-together. Accessed October 19, 2020.
M. Jha. 2020. Eyes in the sky: Indian authorities had to manage 250 million festivalgoers. So they built a high-tech surveillance ministate. *Rest of World*. https://restofworld.org/2020/india-magh-mela/. Accessed October 19, 2020.

21 T. Cusack. 2010. *Riverscapes and National Identities*. Syracuse, NY: Syracuse University Press.

22 L.B. Leopold. 1994. *A View of the River.* Cambridge, MA: Harvard University Press, p. 3.

23 L.B. Leopold. 1994. *A View of the River.* Cambridge, MA: Harvard University Press, p. 2.

24 L.C. Smith. 2020. *Rivers of Power: How a Natural Force Raised Kingdoms, Destroyed Civilizations, and Shapes Our World.* New York: Little, Brown Spark, p.5.

25 L.B. Leopold. 1994. *A View of the River.* Cambridge, MA: Harvard University Press, p. 281.

26 R.E. Horton. 1945. Erosional development of streams and their drainage basins: Hydrophysical approach to quantitative morphology. *Bulletin of the Geological Society of America* 56: 275–370.
    A.N. Strahler. 1957. Quantitative analysis of watershed geomorphology. *Transactions of the American Geophysical Union* 38: 913–20.

27 Benscreek Canoe Club. 2001. Rivers, Stoneycreek Canyon (Class III–IV). http://benscreekcanoeclub.com/river-talk/rivers/. Accessed October 13, 2020.

28 E. Wohl. 2004. *Disconnected Rivers: Linking Rivers to Landscapes.* New Haven, CT: Yale University Press, p. 1.

29 L.C. Smith. 2020. *Rivers of Power: How a Natural Force Raised Kingdoms, Destroyed Civilizations, and Shapes Our World.* New York: Little, Brown Spark.

30 J.C. Davis. 2017. *The Gulf: The Making of an American Sea.* New York: Liveright, p. 5.

31 R. White. 1996. *The Organic Machine: The Remaking the Columbia River.* New York: Hill & Wang, p. ix.

32 D.K. Goodwin. 2018. *Leadership: In Turbulent Times.* New York: Simon & Schuster, p. 368.

33 M. Doyle. 2019. *The Source: How Rivers Made America and America Remade Its Rivers.* New York: W.W. Norton.
    This figure is based on the estimated 250,000 rivers in the USA and then estimating the number in North America by, conservatively, doubling the number, taking into account the relative areas of Canada and Mexico.

34 P.J. Ashworth and J. Lewin. 2012. How do big rivers come to be different? *Earth Sciences Review* 114: 84–107.

35 F. Braudel. 1995. *The Mediterranean and the Mediterranean World in the Age of Philip II*, vol. 2. Berkeley: University of California Press, p. 902.

36 I employ the international system of units (or metric units) throughout this book but give a conversion to American or customary units at first use. 1 km = 0.62 mi.

37 S. McCutcheon. 1991. *Electric Rivers: The Story of the James Bay Project.* New York: Black Rose Books.

38 E.W. Nuffield. 2001. *Samuel Hearne: Journey to the Coppermine River, 1769–1772.* Vancouver: Haro Books.

39 H. MacLennan. 1961. *Seven Rivers of Canada.* Toronto: Macmillan of Canada, p. 9.

40 M. Doyle. 2019. *The Source: How Rivers Made America and America Remade Its Rivers.* New York: W.W. Norton, p. 1.

41 C. Mauch and T. Zeller (eds.). 2008. *Rivers in History: Perspectives on Waterways in Europe and North America.* Pittsburgh: University of Pittsburgh Press.

42 C. Mauch and T. Zeller (eds.). 2008. Rivers in History: Perspectives on Waterways in Europe and North America. Pittsburgh: University of Pittsburgh Press.

43 L. Kriegel. 1961. Afterword to *Life on the Mississippi* (M. Twain). New York: Signet Classics, p. 376.

44 L. Kriegel. 1961. Afterword to *Life on the Mississippi* (M. Twain). New York: Signet Classics, p. 377.

45 C. Darwin. 1889. *A Naturalist's Voyage: Journal of Researches Into The Natural History and Geology of the Countries Visited During the Voyage of the H.M.S. 'Beagle' Round the World*. London: John Murray, p. 127.

46 T.S. McMillin. 2011. *The Meaning of Rivers: Flow and Reflection in American Literature*. Iowa City: University of Iowa Press, p. xviii.

L.B. Leopold. 1994. *A View of the River*. Cambridge, MA: Harvard University Press.

E. Wohl. 2004. *Disconnected Rivers: Linking Rivers to Landscapes*. New Haven, CT: Yale University Press.

Smith, L.C. 2020. *Rivers of Power: How a Natural Force Raised Kingdoms, Destroyed Civilizations, and Shapes Our World*. New York: Little, Brown Spark.

47 P. Horgan. 1954. *Great River: The Rio Grande in American History*, vol. 1, *Indians and Spain*. New York: Reinhart, p. 7.

ONE: The North American Family of Rivers.

1 R.G. Wetzel. 2001. *Limnology: Lake and River Ecosystems*. San Diego: Academic Press.

2 R. Abell et al. 2008. Freshwater ecoregions of the world: A new map of biogeographic units for freshwater biodiversity conservation. *BioScience* 58: 403–14.

3 Natural Resources Canada. 2017. Atlas of Canada. https://www.nrcan.gc.ca/maps-tools-publications/tools/geodetic-reference-systems/water/16888. Accessed October 2, 2020.

4 M.A. Gonzalez. 2003. Continental divides in North Dakota and North America. *North Dakota Geological Survey Newsletter* 30: 1–7.

5 W.E. Galloway, T.L. Whiteaker, and P. Ganey-Curry. 2011. History of Cenozoic North American drainage basin evolution, sediment yield, and accumulation in the Gulf of Mexico basin. *Geosphere* 7: 938–73.

6 P.B. King. 2015. *Evolution of North America*. Princeton, NJ: Princeton University Press, p. 5.

7 S.B. Clark. 2001. *Birth of the Mountains: The Geologic Story of the Southern Appalachian Mountains*. Denver, CO: United States Geological Survey, Information Services.

8 S.M. Stanley and J.A. Luczai. 2015. *Earth System History*, 4th ed. New York: W.H. Freeman.

J.M. English and S.T. Johnston. 2004. The Laramide orogeny: What were the driving forces? *International Geology Review* 46: 833–38.

9 W.E. Galloway, T.L. Whiteaker, and P. Ganey-Curry. 2011. History of Cenozoic North American drainage basin evolution, sediment yield, and accumulation in the Gulf of Mexico basin. *Geosphere* 7: 938–73.

10 E.C. Pielou. 2008. *After the Ice Age: The Return of Life to Glaciated North America*. Chicago: University of Chicago Press.

J. England et al. 2006. The Innuitian Ice Sheet: Configuration, dynamics and chronology. *Quaternary Science Reviews* 25: 689–703.

S.F. Lamoureux and J.H. England. 2000. Late Wisconsinan glaciation of the central sector of the Canadian High Arctic. *Quaternary Research* 54: 182–88.

11 R. Fulton and V. Prest. 1987. Introduction: The Laurentide ice sheet and its significance. *Géographie physique et Quaternaire* 41: 181–86. 1 km² = 0.39 mi.²

12 A.S. Dyke. 2004. An outline of North American deglaciation with emphasis on central and northern Canada. *Developments in Quaternary Sciences* 2: 373–424.

13 Gridded Population of the World, Version 4 (GPWv4): Administrative Unit Center Points with Population Estimates, Center for International Earth Science Information Network – CIESIN – Columbia University. 2016. Gridded Population of the World, Version 4 (GPWv4): Administrative Unit Center Points with Population Estimates. Palisades, NY: NASA Socioeconomic Data and Applications Center (SEDAC). http://dx.doi.org/10.7927/H4F47M2C. Accessed August 24, 2020.

14 H. MacLennan. 1961. *Seven Rivers of Canada*. Toronto: Macmillan of Canada.

15 R. White. 1991. *It's Your Misfortune and None of My Own: A New History of the American West*. Norman: University of Oklahoma Press.

16 C. Gibson and K. Jung. 2005. Historical Census Statistics on Population Totals by Race, 1790 to 1990, and by Hispanic Origin, 1970 to 1990, For Large Cities and Other Urban Places in The United States. US Census Bureau, Population Division Working Paper 76. Washington, DC.

P. Goheen. 1980. Some aspects of Canadian urbanization from 1850 to 1921. In W. Borah, J.E. Hardoy, and G.A. Stelt (eds.), Urbanization in the Americas. *Urban History Review/Revue d'histoire urbaine* (1980): 77–84. https://doi.org/10.7202/1020698ar. Accessed June 11, 2019.

17 H. MacLennan. 1961. *Seven Rivers of Canada*. Toronto: Macmillan of Canada, p. 11.

18 C. Mauch and T. Zeller (eds.). 2008. *Rivers in History: Perspectives on Waterways in Europe and North America*. Pittsburgh: University of Pittsburgh Press, p. 5.

TWO: The Mackenzie River

1 H. Selin. 2003. Introduction. In H. Selin (ed.), *Nature Across Cultures: Views of Nature and the Environment in non-Western Cultures*. Dordrecht: Springer-Science+Business Media, B.V, p. xix.

2 H. Selin. 2003. Introduction. In H. Selin (ed.), *Nature Across Cultures: Views of Nature and the Environment in Non-Western Cultures*. Dordrecht: Springer-Science+Business Media, B.V.

3 L.W. Nielsen. 2004. The "Nature" of 'Nature': The concept of nature and its complexity in a Western cultural and ethical context. *Global Bioethics* 17: 31–38.

F. Berkes. 1999. *Sacred Ecology: Traditional Ecological Knowledge and Resource Management*. London: Taylor & Francis.

4 A.L. Booth. 2003. We are the land: Native American views of nature. In H. Selin (ed.), *Nature Across Cultures: Views of Nature and the Environment in non-Western Cultures*. Dordrecht: Springer-Science+Business Media, B.V, p. 331.

5 A.L. Booth. 2003. We are the land: Native American views of nature. In H. Selin (ed.), *Nature Across Cultures: Views of Nature and the Environment in non-Western Cultures*. Dordrecht: Springer-Science+Business Media, B.V, pp. 329–49.

6 L.C. Smith. 2020. *Rivers of Power: How a Natural Force Raised Kingdoms, Destroyed Civilizations, and Shapes Our World*. New York: Little, Brown Spark, p. 285.

7 D. Groenfeldt. 2006. Water development and spiritual values in western and indigenous societies. In R. Boelens, M. Chiba, and D. Nakashima (eds.), *Water and indigenous peoples*. Knowledge of Nature. No. 2. UNESCO.

8 US National Archives. 2020. American Indian Treaties. https://www.archives.gov/research/native-americans/treaties. Accessed August 16, 2020.

9 Crown-Indigenous Relations and Northern Affairs Canada. 2020. Treaties and Agreements. https://www.rcaanc-cirnac.gc.ca/eng/1100100028574/1529354437231. Accessed August 29, 2020.

10 Crown-Indigenous Relations and Northern Affairs Canada. 2020. Treaties and Agreements. https://www.rcaanc-cirnac.gc.ca/eng/1100100028574/1529354437231. Accessed August 29, 2020.

11 M. Asch. 2018. Dene. *The Canadian Encyclopedia.* Retrieved from https://www.the canadianencyclopedia.ca/en/article/dene. Accessed July 6, 2019.
P.N. Peregrine and M. Ember (eds.). 2001. *Encyclopedia of Prehistory,* vol. 2, *Arctic and Subarctic.* Dordrecht: Springer-Science+Business Media, B.V.
Canada's First Peoples. 2007. Canada's First Peoples Before Contact. https://firstpeoples ofcanada.com/index.html. Accessed September 21, 2020.

12 J.H. Marsh and N. Baker. 2018. Mackenzie Valley Pipeline Proposals. *The Canadian Encyclopedia.* https://www.thecanadianencyclopedia.ca/en/article/mackenzie-valley-pipeline. Accessed October 2, 2020.

13 1 km = 0.62 mile.

14 L. Roberts. 1949. *The Mackenzie.* New York: Rinehart, p. 5.

15 Mackenzie River Basin Board (MRBB). 2003. Mackenzie River Basin. State of the Aquatic Ecosystem Report. 1. Whole Basin Overview. Available from MRBB, Ft. Smith, NT.
Mackenzie River Basin Board. About Us. https://www.mrbb.ca/about-us. August 30, 2020.
M. Morris and R.C. de Loë. 2016. Cooperative and adaptive transboundary water governance in Canada's Mackenzie River Basin: status and prospects. *Ecology and Society* 21: 26. http://dx.doi.org/10.5751/ES-08301-210126.
H. Vaux, Jr. et al. 2013. The Mackenzie River Basin. Rosenberg International Forum on Water Policy. Report of the Rosenberg International Forum's Workshop on Transboundary Relations in the Mackenzie River Basin. http://ciwr.ucanr.edu/files/168679. pdf. Accessed September 21, 2020.

16 L. Roberts. 1949. *The Mackenzie.* New York: Rinehart, p. 6.

17 S.M. Stanley and J.A. Lucsai. 2014. *Earth System History,* 4th ed. New York: W.H. Freeman.

18 NASA Earth Observatory. 2014. The Rocky Mountain Trench. https://earthobservatory. nasa.gov/images/84881/the-rocky-mountain-trench. Accessed June 6, 2018.

19 A. Duk-Rodkin and O.L. Hughes. 1994. Tertiary-Quaternary drainage of the pre-glacial Mackenzie Basin. *Quaternary International* 22: 221–41.

20 D.S. Lemmen, A. Duk-Rodkin, and J.M. Bednarski. 1994. Late glacial drainage systems along the northwestern margin of the Laurentide Ice Sheet. *Quaternary Science Reviews* 13: 805–28.

21 D.S. Lemmen, A. Duk-Rodkin, and J.M. Bednarski. 1994. Late glacial drainage systems along the northwestern margin of the Laurentide Ice Sheet. *Quaternary Science Reviews* 13: 805–28.

22 D. Hopkins. 1959. Cenozoic History of the Bering Land Bridge. *Science* 129: 1519–28.

23 V.V. Pitulko et al. 2004. The Yana RHS site: Humans in the Arctic before the Last Glacial Maximum. *Science* 303: 52–55.

24 C.J. Mulligan and E.J. Szathmáry. 2017. The peopling of the Americas and the origin of the Beringian occupation model. *American Journal of Physical Anthropology* 162: 403–8.

25 R. Gruhn. 2020. Evidence grows that peopling of the Americas began more than 20,000 years ago. *Nature* 584: 47–48.

26 M.Q. Sutton. 2016. How and When: Peopling of the New World. Chapter 2 in M.Q. Sutton, *A Prehistory of North America*. London: Routledge.

27 M.Q. Sutton. 2016. How and When: Peopling of the New World. Chapter 2 in M.Q. Sutton, *A Prehistory of North America*. London: Routledge.
J.F. Hoffecker et al. 2016. Beringia and the global dispersal of modern humans. *Evolutionary Anthropology: Issues, News, and Reviews* 25: 64–78.

28 J.F. Hoffecker et al. 2016. Beringia and the global dispersal of modern humans. *Evolutionary Anthropology: Issues, news, and reviews.* 25: 64–78.

29 D.W. Clark. 1991. Western subarctic prehistory. Gatineau, QC: Canadian Museum of Civilization.

30 J.L. Pilon. 1991. Insights into the Prehistory of the Lower Mackenzie Valley, Anderson Plain Region, Northwest Territories. *Canadian Archaeological Association Occasional Paper* No. 1: 89–111.

31 J.L. Pilon. 1991. Insights into the Prehistory of the Lower Mackenzie Valley, Anderson Plain Region, Northwest Territories. *Canadian Archaeological Association Occasional Paper* No. 1: 89–111.

32 D.S. Lemmen, A. Duk-Rodkin, and J.M. Bednarski. 1994. Late glacial drainage systems along the northwestern margin of the Laurentide Ice Sheet. *Quaternary Science Reviews* 13: 805–28.

33 M.Q. Sutton. 2016. Whales and sleds. Chapter 4 in M.Q. Sutton, *A Prehistory of North America*. London: Routledge.
D.W. Clark. 1991. Western subarctic prehistory. Gatineau, QC: Canadian Museum of Civilization.

34 M.Q. Sutton. 2016. Whales and sleds. Chapter 4 in M.Q. Sutton, *A Prehistory of North America*. London: Routledge.

35 Canada's First Peoples. Undated. The Inuit. https://firstpeoplesofcanada.com/fp_groups/fp_inuit1.html. Accessed October 2, 2019.

36 G. Fedirchuk. 1990. Peter Pond: Map Maker of the Northwest (1780–1807). *Arctic* 43: 184–86.

37 G. Fedirchuk. 1990. Peter Pond: Map Maker of the Northwest (1780–1807). *Arctic* 43: 184–86.

38 T. Marshall and K. Mercer. 2015. Sir Alexander Mackenzie (Explorer). *The Canadian Encyclopedia*. https://www.thecanadianencyclopedia.ca/en/article/sir-alexander-mackenzie-explorer. Accessed October 1, 2020.

39 L. Roberts. 1949. *The Mackenzie*. New York: Rinehart, p. 3.

40 J.K. Smith. 1977. *The Mackenzie River: Yesterday's Fur Frontier, Tomorrow's Energy Battleground*. Agincourt, ON: Gage, p. 25.

41 J.K. Smith. 1977. *The Mackenzie River: Yesterday's Fur Frontier, Tomorrow's Energy Battleground*. Agincourt, ON: Gage.

42 Prince of Wales Heritage Centre. 2020. History of the name of the Northwest Territories. https://www.pwnhc.ca/territorial-evolution-of-the-northwest-territories/. Accessed September 28, 2020.

43 J.K. Smith. 1977. *The Mackenzie River: Yesterday's Fur Frontier, Tomorrow's Energy Battleground*. Agincourt, ON: Gage, p. 202.

44 J.K. Smith. 1977. *The Mackenzie River: Yesterday's Fur Frontier, Tomorrow's Energy Battleground*. Agincourt, ON: Gage, p. 202.

45 Aboriginal Peoples Highlight Tables. 2016 Census. https://www12.statcan.gc.ca/census-recensement/2016/dp-pd/hlt-fst/abo-aut/Table.cfm?Lang=Eng&S=99&O=A&RPP=25. Accessed August 20, 2020.

46 Sir A. Mackenzie. 1802. *Voyages from Montreal, on the River St. Laurence, Through the Continent of North America to the Frozen and Pacific Oceans, in the Years 1789 and 1793*. Philadelphia: John Morgan, p. xxxiii.

47 Sir A. Mackenzie. 1802. *Voyages from Montreal, on the River St. Laurence, Through the Continent of North America to the Frozen and Pacific Oceans, in the Years 1789 and 1793*. Philadelphia: John Morgan, p. xxxiii.

48 1 ha = 2.47 acres.

49 Government of Alberta. 2019. Oil sands facts and statistics. https://www.alberta.ca/oil-sands-facts-and-statistics.aspx. Accessed July 21, 2019.
    F.J. Hein. 2006. Heavy oil and oil (tar) sands in North America: An overview & summary of contributions. *Natural Resources Research* 15: 67–84.

50 Natural Resources Canada. 2020. Oil resources. https://www.nrcan.gc.ca/energy/energy-sources-distribution/crude-oil/oil-resources/18085. Accessed August 31, 2020.
    US Energy Information Administration. 2019. Canada overview. https://www.eia.gov/international/overview/country/CAN. Accessed August 2, 2020.

51 J.K. Smith. 1977. *The Mackenzie River: Yesterday's Fur Frontier, Tomorrow's Energy Battleground*. Agincourt, ON: Gage, p. 206.

52 R.H. Kempthore and J.P.R. Irish. 1981. Norman Wells – A new look at one of Canada's largest oil fields. *Journal of Petroleum Technology* 33: 985–91. https://www.onepetro.org/journal-paper/SPE-9477-PA.

53 Northwest Territories Bureau of Statistics. 2019. Oil and gas. NWT natural gas & crude oil production. https://www.statsnwt.ca/economy/oil-gas/. Accessed August 15, 2020.

54 K.G. Osadetz et al. 2005. Beaufort Sea-Mackenzie Delta Basin: A review of conventional and nonconventional (gas hydrate) petroleum reserves and undiscovered resources. *Scientific Results from Mallik 2002 Gas Hydrate Production Research Well Program, Mackenzie Delta, Northwest Territories, Canada*. Geological Survey of Canada Bulletin 585.

55 W.E. Dean and M.A. Arthur. 1998. Cretaceous Western Interior Seaway drilling project: An overview. Stratigraphy and paleoenvironments of the Cretaceous Western Interior Seaway, USA, SEPM Concepts in Sedimentology and Paleontology. Special Publication of the Society for Sedimentary Geology (SEPM) No. 6: 1–10.
    K.G. Osadetz et al. 2005. Beaufort Sea-Mackenzie Delta Basin: A review of conventional and nonconventional (gas hydrate) petroleum reserves and undiscovered resources. *Scientific Results from Mallik 2002 Gas Hydrate Production Research Well Program, Mackenzie Delta, Northwest Territories, Canada*. Geological Survey of Canada Bulletin 585.

56 Arctic Power. 2013. Background: Prudhoe Bay Oil and Gas Discovery and Development. ANWR.org. http://anwr.org/2013/08/prudhoe-bay-production/. Accessed July 12, 2019.

57 K.G. Osadetz, et al. 2005. Beaufort Sea-Mackenzie Delta Basin: A review of conventional and nonconventional (gas hydrate) petroleum reserves and undiscovered resources. *Scientific Results from Mallik 2002 Gas Hydrate Production Research Well*

Program, Mackenzie Delta, Northwest Territories, Canada. Geological Survey of Canada Bulletin 585.

Canada Energy Regulator (CER). 2014. Energy Briefing Note – Assessment of Discovered Conventional Petroleum Resources in the Northwest Territories and Beaufort Sea. National Energy Board, Calgary, AB. https://www.cer-rec.gc.ca/nrth/archive/pblctn/2014ptrlmrsrc/index-eng.html. Accessed June 20, 2020.

58 C$1 ~ US$0.76.

59 J. Marsh and N. Baker. 2018. Mackenzie Valley Pipeline Proposals. *The Canadian Encyclopedia.* https://www.thecanadianencyclopedia.ca/en/article/mackenzie-valley-pipeline. Accessed October 2, 2020.

60 J.K. Smith. 1977. *The Mackenzie River: Yesterday's Fur Frontier, Tomorrow's Energy Battleground.* Agincourt, ON: Gage, p. 216.

61 C.P. Parham. 2009. *The St. Lawrence Seaway and Power Project: An Oral History of the Greatest Construction Show on Earth.* Syracuse, NY: Syracuse University Press.

62 F. Abele. 2014. The lasting impact of the Berger Inquiry into the construction of a pipeline in the Mackenzie Valley. Chapter 5 in G.J. Inwood and C.M. Johns (eds.), *Commissions of Inquiry and Policy Change: A Comparative Analysis.* Toronto: University of Toronto Press, pp. 88–113.

63 J.K. Smith. 1977. *The Mackenzie River: Yesterday's Fur Frontier, Tomorrow's Energy Battleground.* Agincourt, ON: Gage, p. 213.
    C.A. Dokis. 2015. *Where the Rivers Meet: Pipeline, Participatory Resource Management, and Aboriginal-State Relations in the Northwest Territories.* Vancouver: University of British Columbia Press.

64 D. Torgenson. 1986. Between knowledge and politics: Three faces of policy analysis. *Policy Sciences* 19: 33–59.
    M. Zachariah. 1984. The Berger Commission Inquiry Report and the revitalization of indigenous cultures. *Canadian Journal of Development Studies/Revue canadienne d'études du développement* 5(1): 65–77.

65 J.A. Gray and P.J. Gray. 1977. The Berger Report: Its impact on northern pipelines and decision making in northern development. *Canadian Public Policy* 3: 514–15.
    J.K. Smith. 1977. *The Mackenzie River: Yesterday's Fur Frontier, Tomorrow's Energy Battleground.* Agincourt, ON: Gage.
    M. O'Malley. 1976. *The Past and Future Land: An Account of the Berger Inquiry into the Mackenzie Valley Pipeline.* Toronto: Peter Martin Associates.

66 G. Wynn. 2015. Foreword: The paradoxical politics of participatory praxis. In C.A. Dokis, *Where the Rivers Meet: Pipeline, Participatory Resource Management, and Aboriginal-State Relations in the Northwest Territories.* Vancouver: University of British Columbia Press, p. ix.
    K. Stanton. 2012. Looking forward, looking back: The Canadian truth and reconciliation commission and the Mackenzie Valley pipeline inquiry. *Canadian Journal of Law and Society* 27: 83.

67 T.R. Berger. 1977. *Northern Frontier Northern Homeland. The Report of the Mackenzie Valley Pipeline Inquiry* 1: 1.
    Interview with Justice T.R. Berger. 1973. http://bergerinquiry.ubc.ca/tom-berger/tb-video1.html. indigenousfoundations.arts.ubc.ca. University of British Columbia. Accessed January 18, 2017.

68 J.K. Smith. 1977. *The Mackenzie River: Yesterday's Fur Frontier, Tomorrow's Energy Battleground*. Agincourt, ON: Gage, p. 218.

69 I.G. Waddell. 2018. Kinder Morgan and Lessons from the Berger Inquiry. *The Tyee*. October 2018. https://thetyee.ca/Opinion/2018/10/17/Kinder-Morgan-Lessons-Berger/. Accessed September 1, 2020.

70 J.K. Smith. 1977. *The Mackenzie River: Yesterday's Fur Frontier, Tomorrow's Energy Battleground*. Agincourt, ON: Gage, pp. 219–20.

71 First Nations Study Program. 2009. Berger Inquiry. University of British Columbia. https://indigenousfoundations.arts.ubc.ca/berger_inquiry/. Accessed July 17, 2019.

72 First Nations Study Program. 2009. Berger Inquiry. University of British Columbia. https://indigenousfoundations.arts.ubc.ca/berger_inquiry/. Accessed July 17, 2019.

73 S. Goudge. 2016. The Berger Inquiry in Retrospect: Its Legacy. *Canadian Journal of Women and the Law* 28: 393–407.

74 J.K. Smith. 1977. *The Mackenzie River: Yesterday's Fur Frontier, Tomorrow's Energy Battleground*. Agincourt, ON: Gage, p. 215.

75 First Nations Study Program. 2009. Berger Inquiry. University of British Columbia. https://indigenousfoundations.arts.ubc.ca/berger_inquiry/. Accessed September 3, 2019.

76 J.A. Gray and P.J. Gray. 1977. The Berger Report: Its Impact on Northern Pipelines and Decision Making in Northern Development. *Canadian Public Policy* 3: 514–15.

77 T.R. Berger. 1977. *Northern Frontier Northern Homeland. The Report of the Mackenzie Valley Pipeline Inquiry* 1:xxii.

78 J. Marsh and N. Baker. 2018. Mackenzie Valley Pipeline Proposals. *The Canadian Encyclopedia*. https://www.thecanadianencyclopedia.ca/en/article/mackenzie-valley-pipeline. Accessed October 2, 2020.

79 T.R. Berger. 1977. *Northern Frontier Northern Homeland. The Report of the Mackenzie Valley Pipeline Inquiry* 1:196.

80 J. Marsh and N. Baker. 2018. Mackenzie Valley Pipeline Proposals. *The Canadian Encyclopedia*. https://www.thecanadianencyclopedia.ca/en/article/mackenzie-valley-pipeline. Accessed October 2, 2020.

81 F. Abele. 2014. The lasting impact of the Berger Inquiry into the construction of a pipeline in the Mackenzie Valley. Chapter 5 in G.J. Inwood and C.M. Johns (eds.), *Commissions of Inquiry and Policy Change: A Comparative Analysis*. Toronto: University of Toronto Press, p. 88.
US Energy Information Administration. 2020. Natural Gas. https://www.eia.gov/dnav/ng/hist/n3010us3a.htm. Accessed September 21, 2020.
Inflationdata.com. 2020. Historical crude oil price. Oil prices 1946–2020. https://inflationdata.com/articles/inflation-adjusted-prices/historical-crude-oil-prices-table/. Accessed September 21, 2020.

82 Government of Northwest Territories, Executive and Indigenous Affairs. 2020. Concluding and Implementing Land Claim and Self-Government Agreements. https://www.eia.gov.nt.ca/en/priorities/concluding-and-implementing-land-claim-and-self-government-agreements/gwichin-regional. Accessed September 21, 2020.

83 Crown-Indigenous Relations and Northern Affairs Canada. 2020. Comprehensive Claims. https://www.rcaanc-cirnac.gc.ca/eng/1100100030577/1551196153650. Accessed September 21, 2020.

84 C.A. Dokis. 2015. *Where the Rivers Meet: Pipeline, Participatory Resource Management, and Aboriginal-State Relations in the Northwest Territories.* Vancouver: University of British Columbia Press.

85 Crown-Indigenous Relations and Northern Affairs Canada. 2020. Comprehensive Claims. https://www.rcaanc-cirnac.gc.ca/eng/1100100030577/1551196153650. Accessed September 21, 2020.

86 F. Abele. 2014. The lasting impact of the Berger inquiry into the construction of a pipeline in the Mackenzie Valley. In G.J. Inwood and C.M. Johns (eds.), *Commissions of Inquiry and Policy Change: A Comparative Analysis.* Toronto: University of Toronto Press, pp. 88–112.

87 F. Abele. 2014. The lasting impact of the Berger inquiry into the construction of a pipeline in the Mackenzie Valley. In G.J. Inwood and C.M. Johns (eds.), *Commissions of Inquiry and Policy Change: A Comparative Analysis.* Toronto: University of Toronto Press, pp. 88–112.

88 S. Goudge, S. 2016. The Berger Inquiry in retrospect: Its legacy. *Canadian Journal of Women and the Law* 28: 403.

89 S. Goudge. 2016. The Berger Inquiry in retrospect: Its legacy. Canadian Journal of Women and the Law 28: 403.

90 S. Goudge. 2016. The Berger Inquiry in retrospect: Its legacy. *Canadian Journal of Women and the Law* 28:. 404.

91 S. Goudge. 2016. The Berger Inquiry in retrospect: Its legacy. *Canadian Journal of Women and the Law* 28:. 404.
F. Abele. 2014. The lasting impact of the Berger inquiry into the construction of a pipeline in the Mackenzie Valley. In G.J. Inwood and C.M. Johns (eds.). *Commissions of Inquiry and Policy Change: A Comparative Analysis.* Toronto: University of Toronto Press, pp. 88–112.

92 S. Goudge. 2016. The Berger Inquiry in retrospect: Its legacy. *Canadian Journal of Women and the Law* 28: 393–407.

93 S. Goudge. 2016. The Berger Inquiry in retrospect: Its legacy. *Canadian Journal of Women and the Law* 28: 393–407.

94 CBC News. 2017. Mackenzie Valley pipeline project officially one for the history books. https://www.cbc.ca/news/canada/north/mackenzie-valley-gas-project-no-more-1.4465997. Accessed August 15, 2020.

95 *Canadian Business Journal.* Undated. Aboriginal pipeline group. http://www.cbj.ca/aboriginal_pipeline_group_aboriginal_representation_restarts_lon/. Accessed September 1, 2020.

96 C.A. Dokis. 2015. *Where the Rivers Meet: Pipeline, Participatory Resource Management, and Aboriginal-State Relations in the Northwest Territories.* Vancouver: University of British Columbia Press.
G. Wynn. 2015. Foreword: The paradoxical politics of participatory praxis. In C.A. Dokis, *Where the Rivers Meet: Pipeline, Participatory Resource Management, and Aboriginal-State Relations in the Northwest Territories.* Vancouver: University of British Columbia Press.

THREE: The Yukon River

1   K. Morse. 2009. *The Nature of Gold: An Environmental History of the Klondike Gold Rush*. Seattle: University of Washington Press, p. ix.

2   A. Watt and A. Philip. 2005. *Electroplating and Electrorefining of Metals*. Palm Springs, CA: Wexford College Press, p. 186.

3   K. Morse. 2009. *The Nature of Gold: An Environmental History of the Klondike Gold Rush*. Seattle: University of Washington Press, p. 24.

4   *Gold Rush! El Dorado in British Columbia*, Canadian Museum of History. Gatineau, QC, December 2016 (Notes taken by EBT).

5   World Gold Council. 2020. How much gold has been mined? https://www.gold.org/about-gold/gold-supply/gold-mining/how-much-gold. Accessed August 15, 2020.

6   M. Willbold, T. Elliott, and S. Moorbath. 2011. The tungsten isotopic composition of the Earth's mantle before the terminal bombardment. *Nature* 477: 195–98.

7   J. Kirk et al. 2003. The Origin of Gold in South Africa: Ancient rivers filled with gold, a spectacular upwelling of magma and a colossal meteor impact combined to make the Witwatersrand basin a very special place. *American Scientist* 91: 534–41.

8   P. Berton. 1972. *Klondike: The Last Great Gold Rush, 1896–1899*. Toronto: McClelland & Stewart, p. 5.

9   P. Berton. 1972. *Klondike: The Last Great Gold Rush, 1896–1899*. Toronto: McClelland & Stewart, p. 5.

10 G.W. Lowey. 2006. The origin and evolution of the Klondike goldfields, Yukon, Canada. *Ore Geology Reviews* 28: 431–50.

11 Government of Canada, Culture, History and Sport. 2020. Yukon's territorial symbols. https://www.canada.ca/en/canadian-heritage/services/provincial-territorial-symbols-canada/yukon.html. Accessed August 12, 2020.

12 State of Alaska, Department of Labor and Workforce Development, Research and Analysis. 2020. Population and Census, 2019 Population Estimates by Borough, Census Area, and Economic Region. https://live.laborstats.alaska.gov/pop/index.cfm. Accessed September 23, 2020.
    Government of Yukon. 2020. Yukon Monthly Statistical Review, July 2020. https://yukon.ca/en/yukon-monthly-statistical-review-july-2020. Accessed September 5, 2020.

13 A. Duk-Rodkin et al. 2001. Geologic evolution of the Yukon River: Implications for placer gold. *Quaternary International* 82: 5–31.
    A. Duk-Rodkin et al. 2004. Timing and extent of Plio-Pleistocene glaciations in north-western Canada and east-central Alaska. *Developments in Quaternary Sciences* 2: 313–45.

14 A. Duk-Rodkin et al. 2001. Geologic evolution of the Yukon River: Implications for placer gold. *Quaternary International* 82: 5–31.

15 A. Duk-Rodkin et al. 2001. Geologic evolution of the Yukon River: Implications for placer gold. *Quaternary International* 82: 5–31.

16 A. Duk-Rodkin et al. 2001. Geologic evolution of the Yukon River: Implications for placer gold. *Quaternary International* 82: 5–31.

17 G.W. Lowey. 2006. The origin and evolution of the Klondike goldfields, Yukon, Canada. *Ore Geology Reviews* 28: 431–50.

18 A. Duk-Rodkin et al. 2001. Geologic evolution of the Yukon River: Implications for placer gold. *Quaternary International* 82: 5–31.

A. Duk-Rodkin et al. 2004. Timing and extent of Plio-Pleistocene glaciations in north-western Canada and east-central Alaska. *Developments in Quaternary Sciences* 2: 313–45.

19 A. Duk-Rodkin et al. 2001. Geologic evolution of the Yukon River: Implications for placer gold. *Quaternary International* 82: 5–31.

20 S.L. Bonatto and Francisco M. Salzano. 1997. A single and early migration for the peopling of the Americas supported by mitochondrial DNA sequence data. *Proceedings of the National Academy of Sciences* 94: 1866–87.

E. Tamm et al. 2007. Beringian Standstill and Spread of Native American Founders. *PLoS ONE* 2(9): e829.

A. Kitchen, M.M. Miyamoto, and C.J. Mulligan. 2008. A Three-Stage Colonization Model for the Peopling of the Americas. *PLoS ONE* 3(2): e1596.

21 J.V. Moreno-Mayar et al. 2018. Terminal Pleistocene Alaskan genome reveals first founding population of Native Americans. *Nature* 553(7687): 203.

22 M. Krauss et al. 2011. Indigenous Peoples and Languages of Alaska. Fairbanks and Anchorage: Alaska Native Language Center and UAA Institute of Social and Economic Research. https://www.uaf.edu/anla/collections/map/. Accessed December 4, 2020.

L. Kaplan. 2020. Comparative Yupik and Inuit. Alaska Native Language Center. University of Alaska Fairbanks. https://uaf.edu/anlc/resources/comparative_yupik_and_inuit.php. Accessed September 23, 2020.

G. Holton. 2020. Languages. Alaska Native Language Center. University of Alaska Fairbanks. https://www.uaf.edu/anlc/languages.php. Accessed September 23, 2020.

23 P. Berton. 1972. *Klondike: The Last Great Gold Rush, 1896–1899*. Toronto: McClelland & Stewart.

24 A. Duk-Rodkin et al. 2001. Geologic evolution of the Yukon River: Implications for placer gold. *Quaternary International* 82: 5–31.

25 P. Berton. 1972. *Klondike: The Last Great Gold Rush, 1896–1899*. Toronto: McClelland & Stewart, p. 29.

26 P. Berton. 1972. *Klondike: The Last Great Gold Rush, 1896–1899*. Toronto: McClelland & Stewart, p. 9.

27 K. Morse. 2009. *The Nature of Gold: An Environmental History of the Klondike Gold Rush*. Seattle: University of Washington Press.

C. Gray. 2010. *Gold Diggers: Striking it Rich in the Klondike*. Toronto: HarperCollins.

28 P. Berton. 1972. *Klondike: The Last Great Gold Rush, 1896–1899*. Toronto: McClelland & Stewart, p. 93.

K. Morse. 2009. *The Nature of Gold: An Environmental History of the Klondike Gold Rush*. Seattle: University of Washington Press.

29 P. Berton. 1958. Klondike: The strangest gold rush in history. *Maclean's*. September 27, p. 25.

30 L. Mighetto and M.B. Montgomery. 1998. Hard Drive to the Klondike: Promoting Seattle during the Gold Rush. A Historic Resource Study for the Seattle Unit of the Klondike Gold Rush National Historical Park. National Park Service (Dept. of Interior), Washington, DC, p. 27. https://files.eric.ed.gov/fulltext/ED437334.pdf. Accessed October 24, 2017.

31 Based on the 1897 gold price of US$20.67 per troy ounce (https://onlygold.com/gold-prices/historical-gold-prices/) and a mid-2021 price of US$1732.

M. Lundberg. 2019. Tons of Gold!! Klondike treasure ship passenger lists. http://www.explorenorth.com/klondike/klondike_treasure_ships.html. Accessed September 2, 2020.

32 Government of Yukon. 2009. Klondike gold Rush: Fever pitch. Department of Tourism and Culture. http://www.tc.gov.yk.ca/archives/klondike/en/fever.html. Accessed September 23, 2020.

33 P. Berton. 1972. *Klondike: The Last Great Gold Rush, 1896–1899*. Toronto: McClelland & Stewart.

34 P. Berton. 1972. *Klondike: The Last Great Gold Rush, 1896–1899*. Toronto: McClelland & Stewart.

35 P. Berton. 1972. *Klondike: The Last Great Gold Rush, 1896–1899*. Toronto: McClelland & Stewart.

C. Gray. 2010. *Gold Diggers: Striking it Rich in the Klondike*. Toronto: HarperCollins.

K. Morse. 2009. *The Nature of Gold: An Environmental History of the Klondike Gold Rush*. Seattle: University of Washington Press.

36 R. Mole. 2009. *Gold Fever: Incredible Tales of the Klondike Gold Rush*. Victoria, BC: Heritage House.

C. Porsild. 2011. *Gamblers and Dreamers: Women, Men, and Community in the Klondike*. Vancouver: University of British Columbia Press.

P. Berton. 1972. *Klondike: The Last Great Gold Rush, 1896–1899*. Toronto: McClelland & Stewart, p. 383.

Yukon News. 2010. Klondike King went from rags to riches, to rags. Yukon Nuggets, McBride Museum. https://www.yukon-news.com/letters-opinions/klondike-king-went-from-rags-to-riches-to-rags/. Accessed August 24, 2018.

37 P. Berton. 1972. *Klondike: The Last Great Gold Rush, 1896–1899*. Toronto: McClelland & Stewart.

38 R. Mole. 2009. *Gold Fever: Incredible Tales of the Klondike Gold Rush*. Victoria, BC: Heritage House.

39 P. Berton. 1972. *Klondike: The Last Great Gold Rush, 1896–1899*. Toronto: McClelland & Stewart, p. 391.

40 Yukon Bureau of Statistics. 2020. Population Report, Q1 October 2020. https://yukon.ca/en/population-report-q1-2020. Accessed August 2, 2020.

41 Estimates vary among sources. Yukon Travel suggested $95 million (https://www.travelyukon.com/en/discover/about-yukon/history). *The Canadian Encyclopedia* suggested $29 million to 1899 (M. Gates, Klondike Gold Rush. https://www.thecanadianencyclopedia.ca/en/article/klondike-gold-rush). This estimate was based an intermediate value of $65 million and a price of gold of US$20.7 per troy oz. in 1900 (see endnote 31), converting the dollar value in 1900 to troy oz., and then converting to mid 2020 price of US$1950. The University of Washington suggested a value of more than US$1 billion (adjusted to late 20th century gold prices [~$300/troy oz.]. https://content.lib.washington.edu/extras/goldrush.html).

42 C. Gray. 2010. *Gold Diggers: Striking it Rich in the Klondike*. Toronto: HarperCollins, p. 352.

43 M. Gates. 2015. Klondike Gold Rush. *The Canadian Encyclopedia*. https://www.thecanadianencyclopedia.ca/en/article/klondike-gold-rush.Accessed August 23, 2020.

44 G.W. Lowey. 2006. The origin and evolution of the Klondike goldfields, Yukon, Canada. *Ore Geology Reviews* 28: 431–50.

Government of Yukon. 2008. Gold. Departments of Economic Development & Energy, Mines and Resources. www.geology.gov.yk.ca. Accessed April 17, 2017.

Government of Yukon. 2009–2020. Mining Activity Reports. http://www.emr.gov.yk.ca/mining/statistics.html. Accessed September 23, 2020.

45 US Library of Congress. 2020. Treaty with Russia for the Purchase of Alaska, Primary Documents in American History. https://guides.loc.gov/alaska-treaty. Accessed November 12, 2020.

46 E.P. Oberholtzer. 1917. *A History of the United States since the Civil War.* New York: Macmillan, p. 541 https://archive.org/details/oberholtzerhistorellirich/page/540/mode/2up. Accessed September 23, 2020.

47 Center for Economic Development. 2020. Alaska Macroeconomic Indicators. University of Alaska-Anchorage. https://www.uaa.alaska.edu/academics/business-enterprise-institute/center-for-economic-development/reports/alaska-macroeconomic-indicators.cshtml. Accessed September 23, 2020.

US Department of Commerce, Bureau of Economic Statistics, Bea.gov. Accessed September 23, 2020.

48 US Census Bureau. 2020. State exports from Alaska. Business and Industry, Foreign Trade, US International Trade Data. https://www.census.gov/foreign-trade/statistics/state/data/ak.html. Accessed September 23, 2020.

49 C. Gray. 2010. *Gold Diggers: Striking it Rich in the Klondike.* Toronto: HarperCollins.

50 YukonInfo.com. 2020. Robert Service – The Bard of the Yukon. https://www.yukoninfo.com/dawson-city-yukon/robert-service-the-bard-of-the-yukon/. Accessed September 23, 2020.

51 K. Morse. 2009. *The Nature of Gold: An Environmental History of the Klondike Gold Rush.* Seattle: University of Washington Press.

52 B.C. Willis. 1997. The environmental effects of the Yukon gold rush 1896–1906: Alterations to land, destruction of wildlife, and disease. MA thesis, University of Western Ontario, London, ON.

53 B.C. Willis. 1997. The environmental effects of the Yukon gold rush 1896–1906: Alterations to land, destruction of wildlife, and disease. MA thesis, University of Western Ontario, London, ON.

54 Crown-Indigenous Relations and Northern Affairs Canada. 1998. The Tr'ondëk Hwëch'in Final Agreement. https://www.rcaanc-cirnac.gc.ca/eng/1297209099174/1542826344768. Accessed September 23, 2020.

55 Trondekheritage. 2020. Welcome to Tr'ocheëk. Tr'ondëk Hwëch'in Heritage Sites. http://trondekheritage.com/our-places/trochek/. Accessed September 23, 2020.

56 Yukon News. 2018. Canada withdraws Klondike World Heritage Site Bid. https://www.yukon-news.com/news/canada-withdraws-klondike-world-heritage-site-bid/. Accessed September 23, 2020.

57 P. Berton. 1948. Monsters on the Klondike. *Maclean's.* September 1. https://archive.macleans.ca/article/1948/9/1/monsters-on-the-klondike. Accessed May 4, 2019.

58 B.C. Willis. 1997. The environmental effects of the Yukon gold rush 1896–1906: Alterations to land, destruction of wildlife, and disease. MA thesis, University of Western Ontario, London, ON.

59 B.C. Willis. 1997. The environmental effects of the Yukon gold rush 1896–1906: Alterations to land, destruction of wildlife, and disease. MA thesis, University of Western Ontario, London, ON, p. 32.

C. Pustola. 2014. Impact of the Klondike gold rush. Alaskaweb.org. http://alaskaweb. org/mining/klonimpact.html. Accessed September 23, 2020.

60 National Archives of Canada, *Sessional Papers*. 1904. 22 Report of the Deputy Minister Marine and Fisheries, 34, Edward VII. A Series, p. xxxviii.

61 B.C. Willis. 1997. The environmental effects of the Yukon gold rush 1896–1906: Alterations to land, destruction of wildlife, and disease. MA thesis, University of Western Ontario, p. 61.

62 M.B. Parsons and J.B. Percival. 2005. A brief history of mercury and its environmental impact. *Mercury: Sources, measurements, cycles, and effects* 34: 1–20.

63 B.C. Willis. 1997. The environmental effects of the Yukon gold rush 1896–1906: Alterations to land, destruction of wildlife, and disease. MA thesis, University of Western Ontario, London, ON.
W.L. Lockhart et al. 2005. A history of total mercury in edible muscle of fish from lakes in northern Canada. *Science of the Total Environment* 351: 427–63.

64 B.C. Willis. 1997. The environmental effects of the Yukon gold rush 1896–1906: Alterations to land, destruction of wildlife, and disease. MA thesis, University of Western Ontario, London, ON, p. 55.

65 B.C. Willis. 1997. The environmental effects of the Yukon gold rush 1896–1906: Alterations to land, destruction of wildlife, and disease. MA thesis, University of Western Ontario, London, ON, p. 55.

66 B.C. Willis. 1997. The environmental effects of the Yukon gold rush 1896–1906: Alterations to land, destruction of wildlife, and disease. MA thesis, University of Western Ontario, London, ON, p. 61.

67 *Dawson Daily News*. 1902. To End Season. Big Dredge on Bonanza Creek. Shuts Down Soon. October 3.

68 Government of Yukon. 2017. Yukon State of the Environment. Reporting on Environmental Indicators – 2017. Environment Yukon. https://yukon.ca/sites/yukon.ca/files/ env/env-yukon-state-environment-report-2017.pdf. Accessed September 23, 2020.

69 J.D. Bond and S. van Loon. 2018. *Yukon Placer Mining Industry 2015 to 2017*. Yukon Geological Survey. Government of Yukon. Energy, Mines and Resources.

70 Government of Yukon. 2009–2020. Mining Activity Reports. http://www.emr.gov. yk.ca/mining/statistics.html. Accessed September 23, 2020.

71 World Gold Council. 2020. Gold spot price. www.gold.com. Accessed September 23, 2020.

FOUR: The Fraser River

1 J.A. Endler. 1986. *Natural Selection in the Wild*. Princeton, NJ: Princeton University Press.

2 W.E. Ricker. 1972. Hereditary and environmental factors affecting certain salmonid populations. In *The stock concept in Pacific salmon*. University of British Columbia, H.R. MacMillan Lectures in Fisheries, Vancouver, pp. 19–160.
E.B. Taylor. 1991. A review of local adaptation in Salmonidae, with particular reference to Pacific and Atlantic salmon. *Aquaculture* 98: 185–207.
C.V. Burger. 2000. The needs of salmon and steelhead in balancing their conservation and use. Chapter 2 in E.E. Knudsen et al. (eds.), *Sustainable Fisheries Management: Pacific Salmon*. Boca Raton, FL: Lewis.

D.J. Fraser et al. 2011. Extent and scale of local adaptation in salmonid fishes: Review and meta-analysis. *Heredity* 106: 404–20.

3   F. Neave. 1958. The origin and speciation of *Oncorhynchus*. *Transactions of the Royal Society of Canada* (Series 3) 52: 25–39.

D.R. Montgomery. 2000. Coevolution of the Pacific salmon and Pacific Rim topography. *Geology* 28: 1107–10.

R.S. Waples, G.R. Pess, and T. Beechie. 2008. Evolutionary history of Pacific salmon in dynamic environments. *Evolutionary Applications* 1: 189–206.

4   B.E. Penaluna et al. 2016. Conservation of native Pacific trout diversity in western North America. *Fisheries* 41: 286–300.

C. Groot and L. Margolis. 1991. *Pacific Salmon Life Histories*. Vancouver: University of British Columbia Press.

5   A.K. Fremier, B.J. Yanites, and E.M. Yager. 2018. Sex that moves mountains: The influence of spawning fish on river profiles over geologic timescales. *Geomorphology* 305: 163–72.

6   C.M. Halffman et al. 2015. Early human use of anadromous salmon in North America at 11,500 ÿ ago. *Proceedings of the National Academy of Sciences* 112: 12344–48.

7   M.Q. Sutton. 2017. The "fishing link": Salmonids and the initial peopling of the Americas. *PaleoAmerica* 3: 231–59.

8   See https://www2.gov.bc.ca/gov/content/data/statistics. Accessed March 26, 2021.

9   J.H. Garber. 2011. Tectonic history of British Columbia: Historical and current influences on the Chilko-Chilcotin-Fraser River System. Chapter 1 in J. Mount and P. Moyle (eds.), *Chilko-Chilcotin River Network: A Lakes and Rivers Ecosystem [A field guide]*. Davis: University of California–Davis. Available from www.jmgarber.com/publications.

10 J.S. Nelson and M.J. Paetz. 1992. *The Fishes of Alberta*. Edmonton: University of Alberta Press, p. 53.

11 J.D. McPhail and C.C. Lindsey. 1986. Zoogeography of the freshwater fishes of Cascadia (the Columbia system and rivers north to the Stikine). In C.H. Hocutt and E.O. Wiley (eds.), *The Zoogeography of North American Freshwater Fishes*. New York: Wiley-Interscience, pp. 615–638.

12 G. Mohs. 1985. Spiritual sites, ethnic significance and native spirituality: The heritage and heritage sites of the Sto: lo Indians of British Columbia. PhD diss., Simon Fraser University Vancouver, BC.

13 J. Lichatowich and J.A. Lichatowich. 2001. *Salmon Without Rivers: A History of the Pacific Salmon Crisis*. Washington, DC: Island Press.

Musqueam Indian Band. 2011. CʼƏSNAʔƏM. http://www.musqueam.bc.ca/cʼəsnaʔəm. Accessed September 24, 2020.

M.Q. Sutton. 2016. *A Prehistory of North America*. London: Routledge.

14 D. Sanger. 1967. Prehistory of the Pacific Northwest Plateau as seen from the interior of British Columbia. *American Antiquity* 32: 86–197.

K.R. Fladmark. 1982. An introduction to the prehistory of British Columbia. *Canadian Journal of Archaeology* 1982: 95–196.

15 B. Hutchison. 1950. *The Fraser*. New York: Rinehart.

M.W. Campbell. 1968. *The Savage River: Seventy-one Days with Simon Fraser*. Toronto: Macmillan of Canada.

16 D. Hayes. 2001. *First Crossing: Alexander Mackenzie, His Explorations Across North America, and the Opening of the Continent.* Vancouver/Toronto: Douglas & McIntyre, p. 144.

17 B. Hutchison. 1950. *The Fraser.* New York: Rinehart.
M.W. Campbell. 1968. *The Savage River: Seventy-one Days with Simon Fraser.* Toronto: Macmillan of Canada.

18 H. MacLennan. 1961. *Seven Rivers of Canada.* Toronto: Macmillan of Canada, p. 140.

19 B. Hutchison. 1950. *The Fraser.* New York: Rinehart.
M.W. Campbell. 1968. *The Savage River: Seventy-one Days with Simon Fraser.* Toronto: Macmillan of Canada.

20 K.W. Lamb (ed.). 2007. *The Letters and Journals of Simon Fraser, 1806–1808.* Toronto: Dundurn, p. 129.

21 K.W. Lamb (ed.). 2007. *The Letters and Journals of Simon Fraser, 1806–1808.* Toronto: Dundurn, p. 117.

22 R.S. Macki. 1997. *Trading Beyond the Mountains: The British Fur Trade on the Pacific, 1793–1843.* Vancouver: University of British Columbia Press, p. 58.

23 K.W. Lamb (ed.). 2007. *The Letters and Journals of Simon Fraser, 1806–1808.* Toronto: Dundurn, p. 137.

24 K.W. Lamb (ed.). 2007. *The Letters and Journals of Simon Fraser, 1806–1808.* Toronto: Dundurn, p. 133.

25 B. Hutchison. 1950. *The Fraser.* New York: Rinehart.

26 W.E. Ricker. 1972. Hereditary and environmental factors affecting certain salmonid populations. In *The stock concept in Pacific salmon.* University of British Columbia, H.R. MacMillan Lectures in Fisheries, Vancouver, pp. 19–160.

27 L.B. DeFilippo et al. 2018. Associations of stream geomorphic conditions and prevalence of alternative reproductive tactics among sockeye salmon populations. *Journal of Evolutionary Biology* 3: 239–53.

28 E.L. Brannon et al. 1981. Compass orientation of sockeye salmon fry from a complex river system. *Canadian Journal of Zoology* 59: 1548–53.

29 R.S. Waples, G.R. Pess, and T. Beechie. 2008. Evolutionary history of Pacific salmon in dynamic environments. *Evolutionary Applications* 1: 189–206.

30 M.P. Small et al. 1998. Discriminating coho salmon (*Oncorhynchus kisutch*) populations within the Fraser River, British Columbia, using microsatellite DNA markers. *Molecular Ecology* 7: 141–55.
Q. Rougemont et al. 2020. The role of historical contingency in shaping geographic pattern of deleterious mutation load in a broadly distributed Pacific Salmon. *PLOS Genetics* 17(2): e1009397. https://doi.org/10.1371/journal.pgen.1009397.

31 J.D. McPhail and C.C. Lindsey. 1986. Zoogeography of the freshwater fishes of Cascadia (the Columbia system and rivers north to the Stikine). In C.H. Hocutt and E.O. Wiley (eds.), *The zoogeography of North American freshwater fishes.* New York: Wiley-Interscience, pp. 615–38.

32 J. Lichatowich and J.A. Lichatowich. 2001. *Salmon Without Rivers: A History of the Pacific Salmon Crisis.* Washington, DC: Island Press.

33 D.E. Schindler et al. 2010. Population diversity and the portfolio effect in an exploited species. *Nature* 465: 609–12.

34 W.B. Scott and E.J. Crossman. 1973. *Freshwater Fishes of Canada.* Bulletin of the Fisheries Research Board of Canada, No. 184.

35 W.B. Scott and E.J. Crossman. 1973. *Freshwater Fishes of Canada*. Bulletin of the Fisheries Research Board of Canada, No. 184.
    K.R. Fladmark. 1982. An introduction to the prehistory of British Columbia. *Canadian Journal of Archaeology* 1982: 95–196.

36 J.C. Driver. 1993. Zooarchaeology in British Columbia. *BC Studies* 99: 77–105. B. Hayden and J.M. Ryder. 1991. Prehistoric cultural collapse in the Lillooet area. *American Antiquity* 56: 50–65.

37 A. Stevenson. 1998. Wet-site contributions to developmental models of Fraser River fishing technology. In K. Bernick (ed.), *Hidden Dimensions: The Cultural Significance of Wetland Archaeology. Pacific Rim Archaeology and Wetland Archaeology Research Project*. Occasional Paper 2. University of British Columbia Press.
    J. Lichatowich and J.A. Lichatowich. 2001. *Salmon Without Rivers: A History of the Pacific Salmon Crisis*. Washington, DC: Island Press.

38 K.R. Fladmark. 1982. An introduction to the prehistory of British Columbia. *Canadian Journal of Archaeology* 1982: 95–196.
    J.C. Driver. 1993. Zooarchaeology in British Columbia. *BC Studies* 99: 77–105.

39 H.K. Nesbitt and J.W. Moore. 2016. Species and population diversity in Pacific salmon fisheries underpin indigenous food security. *Journal of Applied Ecology* 53:1489–99.

40 K.T. Carlson (ed.). 1997. *You Are Asked to Witness: The Stó:lō in Canada's Pacific Coast History*. Chilliwack, BC: Stó:lō Heritage Trust.

41 Hon. B.I. Cohen. 2012. *The Uncertain Future of Fraser River Sockeye*, vol. 1, *The Sockeye Fishery*. Commission of Inquiry into the Decline of Sockeye Salmon in the Fraser River. Publishing and Depository Services, Public Works and Government Services Canada.

42 Hon. B.I. Cohen. 2012. *The Uncertain Future of Fraser River Sockeye*, vol. 1, *The Sockeye Fishery*. Commission of Inquiry into the Decline of Sockeye Salmon in the Fraser River. Publishing and Depository Services, Public Works and Government Services Canada, p. 7.

43 Hon. B.I. Cohen. 2012. *The Uncertain Future of Fraser River Sockeye*, vol. 1, *The Sockeye Fishery*. Commission of Inquiry into the Decline of Sockeye Salmon in the Fraser River. Publishing and Depository Services, Public Works and Government Services Canada, p. 7.

44 Hon. B.I. Cohen. 2012. *The Uncertain Future of Fraser River Sockeye*, vol. 1, *The Sockeye Fishery*. Commission of Inquiry into the Decline of Sockeye Salmon in the Fraser River. Publishing and Depository Services, Public Works and Government Services Canada, p. 7.

45 Watershed Watch Salmon Society. 2012. Resource: Cohen Report Card. http://www.watershed-watch.org/issues/salmon-biodiversity/the-fraser-sockeye-inquiry/cohen-report-tracker/. Accessed September 24, 2020.

46 Fisheries and Oceans Canada. 2018. *Cohen Response Status Update – October 2018*. https://www.dfo-mpo.gc.ca/cohen/report-rapport-2018-eng.htm and associated Annex. Accessed August 5, 2020.

47 Watershed Watch Salmon Society. 2016. "Business as usual": A critique of federal update on Cohen. https://watershedwatch.ca/business-as-usual-a-critique-of-federal-update-on-cohen/. Accessed August 5, 2020.

48 Hon. B.I. Cohen. 2012. *The Uncertain Future of Fraser River Sockeye*, vol. 3, *Recommendations – Summary – Process*. Commission of Inquiry into the Decline of Sockeye

Salmon in the Fraser River. Publishing and Depository Services, Public Works and Government Services Canada, p. 64.

Fisheries and Oceans Canada. 2018. *Cohen Response Status Update – October 2018.* https://www.dfo-mpo.gc.ca/cohen/report-rapport-2018-eng.htm and associated Annex. Accessed August 5, 2020.

49 SARA Public Registry. 2021. Species at risk public registry. Environment and Climate Change Canada. https://species-registry.canada.ca/index-en.html#/species?sortBy=commonNameSort&sortDirection=asc&pageSize=10. Accessed March 23, 2021.

50 See also J. Zeman and H. Andrusak. 2020. Hear no evil: Canada's broken Department of Fisheries and Oceans. *The Osprey* 97: 12–14.

51 Alaska Department of Fish and Game. 2020. Inseason Commercial Harvest Estimates. Bristol Bay. http://www.adfg.alaska.gov/index.cfm?adfg=commercialbyareabristolbay.harvestsummary. Accessed August 6, 2020.

52 D.E. Schindler et al. 2008. Climate change, ecosystem impacts, and management for Pacific salmon. *Fisheries* 33: 502–6.

53 Columbia River Inter-Tribal Fish Commission. 2020. Columbia Basin Salmonids. https://www.critfc.org/fish-and-watersheds/columbia-river-fish-species/columbia-river-salmon/. Accessed August 12, 2020.

D.W. Chapman. 1986. Salmon and steelhead abundance in the Columbia River in the nineteenth century. *Transactions of the American Fisheries Society* 115: 662–70.

54 R.M. Yoshiyama et al. 2000. Chinook salmon in the California Central Valley: An assessment. *Fisheries* 25: 6–20.

R.M. Yoshiyama, F.W. Fisher, and P.B. Moyle. 1998. Historical abundance and decline of chinook salmon in the Central Valley region of California. *North American Journal of Fisheries Management* 18: 487–521.

55 T.G. Northcote and D.Y. Atagi. 1997. Pacific salmon abundance trends in the Fraser River watershed compared with other British Columbia systems. In D.J. Stouder, P.A. Bisson, and R. Naiman (eds.), *Pacific Salmon & their Ecosystems: Status and Future Options.* New York: Chapman & Hall, pp. 199–223.

56 Hon. B.I. Cohen. 2012. *The Uncertain Future of Fraser River Sockeye*, vol. 2, *Causes of the Decline.* Commission of Inquiry into the Decline of Sockeye Salmon in the Fraser River. Publishing and Depository Services, Public Works and Government Services Canada.

57 Hon. B.I. Cohen. 2012. *The Uncertain Future of Fraser River Sockeye*, vol. 3, *Recommendations – Summary – Process.* Commission of Inquiry into the Decline of Sockeye Salmon in the Fraser River. Publishing and Depository Services, Public Works and Government Services Canada, p. 88.

58 Hon. B.I. Cohen. 2012. *The Uncertain Future of Fraser River Sockeye*, vol. 2, *Causes of the Decline.* Commission of Inquiry into the Decline of Sockeye Salmon in the Fraser River. Publishing and Depository Services, Public Works and Government Services Canada, p. 123.

59 Hon. B.I. Cohen. 2012. *The Uncertain Future of Fraser River Sockeye*, vol. 2, *Causes of the Decline.* Commission of Inquiry into the Decline of Sockeye Salmon in the Fraser River. Publishing and Depository Services, Public Works and Government Services Canada, p. 123.

E.G. Martins et al. 2011. Effects of river temperature and climate warming on stock-specific survival of adult migrating Fraser River sockeye salmon (*Oncorhynchus nerka*). *Global Change Biology* 17: 99–114.

60 M.C. Healey. 2009. Resilient salmon, resilient fisheries for British Columbia, Canada. *Ecology and Society* 14(1): 2. http://www.ecologyandsociety.org/vol14/iss1/art2/.
R.S. Waples, G.R. Pess, and T. Beechie. 2008. Evolutionary history of Pacific salmon in dynamic environments. *Evolutionary Applications* 1: 189–206.
R.S. Waples, T. Beechie, and G.R. Pess. 2009. Evolutionary history, habitat distur-bance regimes, and anthropogenic changes: What do these mean for resilience of Pacific salmon populations? *Ecology and Society* 14(1): 3. http://www.ecologyandsoci-ety.org/vol14/iss1/art3/.

61 M.C. Healey. 2009. Resilient salmon, resilient fisheries for British Columbia, Canada. *Ecology and Society* 14(1): 2. http://www.ecologyandsociety.org/vol14/iss1/art2/.

62 Fisheries and Oceans Canada. 2018. The 2017 Fraser Sockeye Salmon (*Oncorhynchus nerka*) integrated biological status re-assessment under the Wild Salmon Policy. DFO Can. Sci. Advis. Sec. Sci. Advis. Rep. 2018/017. https://waves-vagues.dfo-mpo.gc.ca/Library/40712163.pdf. Accessed March 23, 2021.

63 Hon. B.I. Cohen. 2012. *The Uncertain Future of Fraser River Sockeye*, vol. 2, *Causes of the Decline*. Commission of Inquiry into the Decline of Sockeye Salmon in the Fraser River. Publishing and Depository Services, Public Works and Government Services Canada, p. 124.

64 Hon. B.I. Cohen. 2012. *The Uncertain Future of Fraser River Sockeye*, vol. 2, *Causes of the Decline*. Commission of Inquiry into the Decline of Sockeye Salmon in the Fraser River. Publishing and Depository Services, Public Works and Government Services Canada, p. 124.

65 D.E. Schindler et al. 2008. Climate change, ecosystem impacts, and management for Pacific salmon. *Fisheries* 33: 502–6.
W.W. Cheung et al. 2015. Projecting future changes in distributions of pelagic fish species of Northeast Pacific shelf seas. *Progress in Oceanography* 130: 19–31.

66 British Columbia Waterfowl Society. 2020. The Fraser River Estuary. http://www.reif-elbirdsanctuary.com/fraser.html. Accessed September 24, 2020.

67 Government of British Columbia. 2020. British Columbia Population Estimates. BC Stats. https://www2.gov.bc.ca/gov/content/data/statistics/people-population-commu-nity/population. Accessed September 24, 2020.

68 Government of British Columbia. 2020. British Columbia Population Projections. BC Stats. https://www2.gov.bc.ca/gov/content/data/statistics/people-population-commu-nity/population. Accessed September 24, 2020.

69 A.K. Hamilton et al. 2020. Seasonal turbidity linked to physical dynamics in a deep lake following the catastrophic 2014 Mount Polley mine tailings spill. *Water Resources Research* 56(8): e2019WR025790.

70 Canadian Centre for Policy Alternatives. 2018. Report on Mount Polley and Bra-zil Tailing spills points to systemic problems with mining industry. https://www.policyalternatives.ca/newsroom/news-releases/report-mount-polley-and-brazil-tail-ings-spills-points-systemic-problems. Accessed August 19, 2020.
E.L. Petticrew et al. 2015. The impact of a catastrophic mine tailings impoundment spill into one of North America's largest fjord lakes: Quesnel Lake, British Columbia, Canada. *Geophysical Research Letters* 42: 3347–55.

71 G.F. Hartman, T.G. Northcote, and C.J. Cederholm. 2006. Human numbers—The alpha factor affecting the future of wild salmon. In R.T. Lackey, D.H. Lach, and S.L.

Duncan (eds.), *Salmon 2100: The Future of Wild Pacific Salmon*. Bethesda, MD: American Fisheries Society, pp. 261–92.

72 R.T. Lackey, D.H. Lach, and S.L. Duncan (eds.). 2006. *Salmon 2100 Project: The Future of Wild Pacific Salmon*. Bethesda, MD: American Fisheries Society.

R.T. Lackey. 2013. The Salmon 2100 Project. http://fw.oregonstate.edu/content/robert-t-lackey. Accessed March 12, 2016.

FIVE: The Columbia River

1 J.D. McPhail, and C.C. Lindsey. 1986. Zoogeography of the freshwater fishes of Cascadia (the Columbia system and rivers north to the Stikine). In C.H. Hocutt and E.O. Wiley (eds.), *The Zoogeography of North American Freshwater Fishes*. New York: Wiley-Interscience, pp. 615–38.

2 Northwest Power and Conservation Council. 2020. David Thompson. https://www.nwcouncil.org/history/ThompsonDavid. Accessed September 30, 2020.

3 D. Worster. 1986. *Rivers of Empire: Water, Aridity, and the Growth of the American West*. New York: Pantheon, p. 7.

4 M. Doyle. 2019. *The Source: How Rivers Made America and America Remade Its Rivers*. New York: W.W. Norton, p. 220.

5 K.A. Wittfogel. 1957. *Oriental Despotism: A Comparative Study of Total Power*. New Haven, CT: Yale University Press, p. 162.

6 K.A. Wittfogel. 1957. *Oriental Despotism: A Comparative Study of Total Power*. New Haven, CT: Yale University Press.

7 D. Worster. 1986. *Rivers of Empire: Water, Aridity, and the Growth of the American West*. New York: Pantheon, pp. 27–28.

8 E.P. Pearkes. 2016. *A River Captured: The Columbia River Treaty and Catastrophic Change*. Victoria, BC: Rocky Mountain Books.

9 B. Harden. 1997. *A River Lost: The Life and Death of the Columbia*. New York: W.W. Norton, p. 25.

10 F.P. Fradkin. 1981. *A River No More: The Colorado River and the West*. Tucson: University of Arizona Press.

11 R. Bilby et al. 2007. Human population impacts on Columbia River Basin Fish and Wildlife. Independent Scientific Advisory Board Human Population Report, ISAB 2007-3. Northwest Power and Conservation Council, Portland. https://www.census.gov/data/datasets/time-series/demo/popest/2010s-counties-total.html. Accessed September 30. 2020.

Columbia Basin Trust. 2020. Columbia Basin Trust Region. https://ourtrust.org/about/basin-map/. Accessed September 30, 2020.

US Census Bureau. 2020. Population estimates by county. https://www.census.gov/data/datasets/time-series/demo/popest/2010s-counties-total.html Accessed September 12, 2020.

12 J.M. English and S.T. Johnston. 2004. The Laramide orogeny: What were the driving forces? *International Geology Review* 46: 833–38.

S.M. Stanley and J.A. Luczaj. 2015. *Earth System History*, 4th ed. New York: W.H. Freeman.

13 P.R. Hooper et al. 2007. The origin of the Columbia River flood basalt province: Plume versus nonplume models. *Geological Society of America Special Papers* 430: 635–68.

14 P.R. Hooper et al. 2007. The origin of the Columbia River flood basalt province: Plume versus nonplume models. *Geological Society of America Special Papers* 430: 635–68.

15 D.B. Booth et al. 2003. The Cordilleran ice sheet. *Developments in Quaternary Sciences* 1: 17–43.

16 J.E. O'Connor et al. 2020. The Missoula and Bonneville floods—A review of ice-age megafloods in the Columbia River basin. *Earth-Science Reviews* 208: 103181.

17 J.E. O'Connor et al. 2020. The Missoula and Bonneville floods—A review of ice-age megafloods in the Columbia River basin. *Earth-Science Reviews* 208: 103181.

18 D.D. Alt and D.W. Hundman. 1995. *Northwest Exposures: A Geologic History of the Northwest.* Missoula, MT: Mountain Press.
   V.R. Baker and R.C. Bunker. 1985. Cataclysmic late Pleistocene flooding from glacial Lake Missoula: A review. *Quaternary Science Reviews* 4: 1–41.

19 V.R. Baker and R.C. Bunker. 1985. Cataclysmic late Pleistocene flooding from glacial Lake Missoula: A review. *Quaternary Science Reviews* 4: 1–41.

20 J.E. O'Connor et al. 2020. The Missoula and Bonneville floods—A review of ice-age megafloods in the Columbia River basin. *Earth-Science Reviews* 208: 103181.

21 Commission for Environmental Cooperation. 1997. Ecological regions of North America. Towards a common perspective. http://www3.cec.org/islandora/en/item/1701-ecological-regions-north-america-toward-common-perspective-en.pdf. Accessed October 1, 2020.

22 Commission for Environmental Cooperation. 1997. Ecological regions of North America. Towards a common perspective. http://www3.cec.org/islandora/en/item/1701-ecological-regions-north-america-toward-common-perspective-en.pdf. Accessed October 1, 2020.

23 Northwest Alliance for Computational Science and Engineering. 2020. Average annual precipitation for Washington State (1981–2010). Prism Climate Group, Oregon State University. https://prism.oregonstate.edu/projects/gallery_view.php?state=WA. Accessed November 10, 2020.

24 J.H. Bretz. 1969. The Lake Missoula floods and the channeled scabland. *Journal of Geology* 77: 505–43.
   J.E. Allen, M. Burns, and S.C. Marjorie. 1986. *Cataclysms on the Columbia: A Layman's Guide to the Features Produced by the Catastrophic Bretz Floods in the Pacific Northwest.* Portland, OR: Timber Press, p. 104.
   J.E. O'Connor et al. 2020. The Missoula and Bonneville floods—A review of ice-age megafloods in the Columbia River basin. *Earth–Science Reviews* 208: 103181.

25 National Research Council (US). 2004. *Managing The Columbia River: Instream Flows, Water Withdrawals, and Salmon Survival.* Washington, DC: National Academies Press, p. 18. https://www.nap.edu/read/10962/chapter/1. Accessed December 4, 2020.
   J.E. O'Connor et al. 2020. The Missoula and Bonneville floods—A review of ice-age megafloods in the Columbia River basin. *Earth–Science Reviews* 208: 103181.

26 M.R. Waters and T.W. Stafford. 2013. The first Americans: A review of the evidence for the Late-Pleistocene peopling of the Americas. In K.E. Graf, C.V. Ketron, and M.R. Waters (eds.), *Paleoamerican Odyssey.* College Station: Texas A&M University Press, pp. 543–62.

27 B.A. Hicks. 2004. *Marmes Rockshelter: A Final Report on 11,000 Years of Cultural Use.* Pullman: Washington State University Press.

28 T.W. Stafford. 2014. Chronology of the Kennewick Man skeleton. Chapter 5 in D.W. Owsley and R.L. Jantz (eds.), *Kennewick Man, The Scientific Investigation of an Ancient American Skeleton.* College Station: Texas A&M University Press, pp. 59–89.

29 Waters, M.R. et al. 2011. Pre-Clovis mastodon hunting 13,800 years ago at the Manis site, Washington. *Science* 334: 351–53.

30 V.L. Butler and J.E. O'Connor. 2004. 9000 years of salmon fishing on the Columbia River, North America. *Quaternary Research* 62: 1–8.

31 National Research Council (US). 2004. *Managing The Columbia River: Instream Flows, Water Withdrawals, and Salmon Survival.* Washington, DC: National Academies Press. https://www.nap.edu/read/10962/chapter/1. Accessed December 4, 2020. P.L. Jackson. 2003. *Atlas of the Pacific Northwest.* Corvallis: Oregon State University Press. K. Barber. 2005. *Death of Celilo Falls.* Seattle: University of Washington Press, pp. 20–21.

32 Columbia River Inter-Tribal Fish Commission. 2014. Columbia River Treaty. https://www.critfc.org/tribal-treaty-fishing-rights/policy-support/columbia-river-treaty/. Accessed October 1, 2020.

33 J.N. Barry. 1932. The first explorers of the Columbia and Snake rivers. *Geographical Review* 22: 443–56.

34 J.N. Barry. 1932. The first explorers of the Columbia and Snake rivers. *Geographical Review* 22: 443–56.

35 C.A. Schwantes. 1996. *The Pacific Northwest: An Interpretive History.* Lincoln: University of Nebraska Press.

36 J. Uldrich. 2004. *Into the Unknown: Leadership Lessons from Lewis & Clark's Daring Westward Adventure.* New York: AMACOM, p. 245. B. Witteman. 2000. *Sacagawea: A Photo-Illustrated Biography.* Mankato, MN: Bridgestone Books/Capstone Press.

37 J. Nisbet. 2002. *Sources of the River: Tracking David Thompson Across North America.* Seattle: Sasquatch Books, p. 151.

38 J.B. Tyrell (ed.). 1916. *David Thompson's Narrative of his Explorations in Western America,* 1784–1812. Toronto: The Champlain Society, p. 297. https://archive.org/details/davidthompsonsna12thom/page/n9/mode/2up. Accessed September 15, 2020.

39 J.B. Tyrell (ed.). 1916. *David Thompson's Narrative of his Explorations in Western America,* 1784–1812. Toronto: The Champlain Society, p. 297. https://archive.org/details/davidthompsonsna12thom/page/n9/mode/2up. Accessed September 15, 2020.

40 US Bureau of Reclamation. 2016. SECURE Water Act section 9503(c) – Reclamation Climate Change and Water 2016. https://www.usbr.gov/climate/secure/. Accessed October 24, 2020. Northwest Power and Conservation Council. 1977. A guide to major hydropower dams of the Columbia River Basin. https://app.nwcouncil.org/ext/storymaps/damguide/index.html. Accessed September 7, 2020.

41 Northwest Power and Conservation Council. 1977. A guide to major hydropower dams of the Columbia River Basin. https://app.nwcouncil.org/ext/storymaps/damguide/index.html. Accessed September 7, 2020.

42 Northwest Power and Conservation Council. 2020. Shad. https://www.nwcouncil.org/history/Shad. Accessed October 1, 2020.

43 Northwest Power and Conservation Council. 2020. Shad. https://www.nwcouncil.org/history/Shad. Accessed October 1, 2020.

44 B.M. Bakke. 2009. Chronology of Salmon Decline in the Columbia River 1779 to the Present. Native Fish Society. Oregon City, OR. http://www.nativefishsociety.org/conservation/ documents/chroncr-nwsalmondecline. Accessed April 23, 2014.

Northwest Power and Conservation Council. 2020. Dams: Impacts on salmon and steelhead. https://www.nwcouncil.org/reports/columbia-river-history/DamsImpacts. Accessed October 1, 2020.

Northwest Power and Conservation Council. 2020. Endangered Species Act, Columbia River salmon and steelhead, and the Biological Opinion. https://www.nwcouncil.org/reports/columbia-river-history/EndangeredSpeciesAct. Accessed October 1, 2020.

COSEWIC. 2018. COSEWIC assessment and status report on the Okanagan Chinook Salmon (*Oncorhynchus tshawytscha*) Okanagan population in Canada. Committee on the Status of Endangered Wildlife in Canada. https://www.canada.ca/en/environment-climate-change/services/species-risk-public-registry/cosewic-assessments-status-reports/chinook-salmon-okanagan-population-2017.html. Accessed October 1, 2020.

45 D.H. Stratton (ed.). 2005. *Spokane & the Inland Empire: An Interior Pacific Northwest Anthology*. Pullman: Washington State University Press.

46 L.B. Reeder. 1902. Open the Columbia to the Sea. *Pendleton Daily Tribune*. https://web.archive.org/web/20080514041723/http://www.ccrh.org/comm/umatilla/primary/opensea.htm. Accessed September 7, 2020.

47 L.B. Reeder. 1902. Open the Columbia to the Sea. *Pendleton Daily Tribune*. https://web.archive.org/web/20080514041723/http://www.ccrh.org/comm/umatilla/primary/opensea.htm. Accessed September 7, 2020.

48 L.B. Reeder. 1902. Open the Columbia to the Sea. *Pendleton Daily Tribune*. https://web.archive.org/web/20080514041723/http://www.ccrh.org/comm/umatilla/primary/opensea.htm. Accessed September 7, 2020.

49 R.M. Boening. 1918. The history of irrigation in the state of Washington. M.Sc. thesis, University of Washington, Seattle.

50 R.M. Boening. 1918. The history of irrigation in the state of Washington. M.Sc. thesis, University of Washington, Seattle, p. 266.

51 L.B. Lee. 1978. 100 years of reclamation historiography. *Pacific Historical Review* 47: 507–64, p. 511.

52 L.B. Lee. 1978. 100 years of reclamation historiography. *Pacific Historical Review* 47: 507–64, p. 511.

53 Touchstones Nelson Museum of Art and History. 2007. Balance of power. Hydroelectric development in southeastern British Columbia. Lower Bonnington Dam. http://www.virtualmuseum.ca/sgc-cms/expositions-exhibitions/hydro/en/dams/?action=lowerbonnington. Accessed October 1, 2020.

54 E.A. Stene. 1996. Shoshone Project. US Bureau of Reclamation. https://www.usbr.gov/projects/pdf.php?id=192. Accessed February 24, 2020.

55 W.D. Miner. 1950. *A History of the Columbia Basin Projects*. Bloomington: University of Indiana Press, p. 167.

56 F.D. Roosevelt. 1934. Fireside chats. September 30. Compiled by Sheba Blake Publishing, 2016.

US National Parks Service. 2015. Franklin Delano Roosevelt Memorial. http://www.nps.gov/frde/learn/photosmultimedia/quotations.htm. Accessed October 2, 2020.

57 B. Harden. 1997. *A River Lost: The Life and Death of the Columbia*. New York: W.W. Norton, p. 25.

58 W.J. Simonds. 1998. The Columbia Basin Project. Bureau of Reclamation History Project. Denver, CO. https://www.usbr.gov/projects/pdf.php?id=88. Accessed September 8, 2020.

59 C. McClung. 2009. The great depression in Washington State. Grand Coulee Dam: Leaving a legacy. Civil Rights and Labor History Consortium. University of Washington. http://depts.washington.edu/depress/grand_coulee.shtml#_edn7. Accessed September 13, 2020.

60 C. McClung. 2009. The great depression in Washington State. Grand Coulee Dam: Leaving a legacy. Civil Rights and Labor History Consortium. University of Washington. http://depts.washington.edu/depress/grand_coulee.shtml#_edn7. Accessed September 13, 2020.

61 G. Bloodworth and J. White. 2008. The Columbia Basin Project: Seventy-five years later. *Yearbook of the Association of Pacific Coast Geographers* 70: 96–111.

62 G. Bloodworth and J. White. 2008. The Columbia Basin Project: Seventy-five years later. *Yearbook of the Association of Pacific Coast Geographers* 70: 99.

63 Columbia Basin Development League. 2020. The Columbia Basin Project. http://www.cbdl.org/. Accessed September 8, 2020.

64 *The Globe & Mail*. 2014. B.C. preparing for flood control talks over Columbia River. June 14. http://www.theglobeandmail.com/news/british-columbia/bc-preparing-for-flood-control-talks-over-columbia-river/article17474772/.
US Department of State. 2018. On the opening of negotiations to modernize the Columbia River Treaty Regime. Department of Western Affairs. https://www.state.gov/on-the-opening-of-negotiations-to-modernize-the-columbia-river-treaty-regime/. Accessed October 2, 2020.

65 Columbia Basin Trust. 2020. Columbia River basin: Dams and hydroelectricity. https://thebasin.ourtrust.org/wp-content/uploads/downloads/2018-07_Trust_Dams-and-Hydroelectricity_Web.pdf. Accessed October 2, 2020.

66 R. White. 1996. *The Organic Machine: The Remaking of the Columbia River*. New York: Hill & Wang.

67 B. Harden. 1997. *A River Lost: The Life and Death of the Columbia*. New York: W.W. Norton.
Data Center Knowledge. 2020. The billion dollar data centers. http://www.datacenterknowledge.com/archives/2013/04/29/the-billion-dollar-data-centers/. Accessed September 20. 2020.

68 Columbia Basin Development League. The Columbia Basin Project. http://www.cbdl.org/. Accessed September 8, 2020.

69 G. Bloodworth and J. White. 2008. The Columbia Basin Project: Seventy-five years later. *Yearbook of the Association of Pacific Coast Geographers* 70: 96–111.

70 G. Bloodworth and J. White. 2008. The Columbia Basin Project: Seventy-five years later. *Yearbook of the Association of Pacific Coast Geographers* 70: 96–111.

71 G. Bloodworth and J. White. 2008. The Columbia Basin Project: Seventy-five years later. *Yearbook of the Association of Pacific Coast Geographers* 70: 105.

72 G. Bloodworth and J. White. 2008. The Columbia Basin Project: Seventy-five years later. *Yearbook of the Association of Pacific Coast Geographers* 70: 105.

73 E. Wohl. 2004. *Disconnected Rivers: Linking Rivers to Landscapes*. New Haven, CT: Yale University Press.

74 G. Bloodworth and J. White. 2008. The Columbia Basin Project: Seventy-five years later. *Yearbook of the Association of Pacific Coast Geographers* 70: 96.

75 G. Bloodworth and J. White. 2008. The Columbia Basin Project: Seventy-five years later. *Yearbook of the Association of Pacific Coast Geographers* 70: 96–111.

76 B. Harden. 1997. *A River Lost: The Life and Death of the Columbia*. New York: W.W. Norton, p. 27.

77 W.E. Ricker. 1972. Hereditary and environmental factors affecting certain salmonid populations. In *The stock concept in Pacific salmon*. University of British Columbia, H.R. MacMillan Lectures in Fisheries, Vancouver, p. 37.

78 Northwest Power and Conservation Council. 2020. Dams: Impacts on salmon and steelhead. https://www.nwcouncil.org/reports/columbia-river-history/DamsImpacts. Accessed October 1, 2020.

79 Northwest Power and Conservation Council. 2020. Dams: Impacts on salmon and steelhead. https://www.nwcouncil.org/reports/columbia-river-history/DamsImpacts. Accessed October 1, 2020.

80 Northwest Power and Conservation Council. 2020. Dams: Impacts on salmon and steelhead. https://www.nwcouncil.org/reports/columbia-river-history/DamsImpacts. Accessed October 1, 2020.

81 Bonneville Power Administration. Undated. Budget submission to Congress. FY 2021. https://www.bpa.gov/Finance/FinancialInformation/Pages/Budget-Submission-to-Congress.aspx. Accessed October 2, 2020.
Bonneville Power Administration. 2017. Correspondence (letter) to US Congresswoman Cathy McMorris Rodgers, June 5. http://www.waterplanet.ws/pdf/FCRPS_BPA_LTR_TO-McMorris-Rodgers_2017-06-05.pdf. Accessed September 9, 2020.

82 Fish and Wildlife Compensation Program. 2020. *Wildbytes*. May 2020. https://fwcp.ca/wildbytes-columbia-region/. Accessed October 2, 2020.
G. Bloodworth and J. White. 2008. The Columbia Basin Project: Seventy-five years later. *Yearbook of the Association of Pacific Coast Geographers* 70: 96–111.

83 G. Bloodworth and J. White. 2008. The Columbia Basin Project: Seventy-five years later. *Yearbook of the Association of Pacific Coast Geographers* 70: 96–111.

84 midcurrent.com. 2007. Bruce Babbitt calls for Snake River dam removals. https://midcurrent.com/2007/09/24/bruce-babbit-calls-for-snake-r/. Accessed October 1, 2020.
Patagonia.com. 2014. Patagonia on dams and dam removal. https://www.patagonia.com/on/demandware.static/Sites-patagonia-us-Site/Library-Sites-PatagoniaShared/en_US/PDF-US/DamNation_Statements_v1.pdf. Accessed October 2, 2020.
WildSalmon.org. 2020. Myths and facts about lower snake River dam removal. http://www.wildsalmon.org/facts-and-information/myths-and-facts-about-lower-snake-river-dam-removal.html. Accessed July 23, 2020.
E. Wohl. 2004. *Disconnected Rivers: Linking Rivers to Landscapes*. New Haven CT: Yale University Press.
American Rivers. 2019. Twenty years of dam removal successes – and what's up next. https://www.americanrivers.org/2019/06/twenty-years-of-dam-removal-successes-and-whats-up-next/. Accessed October 2, 2020.
P. Brewitt. 2019. *Same River Twice: The Politics of Dam Removal and River Restoration*. Corvallis, OR: Oregon State University Press.

85 G.R. Pess et al. 2008. Biological impacts of the Elwha River dams and potential sal-monid responses to dam removal. *Northwest Science* 82: 72–90.

M.J. Kuby et al. 2005. A multiobjective optimization model for dam removal: An example trading off salmon passage with hydropower and water storage in the Willa-mette basin. *Advances in Water Resources* 28: 845–55.

J. Loomis. 2002. Quantifying recreation use values from removing dams and restor-ing free-flowing rivers: A contingent behavior travel cost demand model for the Lower Snake River. *Water Resources Research* 38: 1–8.

E. Whitelaw and E. MacMullan. 2002. A framework for estimating the costs and benefits of dam removal: Sound cost–benefit analyses of removing dams account for subsidies and externalities, for both the short and long run, and place the estimated costs and benefits in the appropriate economic context. *BioScience* 52: 724–30.

J. Leslie. 2019. On the northwest's Snake River, the case for dam removal grows. *Yale Environment 360*. https://e360.yale.edu/features/on-the-northwests-snake-river-the-case-for-dam-removal-grows. Accessed October 2, 2020.

86 US National Parks Service. 2020. Elwha River restoration. http://www.nps.gov/olym/learn/nature/elwha-ecosystem-restoration.htm. Accessed October 2, 2020.

87 E. Whitelaw and E. MacMullan. 2002. A framework for estimating the costs and benefits of dam removal: Sound cost–benefit analyses of removing dams account for subsidies and externalities, for both the short and long run, and place the estimated costs and benefits in the appropriate economic context. *BioScience* 52: 729.

88 M. Nijhus. 2015. Movement to take down thousands of dams goes mainstream. *National Geographic*. http://news.nationalgeographic.com/news/2015/01/150127-white-clay-creek-dam-removal-river-water-environment/. Accessed October 2, 2020.

89 M. Johnson. 2021. Snake River Dams: The Path to Dam Removal. Columbia Riv-erkeeper. https://www.columbiariverkeeper.org/news/2021/2/snake-river-dams. Accessed March 23, 2021.

90 L. Ortolano and K.K. Cushing. 2000. Grand Coulee dam and The Columbia basin project, USA. Case study report prepared as an input to the World Commission on Dams. http://171.67.100.116/courses/2010/ph240/harting2/docs/csusmain.pdf. Ac-cessed October 2, 2020.

91 C. Mauch and T. Zeller (eds.). 2008. *Rivers in History: Perspectives on Waterways in Europe and North America*. Pittsburgh: University of Pittsburgh Press, p. 6.

SIX: The Sacramento–San Joaquin River

1 R.S. Waples. 2006. Distinct population segments. In J.M. Scott, D.D. Goble, and F.W. Davis (eds.), *The Endangered Species Act at Thirty*, vol. 2, *Conserving Biodiversity in Human-Dominated Landscapes*. Washington, DC: Island Press, pp. 127–49.

2 A.P. Williams et al. 2020. Large contribution from anthropogenic warming to an emerging North American megadrought. *Science* 368: 314–18.
National Integrated Drought Information System. 2020. Drought in California. https://www.drought.gov/drought/states/california. Accessed October 3, 2020.

3 J.E. Cloern et al. 2011. Projected evolution of California's San Francisco Bay-Del-ta-River system in a century of climate change. *PloS One* 6(9): e24465.

M.K. Shouse and D.A. Cox. 2013. USGS Science at Work in the San Francisco Bay and Sacramento-San Joaquin Delta Estuary. https://pubs.usgs.gov/fs/2013/3037/pdf/fs2013-3037.pdf. Accessed October 3, 2020.

4   D. Grayson. 2011. *The Great Basin: A Natural Prehistory*. Berkeley: University of California Press.

5   California Department of Water Resources. 2020. State water project. https://water.ca.gov/Programs/State-Water-Project. Accessed October 3, 2020.

6   J.P. Colgan et al. 2011. Oligocene and Miocene arc volcanism in northeastern California: Evidence for post-Eocene segmentation of the subducting Farallon plate. *Geosphere* 7: 733–55.
    T. Atwater. 1970. Implications of plate tectonics for the Cenozoic tectonic evolution of western North America. *Geological Society of America Bulletin* 81: 3513–36.

7   J. Wakabayashi and T.L. Sawyer. 2001. Stream incision, tectonics, uplift, and evolution of topography of the Sierra Nevada, California. *Journal of Geology* 109: 539–62.

8   J. Wakabayashi and T.L. Sawyer. 2001. Stream incision, tectonics, uplift, and evolution of topography of the Sierra Nevada, California. *Journal of Geology* 109: 539–62.

9   G.M. Stock, R.S. Anderson, and R.C. Finkel. 2004. Pace of landscape evolution in the Sierra Nevada, California, revealed by cosmogenic dating of cave sediments. *Geology* 32: 193–96.

10 P.W. Reiners. 2012. Paleotopography in the western US Cordillera. *American Journal of Science* 312: 81–89.

11 D. McPhillips and M.T. Brandon. 2012. Topographic evolution of the Sierra Nevada measured directly by inversion of low-temperature thermochronology. *American Journal of Science* 312: 90–116.

12 C.I. Miller. 2012. Geologic, climatic, and vegetation history of California. In B.G. Baldwin et al. (eds.), *The Jepson Manual: Vascular Plants of California*, 2nd ed. Berkeley: University of California Press, pp. 49–67.

13 B.D. Martin and K.O. Emery. 1967. Geology of Monterey Canyon, California. *American Association of Petroleum Geologists (AAPG) Bulletin* 51: 2281–2304. http://archives.datapages.com/data/bulletns/1965-67/data/pg/0051/0011/2250/2281.htm. Accessed October 4, 2020.

14 M.J. Moratto. 1984. *California Archaeology*. New York: Academic Press.

15 K. Wong. 2006. Carquinez breakthrough. *Bay Nature Magazine*. https://baynature.org/articles/carquinez-breakthrough/. Accessed October 3, 2020.
    J.A. Bartow. 1991. The Cenozoic evolution of the San Joaquin Valley, California. *U.S. Geological Survey Professional Paper* 1501. https://pubs.usgs.gov/pp/1501/report.pdf. accessed November 23, 2020.
    M.J. Moratto. 1984. *California Archaeology*. New York: Academic Press.

16 US Geological Survey. Undated. Central Valley aquifer system. Groundwater Atlas of the United States, Nevada and California. https://pubs.usgs.gov/ha/ha730/ch_b/B-text3.html. Accessed October 4, 2020.

17 M.J. Moratto. 1984. *California Archaeology*. New York: Academic Press.

18 National Conference of State Legislatures. 2020. Federal and state recognized tribes: California. http://www.ncsl.org/research/state-tribal-institute/list-of-federal-and-state-recognized-tribes.aspx. Accessed October 3, 2020.
    B.G. Trigger. 1996. *The Cambridge History of the Native Peoples of the Americas*. Cambridge: Cambridge University Press, p. 66.

19 R.F. Heizer and M.A. Whipple (eds.). 1971. *The California Indians: A Source Book*, 2nd ed. Berkeley: University of California Press.

20 R.M. Yoshiyama, F.W. Fisher, and P.B. Moyle. 1998. Historical abundance and decline of chinook salmon in the Central Valley region of California. *North American Journal of Fisheries Management* 18: 487–521.

P.D. Schulz. 1981. Osteoarchaeology and subsistence change in prehistoric central California. PhD diss., University of California–Davis.

K.W. Gobalet et al. 2004. Archaeological perspectives on Native American fisheries of California, with emphasis on steelhead and salmon. *Transactions of the American Fisheries Society* 133: 801–33.

21 M.J. Rohrbough. 1998. *Days of Gold: The California Gold Rush and the American Nation*. Berkeley: University of California Press.

22 History.com. 2020. California gold rush. https://www.history.com/topics/westward-expansion/gold-rush-of-1849. Accessed October 4, 2020.

750,000 pounds = $1.1x10^7$ troy ounces at \$1732/oz in mid-2021.

23 W.E. Johnston and A.F. McCalla. 2004. A Stylized History of California Agriculture from 1769 to 2000. *Section II Whither California Agriculture: Up, Down or Out*. In Giannini Foundation Special Report 04-1. University of Berkeley Special Report Series. https://escholarship.org/content/qt4232w2sr/qt4232w2sr. Accessed October 4, 2020.

24 W.E. Johnston and A.F. McCalla. 2004. A Stylized History of California Agriculture from 1769 to 2000. *Section II Whither California Agriculture: Up, Down or Out*. In Giannini Foundation Special Report 04-1. University of Berkeley Special Report Series. https://escholarship.org/content/qt4232w2sr/qt4232w2sr. Accessed October 4, 2020.

25 California Department of Water Resources. 2020. California Groundwater Factsheet. Bulletin 118. https://water.ca.gov/Programs/Groundwater-Management/Bulletin-118. M. Kang and R.B. Jackson. 2016. Salinity of deep groundwater in California: Water quantity, quality, and protection. *Proceedings of the National Academy of Sciences* 113: 7768–73.

26 D.J. Pisani. 1984. *From the Family Farm to Agribusiness: The Agricultural Crusade in California and the West, 1850–1931*. Berkeley: University of California Press.

27 A.L. Olmstead and W. Paul. 2004. The Evolution of California Agriculture, 1850–2000. In J. Siebert (ed.), *California Agriculture: Dimensions and Issues*, pp. 1–28. University of California-Berkeley Information Series. https://citeseerx.ist.psu.edu/viewdoc/download?doi=10.1.1.389.2184&rep=rep1&type=pdf. Accessed October 4, 2020.

28 California Department of Food and Agriculture. 2020. California agricultural production statistics. http://www.cdfa.ca.gov/statistics/. Accessed October 4, 2020.

California Department of Food and Agriculture. 2019. Agricultural statistical review. https://www.cdfa.ca.gov/statistics/PDFs/2018-2019AgReportnass.pdf. Accessed October 4, 2020.

29 Almond Board of California. 2019. *Almond Almanac* 2019. https://www.almonds.com/sites/default/files/2020-04/2019_Almanac.pdf. Accessed October 4, 2020.

30 D.J. Pisani. 1984. *From the Family Farm to Agribusiness: The Agricultural Crusade in California and the West, 1850–1931*. Berkeley: University of California Press.

US Department of Agriculture. 2017. 2017 Census of Agriculture. United States Summary and State Data. Vol. 1. Pt. 51. AC-17-A-51. https://www.nass.usda.gov/Publications/AgCensus/2017/Full_Report/Volume_1,_Chapter_2_US_State_Level/usv1.pdf. Accessed October 4, 2020.

31 D.J. Pisani. 1984. *From the Family Farm to Agribusiness: The Agricultural Crusade in California and the West, 1850–1931.* Berkeley: University of California Press, p. 54.

32 D.J. Pisani. 1984. *From the Family Farm to Agribusiness: The Agricultural Crusade in California and the West, 1850–1931.* Berkeley: University of California Press, p. 60.

33 D.J. Pisani. 1984. *From the Family Farm to Agribusiness: The Agricultural Crusade in California and the West, 1850–1931.* Berkeley: University of California Press, p. 61.

34 D.J. Pisani. 1984. *From the Family Farm to Agribusiness: The Agricultural Crusade in California and the West, 1850–1931.* Berkeley: University of California Press.

35 D.J. Pisani. 1984. *From the Family Farm to Agribusiness: The Agricultural Crusade in California and the West, 1850–1931.* Berkeley: University of California Press.

36 CourtListener.com. Undated. *Environmental Defense Fund v. East Bay Municipal Utility Dist.*, 26 Cal. 3d 183 (Cal 1980). https://www.courtlistener.com/opinion/1800972/environmental-defense-fund-v-e-bay-mun-util-dist/. Accessed October 4, 2020.
    D.J. Pisani. 1984. *From the Family Farm to Agribusiness: The Agricultural Crusade in California and the West, 1850–1931.* Berkeley: University of California Press.

37 D.J. Pisani. 1984. *From the Family Farm to Agribusiness: The Agricultural Crusade in California and the West, 1850–1931.* Berkeley: University of California Press, p. 30.

38 M.C. Reheis. 1997. Dust deposition downwind of Owens (dry) Lake, 1991–1994: Preliminary findings. *Journal of Geophysical Research: Atmospheres* 102: 25999–26008.

39 E. Hanak et al. 2011. Managing California's Water: From Conflict to Reconciliation. Public Policy Institute of California, San Francisco. https://www.ppic.org/publication/managing-californias-water-from-conflict-to-reconciliation/. Accessed October 12, 2020.

40 D.J. Pisani. 1984. *From the Family Farm to Agribusiness: The Agricultural Crusade in California and the West, 1850–1931.* Berkeley: University of California Press.

41 Col. R.B. Marshall. 1919. *Irrigation of Twelve Million Acres in the Valley of California.* California State Irrigation Association, Sacramento, p. 6. https://watershed.ucdavis.edu/shed/lund/fun/MarshallWaterPlan1919.pdf. Accessed November 24, 2020.

42 An acre-foot is the volume of water spread across one acre to a depth of 1 foot (= 0.12 ha metres).

43 D.J. Pisani. 1984. *From the Family Farm to Agribusiness: The Agricultural Crusade in California and the West, 1850–1931.* Berkeley: University of California Press, p. 441.

44 R.M.Yoshiyama, F.W. Fisher, and P.B. Moyle. 1998. Historical abundance and decline of chinook salmon in the Central Valley region of California. *North American Journal of Fisheries Management* 18: 487–521.
    D.R. McEwan. 2001. Central valley steelhead. In R.L. Brown, *Contributions to the Biology of Central Valley Salmonids.* Vols. 1 & 2. Fish Bulletin 179: 1–43. Scripps Institution of Oceanography Library, Scripps Institution of Oceanography. University of California–San Diego.

45 National Oceanic and Atmospheric Administration. 2016. 5-Year Status Review: Summary and Evaluation of Sacramento River Winter-Run Chinook Salmon ESU. National Marine Fisheries Service West Coast Region. https://repository.library.noaa.gov/view/noaa/17014. Accessed October 5, 2020.
    National Oceanic and Atmospheric Administration. 2016. 5-Year Status Review: Summary and Central Valley Spring-run Chinook Salmon Evolutionarily Significant Unit. National Marine Fisheries Service West Coast Region. https://repository.library.noaa.gov/view/noaa/17018. Accessed October 5, 2020.

National Oceanic and Atmospheric Administration. 2016. 5-Year Review: Summary and Evaluation California Central Valley Steelhead Distinct Population Segment. National Marine Fisheries Service West Coast Region. https://repository.library.noaa. gov/view/noaa/17019. Accessed October 5, 2020.

46 National Oceanic and Atmospheric Administration. 2014. Recovery Plan for The Evolutionarily Significant Units of Sacramento River Winter-run Chinook Salmon and Central Valley Spring-run Chinook Salmon and the DPS of California Central Valley Steelhead. National Marine Fisheries Service West Coast Region. https:// www.fisheries.noaa.gov/resource/document/recovery-plan-evolutionarily-significant-units-sacramento-river-winter-run. Accessed October 5, 2020.

47 US Bureau of Reclamation (California-Great Basin). 2020. Central Valley Project Improvement Act (CVPIA). http://www.usbr.gov/mp/cvpia/. Accessed October 5, 2020.

48 R. Baxter et al. 2015. An updated conceptual model of Delta Smelt biology: Our evolving understanding of an estuarine fish. Interagency Ecological Program, California Department of Water Resources Technical Report 90. https://pubs.er.usgs.gov/publication/70141018. Accessed October 5, 2020.

49 California Department of Fish and Wildlife. 2020. Spring Kodiak Trawl Catch Distribution Maps. https://www.dfg.ca.gov/delta/data/skt/DisplayMaps.asp. Accessed October 5, 2020.
R. Baxter et al. 2015. An updated conceptual model of Delta Smelt biology: our evolving understanding of an estuarine fish. Interagency Ecological Program, California Department of Water Resources Technical Report 90. https://pubs.er.usgs.gov/publication/70141018. Accessed October 5, 2020.

50 US Department of the Interior, Fish and Wildlife Service. 2010. Endangered and Threatened Wildlife and Plants: 12-Month Finding on a Petition to Reclassify the Delta Smelt From Threatened to Endangered Throughout Its Range. *Federal Register* 75 (66): 17667–80.

51 US Department of the Interior, Fish and Wildlife Service. 2010. Endangered and Threatened Wildlife and Plants: 12-Month Finding on a Petition to Reclassify the Delta Smelt From Threatened to Endangered Throughout Its Range. *Federal Register* 75 (66): 17667–80.

52 US Courts of Appeal, Ninth Circuit. 2014. *San Luis vs. Jewell.* Summary Judgement. Case No. Case: 11-15871. https://law.justia.com/cases/federal/appellate-courts/ca9/11-15871/11-15871-2014-03-13.html. Accessed October 4, 2020.

53 Natural Resources Defense Council. 2007. Judge throws out Biological Opinion for Delta Smelt. http://www.nrdc.org/media/2007/070526.asp. Accessed October 4, 2020.

54 *Wall Street Journal.* 2009. Opinion: California man-made drought. The green war and San Joaquin Valley farmers. http://www.wsj.com/articles/SB100014240529702047318045743847318983756224. Accessed May 6, 2017.

55 US District Court, Ninth Circuit. 2010. Delta smelt consolidated cases, 717 F. Supp. 2d 1021 (E.D. Cal. 2010). https://www.courtlistener.com/opinion/2541272/consolidated-delta-smelt-cases/. Accessed May 6, 2017.

56 US District Court, Ninth Circuit. 2010. Delta smelt consolidated cases, 717 F. Supp. 2d 1021 (E.D. Cal. 2010). https://www.courtlistener.com/opinion/2541272/consolidated-delta-smelt-cases/. Accessed May 6, 2017.

57   US Courts of Appeal, Ninth Circuit. 2014. *San Luis vs. Jewell*. Summary Judgement. Case No. Case: 11-15871. https://law.justia.com/cases/federal/appellate-courts/ca9/11-15871/11-15871-2014-03-13.html. Accessed October 4, 2020.

58   Scotusblog.com. 2015. *State Water Contractors v. Jewell*. Petition for certiorari denied on January 12, 2015. http://www.scotusblog.com/case-files/cases/state-water-contractors-v-jewell/. Accessed May 17, 2017.

59   C.W. Cooke. 2014. Politics & Policy: Green drought. https://www.nationalreview.com/2014/01/green-drought-charles-c-w-cooke/. Accessed May 7, 2017.

60   C.W. Cooke. 2014. Politics & Policy: Green drought. https://www.nationalreview.com/2014/01/green-drought-charles-c-w-cooke/. Accessed May 7, 2017.

61   C.W. Cooke. 2014. Politics & Policy: Green drought. https://www.nationalreview.com/2014/01/green-drought-charles-c-w-cooke/. Accessed May 7, 2017.

62   SFBay.ca. 2011. Supreme court favours fish over farmers. http://sfbay.ca/2015/01/12/supreme-court-favors-fish-over-farmers/. Accessed May 17, 2017.

63   US Geological Survey. Undated. What is drought? California Water Science Center. http://ca.water.usgs.gov/data/drought/. Accessed May 17, 2017.

64   M.K. Hughes and P.M. Brown. 1992. Drought frequency in central California since 101 BC recorded in giant sequoia tree rings. *Climate Dynamics* 6: 161–67.

65   D. Siders, P. Reese, and M. Weiser. 2014. Jerry Brown declares California drought emergency, urges 20 percent cut in water use. *The Sacramento Bee*. January 17. https://www.sacbee.com/news/politics-government/article2589082.html. Accessed May 17, 2017.

66   A. Nagourney. 2015. California imposes first ever water restrictions to deal with drought. *The New York Times*. April 1. http://www.nytimes.com/2015/04/02/us/california-imposes-first-ever-water-restrictions-to-deal-with-drought.html. Accessed May 17, 2017.

67   T.B. Pathak et al. 2018. Climate change trends and impacts on California agriculture: A detailed review. *Agronomy 8*: 21–27.

D.R. Cayan et al. 2008. Climate change scenarios for the California region. *Climatic Change* 87: 21–42.

N.L. Miller, K.E. Bashford, and E. Strem. 2003. Potential impacts of climate change on California hydrology. *Journal of the American Water Resources Association* 39: 771–84.

D.B. Lobell et al. 2006. Impacts of future climate change on California perennial crop yields: Model projections with climate and crop uncertainties. *Agricultural and Forest Meteorology* 141: 208–18.

T. Zhu, M.W. Jenkins, and J.R. Lund. 2005. Estimated impacts of climate warming on California water availability under twelve future climate scenarios. *Journal of the American Water Resources Association* 41: 1027–38.

SEVEN: The Colorado River

1   J.P. Cohn. 2000. Saving the Salton Sea. *Bioscience* 50: 295–301.

2   M.J. Cohen, C. Henges-Jeck, and G. Castillo-Moreno. 2001. A preliminary water balance for the Colorado River delta, 1992–1998. *Journal of Arid Environments* 49: 35–48.

3   M.J. Cohen, C. Henges-Jeck, and G. Castillo-Moreno. 2001. A preliminary water balance for the Colorado River delta, 1992–1998. *Journal of Arid Environments* 49: 35–48.

4   M. Hiltzic. 2010. *Colossus: Hoover Dam and the Making of the American Century*. New York: Free Press, p. 3.

5 US Census Bureau. 2013. A decade of state population change. https://www.census.gov/dataviz/visualizations/043/. Accessed October 8, 2020.
US Census Bureau. 2020. Last census population estimates of the decade preview 2020 census count. https://www.census.gov/library/stories/2020/04/nations-population-growth-slowed-this-decade.html. Accessed October 8, 2020.

6 C. Fletcher. 1997. *River: One Man's Journey Down the Colorado, Source to Sea.* New York: Alfred A. Knopf.

7 C. Fletcher. 1997. *River: One Man's Journey Down the Colorado, Source to Sea.* New York: Alfred A. Knopf.
P.L. Fradkin. 1984. *A River No More: The Colorado River and the West.* Tucson: University of Arizona Press.

8 Public Broadcasting Service. 1997. *Cadillac Desert: Water and the Transformation of Nature.* https://web.archive.org/web/20030212083841/http://www.kteh.org/cadillac-desert/home.html. Accessed October 8, 2020.

9 P.L. Fradkin. 1984. A River No More: The Colorado River and the West. Tucson: University of Arizona Press, p. 16.

10 US Geological Survey. 2019. Boundary Descriptions and Names of Regions, Subregions, Accounting Units and Cataloging Units. http://water.usgs.gov/GIS/huc_name.html. Accessed October 8, 2020.

11 P.L. Fradkin. 1984. *A River No More: The Colorado River and the West.* Tucson: University of Arizona Press, p. 30.

12 P.L. Fradkin, 1984, *A River No More: The Colorado River and the West.* Tucson: University of Arizona Press.

13 P.L. Fradkin. 1984. *A River No More: The Colorado River and the West.* Tucson: University of Arizona Press, p. 31.

14 1 tonne = 1.1 tons.

15 R.W. Adler. 2007. *Restoring Colorado River Ecosystems: A Troubled Sense of Immensity.* Washington, DC: Island Press.

16 J.D. Milliman and M.-e Ren. 1995. River flux to the sea: Impact of human intervention on river systems and adjacent coastal areas. In D. Eisma (ed.), *Climate Change Impact on Coastal Habitation.* Boca Raton, FL: Lewis, pp. 57–83.

17 US Geological Survey. Undated. Colorado River Basin Focus Area study. https://www.usgs.gov/mission-areas/water-resources/science/colorado-river-basin-focus-area-study?qt-science_center_objects=0#qt-science_center_objects. Accessed October 8, 2020.

18 D. Owen. 2017. Where the water goes. *The New Yorker.* April 2. Accessed October 8, 2020.

19 J.L. Pederson. 2008. The mystery of the pre-Grand Canyon Colorado River-results from the Muddy Creek formation. *GSA TODAY* 18: 4–10.

20 I. Lucchitta. 1990. History of the Grand Canyon and of the Colorado River in Arizona. In S.S. Beus and M. Morales (eds.), *Grand Canyon Geology.* New York: Oxford University Press, p. 331.
J.L. Pederson. 2008. The mystery of the pre-Grand Canyon Colorado River – results from the Muddy Creek formation. *GSA TODAY* 18: 4–10.

21 I. Lucchitta. 1990. History of the Grand Canyon and of the Colorado River in Arizona. In S.S. Beus and M. Morales (eds.), *Grand Canyon Geology*. New York: Oxford University Press.

K.E. Karlstrom et al. 2012. Introduction: CRevolution 2: Origin and evolution of the Colorado River system II. *Geosphere* 8: 1170–76.

J.L. Pederson. 2008. The mystery of the pre-Grand Canyon Colorado River–Results from the Muddy Creek formation. *GSA TODAY* 18: 4–10.

22 K.E. Karlstrom et al. 2008. Model for tectonically driven incision of the younger than 6 Ma Grand Canyon. *Geology* 36: 835–38.

K.E. Karlstrom et al. 2014. Formation of the Grand Canyon 5 to 6 million years ago through integration of older palaeocanyons. *Nature Geoscience* 7: 239–44.

23 J.L. Pederson. 2008. The mystery of the pre-Grand Canyon Colorado River – results from the Muddy Creek formation. *GSA TODAY* 18: 4–10.

24 P. House et al. 2005. Birth of the lower Colorado River—Stratigraphic and geomorphic evidence for its inception near the conjunction of Nevada, Arizona, and California. *Interior Western United States: Geological Society of America Field Guide* 6: 357–87.

25 R.J. Dorsey et al. 2007. Chronology of Miocene–Pliocene deposits at Split Mountain Gorge, southern California: A record of regional tectonics and Colorado River evolution. *Geology* 35: 57–60.

26 I. Lucchitta. 1990. History of the Grand Canyon and of the Colorado River in Arizona. In S.S. Beus and M. Morales (eds.), *Grand Canyon Geology*. New York: Oxford University Press, pp. 311–32.

J.E. Spencer and P.A. Pearthree. 2001. Headward erosion versus closed-basin spillover as alternative causes of Neogene capture of the ancestral Colorado River by the Gulf of California. *The Colorado River: Origin and Evolution: Grand Canyon, Arizona, Grand Canyon Association Monograph* 12: 215–19.

R.J. Dorsey et al. 2007. Chronology of Miocene–Pliocene deposits at Split Mountain Gorge, southern California: A record of regional tectonics and Colorado River evolution. *Geology* 35: 57–60.

J.L. Pederson. 2008. The mystery of the pre-Grand Canyon Colorado River – results from the Muddy Creek formation. *GSA TODAY* 18: 4–10.

27 R.C. Brusca et al. 2017. Colorado River flow and biological productivity in the Northern Gulf of California, Mexico. *Earth-Science Reviews* 164: 1–30.

S.M. Nelson et al. 2020. Channel incision by headcut migration: Reconnection of the Colorado River to its estuary and the Gulf of California during the floods of 1979–1988. *Hydrological Processes* 34: 4156–74.

28 P.L. Fradkin. 1984. *A River No More: The Colorado River and the West*. Tucson: University of Arizona Press.

29 P.L. Fradkin. 1984. *A River No More: The Colorado River and the West*. Tucson: University of Arizona Press, p. 21.

30 P.L. Fradkin. 1984. *A River No More: The Colorado River and the West*. Tucson: University of Arizona Press.

31 W.J. Wallace. 1955. Mohave fishing equipment and methods. *Anthropological Quarterly* 28: 87–94.

32 G.P. Winship. 1896. *The Coronado Expedition, 1540–1542.* Fourteenth Annual Report of the Bureau of Ethnology, Washington, pp. 6–638. https://archive.org/details/coronadoexpeditioowinsrich. Accessed October 8, 2020.

33 C.C. Donald. 1990. *The Journey of Coronado.* Wheat Ridge, CO: Fulcrum.

34 W. Davis. 2013. *River Notes: A Natural and Human History of the Colorado River.* Washington, DC: Island Press, p. 29.

35 H.E. Bolton. 2017. *Rim of Christendom: A Biography of Eusebio Francisco Kino: Pacific Coast Pioneer.* Tucson: University of Arizona Press.

36 M. Reisner. 1986. *Cadillac Desert: The American West and its Disappearing Water.* New York: Penguin, p. 120.

37 M. Reisner. 1986. *Cadillac Desert: The American West and its Disappearing Water.* New York: Penguin, p. 34.

38 P.L. Fradkin, 1984, *A River No More: The Colorado River and the West.* Tucson: University of Arizona Press, p. 24.

39 P.L. Fradkin. 1984. *A River No More: The Colorado River and the West.* Tucson: University of Arizona Press, p. 156.

40 M. Reisner. 1986. *Cadillac Desert: The American West and its Disappearing Water.* New York: Penguin, p. 121.

41 M. Reisner. 1986. *Cadillac Desert: The American West and its Disappearing Water.* New York: Penguin, p. 123.

42 US Bureau of Reclamation. 2008. The law of the river. http://www.usbr.gov/lc/region/g1000/lawofrvr.html. Accessed October 8, 2020.

43 Central Arizona Project. 2016. Colorado River shortage. http://www.cap-az.com/departments/planning/colorado-river-programs/shortage. Accessed October 8, 2020.
A.P. Williams et al. 2020. Large contribution from anthropogenic warming to an emerging North American megadrought. *Science* 368: 314–18.

44 P.L. Fradkin. 1984. *A River No More: The Colorado River and the West.* Tucson: University of Arizona Press, p. 188.
Central Arizona Project. 2016. Colorado River shortage. http://www.cap-az.com/departments/planning/colorado-river-programs/shortage. Accessed October 8, 2020.

45 D. Worster. 1986. *Rivers of Empire. Water, Aridity, and the Growth of the American West.* New York: Pantheon, p. 210.

46 M. Reisner. 1986. *Cadillac Desert: The American West and its Disappearing Water.* New York: Penguin, p. 152.

47 M. Reisner. 1986. *Cadillac Desert: The American West and its Disappearing Water.* New York: Penguin, p. 150.

48 G.C. Holdren and K. Turner. 2010. Characteristics of Lake Mead, Arizona-Nevada. *Lake and Reservoir Management* 26: 230–39.
US Bureau of Reclamation. 2018. Hydropower at Hoover Dam. https://www.usbr.gov/lc/hooverdam/faqs/powerfaq.html. Accessed October 2, 2020.
US National Parks Service. 2018. Nevada and Arizona. Hoover Dam. https://www.nps.gov/articles/nevada-and-arizona-hoover-dam.htm. Accessed October 8, 2020.

49 US Bureau of Reclamation. 2015. Hoover Dam Essays: Fatalities at Hoover Dam. http://www.usbr.gov/lc/hooverdam/history/essays/fatal.html. Accessed October 2, 2020.

50 P.L. Fradkin. 1984. *A River No More: The Colorado River and the West*. Tucson: University of Arizona Press.

51 M. Reisner. 1986. *Cadillac Desert: The American West and its Disappearing Water*. New York: Penguin, p. 145.

52 P.L. Fradkin. 1984. *A River No More: The Colorado River and the West*. Tucson: University of Arizona Press, p. 143.

53 P.L. Fradkin. 1984. *A River No More: The Colorado River and the West*. Tucson: University of Arizona Press.
    C.J. Myers. 1966. The Colorado River. *Stanford Law Review* 19: 1–77.
    M.E. Price and G.D. Weatherford. 1976. Indian water rights in theory and practice: Navajo experience in the Colorado River basin. *Law and Contemporary Problems* 40: 97–131.

54 A.R. Summit. 2013. *Contested Waters: An Environmental History of the Colorado River*. Boulder: University Press of Colorado.

55 W.D. Back and J.S. Taylor. 1980. Navajo water rights: Pulling the plug on the Colorado River. *Natural Resources Journal* 20: 71–90.

56 W.D. Back and J.S. Taylor. 1980. Navajo water rights: Pulling the plug on the Colorado River. *Natural Resources Journal* 20: 71–90.

57 M.E. Price and G.D. Weatherford. 1976. Indian water rights in theory and practice: Navajo experience in the Colorado River basin. *Law and Contemporary Problems* 40: 97–131.

58 A.R. Summit. 2013. *Contested Waters: An Environmental History of the Colorado River*. Boulder: University Press of Colorado.

59 A.R. Summit. 2013. *Contested Waters: An Environmental History of the Colorado River*. Boulder: University Press of Colorado.

60 Najavo Nation Water Rights Commission. 2021. Water Rights. https://www.nnwrc.navajo-nsn.gov/Water-Rights. Accessed March 17, 2021.

61 Navajo Nation Department of Justice. Undated. Water rights unit. http://nndoj.org/Water_Rights_Unit.aspx. Accessed October 9, 2020.

62 A.R. Summit. 2013. *Contested Waters: An Environmental History of the Colorado River*. Boulder: University Press of Colorado.
    T.P. Barnett and D.W. Pierce. 2009. Sustainable water deliveries from the Colorado River in a changing climate. *Proceedings of the National Academy of Sciences* 106: 7334–38.

63 P.L. Fradkin. 1984. *A River No More: The Colorado River and the West*. Tucson: University of Arizona Press, p. 292.

64 L. Brun et al. 2010. *Agricultural Value Chains in the Mexicali Valley of Mexico*. Center on Globalization Governance & Competitiveness. Duke University. https://gvcc.duke.edu/wp-content/uploads/Agricultural-Value-Chains-in-the-Mexicali-Valley-of-Mexico_9-15-2010.pdf. Accessed March 17, 2021.

65 A.R. Summit. 2013. *Contested Waters: An Environmental History of the Colorado River*. Boulder: University Press of Colorado, p. 180.

66 R.S. Weinert. 1981. Foreign capital in Mexico. *Proceedings of the Academy of Political Science* 34: 115–24, p. 119.

67 S.C. McCaffrey. 1996. The Harmon Doctrine one hundred years later: Buried, not praised. *Natural Resources Journal* 36: 967.

68 A.R. Summit. 2013. *Contested Waters: An Environmental History of the Colorado River*. Boulder: University Press of Colorado.

69 P.L. Fradkin. 1984. *A River No More: The Colorado River and the West.* Tucson: University of Arizona Press, p. 301.

70 M. Reisner, 1986, *Cadillac Desert: The American West and its Disappearing Water.* New York: Penguin, p. 7.

71 D. Worster. 1986. *Rivers of Empire: Water, Aridity, and the Growth of the American West.* New York: Pantheon, p. 322.

72 US Bureau of Reclamation. 2020. Colorado River Basin Salinity Control Program. https://usbr.gov/uc/progact/salinity/index.html. Accessed October 20, 2020.

73 US Bureau of Reclamation. 2020. Colorado River Basin Salinity Control Program. https://usbr.gov/uc/progact/salinity/index.html. Accessed October 20, 2020.

74 Colorado River Basin Salinity Control Forum. 2020 Review. Water quality Standards for Salinity. Colorado River Basin. http://coloradoriversalinity.org/docs/2020%20RE-VIEW%20-%20June%20Draft%20Complete.pdf. Accessed October 9, 2020.
    P.E. Drusina. 2014. A report on Colorado River salinity operations, under International Boundary and Water Commission Minute 242, January 1 to December 31, 2012. International Boundary Water Commission. United States Section. https://www.ibwc.gov/Files/Annual_Salinity_Report_2012_1.pdf. Accessed October 9, 2020.

75 A.R. Summit. 2013. *Contested Waters: An Environmental History of the Colorado River.* Boulder: University Press of Colorado, p. 191.

76 T. Perry and R. Marosi. 2010. A water-providing marvel – and a 'death trap.' *Los Angeles Times.* November 26. http://articles.latimes.com/2010/nov/26/local/la-me-canal-20101126. Accessed October 9, 2020.

77 K. Rowell et al. 2005. The importance of Colorado River flow to nursery habitats of the Gulf corvina (*Cynoscion othonopterus*). *Canadian Journal of Fisheries and Aquatic Sciences* 62: 2874–85.
    D. Duval and B. Colby. 2017. The influence of Colorado River flows on the upper Gulf of California fisheries economy. *Ecological Engineering* 106: 791–98.
    S.L. Postel, J.I. Morrison, and P.H. Gleick. 1998. Allocating fresh water to aquatic ecosystems: The case of the Colorado River Delta. *Water International* 23: 119–25.

78 A. Leopold. 1949. *A Sand County Almanac and Sketches Here and There.* Oxford: Oxford University Press, p. 135.
    B.C. Howard. 2014. Historic "pulse flow" brings water to parched Colorado River Delta. *National Geographic.* http://news.nationalgeographic.com/news/2014/03/140322-colorado-river-delta-pulse-flow-morelos-dam-minute-319-water/. Accessed November 12, 2020.

79 W. Davis. 2013. *River Notes: A Natural and Human History of the Colorado River.* Washington, DC: Island Press, p. 144.

80 O. Hinojosa-Huerta et al. 2004. Waterbird communities and associated wetlands of the Colorado River delta. Mexico. *Studies in Avian Biology* 27: 52–60.
    M.M. Gomez-Sapiens, E. Soto-Montoya, and O. Hinojosa-Huerta. 2013. Shorebird abundance and species diversity in natural intertidal and non-tidal anthropogenic wetlands of the Colorado River Delta, Mexico. *Ecological Engineering* 59: 74–83.

81 W. Davis. 2013. *River Notes: A Natural and Human History of the Colorado River.* Washington, DC: Island Press.

82 D.F. Luecke et al. 1999. *A Delta Once More: Restoring Riparian and Wetland Habitat in the Colorado River Delta.* Washington, DC: Environmental Defense Publications.

A.R. Summit. 2013. *Contested Waters: An Environmental History of the Colorado River.* Boulder: University Press of Colorado.

83 W. Davis. 2013. *River Notes: A Natural and Human History of the Colorado River.* Washington, DC: Island Press.

A.R. Summit. 2013. *Contested Waters: An Environmental History of the Colorado River.* Boulder: University Press of Colorado.

84 B.C. Howard. 2014. Historic "pulse flow" brings water to parched Colorado River Delta. *National Geographic.* http://news.nationalgeographic.com/news/2014/03/140322-colorado-river-delta-pulse-flow-morelos-dam-minute-319-water/. Accessed November 12, 2020.

85 A. Witze. 2014. Water returns to arid Colorado River delta. *Nature* 507: 286.

P.B. Shafroth et al. 2017. A large-scale environmental flow experiment for riparian restoration in the Colorado River Delta. *Ecological Engineering* 106: 645–60.

86 A.J. Darrah and H.F. Greeney. 2017. Importance of the 2014 Colorado River Delta pulse flow for migratory songbirds: Insights from foraging behavior. *Ecological Engineering* 106: 784–90.

87 W. Davis. 2013. *River Notes: A Natural and Human History of the Colorado River.* Washington, DC: Island Press.

B.C. Howard. 2014. Historic "pulse flow" brings water to parched Colorado River Delta. *National Geographic.* http://news.nationalgeographic.com/news/2014/03/140322-colorado-river-delta-pulse-flow-morelos-dam-minute-319-water/. Accessed November 12, 2020.

88 S.L. Postel. 2012. Grabbing the Colorado from the "People of the River." *National Geographic Newsroom Blog.* https://blog.nationalgeographic.org/2012/12/19/grabbing-the-colorado-from-the-people-of-the-river/. Accessed November 12, 2020.

89 B.C. Howard. 2014. Historic "pulse flow" brings water to parched Colorado River Delta. *National Geographic.* http://news.nationalgeographic.com/news/2014/03/140322-colorado-river-delta-pulse-flow-morelos-dam-minute-319-water/ Accessed November 12, 2020.

A.R. Summit. 2013. *Contested Waters: An Environmental History of the Colorado River.* Boulder: University Press of Colorado.

S.L. Postel, Morrison, J.I., and P.H. Gleick. 1998. Allocating fresh water to aquatic ecosystems: The case of the Colorado River Delta. *Water International* 23: 119–25.

90 A. Leopold. 1949. *A Sand County Almanac and Sketches Here and There.* Oxford: Oxford University Press, p. 192.

91 A. Leopold. 1949. *A Sand County Almanac and Sketches Here and There.* Oxford: Oxford University Press, p. 211.

EIGHT: The Rio Grande/Rio Bravo

1 L.C. Smith. 2020. *Rivers of Power: How a Natural Force Raised Kingdoms, Destroyed Civilizations, and Shapes Our World.* New York: Little, Brown Spark, p. 52.

2 O.J. Martinez (ed.). 1996. *US-Mexico Borderlands: Historical and Contemporary Perspectives.* Lanham, MD: Rowman & Littlefield, p xiii.

L.C. Smith. 2020. *Rivers of Power: How a Natural Force Raised Kingdoms, Destroyed Civilizations, and Shapes Our World.* New York: Little, Brown Spark.

M. Brochmann. 2012. Signing river treaties – does it improve river cooperation? *International Interactions* 38: 141–63.

3   US Census Bureau. 2020. US and World Population Clock. https://www.census.gov/popclock/. Accessed March 29, 2021.

4   The World Bank. 2020. Data. United States. https://data.worldbank.org/country/united-states?view=chart. Accessed March 29, 2021.
    The World Bank. 2020. Data. Mexico. https://data.worldbank.org/country/mexico?view=chart. Accessed March 29, 2021.

5   *The Economist.* 2017. Free exchange. The best policy. Honest campaigns for immigration would advocate much more of it. March 18, p. 76.

6   United Nations Development Programme. 2020. Human Development Reports. http://hdr.undp.org/en/countries/profiles/. Accessed October 13, 2020.

7   G.E. Anzaldúa. 2007. *Borderlands/La Frontera: The New Mestiza.* San Francisco: Aunt Lute Books, p. 25.

8   A. Gonzalez-Barrera and J. Manuel. 2019. What we know about illegal immigration in Mexico. Pew Research Center. FacTTank. https://www.pewresearch.org/fact-tank/2019/06/28/what-we-know-about-illegal-immigration-from-mexico/. Accessed October 13, 2020.

9   J. Durand, D. Massey, and R. Zenteno. 2001. Mexican immigration to the United States: Continuities and changes. *Latin American Research Review* 36: 107–27. http://www.jstor.org/stable/2692076. Accessed October 14, 2020.

10 A. Gonzalez-Barrera and J. Manuel. 2019. What we know about illegal immigration in Mexico. Pew Research Center. FacTTank. https://www.pewresearch.org/fact-tank/2019/06/28/what-we-know-about-illegal-immigration-from-mexico/. Accessed October 13, 2020.

11 R. Bruns. 2019. *Border Towns and Border Crossings: A History of the US-Mexico Divide.* ABC-CLIO. US Dept of Transportation. Bureau of Transportation Statistics. Border Crossing/Entry. Data 2019. https://www.bts.gov/content/border-crossingentry-data. Accessed June 5, 2019.

12 A. Gonzalez-Barrera and J. Manuel. 2019. What we know about illegal immigration in Mexico. Pew Research Center. FacTTank. https://www.pewresearch.org/fact-tank/2019/06/28/what-we-know-about-illegal-immigration-from-mexico/. Accessed October 13, 2020.
    J. Gramlich and L. Noe-Bustamante. 2019. What's happening at the U.S.-Mexico border in 5 charts. Pew Research Center. FacTTank. https://www.pewresearch.org/fact-tank/2019/11/01/whats-happening-at-the-u-s-mexico-border-in-5-charts/. Accessed October 15, 2020.

13 W.S. Baldridge and K.H. Olden. 1989. The Rio Grande rift. *American Scientist* 77: 240–47.

14 W.S. Baldridge and K.H. Olden. 1989. The Rio Grande rift. *American Scientist* 77: 240–47.

15 W.S. Baldridge and K.H. Olden. 1989. The Rio Grande rift. *American Scientist* 77: 240–47.

16 G.H. Mack et al. 2006. Pliocene and Quaternary history of the Rio Grande, the axial river of the southern Rio Grande rift, New Mexico, USA. *Earth-Science Reviews* 79: 141–62.

17 K. Fahey. 2003. *The Rio Grande* (Rivers of North America). Milwaukee, WI: Gareth Stevens Publishing Learning Library.

18 C.L. Riley. 1995. *Rio del Norte: People of the Upper Rio Grande From Earliest Times to the Pueblo Revolt.* Salt Lake City: University of Utah Press.

19 C.L. Riley. 1995. *Rio del Norte: People of the Upper Rio Grande From Earliest Times to the Pueblo Revolt.* Salt Lake City: University of Utah Press.

20 C.L. Riley. 1995. *Rio del Norte: People of the Upper Rio Grande From Earliest Times to the Pueblo Revolt*. Salt Lake City: University of Utah Press.

21 C.L. Riley. 1995. *Rio del Norte: People of the Upper Rio Grande From Earliest Times to the Pueblo Revolt*. Salt Lake City: University of Utah Press.

22 C.L. Riley. 1995. *Rio del Norte: People of the Upper Rio Grande From Earliest Times to the Pueblo Revolt*. Salt Lake City: University of Utah Press.

23 K. Fahey. 2003. *The Rio Grande* (Rivers of North America). Milwaukee, WI: Gareth Stevens Publishing Learning Library.

24 C.L. Riley. 1995. *Rio del Norte: People of the Upper Rio Grande From Earliest Times to the Pueblo Revolt*. Salt Lake City: University of Utah Press, p. 121.

25 P. Horgan. 1954. *Great River: The Rio Grande in American History*, vol. 2, *Mexico and the United States*. New York: Rinehart.

26 C.L. Riley. 1995. *Rio del Norte: People of the Upper Rio Grande From Earliest Times to the Pueblo Revolt*. Salt Lake City: University of Utah Press.

27 G.P. Winship. 1896. *The Coronado Expedition, 1540–1542*. Fourteenth Annual Report of the Bureau of Ethnology, Washington, pp. 6–638. https://archive.org/details/coronadoexpeditioowinsrich. Accessed October 8, 2020.

28 C.L. Riley. 1995. *Rio del Norte: People of the Upper Rio Grande From Earliest Times to the Pueblo Revolt*. Salt Lake City: University of Utah Press, p. 163.

29 C.L. Riley. 1995. *Rio del Norte: People of the Upper Rio Grande From Earliest Times to the Pueblo Revolt*. Salt Lake City: University of Utah Press, p. 163.

30 C.L. Riley. 1995. *Rio del Norte: People of the Upper Rio Grande From Earliest Times to the Pueblo Revolt*. Salt Lake City: University of Utah Press, p. 163.

31 C.L. Riley. 1995. *Rio del Norte: People of the Upper Rio Grande From Earliest Times to the Pueblo Revolt*. Salt Lake City: University of Utah Press, p. 163.

32 C.L. Riley. 1995. *Rio del Norte: People of the Upper Rio Grande From Earliest Times to the Pueblo Revolt*. Salt Lake City: University of Utah Press, p. 163.

33 C.L. Riley. 1995. *Rio del Norte: People of the Upper Rio Grande From Earliest Times to the Pueblo Revolt*. Salt Lake City: University of Utah Press, p. 255.

34 R. St. John. 2011. *Line in the Sand: A History of the Western U.S.–Mexican Border*. Princeton, NJ: Princeton University Press.

35 R. St. John. 2011. *Line in the Sand: A History of the Western U.S.–Mexican Border*. Princeton, NJ: Princeton University Press.

36 R. St. John. 2011. *Line in the Sand: A History of the Western U.S.–Mexican Border*. Princeton, NJ: Princeton University Press.

37 M. Manchaca. 2002. *Recovering History, Constructing Race: The Indian, Black, and White Roots of Mexican Americans*. The Joe R. and Teresa Lozano Long Series in Latin American and Latino Art and Culture. Austin: University of Texas Press, p. 200.

38 R. St. John. 2011. *Line in the Sand: A History of the Western U.S.–Mexican Border*. Princeton, NJ: Princeton University Press.
J.C. Metz. 1989. *Border: The U.S,–Mexico Line*. El Paso, TX: Mangan.

39 R. St. John. 2011. *Line in the Sand: A History of the Western U.S.–Mexican Border*. Princeton, NJ: Princeton University Press.

40 R. St. John. 2011. *Line in the Sand: A History of the Western U.S.–Mexican Border*. Princeton, NJ: Princeton University Press, p. 36.

41 R. St. John. 2011. *Line in the Sand: A History of the Western U.S.–Mexican Border*. Princeton, NJ: Princeton University Press.
J.C. Metz. 1989. *Border: The U.S.–Mexico Line*. El Paso, TX: Mangan.

42 J.E. Mueller, 1975, *Restless River, International Law and the Behavior of the Rio Grande.* El Paso, TX: Texas Western Press, p. 64.

43 J.C. Metz. 1989. *Border: The U.S.–Mexico Line.* El Paso, TX: Mangan.

44 K. Abrams. 2005. Polygamy, prostitution, and the federalization of immigration law. Columbia Law Review *105: 641–716.*
Immigration and Ethnic History Society. 2019. Immigration History. *Page Act* (1875). https://immigrationhistory.org/item/page-act/. Accessed October 12, 2020.

45 R. St. John. 2011. *Line in the Sand. A History of the Western U.S.–Mexican Border.* Princeton, NJ: Princeton University Press.

46 R. St. John. 2011. *Line in the Sand. A History of the Western U.S.–Mexican Border.* Princeton, NJ: Princeton University Press, p. 4.

47 J. Gramlich and L. Noe-Bustamante. 2019. What's happening at the U.S.-Mexico border in 5 charts. Pew Research Center. FacTank. https://www.pewresearch.org/fact-tank/2019/11/01/whats-happening-at-the-u-s-mexico-border-in-5-charts/. Accessed October 15, 2020.

48 G. Hanson and C. McIntosh. 2016. Is the Mediterranean the New Rio Grande? U.S. and EU immigration pressures in the long run. *Journal of Economic Perspectives* 30: 57–82.

49 J. Preston. 2015. Number of migrants illegally crossing Rio Grande rises sharply. *The New York Times.* November 27. http://www.nytimes.com/2015/11/27/us/number-of-migrants-illegally-crossing-rio-grande-rises-sharply.html?_r=0. Accessed October 23, 2016.
Associated Press. 2017. At least 3 drown trying to cross Rio Grande; 7 rescued. https://www.nbcdfw.com/news/local/At-Least-3-Drown-Trying-to-Cross-Rio-Grande-7-Rescued-436633653.html. Accessed October 23, 2016.
J. Gramlich and L. Noe-Bustamante. 2019. What's happening at the U.S.-Mexico border in 5 charts. Pew Research Center. FacTank. https://www.pewresearch.org/fact-tank/2019/11/01/whats-happening-at-the-u-s-mexico-border-in-5-charts/. Accessed October 15, 2020.

50 US Department of Homeland Security. 2020. U.S. Border Patrol Fiscal Year Southwest Border Sector Deaths (FY 1998–FY 2019). https://www.cbp.gov/document/stats/us-border-patrol-fiscal-year-southwest-border-sector-deaths-fy-1998-fy-2019. Accessed October 14, 2020.

51 B. Borrell. 2013. Ghosts of the Rio Grande. *The American Prospect.* http://prospect.org/article/ghosts-rio-grande. *Accessed October 23, 2016.*

52 K. Eschbach et al. 1999. Death at the border. *International Migration Review* 33: 430–54.

53 D.K. Rossmo et al. 2008. Geographic patterns and profiling of illegal crossings of the southern U.S. border. *Security Journal* 21: 29–57.

54 *Eagle Pass Business Journal.* 2016. Eagle Pass border patrol agents rescue man from drowning in Rio Grande. http://www.epbusinessjournal.com/2016/09/eagle-pass-border-patrol-agents-rescue-man-drowning-rio-grande/. Accessed October 14, 2020.

55 *Eagle Pass Business Journal.* 2016. Eagle Pass border patrol agents rescue man from drowning in Rio Grande. http://www.epbusinessjournal.com/2016/09/eagle-pass-border-patrol-agents-rescue-man-drowning-rio-grande/. Accessed October 14, 2020.
P.M. Orrenius. 2001. Illegal immigration and enforcement along the US-Mexico border: An overview. *Economic and Financial Review–Federal Reserve Bank of Dallas* 1: 2–11.
W.A. Cornelius. 2001. Death at the border: Efficacy and unintended consequences of U.S. immigration control policy. *Population and Development Review* 27: 661–85.

56 M. Jimenez. 2009. Humanitarian crisis: Migrant deaths at the U.S.–Mexico border. https://www.aclu.org/files/pdfs/immigrants/humanitariancrisisreport.pdf. Accessed October 14, 2020.

57 M. Jimenez. 2009. Humanitarian crisis: Migrant deaths at the U.S.–Mexico border. https://www.aclu.org/files/pdfs/immigrants/humanitariancrisisreport.pdf. Accessed October 14, 2020.

58 R. St. John. 2011. *Line in the Sand. A History of the Western U.S.–Mexican Border.* Princeton, NJ: Princeton University Press.
J.C. Metz. 1989. *Border: The U.S.–Mexico Line.* El Paso, TX: Mangan.

59 M. Jimenez. 2009. Humanitarian crisis: Migrant deaths at the U.S.–Mexico border. https://www.aclu.org/files/pdfs/immigrants/humanitariancrisisreport.pdf. Accessed October 14, 2020.

NINE: The Mississippi River

1 T. Haning. 2009. Geography of war: The significance of physical and human geography principles. *FOCUS on Geography* 52: 32–36.

2 P. O'Sullivan and J.W. Miller, Jr. 2015. *The Geography of Warfare.* New York: Routledge.

3 M.K. Lawson. 2002. *The Battle of Hastings: 1066.* Stroud, UK: Tempus.
E. Wheeler. 1988. The Battle of Hastings: Math, myth and melee. *Journal of Military History* 52: 28–134.
Sun Tzu. 2019. *The Art of War.* New York: Ixia Press.

4 W.W. Atwood. 1919. Geography factor in war. Fixed line of Hun invasion and forced "war of positions." *The Harvard Crimson.* https://www.thecrimson.com/article/1919/1/30/geography-factor-in-war-pwhen-the/. Accessed October 15, 2020.

5 P. O'Sullivan and J.W. Miller, Jr. 2015. *The Geography of Warfare.* New York: Routledge.

6 *The Economist.* 2015. The South: The present past. April 4.

7 L.B. Leopold. 1994. *A View of the River.* Cambridge, MA: Harvard University Press, p. 3.

8 P.E. Potter. 1978. Significance and origin of big rivers. *Journal of Geology* 86: 13–33.

9 W.E. Galloway, T.L. Whiteaker, and P. Ganey-Curry. 2011. History of Cenozoic North American drainage basin evolution, sediment yield, and accumulation in the Gulf of Mexico basin. *Geosphere* 7: 938–73.

10 A. Aslan, W.J. Autin, and M.D. Blum. 2005. Causes of river avulsion: insights from the late Holocene avulsion history of the Mississippi River, USA. *Journal of Sedimentary Research* 75: 650–64.

11 P.J. Richerson, R. Boyd, and R.L. Bettinger. 2001. Was agriculture impossible during the Pleistocene but mandatory during the Holocene? A climate change hypothesis. *American Antiquity* 66: 387–411.

12 C. Waldman. 2006. *Encyclopedia of Native American Tribes,* 3rd ed. New York: Checkmark Books.

13 S. Morison. 1974. *The European Discovery of America: The Southern Voyages, 1492–1616.* New York: Oxford University Press.

14 ¹⁴H. MacLennan. 1961. *Seven Rivers of Canada.* Toronto: Macmillan of Canada.

15 Z. Cramer. 1801. *The Navigator.* Self-published, p.2.

16 M. Egnal. 2009. *Clash of Extremes: Economic Origins of the Civil War.* New York: Hill & Wang.

D.H. Usner Jr. 1987. The frontier exchange economy of the lower Mississippi valley in the Eighteenth Century. *The William and Mary Quarterly: A Magazine of Early American History and Culture* 44: 166–92.

17 S.N. Dossman. 2014. *Vicksburg 1863: The Deepest Wound*. Santa Barbara, CA: ABC-CLIO.

18 R.L. Ransom. 2018. The Civil War in American economic history. Chapter 10 in L.P. Cain, P.V. Fishback, and P.W. Rhode (eds.), *The Oxford Handbook of the American Economy*, vol. 2. New York: Oxford University Press, p. 372.

19 US National Parks Service. 2020. Mississippi River facts. http://www.nps.gov/miss/riverfacts.htm. Accessed October 15, 2020.

20 S.N. Dossman. 2014. *Vicksburg 1863: The Deepest Wound*. Santa Barbara, CA: ABC-CLIO, p. 2.

21 J. Keegan. 2010. *The American Civil War: A Military History*. New York: Vintage.
J. Keegan. 2012. *Fields of Battle: The Wars for North America*. New York: Vintage.

22 J. Keegan. 2010. *The American Civil War: A Military History*. New York: Vintage.

23 S.N. Dossman. 2014. *Vicksburg 1863: The Deepest Wound*. Santa Barbara, CA: ABC-CLIO, p. 2.

24 J. Keegan. 2010. *The American Civil War: A Military History*. New York: Vintage.

25 S.N. Dossman. 2014. *Vicksburg 1863: The Deepest Wound*. Santa Barbara, CA: ABC-CLIO.
J. Keegan. 2010. *The American Civil War: A Military History*. New York: Vintage.

26 S.N. Dossman. 2014. *Vicksburg 1863: The Deepest Wound*. Santa Barbara, CA: ABC-CLIO, p. 1.

27 M.B. Ballard. 2004. *Vicksburg: The Campaign That Opened The Mississippi*. Chapel Hill: University of North Carolina Press, p. 24.

28 S.N. Dossman. 2014. *Vicksburg 1863: The Deepest Wound*. Santa Barbara, CA: ABC-CLIO, p. 4.

29 W.L. Shea and T.T. Winschel. 2003. *Vicksburg Is the Key: The Struggle for the Mississippi River*. Lincoln: University of Nebraska Press.

30 J. Keegan. 2010. *The American Civil War: A Military History*. New York: Vintage, p. 92.

31 S.N. Dossman. 2014. *Vicksburg 1863: The Deepest Wound*. Santa Barbara, CA: ABC-CLIO.

32 W.L. Shea and T.T. Winschel. 2003. *Vicksburg Is the Key: The Struggle for the Mississippi River*. Lincoln: University of Nebraska Press.

33 S.N. Dossman. 2014. *Vicksburg 1863: The Deepest Wound*. Santa Barbara, CA: ABC-CLIO.

34 W.L. Shea and T.T. Winschel. 2003. *Vicksburg Is the Key: The Struggle for the Mississippi River*. Lincoln: University of Nebraska Press.

35 W.L. Shea and T.T. Winschel. 2003. *Vicksburg Is the Key: The Struggle for the Mississippi River*. Lincoln: University of Nebraska Press, p. 16.

36 W.L. Shea and T.T. Winschel. 2003. *Vicksburg Is the Key: The Struggle for the Mississippi River*. Lincoln: University of Nebraska Press, p. 16.

37 S.N. Dossman. 2014. *Vicksburg 1863: The Deepest Wound*. Santa Barbara, CA: ABC-CLIO, p. 19.

38 W.L. Shea and T.T. Winschel. 2003. *Vicksburg Is the Key: The Struggle for the Mississippi River*. Lincoln: University of Nebraska Press, p. 155.

39 D. McCool. 2014. *River Republic: The Fall and Rise of America's Rivers*. New York: Columbia University Press, p. 139.

40 W.L. Shea and T.T. Winschel. 2003. *Vicksburg Is the Key: The Struggle for the Mississippi River*. Lincoln: University of Nebraska Press, p. 205.

41 W.L. Shea and T.T. Winschel. 2003. *Vicksburg Is the Key: The Struggle for the Mississippi River.* Lincoln: University of Nebraska Press, p. 205.

42 W.L. Shea and T.T. Winschel. 2003. *Vicksburg Is the Key: The Struggle for the Mississippi River.* Lincoln: University of Nebraska Press, p. 205.

TEN: The Hudson River

1 M. Aubert et al. 2019. Earliest hunting scene in prehistoric art. *Nature* 576: 442–45.

2 J.K. Howat. 1987. Introduction. In Rogers, M-A. (ed.). *American Paradise: The World of the Hudson River School.* Metropolitan Museum of Art, p. xvii.

3 J.K. Howat. 1987. Introduction. In Rogers, M-A. (ed.). *American Paradise: The World of the Hudson River School.* Metropolitan Museum of Art, p. xvii.

4 T.S. Wermuth, J.M. Johnson, and C. Pryslopski (eds.). 2009. *America's First River: The History and Culture of the Hudson River Valley.* Albany: State University of New York Press, p. 3.

5 T. Lewis. 2007. *The Hudson: A History.* New Haven, CT: Yale University Press, p. 36.
   F. Dunwell. 2008. *The Hudson: America's River.* New York: Columbia University Press.

6 M.A. Moran and K.E., Limburg. 1986. The Hudson river ecosystem. In K.E. Limberg, M.A. Moran, and W.H. McDowell (eds.), *The Hudson River Ecosystem* New York: Springer, pp. 6–39.

7 Y.W. Isachsen et al. (eds.). 2000. *Geology of New York State: A Simplified Account,* 2nd ed. Albany: New York State Museum Educational Leaflet No. 28.

8 T.S. Wermuth, J.M. Johnson, and C. Pryslopski (eds.). 2009. *America's First River: The History and Culture of the Hudson River Valley.* Albany: State University of New York Press.

9 S. Dawicki. 2005. The great flood of New York. *Oceanus.* Woods Hole Oceanographic Institution. https://www.whoi.edu/oceanus/feature/the-great-flood-of-new-york/. Accessed October 15, 2020.
   J.P. Donnelly et al. 2005. Catastrophic meltwater discharge down the Hudson Valley: A potential trigger for the Intra-Allerød cold period. *Geology* 33: 89–92.

10 Friends of the Pleistocene. 2010. Off New York City's Deep End: A Pleistocene Grand Canyon. https://fopnews.wordpress.com/2010/01/29/off-new-york-citys-deep-end-a-pleistocene-grand-canyon/. Accessed October 16, 2020.

11 R.E. Henshaw (ed.). 2011. *Environmental History of the Hudson River: Human Uses that Changed the Ecology, Ecology that Changed Human Uses.* Albany: State University of New York Press.

12 D.G. Anderson. 1990. The Paleoindian colonization of eastern North America. Early Paleoindian economies of eastern North America. *Research in Economic Anthropology,* Supplement 5: 163–216. JAI Press. http://pidba.org/anderson/cv/Anderson%20 1990%20REAnth.pdf. Accessed October 16, 2020.

13 D.G. Anderson. 1990. The Paleoindian colonization of eastern North America. Early Paleoindian economies of eastern North America. *Research in Economic Anthropology,* Supplement 5: 163–216. JAI Press. http://pidba.org/anderson/cv/Anderson%20 1990%20REAnth.pdf. Accessed October 16, 2020.

14 T.S. Wermuth, J.M. Johnson, and C. Pryslopski (eds.). 2009. *America's First River: The History and Culture of the Hudson River Valley.* Albany: State University of New York Press, p. 42.

15 T. Lewis. 2007. *The Hudson: A History*. New Haven, CT: Yale University Press, p. 37.

16 T. Lewis. 2007. *The Hudson: A History*. New Haven, CT: Yale University Press, p. 46.

17 T.S. Wermuth, J.M. Johnson, and C. Pryslopski (eds.). 2009. *America's First River: The History and Culture of the Hudson River Valley*. Albany: State University of New York Press.

    T. Lewis. 2007. *The Hudson: A History*. New Haven, CT: Yale University Press.

18 T. Lewis. 2007. *The Hudson: A History*. New Haven, CT: Yale University Press.

19 A. Keller, 1997. *Life Along the Hudson*. New York: Fordham University Press.

20 New Netherland Institute. 2016. Peter Schaghen letter. https://web.archive.org/web/20160324021546/http://www.newnetherlandinstitute.org/history-and-heritage/additional-resources/dutch-treats/peter-schagen-letter. Accessed September 16, 2020.

21 T. Lewis. 2007. *The Hudson: A History*. New Haven, CT: Yale University Press, p. 61.

22 S.F. Cooper. 1880. The Hudson River and its names. *Magazine of Natural History* 4(6): 401–418. http://jfcoopersociety.org/susan/hudson.html. Accessed November 4, 2020.

23 T. Lewis. 2007. *The Hudson: A History*. New Haven, CT: Yale University Press.

24 T. Lewis. 2007. *The Hudson: A History*. New Haven, CT: Yale University Press.

25 M.J.T. Pearson. 2015. *Failure Of British Strategy during the Southern Campaign of the American Revolutionary War*. Auckland, NZ: Pickle Partners, Chapter 1.

26 M.J.T. Pearson. 2015. *Failure Of British Strategy during the Southern Campaign of the American Revolutionary War*. Auckland, NZ: Pickle Partners, Chapter 1.

27 A. Keller. 1997. *Life Along the Hudson*. New York: Fordham University Press.

28 A. Keller. 1997. *Life Along the Hudson*. New York: Fordham University Press.

29 T. Lewis. 2007. *The Hudson: A History*. New Haven, CT: Yale University Press, p. 171.

30 T. Lewis. 2007. *The Hudson: A History*. New Haven, CT: Yale University Press, p. 171.

    N. Hawthorne. 1835. The canal boat. *New-England Magazine* 9 (December): 398–409. http://historymatters.gmu.edu/d/6212/. Accessed October 16, 2020.

31 T. Lewis. 2007. *The Hudson: A History*. New Haven, CT: Yale University Press.

    A. Keller. 1997. *Life Along the Hudson*. New York: Fordham University Press.

32 T. Lewis. 2007. *The Hudson: A History*. New Haven, CT: Yale University Press, p. 185.

33 T. Lewis. 2007. *The Hudson: A History*. New Haven, CT: Yale University Press, p. 185.

34 L.S. Leudtke (ed.). 1992. *Making America: The Society & Culture of the United States*. Chapel Hill: University of North Carolina Press, p. 145.

35 J.K. Howat. 1978. *Hudson River and its Painters*. New York: Viking Press, p. 22.

36 J.K. Howat. 1978. *Hudson River and its Painters*. New York: Viking Press.

37 L. Minks. 1999. *The Hudson River School: The Landscape Art of Bierstadt, Cole, Church, Durand, Heade and Twenty Other Artists*. Bexley, OH: Gramercy.

38 J.K. Howat. 1978. *Hudson River and its Painters*. New York: Viking Press, p. 29.

39 J.K. Howat. 1978. *Hudson River and its Painters*. New York: Viking Press.

40 B.B. Millhouse. 2007. *American Wilderness: The Story of the Hudson River School of Painting*. Albany, NY: Black Dome Press, p. 5.

41 B.B. Millhouse. 2007. *American Wilderness: The Story of the Hudson River School of Painting*. Albany, NY: Black Dome Press, p. 8.

42 B.B. Millhouse. 2007. *American Wilderness: The Story of the Hudson River School of Painting*. Albany, NY: Black Dome Press, p. 8.

43 C.N. Philips. 2012. *Epic in American Culture: Settlement To Reconstruction*. Baltimore, MD: Johns Hopkins University Press, p. 117.

44 K.J. Avery. 1987. A historiography of the Hudson River School. In Rogers, M-A. (ed.), *American Paradise: The World of the Hudson River School*. New York: Metropolitan Museum of Art.

45 J.K. Howat. 1978. *Hudson River and its Painters*. New York: Viking Press.

46 K.J. Avery. 1987. A historiography of the Hudson River School. In Rogers, M-A. (ed.). *American Paradise: The World of the Hudson River School*. New York: Metropolitan Museum of Art, p. 5.

47 K.J. Avery. 1987. A historiography of the Hudson River School. In Rogers, M-A. (ed.). *American Paradise: The World of the Hudson River School*. New York: Metropolitan Museum of Art, p. 6.

48 B.B. Lassiter. 1978. *American Wilderness: The Hudson River School of Painting*. New York: Doubleday, p. 147.

49 D.B. Burke and C.H. Voorsanger. 1987. The Hudson River School in eclipse. In M-A. Rogers (ed.), *American Paradise: The World of the Hudson River School*. New York: Metropolitan Museum of Art, p. 71.

50 F. Dunwell. 2008. *The Hudson: America's River*. New York: Columbia University Press, p. 88.

51 A. Keller. 1997. *Life Along the Hudson*. New York: Fordham University Press, pp. 203, 209.

52 A. Keller. 1997. *Life Along the Hudson*. New York: Fordham University Press, p. 105.

53 A. Keller. 1997. *Life Along the Hudson*. New York: Fordham University Press, p. 211.

54 K.J. Avery. 1987. A historiography of the Hudson River School. In M-A. Rogers (ed.), *American Paradise: The World of the Hudson River School*. New York: Metropolitan Museum of Art, p. 6.

55 K.J. Avery. 1987. A historiography of the Hudson River School. In M-A. Rogers (ed.), *American Paradise: The World of the Hudson River School*. New York: Metropolitan Museum of Art, pp. 3–20.

56 K.J. Avery. 1987. A historiography of the Hudson River School. In M-A. Rogers (ed.), *American Paradise: The World of the Hudson River School*. New York: Metropolitan Museum of Art, pp. 3–20.

57 K.J. Avery. 1987. A historiography of the Hudson River School. In M-A. Rogers (ed.), *American Paradise: The World of the Hudson River School*. New York: Metropolitan Museum of Art, pp. 3–20.

58 K.J. Avery. 1987. A historiography of the Hudson River School. In M-A. Rogers (ed.), *American Paradise: The World of the Hudson River School*. New York: Metropolitan Museum of Art, pp. 3–20.

59 R. Pogrebin. 2013. Painting's removal stirs outcry. *The New York Times*. March 17. http://www.nytimes.com/2013/03/18/arts/design/sale-planned-for-thomas-cole-land-scape.html. Accessed October 16, 2020.

60 B.B. Milhouse. 2007. *American Wilderness: The Story of the Hudson River School of Painting*. Albany, NY: Black Dome Press, p. 151.

ELEVEN: The St. Lawrence River

1 Businesswire.com. 2012. Importance of river basins in driving global economic growth to rocket: Top ten basins' GDP to set to exceed that of USA, Japan, and Germany combined by 2050. June 2012. https://www.businesswire.com/news/home/20120611006498/en/Im-portance-River-Basins-Driving-Global-Growth-Rocket. Accessed February 22, 2018.

2   J. Wierenga. 2001. Canoe Van Pesse could really sail (translated from Dutch). http://www.archeoforum.nl/Pesse9.html. Accessed October 16, 2020.

3   US Department of Transportation. 2020. Miles of infrastructure by transportation mode. Bureau of Transportation Statistics. https://www.bts.gov/content/miles-infra-structure-transportation-mode. Accessed October 16, 2020.
    United Nations Economic Commission for Europe. Undated. Total length of inland waterways. https://w3.unece.org/PXWeb/en/Table?IndicatorCode=58. Accessed October 15, 2020.

4   UK–UT. 2014. Inland Navigation in the United States: An Evaluation of Economic Impacts and the Potential Effects of Infrastructure Investment. University of Kentucky and University of Tennessee. http://nationalwaterwaysfoundation.org/documents/INLANDNAVIGATIONINTHEUSDECEMBER2014.pdf. Accessed March 02, 2018.

5   Martin Associates. 2018. *Economic Impacts of Maritime Shipping in the Great Lakes–St. Lawrence Region. Lancaster, PA.* https://greatlakes-seaway.com/wp-content/uploads/2019/10/eco_impact_full.pdf. Accessed October 16, 2020.

6   R.H. Whitbeck. 1914. The St. Lawrence River and its part in the making of Canada. American Association of Geographers 11th Annual Meeting, Chicago, IL, p. 587.

7   H. MacLennan. 1961. *Seven Rivers of Canada.* Toronto: Macmillan of Canada, p. 71.

8   R. MacGregor. 2017. *Original Highways: Travelling the Great Rivers of Canada.* Toronto: Random House Canada, p. 13.
    R.H. Whitbeck. 1914. The St. Lawrence River and its part in the making of Canada. American Association of Geographers 11th Annual Meeting, Chicago, IL.

9   D.G. Creighton. 1956. *The Empire of the St. Lawrence: A Study of Commerce and Politics.* Toronto: Macmillan of Canada, p. 6.

10 C.P. Parham. 2009. *The St. Lawrence Seaway and Power Project: An Oral History of the Greatest Construction Show on Earth.* Syracuse, NY: Syracuse University Press.

11 J. Fuller, K. Shear, and H. Wittig (eds.). 1995. *The Great Lakes: An Environmental Atlas and Resource Book*, 3rd ed. United States Environmental Protection Agency and the Government of Canada. http://publications.gc.ca/site/eng/9.858440/publication.html. Accessed October 16, 2020.

12 Canadian Geographic Online. Undated. Rivers of Canada: St. Lawrence River (Mixedwood Plains). http://www.canadiangeographic.com/atlas/themes.aspx?id=rivers&sub=rivers_east_stlawrence&lang=En. Accessed October 15, 2020.

13 J.C. Kammerer. 1990. Largest rivers in the United States. U.S. Geological Survey. https://pubs.usgs.gov/of/1987/ofr87-242/. Accessed October 16, 2020.

14 Natural Resources Canada. 2007. Rivers. Atlas of Canada. https://web.archive.org/web/20070202064028/http://atlas.nrcan.gc.ca/site/english/learningresources/facts/rivers.html. Accessed October 16, 2020.

15 Great Lakes and St. Lawrence Cities Initiative. Undated. About the Great Lakes and St. Lawrence Cities Initiative. https://glslcities.org/about/. Accessed October 16, 2020.

16 P.S. Kumarapeli and V.A. Saull. 1966. The St. Lawrence valley system: A North American equivalent of the East African rift valley system. *Canadian Journal of Earth Sciences* 3: 639–58.

17 P.S. Kumarapeli and V.A. Saull. 1966. The St. Lawrence valley system: A North American equivalent of the East African rift valley system. *Canadian Journal of Earth Sciences* 3: 639–58.

R.H. Whitbeck. 1914. The St. Lawrence River and its part in the making of Canada. American Association of Geographers 11th Annual Meeting, Chicago, IL, p. 585.

18 Natural Resources Canada. 2021. *The Atlas of Canada*. https://atlas.gc.ca/phys/en/. Accessed March 18, 2021.

19 A. Tremblay and Y. Lemieux. 2001. Supracrustal faults of the St. Lawrence rift system between Cap-Tourmente and Baie-Saint-Paul, Quebec. *Current Research* 2001-D-15. Natural Resources Canada, Geological Survey of Canada.

20 A. Tremblay and Y. Lemieux. 2001. Supracrustal faults of the St. Lawrence rift system between Cap-Tourmente and Baie-Saint-Paul, Quebec. *Current Research* 2001-D-15. Natural Resources Canada, Geological Survey of Canada.

21 F.P. Shepard. 1937. Origin of the Great Lakes basins. *Journal of Geology* 45: 76–88.

22 F.P. Shepard. 1937. Origin of the Great Lakes basins. *Journal of Geology* 45: 76–88. G. Larson and R. Schaetzl. 2001. Origin and evolution of the Great Lakes. *Journal of Great Lakes Research* 27: 518–46.

23 F.P. Shepard. 1937. Origin of the Great Lakes basins. *Journal of Geology* 45: 76–88.

24 F.P. Shepard. 1937. Origin of the Great Lakes basins. *Journal of Geology* 45: 76–88.

25 F. Leverett and F.B. Taylor. 1915. The Pleistocene of Indiana and Michigan and the History of the Great Lakes. *U.S. Geological Survey Monograph* No. 53, Washington, DC.

26 F. Leverett and F.B. Taylor. 1915. The Pleistocene of Indiana and Michigan and the History of the Great Lakes. *U.S. Geological Survey Monograph* No. 53, Washington, DC.

27 M. Parent and S. Occhietti. 2007. Late Wisconsinan deglaciation and Champlain Sea invasion in the St. Lawrence Valley, Québec. *Géographie physique et Quaternaire* 42: 215–46.
T.M. Cronin et al. 2008. Impacts of post-glacial lake drainage events and revised chronology of the Champlain Sea episode 13–9 ka. *Palaeogeography, Palaeoclimatology, Palaeoecology* 262: 46–60.
N.R. Gadd (ed.). 1988. *The Late Quaternary Development of the Champlain Sea Basin*. Geological Association of Canada Special Paper 35.

28 M.J. Dadswell. 1972. Postglacial dispersal of four deepwater fishes on the basis of new distribution records in eastern Ontario and western Quebec. *Journal of the Fisheries Board of Canada* 29: 545–53.
M.J. Dadswell. 1974. Distribution, ecology and postglacial dispersal of certain crustaceans and fishes in eastern North America. National Museum of Canada. *National Museum of Natural Science Publications in Zoology* 11: 1–110.
T.A. Sheldon, N.E. Mandrak, and N.R. Lovejoy. 2008. Biogeography of the deepwater sculpin (*Myoxocephalus thompsonii*), a Nearctic glacial relict. *Canadian Journal of Zoology* 86: 108–15.
T.M. Cronin et al. 2008. Impacts of post-glacial lake drainage events and revised chronology of the Champlain Sea episode 13–9 ka. *Palaeogeography, Palaeoclimatology, Palaeoecology* 262: 46–60.
D.E. McAllister et al. 1988. Paleoenvironmental and biogeographic analyses of fossil fishes in peri-Champlain Sea deposits in eastern Canada. In N.R. Gadd (ed.), *The Late Quaternary Development of the Champlain Sea Basin. Geological Association of Canada Special Paper* 35: 241–58.

29 A.P. Coleman. 1909. Lake Ojibway: Last of the great glacial lakes. *Ontario Bureau of Mines Report* 18: 284–93. http://www.geologyontario.mndmf.gov.on.ca/mndmfiles/pub/data/imaging/ARV18/ARV18.pdf. Accessed October 15, 2015.

A.D. Wickert. 2016. Reconstruction of North American drainage basins and river discharge since the Last Glacial Maximum. *Earth Surface Dynamics* 4: 831–69.

30 J.C Lothrop et al. 2016. Early human settlement of northeastern north America. *PaleoAmerica* 2: 192–251.

T.J. Abel and D.N. Fuerst. 1999. Prehistory of the St. Lawrence River headwaters region. *Archaeology of Eastern North America* 27: 1–53.

D.G. Anderson. 1990. The Paleoindian colonization of eastern North America. Early Paleoindian economies of eastern North America. *Research in Economic Anthropology*, Supplement 5: 163–216. JAI Press. http://pidba.org/anderson/cv/Anderson%20 1990%20REAnth.pdf. Accessed October 16, 2020.

31 Archéo-Québec Network. 2020. Prehistoric Québec. https://www.archeoquebec.com/en/archaeology-quebec/thematic-files/prehistoric-quebec. Accessed October 19, 2020.

32 T.J. Abel and D.N. Fuerst. 1999. Prehistory of the St. Lawrence River headwaters region. *Archaeology of Eastern North America* 27: 1–53.

33 Archéo-Québec Network. 2020. Prehistoric Québec. https://www.archeoquebec.com/en/archaeology-quebec/thematic-files/prehistoric-quebec. Accessed October 19, 2020.

34 Archéo-Québec Network. 2020. Prehistoric Québec. https://www.archeoquebec.com/en/archaeology-quebec/thematic-files/prehistoric-quebec. Accessed October 19, 2020.

35 K.J. Bragdon. 2001. *The Columbia Guide to American Indians of the Northeast.* New York: Columbia University Press.

36 L. Turgeon. Undated. Île aux Basques. *Encyclopedia of French Cultural Heritage in North America.* http://www.ameriquefrancaise.org/en/article-292/%C3%8Ele%20 aux%20Basques. Accessed October 19, 2020.

37 I. Rayburn. 2001. *Naming Canada: Stories about Canadian Place Names.* Toronto: University of Toronto Press, pp. 14–17.

38 Atlas of Canada Online. Undated. Rivers of Canada. St. Lawrence River (Mixedwood Plains). http://www.canadiangeographic.com/atlas/themes.aspx?id=rivers&sub=rivers_east_stlawrence&lang=En. Accessed October 19, 2020.

39 D. Creighton. 1957. *Harold Adams Innis: Portrait of a Scholar.* Toronto: University of Toronto Press, p. 105.

40 D. Macfarlane. 2014. *Negotiating a River: Canada, the US, and the Creation of the St. Lawrence Seaway. Vancouver: University of British Columba Press.*

41 F.M. Carroll. 2001. *A Good and Wise Measure: The Search for the Canadian-American Boundary, 1783–1842.* Toronto: University of Toronto Press.

42 R. Stagg. 2010. *The Golden Dream: A History of the St. Lawrence Seaway.* Toronto: Dundurn, p. 98.

43 R. Stagg. 2010. *The Golden Dream: A History of the St. Lawrence Seaway.* Toronto: Dundurn, p. 98.

44 R. MacGregor. 2017. *Original Highways: Travelling the Great Rivers of Canada.* Toronto: Random House Canada.

H. MacLennan. 1961. *Seven Rivers of Canada.* Toronto: Macmillan of Canada.

45 B.G. Trigger. 1962. Trade and tribal warfare on the St. Lawrence in the sixteenth century. *Ethnohistory* 9: 240–56.

R. Stagg. 2010. *The Golden Dream: A History of the St. Lawrence Seaway.* Toronto: Dundurn.

46 D.G. Creighton. 1956. *The Empire of the St. Lawrence: A Study of Commerce and Politics.* Toronto: Macmillan of Canada, p. 71.

47 R. Stagg. 2010. *The Golden Dream: A History of the St. Lawrence Seaway.* Toronto: Dundurn.

48 R. Stagg. 2010. *The Golden Dream: A History of the St. Lawrence Seaway.* Toronto: Dundurn.

49 R. Stagg. 2010. *The Golden Dream: A History of the St. Lawrence Seaway.* Toronto: Dundurn.

50 D.G. Creighton. 1956. *The Empire of the St. Lawrence: A Study of Commerce and Politics.* Toronto: Macmillan of Canada, p. 198.

51 D. Macfarlane. 2014. *Negotiating a River: Canada, the US, and the Creation of the St. Lawrence Seaway.* Vancouver: University of British Columba Press, p. 31.

52 D.G. Creighton. 1956. *The Empire of the St. Lawrence: A Study of Commerce and Politics.* Toronto: Macmillan of Canada, p. 31.

53 R. Stagg. 2010.*The Golden Dream: A History of the St. Lawrence Seaway.* Toronto: Dundurn, p. 53.

54 D.G. Creighton. 1956. *The Empire of the St. Lawrence: A Study of Commerce and Politics.* Toronto: Macmillan of Canada, p. 254.

55 C.P. Parham. 2009. *The St. Lawrence Seaway and Power Project: An Oral History of the Greatest Construction Show on Earth.* Syracuse, NY: Syracuse University Press.

56 R. Stagg. 2010. *The Golden Dream: A History of the St. Lawrence Seaway.* Toronto: Dundurn.

57 C.P. Parham. 2009. *The St. Lawrence Seaway and Power Project: An Oral History of the Greatest Construction Show on Earth.* Syracuse, NY: Syracuse University Press, p. 3.

58 C.P. Parham. 2009. *The St. Lawrence Seaway and Power Project: An Oral History of the Greatest Construction Show on Earth.* Syracuse, NY: Syracuse University Press.
D. Macfarlane. 2014. *Negotiating a River: Canada, the US, and the Creation of the St. Lawrence Seaway.* Vancouver: University of British Columba Press.
R. Stagg. 2010. *The Golden Dream: A History of the St. Lawrence Seaway.* Toronto: Dundurn, p. 107.

59 R. Stagg. 2010. *The Golden Dream: A History of the St. Lawrence Seaway.* Toronto: Dundurn.

60 C.P. Parham. 2009. *The St. Lawrence Seaway and Power Project: An Oral History of the Greatest Construction Show on Earth.* Syracuse, NY: Syracuse University Press.

61 C.P. Parham. 2009. *The St. Lawrence Seaway and Power Project: An Oral History of the Greatest Construction Show on Earth.* Syracuse, NY: Syracuse University Press, p. 13.

62 C.P. Parham. 2009. *The St. Lawrence Seaway and Power Project: An Oral History of the Greatest Construction Show on Earth.* Syracuse, NY: Syracuse University Press, p. 15.

63 C.P. Parham. 2009. *The St. Lawrence Seaway and Power Project: An Oral History of the Greatest Construction Show on Earth.* Syracuse, NY: Syracuse University Press, p. 18.

64 R. Stagg. 2010. *The Golden Dream: A History of the St. Lawrence Seaway.* Toronto: Dundurn, p. 169.

65 C.P. Parham. 2009. *The St. Lawrence Seaway and Power Project: An Oral History of the Greatest Construction Show on Earth.* Syracuse, NY: Syracuse University Press, p. xxiii.

66 J.H. Brior. 1960. *Taming the Sault: A History of the St. Lawrence Power Development – Heart of the Seaway*. Watertown, NY: Hungerford-Holbrook, p. 14.

67 C.P. Parham. 2009. *The St. Lawrence Seaway and Power Project: An Oral History of the Greatest Construction Show on Earth*. Syracuse, NY: Syracuse University Press, p. 288.

68 R. Stagg. 2010. *The Golden Dream: A History of the St. Lawrence Seaway*. Toronto: Dundurn, p. 161.

69 C.P. Parham. 2009. *The St. Lawrence Seaway and Power Project: An Oral History of the Greatest Construction Show on Earth*. Syracuse, NY: Syracuse University Press.

70 R. Stagg. 2010. *The Golden Dream: A History of the St. Lawrence Seaway*. Toronto: Dundurn, p 181.

71 C.P. Parham. 2009. *The St. Lawrence Seaway and Power Project: An Oral History of the Greatest Construction Show on Earth*. Syracuse, NY: Syracuse University Press.

72 Martin Associates. 2018. *Economic Impacts of Maritime Shipping in the Great Lakes–St. Lawrence Region*. Lancaster, PA. https://greatlakes-seaway.com/wp-content/uploads/2019/10/eco_impact_full.pdf. Accessed October 16, 2020.
    Transport Canada, US Army Corps of Engineers, US Department of Transportation, The St. Lawrence Seaway Management Corporation, Saint Lawrence Seaway Development Corporation, Environment Canada, and US Fish and Wildlife Service. 2007. *Great Lakes St Lawrence Seaway Study: Final Report*. https://greatlakes-seaway.com/wp-content/uploads/2019/10/GLSL-Final-Report-En.pdf. Accessed October 19, 2020.

73 C.P. Parham. 2009. *The St. Lawrence Seaway and Power Project: An Oral History of the Greatest Construction Show on Earth*. Syracuse, NY: Syracuse University Press, p. 26.

74 R. Stagg. 2010. *The Golden Dream: A History of the St. Lawrence Seaway*. Toronto: Dundurn, p. 177.

75 B. Kelly. 2017. A historical St. Lawrence Seaway. *NNY Business*. http://www.nnybizmag.com/index.php/2017/05/22/a-historical-st-lawrence-seaway/. Accessed October 19, 2020.
    R. Stagg. 2010. *The Golden Dream: A History of the St. Lawrence Seaway*. Toronto: Dundurn, p. 202.

76 R. Stagg. 2010. *The Golden Dream: A History of the St. Lawrence Seaway*. Toronto: Dundurn, p. 199.

77 R. Stagg. 2010. *The Golden Dream: A History of the St. Lawrence Seaway*. Toronto: Dundurn, p. 202.

78 R. Stagg. 2010. *The Golden Dream: A History of the St. Lawrence Seaway*. Toronto: Dundurn, p. 225.

79 R. Stagg. 2010. *The Golden Dream: A History of the St. Lawrence Seaway*. Toronto: Dundurn, p. 225.

80 C. Mabee. 1961. *The Seaway Story*. New York: Macmillan, pp. 253–54.

81 R. Stagg. 2010. *The Golden Dream: A History of the St. Lawrence Seaway*. Toronto: Dundurn, p. 230.

82 R. Stagg. 2010. *The Golden Dream: A History of the St. Lawrence Seaway*. Toronto: Dundurn, p. 230.

83 St. Lawrence Seaway Management Corporation. 2014–2020. SLSMC Annual Corporate Summaries. https://greatlakes-seaway.com/en/about-us/slsmc-management/annual-corporate-summaries/. Accessed October 19, 2020.

84 St. Lawrence Seaway Management Corporation. 2014–2020. SLSMC Annual Corporate Summaries. https://greatlakes-seaway.com/en/about-us/slsmc-management/annual-corporate-summaries/. Accessed October 19, 2020.

85 Great Lakes St. Lawrence Seaway System. 2020. 300 Years History. https://great-lakes-seaway.com/en/the-seaway/300-years-history/. Accessed October 20, 2020.

86 Great Lakes St. Lawrence Seaway System. 2020. 300 Years History. https://great-lakes-seaway.com/en/the-seaway/300-years-history/. Accessed October 20, 2020. R.H. Whitbeck. 1914. The St. Lawrence River and its part in the making of Canada. American Association of Geographers 11th Annual Meeting, Chicago, IL.

87 N. Walker. 2019. On the Map: The St. Lawrence Seaway turns 60. *Canadian Geographic*. July/August, pp. 30–31.

88 St. Lawrence Seaway Management Corporation. 2014–2020. SLSMC Annual Corporate Summaries. https://greatlakes-seaway.com/en/about-us/slsmc-management/annual-corporate-summaries/. Accessed October 19, 2020.

89 Great Lakes St. Lawrence Seaway System. 2020. Economic Impacts. https://great-lakes-seaway.com/en/the-seaway/economic-impacts/. Accessed October 20, 2020.

90 St. Lawrence Seaway Management Corporation. 2018. Annual Corporate Summary. https://greatlakes-seaway.com/wp-content/uploads/2019/09/slsmc_ar2018_en.pdf. Accessed March 17, 2021.

91 D.J. Solomon and M.H. Beach. 2003. Fish pass design for eel and elver *(Anguilla anguilla)*. Environment Agency. Technical Report W2–070/TR1, Bristol, UK.

92 R. MacGregor et al. 2010. *DRAFT Recovery Strategy for the American Eel (*Anguilla rostrata*) in Ontario*. Ontario Recovery Strategy Series. Prepared for Ontario Ministry of Natural Resources, Peterborough, ON.

93 COSEWIC. 2012. COSEWIC assessment and status report on the American Eel (*Anguilla rostrata*) in Canada. Committee on the Status of Endangered Wildlife in Canada. Ottawa. www.registrelep-sararegistry.gc.ca/default_e.cfm.

94 M. McClearn. 2020. Flood thy neighbour: As spring arrives, higher Great Lakes water levels pit communities against each other. *The Globe and Mail*. April 2. https://www.theglobeandmail.com/canada/article-flood-thy-neighbour-as-spring-arrives-higher-great-lakes-water/. Accessed October 20, 2020.

95 US Environmental Protection Agency. 2020. Great Lakes Areas of Concerns. https://www.epa.gov/great-lakes-aocs/list-great-lakes-aocs. Accessed Aug. 9, 2019. Environment and Climate Change Canada. 2017. St. Lawrence River: Area of Canada. https://www.canada.ca/en/environment-climate-change/services/great-lakes-protection/areas-concern/st-lawrence-river.html. Accessed Aug. 9, 2020.

96 Transport Canada, US Army Corps of Engineers, US Department of Transportation, The St. Lawrence Seaway Management Corporation, Saint Lawrence Seaway Development Corporation, Environment Canada, and US Fish and Wildlife Service. 2007. *Great Lakes St Lawrence Seaway Study: Final Report*. https://greatlakes-seaway.com/wp-content/uploads/2019/10/GLSL-Final-Report-En.pdf. Accessed October 19, 2020.

97 J. Alexander. 2011. *Pandora's Locks: The Opening of the Great Lakes–St. Lawrence Seaway*. East Lansing: Michigan State University Press, p. xvi.

98 J. Alexander. 2011. *Pandora's Locks: The Opening of the Great Lakes–St. Lawrence Seaway*. East Lansing: Michigan State University Press, p. xvi.

99 A. Ricciardi. 2006. Patterns of invasion in the Laurentian Great Lakes in relation to changes in vector activity. *Diversity and Distributions* 12: 425–33.

100 J. Alexander. 2011. *Pandora's Locks: The Opening of the Great Lakes–St. Lawrence Seaway*. East Lansing: Michigan State University Press.

Transport Canada, US Army Corps of Engineers, US Department of Transportation, The St. Lawrence Seaway Management Corporation, Saint Lawrence Seaway Development Corporation, Environment Canada, and US Fish and Wildlife Service. 2007. *Great Lakes St Lawrence Seaway Study: Final Report*. https://greatlakes-seaway.com/wp-content/uploads/2019/10/GLSL-Final-Report-En.pdf. Accessed October 19, 2020.

101　A. Ricciardi. 2006. Patterns of invasion in the Laurentian Great Lakes in relation to changes in vector activity. *Diversity and Distributions* 12: 425–33.

102　M.L. Johansson et al. 2018. Human-mediated and natural dispersal of an invasive fish in the eastern Great Lakes. *Heredity* 120: 533–46.

103　Joint Ocean Commission Initiative. 2017. Great Lakes: Invasive species threaten the Great lakes economy and ecosystem. https://oceanactionagenda.org/story/invasive-species-threaten-great-lakes-economy-ecosystem/. Accessed Aug. 10, 2019.
J.D. Rothlisberger et al. 2012. Ship-borne nonindigenous species diminish Great Lakes ecosystem services. *Ecosystems* 15: 462–76.

104　G. Santayana. 1905. *The Life of Reason: Or The Phases of Human Progress*, vol. 1. New York: Charles Scribner's Sons, p. 284.

105　Fisheries and Oceans Canada. 2018. *Sea Lamprey: The Battle Continues to Protect Our Great Lakes Fishery*. https://www.dfo-mpo.gc.ca/species-especes/publications/ais-eae/lamprey-lamproie/index-eng.html. Accessed Aug. 10, 2019.

106　K. Bunch. 2017. Sea lamprey: The greatest invasive control success story. Great Lakes Connection. Newsletter of the International Joint Commission. June 2017. https://www.ijc.org/en/sea-lamprey-greatest-invasive-control-success-story#. Accessed September 28, 2020.

107　Great Lakes Fishery Commission. 2019. What is at risk? http://www.glfc.org/what-is-at-risk.php. Accessed August 10, 2019.

108　R.E. Kinnunen. 2015. Sea lamprey control in the Great Lakes. Michigan State University Extension. https://www.canr.msu.edu/news/sea_lamprey_control_in_the_great_lakes. Accessed September 10, 2019.
Great Lakes Fishery Commission. 2019. Budget. http://www.glfc.org/budget.php. Accessed November 5, 2020.

109　J. Alexander. 2011. *Pandora's Locks: The Opening of the Great Lakes-St. Lawrence Seaway*. East Lansing: Michigan State University Press, p. 35.

110　D. Macfarlane. 2014. *Negotiating a River: Canada, the US, and the Creation of the St. Lawrence Seaway. Vancouver: University of British Columba Press*, p. 218.

111　R. Stagg. 2010. *The Golden Dream: A History of the St. Lawrence Seaway*. Toronto: Dundurn.
D. Macfarlane. 2014. *Negotiating a River: Canada, the US, and the Creation of the St. Lawrence Seaway. Vancouver: University of British Columba Press*.
D. Jenish. 2009. *The St. Lawrence Seaway: Fifty years and Counting*. Newcastle, ON: Penumbra Press.
R. MacGregor. 2017. *Original Highways: Travelling the Great Rivers of Canada*. Toronto: Random House Canada.

112　St. Lawrence Seaway Management Corporation. 2020. SLSMC Annual Corporate Summaries. https://greatlakes-seaway.com/wp-content/uploads/2020/07/slsmc_ar2020_en.pdf. Accessed March 17, 2021.

St Lawrence Seaway Development Corporation. 2019. SLSDC Annual Reports https:// greatlakes-seaway.com/en/about-us/slsdc-management/annual-reports/. Accessed October 19, 2020.

113 Transport Canada, US Army Corps of Engineers, US Department of Transportation, The St. Lawrence Seaway Management Corporation, Saint Lawrence Seaway Development Corporation, Environment Canada, and US Fish and Wildlife Service. 2007. *Great Lakes St Lawrence Seaway Study: Final Report*. https://greatlakes-seaway.com/ wp-content/uploads/2019/10/GLSL-Final-Report-En.pdf. Accessed October 19, 2020.

114 Statista.com. 2020. Projected global container market growth between 2015 and 2021. https://www.statista.com/statistics/253931/global-container-market-demand-growth/. Accessed March 18, 2021.

115 Great Lakes St. Lawrence Seaway System. 2021. Tonnage Reports. https://greatlakes-seaway.com/en/the-seaway/facts-figures/tonnage/. Accessed March 18, 2021.

116 Martin Associates. 2018. *Economic Impacts of Maritime Shipping in the Great Lakes– St. Lawrence Region. Lancaster, PA*. https://greatlakes-seaway.com/wp-content/ uploads/2019/10/eco_impact_full.pdf. Accessed October 16, 2020.

TWELVE: The Future of North America's Great Rivers

1 R. MacGregor. 2017. *Original Highways: Travelling the Great Rivers of Canada*. Toronto: Random House Canada, p. 194.

2 L.C. Smith. 2020. *Rivers of Power: How a Natural Force Raised Kingdoms, Destroyed Civilizations, and Shapes Our World*. New York: Little, Brown Spark.

3 M. Meybeck. 2003. Global analysis of river systems: From Earth system controls to Anthropocene syndromes. *Philosophical Transactions of the Royal Society of London. Series B: Biological Sciences* 358: 1935–55.

4 M. Meybeck. 2003. Global analysis of river systems: From Earth system controls to Anthropocene syndromes. *Philosophical Transactions of the Royal Society of London. Series B: Biological Sciences* 358: 1935–55.

5 M. Meybeck. 2003. Global analysis of river systems: From Earth system controls to Anthropocene syndromes. *Philosophical Transactions of the Royal Society of London. Series B: Biological Sciences* 358: 1935–55.

6 T. Moon. 2017. Climate change: Saying goodbye to glaciers. *Science* 356: 580–81.

7 A. Hsu and W. Miao. 2013. 28,000 rivers disappeared in China. What happened? *The Atlantic*. April 29.

8 J. Gao et al. 2019. Collapsing glaciers threaten Asia's water supplies. *Nature* 565: 19–21.

9 P.H. Gleick, 2003, Global freshwater resources: Soft-path solutions for the 21st Century. *Science* 302: 1524–29.

10 S. Long. 2019. Thirsty planet. *The Economist*. Special Report. March 2.
A. Roussi. 2019. Africa's nations clash over giant Nile dam: Egypt says the Grand Ethiopian Renaissance Dam will cause water shortages – but Ethiopia stands firm. *Nature* 574: 159–60.
W.W. Immerzeel et al. 2020. Importance and vulnerability of the world's water towers. *Nature* 577: 364–69.

11 I. Semeniuk. 2017. Climate change stole a Yukon river almost overnight, scientists say. Here's how. *The Globe and Mail*. April 17.

W.W. Immerzeel et al. 2020. Importance and vulnerability of the world's water towers. *Nature* 577: 364–69.

12 J. Best. 2019. Anthropogenic stresses on the world's big rivers. *Nature Geoscience* 12: 7–21.

13 J. Eliasson. 2015. The rising pressure of global water shortages. *Nature* 517: 6.
W.W. Immerzeel et al. 2020. Importance and vulnerability of the world's water towers. *Nature* 577: 364–69.

14 J. Eliasson. 2015. The rising pressure of global water shortages. *Nature* 517: 6.
W.W. Immerzeel et al. 2020. Importance and vulnerability of the world's water towers. *Nature* 577: 364–69.

15 J. Eliasson. 2015. The rising pressure of global water shortages. *Nature* 517: 6.

16 American Rivers. 2019. *America's Most Endangered Rivers 2019*. https://www.americanrivers.org/wp-content/uploads/2019/04/MER-Report-2019_Full-Layout_FNL1.pdf. Accessed October 20, 2020.

17 US Geological Survey. 2017. First-of-its-kind interactive map brings together 40 Years of water-quality data. https://www.usgs.gov/news/first-its-kind-interactive-map-brings-together-40-years-water-quality-data. Accessed October 20, 2020.

18 *National Geographic*. 2016. America's ten most endangered rivers of 2016. https://blog.nationalgeographic.org/2016/04/13/americas-ten-most-endangered-rivers-of-2016/ Accessed August 25, 2019.

19 International Joint Commission. 2014. *Lake Ontario St. Lawrence River Plan 2014: Protecting against extreme water levels, restoring wetlands and preparing for climate change.* https://legacyfiles.ijc.org/tinymce/uploaded/LOSLR/IJC_LOSR_EN_Web.pdf Accessed August 28, 2019.

20 International Lake Ontario–St. Lawrence Regulation Board. 2020. Lake Ontario St. Lawrence River Regulation. https://ijc.org/en/loslrb/who/regulation Accessed September 12, 2019.

21 International Joint Commission. 2006. *Final Report, Options for Managing Lake Ontario and St. Lawrence River Water Levels and Flows.* Prepared by the International Lake Ontario-St. Lawrence River Study Board. March 2006.

22 International Joint Commission. 2006. *Final Report, Options for Managing Lake Ontario and St. Lawrence River Water Levels and Flows.* Prepared by the International Lake Ontario-St. Lawrence River Study Board. March 2006.

23 C. Reynolds. 2019. Rising waters in St. Lawrence Seaway could cost economy more than $1-billion, report says. June 27. https://www.theglobeandmail.com/business/article-report-claims-rising-waters-in-st-lawrence-seaway-could-cost-economy/ Accessed May 2, 2020.
M. McClearn. 2020. Flood thy neighbour: As spring arrives, higher Great Lakes water levels pit communities against each other. *The Globe and Mail*. April 2. https://www.theglobeandmail.com/canada/article-flood-thy-neighbour-as-spring-arrives-higher-great-lakes-water/. Accessed May 2, 2020.
St. Catherines Standard. 2020. December seaway closure would cost millions of dollars each week: Chamber of Marine Commerce. June 2. https://www.stcatharinesstandard.ca/business/2019/12/04/december-seaway-closure-would-cost-millions-of-dollars-each-week-chamber-of-marine-commerce.html. Accessed October 22, 2020.

24 US Environmental Protection Agency. 2019. Facts and figures about the Great Lakes. https://www.epa.gov/greatlakes/facts-and-figures-about-great-lakes. Accessed Aug. 20, 2019.

25 US Environmental Protection Agency. 2020. Great Lakes Areas of Concern. https://www.epa.gov/great-lakes-aocs. Accessed October 22, 2020.

26 US Environmental Protection Agency. 2020. Great Lakes Areas of Concern: Beneficial Use Impairments for the Great Lakes AOCs. https://www.epa.gov/great-lakes-aocs/beneficial-use-impairments-great-lakes-aocs. Accessed October 22, 2020.

27 US Environmental Protection Agency. 2020. Great Lakes Areas of Concern: St. Lawrence River Area of Concern at Massena/Akwesasne. https://www.epa.gov/great-lakes-aocs/st-lawrence-river-area-concern-massenaakwesasne. Accessed October 22, 2020.

28 National Oceanic and Atmospheric and Administration. 2020. Great Lakes region: Invasive species. https://www.regions.noaa.gov/great-lakes/index.php/great_lakes-restoration-initiative/invasive-species/. Accessed October 22, 2020.

29 Center for Invasive Species and Ecosystem Health. 2018. Invasive species in the Great Lakes: costing us our future. University of Georgia, Center for Invasive Species and Ecosystem Health, USDA Animal and Plant Health Inspection Service, USDA Forest Service, USDA Identification Technology Program, and USDA National Institute of Food and Agriculture. https://www.invasive.org/gist/products/library/lodge_factsheet.pdf. Accessed September 12, 2019.

30 Great Lakes Fishery Commission. 2019. Asian carp. http://www.glfc.org/asian-carp.php Accessed September 12, 2019.

31 American Rivers. 2019. America's most endangered rivers of 2019 spotlights climate change threats. https://www.americanrivers.org/2019/04/americas-most-endangered-rivers-of-2019-spotlights-climate-change-threats/. Accessed October 22, 2020.

32 M. Beck. 2019. Months of flooding on Mississippi River marooned midwest trade. National Public Radio. August 16. https://www.npr.org/2019/08/16/750487354/months-of-flooding-on-mississippi-river-marooned-midwest-trade. Accessed Aug. 28, 2019. C. Corley. 2019. Wet, wild and high: Lakes and rivers wreak havoc across Midwest, South. National Public Radio. August 14. https://www.npr.org/2019/08/14/749062901/wet-wild-and-high-lakes-and-rivers-wreak-havoc-across-midwest-south. Accessed August 28, 2020.

33 American Rivers. 2020. America's most endangered rivers 2020. https://endangeredrivers.americanrivers.org/. Accessed October 14, 2020.

34 US Department of Agriculture. 2014. Easements. Natural Resources Conservation Service. https://www.nrcs.usda.gov/wps/portal/nrcs/main/national/programs/easements/. Accessed August 28, 2019.

35 R. Kerth and S. Vineyard. 2012. Wasting our waterways 2012: Toxic Industrial Pollution and the Unfulfilled Promise of the Clean Water Act. Frontier Group and Environment American Research and Policy Center. https://environmentamerica.org/sites/environment/files/reports/Wasting%20Our%20Waterways%20vUS.pdf. Accessed October 20, 2020.

36 M. Weller and T.A. Russell. 2016. State of the river report. 2016. Water quality and river health in the metro Mississippi River. Friends of the Mississippi River and US National Parks Service, Mississippi National River and Recreation Area. http://stateoftheriver.com/state-of-the-river-report/. Accessed August 24, 2019.

37 National Oceanic and Atmospheric Administration. 2019. NOAA forecasts very large 'dead zone' for Gulf of Mexico. https://www.noaa.gov/media-release/noaa-forecasts-very-large-dead-zone-for-gulf-of-mexico. Accessed October 20, 2020.

38 World Wildlife Fund. 2020. WWF's top ten rivers at risk, Rio Grande makes list. https://www.worldwildlife.org/press-releases/wwf-s-top-10-rivers-at-risk-rio-grande-makes-list. Accessed October 20, 2020.

39 World Wildlife Fund. 2020. WWF's top ten rivers at risk, Rio Grande makes list. https://www.worldwildlife.org/press-releases/wwf-s-top-10-rivers-at-risk-rio-grande-makes-list. Accessed October 20, 2020.

40 K. Wahl. 2012. Salt cedar establishment in the lower Rio Grande. Presentation to the Lower Rio Grande Citizens Forum. International Boundary and Water Commission Lower Rio Grande Field Office. https://www.ibwc.gov/Files/CF_LRG_Salt_Cedar_Est_071812.pdf. Accessed October 20, 2020.

41 International Boundary and Water Commission (IBWC). 2020. Rio Grande discharge data. IWBC United States and Mexico. United States Section. https://www.ibwc.gov/Water_Data/rtdata.htm. Accessed October 20, 2020.

42 International Boundary and Water Commission (IBWC). Undated. About the Rio Grande. IWBC United States and Mexico. United States Section. https://www.ibwc.gov/CRP/riogrande.htm. Accessed October 20, 2020.

43 American Rivers. 2018. Lower Rio Grande (Rio Bravo) [TX]. https://www.american-rivers.org/endangered-rivers/lower-rio-grande-tx/. Accessed October 20, 2020.

44 D. Owen. 2017. *Where the Water Goes: Life and Death Along the Colorado River.* New York: Riverhead, p. 228.

45 Save the Colorado. Undated. Dams and diversions. http://savethecolorado.org/threats/dams-and-diversions. Accessed August 23, 2019.

46 S.W. Cooley et al. 2021. Human alteration of global surface water storage variability. *Nature* 591:78–81. https://doi.org/10.1038/s41586-021-03262-3.

47 Earthobservatory. Undated. Visualizing the highs and lows of Lake Mead. https://earthobservatory.nasa.gov/images/88099/visualizing-the-highs-and-lows-of-lake-mead. Accessed August 23, 2019.

48 Save the Colorado. Undated. Dams and diversions. http://savethecolorado.org/threats/dams-and-diversions. Accessed August 23, 2019.
D. Owen. 2017. *Where the Water Goes: Life and Death Along the Colorado River.* New York: Riverhead, p. 120.

49 J. Robbins. 2019. Crisis on the Colorado: Part I. The West's great river hits its limits: Will the Colorado run dry? *Yale Environment 360.* January 14. https://e360.yale.edu/features/the-wests-great-river-hits-its-limits-will-the-colorado-run-dry. Accessed May 24, 2020.

50 P.C. Milly and K.A. Dunne. 2020. Colorado River flow dwindles as warming-driven loss of reflective snow energizes evaporation. *Science* 367: 1252–55.

51 D. Owen. 2017. *Where the Water Goes: Life and Death Along the Colorado River.* New York: Riverhead, p. 246.

52 M. Reisner. 1986. *Cadillac Desert: The American West and its Disappearing Water.* New York: Penguin.

53 C. Melino. 2015. Grand Canyon stretch of the Colorado River threatened by mercury pollution. *EcoWatch.* https://www.ecowatch.com/grand-canyon-stretch-of-the-colorado-river-threatened-by-mercury-pollu-1882089088.html. Accessed August 23, 2019.
J. Thompson. 2017.

The 26,000 tons of radioactive waste under Lake Powell. *High Country News.* December 18. https://www.hcn.org/articles/pollution-a-26-000-ton-pile-of-radioac-tive-waste-lies-under-the-waters-and-silt-of-lake-powell. Accessed August 23, 2019.

54 R.J. Behnke and D.E. Benson. 1983. Endangered and threatened fishes of the upper Colorado River basin." *Bulletin (Colorado State University. Cooperative Extension Service)* 503A.

L.M. Page, E.C. Beckham, and B.M. Curr. 1991. *Freshwater fishes: North America north of Mexico.* Norwalk, CT: Easton Press.

B.M. Burr and R.L. Mayden. 1992. Phylogenetics and North American freshwater fishes. In R.L. Mayden (ed.), *Systematics, Historical Ecology, and North American Freshwater Fishes.* Stanford, CA: Stanford University Press, pp. 18–75.

55 US Bureau of Reclamation. 2020. Quagga and zebra mussels. https://www.usbr.gov/mussels/. Accessed August 24, 2019.

Save the Colorado. Undated. Invasive species. http://savethecolorado.org/threats/invasive-species/. Accessed August 23, 2019.

56 J.R. Patton, R. Stein, and V. Sevilgen. 2018. When the levee breaks: Cascading failures in the Sacramento-San Joaquin River Delta, California. *Tremblor, Inc.* http://temblor.net/earthquake-insights/when-the-levee-breaks-cascading-failures-in-the-sacramen-to-san-joaquin-river-delta-california-7959/. Accessed August 24, 2019.

57 J. Michael. 2016. *Benefit-Costs Analysis of the California WaterFix.* Center for Business and Policy Research. University of the Pacific. Sacramento. https://a11.asmdc.org/sites/a11.asmdc.org/files/pdf/Dr.%20Jeffrey%20Michael%20Benefit-Cost%20Analy-sis%20of%20The%20California%20WaterFix.pdf. Accessed August 25, 2019.

58 E. Wesselman and R. Wright. 2018. Op-Ed: California's WaterFix was always a dangerous deal. Now the Trump administration is making it worse. *Los Angeles Times.* September 7. https://www.latimes.com/opinion/op-ed/la-oe-wesselman-wright-delta-tunnels-in-washington-hands-20180907-story.html. Accessed August 25, 2019.

59 Friends of the River. 2016. San Joaquin Threat: The San Joaquin River is threatened by a plan to build the Temperance Flat Dam. https://www.friendsoftheriver.org/our-work/rivers-under-threat/san-joaquin-threat/. Accessed August 25, 2019.

60 *National Geographic.* 2016. America's ten most endangered rivers of 2016. https://blog.nationalgeographic.org/2016/04/13/americas-ten-most-endangered-rivers-of-2016/. Accessed August 25, 2019.

61 *The Columbian.* 2015. Environmental issues to be key in Columbia River talks: N.W. groups anxious to begin on treat with Canada. https://www.columbian.com/news/2015/jun/11/environmental-issues-to-be-key-in-columbia-river-t/. Accessed August 26, 2019.

62 A.E. Kohler et al. 2013. Salmon-mediated nutrient flux in selected streams of the Columbia River basin, USA. *Canadian Journal of Fisheries and Aquatic Sciences* 70: 502–12.

G. Utzig and D. Schmidt. 2011. Dam Footprint Impact Summary – BC Hydro Dams in the Columbia Basin. Unpublished Report for Fish and Wildlife Compensation Program: Col. Basin, Nelson, BC. http://a100.gov.bc.ca/appsdata/acat/documents/r23145/FWCP_Impacts_Summary_14250549764 35_5053647442.pdf. Accessed August 23, 2019.

63 Columbia River Inter-Tribal Fish Commission. 2012. Ecosystem function integration into the Columbia River Treaty. https://critfc.org/wp-content/uploads/2014/12/eco-system-booklet-single-page.pdf Portland. Accessed Aug. 26, 2019.

64 Radio-Canada International. 2019. B.C. Indigenous groups get a say in Columbia River Treaty renegotiation. https://www.rcinet.ca/en/2019/04/26/b-c-indigenous-groups-get-a-say-in-columbia-river-treaty-renegotiation/. Accessed March 25, 2021.

65 J. Osborn. 2015. State Department to include ecosystem function in Columbia River Treaty. Center for Environmental Law & Policy (CELP), Seattle. https://www.celp.org/2015/06/04/news-columbia-river-treaty-state-department-to-include-ecosys-tem-function/. Accessed August 26, 2019.

66 B. Plumer. 2020. Environmentalists and dam operators, at war for years, start making peace. *The New York Times.* October 13. https://www.nytimes.com/2020/10/13/climate/environmentalists-hydropower-dams.html.

67 World Wildlife Fund. 2020. Watershed reports: Methodology. http://watershedreports.wwf.ca/page/methodology/#canada/by/threat-overall/profile/?page=methodology. Accessed October 21, 2020.

68 US Environmental Protection Agency. 2009. 2009 State of the River Report for Toxics. https://www.epa.gov/columbiariver/2009-state-river-report-toxics. Accessed October 29, 2019.

69 M. Church. 2017. Fraser River: History in a changing landscape. Chapter 27 in O. Slay-maker (ed.), *Landscapes and Landforms of Western Canada. World Geomorphological Landscapes.* Basel: Springer International, pp. 381–93.

70 M.L. Rosenau and M. Angelo. 2007. *Saving the Heart of the Fraser: Addressing Human Impacts to the Aquatic Ecosystem of the Fraser River, Hope to Mission, British Colum-bia.* Report to The Pacific Fisheries Resource Conservation Council, Vancouver, BC. https://www.psf.ca/sites/default/files/SavingHeart-of-the-Fraser_2007_0_Complete.pdf. Accessed August 26, 2019.

71 M.L. Rosenau and M. Angelo. 2007. *Saving the Heart of the Fraser: Addressing Human Impacts to the Aquatic Ecosystem of the Fraser River, Hope to Mission, British Colum-bia.* Report to The Pacific Fisheries Resource Conservation Council, Vancouver, BC. https://www.psf.ca/sites/default/files/SavingHeart-of-the-Fraser_2007_0_Complete.pdf. Accessed August 26, 2019.

72 M.L. Rosenau and M. Angelo. 2007. *Saving the Heart of the Fraser: Addressing Human Impacts to the Aquatic Ecosystem of the Fraser River, Hope to Mission, British Colum-bia.* Report to The Pacific Fisheries Resource Conservation Council, Vancouver, BC. https://www.psf.ca/sites/default/files/SavingHeart-of-the-Fraser_2007_0_Complete.pdf. Accessed August 26, 2019.

M. Church. 2017. Fraser River: History in a changing landscape. Chapter 27 in O. Slay-maker (ed.), *Landscapes and Landforms of Western Canada. World Geomorphological Landscapes.* Basel: Springer International, pp. 381–93.

73 M. Church. 2017. Fraser River: History in a changing landscape. Chapter 27 in O. Slay-maker (ed.), *Landscapes and Landforms of Western Canada. World Geomorphological Landscapes.* Basel: Springer International, pp. 381–93.

74 M. Church. 2017. Fraser River: History in a changing landscape. Chapter 27 in O. Slay-maker (ed.), *Landscapes and Landforms of Western Canada. World Geomorphological Landscapes.* Basel: Springer International, p. 390.

75 Heart of the Fraser. 2020. Defend the Heart of the Fraser. https://www.heartofthefraser.ca/. Accessed August 26, 2019.

76 M.L. Rosenau and M. Angelo. 2007. *Saving the Heart of the Fraser: Addressing Human Impacts to the Aquatic Ecosystem of the Fraser River, Hope to Mission, British Columbia*. Report to The Pacific Fisheries Resource Conservation Council, Vancouver, BC. https://www.psf.ca/sites/default/files/SavingHeart-of-the-Fraser_2007_0_Complete.pdf. Accessed August 26, 2019.

77 R. Dyok. 2020. B.C. First Nation adopts historic law to protect Fraser River. *Toronto Star*. May 28. https://www.thestar.com/news/canada/2020/05/28/bc-first-nation-adopts-historic-law-to-protect-fraser-river.html. Accessed Aug. 22, 2020.

78 Newswire.ca. 2015. Yukon River watershed threatened by climate change and habitat loss. https://www.newswire.ca/news-releases/yukon-river-watershed-threatened-by-climate-change-and-habitat-loss-560004851.html. Accessed August 27, 2019.

79 Newswire.ca. 2015. Yukon River watershed threatened by climate change and habitat loss. https://www.newswire.ca/news-releases/yukon-river-watershed-threatened-by-climate-change-and-habitat-loss-560004851.html. Accessed August 27, 2019.

80 World Wildlife Federation. 2020. Watershed Reports: Yukon. http://watershedreports.wwf.ca/page/about/#ws-5/by/threat-habitat-loss/threat. Accessed Aug. 27, 2019.

81 M. Reisner. 1986. *Cadillac Desert: The American West and its Disappearing Water*. New York: Penguin.

82 D. Fischer. 2011. Yukon River dumping more mercury thanks to climate change. *Scientific American*. October 25. https://www.scientificamerican.com/article/yukon-river-dumping-more-mercury-climate-change/. Accessed August 27, 2019.
    P.F. Schuster et al. 2011. Mercury export from the Yukon River Basin and potential response to a changing climate. *Environmental Science & Technology* 45: 9262–67.

83 J. Best. 2019. Anthropogenic stresses on the world's large rivers. *Nature Geoscience* 12: 7–21.

84 UNEP-DHI and UNEP. 2016. *Transboundary River Basins: Status and Trends*. United Nations Environment Programme (UNEP), Nairobi. http://geftwap.org/publications/river-basins-technical-report. Accessed December 12, 2020.

85 T. Loo. 2007. Disturbing the Peace: Environmental change and the scales of justice on a northern river. *Environmental History* 12: 895–919.

86 I. Austen. 2016. Canada's big dams produce clean energy, and high levels of mercury. *The New York Times*. November 10. https://www.nytimes.com/2016/11/11/world/canada/clean-energy-dirty-water-canadas-hydroelectric-dams-have-a-mercury-problem.html. Accessed Aug. 27, 2019.

87 Joint Review Panel Site C Project. 2014. *Report of the Joint Review Panel: Site C Clean Energy Project BC Hydro*. https://www.ceaa-acee.gc.ca/050/documents/p63919/99173E.pdf. Accessed October 22, 2020.

88 E.W. Allen. 2008. Process water treatment in Canada's oil sands industry: I. Target pollutants and treatment objectives. *Journal of Environmental Engineering and Science* 7: 123–38.

89 G. Kent. 2017. Tailings ponds a critical part of Alberta's oilsands legacy. *Calgary Herald*. September 28. https://calgaryherald.com/business/energy/tailings-ponds-a-critical-part-of-albertas-oilsands-legacy. Accessed October 13, 2020.

90 Natural Resources Defense Council. 2017. One trillion litres of toxic waste and growing: Alberta's tailings ponds. https://environmentaldefence.ca/wp-content/uploads/2017/06/EDC-and-NRDC-One-trillion-litres-of-toxic-waste-and-growing-Albertas-tailings-ponds-June-2017.pdf. Accessed August 28, 2019.

91 J. Kurek et al. 2013. Legacy of a half century of Athabasca oil sands development recorded by lake ecosystems. *Proceedings of the National Academy of Sciences* 110: 1761–66.

92 Canada Energy Regulator. 2020. Canada's energy future 2019: An energy market assessment. https://www.cer-rec.gc.ca/en/data-analysis/canada-energy-future/2019/2019nrgftr-eng.pdf. Accessed October 28, 2019.

93 One degree Celsius equals a change of 1.8 degrees Fahrenheit.

94 Intergovernmental Panel on Climate Change (IPCC). 2014. *Climate Change 2014: Synthesis Report. Contribution of Working Groups I, II and III to the Fifth Assessment Report of the Intergovernmental Panel on Climate Change* [Core Writing Team, R.K. Pachauri, and L.A. Meyer (eds.)]. IPCC, Geneva, Switzerland.
A.P. Williams et al. 2020. Large contribution from anthropogenic warming to an emerging North American megadrought. *Science* 368: 314–18.

95 P.W. Mote et al. 2005. Declining mountain snowpack in western North America. *Bulletin of the American Meteorological Society* 86: 39–50.
T. Barnett et al. 2004. The effects of climate change on water resources in the west: Introduction and overview. *Climatic Change* 62: 1–11.
J.C. Adam, A.F. Hamlet, and D.P. Lettenmaier. 2009. Implications of global climate change for snowmelt hydrology in the twenty-first century. *Hydrological Processes: An International Journal* 23: 962–72.

96 G.T. Pederson et al. 2011. The unusual nature of recent snowpack declines in the North American Cordillera. *Science* 333: 332–35.

97 T. Barnett et al. 2004. The effects of climate change on water resources in the west: Introduction and overview. *Climatic Change* 62: 1–11.
J.C. Adam, A.F. Hamlet, and D.P. Lettenmaier. 2009. Implications of global climate change for snowmelt hydrology in the twenty-first century. *Hydrological Processes: An International Journal* 23: 962–72.

98 R.H. Moss et al. 2010. The next generation of scenarios for climate change research and assessment. *Nature* 463: 747–56.

99 E. Bush and D.S. Lemmen (eds.). 2019. *Canada's Changing Climate Report.* Government of Canada, Ottawa, ON. https://changingclimate.ca/site/assets/uploads/sites/2/2020/06/CCCR_FULLREPORT-EN-FINAL.pdf. Accessed October 22, 2020.

100 Intergovernmental Panel on Climate Change (IPCC). 2014. *Climate Change 2014: Synthesis Report. Contribution of Working Groups I, II and III to the Fifth Assessment Report of the Intergovernmental Panel on Climate Change* [Core Writing Team, R.K. Pachauri, and L.A. Meyer (eds.)]. IPCC, Geneva, Switzerland.

101 E. Bush and D.S. Lemmen (eds.). 2019. *Canada's Changing Climate Report.* Government of Canada, Ottawa, ON. https://changingclimate.ca/site/assets/uploads/sites/2/2020/06/CCCR_FULLREPORT-EN-FINAL.pdf. Accessed October 22, 2020.
US Global Change Research Program (USGCRP). 2018. *Impacts, Risks, and Adaptation in the United States: Fourth National Climate Assessment*, vol. 2 [D.R. Reidmiller et al. (eds.)]. US Global Change Research Program, Washington, DC. https://nca2018.globalchange.gov/chapter/front-matter-about/. Accessed August 23, 2020.

102 R.H. Moss et al. 2010. The next generation of scenarios for climate change research and assessment. *Nature* 463: 747–56.

103 US Bureau of Reclamation. 2016. West-wide climate risk assessments: Hydro-climate projections. Technical Memorandum No. 86-68210-2016-01. Denver, CO. https://www.usbr.gov/climate/secure/docs/2016secure/wwcra-hydroclimateprojections.pdf. Accessed October 12, 2020.

104 E. Bush and D.S. Lemmen (eds.). 2019. *Canada's Changing Climate Report*. Government of Canada, Ottawa, ON. https://changingclimate.ca/site/assets/uploads/sites/2/2020/06/CCCR_FULLREPORT-EN-FINAL.pdf Accessed October 22, 2020.

105 E. Bush and D.S. Lemmen (eds.). 2019. *Canada's Changing Climate Report*. Government of Canada, Ottawa, ON. https://changingclimate.ca/site/assets/uploads/sites/2/2020/06/CCCR_FULLREPORT-EN-FINAL.pdf.
US Global Change Research Program (USGCRP). 2017. *Climate Science Special Report: Fourth National Climate Assessment*, vol. 1 [D.J. Wuebbles et al. (eds.)]. US Global Change Research Program, Washington. https://science2017.globalchange.gov/chapter/front-matter-about/. Accessed August 2, 2019.

106 E. Bush and D.S. Lemmen (eds.). 2019. *Canada's Changing Climate Report*. Government of Canada, Ottawa. https://changingclimate.ca/site/assets/uploads/sites/2/2020/06/CCCR_FULLREPORT-EN-FINAL.pdf Accessed October 22, 2020.
US Global Change Research Program (USGCRP). 2017. *Climate Science Special Report: Fourth National Climate Assessment*, vol. 1 [D.J. Wuebbles et al. (eds.)]. US Global Change Research Program, Washington, DC. https://science2017.globalchange.gov/chapter/front-matter-about/. Accessed August 2, 2019.

107 C. Corley. 2019. Wet, wild and high: Lakes and rivers wreak havoc across Midwest, South. National Public Radio, August 14. https://www.npr.org/2019/08/14/749062901/wet-wild-and-high-lakes-and-rivers-wreak-havoc-across-midwest-south. Accessed August 25, 2019.
US Global Change Research Program (USGCRP), 2017, *Climate Science Special Report: Fourth National Climate Assessment*, vol. 1 [D.J.Wuebbles et al. (eds.)]. US Global Change Research Program, Washington, DC. https://science2017.globalchange.gov/chapter/front-matter-about/. Accessed August 2, 2019.

108 E. Bush and D.S. Lemmen (eds.). 2019. *Canada's Changing Climate Report*. Government of Canada, Ottawa, ON. https://changingclimate.ca/site/assets/uploads/sites/2/2020/06/CCCR_FULLREPORT-EN-FINAL.pdf. Accessed October 22, 2020.

109 J.C. Adam, A.F. Hamlet, and D.P. Lettenmaier. 2009. Implications of global climate change for snowmelt hydrology in the twenty-first century. *Hydrological Processes: An International Journal* 23: 962–72.
P.C. Milly, K.A. Dunne, and A.V. Vecchia. 2005. Global pattern of trends in streamflow and water availability in a changing climate. *Nature* 438: 347–50.
M.A. Palmer et al. 2009. Climate change and river ecosystems: Protection and adaptation options. *Environmental Management* 44: 1053–68.

110 L. Gudmundsson et al. 2021. Globally observed trends in mean and extreme river flow attributed to climate change. *Science* 371:1159–62.

111 S. Jaeschko et al. 2021. Widespread potential loss of streamflow into underlying aquifers across the USA. *Science* 591: 391–97.

112 J.C. Adam, A.F. Hamlet, and D.P. Lettenmaier. 2009. Implications of global climate change for snowmelt hydrology in the twenty-first century. *Hydrological Processes: An International Journal* 23: 962–72.

113 M.A. Palmer et al. 2008. Climate change and the world's river basins: Anticipating management options. *Frontiers in Ecology and the Environment* 6: 81–89.

114 M.A. Palmer et al. 2008. Climate change and the world's river basins: Anticipating management options. *Frontiers in Ecology and the Environment* 6: 81–89.

115 A.B. Smith. 2020. 2010–2019: A landmark decade of U.S. billion-dollar weather and climate disasters. National Oceanic and Atmospheric Administration, Climate.gov. https://www.climate.gov/news-features/blogs/beyond-data/2010-2019-landmark-de-cade-us-billion-dollar-weather-and-climate. Accessed October 22, 2020.

116 J.H. Knouft and D.L. Ficklin. 2017. The potential impacts of climate change on biodiversity in flowing freshwater systems. *Annual Review of Ecology and Systematics* 48: 111–33.

117 J.H. Knouft and D.L. Ficklin. 2017. The potential impacts of climate change on biodiversity in flowing freshwater systems. *Annual Review of Ecology and Systematics* 48: 111–33.

118 M.A. Palmer et al. 2008. Climate change and the world's river basins: Anticipating management options. *Frontiers in Ecology and the Environment* 6: 81–89.

119 M.A. Palmer et al. 2008. Climate change and the world's river basins: Anticipating management options. *Frontiers in Ecology and the Environment* 6: 81–89.

120 M.A. Palmer et al. 2008. Climate change and the world's river basins: Anticipating management options. *Frontiers in Ecology and the Environment* 6: 81–89.

121 M.A. Palmer et al. 2008. Climate change and the world's river basins: Anticipating management options. *Frontiers in Ecology and the Environment* 6: 81–89.

122 M. Reisner. 1986. *Cadillac Desert: The American West and Its Disappearing Water.* New York: Penguin, p. 264.

123 M. Reisner. 1986. *Cadillac Desert: The American West and Its Disappearing Water.* New York: Penguin, p. 301.

124 M. Reisner. 1986. *Cadillac Desert: The American West and Its Disappearing Water.* New York: Penguin, p. 112.

125 F.P. Fradkin. 1981. *A River No More: The Colorado River and the West.* Tucson: University of Arizona Press, p. 42.
D. Owen. 2017. *Where the Water Goes: Life and Death Along the Colorado River.* New York: Riverhead, p. 3.

126 M. Reisner. 1986. *Cadillac Desert: The American West and its Disappearing Water.* New York: Penguin, p. 279.

127 M. Reisner. 1986. *Cadillac Desert: The American West and its Disappearing Water.* New York: Penguin.

128 M. Reisner. 1986. *Cadillac Desert: The American West and its Disappearing Water.* New York: Penguin, p. 487.

129 M. Reisner. 1986. *Cadillac Desert: The American West and its Disappearing Water.* New York: Penguin.
J. Benidickson. 2017. The evolution of Canadian water law and policy: Securing safe and sustainable abundance. *McGill Journal of Sustainable Development Law* 13: 59–104.

130 M. Reisner. 1986. *Cadillac Desert: The American West and its Disappearing Water.* New York: Penguin, p. 492.

131 M. Reisner. 1986. *Cadillac Desert: The American West and its Disappearing Water.* New York: Penguin, p. 493.

132 M. Reisner. 1986. *Cadillac Desert: The American West and its Disappearing Water.* New York: Penguin, p. 491.

133 J. Benidickson. 2017. The evolution of Canadian water law and policy: Securing safe and sustainable abundance. *McGill Journal of Sustainable Development Law* 13: 59–104.

134 W.A. deBuys. 2011. *A Great Aridness: Climate Change and the Future of the American Southwest.* Oxford: Oxford University Press, p. 32.

135 LaRouchePAC. 2012. NAWAPA XXI. https://www.youtube.com/watch?v=1NdKsZ-rG9RA Accessed August 21, 2019.

136 S. Rogers et al. 2020. An integrated assessment of China's South—North Water Transfer Project. *Geographical Research* 58: 49–63.

137 M. Reisner. 1986. *Cadillac Desert: The American West and its Disappearing Water.* New York: Penguin, p. 14.

138 S. Postel, and B. Richter. 2003. *Rivers for Life: Managing Water for People and Nature.* Washington, DC: Island Press, p. 37.

139 J. Robbins. 2017. A new way of understanding what makes a river healthy. *Yale Environment 360.* January 4. https://e360.yale.edu/features/new_look_at_rivers_reveals_toll_of_human_activity_yellowstone_river. Accessed December 29, 2018.

140 S. Postel and B. Richter. 2003. *Rivers for Life: Managing Water for People and Nature.* Washington, DC: Island Press, p. 37.

141 S. Postel and B. Richter. 2003. *Rivers for Life: Managing Water for People and Nature.* Washington, DC: Island Press, p. 38.

142 J.W. Moore. 2015. Bidirectional connectivity in rivers and implications for watershed stability and management. *Canadian Journal of Fisheries and Aquatic Sciences* 72: 785–95.
P. Brewitt. 2019. *Same River Twice: The Politics of Dam Removal and River Restoration.* Corvallis: Oregon State University Press, p. 196.

143 D. McCool. 2014. *River Republic: The Fall and Rise of America's Rivers.* New York: Columbia University Press, p. 84.

144 S. Postel and B. Richter. 2003. *Rivers for Life: Managing Water for People and Nature.* Washington, DC: Island Press.

145 S. Postel and B. Richter. 2003. *Rivers for Life: Managing Water for People and Nature.* Washington, DC: Island Press, p. 51.

146 D. Takacs, 2016. South Africa and the human right to water: Equity, ecology, and the public trust doctrine. *Berkeley Journal of International Law* 34: 55–108.

147 D. McCool. 2014. *River Republic: The Fall and Rise of America's Rivers.* New York: Columbia University Press, p. xiii.

148 International River Foundation. 2017. The Brisbane Declaration (2007). http://riverfoundation.org.au/wp-content/uploads/2017/02/THE-BRISBANE-DECLARATION.pdf. Accessed December 29, 2020.

149 A.H. Arthington et al. 2018. The Brisbane Declaration and global action agenda on environmental flows (2018). *Frontiers in Environmental Science* 6: 1–13.

150 Personal communication from S. Postel to EBT (via email). September 10, 2019.

151 National Wild and Scenic Rivers System. 2020. About the *Wild and Scenic Rivers Act.* https://rivers.gov. Accessed Dec. 30, 2020.

152 Canada Water Act. R.S.C. 1985, c. C-11. https://laws-lois.justice.gc.ca/eng/acts/c-11/page-1.html#h-61099. Accessed September 2, 2019.
J. Benidickson. 2017. The evolution of Canadian water law and policy: Securing safe and sustainable abundance. *McGill Journal of Sustainable Development Law* 13: 59–104.
L. Booth and F. Quinn. 1995. Twenty-five years of the Canada Water Act. *Canada Water Resources Journal* 20: 65–90.

153 J. Benidickson. 2017. The evolution of Canadian water law and policy: Securing safe and sustainable abundance. *McGill Journal of Sustainable Development Law* 13: 59–104.

154 BC Water Sustainability Act 2016, s. 15. https://www.bclaws.ca/civix/document/id/complete/statreg/14015. Accessed September 13, 2020.

155 J. Benidickson. 2017. The evolution of Canadian water law and policy: Securing safe and sustainable abundance. *McGill Journal of Sustainable Development Law* 13: 59–104.

156 J. Best. 2019. Anthropogenic stresses on the world's big rivers. *Nature Geoscience* 12: 7–21.

157 S. Postel and B. Richter. 2003. *Rivers for Life: Managing Water for People and Nature.* Washington, DC: Island Press.

158 US National Parks Service. 2020. Elwha River restoration. http://www.nps.gov/olym/learn/nature/elwha-ecosystem-restoration.htm. Accessed October 2, 2020.

159 S.L. Postel, J.I. Morrison, and P.H. Gleick. 1998. Allocating fresh water to aquatic ecosystems: The case of the Colorado River Delta. *Water International* 23: 119–25.

160 Businesswire.com. 2012. Importance of river basins in driving global economic growth to rocket: Top ten basins' GDP to set to exceed that of USA, Japan, and Germany combined by 2050. June 2012. https://www.businesswire.com/news/home/20120611006498/en/Importance-River-Basins-Driving-Global-Growth-Rocket. Accessed February 22, 2018.

161 D. McCool. 2014. *River Republic: The Fall and Rise of America's Rivers.* New York: Columbia University Press, p. 299.

162 R.W. Davis. 1980. Public trust and protection of stream flows and lake water levels. *University of California-Davis Law Journal* 14: 233–267.
R.Q. Grafton and S.A. Wheeler. 2018. Economics of water recovery in the Murray-Darling Basin, Australia. *Annual Review of Resource Economics* 10: 487–510.

163 J. Benidickson. 2017. The evolution of Canadian water law and policy: Securing safe and sustainable abundance. *McGill Journal of Sustainable Development Law* 13: 59–104.

164 R. Pentland. 2009. The future of Canada-US water relations: The need for modernization. *Policy Options Politique.* July 9. https://policyoptions.irpp.org/magazines/canadas-water-challenges/the-future-of-canada-us-water-relations-the-need-for-modernization/. Accessed October 21, 2020.

165 The Council of Canadians. 2017. Getting it right: A People's guide to renegotiating NAFTA. Water: Fact Sheet. https://canadians.org/sites/default/files/publications/fact-sheet-nafta-water.pdf. Accessed September 12, 2019.

166 D.L. Johansen. 2002. Bulk water removals, water exports and the NAFTA. Government of Canada Publications. http://publications.gc.ca/Collection-R/LoPBdP/BP/prb0041-e.htm. Accessed September 2, 2019.

167 Earnscliffe Strategy Group. 2018. A new chapter for North American trade. https://earnscliffe.ca/en/news-and-insight/new-chapter-for-north-american-trade/. Accessed September 2, 2019.

168 S. Dey. 2018. The good, the bad, and the ugly for NAFTA 2.0. The Council of Canadians. https://canadians.org/blog/good-bad-and-ugly-nafta-20. Accessed September 2, 2019.

169 B.R. Howe. 2021. Wall Street eyes billions in the Colorado's water. *New York Times*. January 3.

D.E. Garrick, N. Hernández-Mora, and E. O'Donnell. 2018. Water markets in federal countries: Comparing coordination institutions in Australia, Spain and the western USA. *Regional Environmental Change* 18: 1593–1606.

S.A. Wheeler and D.E. Garrick. 2020. A tale of two water markets in Australia: Lessons for understanding participation in formal water markets. *Oxford Review of Economic Policy* 36: 132–53.

170 Community Environmental Legal Defense Fund. 2020. Champion the Rights of Nature. https://celdf.org/advancing-community-rights/rights-of-nature/. Accessed October 22, 2020.

171 J. Benhör and P.J. Lynch. 2018. Should rivers have rights? A growing movement says it's about time. *Yale Environment 360*. August 14. https://e360.yale.edu/features/should-rivers-have-rights-a-growing-movement-says-its-about-time. Accessed October 22, 2020.

E.L. O'Donnell and J. Talbot-Jones. 2018. Creating legal rights for rivers: Lessons from Australia. New Zealand, and India. *Ecology and Society* 23(1): 7. https://doi.org/10.5751/ES-09854-230107.

172 US District Court, Colorado Division. 2017. Case 1:17-cv-02316-NYW. http://blogs2.law.columbia.edu/climate-change-litigation/wp-content/uploads/sites/16/case-documents/2017/20171204_docket-117-cv-02316_order.pdf. Accessed October 22, 2020.

J. Turkewitz. 2017. Corporations have rights. Why shouldn't rivers? *The New York Times*. September 26. https://www.nytimes.com/2017/09/26/us/does-the-colorado-river-have-rights-a-lawsuit-seeks-to-declare-it-a-person.html. Accessed October 22, 2020.

173 E. L. O'Donnell and J. Talbot-Jones. 2018. Creating legal rights for rivers: Lessons from Australia, New Zealand, and India. *Ecology and Society* 23(1): 7. https://doi.org/10.5751/ES-09854-230107.

174 Victorian Environmental Water Holder. 2020. About VEWH. https://www.vewh.vic.gov.au/about-vewh. Accessed December 30, 2020.

175 L. Leopold. 1977. A reverence for rivers. *Geology* 5: 429-430.

176 S. Postel and B. Richter. 2003. *Rivers for Life: Managing Water for People and Nature*. Washington, DC: Island Press, p. 51.

177 United Nations. 2019. International decades. Resolution 73/284. United Nations Decade on Ecosystem Restoration (2021–2030). https://undocs.org/A/RES/73/284. Accessed October 22, 2020.

United Nations Decade on Ecosystem Restoration. 2021–2030. Undated. Preventing, halting and reversing the degradation of ecosystems worldwide. https://www.decadeonrestoration.org/. Accessed October 22, 2020.

Bibliography

Abel, T.J., and D.N. Fuerst. 1999. Prehistory of the St. Lawrence River Headwaters Region. *Archaeology of Eastern North America* 27: 1–53.

Abele, F. 2014. The lasting impact of the Berger Inquiry into the construction of a pipeline in the Mackenzie Valley. Chapter 5 in G.J. Inwood and C.M. Johns (eds.), *Commissions of Inquiry and Policy Change: A Comparative Analysis*, pp. 88–113. Toronto: University of Toronto Press.

Abell, R., M.L. Thieme, C. Revenga, M. Bryer, M. Kottelat, N. Bogutskaya, B. Coad, N. Mandrak, S.C. Balderas, W. Bussing, and M.L. Stiassny. 2008. Freshwater ecoregions of the world: A new map of biogeographic units for freshwater biodiversity conservation. *BioScience* 58: 403–414.

Abrams, K. 2005. Polygamy, prostitution, and the federalization of immigration law. *Columbia Law Review* 105: 641–716.

Adam, J.C., A.F. Hamlet, and D.P. Lettenmaier. 2009. Implications of global climate change for snowmelt hydrology in the twenty-first century. *Hydrological Processes: An International Journal* 23: 962–72.

Adler, R.W. 2007. *Restoring Colorado River Ecosystems: A Troubled Sense of Immensity*. Washington, DC: Island Press.

Alaska Department of Fish and Game. 2020. Inseason Commercial Harvest Estimates. Bristol Bay. http://www.adfg.alaska.gov/index.cfm?adfg=commercialbyareabristolbay. harvestsummary. Accessed August 6, 2020.

Alexander, J. 2011. *Pandora's Locks: The Opening of the Great Lakes–St. Lawrence Seaway*. East Lansing: Michigan State University Press.

Allen, E.W. 2008. Process water treatment in Canada's oil sands industry: I. Target pollutants and treatment objectives. *Journal of Environmental Engineering and Science* 7: 123–38.

Allen, J.E., M. Burns, and S.C. Marjorie. 1986. *Cataclysms on the Columbia: A Layman's Guide to the Features Produced by the Catastrophic Bretz Floods in the Pacific Northwest*. Portland, OR: Timber Press.

Almond Board of California. 2019. *Almond Almanac 2019*. https://www.almonds.com/sites/ default/files/2020-04/2019_Almanac.pdf. Accessed October 4, 2020.

Alt, D.D., and D.W. Hundman. 1995. *Northwest Exposures: A Geologic History of the Northwest*. Missoula, MT: Mountain Press.

American Rivers. 2018. Lower Rio Grande (Rio Bravo) [TX]. https://www.americanrivers. org/endangered-rivers/lower-rio-grande-tx/. Accessed October 20, 2020.

American Rivers. 2019. *America's Most Endangered Rivers 2019*. https://www.american-rivers.org/wp-content/uploads/2019/04/MER-Report-2019_Full-Layout_FNL1.pdf. Accessed October 20, 2020.

American Rivers. 2019. America's Most Endangered Rivers of 2019 spotlights climate change threats. https://www.americanrivers.org/2019/04/americas-most-endangered-rivers-of-2019-spotlights-climate-change-threats/. Accessed October 22, 2020.

American Rivers. 2019. Twenty years of dam removal successes – and what's up next. https://www.americanrivers.org/2019/06/twenty-years-of-dam-removal-successes-and-whats-up-next/. Accessed October 2, 2020.

American Rivers. 2020. America's most endangered rivers 2020. https://endangeredrivers. americanrivers.org/. Accessed October 14, 2020.

Anderson, D.G. 1990. The Paleoindian colonization of eastern North America. Early Paleoindian economies of eastern North America. *Research in Economic Anthropology*, Supplement 5: 163–216. JAI Press. http://pidba.org/anderson/cv/Anderson%201990%20 REAnth.pdf. Accessed October 16, 2020.

Anzaldúa, G.E. 2007. *Borderlands/La Frontera: The New Mestiza*. San Francisco: Aunt Lute.

Archéo-Québec Network. 2020. Prehistoric Québec. https://www.archeoquebec.com/en/archaeology-quebec/thematic-files/prehistoric-quebec. Accessed October 19, 2020.

Arctic Power. 2013. Background: Prudhoe Bay Oil and Gas Discovery and Development. ANWR.org. http://anwr.org/2013/08/prudhoe-bay-production/. Accessed July 12, 2019.

Arthington, A.H., A. Bhaduri, S.E. Bunn, S.E. Jackson, R.E. Tharme, D. Tickner, B. Young, M. Acreman, N. Baker, S. Capon, and A.C. Horne. 2018. The Brisbane Declaration and global action agenda on environmental flows (2018). *Frontiers in Environmental Science* 6: 1–13.

Asch, M. 2018. Dene. *The Canadian Encyclopedia*. https://www.thecanadianencyclopedia. ca/en/article/dene. Accessed July 6, 2019.

Ashworth, P.J., and J. Lewin. 2012. How do big rivers come to be different? *Earth Sciences Review* 114: 84–107.

Aslan, A., W.J. Autin, and M.D. Blum. 2005. Causes of river avulsion: Insights from the late Holocene avulsion history of the Mississippi River, USA. *Journal of Sedimentary Research* 75: 650–64.

Atwater, T. 1970. Implications of plate tectonics for the Cenozoic tectonic evolution of western North America. *Geological Society of America Bulletin* 81: 3513–36.

Atwood, W.W. 1919. Geography factor in war. Fixed line of Hun invasion and forced "war of positions." *The Harvard Crimson*. https://www.thecrimson.com/article/1919/1/30/geography-factor-in-war-pwhen-the/. Accessed October 15, 2020.

Aubert, M., R. Lebe, A.A. Oktaviana, M. Tang, B. Burhan, Hamrullah, A. Jsudi, Abdullah, B. Hakim, J-x Zhao, I.M. Geria, P.H. Sulistyarto, R. Sardi, and A. Brumm. 2019. Earliest hunting scene in prehistoric art. *Nature* 576: 442–45.

Avery, K.J. 1987. A historiography of the Hudson River School. In M-A. Rogers (ed.), *American Paradise: The World of the Hudson River School*, pp. 3–20. New York: Metropolitan Museum of Art.

Back, W.D., and J.S. Taylor. 1980. Navajo water rights: Pulling the plug on the Colorado River. *Natural Resources Journal* 20: 71–90.

Baker, V.R., and R.C. Bunker. 1985. Cataclysmic late Pleistocene flooding from glacial Lake Missoula: A review. *Quaternary Science Reviews* 4: 1–41.

Bakke, B.M. 2009. Chronology of Salmon Decline in the Columbia River 1779 to the Present. Native Fish Society. Oregon City, OR. http://www.nativefishsociety.org/conservation/ documents/chroncr-nwsalmondecline. Accessed April 23, 2014.

Baldridge, W.S., and K.H. Olden. 1989. The Rio Grande rift. *American Scientist* 77: 240–47.

Ball, P. 2016. *The Water Kingdom: A Secret History of China*. Chicago: University of Chicago Press.

Ballard, M.B. 2004. *Vicksburg: The Campaign That Opened The Mississippi.* Chapel Hill: University of North Carolina Press.

Barber, K. 2005. *Death of Celilo Falls.* Seattle: University of Washington Press.

Barlow, M. 2014. *Blue Future: Protecting Water for People and the Planet Forever.* New York: The New Press.

Barnett, T., R. Malone, W. Pennell, D. Stammer, B. Semtner, and W. Washington. 2004. The effects of climate change on water resources in the west: Introduction and overview. *Climatic Change* 62: 1–11.

Barnett, T.P., and D.W. Pierce. 2009. Sustainable water deliveries from the Colorado River in a changing climate. *Proceedings of the National Academy of Sciences* 106: 7334–38.

Barry, J.N. 1932. The first explorers of the Columbia and Snake rivers. *Geographical Review* 22: 443–56.

Bartow, J.A. 1991. The Cenozoic evolution of the San Joaquin Valley, California. *U.S. Geological Survey Professional Paper* 1501. https://pubs.usgs.gov/pp/1501/report.pdf. Accessed November 23, 2020.

Baxter, R., L.R. Brown, G. Castillo, L. Conrad, S.D. Culberson, M.P. Dekar, M. Dekar, F. Feyrer, T. Hunt, K. Jones, and J. Kirsch. 2015. An updated conceptual model of Delta Smelt biology: our evolving understanding of an estuarine fish. Interagency Ecological Program. California Department of Water Resources Technical Report 90. https://pubs.er.usgs.gov/publication/70141018. Accessed October 5, 2020.

Behnke, Robert J., and D.E. Benson. 1983. Endangered and threatened fishes of the upper Colorado River basin." *Bulletin (Colorado State University. Cooperative Extension Service)* 503A.

Benhör, J., and P.J. Lynch. 2018. Should rivers have rights? A growing movement says it's about time. *Yale Environment 360.* August 14. https://e360.yale.edu/features/should-rivers-have-rights-a-growing-movement-says-its-about-time. Accessed October 22, 2020.

Benidickson, J. 2017. The evolution of Canadian water law and policy: Securing safe and sustainable abundance. *McGill Journal of Sustainable Development Law* 13: 59–104.

Benke, A.C., and C.E. Cushing. 2005. *Rivers of North America.* Boston: Academic Press.

Benscreek Canoe Club. 2001. Rivers. Stoneycreek Canyon (Class III–IV). http://benscreek-canoeclub.com/river-talk/rivers/. Accessed October 13, 2020.

Berger, T.R. Interview. 1973. http://bergerinquiry.ubc.ca/tom-berger/tb-video1.html. indigenousfoundations.arts.ubc.ca. University of British Columbia. Accessed January 18, 2017.

Berger, T.R. 1977. *Northern Frontier Northern Homeland. The Report of the Mackenzie Valley Pipeline Inquiry.*

Berkes, F. 1999. *Sacred Ecology: Traditional Ecological Knowledge and Resource Management.* London: Taylor & Francis.

Berton, P. 1948. Monsters on the Klondike. *Maclean's.* September 1. https://archive.macleans.ca/article/1948/9/1/monsters-on-the-klondike. Accessed May 4, 2019.

Berton, P. 1958. Klondike: The strangest gold rush in history. *Maclean's.* September 27. https://archive.macleans.ca/article/1958/9/27/klondike-the-strangest-gold-rush-in-history. Accessed March 17, 2020.

Berton, P. 1972. *Klondike: The Last Great Gold Rush, 1896–1899.* Toronto: McClelland & Stewart.

Best, J. 2019. Anthropogenic stresses on the world's large rivers. *Nature Geoscience* 12: 7–21.

Bilby, R., S. Hanna, S. Huntly, R. Lamberson, C.D. Levings, W. Pearcy, T.P. Poe, and R. Smouse. 2007. Human population impacts on Columbia River Basin Fish and Wildlife. Independent Scientific Advisory Board Human Population Report, ISAB 2007-3.

Northwest Power and Conservation Council, Portland. https://www.census.gov/data/datasets/time-series/demo/popest/2010s-counties-total.html. Accessed September 30. 2020.

Bloodworth, G., and J. White. 2008. The Columbia Basin Project: Seventy-five years later. *Yearbook of the Association of Pacific Coast Geographers* 70: 96–111.

Boening, R.M. 1918. The history of irrigation in the state of Washington. M.Sc. thesis, University of Washington, Seattle.

Bolton, H.E. 2017. *Rim of Christendom: A Biography of Eusebio Francisco Kino: Pacific Coast Pioneer.* Tucson: University of Arizona Press.

Bonatto, S.L., and Francisco M. Salzano. 1997. A single and early migration for the peopling of the Americas supported by mitochondrial DNA sequence data. *Proceedings of the National Academy of Sciences* 94: 1866–87.

Bond, J.D., and S. van Loon. 2018. *Yukon Placer Mining Industry 2015 to 2017.* Yukon Geological Survey. Government of Yukon. Energy, Mines and Resources.

Bonneville Power Administration. 2017. Correspondence (letter) to US Congresswoman Cathy McMorris Rodgers. June 5. http://www.waterplanet.ws/pdf/FCRPS_BPA_LTR_TO-McMorris-Rodgers_2017-06-05.pdf. Accessed September 9, 2020.

Bonneville Power Administration. Undated. Budget submission to Congress. FY 2021. https://www.bpa.gov/Finance/FinancialInformation/Pages/Budget-Submission-to-Congress.aspx. Accessed October 2, 2020.

Booth, A.L. 2003. We are the land: Native American views of nature. In H. Selin (ed.), *Nature Across Cultures: Views of Nature and the Environment in non-Western Cultures,* pp. 329–49. Dordrecht: Springer-Science+Business Media, B.V.

Booth, D.B., K.G. Troost, J.J. Clague, and R.B. Waitt. 2003. The Cordilleran ice sheet. *Developments in Quaternary Sciences* 1: 17–43.

Booth, L., and F. Quinn. 1995. Twenty-five years of the Canada Water Act. *Canada Water Resources Journal* 20: 65–90.

Borrell, B. 2013. Ghosts of the Rio Grande. *The American Prospect.* http://prospect.org/article/ghosts-rio-grande. *Accessed October 23, 2016.*

Bragdon, K.J. 2001. *The Columbia Guide to American Indians of the Northeast.* New York: Columbia University Press.

Brannon, E.L., T.P. Quinn, G.L. Lucchetti, and B.D. Ross. 1981. Compass orientation of sockeye salmon fry from a complex river system. *Canadian Journal of Zoology* 59: 1548–53.

Braudel, F. 1995. *The Mediterranean and the Mediterranean World in the Age of Philip II.* Vol. 2. Berkeley: University of California Press.

Bretz, J.H. 1969. The Lake Missoula floods and the channeled scabland. *Journal of Geology* 77: 505–43.

Brewitt, P. 2019. *Same River Twice: The Politics of Dam Removal and River Restoration.* Corvallis: Oregon State University Press.

Brior, J.H. 1960. *Taming of the Sault: A History of the St. Lawrence Power Development – Heart of the Seaway.* Watertown, NY: Hungerford-Holbrook.

British Columbia Waterfowl Society. 2020. The Fraser River Estuary. http://www.reifelbird-sanctuary.com/fraser.html. Accessed September 24, 2020.

Brochmann, M. 2012. Signing river treaties – does it improve river cooperation? *International Interactions* 38: 141–63.

Brun, L., A. Abdulsamad, C. Geurtsen, and G. Gereffi. 2010. *Agricultural Value Chains in the Mexicali Valley of Mexico.* Center on Globalization Governance &

Competitiveness. Duke University. https://gvcc.duke.edu/wp-content/uploads/Agricultur-al-Value-Chains-in-the-Mexicali-Valley-of-Mexico_9-15-2010.pdf. Accessed March 17, 2021.

Bruns, R. 2019. *Border Towns and Border Crossings: A History of the US-Mexico Divide.* ABC-CLIO. US Dept of Transportation. Bureau of Transportation Statistics. Border Crossing/Entry. Data 2019. https://www.bts.gov/content/border-crossingentry-data. Accessed June 5, 2019.

Brusca, R.C., S. Álvarez-Borrego, P.A. Hastings, and L.T. Findley. 2017. Colorado River flow and biological productivity in the Northern Gulf of California, Mexico. *Earth-Science Reviews* 164: 1–30.

Bunch, K. 2017. Sea lamprey: The greatest invasive control success story. Great Lakes Connection. Newsletter of the International Joint Commission. June. https://www.ijc.org/en/sea-lamprey-greatest-invasive-control-success-story#. Accessed September 28, 2020.

Burger, C.V. 2000. The needs of salmon and steelhead in balancing their conservation and use. Chapter 2 in E.E. Knudsen, C.R. Stewart, D.D. MacDonald, J.E. Williams, and D.W. Reiser (eds.), *Sustainable Fisheries Management: Pacific Salmon.* Boca Raton, FL: Lewis.

Burke, D.B., and C.H. Voorsanger. 1987. The Hudson River School in eclipse. In M-A. Rogers (ed.), *American Paradise: The World of the Hudson River School,* pp. 71–90. New York: Metropolitan Museum of Art.

Burr, B.M., and R.L. Mayden. 1992. Phylogenetics and North American freshwater fishes. In R.L. Mayden (ed.), *Systematics, Historical Ecology, and North American Freshwater Fishes,* pp. 18–75. Stanford, CA: Stanford University Press.

Bush, E., and D.S. Lemmen (eds.). 2019. *Canada's Changing Climate Report.* Government of Canada, Ottawa, ON. https://changingclimate.ca/site/assets/uploads/sites/2/2020/06/CCCR_FULLREPORT-EN-FINAL.pdf. Accessed October 22, 2020.

Businesswire.com. 2012. Importance of river basins in driving global economic growth to rocket: Top ten basins' GDP to set to exceed that of USA, Japan, and Germany combined by 2050. June. https://www.businesswire.com/news/home/20120611006498/en/Importance-River-Basins-Driving-Global-Growth-Rocket. Accessed February 22, 2018.

Butler, V.L., and J.E O'Connor. 2004. 9000 years of salmon fishing on the Columbia River, North America. *Quaternary Research* 62: 1–8.

California Department of Fish and Wildlife. 2020. Spring Kodiak Trawl Catch Distribution Maps. https://www.dfg.ca.gov/delta/data/skt/DisplayMaps.asp. Accessed October 5, 2020.

California Department of Food and Agriculture. 2019. Agricultural statistical review. https://www.cdfa.ca.gov/statistics/PDFs/2018-2019AgReportnass.pdf. Accessed October 4, 2020.

California Department of Food and Agriculture. 2020. California agricultural production statistics. http://www.cdfa.ca.gov/statistics/. Accessed October 4, 2020.

California Department of Water Resources. 2020. California Groundwater Factsheet. Bulletin 118. https://water.ca.gov/Programs/Groundwater-Management/Bulletin-118.

California Department of Water Resources. 2020. State water project. https://water.ca.gov/Programs/State-Water-Project. Accessed October 3, 2020.

Campbell, B. 2012. *Rivers and the Power of Ancient Rome.* Chapel Hill: University of North Carolina Press.

Campbell, M.W. 1968. *The Savage River: Seventy-one Days with Simon Fraser.* Toronto: Macmillan of Canada.

Canada Energy Regulator (CER). 2014. Energy Briefing Note – Assessment of Discovered Conventional Petroleum Resources in the Northwest Territories and Beaufort Sea. National Energy Board, Calgary, AB. https://www.cer-rec.gc.ca/nrth/archive/pblct-n/2014ptrlmrsrc/index-eng.html. June 20, 2020.

Canada Energy Regulator (CER). 2020. Canada's energy future 2019: An energy market assessment. https://www.cer-rec.gc.ca/en/data-analysis/canada-energy-future/2019/2019nrgftr-eng.pdf. Accessed October 28, 2019.

Canada's First Peoples. 2007. Canada's First Peoples Before Contact. https://firstpeoplesofcanada.com/index.html. Accessed September 21, 2020.

Canada's First Peoples. Undated. The Inuit. https://firstpeoplesofcanada.com/fp_groups/fp_inuit1.html. Accessed October 2, 2019.

Canadian Atlas Online. Undated. Rivers of Canada. St. Lawrence River (Mixedwood Plains). http://www.canadiangeographic.com/atlas/themes.aspx?id=rivers&sub=rivers_east_stlawrence&lang=En. Accessed October 19, 2020.

Canadian Business Journal. Undated. Aboriginal pipeline group. http://www.cbj.ca/aboriginal_pipeline_group_aboriginal_representation_restarts_lon/. Accessed September 1, 2020.

Canadian Centre for Policy Alternatives. 2018. Report on Mount Polley and Brazil Tailing spills points to systemic problems with mining industry. https://www.policyalternatives.ca/newsroom/news-releases/report-mount-polley-and-brazil-tailings-spills-points-systemic-problems. Accessed August 19, 2020.

Canadian Geographic Online. Undated. Rivers of Canada: St. Lawrence River (Mixedwood Plains). http://www.canadiangeographic.com/atlas/themes.aspx?id=rivers&sub=rivers_east_stlawrence&lang=En. Accessed October 15, 2020.

Carlson, K.T. (ed.). 1997. *You Are Asked to Witness: The Stó:lō in Canada's Pacific Coast History.* Chilliwack, BC: Stó:lō Heritage Trust.

Carroll, F.M. 2001. *A Good and Wise Measure: The Search for the Canadian-American Boundary, 1783–1842.* Toronto: University of Toronto Press.

Cayan, D.R., E.P. Maurer, M.D. Dettinger, M. Tyree, and K. Hayhoe. 2008. Climate change scenarios for the California region. *Climatic Change* 87: 21–42.

CBC News. 2017. Mackenzie Valley pipeline project officially one for the history books. https://www.cbc.ca/news/canada/north/mackenzie-valley-gas-project-no-more-1.4465997. Accessed August 15, 2020.

Center for Economic Development. 2020. Alaska Macroeconomic Indicators. University of Alaska-Anchorage. https://www.uaa.alaska.edu/academics/business-enterprise-institute/center-for-economic-development/reports/alaska-macroeconomic-indicators.cshtml. Accessed September 23, 2020.

Center for Invasive Species and Ecosystem Health. 2018. Invasive species in the Great Lakes: costing us our future. University of Georgia, Center for Invasive Species and Ecosystem Health, USDA Animal and Plant Health Inspection Service, USDA Forest Service, USDA Identification Technology Program, and USDA National Institute of Food and Agriculture. https://www.invasive.org/gist/products/library/lodge_factsheet.pdf. Accessed September 12, 2019.

Central Arizona Project. 2016. Colorado River shortage. http://www.cap-az.com/departments/planning/colorado-river-programs/shortage. Accessed October 8, 2020.

Chapman, D.W. 1986. Salmon and steelhead abundance in the Columbia River in the nineteenth century. *Transactions of the American Fisheries Society* 115: 662–70.

Cheung, W.W., R.D. Brodeur, T.A. Okey, and D. Pauly. 2015. Projecting future changes in distributions of pelagic fish species of Northeast Pacific shelf seas. *Progress in Oceanography* 130: 19–31.

Church, M. 2017. Fraser River: History in a changing landscape. Chapter 27 in O. Slaymaker (ed.), *Landscapes and Landforms of Western Canada. World Geomorphological Landscapes*, pp. 381–93. Basel: Springer International.

Clark, D.W. 1991. Western subarctic prehistory. Gatineau, QC: Canadian Museum of Civilization.

Clark, S.B. 2001. *Birth of the Mountains: The Geologic Story of the Southern Appalachian Mountains.* Denver, CO: United States Geological Survey, Information Services.

Cloern, J.E., N. Knowles, L.R. Brown, D. Cayan, M.D. Dettinger, T.L. Morgan, D.H. Schoellhamer, M.T. Stacey, M. Van der Wegen, R.W. Wagner, and A.D. Jassby. 2011. Projected evolution of California's San Francisco Bay-Delta-River system in a century of climate change. *PloS One* 6(9): e24465.

Cohen, B.I. (Hon.). 2012. *The Uncertain Future of Fraser River Sockeye*, vol. 1, *The Sockeye Fishery.* Commission of Inquiry into the Decline of Sockeye Salmon in the Fraser River. Publishing and Depository Services, Public Works and Government Services Canada.

Cohen, B.I (Hon.). 2012. *The Uncertain Future of Fraser River Sockeye*, vol. 2, *Causes of the Decline.* Commission of Inquiry into the Decline of Sockeye Salmon in the Fraser River. Publishing and Depository Services, Public Works and Government Services Canada.

Cohen, B.I. (Hon.). 2012. *The Uncertain Future of Fraser River Sockeye*, vol. 3, *Recommendations – Summary – Process.* Commission of Inquiry into the Decline of Sockeye Salmon in the Fraser River. Publishing and Depository Services, Public Works and Government Services Canada.

Cohen, M.J., C. Henges-Jeck, and G. Castillo-Moreno. 2001. A preliminary water balance for the Colorado River delta, 1992–1998. *Journal of Arid Environments* 49: 35–48.

Cohn, J.P. 2000. Saving the Salton Sea. *Bioscience* 50: 295–301.

Coleman, A.P. 1909. Lake Ojibway: Last of the great glacial lakes. *Ontario Bureau of Mines Report* 18: 284–93. http://www.geologyontario.mndmf.gov.on.ca/mndmfiles/pub/data/imaging/ARV18/ARV18.pdf. Accessed October 15, 2015.

Colgan, J.P., A.E. Egger, D.A. John, B. Cousens, R.J. Fleck, and C.D. Henry. 2011. Oligocene and Miocene arc volcanism in northeastern California: Evidence for post-Eocene segmentation of the subducting Farallon plate. *Geosphere* 7: 733–55.

Colorado River Basin Salinity Control Forum. 2020 Review. Water quality Standards for Salinity. Colorado River Basin. http://coloradoriversalinity.org/docs/2020%20REVIEW%20-%20June%20Draft%20Complete.pdf. Accessed October 9, 2020.

Columbia Basin Development League. 2020. The Columbia Basin Project. http://www.cbdl.org/. Accessed September 8, 2020.

Columbia Basin Trust. 2020. Columbia Basin Trust Region. https://ourtrust.org/about/basin-map/. Accessed September 30, 2020.

Columbia Basin Trust. 2020. Columbia River basin: Dams and hydroelectricity. https://thebasin.ourtrust.org/wp-content/uploads/downloads/2018-07_Trust_Dams-and-Hydroelectricity_Web.pdf. Accessed October 2, 2020.

Columbia River Inter-Tribal Fish Commission. 2012. Ecosystem function integration into the Columbia River Treaty. https://critfc.org/wp-content/uploads/2014/12/ecosystem-booklet-single-page.pdf Portland. Accessed August 26, 2019.

Columbia River Inter-Tribal Fish Commission. 2014. Columbia River Treaty. https://www.critfc.org/tribal-treaty-fishing-rights/policy-support/columbia-river-treaty/. Accessed October 1, 2020.

Columbia River Inter-Tribal Fish Commission. 2020. Columbia Basin Salmonids. https://www.critfc.org/fish-and-watersheds/columbia-river-fish-species/columbia-river-salmon/. Accessed August 12, 2020.

Commission for Environmental Cooperation. 1997. Ecological regions of North America. Towards a common perspective. http://www3.cec.org/islandora/en/item/1701-ecological-regions-north-america-toward-common-perspective-en.pdf. Accessed October 1, 2020. .

Community Environmental Legal Defense Fund. 2020. Champion the Rights of Nature. https://celdf.org/advancing-community-rights/rights-of-nature/. Accessed October 22, 2020.

Cooke, C.W. 2014. Politics & Policy: Green drought. https://www.nationalreview.com/2014/01/green-drought-charles-c-w-cooke/. Accessed May 7, 2017.

Cooper, S.F. 1880. The Hudson River and its names. *Magazine of Natural History* 4(6): 401–18. http://jfcoopersociety.org/susan/hudson.html. Accessed November 4, 2020.

Corley, C. 2019. Wet, wild and high: Lakes and rivers wreak havoc across Midwest, South. National Public Radio. August 14. https://www.npr.org/2019/08/14/749062901/wet-wild-and-high-lakes-and-rivers-wreak-havoc-across-midwest-south. Accessed August 28, 2020.

Cornelius, W.A. 2001. Death at the border: Efficacy and unintended consequences of U.S. immigration control policy. *Population and Development Review* 27: 661–85.

COSEWIC. 2012. COSEWIC assessment and status report on the American Eel (*Anguilla rostrata*) in Canada. Committee on the Status of Endangered Wildlife in Canada. Ottawa. www.registrelep-sararegistry.gc.ca/default_e.cfm.

COSEWIC. 2018. COSEWIC assessment and status report on the Okanagan Chinook Salmon (*Oncorhynchus tshawytscha*) Okanagan population in Canada. Committee on the Status of Endangered Wildlife in Canada. https://www.canada.ca/en/environment-climate-change/services/species-risk-public-registry/cosewic-assessments-status-reports/chinook-salmon-okanagan-population-2017.html. Accessed October 1, 2020.

Council of Canadians. 2017. Getting it right: A People's guide to renegotiating NAFTA. Water: Fact Sheet. https://canadians.org/sites/default/files/publications/factsheet-nafta-water.pdf. Accessed September 12, 2019.

CourtListener.com. Undated. *Environmental Defense Fund v. East Bay Municipal Utility Dist.*, 26 Cal. 3d 183 (Cal 1980). https://www.courtlistener.com/opinion/1800972/environmental-defense-fund-v-e-bay-mun-util-dist/. Accessed October 4, 2020.

Cramer, Z. 1801. *The Navigator.* Self-published.

Creighton, D. 1957. *Harold Adams Innis: Portrait of a Scholar.* Toronto: University of Toronto Press.

Creighton, D.G. 1956. *The Empire of the St. Lawrence: A Study of Commerce and Politics.* Toronto: Macmillan of Canada.

Cronin, T.M., P.L. Manley, S. Brachfeld, T.O. Manley, D.A. Willard, J.P. Guilbault, L.A. Rayburn, R. Thunell, and M. Berke. 2008. Impacts of post-glacial lake drainage events and revised chronology of the Champlain Sea episode 13–9 ka. *Palaeogeography, Palaeoclimatology, Palaeoecology* 262: 46–60.

Crown-Indigenous Relations and Northern Affairs Canada. 1998. The Tr'ondëk Hwëch'in Final Agreement. https://www.rcaanc-cirnac.gc.ca/eng/1297209099174/1542826344768. Accessed September 23, 2020.

Crown-Indigenous Relations and Northern Affairs Canada. 2020. Comprehensive Claims. https://www.rcaanc-cirnac.gc.ca/eng/1100100030577/1551196153650. Accessed September 21, 2020.

Crown-Indigenous Relations and Northern Affairs Canada. 2020. Treaties and Agreements. https://www.rcaanc-cirnac.gc.ca/eng/1100100028574/1529354437231. Accessed August 29, 2020.

Cusack, T. 2010. *Riverscapes and National Identities*. Syracuse, NY: Syracuse University Press.

Dadswell, M.J. 1972. Postglacial dispersal of four deepwater fishes on the basis of new distribution records in eastern Ontario and western Quebec. *Journal of the Fisheries Board of Canada* 29: 545–53.

Dadswell, M.J. 1974. Distribution, ecology and postglacial dispersal of certain crustaceans and fishes in eastern North America. *National Museum of Natural Science Publications in Zoology*. National Museum of Canada 11: 1–110.

Darrah, A.J., and H.F. Greeney. 2017. Importance of the 2014 Colorado River Delta pulse flow for migratory songbirds: Insights from foraging behavior. *Ecological Engineering* 106: 784–90.

Darwin, C. 1889. *A Naturalist's Voyage: Journal of Researches Into The Natural History and Geology of the Countries Visited During the Voyage of the H.M.S. 'Beagle' Round the World*. London: John Murray.

Data Center Knowledge. 2020. The billion dollar data centers. http://www.datacenterknowledge.com/archives/2013/04/29/the-billion-dollar-data-centers/. Accessed September 20. 2020.

Davis, J.C. 2017. *The Gulf: The Making of an American Sea*. New York: Liveright.

Davis, R.W. 1980. Public trust and protection of stream flows and lake water levels. *University of California-Davis Law Journal* 14: 233–67.

Davis, W. 2013. *River Notes: A Natural and Human History of the Colorado River*. Washington, DC: Island Press.

Dawicki, S. 2005. The great flood of New York. *Oceanus*. Woods Hole Oceanographic Institution. https://www.whoi.edu/oceanus/feature/the-great-flood-of-new-york/. Accessed October 15, 2020.

Dean, W.E., and M.A. Arthur, 1998. Cretaceous Western Interior Seaway drilling project: An overview. Stratigraphy and paleoenvironments of the Cretaceous Western Interior Seaway, USA, SEPM Concepts in Sedimentology and Paleontology. Special Publication of the Society for Sedimentary Geology (SEPM) No. 6: 1–10.

deBuys, W.A. 2011. *A Great Aridness: Climate Change and the Future of the American Southwest*. Oxford: Oxford University Press.

DeFilippo, L.B., D.E. Schindler, J.L. Carter, T.E. Walsworth, T.J. Cline, W.A. Larson, and T. Buehrens. 2018. Associations of stream geomorphic conditions and prevalence of alternative reproductive tactics among sockeye salmon populations. *Journal of Evolutionary Biology* 3: 239–53.

Dey, S. 2018. The good, the bad, and the ugly for NAFTA 2.0. The Council of Canadians. https://canadians.org/blog/good-bad-and-ugly-nafta-20. Accessed September 2, 2019.

Dokis, C.A. 2015. *Where the Rivers Meet: Pipeline, Participatory Resource Management, and Aboriginal-State Relations in the Northwest Territories.* Vancouver: University of British Columbia Press.

Donald, C.C. 1990. *The Journey of Coronado.* Wheat Ridge, CO: Fulcrum.

Donnelly, J.P., N.W. Driscoll, E. Uchupi, L.D. Keigwin, W.C. Schwab, E.R. Thieler, and S.A. Swift. 2005. Catastrophic meltwater discharge down the Hudson Valley: A potential trigger for the Intra-Allerød cold period. *Geology* 33: 89–92.

Dorsey, R.J., A. Fluette, K. McDougall, B.A. Housen, S.U. Janecke, G.J. Axen, and C.R. Shirvell. 2007. Chronology of Miocene–Pliocene deposits at Split Mountain Gorge, southern California: A record of regional tectonics and Colorado River evolution. *Geology* 35: 57–60.

Dossman, S.N. 2014. *Vicksburg 1863: The Deepest Wound.* Santa Barbara, CA: ABC-CLIO.

Doyle, M. 2019. *The Source: How Rivers Made America and America Remade Its Rivers.* New York: W.W. Norton.

Driver, J.C. 1993. Zooarchaeology in British Columbia. *BC Studies* 99: 77–105.

Drusina, P.E. 2014. A report on Colorado River salinity operations, under International Boundary and Water Commission Minute 242, January 1 to December 31, 2012. International Boundary Water Commission. United States Section. https://www.ibwc.gov/Files/Annual_Salinity_Report_2012_1.pdf. Accessed October 9, 2020.

Duk-Rodkin, A., and O.L. Hughes. 1994. Tertiary-Quaternary drainage of the pre-glacial Mackenzie Basin. *Quaternary International* 22: 221–41.

Duk-Rodkin, A., R.W. Barendregt, J.M. White, and V.H. Singhroy. 2001. Geologic evolution of the Yukon River: Implications for placer gold. *Quaternary International* 82: 5–31.

Duk-Rodkin, A., R.W. Barendregt, D.G. Froese, F. Weber, R. Enkin, I.R. Smith, G.D. Zazula, P. Waters, and R. Klassen. 2004. Timing and extent of Plio-Pleistocene glaciations in north-western Canada and east-central Alaska. *Developments in Quaternary Sciences* 2: 313–45.

Dunwell, F. 2008. *The Hudson: America's River.* New York: Columbia University Press.

Durand, J., D. Massey, and R. Zenteno. 2001. Mexican immigration to the United States: Continuities and changes. *Latin American Research Review* 36: 107–27. http://www.jstor.org/stable/2692076. Accessed October 14, 2020.

Duval, D., and B. Colby. 2017. The influence of Colorado River flows on the upper Gulf of California fisheries economy. *Ecological Engineering* 106: 791–98.

Dyke, A.S. 2004. An outline of North American deglaciation with emphasis on central and northern Canada. *Developments in Quaternary Sciences* 2: 373–424.

Earnscliffe Strategy Group. 2018. A new chapter for North American trade. https://earnscliffe.ca/en/news-and-insight/new-chapter-for-north-american-trade/. Accessed September 2, 2019.

Earthobservatory. Undated. Visualizing the highs and lows of Lake Mead. https://earthobservatory.nasa.gov/images/88099/visualizing-the-highs-and-lows-of-lake-mead. Accessed August 23, 2019.

Economist. 2013. Kumbh together: The world's biggest gatherings. Graphic detail. January 15. https://www.economist.com/graphic-detail/2013/01/15/kumbh-together. Accessed October 19, 2020.

Economist. 2015. The South: The present past. April 4. https://www.economist.com/united-states/2015/04/04/the-present-past. Accessed March 17, 2020.

Economist. 2017. Free Exchange. The Best Policy. Honest campaigns for immigration would advocate much more of it. March 18.

Egnal, M. 2009. *Clash of Extremes: Economic Origins of the Civil War.* New York: Hill & Wang.

Eliasson, J. 2015. The rising pressure of global water shortages. *Nature* 517: 6.

Endler, J.A. 1986. *Natural Selection in the Wild.* Princeton, NJ: Princeton University Press.

England, J., N. Atkinson, J. Bednarski, A.S. Dyke, D.A. Hodgson, and C.Ó. Cofaigh. 2006. The Innuitian Ice Sheet: Configuration, dynamics and chronology. *Quaternary Science Reviews* 25: 689–703.

English, J.M., and S.T. Johnston. 2004. The Laramide orogeny: What were the driving forces? *International Geology Review* 46: 833–38.

Environment and Climate Change Canada. 2017. St. Lawrence River: Area of Canada. https://www.canada.ca/en/environment-climate-change/services/great-lakes-protection/areas-concern/st-lawrence-river.html. Accessed Aug. 9, 2020.

Eschbach, K., J. Hagan, N. Rodriguez, R. Hernandez-Leon, and S. Bailey. 1999. Death at the border. *International Migration Review* 33: 430–54.

Fahey, K. 2003. *The Rio Grande* (Rivers of North America). Milwaukee, WI: Gareth Stevens Publishing Learning Library.

Fedirchuk, G. 1990. Peter Pond: Map Maker of the Northwest (1780–1807). *Arctic* 43: 184–86.

First Nations Study Program. 2009. Berger Inquiry. University of British Columbia. https://indigenousfoundations.arts.ubc.ca/berger_inquiry/. Accessed September 3, 2019.

Fischer, D. 2011. Yukon River dumping more mercury thanks to climate change. *Scientific American.* October 25.

Fish and Wildlife Compensation Program. 2020. *Wildbytes.* May 2020. https://fwcp.ca/wildbytes-columbia-region/. Accessed October 2, 2020.

Fisheries and Oceans Canada. 2018. *Cohen Response Status Update – October 2018.* https://www.dfo-mpo.gc.ca/cohen/report-rapport-2018-eng.htm and associated Annex. Accessed August 5, 2020.

Fisheries and Oceans Canada. 2018. *Sea Lamprey: The Battle Continues to Protect Our Great Lakes Fishery.* https://www.dfo-mpo.gc.ca/species-especes/publications/ais-eae/lamprey-lamproie/index-eng.html. Accessed Aug. 10, 2019.

Fladmark, K.R. 1982. An introduction to the prehistory of British Columbia. *Canadian Journal of Archaeology* 1982: 95–196.

Fletcher, C. 1997. *River: One Man's Journey Down the Colorado, Source to Sea.* New York: Alfred A. Knopf.

Fradkin, P.L. 1984. *A River No More: The Colorado River and the West.* Tucson: University of Arizona Press.

Fraser, D.J., L.K. Weir, L. Bernatchez, M.M. Hansen, and E.B. Taylor. 2011. Extent and scale of local adaptation in salmonid fishes: Review and meta-analysis. *Heredity* 106: 404–20.

Fremier, A.K., B.J. Yanites, and E.M. Yager. 2018. Sex that moves mountains: The influence of spawning fish on river profiles over geologic timescales. *Geomorphology* 305: 163–72.

Friends of the Pleistocene. 2010. Off New York City's deep end: A Pleistocene grand canyon. https://fopnews.wordpress.com/2010/01/29/off-new-york-citys-deep-end-a-pleistocene-grand-canyon/. Accessed October 16, 2020.

Friends of the River. 2016. San Joaquin Threat; The San Joaquin River is threatened by a plan to build the Temperance Flat Dam. https://www.friendsoftheriver.org/our-work/rivers-under-threat/san-joaquin-threat/. Accessed August 25, 2019.

Fuller, J., K. Shear, and H. Wittig (eds.). 1995. *The Great Lakes: An Environmental Atlas and Resource Book*, 3rd ed. United States Environmental Protection Agency and the Government of Canada. http://publications.gc.ca/site/eng/9.858440/publication.html. Accessed October 16, 2020.

Fulton, R., and V. Prest. 1987. Introduction: The Laurentide ice sheet and its significance. *Géographie physique et Quaternaire* 41: 181–86.

Gadd, N.R. (ed.). 1988. *The Late Quaternary Development of the Champlain Sea Basin*. Geological Association of Canada Special Paper. Vol. 35.

Galloway, W.E., T.L. Whiteaker, and P. Ganey-Curry. 2011. History of Cenozoic North American drainage basin evolution, sediment yield, and accumulation in the Gulf of Mexico basin. *Geosphere* 7: 938–73.

Garrick, D.E., N. Hernández-Mora, and E. O'Donnell. 2018. Water markets in federal countries: Comparing coordination institutions in Australia, Spain and the western USA. *Regional Environmental Change* 18: 1593–1606.

Gao, J., T.V. Yao, V. Masson-Delmotte, H.C. Steen-Larson, and W. Wang. 2019. Collapsing glaciers threaten Asia's water supplies. *Nature* 565: 19–21.

Garber, J.H. 2011. Tectonic History of British Columbia: Historical and Current Influences on the Chilko-Chilcotin-Fraser River System. Chapter 1 in J. Mount and P. Moyle (eds.), *Chilko-Chilcotin River Network: A Lakes and Rivers Ecosystem [A field guide]*. Davis: University of California–Davis. Available from www.jmgarber.com/publications.

Gates, M. 2015. Klondike Gold Rush. *The Canadian Encyclopedia*. https://www.thecanadianencyclopedia.ca/en/article/klondike-gold-rush. Accessed August 23, 2020.

Gibson, C., and K. Jung. 2005. Historical Census Statistics on Population Totals by Race, 1790 to 1990, and by Hispanic Origin, 1970 to 1990, For Large Cities and Other Urban Places in The United States. U.S. Census Bureau, Population Division Working Paper 76. Washington, DC.

Gleick, P.H. 2003. Global freshwater resources: Soft-path solutions for the 21st Century. *Science* 302: 1524–29.

Gobalet, K.W., P.D. Schulz, T.A. Wake, and N. Siefkin. 2004. Archaeological perspectives on Native American fisheries of California, with emphasis on steelhead and salmon. *Transactions of the American Fisheries Society* 133: 801–33.

Goheen, P. 1980. Some aspects of Canadian urbanization from 1850 to 1921. In W. Borah, W., J.E. Hardoy, and G.A. Stelt (eds.), Urbanization in the Americas. *Urban History Review/Revue d'histoire urbaine* (1980): 77–84. https://doi.org/10.7202/1020698ar. Accessed June 11, 2019.

Gomez-Sapiens, M.M., E. Soto-Montoya, and O. Hinojosa-Huerta. 2013. Shorebird abundance and species diversity in natural intertidal and non-tidal anthropogenic wetlands of the Colorado River Delta, Mexico. *Ecological Engineering* 59: 74–83.

Gonzalez, M.A. 2003. Continental divides in North Dakota and North America. *North Dakota Geological Survey Newsletter* 30: 1–7.

Gonzalez-Barrera, A., and J. Manuel. 2019. What we know about illegal immigration in Mexico. Pew Research Center. FacTTank. https://www.pewresearch.org/facttank/2019/06/28/what-we-know-about-illegal-immigration-from-mexico/. Accessed October 13, 2020.

Goodwin, D.K. 2018. *Leadership: In Turbulent Times*. New York: Simon & Schuster.

Goudge, S. 2016. The Berger Inquiry in retrospect: Its legacy. *Canadian Journal of Women and the Law* 28: 393–400.

Government of Alberta. 2019. Oil sands facts and statistics. https://www.alberta.ca/oil-sands-facts-and-statistics.aspx. Accessed July 21, 2019.

Government of British Columbia. 2020. British Columbia Population Estimates. BC Stats. https://www2.gov.bc.ca/gov/content/data/statistics/people-population-community/population. Accessed September 24, 2020.

Government of Canada. Culture, History and Sport. 2020. Yukon's territorial symbols. https://www.canada.ca/en/canadian-heritage/services/provincial-territorial-symbols-canada/yukon.html. Accessed August 12, 2020.

Government of Northwest Territories. Executive and Indigenous Affairs. 2020. Concluding and Implementing Land Claim and Self-Government Agreements. https://www.eia.gov.nt.ca/en/priorities/concluding-and-implementing-land-claim-and-self-government-agreements/gwichin-regional. Accessed September 21, 2020.

Government of Yukon. 2008. Gold. Departments of Economic Development & Energy, Mines and Resources. www.geology.gov.yk.ca. Accessed April 17, 2017.

Government of Yukon. 2009. Klondike gold rush. Fever pitch. Department of Tourism and Culture. http://www.tc.gov.yk.ca/archives/klondike/en/fever.html. Accessed September 23, 2020.

Government of Yukon. 2009–2020. Mining Activity Reports. http://www.emr.gov.yk.ca/mining/statistics.html. Accessed September 23, 2020.

Government of Yukon. 2017. Yukon State of the Environment. Reporting on Environmental Indicators – 2017. Environment Yukon. https://yukon.ca/sites/yukon.ca/files/env/env-yukon-state-environment-report-2017.pdf. Accessed September 23, 2020.

Government of Yukon. 2020. Yukon Monthly Statistical Review, July 2020. https://yukon.ca/en/yukon-monthly-statistical-review-july-2020. Accessed September 5, 2020

Grafton, R.Q., and S.A. Wheeler. 2018. Economics of water recovery in the Murray-Darling Basin, Australia. *Annual Review of Resource Economics* 10: 487–510.

Gramlich, J., and L. Noe-Bustamante. 2019. What's happening at the U.S.-Mexico border in 5 charts. Pew Research Center. FacTTank. https://www.pewresearch.org/fact-tank/2019/11/01/whats-happening-at-the-u-s-mexico-border-in-5-charts/. Accessed October 15, 2020.

Gray, C. 2010. *Gold Diggers: Striking it Rich in the Klondike*. Toronto: HarperCollins.

Gray, J.A., and P.J. Gray. 1977. The Berger Report: Its impact on northern pipelines and decision making in northern development. *Canadian Public Policy* 3: 514–15.

Grayson, D. 2011. *The Great Basin: A Natural Prehistory*. Berkeley: University of California Press.

Great Lakes and St. Lawrence Cities Initiative. Undated. About the Great Lakes and St. Lawrence Cities Initiative. https://glslcities.org/about/. Accessed October 16, 2020.

Great Lakes Fishery Commission. 2019. Asian carp. http://www.glfc.org/asian-carp.php Accessed September 12, 2019.

Great Lakes Fishery Commission. 2019. Budget. http://www.glfc.org/budget.php. Accessed November 5, 2020.

Great Lakes Fishery Commission. 2019. What is at risk? http://www.glfc.org/what-is-at-risk.php. Accessed August 10, 2019.

Great Lakes St. Lawrence Seaway System. 2020. 300 Years History. https://greatlakes-seaway.com/en/the-seaway/300-years-history/. Accessed October 20, 2020.

Great Lakes St. Lawrence Seaway System. 2020. Economic Impacts. https://greatlakes-seaway.com/en/the-seaway/economic-impacts/. Accessed October 20, 2020.

Groenfeldt, D. 2006. Water development and spiritual values in western and indigenous societies. In R. Boelens, M. Chiba, and D. Nakashima (eds.), *Water and Indigenous Peoples*. Knowledge of Nature. No. 2. UNESCO.

Groot, C., and L. Margolis. 1991. *Pacific Salmon Life Histories*. Vancouver: University of British Columbia Press.

Gruhn, R. 2020. Evidence grows that peopling of the Americas began more than 20,000 years ago. *Nature* 584: 47–48.

Gudmundsson, L., J. Boulange, H.X. Do, S.N. Gosling, M.G. Grillakis, AG., Koutroulis, M. Leonard, J. Liu, H.M. Schmied, L. Papadimitriou, Y. Pokhrel, O.I. Seneviratne, Y. Satoh, W. Thiery, S. Westra, X. Zhang, and F. Zhao. 2021. Globally observed trends in mean and extreme river flow attributed to climate change. *Science* 371: 1159–62.

Haidvogl, G. 2018. Historic milestones of human river uses and ecological impacts. In S. Schmutz and J. Sendzimir (eds.), *Riverine Ecosystem Management: Science for Governing Towards a Sustainable Future*, pp. 19–39. Aquatic Ecology Series 8. Cham, Switzerland: Springer.

Halffman, C.M., B.A. Potter, H.J. McKinney, B.P. Finney, A.T. Rodrigues, D.Y. Yang, and B.M. Kemp. 2015. Early human use of anadromous salmon in North America at 11,500 y ago. *Proceedings of the National Academy of Sciences* 112: 12344–48.

Hamilton, A.K., B.E. Laval, E.L. Petticrew, S.J. Albers, M. Allchin, S.A. Baldwin, E.C. Carmack, S.J. Déry, T.D. French, B. Granger, and K.E. Graves. 2020. Seasonal turbidity linked to physical dynamics in a deep lake following the catastrophic 2014 Mount Polley mine tailings spill. *Water Resources Research* 56(8): e2019WR025790.

Hanak, E., J. Lund, A.B. Gray, R. Howitt, J. Mount, P. Moyle, and B. Thompson. 2011. Managing California's Water: From Conflict to Reconciliation. Public Policy Institute of California, San Francisco. https://www.ppic.org/publication/managing-californias-water-from-conflict-to-reconciliation/. Accessed October 12, 2020.

Haning, T. 2009. Geography of war: The significance of physical and human geography principles. *FOCUS on Geography* 52: 32–36.

Hanson, G., and C. McIntosh. 2016. Is the Mediterranean the New Rio Grande? U.S. and EU immigration pressures in the long run. *Journal of Economic Perspectives* 30: 57–82.

Harden, B. 1997. *A River Lost: The Life and Death of the Columbia*. New York: W.W. Norton.

Hartman, G.F., T.G. Northcote, and C.J. Cederholm. 2006. Human numbers—The alpha factor affecting the future of wild salmon. In R.T. Lackey, D. Lach, and S.L. Duncan (eds.), *Salmon 2100: The Future of Wild Pacific Salmon*, pp. 261–92. Bethesda, MD: American Fisheries Society.

Hawthorne, N. 1835. The canal boat. *New-England Magazine* 9 (December): 398–409. http://historymatters.gmu.edu/d/6212/. Accessed October 16, 2020.

Hayden, B., and J.M. Ryder. 1991 Prehistoric Cultural Collapse in the Lillooet Area. *American Antiquity* 56: 50–65.

Hayes, D. 2001. First Crossing: Alexander Mackenzie, His Explorations Across North America, and the Opening of the Continent. Vancouver/Toronto: Douglas & McIntyre.

Healey, M.C. 2009. Resilient salmon, resilient fisheries for British Columbia, Canada. *Ecology and Society* 14(1): 2. http://www.ecologyandsociety.org/vol14/iss1/art2/.

Heart of the Fraser. 2020. Defend the Heart of the Fraser. https://www.heartofthefraser.ca/. Accessed August 26, 2019.

Hein, F.J. 2006. Heavy oil and oil (tar) sands in North America: An overview & summary of contributions. *Natural Resources Research* 15: 67–84.

Heizer, R.F., and M.A. Whipple (eds.). 1971. *The California Indians: A Source Book*, 2nd ed. Berkeley: University of California Press.

Henshaw, R.E. (ed.). 2011. *Environmental History of the Hudson River: Human Uses that Changed the Ecology, Ecology that Changed Human Uses*. Albany: State University of New York Press.

Hicks, B.A. 2004. *Marmes Rockshelter: A Final Report on 11,000 Years of Cultural Use*. Pullman: Washington State University Press.

Hiltzic, M. 2010. *Colossus: Hoover Dam and the Making of the American Century*. New York: Free Press.

Hinojosa-Huerta, O., S. DeStefano, Y. Carrillo-Guerrero, W.W. Shaw, and C. Valdés-Casillas. 2004. Waterbird communities and associated wetlands of the Colorado River delta, Mexico. *Studies in Avian Biology* 27: 52–60.

History.com. 2020. California gold rush. https://www.history.com/topics/westward-expansion/gold-rush-of-1849. Accessed October 4. 2020.

Hoffecker, J.F., S.A. Elias, D.H. O'Rourke, G.R. Scott, and N.H. Bigelow. 2016. Beringia and the global dispersal of modern humans. *Evolutionary anthropology: Issues, News, and Reviews*. 25: 64–78.

Holdren, G.C., and K. Turner. 2010. Characteristics of Lake Mead, Arizona-Nevada. *Lake and Reservoir Management* 26: 230–39.

Holton, G. 2020. Languages. Alaska Native Language Center. University of Alaska Fairbanks. https://www.uaf.edu/anlc/languages.php. Accessed September 23, 2020.

Hooper, P.R., V.E. Camp, S.P. Reidel, and M.E. Ross. 2007. The origin of the Columbia River flood basalt province: Plume versus nonplume models. *Geological Society of America Special Papers* 430: 635–68.

Hopkins, D. 1959. Cenozoic History of the Bering Land Bridge. *Science* 129: 1519–28.

Horgan, P. 1954. *Great River: The Rio Grande in American History*, vol. 1, *Indians and Spain*. New York: Rinehart.

Horgan, P. 1954. *Great River: The Rio Grande in American History*, vol. 2, *Mexico and the United States*. New York: Rinehart.

Horton, R.E. 1945. Erosional development of streams and their drainage basins; Hydrophysical approach to quantitative morphology. *Bulletin of the Geological Society of America*. 56: 275–370.

House, P., P.A. Pearthree, K.A. Howard, J.W. Bell, M.E. Perkins, J.E. Faulds, A.L. Brock, J. Pederson, and C.M. Dehler. 2005. Birth of the lower Colorado River—Stratigraphic and geomorphic evidence for its inception near the conjunction of Nevada, Arizona, and California. *Interior Western United States: Geological Society of America Field Guide* 6: 357–87.

Howard, B.C. 2014. Historic "pulse flow" brings water to parched Colorado River Delta. *National Geographic*. http://news.nationalgeographic.com/news/2014/03/140322-colorado-river-delta-pulse-flow-morelos-dam-minute-319-water/. Accessed November 12, 2020.

Howat, J.K. 1978. *Hudson River and its Painters*. New York: Viking Press.

Howat, J.K. 1987. Introduction. In M-A. Rogers (ed.), *American Paradise: The World of the Hudson River School*. Metropolitan Museum of Art.

Hsu, A., and W. Miao. 2013. 28,000 rivers disappeared in China. What happened? *The Atlantic*. April 29.

Hughes, M.K., and P.M. Brown. 1992. Drought frequency in central California since 101 BC recorded in giant sequoia tree rings. *Climate Dynamics* 6: 161–67.

Hutchison, B. 1950. *The Fraser*. New York: Rinehart.

Immerzeel, W.W., A.F. Lutz, M. Andrade, A. Bahl, H. Biemans, T. Bolch, S. Hyde, S. Brumby, B.J. Davies, A.C. Elmore, and A. Emmer. 2020. Importance and vulnerability of the world's water towers. *Nature* 577: 364–69.

Immigration and Ethnic History Society. 2019. Immigration History. *Page Act* (1875). https://immigrationhistory.org/item/page-act/. Accessed October 12, 2020.

Inflationdata.com. 2020. Historical crude oil price. Oil prices 1946–2020. https://inflation-data.com/articles/inflation-adjusted-prices/historical-crude-oil-prices-table/. Accessed September 21, 2020.

Intergovernmental Panel on Climate Change (IPCC). 2014. *Climate Change 2014: Synthesis Report. Contribution of Working Groups I, II and III to the Fifth Assessment Report of the Intergovernmental Panel on Climate Change* [Core Writing Team, R.K. Pachauri, and L.A. Meyer (eds.)]. IPCC, Geneva, Switzerland.

International Boundary and Water Commission (IBWC). 2020. Rio Grande discharge data. IWBC United States and Mexico. United States Section. https://www.ibwc.gov/Water_Data/rtdata.htm. Accessed October 20, 2020.

International Boundary and Water Commission (IBWC). Undated. About the Rio Grande. IWBC United States and Mexico. United States Section. https://www.ibwc.gov/CRP/riogrande.htm. Accessed October 20, 2020.

International Joint Commission. 2006. *Final Report, Options for Managing Lake Ontario and St. Lawrence River Water Levels and Flows*. Prepared by the International Lake Ontario–St. Lawrence River Study Board. March 2006.

International Joint Commission. 2014. Lake Ontario St. Lawrence River Plan 2014: Protecting against extreme water levels, restoring wetlands and preparing for climate change. https://legacyfiles.ijc.org/tinymce/uploaded/LOSLR/IJC_LOSR_EN_Web.pdf Accessed August 28, 2019.

International Lake Ontario–St. Lawrence Regulation Board. 2020. Lake Ontario St. Lawrence River Regulation. https://ijc.org/en/loslrb/who/regulation Accessed September 12, 2019.

International River Foundation. 2017. The Brisbane Declaration (2007). http://riverfoundation.org.au/wp-content/uploads/2017/02/THE-BRISBANE-DECLARATION.pdf. Accessed December 29, 2020.

Isachsen, Y.W., E. Landing, J.M. Lauber, L.V. Rickard, and W.B. Rogers (eds.). 2000. *Geology of New York State: A Simplified Account*, 2nd ed. Albany: New York State Museum Educational Leaflet No. 28.

Jackson, P.L. 2003. *Atlas of the Pacific Northwest*. Corvallis: Oregon State University Press.

Jaeschko, S., et al. 2021. Widespread potential loss of streamflow into underlying aquifers across the USA. *Science* 591: 391–97.

Jenish, D. 2009. *The St. Lawrence Seaway: Fifty years and Counting*. Newcastle, ON: Penumbra Press.

Jha, M. 2020. Eyes in the sky: Indian authorities had to manage 250 million festivalgoers. So they built a high-tech surveillance ministate. *Rest of World*. https://restofworld.org/2020/india-magh-mela/. Accessed October 19, 2020.

Jiang, Z.L., G.S. Kassab, and Y.C. Fung. 1994. Diameter-defined Strahler system and connectivity matrix of the pulmonary arterial tree. *Journal of Applied Physiology* 76: 882–92.

Jimenez, M. 2009. Humanitarian crisis: Migrant deaths at the U.S.–Mexico border. https://www.aclu.org/files/pdfs/immigrants/humanitariancrisisreport.pdf. Accessed October 14, 2020.

Johansen, D.L. 2002. Bulk water removals, water exports and the NAFTA. Government of Canada Publications. http://publications.gc.ca/Collection-R/LoPBdP/BP/prb0041-e.htm. Accessed September 2, 2019.

Johansson, M.L., B.A. Dufour, K.W. Wellband, L.D. Corkum, H.J. MacIsaac, and D.D. Heath. 2018. Human-mediated and natural dispersal of an invasive fish in the eastern Great Lakes. *Heredity* 120: 533–46.

Johnson, M. 2021. Snake River Dams: The Path to Dam Removal. Columbia Riverkeeper. https://www.columbiariverkeeper.org/news/2021/2/snake-river-dams. Accessed March 23, 2021.

Johnston, W.E., and A.F. McCalla. 2004. A Stylized History of California Agriculture from 1769 to 2000. *Section II Whither California Agriculture: Up, Down or Out*. In Giannini Foundation Special Report 04-1. University of Berkeley Special Report Series. https://escholarship.org/content/qt4232w2sr/qt4232w2sr. Accessed October 4, 2020.

Joint Ocean Commission Initiative. 2017. Great Lakes: Invasive species threaten the Great lakes economy and ecosystem. https://oceanactionagenda.org/story/invasive-species-threaten-great-lakes-economy-ecosystem/. Accessed Aug. 10, 2019.

Joint Review Panel Site C Project. 2014. *Report of the Joint Review Panel: Site C Clean Energy Project BC Hydro*. https://www.ceaa-acee.gc.ca/050/documents/p63919/99173E.pdf. Accessed October 22, 2020.

Kammerer, J.C. 1990. Largest rivers in the United States. US Geological Survey. https://pubs.usgs.gov/of/1987/ofr87-242/. Accessed October 16, 2020.

Kang, M., and R.B. Jackson. 2016. Salinity of deep groundwater in California: Water quantity, quality, and protection. *Proceedings of the National Academy of Sciences* 113: 7768–73.

Kaplan, L. 2020. Comparative Yupik and Inuit. Alaska Native Language Center. University of Alaska Fairbanks. https://uaf.edu/anlc/resources/comparative_yupik_and_inuit.php. Accessed September 23, 2020.

Karlstrom, K.E., L.S. Beard, K. House, R.A. Young, A. Aslan, G. Billingsley, and J. Pederson. 2012. Introduction: CRevolution 2: Origin and evolution of the Colorado River system II. *Geosphere* 8: 1170–76.

Karlstrom, K.E., R. Crow, L.J. Crossey, D. Coblentz, and J.W. Van Wijk. 2008. Model for tectonically driven incision of the younger than 6 Ma Grand Canyon. *Geology* 36: 835–38.

Karlstrom, K.E., J.P. Lee, S.A. Kelley, R.S. Crow, L.J. Crossey, R.A. Young, G. Lazear, L.S. Beard, J.W. Ricketts, M. Fox, and D.L. Shuster. 2014. Formation of the Grand Canyon 5 to 6 million years ago through integration of older palaeocanyons. *Nature Geoscience* 7: 239–44.

Keegan, J. 2010. *The American Civil War: A Military History*. New York: Vintage.

Keegan, J. 2012. *Fields of Battle: The Wars for North America*. New York: Vintage.

Keller, A. 1997. *Life Along the Hudson*. New York: Fordham University Press.

Kelly, B. 2017. A historical St. Lawrence Seaway. *NNY Business*. http://www.nnybizmag.com/index.php/2017/05/22/a-historical-st-lawrence-seaway/. Accessed October 19, 2020.

Kempthore, R.H., and J.P.R. Irish. 1981. Norman Wells – A new look at one of Canada's largest oil fields. *Journal of Petroleum Technology* 33: 985–91. https://www.onepetro.org/journal-paper/SPE-9477-PA.

Kerth, R., and S. Vineyard. 2012. 2012. Wasting our waterways 2012: Toxic Industrial Pollution and the Unfulfilled Promise of the Clean Water Act. Frontier Group and Environment American Research and Policy Center. https://environmentamerica.org/sites/environment/files/reports/Wasting%20Our%20Waterways%20vUS.pdf. Accessed October 20, 2020.

King, P.B. 2015. *Evolution of North America*. Princeton, NJ: Princeton University Press.

Kinnunen, R.E. 2015. Sea lamprey control in the Great Lakes. Michigan State University Extension. https://www.canr.msu.edu/news/sea_lamprey_control_in_the_great_lakes. Accessed September 10, 2019.

Kirk, J., J. Ruiz, J. Chesley, and S. Titley. 2003. The Origin of Gold in South Africa: Ancient rivers filled with gold, a spectacular upwelling of magma and a colossal meteor impact combined to make the Witwatersrand basin a very special place. *American Scientist* 91: 534–41.

Kitchen, A., M.M. Miyamoto, and C.J. Mulligan. 2008. A Three-Stage Colonization Model for the Peopling of the Americas. *PLoS ONE* 3(2): e1596.

Knouft, J.H., and D.L. Ficklin. 2017. The potential impacts of climate change on biodiversity in flowing freshwater systems. *Annual Review of Ecology and Systematics* 48: 111–33.

Kohler, A.E., P.C. Kusnierz, T. Copeland, D.A. Venditti, L. Denny, J. Gable, B.A. Lewis, R. Kinzer, B. Barnett, and M.S. Wipfli. 2013. Salmon-mediated nutrient flux in selected streams of the Columbia River basin, USA. *Canadian Journal of Fisheries and Aquatic Sciences* 70: 502–12.

Krauss, M., G. Holton, J. Kerr, and C.T. West. 2011. Indigenous Peoples and Languages of Alaska. Fairbanks and Anchorage: Alaska Native Language Center and UAA Institute of Social and Economic Research. https://www.uaf.edu/anla/collections/map/. Accessed December 4, 2020.

Kriegel, L. 1961. Afterword to *Life on the Mississippi* (M. Twain). New York: Signet Classics.

Kuby, M.J., W.F. Fagan, C.S. ReVelle, and W.L. Graf. 2005. A multiobjective optimization model for dam removal: An Example trading off salmon passage with hydropower and water storage in the Willamette basin. *Advances in Water Resources* 28: 845–55.

Kumarapeli, P.S., and V.A. Saull. 1966. The St. Lawrence valley system: A North American equivalent of the East African rift valley system. *Canadian Journal of Earth Sciences* 3: 639–58.

Kurek, J., J.L. Kirk, D.C. Muir, X. Wang, M.S. Evans, and J.P. Smol. 2013. Legacy of a half century of Athabasca oil sands development recorded by lake ecosystems. *Proceedings of the National Academy of Sciences* 110: 1761–66.

Lackey, R.T. 2013. *The Salmon 2100 Project*. http://fw.oregonstate.edu/content/robert-t-lackey. Accessed March 12, 2016.

Lackey, R.T., D.H. Lach, and S.L. Duncan (eds.). 2006. *Salmon 2100 Project: Future of Wild Pacific Salmon*. Bethesda, MD: American Fisheries Society.

Lamb, K.W. (ed.). 2007. *The Letters and Journals of Simon Fraser, 1806–1808*. Toronto: Dundurn.

Lamoureux, S.F., and J.H. England. 2000. Late Wisconsinan glaciation of the central sector of the Canadian High Arctic. *Quaternary Research* 54: 182–88.

Larson, G., and R. Schaetzl. 2001. Origin and evolution of the Great Lakes. *Journal of Great Lakes Research* 27: 518–46.

Lassiter, B.B. 1978. *American Wilderness: The Hudson River School of Painting*. New York: Doubleday.

Lawson, M.K. 2002. *The Battle of Hastings: 1066*. Stroud, UK: Tempus.

Lee, L.B. 1978. 100 years of reclamation historiography. *Pacific Historical Review* 47: 507–64.

Lemmen, D.S., A. Duk-Rodkin, and J.M. Bednarski. 1994. Late glacial drainage systems along the northwestern margin of the Laurentide Ice Sheet. *Quaternary Science Reviews* 13: 805–28.

Leopold, A. 1949. *A Sand County Almanac and Sketches Here and There.* Oxford: Oxford University Press.

Leopold, L.B. 1994. *A View of the River.* Cambridge, MA: Harvard University Press.

Leslie, J. 2019. On the northwest's Snake River, the case for dam removal grows. *Yale Environment 360.* https://e360.yale.edu/features/on-the-northwests-snake-river-the-case-for-dam-removal-grows. Accessed October 2, 2020.

Leudtke, L.S. (ed.). 1992. *Making America: The Society & Culture of the United States.* Chapel Hill: University of North Carolina Press.

Leverett, F., and F.B. Taylor. 1915. The Pleistocene of Indiana and Michigan and the History of the Great Lakes. *US Geological Survey Monograph* No. 53. Washington, DC.

Lewis, T. 2007. *The Hudson: A History.* New Haven, CT: Yale University Press.

Lichatowich, J., and J.A. Lichatowich. 2001. *Salmon Without Rivers: A History of the Pacific Salmon Crisis.* Washington, DC: Island Press.

Lobell, D.B., C.B. Field, K.N. Cahill, and C. Bonfils. 2006. Impacts of future climate change on California perennial crop yields: Model projections with climate and crop uncertainties. *Agricultural and Forest Meteorology* 141: 208–18.

Lockhart, W.L., G.A. Stern, G. Low, M. Hendzel, G. Boila, P. Roach, P., M.S. Evans, B.N. Billeck, J. DeLaronde, S. Friesen, and K. Kidd. 2005. A history of total mercury in edible muscle of fish from lakes in northern Canada. *Science of the Total Environment* 351: 427–63.

Long, S. 2019. Thirsty planet. *The Economist.* Special Report. March 2.

Loo, T. 2007. Disturbing the Peace: Environmental change and the scales of justice on a northern river. *Environmental History* 12: 895–919.

Loomis, J. 2002. Quantifying recreation use values from removing dams and restoring free-flowing rivers: A contingent behavior travel cost demand model for the Lower Snake River. *Water Resources Research* 38: 1–8.

Lothrop, J.C., D.L. Lowery, A.E. Spiess, and C.J. Ellis. 2016. Early human settlement of northeastern north America. *PaleoAmerica* 2: 192–251.

Lowey, G.W. 2006. The origin and evolution of the Klondike goldfields, Yukon, Canada. *Ore Geology Reviews* 28: 431–50.

Lucchitta, I. 1990. History of the Grand Canyon and of the Colorado River in Arizona. In S.S. Beus, and M. Morales (eds.), *Grand Canyon Geology,* pp. 311–32. New York: Oxford University Press.

Luecke, D.F., J. Pitt, C. Congdon, E. Glenn, C. Valdés-Casillas, and M. Briggs. 1999. A Delta once more: Restoring riparian and wetland habitat in the Colorado River Delta. Washington, DC: Environmental Defense Publications.

Lundberg, M. 2019. Tons of Gold!! Klondike treasure ship passenger lists. http://www.explorenorth.com/klondike/klondike_treasure_ships.html. Accessed September 2, 2020.

Mabee, C. 1961. *The Seaway Story.* New York: Macmillan

Macfarlane, D. 2014. *Negotiating a River: Canada, the US, and the Creation of the St. Lawrence Seaway. Vancouver: University of British Columba Press.*

MacGregor, R. 2017. *Original Highways: Travelling the Great Rivers of Canada.* Toronto: Random House Canada.

MacGregor, R., J. Casselman, L. Greig, W.A. Allen, L. McDermott, and T. Haxton. 2010. *DRAFT Recovery Strategy for the American Eel (*Anguilla rostrata*) in Ontario.* Ontario Recovery Strategy Series. Prepared for Ontario Ministry of Natural Resources, Peterborough, ON.

Mack, G.H., W.R. Seager, M.R. Leeder, M. Perez-Arlucea, and S.L. Salyards. 2006. Pliocene and Quaternary history of the Rio Grande, the axial river of the southern Rio Grande rift, New Mexico, USA. *Earth-Science Reviews* 79: 141–62.

Mackenzie River Basin Board (MRBB). 2003. Mackenzie River Basin. State of the Aquatic Ecosystem Report. 1. Whole Basin Overview. Available from MRBB, Ft. Smith, NT.

Mackenzie, Sir A. 1802. *Voyages from Montreal, on the River St. Laurence, Through the Continent of North America to the Frozen and Pacific Oceans, in the Years 1789 and 1793.* Philadelphia: John Morgan.

Macki, R.S. 1997. *Trading Beyond the Mountains: The British Fur Trade on the Pacific, 1793–1843.* Vancouver: University of British Columbia Press.

MacLennan, H. 1961. *Seven Rivers of Canada.* Toronto: Macmillan of Canada.

Manchaca, M. 2002. *Recovering History, Constructing Race: The Indian, Black, and White Roots of Mexican Americans.* The Joe R. and Teresa Lozano Long Series in Latin American and Latino Art and Culture. Austin: University of Texas Press.

Marsh, J., and N. Baker. 2018. Mackenzie Valley Pipeline Proposals. *The Canadian Encyclopedia.* https://www.thecanadianencyclopedia.ca/en/article/mackenzie-valley-pipeline. Accessed October 2, 2020.

Marshall, Col. R.B. 1919. *Irrigation of Twelve Million Acres in the Valley of California.* California State Irrigation Association, Sacramento. https://watershed.ucdavis.edu/shed/lund/fun/MarshallWaterPlan1919.pdf. Accessed November 24, 2020.

Marshall, T., and K. Mercer. 2015. Sir Alexander Mackenzie (Explorer). *The Canadian Encyclopedia.* https://www.thecanadianencyclopedia.ca/en/article/sir-alexander-mackenzie-explorer. Accessed October 1, 2020.

Martin Associates. 2018. *Economic Impacts of Maritime Shipping in the Great Lakes–St. Lawrence Region.* Lancaster, PA. https://greatlakes-seaway.com/wp-content/uploads/2019/10/eco_impact_full.pdf. Accessed October 16, 2020.

Martin, B.D., and K.O. Emery. 1967. Geology of Monterey Canyon, California. *American Association of Petroleum Geologists (AAPG) Bulletin* 51: 2281–2304. http://archives.datapages.com/data/bulletns/1965-67/data/pg/0051/0011/2250/2281.htm. Accessed October 4, 2020.

Martinez, O.J. (ed.). 1996. *US-Mexico Borderlands: Historical and Contemporary Perspectives.* Lanham, MD: Rowman & Littlefield.

Martins, E.G., S.G. Hinch, D.A. Patterson, M.J. Hague, S.J. Cooke, K.M. Miller, M.F. Lapointe, K.K. English, and A.P. Farrell. 2011. Effects of river temperature and climate warming on stock-specific survival of adult migrating Fraser River sockeye salmon (*Oncorhynchus nerka*). *Global Change Biology* 17: 99–114.

Mauch, C., and T. Zeller (eds.). 2008. *Rivers in History: Perspectives on Waterways in Europe and North America.* Pittsburgh: University of Pittsburgh Press.

McAllister, D.E., C.R. Harington, S.L. Cumbaa, and C.B. Renaud. 1988. Paleoenvironmental and biogeographic analyses of fossil fishes in peri-Champlain Sea deposits in eastern Canada. In N.R. Gadd (ed.), *The Late Quaternary Development of the Champlain Sea Basin.* Geological Association of Canada Special Paper 35: 241–58.

McCaffrey, S.C. 1996. The Harmon Doctrine one hundred years later: Buried, not praised. *Natural Resources Journal* 36: 965–1007.

McClung, C. 2009. The great depression in Washington State. Grand Coulee Dam: Leaving a legacy. Civil Rights and Labor History Consortium. University of Washington. http://depts.washington.edu/depress/grand_coulee.shtml#_edn7. Accessed September 13, 2020.

McCool, D. 2014. *River Republic: The Fall and Rise of America's Rivers.* New York: Columbia University Press.

McCutcheon, S. 1991. *Electric Rivers: The Story of the James Bay Project.* New York: Black Rose.

McEwan, D.R. 2001. Central valley steelhead. In R.L. Brown, *Contributions to the Biology of Central Valley Salmonids.* Vols. 1 & 2. *Fish Bulletin* 179: 1–43. Scripps Institution of Oceanography Library, Scripps Institution of Oceanography, University of California–San Diego.

McMillin, T.S. 2011. The Meaning of Rivers: Flow and Reflection in American Literature. Iowa City: University of Iowa Press.

McPhail, J.D., and C.C. Lindsey. 1986. Zoogeography of the freshwater fishes of Cascadia (the Columbia system and rivers north to the Stikine). In C.H. Hocutt and E.O. Wiley (eds.), *The Zoogeography of North American Freshwater Fishes,* pp. 615–37. New York: Wiley-Interscience.

McPhillips, D., and M.T. Brandon. 2012. Topographic evolution of the Sierra Nevada measured directly by inversion of low-temperature thermochronology. *American Journal of Science* 312: 90–116.

Melino, C. 2015. Grand Canyon stretch of the Colorado River threatened by mercury pollution. *EcoWatch.* https://www.ecowatch.com/grand-canyon-stretch-of-the-colorado-river-threatened-by-mercury-pollu-1882089088.html. Accessed August 23, 2019.

Metz, J.C. 1989. *Border: The U.S,–Mexico Line.* El Paso, TX: Mangan.

Meybeck, M. 2003. Global analysis of river systems: From Earth system controls to Anthropocene syndromes. *Philosophical Transactions of the Royal Society of London. Series B: Biological Sciences* 358: 1935–55.

Michael, J. 2016. Benefit-costs analysis of the California WaterFix. Center for Business and Policy Research. University of the Pacific. Sacramento. https://a11.asmdc.org/sites/a11.asmdc.org/files/pdf/Dr.%20Jeffrey%20Michael%20Benefit-Cost%20Analysis%20of%20The%20California%20WaterFix.pdf. Accessed August 25, 2019.

midcurrent.com. 2007. Bruce Babbitt calls for Snake River dam removals. https://midcurrent.com/2007/09/24/bruce-babbit-calls-for-snake-r/. Accessed October 1, 2020.

Mighetto, L., and M.B. Montgomery. 1998. Hard Drive to the Klondike: Promoting Seattle during the Gold Rush. A Historic Resource Study for the Seattle Unit of the Klondike Gold Rush National Historical Park. National Park Service (Dept. of Interior), Washington, DC. https://files.eric.ed.gov/fulltext/ED437334.pdf. Accessed October 24, 2017.

Millhouse, B.B. 2007. *American Wilderness: The Story of the Hudson River School of Painting.* Albany, NY: Black Dome Press.

Miller, C.I. 2012. Geologic, climatic, and vegetation history of California. In B.G. Baldwin, D.H. Goldman, D.J. Keil, R. Patterson, T.J. Rosatti, and D.H. Wilken (eds.), *The Jepson Manual: Vascular Plants of California,* 2nd ed., pp. 49–67. Berkeley: University of California Press.

Miller, N.L., K.E. Bashford, and E. Strem. 2003. Potential impacts of climate change on California hydrology. *Journal of the American Water Resources Association* 39: 771–84.

Milliman, J.D., and M.-e Ren. 1995. River flux to the sea: Impact of human intervention on river systems and adjacent coastal areas. In D. Eisma (ed.), *Climate Change Impact on Coastal Habitation*, pp. 57–83. Boca Raton, FL: Lewis.

Milly, P.C., and K.A. Dunne. 2020. Colorado River flow dwindles as warming-driven loss of reflective snow energizes evaporation. *Science* 367: 1252–55.

Milly, P.C., K.A. Dunne, and A.V. Vecchia. 2005. Global pattern of trends in streamflow and water availability in a changing climate. *Nature* 438: 347–50.

Miner, W.D. 1950. *A History of the Columbia Basin Projects*. Bloomington: University of Indiana Press.

Minks, L. 1999. *The Hudson River School: The Landscape Art of Bierstadt, Cole, Church, Durand, Heade and Twenty Other Artists*. Bexley, OH: Gramercy.

Mohs, G. 1985. Spiritual sites, ethnic significance and native spirituality: The heritage and heritage sites of the Sto:lo Indians of British Columbia. PhD diss., Simon Fraser University, Vancouver, BC.

Mole, R. 2009. *Gold Fever: Incredible Tales of the Klondike Gold Rush*. Victoria, BC: Heritage House.

Montgomery, D.R. 2000. Coevolution of the Pacific salmon and Pacific Rim topography. *Geology* 28: 1107–10.

Moon, T. 2017. Climate change: Saying goodbye to glaciers. *Science* 356: 580–81.

Moore, J.W. 2015. Bidirectional connectivity in rivers and implications for watershed stability and management. *Canadian Journal of Fisheries and Aquatic Sciences* 72: 785–95.

Moran, M.A., and K.E. Limburg. 1986. The Hudson river ecosystem. In K.E. Limberg, M.A. Moran, and W.H. McDowell (eds.), *The Hudson River Ecosystem*, pp. 6–39. New York: Springer.

Moratto, M.J. 1984. *California Archaeology*. New York: Academic Press.

Moreno-Mayar, J.V., B.A. Potter, L. Vinner, M. Steinrücken, S. Rasmussen, J. Terhorst, J.A. Kamm, A. Albrechtsen, A.S. Malaspinas, M. Sikora, and J.D. Reuther. 2018. Terminal Pleistocene Alaskan genome reveals first founding population of Native Americans. *Nature* 553(7687): 203.

Morison, S. 1974. *The European Discovery of America: The Southern Voyages, 1492–1616*. New York: Oxford University Press.

Morris, M., and R.C. de Loë. 2016. Cooperative and adaptive transboundary water governance in Canada's Mackenzie River Basin: Status and prospects. *Ecology and Society* 21: 26. http://dx.doi.org/10.5751/ES-08301-210126.

Morse, K. 2009. *The Nature of Gold: An Environmental History of the Klondike Gold Rush*. Seattle: University of Washington Press.

Moss, R.H., J.A. Edmonds, K.A. Hibbard, M.R. Manning, S.K. Rose, D.P. van Vuuren, T.R. Carter, S. Emori, M. Kainuma, T. Kram, G.A. Meehl, J.F.B. Mitchell, N. Nakicenovic, K. Riahi, S.J. Smith, R.J. Stouffer, A.M. Thomson, J.P. Weyant, and T.J. Wilbanks. 2010. The next generation of scenarios for climate change research and assessment. *Nature* 463: 747–56.

Mote, P.W., A.F. Hamlet, M.P. Clark, and D.P. Lettenmaier. 2005. Declining mountain snowpack in western North America. *Bulletin of the American Meteorological Society* 86: 39–50.

Mueller, J.E. 1975. *Restless River, International Law and the Behavior of the Rio Grande*. El Paso: Texas Western Press.

Mulligan, C.J., and E.J. Szathmáry. 2017. The peopling of the Americas and the origin of the Beringian occupation model. *American Journal of Physical Anthropology* 162: 403–8.

Musqueam Indian Band. 2011. CʼƏSNAʔƏM. http://www.musqueam.bc.ca/cʼəsnaʔəm. Accessed September 24, 2020.

Myers, C.J. 1966.The Colorado River. *Stanford Law Review* 19: 1–77.

NASA Earth Observatory. 2014. The Rocky Mountain Trench. https://earthobservatory.nasa.gov/images/84881/the-rocky-mountain-trench. Accessed June 6, 2018.

NASA Socioeconomic Data and Applications Center (SEDAC). Undated. Gridded Population of the World, Version 4 (GPWv4): Administrative Unit Center Points with Population Estimates. Center for International Earth Science Information Network – CIESIN – Columbia University. 2016. Gridded Population of the World, Version 4 (GPWv4): Administrative Unit Center Points with Population Estimates. http://dx.doi.org/10.7927/H4F47M2C. Accessed March 18, 2020.

National Archives of Canada. 1904. *Sessional Papers*, 1904. 22 Report of the Deputy Minister Marine and Fisheries, 34, Edward VII. A Series.

National Archives (US). 2020. American Indian Treaties. https://www.archives.gov/research/native-americans/treaties. Accessed August 16, 2020.

National Conference of State Legislatures. 2020. Federal and state recognized tribes; California. http://www.ncsl.org/research/state-tribal-institute/list-of-federal-and-state-recognized-tribes.aspx. Accessed October 3, 2020.

National Geographic. 2016. America's ten most endangered rivers of 2016. https://blog.nationalgeographic.org/2016/04/13/americas-ten-most-endangered-rivers-of-2016/ Accessed August 25, 2019.

National Geographic. 2016. America's ten most endangered rivers of 2016. https://blog.nationalgeographic.org/2016/04/13/americas-ten-most-endangered-rivers-of-2016/. Accessed August 25, 2019.

National Integrated Drought Information System. 2020. Drought in California. https://www.drought.gov/drought/states/california. Accessed October 3, 2020.

National Oceanic and Atmospheric Administration. 2014. Recovery Plan for The Evolutionarily Significant Units of Sacramento River Winter-run Chinook Salmon and Central Valley Spring-run Chinook Salmon and the DPS of California Central Valley Steelhead. National Marine Fisheries Service West Coast Region. https://www.fisheries.noaa.gov/resource/document/recovery-plan-evolutionarily-significant-units-sacramento-river-winter-run. Accessed October 5, 2020.

National Oceanic and Atmospheric Administration. 2016. 5-Year Review: Summary and Evaluation California Central Valley Steelhead Distinct Population Segment. National Marine Fisheries Service West Coast Region. https://repository.library.noaa.gov/view/noaa/17019. Accessed October 5, 2020.

National Oceanic and Atmospheric Administration. 2016. 5-Year Status Review: Summary and Evaluation of Sacramento River Winter-Run Chinook Salmon ESU. National Marine Fisheries Service West Coast Region. https://repository.library.noaa.gov/view/noaa/17014. Accessed October 5, 2020.

National Oceanic and Atmospheric Administration. 2016. 5-Year Status Review: Summary and Central Valley Spring-run Chinook Salmon Evolutionarily Significant Unit. National Marine Fisheries Service West Coast Region. https://repository.library.noaa.gov/view/noaa/17018. Accessed October 5, 2020.

National Oceanic and Atmospheric Administration. 2019. NOAA forecasts very large 'dead zone' for Gulf of Mexico. https://www.noaa.gov/media-release/noaa-forecasts-very-large-dead-zone-for-gulf-of-mexico. Accessed October 20, 2020.

National Oceanic and Atmospheric and Administration. 2020. Great Lakes Region: Invasive species. https://www.regions.noaa.gov/great-lakes/index.php/great_lakes-res-toration-initiative/invasive-species/. Accessed October 22, 2020.

National Research Council (US). 2004. *Managing The Columbia River: Instream Flows, Water Withdrawals, and Salmon Survival.* Washington, DC: National Academies Press. https://www.nap.edu/read/10962/chapter/1. Accessed Dec. 4, 2020.

Natural Resources Canada. 2007. Rivers. Atlas of Canada. https://web.archive.org/web/20070202064028/http://atlas.nrcan.gc.ca/site/english/learningresources/facts/rivers.html. Accessed October 16, 2020.

Natural Resources Canada. 2017. Atlas of Canada. https://www.nrcan.gc.ca/maps-tools-pub-lications/tools/geodetic-reference-systems/water/16888 Accessed October 2, 2020.

Natural Resources Canada. 2020. Oil Resources. https://www.nrcan.gc.ca/energy/ener-gy-sources-distribution/crude-oil/oil-resources/18085. Accessed August 31, 2020.

Natural Resources Defense Council. 2007. Judge throws out Biological Opinion for Delta Smelt. http://www.nrdc.org/media/2007/070526.asp. Accessed October 4, 2020.

Natural Resources Defense Council. 2017. One trillion litres of toxic waste and growing: Alberta's tailings ponds. https://environmentaldefence.ca/wp-content/uploads/2017/06/EDC-and-NRDC-One-trillion-litres-of-toxic-waste-and-growing-Albertas-tailings-ponds-June-2017.pdf. Accessed August 28, 2019.

National Wild and Scenic Rivers System. 2020. About the *Wild and Scenic Rivers Act.* https://rivers.gov. Accessed December 30, 2020.

Navajo Nation Department of Justice. Undated. Water rights unit. http://nndoj.org/Wa-ter_Rights_Unit.aspx. Accessed October 9, 2020.

Najavo Nation Water Rights Commission. 2021. Water Rights. https://www.nnwrc.nava-jo-nsn.gov/Water-Rights. Accessed March 17, 2021.

Neave, F. 1958. The origin and speciation of *Oncorhynchus. Transactions of the Royal Society of Canada* (Series 3) 52: 25–39.

Nelson, S.M., E. Kendy, K.W. Flessa, J.E. Rodríguez-Burgueño, J. Ramírez-Hernández, and T.E. Rivas-Salcedo. 2020. Channel incision by headcut migration: Reconnection of the Colorado River to its estuary and the Gulf of California during the floods of 1979–1988. *Hydrological Processes* 34: 4156–74.

Nesbitt, H.K., and J.W. Moore. 2016. Species and population diversity in Pacific salmon fisheries underpin indigenous food security. *Journal of Applied Ecology* 53:1489–99.

New Netherland Institute. 2016. Peter Schaghen letter. https://web.archive.org/web/20160324021546/http://www.newnetherlandinstitute.org/history-and-heritage/additional-resources/dutch-treats/peter-schagen-letter. Accessed September 16, 2020.

Nielsen, L.W. 2004. The "Nature" of 'Nature': The concept of nature and its complexity in a Western cultural and ethical context. *Global Bioethics* 17: 31–38.

Nijhus, M. 2015. Movement to take down thousands of dams goes mainstream. *National Geographic.* http://news.nationalgeographic.com/news/2015/01/150127-white-clay-creek-dam-removal-river-water-environment/. Accessed October 2, 2020.

Nisbet, J. 2002. *Sources of the River: Tracking David Thompson Across North America.* Se-attle: Sasquatch.

Northcote, T.G., and D.Y. Atagi. 1997. Pacific Salmon Abundance Trends in the Fraser River Watershed Compared with Other British Columbia Systems. In D.J. Stouder, P.A. Bisson, and R. Naiman (eds.), *Pacific Salmon & their Ecosystems: Status and Future Options*, pp. 199–223. New York: Chapman & Hall.

Northwest Alliance for Computational Science and Engineering. 2020. Average annual precipitation for Washington State (1981–2010). Prism Climate Group, Oregon State University. https://prism.oregonstate.edu/projects/gallery_view.php?state=WA. Accessed November 10, 2020.

Northwest Power and Conservation Council. 1977. A guide to major hydropower dams of the Columbia River Basin. https://app.nwcouncil.org/ext/storymaps/damguide/index.html. Accessed September 7, 2020.

Northwest Power and Conservation Council. 2020. Dams: Impacts on salmon and steelhead. https://www.nwcouncil.org/reports/columbia-river-history/DamsImpacts. Accessed October 1, 2020.

Northwest Power and Conservation Council. 2020. David Thompson. https://www.nwcouncil.org/history/ThompsonDavid. Accessed September 30, 2020.

Northwest Power and Conservation Council. 2020. Endangered Species Act, Columbia River salmon and steelhead, and the Biological Opinion. https://www.nwcouncil.org/reports/columbia-river-history/EndangeredSpeciesAct. Accessed October 1, 2020.

Northwest Power and Conservation Council. 2020. Shad. https://www.nwcouncil.org/history/Shad. Accessed October 1, 2020.

Northwest Territories Bureau of Statistics. 2019. Oil and gas. NWT natural gas & crude oil production. https://www.statsnwt.ca/economy/oil-gas/. Accessed August 15, 2020.

Nuffield, E.W. 2001. *Samuel Hearne: Journey to the Coppermine River, 1769–1772.* Vancouver: Haro.

Oberholtzer, E.P. 1917. *A History of the United States since the Civil War.* New York: MacMillan. https://archive.org/details/oberholtzerhisto1ellirich/page/540/mode/2up. Accessed September 23, 2020.

O'Connor, J.E., V.R. Baker, R.B. Waitt, L.N. Smith, C.M. Cannon, D.L. George, and R.P. Denlinger. 2020. The Missoula and Bonneville floods—A review of ice-age megafloods in the Columbia River basin. *Earth-Science Reviews* 208: 103181.

O'Donnell, E., and J. Talbot-Jones. 2017. Three rivers are now legally people – but that's just the start of looking after them. *The Conversation.* March 23. https://theconversation.com/three-rivers-are-now-legally-people-but-thats-just-the-start-of-looking-after-them-74983?utm_source=twitter&utm_medium=twitterbutton Accessed August 12, 2019.

O'Donnell, E.L., and J. Talbot-Jones. 2018. Creating legal rights for rivers: Lessons from Australia, New Zealand, and India. *Ecology and Society* 23(1): 7. https://doi.org/10.5751/ES-09854-230107.

Olmstead, A.L., and W. Paul. 2004. The Evolution of California Agriculture, 1850–2000. In J. Siebert (ed.), *California Agriculture: Dimensions and Issues,* pp. 1–28. University of California-Berkeley Information Series. https://citeseerx.ist.psu.edu/viewdoc/download?doi=10.1.1.389.2184&rep=rep1&type=pdf. Accessed October 4, 2020.

O'Malley, M. 1976. *The Past and Future Land: An Account of the Berger Inquiry into the Mackenzie Valley Pipeline.* Toronto: Peter Martin Associates.

Orrenius, P.M. 2001. Illegal immigration and enforcement along the US-Mexico border: An overview. *Economic and Financial Review–Federal Reserve Bank of Dallas* 1: 2–11.

Ortolano, L., and K.K. Cushing. 2000. Grand Coulee dam and The Columbia basin project, USA. Case study report prepared as an input to the World Commission on Dams. http://171.67.100.116/courses/2010/ph240/harting2/docs/csusmain.pdf. Accessed October 2, 2020.

Osadetz, K. G., G. R. Morrell, J. Dixon, J.R. Dietrich, L.R. Snowdon, S.R. Dallimore, and J.A. Majorowicz. 2005. Beaufort Sea-Mackenzie Delta Basin: A review of conventional and nonconventional (gas hydrate) petroleum reserves and undiscovered resources. *Scientific Results from Mallik 2002 Gas Hydrate Production Research Well Program, Mackenzie Delta, Northwest Territories, Canada.* Geological Survey of Canada Bulletin 585.

Osborn, J. 2015. State Department to include ecosystem function in Columbia River Treaty. Center for Environmental Law & Policy (CELP), Seattle. https://www.celp.org/2015/06/04/news-columbia-river-treaty-state-department-to-include-ecosystem-function/. Accessed August 26, 2019.

O'Sullivan, P., and J.W. Miller, Jr. 2015. *The Geography of Warfare.* New York: Routledge

Owen, D. 2017. Where the water goes. *The New Yorker.* April 2. Accessed October 8, 2020.

Page, L.M., E.C. Beckham, and B.M. Curr. 1991. *Freshwater Fishes: North America North of Mexico.* Norwalk, CT: Easton Press.

Palmer, M.A., C.A. Reidy Liermann, C. Nilsson, M. Flörke, J. Alcamo, P.S. Lake, and N. Bond. 2008. Climate change and the world's river basins: Anticipating management options. *Frontiers in Ecology and the Environment* 6: 81–89.

Palmer, M.A., D.P. Lettenmaier, N.L. Poff, S.L. Postel, B. Richter, and R. Warner. 2009. Climate change and river ecosystems: Protection and adaptation options. *Environmental Management* 44: 1053–68.

Parent, M., and S. Occhietti. 2007. Late Wisconsinan Deglaciation and Champlain Sea Invasion in the St. Lawrence Valley, Québec. *Géographie physique et Quaternaire* 42: 215–46.

Parham, C.P. 2009. *The St. Lawrence Seaway and Power Project: An Oral History of the Greatest Construction Show on Earth.* Syracuse, NY: Syracuse University Press.

Parkes, M.W., K.E. Morrison, M.J. Bunch, L.K. Hallström, R.C. Neudoerffer, H.D. Venema and D. Waltner-Toews. 2010. Towards integrated governance for water, health and social–ecological systems: The watershed governance prism. *Global Environmental Change* 20: 693–704.

Parsons, M.B., and J.B. Percival. 2005. A brief history of mercury and its environmental impact. *Mercury: Sources, Measurements, Cycles, and Effects* 34: 1–20.

Patagonia.com. 2014. Patagonia on dams and dam removal. https://www.patagonia.com/on/demandware.static/Sites-patagonia-us-Site/Library-Sites-PatagoniaShared/en_US/PDF-US/DamNation_Statements_v1.pdf. Accessed October 2, 2020.

Pathak, T.B., M.L. Maskey, J.A. Dahlberg, F. Kearns, K.M. Bali, and D. Zaccaria. 2018. Climate change trends and impacts on California agriculture: A detailed review. *Agronomy* 8: 21–27.

Patton, J.R., R. Stein, and V. Sevilgen. 2018. When the levee breaks: Cascading failures in the Sacramento-San Joaquin River Delta, California. *Tremblor, Inc.* http://temblor.net/earthquake-insights/when-the-levee-breaks-cascading-failures-in-the-sacramento-san-joaquin-river-delta-california-7959/. Accessed August 24, 2019.

Pearkes, E.P. 2016. *A River Captured: The Columbia River Treaty and Catastrophic Change.* Victoria, BC: Rocky Mountain Books.

Pearson, M.J.T. 2015. *Failure Of British Strategy during the Southern Campaign of the American Revolutionary War.* Auckland, NZ: Pickle Partners. Chapter 1.

Pederson, G.T., S.T. Gray, C.A. Woodhouse, J.L. Betancourt, D.B. Fagre, J.S. Littell, E. Watson, B.H. Luckman, and L.J. Graumlich. 2011. The unusual nature of recent snowpack declines in the North American Cordillera. *Science* 333: 332–35.

Pederson, J.L. 2008. The mystery of the pre-Grand Canyon Colorado River-results from the Muddy Creek formation. *GSA TODAY* 18: 4–10.

Penaluna, B.E., A. Abadía-Cardoso, J.B. Dunham, F.J. Garcia-De Leon, R.E. Gresswell, A.R. Luna, E.B. Taylor, B.B. Shepard, R. Al-Chokhachy, C.C. Muhlfeld, and K.R. Bestgen. 2016. Conservation of native Pacific trout diversity in western North America. *Fisheries* 41: 286–300.

Pentland, R. 2009. The future of Canada-US water relations: The need for modernization. *Policy Options Politique.* July 9. https://policyoptions.irpp.org/magazines/canadas-water-challenges/the-future-of-canada-us-water-relations-the-need-for-modernization/. Accessed October 21, 2020.

Peregrine, P.N., and M. Ember (eds.). 2001. *Encyclopedia of Prehistory,* vol. 2, *Arctic and Subarctic.* Dordrecht: Springer-Science+Business Media, B.V.

Perry, T., and R. Marosi. 2010. A water-providing marvel – and a 'death trap.' *Los Angeles Times.* November 26. http://articles.latimes.com/2010/nov/26/local/la-me-canal-20101126. Accessed October 9, 2020.

Pess, G.R., M.L. McHenry, T.J. Beechie, and J. Davies. 2008. Biological impacts of the Elwha River dams and potential salmonid responses to dam removal. *Northwest Science* 82: 72–90.

Petticrew, E.L., S.J. Albers, S.A. Baldwin, S.A., E.C. Carmack, S.J. Déry, N. Gantner, K.E. Graves, B. Laval, J. Morrison, P.N. Owens, and D.T. Selbie. 2015. The impact of a catastrophic mine tailings impoundment spill into one of North America's largest fjord lakes: Quesnel Lake, British Columbia, Canada. *Geophysical Research Letters* 42: 3347–55.

Philips, C.N. 2012. *Epic in American Culture: Settlement To Reconstruction.* Baltimore, MD: Johns Hopkins University Press.

Pielou, E.C. 2008. *After the Ice Age: The Return of Life to Glaciated North America.* Chicago: University of Chicago Press.

Pilon, J.L. 1991. Insights into the Prehistory of the Lower Mackenzie Valley, Anderson Plain Region, Northwest Territories. *Canadian Archaeological Association Occasional Paper* 1: 89–111.

Pisani, D.J. 1984. *From the Family Farm to Agribusiness: The Agricultural Crusade in California and the West, 1850–1931.* Berkeley: University of California Press.

Pitulko, V.V., P.A. Nikolsky, Yu. E. Girya, A.E.Basilyan, V.E. Tumskoy, S.A. Koulakov, S.N.Astakhov, E. Yu. Pavlova, and M.A. Anisimov. 2004. The Yana RHS site: Humans in the Arctic before the Last Glacial Maximum. *Science* 303: 52–55.

Porsild, C. 2011. *Gamblers and Dreamers: Women, Men, and Community in the Klondike.* Vancouver: University of British Columbia Press.

Postel, S. 2020. *Replenish: The Virtuous Cycle of Water and Prosperity.* Washington, DC: Island Press.

Postel, S., and B. Richter. 2003. *Rivers for Life: Managing Water for People and Nature.* Washington, DC: Island Press.

Postel, S.L., J.I. Morrison, and P.H. Gleick. 1998. Allocating fresh water to aquatic ecosystems: The case of the Colorado River Delta. *Water International* 23: 119–25.

Potter, P.E. 1978. Significance and origin of big rivers. *Journal of Geology* 86: 13–33.

Powell, J.W., et al. 1878. Report on the lands of the arid region of the United States: with a more detailed account of the lands of Utah: with maps. Washington, DC: Government Printing Office.

Price, M.E., and G.D. Weatherford. 1976. Indian water rights in theory and practice: Navajo experience in the Colorado River basin. *Law and Contemporary Problems* 40: 97–131.

Prince of Wales Heritage Centre. 2020. History of the name of the Northwest Territories. https://www.pwnhc.ca/territorial-evolution-of-the-northwest-territories/. Accessed September 28, 2020.

Pustola, C. 2014. Impact of the Klondike gold rush. Alaskaweb.org. http://alaskaweb.org/mining/klonimpact.html. Accessed September 23, 2020.

Ransom, R.L. 2018. The Civil War in American economic history. Chapter 10 in L.P. Cain, P.V. Fishback, and P.W. Rhode (eds.), *The Oxford Handbook of the American Economy*, vol. 2. New York: Oxford University Press.

Rayburn, I. 2001. *Naming Canada: Stories about Canadian Place Names*. Toronto: University of Toronto Press.

Reheis, M.C. 1997. Dust deposition downwind of Owens (dry) Lake, 1991–1994: Preliminary findings. *Journal of Geophysical Research: Atmospheres* 102: 25999–26008.

Reiners, P.W. 2012. Paleotopography in the western U.S. Cordillera. *American Journal of Science* 312: 81–89.

Reisner, M. 1986. *Cadillac Desert: The American West and its Disappearing Water*. New York: Penguin.

Ricciardi, A. 2006. Patterns of invasion in the Laurentian Great Lakes in relation to changes in vector activity. *Diversity and Distributions* 12: 425–33.

Richerson, P.J., R. Boyd, and R.L. Bettinger. 2001. Was agriculture impossible during the Pleistocene but mandatory during the Holocene? A climate change hypothesis. *American Antiquity* 66: 387–411.

Ricker, W.E. 1972. Hereditary and environmental factors affecting certain salmonid populations. In *The stock concept in Pacific salmon*, pp. 19–160. University of British Columbia, H.R. MacMillan Lectures in Fisheries, Vancouver.

Riley, C.L. 1995. *Rio del Norte: People of the Upper Rio Grande From Earliest Times to the Pueblo Revolt*. Salt Lake City: University of Utah Press.

Robbins, J. 2017. A new way of understanding what makes a river healthy. *Yale Environment 360*. January 4. https://e360.yale.edu/features/new_look_at_rivers_reveals_toll_of_human_activity_yellowstone_river. Accessed December 29, 2018.

Robbins, J. 2019. Crisis on the Colorado: Part I. The West's great river hits its limits: Will the Colorado run dry? *Yale Environment 360*. January 14. https://e360.yale.edu/features/the-wests-great-river-hits-its-limits-will-the-colorado-run-dry. Accessed May 24, 2020.

Roberts, L. 1949. *The Mackenzie*. New York: Rinehart.

Rogers, S., D. Chen, H. Jiang, I. Rutherfurd, M. Wang, M. Webber, B. Crow-Miller, J. Barnett, B. Finlayson, M. Jiang, and C. Shi. 2020. An integrated assessment of China's South—North Water Transfer Project. *Geographical Research* 58: 49–63.

Rohrbough, M.J. 1998. *Days of gold: The California Gold Rush and the American Nation*. Berkeley: University of California Press.

Roosevelt, F.D. 1934. Fireside chats. September 30. Compiled by Sheba Blake Publishing, 2016.

Rosenau, M.L., and M. Angelo. 2007. *Saving the Heart of the Fraser: Addressing Human Impacts to the Aquatic Ecosystem of the Fraser River, Hope to Mission, British Columbia*. Report to The Pacific Fisheries Resource Conservation Council, Vancouver, British

Columbia. https://www.psf.ca/sites/default/files/SavingHeart-of-the-Fraser_2007_0_ Complete.pdf. Accessed August 26, 2019.

Rossmo, D.K., Q.C. Thurman, J.D. Jamieson, and J. Egan. 2008. Geographic patterns and profiling of illegal crossings of the southern U.S. border. *Security Journal* 21: 29–57.

Rothlisberger, J.D., D.C. Finnoff, R.M. Cooke, and D.M. Lodge. 2012. Ship-borne nonindigenous species diminish Great Lakes ecosystem services. *Ecosystems* 15: 462–76.

Rougemont, Q., J-S. Moore, T. Leroy, E. Normandeau, E.B. Rondeau, R.E. Withler, D.M. Van Doornik, P.A. Crane, K.A. Naish, J.C. Garza, T.D. Beacham, B.F Koop, and L. Bernatchez. 2020. The role of historical contingency in shaping geographic pattern of deleterious mutation load in a broadly distributed Pacific Salmon. *PLOS Genetics* 17(2): e1009397.

Roussi, A. 2019. Africa's nations clash over giant Nile dam: Egypt says the Grand Ethiopian Renaissance Dam will cause water shortages — but Ethiopia stands firm. *Nature* 574: 159–60.

Rowell, K., K.W. Flessa, D.L. Dettman, and M. Román. 2005. The importance of Colorado River flow to nursery habitats of the Gulf corvina (*Cynoscion othonopterus*). *Canadian Journal of Fisheries and Aquatic Sciences* 62: 2874–85.

Sanger, D. 1967. Prehistory of the Pacific Northwest Plateau as seen from the interior of British Columbia. *American Antiquity* 32: 86–197.

Santayana, G. 1905. *The Life of Reason: Or The Phases of Human Progress*, vol. 1. New York: Charles Scribner's Sons.

SARA Public Registry. 2021. Species at risk public registry. Environment and Climate Change Canada. https://species-registry.canada.ca/index-en.html#/species?sortBy=commonNameSort&sortDirection=asc&pageSize=10. Accessed March 23, 2021.

Save the Colorado. Undated. Dams and diversions. http://savethecolorado.org/threats/ dams-and-diversions. Accessed August 23, 2019.

Save the Colorado. Undated. Invasive species. http://savethecolorado.org/threats/invasive-species/ Accessed August 23, 2019.

Schindler, D.E., R. Hilborn, B. Chasco, B., C.P. Boatright, T.P. Quinn, L.A. Rogers, and M.S. Webster. 2010. Population diversity and the portfolio effect in an exploited species. *Nature* 465: 609–12.

Schindler, D.E., X. Augerot, E. Fleishman, N.J. Mantua, B. Riddell, M. Ruckelshaus, J. Seeb, and M. Webster. 2008. Climate change, ecosystem impacts, and management for Pacific salmon. *Fisheries* 33: 502–6.

Schulz, P.D. 1981. Osteoarchaeology and subsistence change in prehistoric central California. PhD diss., University of California–Davis.

Schuster, P.F., R.G. Striegl, G.R. Aiken, D.P. Krabbenhoft, J.F. Dewild, K. Butler, B. Kamark, and M. Dornblaser. 2011. Mercury export from the Yukon River Basin and potential response to a changing climate. *Environmental Science & Technology* 45: 9262–67.

Schwantes, C.A. 1996. *The Pacific Northwest: An Interpretive History*. Lincoln: University of Nebraska Press.

Schwatka, F. 1885. *Along Alaska's great river: A Popular account of the travels of the Alaska exploring expedition of 1883, along the great Yukon River, from its source to its mouth, in the British North-West territory, and in the territory of Alaska*. New York: Cassels.

Scott, W.B., and E.J. Crossman. 1973. *Freshwater Fishes of Canada*. Bulletin of the Fisheries Research Board of Canada, No. 184.

Scotusblog.com. 2015. State Water Contractors v. Jewell. Petition for certiorari denied on January 12, 2015 http://www.scotusblog.com/case-files/cases/state-water-contractors-v-jewell/. Accessed May 17, 2017.

Selin, H. 2003. Introduction. In H. Selin (ed.), *Nature Across Cultures: Views of Nature and the Environment in non-Western Cultures.* Dordrecht: Springer-Science+Business Media, B.V.

Shafroth, P.B., K.J. Schlatter, M. Gomez-Sapiens, E. Lundgren, M.R. Grabau, J. Ramírez-Hernández, J.E. Rodríguez-Burgueño, and K.W. Flessa. 2017. A large-scale environmental flow experiment for riparian restoration in the Colorado River Delta. *Ecological Engineering* 106: 645–60.

Shea, W.L., and T.T. Winschel. 2003. Vicksburg Is the Key: The Struggle for the Mississippi River. Lincoln: University of Nebraska Press.

Sheldon, T.A., N.E. Mandrak, and N.R. Lovejoy. 2008. Biogeography of the deepwater sculpin (*Myoxocephalus thompsonii*), a Nearctic glacial relict. *Canadian Journal of Zoology* 86: 108–15.

Shepard, F.P. 1937. Origin of the Great Lakes basins. *Journal of Geology* 45: 76–88.

Shouse, M.K., and D.A. Cox. 2013. USGS Science at Work in the San Francisco Bay and Sacramento-San Joaquin Delta Estuary. https://pubs.usgs.gov/fs/2013/3037/pdf/fs2013-3037.pdf. Accessed October 3, 3030.

Simonds, W.J. 1998. The Columbia Basin Project. Bureau of Reclamation History Project, Denver, CO. https://www.usbr.gov/projects/pdf.php?id=88. Accessed September 8, 2020.

Small, M.P., T.D. Beacham, R.E. Withler, and R.J. Nelson. 1998. Discriminating coho salmon (*Oncorhynchus kisutch*) populations within the Fraser River, British Columbia, using microsatellite DNA markers. *Molecular Ecology* 7: 141–55.

Smith, A.B. 2020. 2010–2019: A landmark decade of U.S. billion-dollar weather and climate disasters. National Oceanic and Atmospheric Administration, Climate.gov. https://www.climate.gov/news-features/blogs/beyond-data/2010-2019-landmark-decade-us-billion-dollar-weather-and-climate. Accessed October 22, 2020.

Smith, J.K. 1977. *The Mackenzie River: Yesterday's Fur Frontier, Tomorrow's Energy Battleground.* Agincourt, ON: Gage.

Smith, L.C. 2020. *Rivers of Power: How a Natural Force Raised Kingdoms, Destroyed Civilizations, and Shapes Our World.* New York: Little, Brown Spark.

Solomon, D.J., and M.H. Beach. 2003. Fish pass design for eel and elver *(Anguilla anguilla).* Environment Agency. Technical Report W2–070/TR1. Bristol, UK.

Spencer, J.E., and P.A. Pearthree. 2001. Headward erosion versus closed-basin spillover as alternative causes of Neogene capture of the ancestral Colorado River by the Gulf of California. *The Colorado River: Origin and Evolution: Grand Canyon, Arizona, Grand Canyon Association Monograph* 12: 215–19.

Stafford, T.W. 2014. Chronology of the Kennewick Man skeleton. Chapter 5 in D.W. Owsley and R.L. Jantz (eds.), *Kennewick Man, The Scientific Investigation of an Ancient American Skeleton,* pp. 59–89. College Station: Texas A&M University Press.

Stagg, R. 2010. *The Golden Dream: A History of the St. Lawrence Seaway.* Toronto: Dundurn.

Stanley, S.M., and J.A. Luczaj. 2015. *Earth System History,* 4th ed. New York: W.H. Freeman.

Stanton, K. 2012. Looking forward, looking back: The Canadian truth and reconciliation commission and the Mackenzie Valley pipeline inquiry. *Canadian Journal of Law and Society* 27: 81–99.

State of Alaska. Department of Labor and Workforce Development, Research and Analysis. 2020. Population and Census, 2019 Population Estimates by Borough, Census Area, and Economic Region. https://live.laborstats.alaska.gov/pop/index.cfm. Accessed September 23, 2020.

Statista.com. 2020. International seaborne trade carried by container ships from 1980 to 2017. https://www.statista.com/statistics/253987/international-seaborne-trade-carried-by-containers/. Accessed May 3, 2020.

Statista.com. 2020. Projected global container market growth between 2015 and 2021. https://www.statista.com/statistics/253931/global-container-market-demand-growth/. Accessed March 18, 2021.

Statistics Canada. 2016. Aboriginal Peoples Highlight Tables, 2016 Census. https://www12.statcan.gc.ca/census-recensement/2016/dp-pd/hlt-fst/abo-aut/Table.cfm?Lang=Eng&S=99&O=A&RPP=25. Accessed August 20, 2020.

Stene, E.A. 1996. Shoshone Project. US Bureau of Reclamation. https://www.usbr.gov/projects/pdf.php?id=192. Accessed February 24, 2020.

Stevenson, A. 1998. Wet-site contributions to developmental models of Fraser River fishing technology. In K. Bernick (ed.), *Hidden Dimensions: The Cultural Significance of Wetland Archaeology. Pacific Rim Archaeology and Wetland Archaeology Research Project*, pp. 220–38. Occasional Paper 2. Vancouver: University of British Columbia Press.

St. John, R. 2011. *Line in the Sand. A History of the Western U.S.–Mexican Border*. Princeton, NJ: Princeton University Press.

St. Lawrence Seaway Development Corporation. 2019. SLSDC Annual Reports. https://greatlakes-seaway.com/en/about-us/slsdc-management/annual-reports/. Accessed October 19, 2020.

St. Lawrence Seaway Management Corporation. 2014–2020. SLSMC Annual Corporate Summaries. https://greatlakes-seaway.com/en/about-us/slsmc-management/annual-corporate-summaries/. Accessed October 19, 2020.

St. Lawrence Seaway Management Corporation. 2018. Annual Corporate Summary. https://greatlakes-seaway.com/wp-content/uploads/2019/09/slsmc_ar2018_en.pdf. Accessed March 17, 2021.

St. Lawrence Seaway Management Corporation. 2020. SLSMC Annual Corporate Summary. https://greatlakes-seaway.com/wp-content/uploads/2020/07/slsmc_ar2020_en.pdf. Accessed March 17, 2021.

Stock, G.M., R.S. Anderson, and R.C. Finkel. 2004. Pace of landscape evolution in the Sierra Nevada, California, revealed by cosmogenic dating of cave sediments. *Geology* 32: 193–96.

Strahler, A.N. 1957. Quantitative analysis of watershed geomorphology. *Transactions of the American Geophysical Union* 38: 913–20.

Stratton, D.H. (ed.). 2005. *Spokane & the Inland Empire: An Interior Pacific Northwest Anthology*. Pullman: Washington State University Press.

Summit, A.R. 2013. *Contested Waters: An Environmental History of the Colorado River*. Boulder: University Press of Colorado.

Sunil, A. 2018. *Unruly Waters: How Rains, Rivers, Coasts, and Seas Have Shaped Asia's History*. New York: Basic Books.

Sun Tzu. 2019. *The Art of War*. New York: Ixia Press.

Sutton, M.Q. 2016. *A Prehistory of North America*. London: Routledge.

Sutton, M.Q. 2016. How and when: Peopling of the New World. Chapter 2 in M.Q. Sutton, A Prehistory of North America. London: Routledge.

Sutton, M.Q. 2016. Whales and sleds. Chapter 4 in M.Q. Sutton, *A Prehistory of North America*. London: Routledge.

Sutton, M.Q. 2017. The "fishing link": Salmonids and the initial peopling of the Americas. *PaleoAmerica* 3: 231–59.

Takacs, D. 2016. South Africa and the human right to water: Equity, ecology, and the public trust doctrine. *Berkeley Journal of International Law* 34: 55–108.

Tamm, E., T. Kivisild, M. Reidla, M. Metspalu, D.G. Smith, C.J. Mulligan, C.M. Bravi, O. Rickards, C. Martinez-Labarga, E.K. Khusnutdinova, S.A. Fedorova, M.V. Golubenko, V.A. Stepanov, M.A. Gubina, S.I. Zhadanov, L.P. Ossipova, L. Damba, M.I. Voevoda, J.E. Dipierri, R. Villems, and R.S. Malh. 2007. Beringian Standstill and Spread of Native American Founders. *PLoS ONE* 2(9): e829.

Taylor, E.B. 1991. A review of local adaptation in Salmonidae, with particular reference to Pacific and Atlantic salmon. *Aquaculture* 98: 185–207.

Thompson, J. 2017. The 26,000 tons of radioactive waste under Lake Powell. *High Country News*. December 18. https://www.hcn.org/articles/pollution-a-26-000-ton-pile-of-radioactive-waste-lies-under-the-waters-and-silt-of-lake-powell. Accessed August 23, 2019.

Torgenson, D. 1986. Between knowledge and politics: Three faces of policy analysis. *Policy Sciences* 19: 33–59.

Touchstones Nelson Museum of Art and History. 2007. Balance of power. Hydroelectric development in southeastern British Columbia. Lower Bonnington Dam. http://www.virtualmuseum.ca/sgc-cms/expositions-exhibitions/hydro/en/dams/?action=lower-bonnington. Accessed October 1, 2020.

Transport Canada, US Army Corps of Engineers, US Department of Transportation, The St. Lawrence Seaway Management Corporation, Saint Lawrence Seaway Development Corporation, Environment Canada, and US Fish and Wildlife Service. 2007. *Great Lakes St Lawrence Seaway Study: Final Report.* https://greatlakes-seaway.com/wp-content/uploads/2019/10/GLSL-Final-Report-En.pdf. Accessed October 19, 2020.

Tremblay, A., and Y. Lemieux. 2001. Supracrustal faults of the St. Lawrence rift system between Cap-Tourmente and Baie-Saint-Paul, Quebec. *Current Research* 2001-D-15. Natural Resources Canada, Geological Survey of Canada.

Tribot, A.S., J. Deter, and N. Mouquet. 2018. Integrating the aesthetic value of landscapes and biological diversity. *Proceedings of the Royal Society B: Biological Sciences* 285: 20180971.

Trigger, B.G. 1962. Trade and tribal warfare on the St. Lawrence in the sixteenth century. *Ethnohistory* 9: 240–56.

Trigger, B.G. 1996. *The Cambridge History of the Native Peoples of the Americas.* Cambridge: Cambridge University Press.

Trondekheritage. 2020. Welcome to Tr'ocheëk. Tr'ondëk Hwëch'in Heritage Sites. http://trondekheritage.com/our-places/trochek/. Accessed September 23, 2020.

Turgeon, L. Undated. Île aux Basques. *Encyclopedia of French Cultural Heritage in North America.* http://www.ameriquefrancaise.org/en/article-292/%C3%8Ele%20aux%20Basques. Accessed October 19, 2020.

Tyrell, J.B. (ed.). 1916. *David Thompson's Narrative of his Explorations in Western America, 1784–1812.* Toronto: The Champlain Society. https://archive.org/details/davidthompsonsna12thom/page/n9/mode/2up. Accessed September 15, 2020.

UK–UT. 2014. Inland Navigation in the United States: An Evaluation of Economic Impacts and the Potential Effects of Infrastructure Investment. University of Kentucky and University of Tennessee. http://nationalwaterwaysfoundation.org/documents/INLANDNAVIGATIONINTHEUSDECEMBER2014.pdf. Accessed March 02, 2018.

Uldrich, J. 2004. *Into the Unknown: Leadership Lessons from Lewis & Clark's Daring Westward Adventure.* New York: AMACOM.

UNEP-DHI and UNEP. 2016. *Transboundary River Basins: Status and Trends.* United Nations Environment Programme (UNEP), Nairobi. http://geftwap.org/publications/river-basins-technical-report. Accessed December 12, 2020.

United Nations. 2019. International decades. Resolution 73/284. United Nations Decade on Ecosystem Restoration (2021–2030). https://undocs.org/A/RES/73/284. Accessed October 22, 2020.

United Nations Decade on Ecosystem Restoration 2021–2030. Undated. Preventing, halting and reversing the degradation of ecosystems worldwide. https://www.decadeonrestoration.org/. Accessed October 22, 2020.

United Nations Development Programme. 2020. Human Development Reports. http://hdr.undp.org/en/countries/profiles/. Accessed October 13, 2020.

United Nations Economic Commission for Europe. Undated. Total length of inland waterways. https://w3.unece.org/PXWeb/en/Table?IndicatorCode=58. Accessed October 15, 2020.

US Bureau of Reclamation. 2008. The law of the river. http://www.usbr.gov/lc/region/g1000/lawofrvr.html. Accessed October 8, 2020.

US Bureau of Reclamation. 2015. Hoover dam essays: Fatalities at Hoover Dam. http://www.usbr.gov/lc/hooverdam/history/essays/fatal.html. Accessed October 2, 2020.

US Bureau of Reclamation. 2016. West-wide climate risk assessments: Hydro-climate projections. Technical Memorandum No. 86-68210-2016-01. Denver, CO. https://www.usbr.gov/climate/secure/docs/2016secure/wwcra-hydroclimateprojections.pdf. Accessed October 12, 2020.

US Bureau of Reclamation. 2016. SECURE Water Act section 9503(c) – Reclamation Climate Change and Water 2016. https://www.usbr.gov/climate/secure/. Accessed October 24, 2020.

US Bureau of Reclamation. 2018. Hydropower at Hoover Dam. https://www.usbr.gov/lc/hooverdam/faqs/powerfaq.html. Accessed October 2, 2020.

US Bureau of Reclamation. 2020. Quagga and zebra mussels. https://www.usbr.gov/mussels/. Accessed August 24, 2019.

US Bureau of Reclamation. 2020. Colorado River Basin Salinity Control Program. https://usbr.gov/uc/progact/salinity/index.html. Accessed October 20, 2020.

US Bureau of Reclamation (California-Great Basin). 2020. Central Valley Project Improvement Act (CVPIA). http://www.usbr.gov/mp/cvpia/. Accessed October 5, 2020.

US Census Bureau. 2013. A decade of state population change. https://www.census.gov/dataviz/visualizations/043/. Accessed October 8, 2020.

US Census Bureau. 2020. Last census population estimates of the decade preview 2020 census count. https://www.census.gov/library/stories/2020/04/nations-population-growth-slowed-this-decade.html. Accessed October 8, 2020.

US Census Bureau. 2020. Population estimates by county. https://www.census.gov/data/datasets/time-series/demo/popest/2010s-counties-total.html Accessed September 12, 2020.

US Census Bureau. 2020. State exports from Alaska. Business and Industry, Foreign Trade, US International Trade Data. https://www.census.gov/foreign-trade/statistics/state/data/ak.html. Accessed September 23, 2020.

US Census Bureau. 2020. US and World Population Clock. https://www.census.gov/popclock/. Accessed October 13, 2020.

US Department of Agriculture. 2014. Easements. Natural resources Conservation Service. https://www.nrcs.usda.gov/wps/portal/nrcs/main/national/programs/easements/. Accessed August 28, 2019.

US Department of Agriculture. 2017. 2017 Census of Agriculture. United States Summary and State Data. Vol. 1, Pt. 51. AC-17-A-51. https://www.nass.usda.gov/Publications/Ag-Census/2017/Full_Report/Volume_1,_Chapter_2_US_State_Level/usv1.pdf. Accessed October 4, 2020.

US Department of Homeland Security. 2020. US Border Patrol Fiscal Year Southwest Border Sector Deaths (FY 1998–FY 2019). https://www.cbp.gov/document/stats/us-border-patrol-fiscal-year-southwest-border-sector-deaths-fy-1998-fy-2019. Accessed October 14, 2020.

US Department of State. 2018. On the opening of negotiations to modernize the Columbia River Treaty Regime. Department of Western Affairs. https://www.state.gov/on-the-opening-of-negotiations-to-modernize-the-columbia-river-treaty-regime/. Accessed October 2, 2020.

US Department of the Interior, Fish and Wildlife Service. 2010. Endangered and Threatened Wildlife and Plants; 12-Month Finding on a Petition to Reclassify the Delta Smelt From Threatened to Endangered Throughout Its Range. *Federal Register* 75(66): 17667–80.

US Department of Transportation. 2020. Miles of infrastructure by transportation mode. Bureau of Transportation Statistics. https://www.bts.gov/content/miles-infrastructure-transportation-mode. Accessed October 16, 2020.

US District Court, Colorado Division. 2017. Case 1:17-cv-02316-NYW. http://blogs2.law.columbia.edu/climate-change-litigation/wp-content/uploads/sites/16/case-documents/2017/20171204_docket-117-cv-02316_order.pdf. Accessed October 22, 2020.

US District Court, Ninth Circuit. 2010. Delta smelt consolidated cases, 717 F. Supp. 2d 1021 (E.D. Cal. 2010). https://www.courtlistener.com/opinion/2541272/consolidated-delta-smelt-cases/. Accessed May 6, 2017.

US Energy Information Administration. 2019. Canada Overview. https://www.eia.gov/international/overview/country/CAN). Accessed August 2, 2020.

US Energy Information Administration. 2020. Natural Gas. https://www.eia.gov/dnav/ng/hist/n3010us3a.htm. Accessed September 21, 2020.

US Environmental Protection Agency. 2009. 2009 State of the River Report for Toxics. https://www.epa.gov/columbiariver/2009-state-river-report-toxics. Accessed October 29, 2019.

US Environmental Protection Agency. 2019. Facts and figures about the Great Lakes. https://www.epa.gov/greatlakes/facts-and-figures-about-great-lakes. Accessed Aug. 20, 2019.

US Environmental Protection Agency. 2020. Great Lakes Areas of Concern. https://www.epa.gov/great-lakes-aocs Accessed October 22, 2020.

US Environmental Protection Agency. 2020. Great Lakes Areas of Concern: Beneficial Use Impairments for the Great Lakes AOCs. https://www.epa.gov/great-lakes-aocs/beneficial-use-impairments-great-lakes-aocs Accessed October 22, 2020.

US Environmental Protection Agency. 2020. Great Lakes Areas of Concern: St. Lawrence River Area of Concern at Massena/Akwesasne. https://www.epa.gov/great-lakes-aocs/st-lawrence-river-area-concern-massenaakwesasne. Accessed October 22, 2020.

US Geological Survey. 2017. First-of-its-kind interactive map brings together 40 Years of water-quality data. https://www.usgs.gov/news/first-its-kind-interactive-map-brings-together-40-years-water-quality-data. Accessed October 20, 2020.

US Geological Survey. 2019. Boundary Descriptions and Names of Regions, Subregions, Accounting Units and Cataloging Units. http://water.usgs.gov/GIS/huc_name.html. Accessed October 8, 2020.

US Geological Survey. Undated. Central Valley aquifer system. Groundwater Atlas of the United States, Nevada and California. https://pubs.usgs.gov/ha/ha730/ch_b/B-text3.html. Accessed October 4, 2020.

US Geological Survey. Undated. What is drought? California Water Science Center. http://ca.water.usgs.gov/data/drought/. Accessed May 17, 2017.

US Geological Survey. Undated. Colorado River Basin Focus Area study. https://www.usgs.gov/mission-areas/water-resources/science/colorado-river-basin-focus-area-study?qt-science_center_objects=0#qt-science_center_objects. Accessed October 8, 2020.

US Global Change Research Program (USGCRP). 2017. *Climate Science Special Report: Fourth National Climate Assessment*, vol. 1 [D.J. Wuebbles, D.W. Fahey, K.A. Hibbard, D.J. Dokken, B.C. Stewart, and T.K. Maycock (eds.)]. US Global Change Research Program, Washington, DC. https://science2017.globalchange.gov/chapter/front-matter-about/. Accessed August 2, 2019.

US Global Change Research Program (USGCRP). 2018. *Impacts, Risks, and Adaptation in the United States: Fourth National Climate Assessment*, vol. 2 [D.R. Reidmiller, C.W. Avery, D.R. Easterling, K.E. Kunkel, K.L.M. Lewis, T.K. Maycock, and B.C. Stewart (eds.)]. US Global Change Research Program, Washington, DC. https://nca2018.globalchange.gov/chapter/front-matter-about/. Accessed August 23, 2020.

US Library of Congress. 2020. Treaty with Russia for the Purchase of Alaska, Primary Documents in American History. https://guides.loc.gov/alaska-treaty Accessed November 12, 2020.

US National Parks Service. 2015. Franklin Delano Roosevelt Memorial. http://www.nps.gov/frde/learn/photosmultimedia/quotations.htm. Accessed October 2, 2020.

US National Parks Service. 2018. Nevada and Arizona. Hoover Dam. https://www.nps.gov/articles/nevada-and-arizona-hoover-dam.htm. Accessed October 8, 2020.

US National Parks Service. 2020. Elwha River restoration. http://www.nps.gov/olym/learn/nature/elwha-ecosystem-restoration.htm. Accessed October 2, 2020.

US National Parks Service. 2020. Mississippi River facts. http://www.nps.gov/miss/riverfacts.htm. Accessed October 15, 2020.

Usner Jr., D.H., 1987. The frontier exchange economy of the lower Mississippi valley in the Eighteenth Century. *The William and Mary Quarterly: A Magazine of Early American History and Culture* 44: 166–92.

Utzig, G., and D. Schmidt. 2011. Dam Footprint Impact Summary – BC Hydro Dams in the Columbia Basin. Unpublished Report for Fish and Wildlife Compensation Program: Columbia Basin, Nelson, BC. http://www.sgrc.selkirk.ca/bioatlas/pdf/FWCP-CB_Impacts_Summary.pdf. Accessed March 18, 2020.

Vaux, H. Jr. et al. 2013. The Mackenzie River Basin. Rosenberg International Forum on Water Policy. Report of the Rosenberg International Forum's Workshop on Transboundary Relations in the Mackenzie River Basin. http://ciwr.ucanr.edu/files/168679.pdf. Accessed September 21, 2020.

Waddell, I.G. 2018. Kinder Morgan and Lessons from the Berger Inquiry. *The Tyee*. October 2018. https://thetyee.ca/Opinion/2018/10/17/Kinder-Morgan-Lessons-Berger/. Accessed September 1, 2020.

Wahl, K. 2012. Salt cedar establishment in the lower Rio Grande. Presentation to the Lower Rio Grande Citizens Forum. International Boundary and Water Commission Lower Rio Grande Field Office. https://www.ibwc.gov/Files/CF_LRG_Salt_Cedar_Est_071812. pdf. Accessed October 20, 2020.

Wakabayashi, J., and T.L. Sawyer. 2001. Stream incision, tectonics, uplift, and evolution of topography of the Sierra Nevada, California. *Journal of Geology* 109: 539–62.

Waldman, C. 2006. *Encyclopedia of Native American Tribes*, 3rd ed. New York: Checkmark Books.

Walker, N. 2019. On the Map: The St. Lawrence Seaway turns 60. *Canadian Geographic*. July/August.

Wallace, W.J. 1955. Mohave fishing equipment and methods. *Anthropological Quarterly* 28: 87–94.

Waples, R.S. 2006. Distinct population segments. In J.M. Scott, D.D. Goble, and F.W. Davis (eds.), *The Endangered Species Act at Thirty*, vol. 2: *Conserving Biodiversity in Human-Dominated Landscapes*, pp. 127–49. Washington, DC: Island Press.

Waples, R.S., T. Beechie, and G.R. Pess. 2009. Evolutionary history, habitat disturbance regimes, and anthropogenic changes: What do these mean for resilience of Pacific salmon populations? *Ecology and Society* 14(1): 3. http://www.ecologyandsociety.org/vol14/iss1/art3/.

Waples, R.S., G.R. Pess, and T. Beechie. 2008. Evolutionary history of Pacific salmon in dynamic environments. *Evolutionary Applications* 1: 189–206.

Waters, M.R., and T.W. Stafford. 2013. The first Americans: A review of the evidence for the Late-Pleistocene peopling of the Americas. In K.E. Graf, C.V. Ketron, and M.R. Waters (eds.), *Paleoamerican Odyssey*, pp. 543–62. College Station: Texas A&M University Press.

Waters, M.R., T.W. Stafford, H.G. McDonald, C. Gustafson, M. Rasmussen, E. Cappellini, J.V. Olsen, D. Szklarczyk, L.J. Jensen, M.T.P. Gilbert and E. Willerslev. 2011. Pre-Clovis mastodon hunting 13,800 years ago at the Manis site, Washington. *Science* 334: 351–53.

Watershed Watch Salmon Society. 2012. Resource: Cohen Report Card. http://www. watershed-watch.org/issues/salmon-biodiversity/the-fraser-sockeye-inquiry/cohen-report-tracker/. Accessed September 24, 2020.

Watershed Watch Salmon Society. 2016. "Business as usual": A critique of federal update on Cohen. https://watershedwatch.ca/business-as-usual-a-critique-of-federal-update-on-cohen/. Accessed August 5, 2020.

Watt, A., and A. Philip. 2005. *Electroplating and Electrorefining of Metals*. Palm Springs, CA: Wexford College Press.

Weinert, R.S. 1981. Foreign capital in Mexico. *Proceedings of the Academy of Political Science* 34: 115–24.

Weller, M., and T.A. Russell. 2016. State of the river report. 2016. Water quality and river health in the metro Mississippi River. Friends of the Mississippi River and US National Parks Service, Mississippi National River and Recreation Area. http://stateoftheriver. com/state-of-the-river-report/. Accessed August 24, 2019.

Wermuth, T.S., J.M. Johnson, and C. Pryslopski (eds.). 2009. *America's First River: The History and Culture of the Hudson River Valley*. Albany: State University of New York Press.

Wetzel, R.G. 2001. *Limnology: Lake and River Ecosystems*. San Diego: Academic Press.

Wheeler, E. 1988. The Battle of Hastings: Math, myth and melee. *Journal of Military History* 52: 28–134.

Wheeler, S.A., and D.E. Garrick. 2020. A tale of two water markets in Australia: Lessons for understanding participation in formal water markets. *Oxford Review of Economic Policy* 36: 132–53.

Whitbeck, R.H. 1914. The St. Lawrence River and its part in the making of Canada. American Association of Geographers 11th Annual Meeting, Chicago, IL.

White, R. 1991. *It's Your Misfortune and None of My Own: A New History of the American West.* Norman: University of Oklahoma Press.

White, R. 1996. *The Organic Machine: The Remaking the Columbia River.* New York: Hill & Wang.

Whitelaw, E., and E. MacMullan. 2002. A framework for estimating the costs and benefits of dam removal: Sound cost–benefit analyses of removing dams account for subsidies and externalities, for both the short and long run, and place the estimated costs and benefits in the appropriate economic context. *BioScience* 52: 724–30.

Wickert, A.D. 2016. Reconstruction of North American drainage basins and river discharge since the Last Glacial Maximum. *Earth Surface Dynamics* 4: 831–69.

WildSalmon.org. 2020. Myths and facts about lower snake River dam removal. http://www.wildsalmon.org/facts-and-information/myths-and-facts-about-lower-snake-river-dam-removal.html. Accessed July 23, 2020.

Wilkinson, T.J., L. Rayne, and J. Jotheri. 2015. Hydraulic landscapes in Mesopotamia: The role of Human Niche Construction. *Water History* 7: 397–418

Willbold, M., T. Elliott, and S. Moorbath. 2011. The tungsten isotopic composition of the Earth's mantle before the terminal bombardment. *Nature* 477: 195–98.

Williams, A.P., E.R. Cook, J.E. Smerdon, B.I. Cook, and J.T. Abatzoglou. 2020. Large contribution from anthropogenic warming to an emerging North American megadrought. *Science* 368: 314–18.

Willis, B.C. 1997. The environmental effects of the Yukon gold rush 1896–1906: Alterations to land, destruction of wildlife, and disease. MA thesis, University of Western Ontario, London, ON.

Winship, G.P. 1896. *The Coronado Expedition, 1540–1542.* Fourteenth Annual Report of the Bureau of Ethnology, Washington. pp. 6–638. https://archive.org/details/coronadoexpeditioowinsrich. Accessed October 8, 2020.

Witteman, B. 2000. *Sacagawea: A Photo-Illustrated Biography.* Mankato, MN: Bridgestone Books/Capstone Press.

Wittfogel, K.A. 1957. *Oriental Despotism: A Comparative Study of Total Power.* New Haven, CT: Yale University Press.

Witze, A. 2014. Water returns to arid Colorado River delta. *Nature* 507: 286.

Wohl, E. 2004. *Disconnected Rivers: Linking Rivers to Landscapes.* New Haven, CT: Yale University Press.

Wong, K. 2006. Carquinez breakthrough. *Bay Nature Magazine.* https://baynature.org/articles/carquinez-breakthrough/. Accessed October 3, 2020.

World Bank. 2020. Data. Mexico. https://data.worldbank.org/country/mexico?view=chart. Accessed October 13, 2020.

World Bank. 2020. Data. United States. https://data.worldbank.org/country/united-states?view=chart. Accessed October 13, 2020.

World Gold Council. 2020. Gold spot price. www.gold.com. Accessed September 23, 2020.

World Gold Council. 2020. How much gold has been mined? https://www.gold.org/about-gold/gold-supply/gold-mining/how-much-gold. Accessed August 15, 2020.

World Wildlife Federation. 2020. Watershed Reports: Yukon. http://watershedreports.wwf. ca/page/about/#ws-5/by/threat-habitat-loss/threat. Accessed Aug. 27, 2019.

World Wildlife Fund. 2020. Watershed reports: Methodology. http://watershedreports. wwf.ca/page/methodology/#canada/by/threat-overall/profile/?page=methodology. Accessed October 21, 2020.

World Wildlife Fund. 2020. WWF's top ten rivers at risk, Rio Grande makes list. https:// www.worldwildlife.org/press-releases/wwf-s-top-10-rivers-at-risk-rio-grande-makes-list. Accessed October 20, 2020.

Worster, D. 1986. *Rivers of Empire. Water, Aridity, & the Growth of the American West.* New York: Pantheon.

Wynn, G. 2015. Foreword: The paradoxical politics of participatory praxis. In C.A. Dokis, *Where the Rivers Meet: Pipeline, Participatory Resource Management, and Aboriginal-State Relations in the Northwest Territories.* Vancouver: University of British Columbia Press.

Yoshiyama, R.M., F.W. Fisher, and P.B. Moyle. 1998. Historical abundance and decline of chinook salmon in the Central Valley region of California. *North American Journal of Fisheries Management* 18: 487–521.

Yoshiyama, R.M., P.B. Moyle, E.R. Gerstung, and F.W. Fisher. 2000. Chinook salmon in the California Central Valley: An assessment. *Fisheries* 25: 6–20.

Yukon Bureau of Statistics. 2020. Population Report, Q1 October 2020. https://yukon.ca/ en/population-report-q1-2020. Accessed August 2, 2020.

YukonInfo.com. 2020. Robert Service – The Bard of the Yukon. https://www.yukoninfo. com/dawson-city-yukon/robert-service-the-bard-of-the-yukon/. Accessed September 23, 2020.

Zachariah, M. 1984. The Berger Commission Inquiry Report and the revitalization of indigenous cultures. *Canadian Journal of Development Studies/Revue canadienne d'études du développement* 5(1): 65–77.

Zeman, J., and H. Andrusak. 2020. Hear no evil. Canada's broken Department of Fisheries and Oceans. *The Osprey* 97: 12–14.

Zhu, T., M.W. Jenkins, and J.R. Lund. 2005. Estimated impacts of climate warming on California water availability under twelve future climate scenarios. *Journal of the American Water Resources Association* 41: 1027–38.

Illustration credits

1 Three stages of Sumerian irrigation. Drafted by Derek Tan, Beaty Biodiversity Museum, University of British Columbia.
2 River watershed. Drafted by Derek Tan, Beaty Biodiversity Museum, University of British Columbia.
3 Justice Thomas Berger (seated at table) conducting an inquiry session. Photo by Peter Gorrie.
4 Dawson City, Yukon. Photo by Eric Hegg.
5 Klondike mine tailings. Google Earth.
6 Sockeye salmon. Photo by Thomas Quinn.
7 Grand Coulee Dam. Photo by US Bureau of Reclamation.
8 Central Valley agriculture. Photo by Ken Lund.
9 The Colorado River Delta. LANDSAT image courtesy of Alejandro Hinojosa-Corona (CICESE, Ensenada, México).
10 US National Guard. Photo by Staff Sgt. Roberto Di Giovine.
11 Vicksburg, Mississippi. US Library of Congress.
12 *Kaaterskill Falls*, Thomas Cole (1826)
13 *Portage Falls on the Genesee,* Thomas Cole (1839)
14 The Eisenhower Lock on the American side of the St. Lawrence Seaway looking west towards Massena, NY. Photo by: Robert Estall.
15 Zebra mussels. Photo by: Dan Schloesser, USGS, Biological Resources Division.
16 Projected changes in annual air temperatures. Courtesy of US Global Change Research Program.
17 Projected average change (%) in total seasonal precipitation. Courtesy of US Global Change Research Program.
18 NAWAPAXXI. Drafted by Derek Tan, Beaty Biodiversity Museum, University of British Columbia.

Maps

All maps were drafted by Eric Leinberger, University of British Columbia Department of Geography.

Index